Foundation Grants to Individuals
6th Edition

Stan Olson
Editor

Margaret Mary Feczko
Assistant Editor

The Foundation Center
New York
1988

CONTRIBUTING STAFF

Director of Information Systems	Martha David
Assistant Director of Information Systems	Sarah Johnson
Production Manager	Rick Schoff
Information Control Coordinator	Ted Murphy
Editorial Associates	Maria Ricardo Ben-Ali Margaret B. Jung Darryl Mitteldorf M. Lara Brock Tim Cockey
Editorial Assistant	Joan Seabourne

The Editor gratefully acknowledges the many other Foundation Center staff whose support and encouragement made this volume possible. Our thanks also go to the many foundations which cooperated fully in updating and verifying information for the sixth edition.

Contents

Introduction

Foundation Grants to Individuals is the most comprehensive listing available of private U.S. foundations which provide financial assistance to individuals. The *Sixth Edition* contains those 1,233 foundations, out of approximately 30,000 active private grantmaking U.S. foundations, that The Foundation Center has identified as conducting ongoing grantmaking programs for individuals. It describes giving for a variety of purposes including scholarships, student loans, fellowships, foreign recipients, travel, internships, residencies, arts and cultural projects, and general welfare. It is intended to be both a grantseeker's guide and a reference tool for those interested in foundation giving to individuals.

The *Sixth Edition* includes the most current information available at press time for 988 foundations listed in previous editions and 245 foundation programs new to this edition. To prepare the *Sixth Edition*, Foundation Center staff researched public records, especially IRS Form 990-PF which all foundations are required to file, annual reports, newsletters, and other published information about the foundations. Entries were mailed to all potential *Sixth Edition* foundations for review and correction and were revised according to the information supplied by the foundations. Entries for foundations that responded to our mailing, updating and verifying our research, are indicated with a star (★).

It is important to note that this directory describes only those foundation programs open to individuals. Most foundations have funding programs for nonprofit organizations and institutions, often much more substantial than their programs for individuals. Information about these programs is available in The Foundation Center's *The Foundation Directory* and in *Source Book Profiles*, as well as other

publications. Many of the programs that foundations finance through nonprofit organizations are geared to individual recipients, such as funds given by foundations to colleges and universities to set up scholarship programs, but are not included in this volume because applicants must apply to the school and not to the foundation for assistance. They are, however, sources of funds that should be explored, and information on them can be obtained through the appropriate financial aid offices.

Keep in mind also that many alternative sources of funding for individuals are available in the United States. Government grants, scholarships offered directly by colleges and universities, scholarships offered directly from corporations, research funds from nonprofit institutions, and other awards should be fully investigated in your search for money to attend school, do research, or gain assistance. To help individual grantseekers of all kinds learn about alternative funding, we have provided a bibliography of reference guides to grants other than those made by foundations. This bibliography may be as useful to you as the descriptions of the foundations listed in this book.

Criteria for Inclusion

For inclusion in *Foundation Grants to Individuals* a foundation must meet three criteria:

1. It must make grant awards to or for individuals of at least $2,000 a year. Whenever possible, financial information for the years 1986 or 1987 was used. In the absence of timely delivery of tax reporting forms from the IRS, however, 1984 information or the most recent reporting year available has been presented. If a foundation made less than $2,000 in grant

awards in the latest year available, financial data from the previous year was reviewed and the foundation was included if it qualified in that year.

2. It must select the recipients of its grants by its governing board or an independent selection committee.

3. It must accept applications from individuals directly or through an intermediary. The one exception to this requirement is a special category, "Awards, Prizes, and Grants by Nomination," where information is given on awards programs sponsored by foundations and programs which require nominations from sources other than the individuals themselves, such as institutions or organizations affiliated with the foundation. This section has been included for those interested in reviewing the full spectrum of foundation support for individuals. **Individuals cannot apply directly to those foundations described as accepting only nominations.**

Arrangement

The *Sixth Edition* divides foundation awards to individuals into three major categories—educational support, general welfare, and arts and culture. These three sections account for 949 entries or about 74 percent of the entries in the book. Three additional sections cover grants to foreign individuals; awards, prizes, and grants by nomination; and company employee grants. This last section is subdivided into educational and general welfare listings. Arrangement within each section or subsection is alphabetical by foundation name.

Several foundations have grantmaking programs of more than one type. For example, they make scholarship awards and also give support to needy, aged persons. Where breakdowns are available

and both programs are of substantial size (usually over $2,000 in grant awards in each program) two entries are provided. When only one of the two programs makes grant awards of at least $2,000, there is only one entry.

Each entry includes, as available, the following information:

1. Foundation name and address
2. Telephone number—most smaller size foundations do not have full-time staff and do not list a telephone number
3. Name and title of person to whom inquiries, applications, and proposals should be sent
4. Limitations statement describing restrictions on giving made by the foundation
5. Financial information, including
   a. Assets at market value (unless otherwise indicated) for the specified fiscal year
   b. Total amount of the foundation's grants, including awards to organizations as well as individuals
   c. Subtotal of the foundation's grants or loans which were awarded either directly to individuals or to institutions for the benefit of individuals
   d. Number of individuals receiving grants
6. Application information, including whether formal application is required, whether interviews are required or granted upon request, and deadlines (if only past deadlines are known or if current deadlines were unspecified, the reader should contact the foundation for current information)
7. Information on any available foundation publications, such as annual reports, program guidelines, or

application information which would be of primary interest to any potentially qualified grantseeker

8. The body of the entry includes, as available, the name of the grant or award, purpose, terms and conditions of the grants such as duration, activities funded, and accountability to the foundation.

The absence of certain pieces of information in an entry indicates that such information is not pertinent for that foundation or was not available. Where full information is not provided, it is advisable to write to the foundation if available data seems to indicate that you might be eligible. If no foundation officer is listed as a contact person and no specific program is named or described, inquiries should simply be addressed to the foundation.

Indexes

In order to facilitate research and provide access to the many entries in this volume, six indexes have been developed. They are the best place to begin when using this book.

The numbers listed in these indexes refer to the sequence number corresponding to each entry, found in the left-hand corner. In the Index of Foundations the letter "A" refers to the Appendix which lists those foundations from the *Fifth Edition* of *Foundation Grants to Individuals* which have not been included in this *Sixth Edition*. There are 74 foundations in the *Fifth Edition* that are not included in the *Sixth Edition*. The foundations listed in the Appendix have either terminated or no longer meet our criteria for inclusion. These foundations should not be considered as possible sources of grants to individuals and should not be contacted.

The indexes include the following:

1. **Index of Foundations.** This index provides access by foundation name to entries in the main section of this book as well as those foundations listed in the Appendix.

2. **Subject Index.** This index provides access to foundations making grants in specific subject areas. Entries are indexed under the applicable terms. However, related subjects should be checked to make certain all entries are reviewed as possibilities.

Entry numbers for foundations that give nationally or regionally are given in boldface type following the states in which they are located. Entries describing foundations that restrict their giving to particular states are listed in lighter type following the states in which they give.

3. **Types of Support Index.** This index provides access to foundations according to the particular kinds of grants awarded, such as scholarships, pensions, or publishing support. Entries are indexed under the applicable terms. However, related types of support should be checked to make certain all entries are reviewed as possibilities.

Entry numbers for foundations that give nationally or regionally are given in boldface type following the states in which they are located. Entries describing foundations that restrict their giving to particular states are listed in lighter type following the states in which they give.

4. **Geographic Focus Index.** This index provides access by state to all foundation entries in which a geographic preference or restriction is stated. Listings are further subdivided into categories of giving to provide more rapid access.

5. **Index of Company Employee Grants.** This index provides access by company name to foundation grant programs that are open to that company's employees, former employees, families of employees, or those

residing in areas where the company operates plants.

6. **Index of Specific Educational Institutions.** This index provides access to foundations making grants to individuals who must attend or have attended specific educational institutions.

TO THE GRANTSEEKER

Researching Foundation Grantmaking

Foundation Grants to Individuals is a primary tool in the construction of a methodical research scheme to uncover those foundations which might be able to fulfill your funding needs. It is as much a guide to those programs to which you should not apply as it is a guide to those for which you may qualify. Many foundations making grants to individuals are small, have limited assets, and make a limited number of grants each year. Federal laws outline specific restrictions and requirements for foundation giving to individuals and have limited the extent and nature of such programs. An excellent analysis of these laws is provided in this book by Edward Thomson.

Remember that most of the foundations in this volume place specific limitations on their giving by subject area, types of recipients, and geographic location. Finding out about those limitations before submitting applications will save you time and increase your chances of obtaining assistance. A foundation will automatically reject any applicant who does not qualify under its restrictions. For example, a foundation will reject you immediately if it gives only to residents of Kansas and you live in California.

Do not waste time applying to inappropriate foundations. The law of averages does not apply when seeking grants. One hundred applications sent to one hundred foundations whose qualifications you do not meet will result in either one hundred rejections or in no responses at all. By demonstrating your knowledge of the foundation's programs and your qualifications for them, however, you have a better chance of getting that important first step in the door. Foundations can grant only a limited amount of money and have a large number of applications from which to choose and foundation personnel who will review your application will be looking for the candidate who best meets the standards and purposes of their programs.

Each entry in this book includes a statement of limitations showing the specific constraints on the foundation's giving program for individuals. In addition, geographic limitations are indicated in the Subject Index, Types of Support Index, and Geographic Focus Index.

REMEMBER; IF YOU DON'T QUALIFY, DON'T APPLY.

Identifying Funding Possibilities

As with all grantseeking, the key to obtaining grants is preparation. Preparation means identifying the foundations which make grants in your area and determining if you fall within their restrictions. It is important to pay close attention to their limitations, their giving patterns, their areas of interest, and the amount of awards they make each year. Applying to a foundation outside your field of study or to one which only makes grants of a few hundred dollars when you need thousands, will prove futile. Learn as much as you can about the foundation. Do your homework! Use as many resources as you have access to.

Identify funding possibilities using the indexes provided in this book. These indexes will give you access to the foundation's entries by subject, types of support, geographic focus, company-related grantmaking, and specific educational institutions. Once the foundations that are likely to consider your request are identified, try to find out more about their particular programs. Visit one of The Foundation Center's cooperating libraries listed following this introduction. There you will find a variety of resources about foundations and their grantmaking activities, as well as have access to the IRS Form 990 that all foundations are required to file. These forms provide the financial information that can help you determine whether a foundation's grantmaking activities meet your needs. Inquire at your local collection as to the availability of these resources. A librarian will also be available to help answer your questions.

If you meet the qualifications of the foundation and believe the foundation may be receptive to your request, prepare the application or proposal along the guidelines set up by the foundation. Be thorough. Provide all the information asked for, give references if required, and provide carefully planned budgets, letting the foundation know how the money will be used.

Approach the application procedure as you would a job application. Explain why you are the best person for this foundation to support, emphasizing your qualifications. Remember there are more talented people around than there is foundation money available, so you must prove that the money should go to you and not others.

With these things in mind you are ready to use this book to begin the process that could lead to the funding you seek.

Federal Laws and Private Foundation Grants to Individuals

by Edward G. Thomson, Executive Assistant, The Foundation Center

This II makes no sense!

In general, careful foundation grantmaking involves choices based on the capabilities of individuals, even though the foundation is *not* making a grant to an individual in the tax law sense. General support grants to colleges and universities, for example, may be based on perceptions of the capacities of the school's administrative leadership and faculty. Grantee selection for more specialized programs is all the more likely related to an applicant organization's leadership and staff. If, for example, a foundation wants to support an organization with programs that will provide housing and supporting services for homeless people, the foundation will take a good look at the background, experience and track record of the individuals who determine the prospective grantee's policies, priorities, and directions. Foundations, it is frequently said, "bet on individuals," and this applies whether a foundation is making a grant to an individual or an organization.

Some Background Information

Provisions of the Internal Revenue Code establish some special requirements that certain foundation individual grant programs must meet. Individual grantees should be generally familiar with these rules, because they affect the grantee as well as the foundation grantor.

Charitable organizations in general and foundations in particular have traditionally enjoyed favorable treatment in the individual grants area not enjoyed to the same extent by individual contributors. If you as an individual know a deserving and needy student, assuming you are financially able to do so, you can give that student the necessary funds for a college education,

graduate degree, or research project as the case may be—but you won't get the benefit of a charitable contribution for doing so. However, charitable organizations, including foundations, whose funds are already exempt from income taxes and to which tax deductible contributions can be made, have long been able to make individual grants without adversely affecting their tax status.

Legislative History

This right came under close scrutiny in 1969, when the current elaborate private foundation rules and restrictions were first under consideration in Congress. The House Ways and Means Committee at one point tentatively decided that, with certain limited exceptions, private foundations should be denied the right to make grants directly to individuals for travel, study, or similar purposes. But the Committee changed its mind and reported a proposed bill allowing private foundations to award individual grants for travel, study, or similar purposes provided selection procedures for these grants were approved in advance by the Treasury Department on a one-time approval basis. This approach was enacted into law and remains in effect.

Some Ground Rules and Some Questions

Internal Revenue Code section 4945 and the regulations to it provide the ground rules that private foundations must follow. A grant to an individual for travel, study, or similar purposes is proscribed, unless the grant is awarded on an objective and nondiscriminatory basis under an approved procedure and the grant:

xii

(1) is a scholarship or fellowship as specially defined for study at an educational institution;
(2) is a prize or award given for the achievement of exempt charitable purposes, where the recipient did not enter a contest or other proceedings leading to the award and no substantial future services are required of the recipient as a condition to the prize or award; or
(3) achieves a specific objective; produces a report or other similar product, or improves or enhances an artistic, scientific, or teaching capacity, skill, or talent of the grantee.

Though few foundations make such grants, the law also permits private foundations to provide direct support to needy individuals. Thus, the regulations to section 4945 provide that, for example, a private foundation may make grants to indigent individuals enabling them to purchase furniture, without regard to whether the criteria just cited are met.

Let's take a closer look at the "objective and nondiscriminatory" and "approved procedure" requirements.

A question that has arisen with increasing frequency in other contexts is whether an educational program can be nondiscriminatory if it benefits limited classes of people (women, blacks, other specified groups, the residents of a particular community or region, etc.). In the case of foundation individual grant programs, it still seems clear that prospective recipients can be limited to a group sufficiently broad to be recognized as a charitable class. The purpose of the individual grant rules was to ensure against arbitrary, whimsical, or personally motivated grants. If a foundation maintains a program of scholarship aids for residents

of a particular county or state, or for a particular group that has been victimized by discrimination, the tax law rules do not require the foundation to change that focus so long as the program is administered in an objective and nondiscriminatory fashion within the group or class for whom benefits are available. The regulations also recognize that for grants to "achieve a specific objective" as noted in subparagraph (3) above, selection from a group is not necessary where, taking the grant's purposes into account, one or more persons are selected because they are exceptionally qualified to accomplish these purposes.

A foundation and its individual grantees have additional responsibilities. Leaving aside prizes and awards, the foundation must follow up to see to it that the funds are being used by the individual grantee for the intended purposes. The foundation must obtain reports at least annually, though reporting and recordkeeping burdens can be lessened where the grants are paid to the educational institution for the benefit of the grantee rather than to the grantee directly.

A foundation also has a duty to investigate situations where there are indications that the grant is not being used for the purposes intended or is being diverted to improper purposes. A foundation would normally withhold any further funds under the grant until the situation is corrected and, where a diversion occurs, it is obliged to take all reasonable and appropriate steps to recover or to otherwise ensure the restoration of those funds.

Failure to comply with the requirements is sanctioned by a series of penalty excise taxes that can be imposed on the foundation and, in limited circumstances, on its managers. In flagrant cases, the foundation can lose its tax-exempt status.

Income Tax Considerations

There is a substantial amount of law on the subject of whether scholarships and similar payments are taxable, or tax-exempt, income—a subject that is beyond the scope of this publication. Only a few general observations will be made here.

Under prior law, private foundation scholarship and fellowship grants were generally income-tax free to the recipient. This rule, however, was very substantially curtailed by the Tax Reform Act of 1986. The income-tax exemption is now generally limited to scholarships for degree candidates at educational institutions (also specially defined), and then only for amounts spent for tuition, fees, books and supplies. Amounts spent for room, board and other "personal expenses" are subject to tax. Similarly, prizes and awards are excluded from the recipient's income only if turned over to another charity or to government.

Individuals lucky enough to receive a private foundation grant should surely not assume that their grant is nontaxable. They should be on notice that tax-exempt treatment is limited to a narrow area.

Other Programs

Bear in mind that many foundations provide substantial scholarship dollars, but make these funds available to schools and other public charities, farming out to them the responsibility for selecting grant recipients. Students will often find that the source of the money for the scholarship awarded by the school or college of their choice is a foundation grant. The foundation community is a major source of support for organizations such as A Better Chance, the Woodrow Wilson Scholarship and Fellowship Program, the National Merit Scholarship Program, and many others. Such grant programs are generally treated, however, as grants to organizations, and the detailed requirements for grants to individuals described here do not apply.

Conclusion

A relatively small number of foundations make "grants to individuals" as defined by federal law. For these foundations, however, the general consensus is that the rules are reasonable and provide assurance that individual grants by foundations will be rational rather than whimsical, fair rather than arbitrary, and very much in the public interest.

How about the foundations that do not make grants to individuals? Do they think the requirements are reasonable?

Scholarships and Grants for Individuals: Where to Find Them

by Zeke Kilbride and Marie Lawrence

How can you get a grant to help pay for your education, write a book, make a film, do research or for any purpose?

There are not easy answers but there are resources that can help you. *Foundation Grants to Individuals* is an excellent starting point. The purpose of this article is to suggest additional resources that can lead you to scholarships and grants.

Financial Aid for Education

If you are a student and need financial support to further your education, your first stop should be the financial aid office of the school you plan to attend. Financial aid officers often have information about special scholarships or awards given by government agencies, local corporations or foundations. Their advice can get you started in the right direction. You might also research the various financial aid directories available to you. A representative list of resources appears at the end of this article. The best approach is to consider your own attributes and the connections you have to associations, corporations or other organizations. Many scholarships are not based solely on academic merit or financial need. For example, there are scholarships of a particular county, scholarships for art history majors, scholarships for the physically handicapped, scholarships for women, etc. Consider your background, the type of support you need and apply to those programs for which you qualify. Some of the more useful directories include: *The College Blue Book* (New York: MacMillan Information, published annually), *The Graduate Scholarship Book: The Complete Guide to Scholarships, Fellowships, Grants and Loans for Graduate*

and Professional Study (Englewood Cliffs, NJ: Prentice-Hall, Inc., 1988), *Financial Aids for Higher Education Catalog* (Dubuque, Iowa: William C. Brown Company, published biennially) and *The Chronicle Student Aid Annual* (Moravia, NY: Chronicle Guidance Publications, published annually). These books are well-indexed and may suggest additional funding possibilities to you.

General Resources for Grantseekers

In addition to the directories of financial aid for education, there are directories covering noneducational funding possibilities too. For example, *The Annual Register of Grant Support* (Chicago: Marquis Academic Media, published annually) covers grants for academic and scientific research, project development, travel and exchange programs, publication support, equipment and construction, in-service training, and competitive awards and prizes in a variety of fields. *The Grants Register* (New York: St. Martin's Press, published biennially) is tailored more toward grantseekers at or above the graduate level and for all who require further professional or advanced vocational training. It is international in scope and is especially useful to students from other countries seeking exchange opportunities or international scholarships. Volume 1 of *Awards, Honors and Prizes* (Detroit: Gale Research, published annually) contains details about more than 6,000 prizes and awards for all types of service and special achievement in the United States and Canada. Volume 2 covers awards in more than 58 foreign countries. *The Directory of Research Grants* (Phoenix: Oryx Press, annual) is a useful source for scholars, grant administrators, faculty members and others seeking support for research projects. Over 2,000 programs are listed, including programs supported by private foundations, corporations, professional organizations, and a few state and foreign governments. Also of interest to the researcher is the *Research Centers Directory*, (Detroit: Gale Research Company, published annually) which lists over 8,300 university-related and other nonprofit research organizations in the U.S. and Canada.

Specialized Resources for Grantseekers

In addition to the general directories, there are specialized resources written for specific groups of people (women, minorities, etc.) or for specific disciplines and professional fields (grants in the arts, medicine, sciences, etc). Some of the titles include: the *Directory of Financial Aids for Women* (Los Angeles: Reference Service Press, 1987), the *Directory of Financial Aids for Minorities* (Los Angeles: Reference Service Press, biennial), *Grants in the Humanities*, 2nd Edition (New York: Neal-Schuman, 1984), *1988 Resource Guide to New England Galleries, Grants and Services* (Boston: The Artists Foundation, 1988), *Grants and Awards Available to American Writers* (New York: PEN American Center, 1987), *Fellowships and Grants of Interest to Historians* (Washington, DC: American Historical Association, annual) and *The ARIS Funding Messengers* (San Francisco: Academic Research Information System, subscription service). There are three separate ARIS Messengers: "Creative Arts and Humanities", "Bio-Medical Sciences Report" and "Social and Natural Sciences Report", issued 8 times a year. For information on federal funding, the main source is the *Catalog of Federal Domestic Assistance* (Washington, DC: U.S. Superintendent of Documents, Government Printing Office, annual). Use this catalog as a starting point because much of the information is dated by the time it's published. Follow-up by calling the local or regional office listed under "Information Contacts".

Typically, these publications provide addresses of funders, program descriptions, financial data and deadline dates. Keep in mind that researching takes time and effort. You will need to carefully read each book's introduction, scan indexes, and study program descriptions to identify grant programs for which you qualify. Always request guidelines or applications before submitting a proposal.

Affiliating with a Tax-Exempt Organization

If you are seeking support other than for your education, you should know that few private foundations and corporations make grants directly to individuals. Most only make grants to nonprofit tax-exempt organizations (universities, hospitals, museums and other organizations with educational, scientific, religious or other charitable purposes) to whom contributions are deductible. Some individual grantseekers such as artists or writers seek to become affiliated with tax-exempt organizations to obtain the federal tax-exempt status that funders require. This may also lead to additional credibility and exposure for their work. For a list of organizations to whom contributions are deductible, see the *Cumulative List of Organizations* published annually by the U.S. Internal Revenue Service, Publication 78. Order from the U.S. Government Printing Office, Washington, DC. For agood discussion of affiliation and of grantseeking generally, see Judith Margolin's *The*

Individual's Guide to Grants (New York: Plenum Press, 1983) and Ron Gross' *Independent Scholar's Handbook* (Reading, MA: Addison-Wesley, 1982). Margolin suggests a number of affiliation possibilities including: forming a consortium with other individuals interested in the same subject, finding a temporary "in name only" tax-exempt sponsor or umbrella group to serve as a fiscal agent for your project, making use of your current affiliations to professional societies, trade associations, clubs, alumni groups, etc., or becoming an employee of a nonprofit institution. Gross offers suggestions like teaching in a college or university continuing education program on a part-time basis, developing a "scholar-in-residence" role, etc.

If you don't have organizational affiliations, there are a number of directories of nonprofit organizations that might help you find them. One, for example, is *The Encyclopedia of Associations*, Volume 5: Research Activities and Funding Programs (Detroit: Gale Research, updated biennially in 3 vols.). Let's say, for example, that you are writing a book on the contributions of Hispanic Americans to American society. Looking in the index of the *Encyclopedia of Associations*, you'll find under "Hispanic" an organization called "The Institute for the Study of the Hispanic American in U.S. Life and History". It says "research is conducted both in-house and through the awarding of research contracts, project grants, scholarships, fellowships, and institutional grants". Perhaps The Institute or a similar organization would be worth affiliating with. Some of the organizationsmight fund your project directly or serve as "conduits" for your funding. A "conduit" is an organization which will accept funds on your behalf. It makes formal application for the grant and

retains fiscal responsibility over the project. If you choose to work with a conduit organization, be sure that it has federal tax-exempt status and be aware that there may be strings attached. For example, the organization might impose administrative controls on your work; it might want a percentage of your grant; it might want rights as a joint author, etc. No two conduit relationships are exactly alike. Proceed with caution.

Forming Your Own Nonprofit Organization

Still a third option is to consider forming your own nonprofit, tax-exempt organization. This will require careful thought and a good deal of administrative work on your part. It also entails legal and financial responsibilities requiring a lawyer. Don't try it alone. If you'd like to learn more about what's involved in incorporating or in forming an unincorporated association, there are a number of useful sources including: *Starting and Running a Nonprofit Organization* (Minneapolis, MN: University of Minnesota Press, 1980), *To Be or Not To Be: An Artist's Guide to Not-for-Profit Incorporation* (New York: Volunteer Lawyers for the Arts, 1986), *The Nonprofit Organization Handbook*, 2nd ed. (New York: McGraw-Hill, 1988) and *Arts Money: Raising It, Saving It, and Earning It*, by Joan Jeffri (New York: Neal-Schuman, 1983). Books covering incorporation for your particular state can be even more useful, for example, *The California Non-Profit Corporation Handbook*, 4th Edition(Berkeley, CA: Nolo Press, 1988) or *The New York Not-for-Profit Organization Manual* (New York: Council of New York Law Associates, Volunteer Lawyers for the Arts, 1985).

Keep in mind that forming a nonprofit organization is not the same as getting tax-exempt, tax deductible status. Nonprofit incorporation is a procedure handled on the state level; tax-exempt status is a federal procedure. For information on getting federal tax-exempt status, see IRS publication 557, *Tax Exempt Status for Your Organization*. You can obtain copies from the U.S. Government Printing Office, Washington, DC or by calling the Tax Information number in the phone book listed under "United States Government," Internal Revenue Service. Forming a nonprofit organization is not for everyone. In fact, many nonprofit organizations fail in their first few years because the people who formed them did not understand what they were getting into. By reviewing the resources mentioned and discussing your options with a lawyer, you should be able to better decide if this approach is right for you.

This article has discussed a number of ideas and resources for individual grantseekers to consider. It's meant as a starting point for further research. The following is a list of representative resources that can be valuable to you as you research further. The categories are not mutually exclusive. When grantseeking, a good approach is to scan the general resources first. Then, check to see if there are specific resources related to your interests.

Publishers' addresses, book prices and editions are constantly changing. Before ordering a particular title, check with the publisher to verify that you have the most current information. Copies of many of the works are available for free reference use in The Foundation Center's New York, Washington, DC, Cleveland and San Francisco libraries and in many of its cooperating libraries. Many publications are also available in local libraries and college financial aid offices.

GENERAL SOURCES OF INFORMATION ON GRANTS TO INDIVIDUALS

Annual Register of Grant Support, 1987–88. 21st ed. Chicago, IL: Marquis Academic Media, Annual. 998 p. (200 East Ohio St., 60611)

Includes information on programs sponsored by funding sources, including government agencies, public and private foundations, educational and professional associations, special interest organizations and corporations. Covers a broad range of interests including academic and scientific research, publication support, equipment and construction support, in-service training, competitions and prizes, and travel and exchange programs. Organized by broad subject areas with four indexes: subject, organization and program, geographic, and personnel.

Awards, Honors, and Prizes: Volume I: United States and Canada. 7th ed. Paul Wasserman, ed. Detroit, MI: Gale Research Co., 1987. 1000 p. (Book Tower, 48226) $155.00

Directory of awards in advertising, public relations, art, business, government, finance, science, education, engineering, literature, technology, sports, religion, public affairs, radio and television, politics, librarianship, fashion, medicine, law, publishing, international affairs, transportation, architecture, journalism, motion pictures, music, photography, and theater and performing arts.

Catalog of Federal Domestic Assistance. U.S. Office of Management and Budget. Washington, DC: Government Printing Office, Annual. Looseleaf, various pages (Superintendent of Documents, 20402) approx. $36.00

Official compendium of federal programs, projects, services, and activities which provide assistance or benefits to American organizations, institutions, and individuals. Includes programs open to individual applicants or for individual beneficiaries in the areas of agriculture, commerce, community development, consumer protection, cultural affairs, disaster prevention and relief, education, employment, energy, environmental quality, nutrition, health, housing, social services, information sciences, law, natural resources, regional development, science and technology, and transportation.

Directory of Research Grants, 1988. Phoenix, AZ: The Oryx Press, Annual, 1078 p. (2214 North Central at Encanto, 85004) approx. $80.00

Information about 3,000 grants, contracts, and fellowships available from federal and state governments, private foundations, professional organizations, and corporations for research projects. Lists grants programs by specific funding areas; indexed by sponsoring organization and grant name.

Foundation Grants to Individuals. 6th ed. New York, NY: Foundation Center, 1988. (79 Fifth Ave., 10003) $24.00

Profiles the programs of foundations that make grants to individuals. The foundations described have made grants to students, artists, scholars, foreign individuals, minorities, musicians, scientists and writers. The book includes information on foundation sources of funds for scholarships, fellowships, internships, medical and emergency assistance, residencies and travel programs.

The Grants Register, 1987–1989. Roland Turner, ed. New York, NY: St. Martin's Press, Bi-annual. 744 p. (175 Fifth Ave., 10010) approx. $40.00

Lists scholarships and fellowships at all levels of graduate study, from regional, national and international sources. Also includes research grants, exchange opportunities, vacation study awards, travel grants, all types of grants-in-aid, project grants, competitions, prizes and honoraria—including awards in recognition or support of creative work, professional and vocational awards, and special awards—for refugees, war veterans, minority groups, and students in unexpected financial difficulties, etc.

The Independent Scholar's Handbook. Ronald Gross. Reading, MA: Addison-Wesley Publishing Co., Inc., 1982. 256 p. (01867) Out of print but available in libraries.

Designed to give direction and advice to anyone who wishes to become an independent scholar or a more effective researcher. There is also information on how to obtain grants and funding, rather than listings of specific sources of funding.

The Individual's Guide to Grants. Judith B. Margolin. New York, NY: Plenum Press, 1983. 295 p. (233 Spring St., 10013) $15.95

Aimed at a wide audience of individual grantseekers, it discusses getting a sponsor, finding the right funder, refining your idea, facts about funders and preparing the proposal, and follow-up information. It is an excellent source to start with.

SOURCES OF SCHOLARSHIPS, FELLOWSHIPS, AND LOANS

ARIS Funding Messenger: Creative Arts and Humanities Report. 8 issues per year. Special rates for individuals.

ARIS Funding Messenger: Bio-Medical Sciences Report. 8 issues per year + 8 supplements.

ARIS Funding Messenger: Social and Natural Sciences Report. 8 issues per year + 8 supplements. Academic Research Information System. San Francisco, 1976–. (2940 16th St., Suite 314, 94103)

Reports which provide up-to-date information about grant opportunities, current agency activities, new programs, and funding policies. Includes addresses, telephone numbers of relevant program personnel, concise guidelines, and deadline dates.

After Scholarships, What? Creative Ways to Lower Your College Costs—and the Colleges That Offer Them. Princeton, NJ: Peterson's Guides, 1981. x, 385 p. (P.O. Box 2123, 08540) Out of print but available in libraries.

Aids to Individual Scholars: Competitions to Be Held 1987–1988. New York, NY: American Council of Learned Societies, Annual. (228 E. 45th St., 10017) free

Annual guide to ACLS fellowships and grant programs; awards mainly to support postdoctoral humanistic research.

Arco's Financial Aid Annual. John Schwartz. New York, NY: Arco Publishing, Inc., 1987. 608 p. (215 Park Ave. South, 10003) $14.95

Bear's Guide to Finding Money for College. John Bear. Berkeley, CA: Ten Speed Press, 1984. vii, 157 p. (P.O. Box 7123, 94707) $5.95

Chronicle Student Aid Annual. Moravia, NY: Chronicle Guidance Publications, Inc., 1988. (13118) approx. $17.00
　　Contains information on financial aid programs offered nationally or regionally, primarily by non-collegiate organizations. Awards are for undergraduate, graduate and postdoctoral students.

The College Blue Book: Vol. 5: Scholarships, fellowships, grants, and loans. 21st ed. New York, NY: Macmillan Information, 1987. xv, 718 p. (866 Third Ave., 10022) $46.00
　　Lists financial aid programs offered by agencies and institutions, excluding colleges and universities. Individual programs listed by grant-making organization and arranged under broad and specific subject areas.

College Checkmate: Innovative Tuition Plans That Make You a Winner. 2nd ed. Priscilla S. Goeller, Alexandria, VA: Octameron Associates, 1987. (4805A Eisenhower Ave., 22304) $5.00

The College Cost Book, 1987–88. College Scholarship Service. New York, NY: College Board, 1985. vii, 244 p. (888 Seventh Ave., 10106) $10.95
　　Explains how college financial planning can be done in advance and how to estimate your need and eligibility for financial aid.

The College Financial Aid Emergency Kit. Joyce Lain Kennedy, Dr. Herm Davis and Dr. Sharon Bob. Cardiff, CA: Sun Features, Inc., 1988. 40 p. (Box 368-F, 92007) $4.50

College Grants from Uncle Sam: Am I eligible—and for how much? 1989–90. Alexandria, VA: Octameron Associates, 1987. (4805A Eisenhower Ave., 22304) $3.00

College Loans from Uncle Sam: The borrower's guide that explains it all—from locating lenders to loan forgiveness. 1989–90. Alexandria, VA: Octameron Associates, 1987. (4805A Eisenhower Ave., 22304) $3.00

College Money Handbook: The Complete Guide to Expenses, Scholarships, Loans, Jobs and Special Aid Programs at Four-Year Colleges. Princeton, NJ: Peterson's Guides. 1988, 599 p. (P.O. Box 2123, 08540) $18.95 paper

Complete Grants Sourcebook for Higher Education, 2nd ed. American Council on Education. New York, NY: Macmillan Publishing Co. 1985. 608 p. (866 Third Ave., New York, NY 10022) $85.00
　　A guide to grantsmanship and a directory to more than 500 funding sources for higher education.

Don't Miss Out: The Ambitious Student's Guide to Financial Aid, 1989–90. 13th ed. Robert Leider. Alexandria, VA: Octameron Associates, 1987. 86 p. (4805A Eisenhower Ave., 22304) $5.00
　　Planning guide suggesting procedures and strategies for students seeking financial aid. Updated annually in September.

The Dow Jones-Irwin Guide to College Financial Planning. Paul M. Lane. Homewood, IL: Dow Jones-Irwin, 1981. xii, 260 p. (60430) Out of print but available in libraries.

Earn and Learn: Cooperative education opportunities offered by the federal government. 10th ed. 1989–90. Alexandria, VA: Octameron Associates, Inc. 1987. approx. 20 p. (4805A Eisenhower Ave., 22304) $3.00

Includes sponsors, occupational fields, and participating colleges.

Financial Aid for College-Bound Athletes. Marlene Lazar and Dr. Stephen H. Lazar. New York, NY: Arco Publishing, Inc., 1982. x, 323 p. (215 Park Ave. South, 10003) Out of print but available in libraries.

850 colleges and universities covered. Entries include name of school, address, athletic director's name, teams (both men's and women's), conferences participated in, deadlines, and other scholarship information. Also an index by sport—under name of sport are the schools with awards in that sport.

Financial Aid for Veterans, Military Personnel, and Their Dependents, 1988–1989. Gail Schlachter and R. David Weber. Redwood City, CA: Reference Service Press, 1988. 238 p. (10 Twin Dolphin Dr., Suite B-308) $32.50

Contains more than 600 references to programs open to applicants at all levels (from high school through postdoctoral) for education, research, travel, training, career development, or emergency situations.

Financial Aids for Higher Education Catalog: A Catalog for Undergraduates. 13th ed. Oreon Keesler. Dubuque, IA: William C. Brown Company Publishers, 1987. 758 p. (2460 Kerper Blvd., 52001) $36.95

Lists programs intended for both college freshmen and advanced students. Index includes donor agencies and foundations, common program names, subject areas, types of awards, and special eligibility characteristics. Updated every two years.

Five Federal Financial Aid Programs, 1987–1988: A Student Consumer's Guide. Washington, DC: US Department of Education, Annual (Box 84, 20044) free.

Grants for Graduate Students, 1986–1988: A directory of grants and fellowships. Andrea Leskes, ed. Princeton, NJ: Peterson's Guides, 1986. ix, 385 p. $29.95

How to Find Out about Financial Aid: A Guide to over 700 Directories Listing Scholarships, Fellowships, Loans, Grants, Awards, and Internships. Gail Ann Schlachter. Redwood City, CA: Reference Service Press, 1987. 334 p. (10 Twin Dolphin Drive, Suite B-308) $32.50

Identifies, classifies, describes, evaluates, and compares the more than 700 print and online directories that provide current information on financial aid opportunities.

Lovejoy's Guide to Financial Aid. 3rd ed. Robert Leider and Hanna Leider. Alexandria, VA: Octameron Associates, 1988. (4805A Eisenhower Ave., 22304) $10.95

Need a Lift? To Educational Opportunities, Careers, Loans, Scholarships, Employment. Indianapolis, IN: American Legion Education and Scholarship Program, Fall, 1986. 144 p. (The American Legion, Need a Lift? P.O. Box 1055, 46206) $1.00 prepaid

Paying for Your Education: A Guide for Adult Learners. 2nd ed. New York, NY: College Board Publications, 1983. 160 p. (Box 886, 10101) $7.95

The Right College: 1988. College Research Group of Concord, MA. West Nyack, NY: Prentice-Hall Press, 1987. xxxviii, 1545 p. (Simon and Schuster, Route 59 at Brook Hill Dr., 10994) $14.95

The Scholarship Book. Englewood Cliffs, NJ: Prentice-Hall, Inc., 1987. approx. 400 p. (West Nyack, NY 10995) $19.95
    Directory of over 1,100 potential sources of aid for undergraduates. Describes scholarships awarded by foundations, associations, armed forces, state and local governments, and individual colleges. Entries include scholarship name, address, phone number, amount of award, deadline, subject area, and an abridged description. Provides a list of over 300 career organizations and a bibliography. Includes indexes by major fields of study and by scholarship name.

Scholarships, Fellowships, and Loans: Volume 7. S. Norman Feingold and Marie Feingold. Arlington, MA: Bellman Publishing Co., 1982. 800 p. (02174-0164) $75.00/volume
    Lists a wide range of scholarships, fellowships, loans, grants, and awards not controlled by the college or university. Includes index which lists awards according to specific educational or occupational goals. Material is dated. Check with funder before applying.

Scholarships, Fellowships, and Loans: Volume 8. S. Norman Feingold and Marie Feingold. Arlington, MA: Bellman Publishing Co., 1987. (02174-0164) $80.00
    Similar to Volume 7 in format but includes different awards.

The Student Guide: Five Federal Financial Aid Programs 87–88. Washington, DC: Government Printing Office, 1987. 61 p. (Superintendent of Documents, 20402) free.

Winning Money for College: The High School Student's Guide to Scholarship Contests. Allen Deutschman. Princeton, NJ: Peterson's Guides, 1987. 219 p. (P.O. Box 2123, 08540) $8.95

GRANTS FOR MINORITIES AND WOMEN

Better Late Than Never: Financial Aid for Older Women Seeking Education and Training. Washington, DC: Women's Equity Action League, 1985. 43 p. (1250 I St., NW, Suite 305, 20005) $8.00
    Focuses on programs that provide financial aid for women who need to train or retrain for a career. Apprenticeships are also included.

Directory of Financial Aids for Minorities, 1988–89. Gail A. Schlachter, ed. with Sandra E. Goldstein. Redwood City, CA: Reference Service Press, 1988. 440 p. (10 Twin Dolphin Drive, Suite B-308, 94065) $42.50
    The Directory is divided into four separate sections: financial aids designed primarily or exclusively for minorities, a list of state sources for educational benefits, an annotated bibliography of directories and five sets of indexes by program title, sponsoring organization, geographic, subject and calendar filing dates. Over 1,800 references and cross references to scholarships, fellowships, loans, grants, awards, internships, state sources of educational benefits and general financial aid directories are included.

Directory of Financial Aids for Women, 1987–1988. Gail Ann Schlachter, ed. with Sandra E. Goldstein, Redwood City, CA: Reference Service Press, 1987. 420 p. (10 Twin Dolphin Drive, Suite B-308, 94065) $35.00

Lists scholarships, fellowships, loans, grants, internships, awards, and prizes designed for women. Also includes women's credit unions and sources of state educational benefits. Also includes international programs, more than 1,700 references to scholarships, etc. Annotated bibliography; indexed by sponsoring organization, geographic location, and subject.

Directory of Special Programs for Minority Group Members: Career Information Services, Employment Skills Banks, Financial Aid Sources. Willis L. Johnson, ed. 4th ed. Garrett Park, MD: Garrett Park Press, 1986. 348 p. (20896)

Lists financial assistance available to undergraduate, graduate and postgraduate women.

Financial Aid for the Disabled and Their Families, 1988–1989. Gail Ann Schlachter and R. David Weber. Redwood City, CA: Reference Service Press, 1988. 230 p. (10 Twin Dolphin Dr., Suite B-308) $32.50

All disabilities are covered, including visual impairments, hearing impairments, development disabilities, learning disabilities, and multiple disabilities. Also identifies state educational offices, state agencies concerned with the disabled and the 75 key directories to locate additional sources of financial aid.

Financial Aid for Minorities in Health Fields. Garrett Park, MD: Garrett Park Press, 1987. (20896) $4.00

Financial Aid for Minorities in Business and Law. Garrett Park, MD: Garrett Park Press, 1987. (20896) $4.00

Financial Aid for Minorities in Education. Garrett Park, MD: Garrett Park Press, 1987. (20896) $4.00

Financial Aid for Minorities in Journalism and Mass Communications. Garrett Park, MD: Garrett Park Press, 1987. (20896) $4.00

Financial Aid: A Partial List of Resources for Women. Washington, DC: Project on the Status and Education of Women, Association of American Colleges, Jan., 1987. 18 p. (1818 R St., NW, 20009) $3.50

Includes programs geared toward older women, returning students, minority women, and those in professional and technical programs, as well as programs open to students of both sexes. Selected bibliography.

Higher Education Opportunities for Minorities and Women: Annotated Selections. Washington, DC: U.S. Education Department, 1985, 103 p. (20402) $5.50

Includes specific loan, scholarship, and fellowship opportunities, as well as information on how to seek guidance about educational and career goals.

How to Get Money for Research. Mary Rubin and the Business and Professional Women's Foundation. Westbury, NY: The Feminist Press, 1983. xiii, 78 p. (P.O. Box 334, 11568) $6.95

A guide to research funding opportunities for and about women at the pre- and post-doctoral levels. This book was compiled for women scholars, researchers, and others pursuing research questions about women.

Minority Student Opportunities in United States Medical Schools 1988–89. 10th ed. Mary T. Cureton, ed. Washington, DC: Association of American Medical Colleges, 1988. approx. 317 p. (One Dupont Circle, NW, 20036) $7.50

"1988 Scholarship Guide." *Women's Sports.* New York, NY: Women's Sports Foundation, 1984. 12 p. (342 Madison Ave., Suite 728, 10173) $2.00
    Lists institutions offering financial aid to women athletes.

NSF Visiting Professorships for Women. Washington, DC: National Science Foundation, 1985. 20 p.

Women of Color. Sasha Hohri and Adisa Douglas. Washington, DC: National Network for Grantmakers, 1986. 24 p. (2000 P Street, NW, Suite 410 Washington, DC 20036) $5.00

Women's Organizations: A National Directory. Martha Merrill Doss, ed. Garrett Park, MD: Garrett Park Press, 1986. 302 p. (Garrett Park, MD 20896) $18.00
    Lists over 1,000 funding sources for women seeking educational and career opportunities.

GRANTS IN PARTICULAR SUBJECT FIELDS

Arts

A Tax Guide for Artists and Arts Organizations. Herrick Lidstone ed. Lexington, MA: Lexington Books, 1979, xi, 378 p.

American Art Directory. New York, NY: Jaques Cattell Press, R.R. Bowker Co., 1988. x, 740 p. (245 W. 17th St., 10011)
    Includes a section listing art scholarships and fellowships available through various organizations including museums and colleges.

Artist Colonies. John Thompson. New York, NY: Center for Arts Information, 1986. 19 p. (1285 Ave. of the Americas, 3rd Floor, 10019) $4.00
    Artists colonies are briefly covered including the name of the colony, address, and phone number. Also included is information on the residency season, application deadline and financial assistance available.

Artsmoney: Raising It, Saving It, and Earning It. Joan Jeffri. New York, NY: Neal-Schuman Publishers, Inc., 1983. 291 p. (23 Cornelia St. 10014) $24.95

Dance Magazine's Performing Arts Directory. New York, NY: Dance Magazine, Inc., 1988. approx. 500 p. (33 W. 60th St., 10023) $37.89
    Emphasis on all aspects of dance, but of particular interest are sections on funding agencies and programs, sponsors and spaces for dance, organizations and councils for

dance and the arts, sources and resources (information and merchandise for the dance world), and dance education directory.

Dramatists Sourcebook, 1986–87 Edition. New York, NY: Theatre Communications Group, Inc., 1985. 230 p. (355 Lexington Ave., 10017) approx. $12.00
    A guide to fellowships and grants, contests and awards, emergency funds, artist colonies for translators, lyricists, librettists, composers, as well as playwrights. Also includes information on conferences, festivals, workshops, residencies and artist colonies.

Guide to Women's Art Organizations and Directory for the Arts. Cynthia Navaretta. New York, NY: Midmarch Associates, 1983. vi, 174 p. Has inserts for successive years. (Box 3304, Grand Central Station, 10163) $8.50
    Information on visual and performing arts, crafts, writing, film. The financial help and work opportunities section has information on emergency funds, artists' colonies and residences, studying abroad, and grants, awards, fellowship resources.

Guide to NEA. Washington, DC: National Endowment for the Arts, Annual. 52 p. (1100 Pennsylvania Ave., Washington, DC 20506) free
    Overview of funding programs offered by the NEA.

Money Business: Grants and Awards for Creative Artists. Boston, MA: The Artists Foundation, Inc., Revised ed. 1982. 130 p. (110 Broad St., 02110) Out of print but available in some libraries.
    Directory of organizations that offer financial assistance to poets, fiction writers, playwrights, filmmakers, video artists, composers, choreographers, painters, printmakers, sculptors, craftsmen and photographers. Aid is for both independent artists and students for special projects.

Money for Artists: A guide to grants and awards for individual artists. Laura Green, ed. New York, NY: Center for Arts Information, 1983. 6 p. (625 Broadway, 10012) $3.00

National Directory of Grants and Aid to Individuals in the Arts, International. Washington, DC: Washington International Arts Letter, Annual. approx 230 p. (Box 12010, Des Moines, IA 50312) $25.00
    Brief listings of grants, prizes, and awards for professional work in the U.S. and abroad; includes information about universities and schools with special aid to students.

New York City Arts Funding Guide. New York, NY: Center for Arts Information, 1985. 91 p. (625 Broadway, 10012) $13.95

Supporting Yourself as an Artist. Deborah A. Hoover. New York, NY: Oxford University Press, 1985. x, 246 p. (200 Madison Ave., 10016) $6.95 paper

Whole Arts Directory. Cynthia Nararetta. New York, NY: Midmarch Associates, 1987. (Box 3304, Grand Central Station, 10163) $12.95

Crafts

The Crafts Business Encyclopedia: Marketing, Management, and Money. Michael Scott. New York, NY: Harcourt Brace Jovanovich, 1979. xviii, 286 p. (465 S. Lincoln Drive, Troy, MO 63379) $4.95 + $.75 postage and handling.

Focuses primarily on managing a crafts business with such areas as management, insurance, labor and employees, legal affairs, accounting, banking, pricing, taxes, selling and marketing. A section on organizations of interest to craftspeople and a chapter on grants is included.

How to Enter and Win Fabric and Fiber Crafts Contests. Alan Gadney. New York, NY: Facts on File Publications, 1983. xviii, 202 p. (460 Park Ave. South, 10016) Out of print but available in some libraries.

How to Enter and Win Jewelry and Metal Crafts Contests. Alan Gadney. New York, NY: Facts on File Publications, 1983. xviii, 204 p. (460 Park Ave. South, 10016) Out of print but available in some libraries.

Engineering (See also Internships/Employment, Mathematics and Sciences)

Official Register 1988. New York, NY: American Society of Civil Engineers, 1988. 332 p. (345 E. 47th St., 10017) free

History

Fellowships and Grants of Interest to Historians, 1988–89. Washington, DC: American Historical Association, Annual. approx. 154 p. (400 A St., SE, 20003) $6.00

Lists sources of funding for graduate students, postdoctoral researchers and scholars in history. Published in June.

Humanities

Directory of Grants in the Humanities: 1987. Phoenix, AZ: Oryx Press, Annual. vi, 426 p. (2214 N. Central, 85004-1483) $74.50

Contains over 2,500 programs by foundations, federal and state government agencies, corporations, professional organizations and associations which fund both research and performance projects.

Grants in the Humanities: A scholar's guide to funding sources, 2nd ed. William E. Coleman. New York, NY: Neal-Schuman Publishers, Inc., 1984. xiv, 152 p. (23 Leonard Place 10013) $26.50

This publication focuses on grantsmanship for the individual grantseeker and covers preparation of the essential parts of a proposal, along with a sample proposal and budget. Coverage of funders in the humanities is provided. The audience for which this book was compiled is the humanities scholar interested in sources of funding for postdoctoral research.

Overview of Endowment Programs. Washington, DC: National Endowment for the Humanities, Annual. (1100 Pennsylvania Ave., NW, 20506) free
　　Annual overview of funding programs offered by the NEH.

Internships/Employment

1988 Internships: On-the-job training opportunities for all types of careers. Kathy Jobst, ed. Cincinnati, OH: Writer's Digest Books, 1988, approx. 423 p. (1507 Dana Ave., 45207) $14.95

National Directory of Arts Internships. Warren Christensen. Valencia, CA: California Institute of the Arts, 1986. 373 p. (Office of Career Development and Placement 24700 McBean Parkway, 91355) $25

Peterson's Guide to Engineering, Science, and Computer Jobs, 1988. Sandra Grundfest, ed. Princeton, NJ: Peterson's Guides, Annual. (P.O. Box 2123, 08540) $19.95
　　This guide is more career-oriented and includes information on job-related graduate study, postdoctoral appointments, summer employment, co-op education programs, and advice on getting a job.

1988 Summer Employment Directory of the United States. Barbara Norton Kuroff, ed. Cincinnati, OH: Writer's Digest Books, 1988. (1507 Dana Ave., 45207) $9.95
　　Lists paying jobs including summer, seasonal, part-time and some full-time. An international section lists jobs abroad for U.S. students.

Library Sciences

Financial Assistance for Library Education, Academic Year 1988–89. Chicago, IL: American Library Association, Annual. approx. 52 p. (Standing Committee on Library Education, 50 East Huron St., 60611) $1.00
　　Annually revised list of awards from state library agencies, national and state library associations, local libraries, academic institutions, national associations, foundations, and other agencies giving financial assistance for library education.

Mathematics and Sciences

"Assistantships and Fellowships in the Mathematical Sciences" 1987–1988 in *NOTICES of the American Mathematical Society*, December issue annually. (American Mathematical Society, P.O. Box 1571, Annex Station, Providence, RI 02901) $9.00 prepaid

Directory of Grants in the Physical Sciences 1987. Phoenix, AZ: Oryx Press, Annual. 299 p. (2214 N. Central, 85004-1483).

Free Money for Science Students. Laurie Blum. New York, NY: Harper and Row, 1985. 204 p. (10 E. 53rd St., 10022) Out of print but available in some libraries.
　　State-by-state listings of scholarships and grants from over 1,000 foundations. Some are "science" oriented but many are general.

Graduate Assistantships Directory in the Computer Sciences. New York, NY: Association for Computing Machinery. Biennial. (Association for Computing Machinery, P.O. Box 64145, Baltimore, MD 21264) approx. $10.00/nonmembers

 Lists U.S. universities that offer fellowships and scholarships for the study of computer science.

Grants for Scientific and Engineering Research. Washington, DC: National Science Foundation, 1985. iv, 32 p.

National Science Foundation Guide to Programs. Washington, DC: National Science Foundation. Annual. (Publications Office, 1800 G St., NW, 20550) free

 Lists foundation programs in various areas of scientific research. Describes NSF criteria for selection of research projects.

Media and Communications

Fact File #3—Film/Video Festivals and Awards. Washington, DC: The American Film Institute. Education Services. 1985. 109 p. (2021 N. Western, P.O. Box 27999, Los Angeles, CA 90027) $5.00 members, $6.00 non-members prepaid

Gadney's Guide to 1800 International Contests, Festivals and Grants in Film and Video, Photography, TV-Radio Broadcasting, Writing, Poetry, Playwriting, and Journalism. Alan Gadney. Glendale, CA: Festival Publications, 1980. xv, 578 p. (P.O. Box 10180, 91209) $15.95 plus $1.75 postage

 Includes national and international contests, festivals, competitions, exhibitions, markets, and award/sales events, as well as grants, loans, scholarships, fellowships, residencies, apprenticeships, internships, and training programs. Indexed by event, sponsor, award, and subject area. Awarded Outstanding Reference Book of the Year by the American Library Association.

Get the Money and Shoot: The DRI guide to funding documentary films. Bruce Jackson and Diane Christian. Buffalo, NY: Documentary Research, Inc., 1987. v, 161 p. (96 Rumsey Road, 14209) $20.00 plus $2.00 postage

 This volume, aimed at filmmakers, covers how to find out about money, getting a sponsor, and preparing your budget and proposal.

1988 Journalism Career and Scholarship Guide. Princeton, NJ: The Newspaper Fund, Annual. 172 p. (P.O. Box 300, 00543-0300) Single copies free; two or more at $2.50/copy

 Annual guide to aid offered through schools and departments of journalism in U.S. and Canadian colleges and universities, by newspapers, professional societies, and miscellaneous sources. Section on grants specifically designed for minority students.

Making Films Your Business. Mollie Gregory. New York, NY: Schocken Books, 1979. xiv, 256 p. (201 E. 50th St., 10022) $8.95 paper

 Briefly covers writing proposals to foundations, foundations as sources of support, and the appendix mentions foundations which have an interest in funding films.

Sponsors: A Guide for Video and Filmmakers. Debra Goldman and Laura Green. New York, NY: Clearinghouse for Arts Information, Inc., 1987. 45 p. (Center for Arts Information, 1285 Ave. of Americas, 3rd fl., 10019) $6.00

What a sponsor is, how to find one, and how to interview one for a project.

Medicine/Health

Arthritis Fellowships and Research Grants for Non-Physician Health Professionals: Information for applicants. Atlanta, GA: Arthritis Foundation, brochure. (3400 Peachtree Road, NE, 30326)

Medical School Admission Requirements 1989–90, United States and Canada. Washington, DC: Association of American Medical Colleges, Annual. 366 p. (One Dupont Circle, NW, 20036) $10.00

Includes information on undergraduate financial planning, sources of financial aid at the medical school and post-M.D. levels, and financial resources for minority and disadvantaged students.

Research Fellowships Related to the Rheumatic Diseases: Information for applicants. Atlanta, GA: Arthritis Foundation, brochure. (3400 Peachtree Road, NE, 30326)

Scholarships and Loans for Nursing Education. New York, NY: National League for Nursing. 1987–88. approx. 30 p. (10 Columbus Circle, 10019) $8.95

Music

Career Guide for Young American Singers from the US and Canada. Central Opera Service Bulletin. New York, NY: Central Opera Service, 1985. approx. 70 p. (Metropolitan Opera, Lincoln Center, 10023) $9.50 (Includes update). Updates published biennially.

Provides information on grants for American singers, grants for study abroad, American vocal competitions, foreign vocal competitions, apprenticeships. A section on American and Canadian opera companies is also provided.

Music Industry Directory. 7th ed., 1983. Chicago, IL: Marquis Academic Media, 1983. 678 p. (Marquis Who's Who, Inc., 200 E. Ohio St., 60611) Out of print but available in libraries.

Has sections on foundations, music competitions and festivals, and information on scholarships and awards.

Opportunities for Composers. Ellen Schantz. New York, NY: American Music Center, 1987. 25 p. (250 W. 54th St., Suite 300, 10019) $8.00

Songwriter's Market: 1988: Where to sell your songs. Cincinnati, OH: Writer's Digest Books, 1988. 432 p. (1507 Dana Ave., 45207) $16.95

Focuses on music publishers, record companies and record producers, managers and booking agencies, but does include a section on awards and contests.

Pharmacology

Clinical Pharmacology: A Guide to Training Programs. 6th ed. Barbara C. Ready, ed. Princeton, NJ: Peterson's Guides, 1985. 150 p. (Box 2123, 08540)

Philosophy

Grants and Fellowship Opportunities of Interest to Philosophers. Vol. 60, #5, June 1987. Newark, DE: American Philosophical Association, 1986. approx. 50 p. (University of Delaware, 19716) approx. $5.00 prepaid
    Annual publication lists fellowships and grant opportunities available from sixty different sources.

Photography

Photographer's Market: 1988: Where to sell your photography. Cincinnati, OH: Writer's Digest Books, 1985. 567 p. (1507 Dana Ave., 45207) $18.95

Political Science

Guide to Graduate Study in Political Science, 1986. rev. 12th ed. Patricia Spellman, comp. Washington, DC: American Political Science Association, 1986. 430 p. (1527 New Hampshire Ave., NW, 20036) $20.00 for non-APSA members
    Describes approximately 300 masters and doctoral programs in political science; includes financial aid information and faculty listings for each program.

Research Support for Political Scientists: A Guide to Sources of Funds for Research Fellowships, Grants, and Contracts. Compiled by Stephen F. Szabo. Washington, DC: American Political Science Association, 1981. viii, 126 p. (Departmental Services program, 1527 New Hampshire Ave., NW, 20036) $6.00
    Includes information on research fellowships, doctoral dissertation grants and fellowships, foundation research grants and U.S. government grants and contracts.

Psychology

Supplement may recces?

APA Guide to Research Support. 2nd ed. Ralph E. Dusek, et al., eds. Washington, DC: American Psychological Association, 1984. 376 p. (1200 17th St., NW, 20036) $25.00
    Covers over 150 federally-funded programs for behavioral science research.

Sciences (See Mathematics and Sciences)

Social Sciences

Fellowships and Grants for Training and Research: To Be Offered in 1987–88. New York, NY: Social Science Research Council, 1987. 64 p. (605 Third Ave., 10158) free
    Describes the several foreign area fellowship and grant programs the Council sponsors jointly with American Council of Learned Societies. Research Training Fellowships offer support for training in the Social Sciences. Foreign area programs offer dissertation fellowships and postdoctoral research grants in both the social sciences and the humanities.

Writing

Grants and Awards Available to American Writers. 14th ed. New York, NY: P.E.N. American Center, 1987. approx. 90 p. (47 Fifth Ave., 10003)

A comprehensive list of awards available to American and Canadian writers for use in the U.S. or abroad. Appendix of American State Arts Councils.

Literary and Library Prizes. New York, NY: R.R. Bowker Co., 1984. x, 651 p. (1180 Ave. of the Americas, 10036) $26.95

Literary Market Place 1988: The Directory of American Book Publishing. New York, NY: R.R. Bowker Co., 1987. 1181 p. (245 W. 17th St., 10011) $85.00

Includes literary awards, contests, fellowships, and grants.

Writer's Market: 1988. Cincinnati, OH: Writer's Digest Books, 1988. 1,056 p. (1507 Dana Ave., 45207) $21.95

GRANTS FOR INTERNATIONAL STUDY, TRAVEL, AND STUDY ABROAD

AAASS Directory of Programs in Soviet and East European Studies, 1987–89. Stanford, CA: American Association for the Advancement of Slavic Studies, 1987. 270 p. (Stanford University, 128 Encina Commons, 94305-6029)

Awards, Honors and Prizes. 7th ed. Volume 2. International and Foreign. Paul Wasserman, ed. Detroit, MI: Gale Research Company, 1987. 640 p. (Order Department, Book Tower, 48226-9948) $180

Basic Facts on Foreign Study. New York, NY: Institute of International Education, 1987. approx 32 p. (809 United Nations Plaza, 10017) Single copies free.

A guide for U.S. students planning study abroad.

Directory of Financial Aids for International Activities. 4th ed. Minneapolis, MN: Office of International Programs, University of Minnesota, 1985. approx 440 p. (201 Nolte West, 315 Pillsbury Drive, SE, 55455) $20.00

Covers grants to individuals interested in international activities or in studying abroad.

Fellowship Guide to Western Europe. 6th ed. New York, NY: Council for European Studies, 1985. approx. 100 p. (1509 International Affairs, Columbia University, 10027) $5.00

Fellowships, Scholarships, and Related Opportunities in International Education. Knoxville, TN: University of Tennessee, 1985. unpaged. (Division of International Education, 205 Alumni Hall, 37916) $5.00 + $1.45 postage and handling

Fulbright Grants and Other Grants for Graduate Study Abroad. New York, NY: Institute of International Education, Annual. (809 United Nations Plaza, 10017) free

Lists 11E-administered financial assistance programs available to U.S. graduate students for study abroad.

Funding for Research, Study and Travel: The People's Republic of China. Denise Wallen and Karen Cantrell eds. Phoenix, AZ: Oryx Press, 1987. 230 p. (2214 N. Central, 85004-1483) $27.50

Organizations which sponsor research, study and travel support for students and professional scholars in the People's Republic of China. Approximately 300 programs are alphabetically listed by sponsor's name.

Scholarships for International Students: A Complete Guide to Colleges and Universities in the United States 1986–88. Middleburg Hts, OH: Scholarship Research Group, 1986. vi, 271 p. (16600 Sprague Rd., Suite 110, 44130) $14.95

Study Abroad, 1988–89. Paris: UNESCO, 1988. approx. 1,000 p. (Bernan-Unipub, 4611-F Assembly Dr., Lanham, MD 20706-4391) approx. $15.00
Listing in three languages of scholarships and courses offered by foreign universities and international and national organizations and institutions. The term scholarship is used to include all forms of financial or material aid for study abroad.

The Learning Traveler: Volume 1. Academic Year Abroad. Howard Edrice, ed. New York, NY: Institute of International Education, Annual. (809 United Nations Plaza, 10017) $19.95
Lists by country over 800 semester and academic-year study programs abroad (for undergraduates) that are sponsored by accredited U.S. colleges and universities.

The Learning Traveler: Volume II. Vacation Study Abroad. Howard Edrice, ed. New York, NY: Institute of International Education, Annual. (809 United Nations Plaza, 10017) $19.95
Lists by country about 900 spring, summer, and early fall study programs offered in countries around the world by U.S. and foreign institutions and private organizations.

The Young American's Scholarship Guide to Travel and Learning Abroad. Joseph Lurie ed. New York, NY: Intravco Press, 1986. 204 p. (211 E. 43rd St., Suite 1303, 10017) $12.95
Comprehensive guide designed for young Americans seeking pre-college learning experience abroad. Examines descriptions of more than 4,000 scholarship opportunities offered by 70 organizations in over 80 countries.

SOURCES FOR AFFILIATING WITH OR FORMING A NONPROFIT ORGANIZATION

Arts Money: Raising It, Saving It, and Earning It. Joan Jeffri. New York, NY: Neal-Schuman Publishers, 1983. 291 p. (23 Leonard St., 10013) $24.95
As the title suggests, plus useful advice on considering and choosing an organizational format.

The California Non-Profit Corporation Handbook. Anthony Mancuso. Berkeley, CA: Nolo Press, 1988. 288 p. (950 Parker St., 94710) $24.95
A guide to preparing articles and bylaws, obtaining exempt status, keeping legal records, choosing a lawyer, etc.

Cumulative List of Organizations. Department of the Treasury. Internal Revenue Service. Publication number 78. Washington, DC: U.S. Government Printing Office, Annual. (Superintendent of Documents, 20402) approx. $38.00. Subscription includes three yearly updates.
Lists organizations to whom contributions are deductible. The list is not all-inclusive. If an organization is not listed but has a ruling or an IRS determination letter holding

contributions to be deductible, generally the letter will serve as evidence to contributors of the deductibility of their contributors.

Encyclopedia of Associations, Volume 1: National Organizations of the United States. 1988, Detroit, MI: Gale Research, Biannual. (Book Tower, 48226) $210.00
    Updated every two years in three volumes. Includes about 20,000 organizations with 17 broad subject categories, e.g., scientific, cultural, social welfare, fraternal, etc. Many associations can offer or suggest funding possibilities and other types of support for your work.

How to Set Up and Operate a Non-Profit Organization. Carole C. Upshur. Englewood Cliffs, NJ: Prentice-Hall, Inc., 1982. 252 p. (07632) Out of print but available in some libraries.
    Guidelines for incorporating, raising funds and writing grant proposals.

Instructions for Form 990, 1987: Return of Organization Exempt from Income Tax. Washington, DC: Government Printing Office, Annual. 12 p. (Superintendent of Documents, 20402)

National VLA Directory, 1987. Volunteer Lawyers for the Arts. New York, NY: Volunteer Lawyers for the Arts, 1987. (1285 Ave. of the Americas, 10019) $5.00
    Describes Volunteer Lawyers for the Arts program throughout the U.S.—and one in Canada. VLAs are groups of lawyers that will provide legal services for free or at a reduced rate to artists and nonprofit groups.

New York Not-for-Profit Organization Manual. rev. ed. New York, NY: Council of New York Law Associates, 1985. 190 p. (99 Hudson St., 10013) $25.00
    An attorney's guide to incorporating in New York State and gaining tax-exempt status.

The Nonprofit Organization Handbook. 2nd ed. New York, NY: McGraw-Hill, 1988. 800 p. (1221 Ave. of the Americas, 10020) $64.95
    A desk reference on organizing and operating nonprofit organizations.

Research Centers Directory. Detroit, MI: Gale Research, Annual. (Book Tower, 48226)
    A guide to approximately 8,300 university-related and other nonprofit research organizations in 17 broad subject areas. An excellent guide to finding out what's being done where.

Securing Your Organization's Future: A Complete Guide to Fundraising Strategies. Michael Seltzer. New York, NY: Foundation Center, 1987. xiv, 514 p. (79 Fifth Ave., 10003) $19.95

Starting and Running a Nonprofit Organization. Joan Hummel. Minneapolis, MN: University of Minnesota Press, 1980. 147 p. (2037 University Ave. Southeast, 55414) $20.00 cloth, $11.95 paper
    Basic guide for putting together a small, nonprofit organization.

Tax Exempt Status for Your Organization. Publication 557. Department of the Treasury. Internal Revenue Service. Washington, DC: U.S. Government Printing Office. (Superintendent of Documents, 20402) free

To Be or Not to Be: An Artist's Guide to Not-for-Profit Incorporation. Volunteer Lawyers for the Arts. New York, NY: Volunteer Lawyers for the Arts, 1986. 12 p. (1560 Broadway, Suite 711, 10036) $3.00 plus postage

Covers the critical questions you should ask yourself and your attorney about nonprofit incorporation.

Publications and Services of The Foundation Center

The Foundation Center is a national service organization founded and supported by foundations to provide a single authoritative source of information on foundation giving. The Center's programs are designed to help grantseekers as they begin to select from over 25,000 active U.S. foundations those which may be most interested in their projects. Among its primary activities toward this end are publishing reference books on foundations and foundation grants and disseminating information on foundations through a nationwide public service program.

Publications of The Foundation Center are the primary working tools of every serious grantseeker. They are also used by grantmakers, scholars, journalists, regulators, and legislators—in short, everyone seeking any type of factual information on foundation philanthropy. All private foundations actively engaged in grantmaking, regardless of size or geographic location, are included in one or more of the Center's publications. The publications are of three kinds: directories that describe specific foundations, characterizing their program interests and providing fiscal and personnel data; grants indexes that list and classify by subject recent foundation awards; and guides, brochures, and bibliographies which introduce the reader to funding research, elements of proposal writing, as well as other sources of information.

Foundation Center publications may be ordered from The Foundation Center, 79 Fifth Avenue, New York, NY 10003. For more information about any aspect of the Center's program or for the name of the Center's library collection nearest you, call toll-free (800) 424-9836.

THE FOUNDATION DIRECTORY, 11th EDITION

The Foundation Directory has been widely known and respected in the field for 25 years. It includes the latest information on all foundations whose assets exceed $1 million or whose annual grant total is $100,000 or more. The new 11th Edition is the biggest ever: 5148 foundations are included, 983 of which are new to the *Directory* this year, and 781 of which are corporate foundations. *Directory* foundations hold over $89 billion in assets and award $5.3 billion in grants annually, accounting for 92% of all U.S. foundation dollars awarded in 1985 and 1986. The 11th Edition documents a period of remarkable growth in the foundation field and a resurgence in the creation of *Directory* foundations. It lists entries on 446 foundations created in the 1980s, including 5 with assets in excess of $100 million.

Each *Directory* entry now contains more precise information on application procedures, giving limitations, types of support awarded, the publications of each foundation, and foundation staff—all this in addition to such vital data as the grantmakers' giving interests, financial data, grant amounts, addresses and telephone numbers. The Foundation Center works closely with foundations to ensure the accuracy and timeliness of the information provided. Among the largest foundations, the response rate to requests for information for the 11th Edition exceeded 85 percent and nearly 80 percent provided 1986 or early 1987 data.

The *Directory* includes indexes by foundation name; subject areas of interest; names of donors, trustees, and officers; geographic location; and the types of support awarded. Also included are analyses of the foundation community by geography, asset and grant size, different types of foundations, trends in foundation establishment, and information on the effects of inflation on the field since 1975.

11th Edition, Oct. 1987. 1001 pages. ISBN 0-87954-199-7. $85

COMSEARCH PRINTOUTS
This popular series of computer-produced guides to foundation giving derived from The Foundation Center Database is now issued in four separate categories:

COMSEARCH: Broad Topics
This series indexes and analyzes recent foundation grants in 27 broad subject categories. Each listing includes all grants in the particular subject area reported to The Foundation Center during the preceding year, along with an index listing name and geographic location of organizations which have received grants, a geographic index arranged by state of the organization which received grants, and a key word index listing descriptive words and phrases which link a foundation's giving interests with your organization's field. *COMSEARCH: Broad Topics* includes grants for:

Aged
Arts & Cultural Programs
Business & Employment
Children & Youth
Community & Urban Development
Crime & Law Enforcement
Elementary & Secondary Education (Public & Private Schools)
Environmental Law, Protection & Education
Family Services
Film, Media & Communications
Higher Education
Hospitals
International & Foreign Programs
Libraries & Information Services
Matching & Challenge Support
Medical & Professional Health Education

Minorities
Museums
Physically & Mentally Disabled
Professional Associations & Societies
Public Health
Public Policy & Political Science
Recreation
Religion & Religious Education
Science Programs
Social Science Programs
Women & Girls

Series published annually in July. $40 each

COMSEARCH: Subjects
This series includes 31 specially focused subject listings of grants reported to The Foundation Center during the preceding year. Listings are arranged by the state where the foundation is located and then by foundation name, and include complete information on the name and location of the grant recipient, the amount awarded, and the purpose of the grant. *COMSEARCH: Subjects* may be purchased as a complete set on microfiche or individually by particular subject area of interest in paper or microfiche form. A full list of categories follows:

Order Number/Title
Education
  15. Adult & Continuing Education
  18. Higher Education—Capital Support
  19. Higher Education—Endowments
  20. Higher Education—Faculty and Professorships
  22. Scholarships, Student Aid & Loans
  24. Educational Research
  25. Vocational Education, Career Development & Employment
  26. International Studies, Education & Exchange
Health
  30. Health & Medical Care—Cost Containment
  32. Medical Research & Advancement
  34. Nursing

37. Mental Health
39. Alcohol & Drug Abuse
40. Cancer Care & Research
41. Hospices
43. Children & Youth—Health Programs

Cultural Activities

47. Theater
50. Architecture, Historical Preservation &
    Historical Societies

Welfare

91. Legal Services
95. Child Abuse
101. Animal Welfare & Wildlife
102. Rural Development
107. Volunteer Programs
108. Homeless

Other

3. Language, Literature & Journalism
66. Hispanics
79. Computer Science & Systems
110. Nonprofit Management
111. Philanthropy & Nonprofit Sector
     Research
112. Governmental Agencies
114. Conferences & Seminars

Series published annually in July. $125 micro-
fiche set; $20 per subject on paper; $8 per
subject on microfiche

COMSEARCH: Geographics

This series provides customized listings of
grants received by organizations in two cities,
eleven states, and seven regions. These listings
make it easy to see which major foundations
have awarded grants in your area, to which
nonprofit organizations, and what each grant
was intended to accomplish. Listings are
available for Washington, D.C., New York City,
California, Illinois, Massachusetts, Michigan,
Minnesota, New Jersey, New York State
(excluding New York City), North Carolina,
Ohio, Pennsylvania, Texas, the Northeast
(Maine, New Hampshire, Rhode Island,
Vermont, Connecticut), Southeast (Florida,

Georgia, Alabama, Mississippi, Louisiana, South
Carolina, Tennessee), Northwest (Alaska,
Hawaii, Washington and Oregon), the Rocky
Mountains (Arizona, New Mexico, Colorado,
Utah, Nevada, Idaho, Montana, Wyoming),
South Atlantic (Delaware, Maryland, Virginia),
Central Midwest (Arkansas, Indiana, Iowa,
Kansas, Kentucky, Missouri, Oklahoma, West
Virginia), Upper Midwest (Nebraska, North
Dakota, South Dakota, Wisconsin).

Series published annually in July. $35 each

COMSEARCH: Special Topics

These are three of the most frequently requested special listings from the Center's computer databases. The three special listings are:

- The 1,000 Largest U.S. Foundations by
  Asset Size,
- The 1,000 Largest U.S. Foundations by
  Annual Grants Total,
- The over 2,000 Operating Foundations
  that Administer Their Own Projects or
  Programs.

Series published annually in July. $20 each

THE FOUNDATION GRANTS INDEX ANNUAL, 17TH EDITION

The Foundation Grants Index Annual lists the
grants of $5,000 or more awarded to nonprofit
organizations by 465 foundations. It is the
most thorough subject index available to the
actual grants of major U.S. foundations, including the top 100 grantmakers.

The 17th Edition is the largest annual
Index ever, with an expanded analytical introduction, an improved and enlarged subject
index, and more grant descriptions than ever
before—more than 43,000 grants of $5,000 or
more made to nonprofit organizations reported to the Center in 1986/1987. The
volume is arranged alphabetically by state,
then by foundation name. Each entry includes
the amount and date of the grant, name and

location of the recipient, a description of the grant, and any known limitations of the foundation's giving pattern. The grants are indexed by subject and geographic location, by the names of the recipient organizations, and by a multitude of key words describing all aspects of each grant. The grants total over $2 billion and represent about 45% of all foundation giving, making this the most comprehensive grants compilation available.

The Foundation Grants Index Annual is the reference used by educators, librarians, fundraisers, medical personnel, and other professionals interested in learning about foundation grants. It shows you what kind of organizations and programs the major foundations have been funding.

17th Edition, 1988. ISBN 0-87954-241-1. $55

THE FOUNDATION GRANTS INDEX BIMONTHLY

This unique subscription service keeps your fundraising program up-to-date, bringing you important new information on foundation funding every other month. Each issue of *The Foundation Grants Index Bimonthly* brings you descriptions of over 2,000 recent foundation grants, arranged by state and indexed by subjects and recipients. This enables you to zero in on grants made in your subject area within your geographic region. You can use the *Bimonthly* to target potential sources of funding for medical schools in Washington D.C., for example, modern dance troupes in New York, or any other combination of factors.

The *Bimonthly* also contains updates on grantmakers, noting changes in foundation address, personnel, program interests, and application procedures. Also included is a list of grantmakers' publications—annual reports, information brochures, grants lists, and newsletters. *The Foundation Grants Index*

Bimonthly is a trusted current-awareness tool used by professional fundraisers.

Annual subscription $32 /6 issues
ISSN 0735-2522

SOURCE BOOK PROFILES

Source Book Profiles is an annual subscription service offering detailed descriptions of the 1,000 largest foundations, analyzing giving patterns by subject area, type of support, and type of recipient. The service operates on a two-year publishing cycle, with each one-year series covering 500 foundations. Each quarterly installment includes 125 new profiles as well as information on changes in address, telephone, personnel, or program, and a revised, cumulative set of indexes to all 1,000 foundations covered in the two-year cycle by name, subject interest, type of grants awarded, and city and state location or concentration of giving.

1988 Series / $295 annual subscription /
ISBN 0-87954-235-7
1987 Cumulative Volume (500 Profiles) /
$285 / ISBN 0-87954-195-4

CORPORATE FOUNDATION PROFILES, 5TH EDITION

This newly updated volume includes comprehensive information on corporate direct giving programs *and* company-sponsored foundations. A total of 720 grantmakers with assets of $1 million or annual giving of $100,000 or more are listed with full subject, type of support, and geographic indexes. Detailed profiles of the largest corporate foundations and timely information on foundation policies, guidelines, representative grants, and application procedures are included in the listing. Financial data provides a summary of the size and granting capacity of each foundation and contains a list of assets, gifts or contributions, grants paid, operating programs, expenditures, scholarships, and loans.

5th Edition, Feb. 1988. ISBN 0-87954-237-3. $75

NATIONAL DIRECTORY OF CORPORATE CHARITY

This ambitious and exhaustively researched directory describes the charitable activities of 1,600 major U.S. corporations, with an emphasis on direct giving programs in corporations.

Used as a companion reference with *Corporate Foundation Profiles*, the *National Directory of Corporate Charity* gives researchers the most comprehensive picture of corporate giving in the U.S. All profiles included in the *National Directory of Corporate Charity* cover U.S. corporations with annual sales of $200 million or more. Included in each corporation entry is information on subject areas of giving; sample grant recipients; financial data on average, high, and low dollar awards; policies regarding giving program; and application guidelines and procedures.

Special features that facilitate research include a complete subject index and state index for ready access to corporations that give in your field and geographic location. Excellent introduction analyzes corporate giving trends.

Originally published by the Regional Young Adult Project, this volume is now distributed and published exclusively by The Foundation Center.

August 1984. 613 pages. ISBN 0-87954-189-X. $80

THE NATIONAL GUIDE TO FUNDING IN AGING

This comprehensive reference is the result of a unique collaborative effort between The Foundation Center, Long Island University, and the Nassau County, New York, Department of Senior Citizen Affairs. Carefully researched, up-to-date, and truly comprehensive, *The National Guide to Funding in Aging* is the only funding tool to cover all public and private sources of funding support and technical assistance for programs for the aging. Areas of support categorized are: Federal Funding Programs, with detailed profiles of 99 funding programs in 15 areas of service; State Government Funding Programs, including programs and up-to-date listings for all 50 states and U.S. territories; Foundations, covering 369 private and community grantmakers with an expressed interest in the field of the aging *plus* a complete list of all grants reported to The Foundation Center for aging in 1985; and *Private Organizations*, with 78 profiles of academic, religious, and service agencies offering funding and technical aid.

January 1987. 288 pages. ISBN 0-87954-191. $35

FOUNDATION GRANTS TO INDIVIDUALS, 6TH EDITION

The only publication devoted entirely to specialized foundation grant opportunities for qualified individual applicants. The 6th Edition provides full descriptions of the programs for individuals of over 1,000 foundations. Entries also include foundation addresses and telephone numbers, names of trustees and staff, financial data, and sample grants. This volume can save individuals seeking grants countless hours of research.

July 1988. ISBN 0-87954-238-1. $24

AMERICA'S VOLUNTARY SPIRIT: A BOOK OF READINGS

In this thoughtful collection, Brian O'Connell, President of INDEPENDENT SECTOR, brings together 45 selections which celebrate and examine the richness and variety of America's unique voluntary sector. O'Connell researched nearly 1,000 selections spanning over 300 years of writing to identify those speeches, articles, chapters, and papers which best define and characterize the role that philanthropy and voluntary action play in our society. Contributors as diverse as de Tocqueville and John D. Rockefeller, Thoreau and Max Lerner, Erma Bombeck and Vernon Jordan are unified in a common examination of this unique dimension of American life. The anthology includes a bibliography of over 500 important writings and a detailed subject index.

October 1983. ISBN 0-87954-079-6 (hardcover). $19.95 ISBN 0-87954-081-8 (softcover). $14.95

PHILANTHROPY IN AN AGE OF TRANSITION

The Essays of Alan Pifer

This is a collection of essays by one of the most respected and well-known individuals in philanthropy. In these essays, Alan Pifer analyzes issues of great concern to all Americans; the responsibilities of higher education, charitable tax deductions, women in the work force, the financial straits of the nonprofit sector, the changing age composition of the American population, bilingual education, the progress of blacks, and more. The essays have been collected from the annual reports of Carnegie Corporation, from 1966-82, some of the most turbulent years in American history.

Alan Pifer is President Emeritus of Carnegie Corporation of New York where he was President for over seventeen years.

April 1984. 270 pages. ISBN 0-87954-104-0. $12.50

THE BOARD MEMBER'S BOOK

by Brian O'Connell, President, INDEPENDENT SECTOR

Based on his extensive experience working with and on the boards of voluntary organizations, Brian O'Connell has developed this practical guide to the essential functions of voluntary boards. O'Connell offers practical advice on how to be a more effective board member and how board members can help their organizations make a difference. This is an invaluable instructional and inspirational tool for anyone who works on or with a voluntary board. Includes an extensive reading list.

May 1985. 208 pages. ISBN 0-87954-133-4. $16.95

MANAGING FOR PROFIT IN THE NONPROFIT WORLD

by Paul B. Firstenberg

How can service-oriented nonprofits expand their revenue bases? In this title in our series on nonprofit management, author Paul B. Firstenberg shares his view that a vital nonprofit is an entrepreneurial nonprofit. Drawing upon his 14 years of experience as a professional in the nonprofit sector—at the Ford Foundation, Princeton, Tulane, and Yale Universities, and Children's Television Workshop—as well as his extensive for-profit experience, Firstenberg outlines innovative ways in which nonprofit managers can utilize the state-of-the-art management techniques as our most successful for-profit enterprises.

September 1986. 253 pages. ISBN 0-87954-159-8. $19.95

SECURING YOUR ORGANIZATION'S FUTURE: A COMPLETE GUIDE TO FUNDRAISING STRATEGIES

by Michael Seltzer

Michael Seltzer, a well-known pioneer in the field of nonprofit management, uses compelling case studies and bottom-line facts to demonstrate how fundraisers—whether beginner or seasoned pro—can help their nonprofit organizations achieve long-term financial well-being. Seltzer uses a step-by-step approach to guide fundraisers through the world of money and shows how to build a network of support from among the wide variety of funding sources available today. Seltzer's work is supplemented with easy-to-follow worksheets and an extensive bibliography of selected readings and resource organizations. Highly recommended for use as a text in nonprofit management programs at colleges and universities.

January 1987. 52 pages. ISBN 0-87954-190-3. $19.95

THE NONPROFIT ENTREPRENEUR: CREATING VENTURES TO EARN INCOME

Edited by Edward Skloot

Nonprofit consultant and entrepreneur Edward Skloot, in a well-organized topic-by-topic analytical approach to nonprofit venturing, demonstrates how nonprofits can launch successful earned income enterprises without compromising their missions. Skloot has compiled a collection of writings by the nation's top practitioners and advisors in

nonprofit enterprise. Topics covered include legal issues, marketing techniques, business planning, avoiding the pitfalls of venturing for smaller nonprofits, and a special section on museums and their retail operations.

March 1988. 170 pages. ISBN 0-87954-239-X. $19.95

WORKING IN FOUNDATIONS: CAREER PATTERNS OF WOMEN AND MEN

By Teresa Jean Odendahl, Elizabeth Trocolli Boris, and Arlene Kaplan Daniels

This publication is the result of a ground-breaking study of foundation career paths of women and men undertaken by Women and Foundations/Corporate Philanthropy with major funding from the Russell Sage Foundation. This book offers a detailed picture of the roles and responsibilities of foundation staff members, employment opportunities in philanthropy, and the management styles and grantmaking processes within foundations.

April 1985. 115 pages. ISBN 0-87954-134-2. $12.95

FOUNDATION FUNDAMENTALS: A RESOURCE GUIDE FOR GRANTSEEKERS

This comprehensive, easy-to-read guidebook written by Patricia Read presents the facts you need to understand the world of foundations and to identify foundation funding sources for your organization. Over 45 illustrations take you step-by-step through the funding research process. Worksheets and checklists are provided to help you get started in your search for funding. Comprehensive bibliographies and detailed research examples are also supplied.

Revised edition, September 1986. 239 pages. ISBN 0-87954-100-8. $9.95

PROMOTING ISSUES AND IDEAS: A GUIDE TO PUBLIC RELATIONS FOR NONPROFIT ORGANIZATIONS

by Public Interest, Public Relations, Inc. (PIPR)

PIPR, specialists in promoting the issues and ideas of nonprofit groups, present proven strategies that will put your organization on the map and attract the interest of the people you wish to influence and inform. Included are the nuts-and-bolts of advertising, publicity, speech-making, lobbying, and special events; how to write and produce informational literature that leaps off the page; public relations on a shoestring budget; how to plan and evaluate "pr" efforts, and the use of new communication technologies.

March 1987. 183 pages. ISBN 0-87954-192-X. $19.95

AMERICA'S WEALTHY AND THE FUTURE OF FOUNDATIONS

Edited by Teresa J. Odendahl
Co-sponsored by The Council on Foundations and the Yale University Program on Non-Profit Organizations

Recent studies indicate that the "big foundations" with giant assets and high public profiles are declining in popularity as charitable vehicles of the rich. *America's Wealthy* poses the compelling question: What impact will the declining birthrate of "big foundations" have on the future of philanthropy and the social programs it supports? It also takes us behind the scenes for a first-hand look at the culture of the wealthy and reveals a complex set of attitudes, motivations, economic forces, and policy regulations that offer insight into how and why America's wealthy commit their private resources for the public good. A must-read for all concerned with philanthropy in America.

*March 1987. 325 pages. ISBN 0-87954-194-6. $24.95—paperbound
ISBN 0-87954-197-0. $34.95—hardbound*

PHILANTHROPY IN ACTION
by Brian O'Connell, President, INDEPENDENT SECTOR

Goddard's rocketry research. The suffrage and civil rights movements. Salk's polio vaccine. Historic Williamsburg. *Philanthropy in Action* tells the fascinating stories of hundreds of grants which have made a difference, revealing the history, role, and impact of philanthropy in our society. O'Connell captures the remarkable relationships between donors and grantees as he presents philanthropy according to nine roles including discovering new frontiers of knowledge, supporting and encouraging excellence, relieving human misery, and making communities a better place to live. The stories of the invaluable contributions made by community foundations, cooperative benevolence associations, and corporate giving programs are also narrated. Lively, entertaining, and informative, *Philanthropy in Action* is both an essential resource tool for students, teachers, writers, and scholars of philanthropy, and a collection of great stories, masterfully told.
*September 1987. 337 pages. ISBN 0-87954-231-4. $19.95—paperbound
ISBN 0-87954-230-6. $24.95—hardbound*

PHILANTHROPY AND VOLUNTARISM: AN ANNOTATED BIBLIOGRAPHY

by Daphne N. Layton for the Association of American Colleges

Finally, a comprehensive bibliography of philanthropy and voluntarism to aid students, scholars, and the general public in understanding the field. All of the best and most important works can be found here including over 1,600 books and articles that analyze aspects of the philanthropic tradition in the U.S. and abroad. Among these are 250 extensively annotated scholarly works particularly useful as texts or background reading for undergraduate study and research in philanthropy.

June 1987. 308 pages. ISBN 0-87954-198-9. $18.50

MAPPING THE THIRD SECTOR: VOLUNTARISM IN A CHANGING SOCIAL ECONOMY

by Jon Van Til

Over 700,000 nonprofit organizations. Over 15 million volunteers. What impact do they have on society today? Professor Jon Van Til, Editor of the Journal of Voluntary Action Research, raises this compelling question in his scholarly new work as he sets the stage for a coherent view of the voluntary sector. His review of historical and contemporary models of voluntary action paves the way for one that stresses the need for a new conception of how to preserve, extend, and experience community within the interactive web of modern society.

March 1988. 270 pages. ISBN 0-87954-240-3. $24.95

ASSOCIATES PROGRAM

"Direct Line to Fundraising Information"

The Associates Program puts important facts and figures on your desk through a toll-free telephone reference service helping you to:

- identify potential sources of foundation funding for your organization,

- gather important information to target and present your proposals most effectively.

Your annual membership in the Associates Program gives you vital information on a timely basis, saving you hundreds of hours of research time.

- Membership in the Associates Program puts important funding information on your desk, including information from:
  - foundation annual reports, information brochures, press releases, grants lists, and other documents
  - IRS 990-PF information returns for all 25,000 U.S. foundations—often the

only source of information on small foundations
  - books and periodicals chronicling foundation and philanthropic history and regulations
  - files filled with news clippings about foundations
  - The Foundation Center's own publications: *Foundation Directory* and *Supplement, Foundation Grants Index*— annual and bimonthly, *Source Book Profiles, Corporate Foundation Profiles, National Data Book, COMSEARCH Printouts, Foundation Fundamentals, Grants to Individuals,* and *Special Topics.*

- The Associates Program puts this vital information on your desk through a *toll-free telephone call.* The annual fee of $350 for the Associates Program grants you *10 free calls or 2½ hours* worth of answers per month.

- Membership in the Associates Program allows you to request *custom searches of The Foundation Center's computerized databases* which contain information on *all 25,000* active U.S. foundations.

Thousands of professional fundraisers find it extremely cost effective to rely on the Center's Associates Program. Put our staff of experts to work for your fundraising program. For more information call TOLL-FREE 800-424-9836.

FOUNDATION CENTER COMPUTER DATABASES

Foundation and Grants Information Online

As the only nonprofit organization whose sole purpose is to provide information on philanthropic activity, The Foundation Center offers three important databases online—Foundation Directory, Foundation Grants Index, and National Foundations. The databases

xlvi

correspond in form and content to the printed volumes: *The Foundation Directory, The Foundation Grants Index,* and the *National Data Book.* Online retrieval provides vital information on funding sources, philanthropic giving, grant application guidelines, and the financial status of foundations to:

Nonprofit organizations seeking funds
Grantmaking institutions
Corporate contributors
Researchers
Journalists
Legislators

Searches of the Center's databases can provide comprehensive and timely answers to your questions, such as ...

- Which New York foundations support urban projects? Who are their officers and trustees?
- What are the program interests of the ten largest corporate foundations? Which ones publish annual reports?
- Which foundations have given grants in excess of $100,000 in the past two years for continuing education for women?
- Which foundations would be likely to fund a cancer research project at a California hospital?
- Which are the ten largest foundations in Philadelphia by annual grants amount?
- What are the names and addresses of smaller foundations in the 441 zip code area?

The Center's up-to-date and authoritative data is available online through DIALOG Information Services, and on the Telecommunications Cooperative Network's (TCN) DIALCOM System. For additional information about how you may have access to Foundation Center databases, call TOLL-FREE 800-424-9836.

THE FOUNDATION CENTER COOPERATING COLLECTIONS NETWORK

The Foundation Center is an independent national service organization established by foundations to provide an authoritative source of information on private philanthropic giving. In fulfilling its mission, The Center disseminates information on private giving through public service programs, publications and through a national network of library reference collections for free public use. The New York, Washington, DC, Cleveland and San Francisco reference collections operated by The Foundation Center offer a wide variety of services and comprehensive collections of information on foundations and grants. The Cooperating Collections are libraries, community foundations and other nonprofit agencies that provide a core collection of Foundation Center publications and a variety of supplementary materials and services in subject areas useful to grantseekers.

Over 100 of the network members have sets of private foundation information returns (IRS Form 990-PF) for their states or regions which are available for public use. A complete set of U.S. foundation returns can be found at the New York and Washington, DC offices of The Foundation Center. The Cleveland and San Francisco offices contain IRS returns for those foundations in the midwestern and western states, respectively.

Because the collections vary in their hours, materials and services, IT IS RECOMMENDED THAT YOU CALL EACH COLLECTION IN ADVANCE. To check on new locations or current information, call toll-free 1-800-424-9836.

Those collections marked with a bullet (●) have sets of private foundation information returns (IRS Form 990-PF) for their states or regions, available for public reference.

Reference collections operated by The Foundation Center are in **boldface**.

ALABAMA

● Birmingham Public Library
2100 Park Place
Birmingham 35203
205-226-3600

Huntsville-Madison County
Public Library
108 Fountain Circle
P.O. Box 443
Huntsville 35804
205-532-5940

University of South Alabama
Library Building
Reference Department
Mobile 36688
205-460-7025

● Auburn University at
Montgomery Library
Montgomery 36193-0401
205-271-9649

ALASKA

● University of Alaska,
Anchorage Library
3211 Providence Drive
Anchorage 99508
907-786-1848

ARIZONA

● Phoenix Public Library Business
and Sciences Department
12 East McDowell Road
Phoenix 85004
602-262-4636

● Tucson Public Library
Main Library
200 South Sixth Avenue
Tucson 85701
602-791-4393

ARKANSAS

● Westark Community College
Library
Grand Avenue at Waldron Road
Fort Smith 72913
501-785-7000

● Little Rock Public Library
Reference Department
700 Louisiana Street
Little Rock 72201
501-370-5950

CALIFORNIA

● California Community
Foundation Funding Information
Center
3580 Wilshire Blvd., Suite 1660
Los Angeles 90010
213-413-4042

● Community Foundation for
Monterey County
420 Pacific Street
Monterey 93940
408-375-9712

California Community
Foundation
4050 Metropolitan Drive #300
Orange 92668
714-937-9077

Riverside Public Library
3581 7th Street
Riverside 92501
714-782-5201

California State Library
Reference Services, Rm. 309
914 Capital Mall
Sacramento 95814
916-322-4570

● San Diego Community
Foundation
525 "B" Street, Suite 410
San Diego 92101
619-239-8815

● **The Foundation Center**
312 Sutter Street, Room 312
San Francisco 94108
415-397-0902

● Grantsmanship Resource Center
Junior League of San Jose, Inc.
Community Foundation of Santa
Clara County
960 West Hedding, Suite 220
San Jose 95126
408-244-5280

● Orange County Community
Developmental Council
1440 East First Street, 4th Floor
Santa Ana 92701
714-547-6801

● Peninsula Community
Foundation
1204 Burlingame Avenue
Burlingame 94011-0627
415-342-2505

● Santa Barbara Public Library
Reference Section
40 East Anapamu
P.O. Box 1019
Santa Barbara 93102
805-962-7653

Santa Monica Public Library
1343 Sixth Street
Santa Monica 90401-1603
213-458-8603

Tuolomne County Library
465 S. Washington Street
Sonora 95370
209-533-5707

COLORADO

Pikes Peak Library District
20 North Cascade Avenue
Colorado Springs 80901
303-473-2780

● Denver Public Library
Sociology Division
1357 Broadway
Denver 80203
303-571-2190

CONNECTICUT

Danbury Public Library
170 Main Street
Danbury 06810
203-797-4527

● Hartford Public Library
Reference Department
500 Main Street
Hartford 06103
203-525-9121

D.A.T.A.
30 Arbor Street
Hartford 06106
203-232-6619

D.A.T.A.
25 Science Park
Suite 502
New Haven 06511
203-786-5225

DELAWARE

● Hugh Morris Library
University of Delaware
Newark 19717-5267
302-451-2965

DISTRICT OF COLUMBIA

● **The Foundation Center**
1001 Connecticut Avenue, NW
Washington 20036
202-331-1400

FLORIDA

Volusia County Public Library
City Island
Daytona Beach 32014
904-252-8374

● Jacksonville Public Library
Business, Science, and Industry
Department
122 North Ocean Street
Jacksonville 32202
904-633-3926

● Miami-Dade Public Library
Humanities Department
101 W. Flagler St.
Miami 33132
305-375-2665

● Orlando Public Library
101 E. Central Blvd.
Orlando 32801
305-425-4694

Selby Public Library
1001 Boulevard of the Arts
Sarasota 33577
813-366-7303

● Leon County Public Library
Community Funding Resources
Center
1940 North Monroe Street
Tallahassee 32303
904-478-2665

Palm Beach County Community
Foundation
324 Datura Street, Suite 340
West Palm Beach 33401
305-659-6800

GEORGIA

● Atlanta–Fulton Public Library
Ivan Allen Department
1 Margaret Mitchell Square
Atlanta 30303
404-688-4636

HAWAII

- Thomas Hale Hamilton Library
  General Reference
  University of Hawaii
  2550 The Mall
  Honolulu 96822
  808-948-7214

  The Hawaiian Foundation
  Resource Room
  130 Merchant Street
  Bancorp Tower, Suite 901
  Honolulu 96813
  808-538-4540

IDAHO

- Caldwell Public Library
  1010 Dearborn Street
  Caldwell 83605
  208-459-3242

ILLINOIS

Belleville Public Library
121 East Washington Street
Belleville 62220
618-234-0441

DuPage Township
300 Briarcliff Road
Bolingbrook 60439
312-759-1317

- Donors Forum of Chicago
  53 W. Jackson Blvd., Rm. 430
  Chicago 60604
  312-431-0265

- Evanston Public Library
  1703 Orrington Avenue
  Evanston 60201
  312-866-0305

- Sangamon State University
  Library
  Shepherd Road
  Springfield 62708
  217-786-6633

INDIANA

Allen County Public Library
900 Webster Street
Fort Wayne 46802
219-424-7241

Indiana University Northwest
Library
3400 Broadway
Gary 46408
219-980-6580

- Indianapolis–Marion County
  Public Library
  40 East St. Clair Street
  Indianapolis 46204
  317-269-1733

IOWA

- Public Library of Des Moines
  100 Locust Street
  Des Moines 50308
  515-283-4259

KANSAS

- Topeka Public Library
  Adult Services Department
  1515 West Tenth Street
  Topeka 66604
  913-233-2040

- Wichita Public Library
  223 South Main
  Wichita 67202
  316-262-0611

KENTUCKY

Western Kentucky University
Division of Library Services
Helm-Cravens Library
Bowling Green 42101
502-745-3951

- Louisville Free Public Library
  Fourth and York Streets
  Louisville 40203
  502-561-8600

LOUISIANA

- East Baton Rouge Parish Library
  Centroplex Library
  120 St. Louis Street
  Baton Rouge 70821
  504-389-4960

- New Orleans Public Library
  Business and Science Division
  219 Loyola Avenue
  New Orleans 70140
  504-596-2583

- Shreve Memorial Library
  424 Texas Street
  Shreveport 71101
  318-226-5894

MAINE

- University of Southern Maine
  Office of Sponsored Research
  Library
  96 Falmouth Street
  Portland 04103
  207-780-4411

MARYLAND

- Enoch Pratt Free Library
  Social Science and History
  Department
  400 Cathedral Street
  Baltimore 21201
  301-396-5320

MASSACHUSETTS

- Associated Grantmakers of
  Massachusetts
  294 Washington Street
  Suite 501
  Boston 02108
  617-426-2608

- Boston Public Library
  Copley Square
  Boston 02117
  617-536-5400

  Walpole Public Library
  Common Street
  Walpole 02081
  617-668-5497 ext. 340

- Western Massachusetts Funding
  Resource Center
  Campaign for Human
  Development
  Chancery Annex
  73 Chestnut Street
  Springfield 01103
  413-732-3175 ext. 67

- Grants Resource Center
  Worcester Public Library
  Salem Square
  Worcester 01608
  617-799-1655

MICHIGAN

- Alpena County Library
  211 North First Avenue
  Alpena 49707
  517-356-6188

  University of Michigan–Ann
  Arbor
  Reference Department
  209 Hatcher Graduate Library
  Ann Arbor 48109-1205
  313-764-1149

- Henry Ford Centennial Library
  16301 Michigan Avenue
  Dearborn 48126
  313-943-2337

- Purdy Library
  Wayne State University
  Detroit 48202
  313-577-4040

- Michigan State University
  Libraries
  Reference Library
  East Lansing 48824
  517-353-9184

- Farmington Community Library
  32737 West 12 Mile Road
  Farmington Hills 48018
  313-553-0300

- University of Michigan–Flint
  Library
  Reference Department
  Flint 48503
  313-762-3408

- Grand Rapids Public Library
  Sociology and Education Dept.
  Library Plaza
  Grand Rapids 49502
  616-456-4411

- Michigan Technological
  University Library
  Highway U.S. 41
  Houghton 49931
  906-487-2507

MINNESOTA

- Duluth Public Library
  520 Superior Street
  Duluth 55802
  218-723-3802

- Southwest State University
  Library
  Marshall 56258
  507-537-7278

- Minneapolis Public Library
  Sociology Department
  300 Nicollet Mall
  Minneapolis 55401
  612-372-6555

  Rochester Public Library
  Broadway at First Street, SE
  Rochester 55901
  507-285-8002

  Saint Paul Public Library
  90 West Fourth Street
  Saint Paul 55102
  612-292-6311

MISSISSIPPI

Jackson Metropolitan Library
301 North State Street
Jackson 39201
601-944-1120

MISSOURI

- Clearinghouse for Midcontinent
  Foundations
  P.O. Box 22680
  Univ. of Missouri, Kansas City
  Law School, Suite 1-300
  52nd Street and Oak
  Kansas City 64113
  816-276-1176

- Kansas City Public Library
  311 East 12th Street
  Kansas City 64106
  816-221-2685

- Metropolitan Association for
  Philanthropy, Inc.
  5585 Pershing Avenue
  Suite 150
  St. Louis 63112
  314-361-3900

- Springfield–Greene County
  Library
  397 East Central Street
  Springfield 65801
  417-866-4636

MONTANA

- Eastern Montana College Library
  Reference Department
  1500 N. 30th Street
  Billings 59101-0298
  406-657-2262

- Montana State Library
  Reference Department
  1515 E. 6th Avenue
  Helena 59620
  406-444-3004

NEBRASKA

University of Nebraska, Lincoln
106 Love Library
Lincoln 68588-0410
402-472-2526

- W. Dale Clark Library
  Social Sciences Department
  215 South 15th Street
  Omaha 68102
  402-444-4826

NEVADA

- Las Vegas–Clark County Library
  District
  1401 East Flamingo Road
  Las Vegas 89119
  702-733-7810

- Washoe County Library
  301 South Center Street
  Reno 89505
  702-785-4190

NEW HAMPSHIRE

- The New Hampshire Charitable
  Fund
  One South Street
  Concord 03301
  603-225-6641

Littleton Public Library
109 Main Street
Littleton 03561
603-444-5741

NEW JERSEY

Cumberland County Library
800 E. Commerce Street
Bridgeton 08302
609-455-0080

The Support Center
17 Academy Street, Suite 1101
Newark 07102
201-643-5774

County College of Morris
Masten Learning Resource
 Center
Route 10 and Center Grove Rd.
Randolph 07869
201-361-5000 ext. 470

● New Jersey State Library
Governmental Reference
185 West State Street
Trenton 08625
609-292-6220

NEW MEXICO

Albuquerque Community
 Foundation
6400 Uptown Boulevard N.E.
Suite 500-W
Albuquerque 87110
505-883-6240

● New Mexico State Library
325 Don Gaspar Street
Santa Fe 87503
505-827-3824

NEW YORK

● New York State Library
Cultural Education Center
Humanities Section
Empire State Plaza
Albany 12230
518-474-7645

Bronx Reference Center
New York Public Library
2556 Bainbridge Avenue
Bronx 10458
212-220-6575

Brooklyn in Touch
101 Willoughby Street
Room 1508
Brooklyn 11201
718-237-9300

● Buffalo and Erie County Public
 Library
Lafayette Square
Buffalo 14203
716-856-7525

Huntington Public Library
338 Main Street
Huntington 11743
516-427-5165

● Levittown Public Library
Reference Department
One Bluegrass Lane
Levittown 11756
516-731-5728

● **The Foundation Center**
79 Fifth Avenue
New York 10003
212-620-4230

SUNY/College at Old Westbury
 Library
223 Store Hill Road
Old Westbury 11568
516-876-3156

● Plattsburgh Public Library
Adult Services Department
15 Oak Street
Plattsburgh 12901
518-563-0921

Adriance Memorial Library
93 Market Street
Poughkeepsie 12601
914-485-3445

Queens Borough Public Library
89-11 Merrick Boulevard
Jamaica 11432
718-990-0700

● Rochester Public Library
Business and Social Sciences
 Division
115 South Avenue
Rochester 14604
716-428-7328

Staten Island Council on the Arts
One Edgewater Plaza Rm. 311
Staten Island 10305
718-447-4485

● Onondaga County Public Library
335 Montgomery Street
Syracuse 13202
315-473-4493

● White Plains Public Library
100 Martine Avenue
White Plains 10601
914-682-4488

● Suffolk Cooperative Library
 System
627 North Sunrise Service Road
Bellport 11713
516-286-1600

NORTH CAROLINA

● The Duke Endowment
200 S. Tryon Street, Ste. 1100
Charlotte 28202
704-376-0291

Durham County Library
300 N. Roxboro Street
Durham 27701
919-683-2626

● North Carolina State Library
109 East Jones Street
Raleigh 27611
919-733-3270

● The Winston-Salem Foundation
229 First Union National Bank
 Building
Winston-Salem 27101
919-725-2382

NORTH DAKOTA

Western Dakota Grants Resource
 Center
Bismarck Junior College Library
Bismarck 58501
701-224-5450

● The Library
North Dakota State University
Fargo 58105
701-237-8876

OHIO

● Public Library of Cincinnati and
 Hamilton County
Education Department
800 Vine Street
Cincinnati 45202
513-369-6940

● **The Foundation Center**
Kent H. Smith Library
1442 Hanna Building
1422 Euclid Avenue
Cleveland 44115
216-861-1933

The Public Library of Columbus
 and Franklin County
Main Library
96 S. Grant Avenue
Columbus 43215
614-222-7180

● Dayton and Montgomery County
 Public Library
Grants Information Center
215 E. Third Street
Dayton 45402-2103
513-227-9500 ext. 211

● Toledo-Lucas County Public
 Library
Social Science Department
325 Michigan Street
Toledo 43624
419-255-7055 ext. 221

Ohio University–Zanesville
Community Education and
 Development
1425 Newark Road
Zanesville 43701
614-453-0762

Stark County District Library
715 Market Avenue North
Canton 44702-1080
216-452-0665

OKLAHOMA

● Oklahoma City University Library
NW 23rd at North Blackwelder
Oklahoma City 73106
405-521-5072

● Tulsa City–County Library System
400 Civic Center
Tulsa 74103
918-592-7944

OREGON

● Library Association of Portland
Government Documents Room
801 S.W. Tenth Avenue
Portland 97205
503-223-7201

Oregon State Library
State Library Building
Salem 97310
503-378-4274

PENNSYLVANIA

Northampton County Area
 Community College
Learning Resources Center
3835 Green Pond Road
Bethlehem 18017
215-865-5358

● Erie County Public Library
3 South Perry Square
Erie 16501
814-452-2333 ext. 54

● Dauphin County Library System
Central Library
101 Walnut Street
Harrisburg 17101
717-234-4961

Lancaster County Public Library
125 North Duke Street
Lancaster 17602
717-394-2651

● The Free Library of Philadelphia
Logan Square
Philadelphia 19103
215-686-5423

● Hillman Library
University of Pittsburgh
Pittsburgh 15260
412-624-4423

Economic Development Council
 of Northeastern Pennsylvania
1151 Oak Street
Pittston 18640
717-655-5581

James V. Brown Library
12 E. 4th Street
Williamsport 17701
717-326-0536

RHODE ISLAND

● Providence Public Library
Reference Department
150 Empire Street
Providence 02903
401-521-7722

SOUTH CAROLINA

● Charleston County Public Library
404 King Street
Charleston 29403
803-723-1645

● South Carolina State Library
Reader Services Department
1500 Senate Street
Columbia 29201
803-734-8666

SOUTH DAKOTA

● South Dakota State Library
State Library Building
800 North Illinois Street
Pierre 57501
605-773-3131

Sioux Falls Area Foundation
404 Boyce Greeley Building
321 South Phillips Avenue
Sioux Falls 57102-0781
605-336-7055

TENNESSEE

● Knoxville-Knox County Public
 Library
500 West Church Avenue
Knoxville 37902
615-523-0781

● Memphis Shelby County Public
 Library
1850 Peabody Avenue
Memphis 38104
901-725-8876

- Public Library of Nashville and
  Davidson County
  8th Avenue, North and Union
  Street
  Nashville 37203
  615-244-4700

TEXAS

Amarillo Area Foundation
1000 Polk
P.O. Box 25569
Amarillo 79105-269
806-376-4521

- The Hogg Foundation for Mental
  Health
  The University of Texas
  Austin 78712
  512-471-5041

- Corpus Christi State University
  Library
  6300 Ocean Drive
  Corpus Christi 78412
  512-991-6810

- El Paso Community Foundation
  El Paso National Bank Building
  Suite 1616
  El Paso 79901
  915-533-4020

- Funding Information Center
  Texas Christian University Library
  Ft. Worth 76129
  817-921-7664

- Houston Public Library
  Bibliographic & Information
  Center
  500 McKinney Avenue
  Houston 77002
  713-236-1313

- Lubbock Area Foundation
  502 Commerce Bank Building
  Lubbock 79401
  806-762-8061

- Funding Information Library
  507 Brooklyn
  San Antonio 78215
  512-227-4333

- Dallas Public Library
  Grants Information Service
  1515 Young Street
  Dallas 75201
  214-670-1487

- Pan American University
  Learning Resource Center
  1201 W. University Drive
  Edinburg 78539
  512-381-3304

UTAH

- Salt Lake City Public Library
  Business and Science
  Department
  209 East Fifth South
  Salt Lake City 84111
  801-363-5733

VERMONT

- State of Vermont Department of
  Libraries
  Reference Services Unit
  111 State Street
  Montpelier 05602
  802-828-3261

VIRGINIA

- Grants Resources Collection
  Hampton Public Library
  4207 Victoria Blvd.
  Hampton 23669
  804-727-6234

- Richmond Public Library
  Business, Science, & Technology
  Department
  101 East Franklin Street
  Richmond 23219
  804-780-8223

WASHINGTON

- Seattle Public Library
  1000 Fourth Avenue
  Seattle 98104
  206-625-4881

- Spokane Public Library
  Funding Information Center
  West 906 Main Avenue
  Spokane 99201
  509-838-3364

WEST VIRGINIA

- Kanawha County Public Library
  123 Capital Street
  Charleston 25301
  304-343-4646

WISCONSIN

- Marquette University Memorial
  Library
  1415 West Wisconsin Avenue
  Milwaukee 53233
  414-224-1515

- University of Wisconsin–Madison
  Memorial Library
  728 State Street
  Madison 53706
  608-262-3647

WYOMING

- Laramie County Community
  College Library
  1400 East College Drive
  Cheyenne 82007
  307-634-5853

AUSTRALIA

Victorian Community Foundation
94 Queen Street
Melbourne Vic 3000
607-5922

CANADA

Canadian Center for Philanthropy
3080 Yonge Street
Suite 4080
Toronto, Ontario M4N3N1
416-484-4118

ENGLAND

Charities Aid Foundation
18 Doughty Street
London W1N 2 PL
01-831-7798

JAPAN

Foundation Center Library
of Japan
Elements Shinjuku Bldg. 3F
2-1-14 Shinjuku, Shinjuku-ku
Tokyo
03-350-1857

MEXICO

Biblioteca Benjamin Franklin
Londres 16
Mexico City 6, D.F.
525-591-0244

PUERTO RICO

Universidad Del Sagrado
Corazon
M.M.T. Guevarra Library
Correo Calle Loiza
Santurce 00914
809-728-1515 ext. 357

VIRGIN ISLANDS

College of the Virgin Islands
Library
Saint Thomas
U.S. Virgin Islands 00801
809-774-9200 ext. 487

THE FOUNDATION CENTER AFFILIATES PROGRAM

As participants in the cooperating collection network, affiliates are libraries or nonprofit agencies that provide fundraising information or other funding-related technical assistance in their communities. Affiliates agree to provide free public access to a basic collection of Foundation Center publications during a regular schedule of hours, offering free funding research guidance to all visitors. Many also provide a variety of special services for local nonprofit organizations using staff or volunteers to prepare special materials, organize workshops, or conduct library orientations.

The affiliates program began in 1981 to continue the expansion of The Foundation Center's funding information network of 90 funding information collections. Since its inception, over 80 organizations have been designated Foundation Center affiliates. Affiliate collections have been established in a wide variety of host organizations, including public and university libraries, technical assistance agencies, and community foundations. The Center maintains strong ties with its affiliates through regular news bulletins, the provision of supporting materials, the sponsorship of regional meetings, and by referring the many nonprofits that call or write to The Foundation Center to the affiliate nearest them.

The Foundation Center welcomes inquiries from agencies interested in providing this type of public information service. If you are interested in establishing a funding information library for the use of nonprofit agencies in your area or in learning more about the program, we would like to hear from you.

The first step is for the director of your organization to write to Zeke Kilbride, Network Coordinator, explaining why the collection is needed and how the responsibilities of network participation would be met. The Center will contact you to review the details of the relationship. If your agency is designated an affiliate, you will then be entitled to purchase a core collection of Foundation Center materials at a 20% discount rate (annual cost of approx. $500). Center staff will be happy to assist in identifying supplementary titles for funding information libraries. A core collection, which must be maintained from year to year, consists of current editions to the following publications (subject to change):

Corporate Giving Directory
The Foundation Directory
The Foundation Directory Supplement
The Foundation Grants Index
The Foundation Grants Index Bimonthly

Source Book Profiles
The National Data Book
Foundation Fundamentals
Foundation Grants to Individuals

For more information, please write to: Zeke Kilbride, The Foundation Center, 79 Fifth Avenue, New York, NY 10003.

DESCRIPTIVE DIRECTORY

EDUCATIONAL SUPPORT

This largest section of the directory lists sources of educational support for secondary, undergraduate, graduate, or postgraduate study as well as for advanced research.

Major types of educational assistance available include the following:

● **Scholarships -** grants awarded directly to students, or to schools for the benefit of students, to help meet tuition costs, primarily at the undergraduate level

● **Fellowships -** grants awarded to graduate students in colleges, universities, and other institutions

● **Loans -** funds for educational expenses which usually must be repaid to the lending foundation

● **Internships -** to support undergraduate, graduate, or postgraduate students in gaining practical experience

● **Residencies -** for study, research, including advanced training in a medical specialty, or teaching at a college, university or research institute

● **Research grants -** awards to support individuals engaged in independent scholarly projects or medical or scientific investigation

Not included are student aid grants that are company-sponsored for the benefit only of children of employees, or educational support for which individuals are ineligible to apply directly; such programs may be found in the "Company Employee Grants" and "Awards, Prizes, and Grants by Nomination" sections.

Entries are arranged alphabetically by foundation name. Access to grants by the above types of support, as well as specific subject areas and geographic focus is provided in the "Subject," "Types of Support" and "Geographic Focus" indexes in the back of the book. Some foundations provide educational support for study only at named schools, colleges or universities, or for graduates only of named schools. The "Index of Specific Educational Institutions" provides access to these foundation sources.

Limitations on grantmaking are indicated in the entry when available. The limitations statement should be checked carefully as a foundation will reject any application that does not fall within its stated geographic area, recipient type, or area of interest.

Foundation sources requiring affliation with a particular institution or organization are included in this section as long as application for the grant may be made directly by an individual.

REMEMBER: IF YOU DON'T QUALIFY, DON'T APPLY.

1★
Aaron (Mary M.) Memorial Trust Scholarship Fund
P.O. Box 241
Yuba City, CA 95992
Contact: W.D. Chipman, Trustee

Limitations: Undergraduate scholarships to residents of California to attend schools located within the state of California.
Financial data: Year ended 6/30/87. Assets, $1,071,555 (M); Total giving, $40,500; Grants to individuals, 68 grants totaling $40,500, high $750, low $187, general range $375-750, average grant $550.
Employer Identification Number: 941561354
Applications: Deadline March 15th; Completion of formal application required.
Publications: Application guidelines, 990-PF printed copy available upon request.
Program description:
Grants are awarded on the basis of financial need rather than on scholastic grades or courses of study. The fund does not award scholarship grants for graduate studies.

2
Abell (Jennie G. and Pearl) Education Trust
723 1/2 Main Street
P.O. Box 487
Ashland, KS 67831   (316) 635-2228
Contact: Sarah D. Shattuck, Manager

Limitations: Scholarships only to graduates of Clark County, KS, high schools.
Financial data: Year ended 5/31/87. Assets, $1,940,670 (M); Total giving, $149,900; Grants to individuals, 77 grants totaling $149,900, high $5,000, low $500.
Employer Identification Number: 237454791
Applications: Deadline June 15th; Completion of formal application required; Interviews granted upon request.
Program description:
Summer school grants are available and require a separate application. If the student fails to meet the minimum academic standard, the college is instructed not to disburse the next semester's grant.

3
Abernethy (Sally) Charitable Education Fund
c/o NCNB, National Bank of Florida
P.O. Box 1469
Tampa, FL 33601

Limitations: Educational grants to individuals, with preference to residents of Florida attending schools in Florida, especially to students from the Winter Haven, FL, area.

Financial data: Year ended 12/31/84. Assets, $175,530 (M); Total giving, $4,933; Grants to individuals, 6 grants totaling $4,933, high $1,500, low $433, general range $500-1,000.
Employer Identification Number: 591867419
Applications: Initial approach by letter, including statement of academic qualifications and statement of need.

4
Abrahamian (George) Foundation
945 Admiral Street
Providence, RI 02904   (401) 831-0008
Contact: Abraham G. Abraham, Treasurer

Limitations: Scholarships to local students of Armenian ancestry to attend colleges and universities primarily in Rhode Island.
Financial data: Year ended 12/31/86. Assets, $72,324 (M); Total giving, $4,550; Grants to individuals, 5 grants totaling $3,500, high $700, low $275.
Employer Identification Number: 237039366
Applications: Deadline September; Initial approach by in-person visit through the Armenian churches in the area; Completion of formal application required; Interviews required before final selections are made.
Program description:
Scholarship candidates are recommended by Armenian churches in the area. Selection criteria are Armenian ancestry, U.S. citizenship, good character, scholastic ability, and financial need. Periodic follow-ups are made after scholarship is awarded.

5
Abrams (Samuel L.) Foundation
c/o Commonwealth National Bank
P.O. Box 1010
Harrisburg, PA 17108
Contact: Samuel A. Evans, Secretary, or Georgianna R. Hawk, Assistant to the Secretary, 2301 North Third Street, Harrisburg, PA 17110; Tel.: (717) 234-4344

Limitations: Non-interest bearing loans to high school students in the greater Harrisburg, PA, area.
Financial data: Year ended 12/31/86. Assets, $768,734 (M); Expenditures, $43,923; Loans to individuals, 36 loans totaling $35,300, high $1,600, low $100, general range $500-1,000, average loan $1,000.
Employer Identification Number: 236408237
Applications: Deadline May 15th; Completion of formal application required.

6
Adams Scholarship Fund
c/o First Agricultural National Bank
99 West Street
Pittsfield, MA 01201   (413) 499-3000
Contact: Thomas G. Sokop

Limitations: Scholarships only for residents of
Adams-Cheshire, MA, Regional School District.
Financial data: Year ended 12/31/85. Assets, $53,964
(M); Total giving, $3,936; Grants to individuals, 14
grants totaling $3,936, high $300, low, $100, average
grant $300.
Employer Identification Number: 046024006

7
Adelphic Educational Fund, Inc.
c/o United Bank and Trust Company-Tax Dept.
101 Pearl Street, P.O. Box 31317
Hartford, CT 06103-7317
Contact: Herbert A. Arnold, One Edwards Road,
Portland, CT 06480; Tel.: (203) 342-2607

Limitations: Scholarships and honorariums primarily to
undergraduate students at Wesleyan University, CT.
Financial data: Year ended 4/30/85. Assets, $453,041
(M); Total giving, $44,634; Grants to individuals, 14
grants totaling $8,850; Subtotal for scholarships, 11
grants totaling $6,700, high $850, low $200; Subtotal
for honorariums, 3 grants totaling $2,150, high
$1,500, low $150.
Employer Identification Number: 066023615
Applications: Deadline October 1st; Initial approach
by letter requesting application; Completion of formal
application required.
Program description:
Scholarship awards are based on financial need and
scholastic aptitude.

8
AEI Scholarship Fund
c/o Citizens Trust
100 South Main Street
Ann Arbor, MI 48104   (313) 994-5555
Contact: B. Todd Jones, Trust Officer

Limitations: Educational loans only to female students
accepted at or attending accredited medical schools in
the U.S.
Financial data: Year ended 6/30/86. Assets, $153,619
(M); Expenditures, $8,735; Loans to individuals, 2
loans totaling $6,950, each loan $3,475.
Employer Identification Number: 382088329
Applications: Deadline May 1st; Completion of formal
application required; Interviews granted upon request.
Program description:
Loans must be recertified each year and are to be
repaid upon completion of medical school.

9★
Alexander Educational Fund
c/o Wells Fargo Bank
P.O. Drawer H-H
Santa Barbara, CA 93102
Contact: Bonnie Egan, c/o Wells Fargo Bank, 1001
State Street, Santa Barbara, CA; Tel.: (805) 564-2868

Limitations: Student loans only to long-term residents
of Santa Barbara County, CA. Two years of
non-college residence is the minimum requirement.
Financial data: Year ended 12/31/86. Assets, $696,801
(M); Expenditures, $63,615; Loans to individuals, 110
loans totaling $54,525; high $1,000, low $250,
general range $500-750.
Employer Identification Number: 956063291
Applications: Deadline June 1st; Applications
accepted between January 1st and June 1st;
Completion of formal application required; Interviews
required.
Program description:
Loans may be used at any accredited school of the
recipient's choice. Loans are renewable for subsequent
years and must be repayed after completion of
education.

10
Alexander (Thomas L., Myrtle R., Arch and Eva) Scholarship Fund
c/o Posey County National Bank
112 East Third Street
Mount Vernon, IN 47620
Contact: K. Richard Hawley

Limitations: Scholarships limited to graduating
students of Posey County, IN, high schools.
Financial data: Year ended 2/28/87. Assets, $714,336
(M); Total giving, $53,418; Grants to individuals, 64
grants totaling $53,418, high $1,500, low $594,
general range $594-1,500, average grant $594.
Employer Identification Number: 356333739
Applications: Deadline May 1st; Completion of formal
application required; Application forms available at
Posey County, IN, area schools; Submit completed
application to respective high school.
Program description:
Scholarship recipients are selected by their respective
high schools of Posey County, IN. Successful
applicants are required to keep the trustees of the fund
informed regarding their academic progress.

11★
Allen (Rita) Foundation, Inc.
550 Park Avenue
New York, NY 10021
Contact: Milton E. Cassel, President

Limitations: Medical research grants to university
research scientists in the fields of cancer, multiple

sclerosis, cerebral palsy, and euphorics and analgesics related to the terminally ill.
Financial data: Year ended 12/31/86. Assets, $9,395,247 (M); Total giving, $587,041; Grants to individuals amount not specified.
Employer Identification Number: 136116429
Applications: Deadline January 15th.
Program description:
Research grant payments are made to the university with which the individual investigator is affiliated.

12
Allied Educational Fund B
467 Sylvan Avenue
Englewood Cliffs, NJ 07632   (212) 695-7791
Contact: Morris Aarons, Trustee

Limitations: Scholarships only to graduating high school seniors who are family of Union members.
Financial data: Year ended 12/31/85. Assets, $4,740,414 (M); Total giving, $74,500; Grants to individuals, 63 grants totaling $74,500, high $2,000, low $1,000.
Employer Identification Number: 136202432
Applications: Deadline March 15th; Initial approach by letter in the form of an autobiography. See program description below for more specific application information.
Program description:
Applicant should also include a 5"x4" photograph of him or herself, transcripts, a personal letter or recommendation, a letter of recommendation from faculty advisor, professor or teacher, and information on the financial condition of the family, along with the autobiography.
    Awards must be accepted personally and publicly.

13
Allyn (Charles B.) Foundation, Inc.
P.O. Box 214
Mystic, CT 06355
Contact: Alfred J. Goodman, President

Limitations: Educational loans primarily to residents of New London County, CT. Funds are very limited and used for extremely narrow local boundaries. Loans represent approximately one-half of total annual funds.
Financial data: Year ended 9/30/85. Assets, $411,434 (M); Expenditures, $23,226; Loans to individuals, 10 loans totaling $12,450, high $2,400, low $500.
Employer Identification Number: 060391375
Applications: Initial approach by letter; Completion of formal application required; Update by letter including grades.

14
Almanor Scholarship Fund
c/o Collins Pine Company
Chester, CA 96020   (916) 258-2111
Contact: Charles M. Karns, Secretary

Limitations: Scholarships to graduates of Chester High School, Chester, CA.
Financial data: Year ended 12/31/86. Assets, $1,175,989 (M); Total giving, $62,600; Grants to individuals, 73 grants totaling $62,600, high $1,400, low $400, general range $600-1,200.
Employer Identification Number: 946066722
Applications: Deadline September 1st; Completion of formal application required.
Program description:
Scholarships are awarded for undergraduate and graduate study to individuals who will be full-time students and single at the time of registration, have maintained a 3.0 GPA in high school and a 2.5 GPA in college, and have exhibited leadership potential in school and community activities, employment experience, and attitude.

15
Alpert (Ida and Benjamin) Foundation
31275 Northwestern Highway 233
Farmington Hills, MI 48018
Contact: Myron Alpert, Secretary

Limitations: Scholarships to Michigan residents accepted by or enrolled in an accredited law school.
Financial data: Year ended 12/31/86. Assets, $136,817 (M); Total giving, $5,100; Grants to individuals, 10 grants totaling $5,000, high $1,500, low $250, average grant $250.
Employer Identification Number: 386143935
Applications: Completion of formal application required; Submit applications to Judge Frank S. Szymanski, 1215 City County Building, Detroit, MI 48226.
Program description:
The purpose of the foundation is to assist qualified students preparing for a career in law. Selection criteria: need, scholarship and social participation as college students. Upon receipt of applications, ten candidates will be asked to write an essay on a topic set by the foundation.

16
Alsobrooks (Miriam E.) Educational Fund
South Carolina National Bank
1401 Main Street
Columbia, SC 29226   (803) 771-3740
Contact: Trust Department

Limitations: Scholarships to graduates of McColl High School, McColl, SC.
Financial data: Year ended 6/30/86. Assets, $122,362 (M); Total giving, $2,400; Grants to individuals, 2

grants totaling $2,400, each grant $1,200.
Employer Identification Number: 576037000
Program description:
Scholarship awards are paid directly to the
educational institution on behalf of the individual
recipient.

17
Alworth (Marshall H. and Nellie) Memorial Fund

604 Alworth Building
Duluth, MN 55802   (218) 722-9366
Contact: Raymond W. Darland, President

Limitations: Scholarships in basic sciences to high
school graduates who are residents of northern
Minnesota.
Financial data: Year ended 12/31/86. Assets,
$3,343,740 (M); Total giving, $543,180; Grants to
individuals, 468 grants totaling $543,180.
Employer Identification Number: 410797340
Applications: Deadline March 1st; Submit proposal
preferably from December through February; Initial
approach by letter; Completion of formal application
required.
Publications: Program information, application
guidelines.
Program description:
Scholarships in chemistry, physics, mathematics,
engineering, geology, the biological sciences, and
medicine.

18
Amarillo Area Foundation, Inc.

1000 Polk Street
P.O. Box 2569
Amarillo, TX 79105   (806) 376-4521
Contact: Jack Cromartie, Executive Director

Limitations: Scholarships for residents of the 26 most
northern counties of the Texas Panhandle.
Financial data: Year ended 12/31/86. Assets,
$16,140,370; (M); Total giving, $640,662; Grants to
individuals, 39 grants totaling $25,650.
Employer Identification Number: 750978220
Applications: Deadline October 1st; Initial approach
by letter or telephone.
Publications: Annual report.

19
American Association of University Women, Honolulu Branch, Educational Fund

1802 Keeaumoku Street
Honolulu, HI 96822   (808) 537-4702
Contact: Current chairperson

Limitations: Graduate and undergraduate college
scholarships to women in the Pacific region; Awards

to professional working women.
Financial data: Year ended 6/30/86. Assets, $385,065
(M); Total giving, $11,611; Grants to individuals, 16
grants totaling $11,611, high $2,334, low $500,
general range $500-1,000, average grant $500.
Employer Identification Number: 990117668
Applications: Contact foundation for current
application deadline; Initial approach by letter.
Program description:
The fund supports three programs:
   The **Ruth E. Black Scholarship Fund** for
undergraduate study to residents of Hawaii for use
only at an accredited institution in Hawaii.
   The **Pacific Fellowship Fund** for graduate study to
women from the Pacific region, for use only at the
University of Hawaii at Manoa. After study is
completed, grantees must return "to help their own
countries".
   Women Who Make A Difference awards grants to
women already engaged in a profession so they may
enrich their learning with a three- to four-month
sabbatical in Hawaii. Applicants must be employed at
an institution or agency that contributed to the
development of the country; be able to present a
proposal for special study; and contribute, if possible,
to travel expenses.

20
Andalusia Health Services, Inc.

c/o William H. McWhorter
P.O. Box 1418
Andalusia, AL 36420   (205) 222-6591

Limitations: Scholarships only to residents of
Covington County, AL, wishing to attend college to
major in a health-related field, such as nursing,
medicine, medical or laboratory technology.
Financial data: Year ended 6/30/86. Assets,
$2,384,976 (M); Total giving, $273,092; Grants to
individuals, 56 grants totaling $52,092, high $3,334,
low $125.
Employer Identification Number: 630793474
Applications: Deadline March 15th; Completion of
formal application required. Applications may be
mailed to the foundation or submitted by hand to
office of the President, L.B. Wallace State Junior
College, Highway 84 By-Pass, Andalusia, AL 36420.
Program description:
The scholarship committee will consider financial
status, scholastic standing (should have at least a C
average), character and leadership qualities when
selecting recipients. Awards will be made for one year
and will be paid to the college on a semester or
quarterly basis. Recipients are expected to take a full
class load and submit an official transcript to the
committee each term.
   Upon completion of a college program it is
expected that the recipient will return to improve
health services for the Covington County community.

21
Anderson (William P.) Foundation
3552 Bayard Road
Cincinnati, OH 45208   (513) 871-1432
Contact: Paul D. Myers, Secretary

Limitations: Student aid primarily in Cincinnati, OH, and Boston, MA.
Financial data: Year ended 10/31/86. Assets, $3,641,197 (M); Total giving, $172,071; Grants to individuals, 5 grants totaling $24,571, high $14,167, low $720.
Employer Identification Number: 316034059
Applications: Applications accepted throughout the year; Initial approach by letter.

22★
Andrus (Alice A.) Foundation
c/o Wellington High School
629 North Main Street
Wellington, OH 44090
Contact: Robert F. Shaffer Jr., Principal, Wellington High School

Limitations: Scholarships only to graduates of Wellington High School, Wellington, OH.
Financial data: Year ended 3/31/87. Assets, $206,798 (M); Total giving, $13,650; Grants to individuals, 21 grants totaling $13,650, each grant $650.
Employer Identification Number: 346653271
Applications: Deadline April 1st; Initial approach by letter, including amount and purpose.

23
Ann Arbor Area Foundation
125 West Washington, Suite 400
Ann Arbor, MI 48104   (313) 663-0401
Contact: Joan U. Nagy, Executive Director

Limitations: Limited number of academic scholarships only to residents of the Ann Arbor, MI, area.
Financial data: Year ended 12/31/86. Assets, $2,761,609 (M); Total giving, $79,559; Grants to individuals, 2 grants totaling $2,000.
Employer Identification Number: 386087967
Applications: Initial approach by telephone; Completion of formal application required.
Publications: Annual report (including application guidelines).

24
Archer (Virginia A.) Scholarship Trust Fund
920 Spalding Building
Portland, OR 97204
Contact: Ralph J. Shepherd, 319 S.W. Washington, No. 920, Portland, OR 97204; Tel.: (503) 224-3015

Limitations: Scholarships only to graduating seniors of a Multnomah County, OR, high school planning to attend an Oregon college or university.
Financial data: Year ended 6/30/87. Assets, $189,735 (M); Total giving, $11,250; Grants to individuals, 19 grants totaling $11,250, high $800, low $200, general range $400-600.
Employer Identification Number: 936107007
Applications: Deadline April 1st; Initial approach by letter requesting application; Completion of formal application required.

25
Arlington Catholic High School Scholarship Fund
c/o First National Bank of Boston
P.O. Box 1861
Boston, MA 02105
Contact: Sister Ellen Pumphref, C.S.F., Principal, Arlington Catholic High School, 16 Medford Street, Arlington, MA 02174

Limitations: College scholarships for graduating students of Arlington Catholic High School, MA.
Financial data: Year ended 12/31/85. Assets, $127,307 (M); Total giving, $5,400; Grants to individuals, 18 grants totaling $5,400, each grant $300.
Employer Identification Number: 046116950
Applications: Applications accepted throughout the year; Initial approach by letter.

26
Armstrong (Cecil) Foundation
c/o Lake City Bank
P.O. Box 1387
Warsaw, IN 46580   (219) 267-9110
Contact: Trust Department

Limitations: Awards, either a grant or a loan, to Warsaw, IN, area students to improve skills or advance education by attending any properly accredited or certified educational program.
Financial data: Year ended 12/31/86. Assets, $174,518 (M); Total giving, $11,320; Grants to individuals, 50 grants totaling $11,320, high $300, low $16, average grant $300.
Employer Identification Number: 237128298
Applications: Completion of formal application required; Interviews required; Applications available at local schools and Lake City Bank.
Program description:
Grants for tuition, housing, and school expenses are awarded to students attending colleges, universities, vocational schools, rehabilitation training, or any properly accredited course in Indiana. For college-bound applicants, SAT, ACT, PSAT, or equivalent score will be required; no specific rank in class required. For vocational, rehabilitation, or any other type of training, sufficient evidence of skills and ability to pursue such a course of study is required. Applicants applying for assistance to continue a course

in which they are already enrolled must submit transcript of grades and present status from institution or program which they are attending. Applicants may reapply for continuance of this award.

The five-member awards committee is composed of people from the community.

27
A-T Medical Research Foundation
c/o Michael Traiger and Company
16255 Ventura Boulevard, No. 803
Encino, CA 91436   (818) 981-2111
Contact: Michael Traiger, Director

Limitations: Grants for medical research relating to ataxia-telangiectasia.
Financial data: Year ended 9/30/86. Assets, $18,673 (M); Total giving, $215,405; Grants to individuals, 1 grant totaling $25,405.
Employer Identification Number: 953882022
Applications: Applications accepted throughout the year.
Publications: 990-PF printed copy available upon request.

28★
Atherton Family Foundation
c/o Hawaiian Trust Company, Ltd.
111 South King Street
Honolulu, HI 96802   (808) 538-4539
Contact: Jane R. Smith, Secretary, c/o Hawaiian Trust Company, Ltd., P.O. Box 3170, Honolulu, HI 96802

Limitations: Scholarships to Hawaii residents who are children of Protestant ministers, or graduate theological students at a Protestant seminary.
Financial data: Year ended 12/31/86. Assets, $42,000,000 (M); Total giving, $1,687,868; Grants to individuals, 96 grants totaling $247,868; 1987, Grants to individuals, 49 grants totaling $51,635, high $2,000, low $340, general range $500-1,000, average grant $1,000.
Employer Identification Number: 510175971
Applications: Deadline March 1st; Initial approach by contacting the foundation or the financial aid administrator/high school counselor; Completion of formal application required.
Publications: Annual report, application guidelines, informational brochure.
Program description:
The **Juliette M. Atherton Scholarship Fund** is awarded to eligible applicants who have demonstrated financial need and promise of achievement. Scholarship requests are accepted from individuals in the following categories only:
  1. Christian Protestant ministers seeking further education at the postgraduate level.
  2. Children of Protestant ministers attending accredited postsecondary educational institutions.

  3. Individuals desiring to attend Christian Protestant seminaries for graduate theological study.

29
Atwood (Arthur R.) Scholarship Fund
Key Trust Company
60 State Street
Albany, NY 12207
Contact: Secretary; c/o Principal of Champlain Central School, Champlain, NY 12919

Limitations: Scholarships only for male students who have resided in the town of Champlain, NY, or the county of Clinton, NY, for at least seven-years. Preference is given to students accepted to Yale University.
Financial data: Year ended 2/28/86. Assets, $53,332 (M); Total giving, $4,400; Grants to individuals totaling $4,400.
Employer Identification Number: 146014625
Applications: Deadline April 15th; Initial approach by letter; Completion of formal application required.

not education

30★
Auer (Arthur A. and Hazel S.) Scholarship Fund
c/o Summit Bank of Kendallville
P.O. Box 668
Kendallville, IN 46755   (219) 347-0800
Contact: Fred Inniger, Guidance Counselor, East Noble School Corporation, Kendallville, IN 46755; Tel.: (219) 347-2032

Limitations: Scholarships only to seniors and graduates of East Noble High School, Kendallville, IN, for attendance at an accredited institution of higher learning.
Financial data: Year ended 12/31/86. Assets, $89,479 (M); Total giving, $8,442; Grants to individuals, 5 grants totaling $8,442, high $2,150, low $996.
Employer Identification Number: 356245200
Applications: Deadline first Friday in February; Completion of formal application required.
Program description:
Applicants considered on basis of academic standing, extracurricular activities, and citizenship.

31
Aurora Foundation, The
P.O. Box 1848
Bradenton, FL 33506   (813) 748-4100
Contact: Anthony T. Rossi, Chairman

Limitations: Scholarships for education and training of Christian ministers, missionaries, or those otherwise engaged in Christian service.
Financial data: Year ended 6/30/87. Assets, $59,517,881 (M); Total giving, $4,347,297; Grants to individuals, 58 grants totaling $126,547.

Employer Identification Number: 237044641
Applications: Applications accepted throughout the
year; Initial approach by letter.

32
Aurora Foundation, The
111 West Downer Place, Suite 312
Aurora, IL 60507-5136   (312) 896-7800
Contact: Sharon Stredde, Corporate Secretary

Limitations: Scholarships and loans to students
residing in or near Aurora, IL.
Financial data: Year ended 9/30/86. Assets,
$4,298,671 (M); Total giving $263,372; Grants to
individuals totaling $134,958.
Employer Identification Number: 366086742
Applications: Applications accepted throughout the
year; Interviews usually required.
Publications: Annual report.
Program description:
Awards are made on the basis of merit and need for
undergraduate, vocational, and graduate study.
Consideration is given to the applicant's academic
record, achievements outside the classroom, plus an
indicated ability to carry and to benefit from
academically demanding studies.

33★
Ayres (Mildred L.) Trust
c/o First National Bank of Kansas City
14 West Tenth Street
Kansas City, MO 64105   (816) 234-7481
Contact: David P. Ross

Limitations: Student loans and scholarships to
residents of Missouri attending Midwestern Baptist
Seminary, William Jewell College, or the University of
Missouri at Columbia to assist with theological and
medical training and living expenses. Preference is
given to residents of metropolitan Kansas City.
Financial data: Year ended 12/31/87. Assets, $221,340
(M); Grants to individuals, 8 grants totaling $12,000,
high $1,500, low $500, general range $500-1,500;
Loans to individuals amount not specified.
Employer Identification Number: 446008191
Applications: Applications accepted throughout the
year; Completion of formal application required;
Application available from applicant's high school
financial aid office or trust office; Interviews required.
Program description:
The student's application file should include:
   1. Formal application
   2. Financial statement
   3. Personal statement (reason for wanting further
   education and need for loan)
   4. Picture
   5. Transcript
   6. Four letters of reference (two personal and two
   from instructors or advisors).

34
Babcock (Charles C. and Elizabeth V.) Memorial Scholarship Fund
c/o Bank One of Indianapolis N.A.
101 Monument Circle
Indianapolis, IN 46277   (317) 639-8145
Contact: W. Francis Brezette

Limitations: Scholarships only to graduates of
Rochester High School, Rochester, IN.
Financial data: Year ended 6/30/87. Assets, $492,487
(M); Total giving, $42,350; Grants to individuals, 90
grants totaling $42,350, high $1,500, low $100.
Employer Identification Number: 356275255
Applications: Deadlines May and November; Initial
approach by letter requesting application; Completion
of formal application required; Interviews required.

35★
Baber (Weisell) Foundation, Inc.
535 South Broadway
Peru, IN 46970   (317) 473-7526
Contact: Roger D. Baber, President

Limitations: Student loans to graduates of one of the
Miami County high schools only.
Financial data: Year ended 12/31/86. Assets,
$2,559,088 (M); Expenditures, $172,393; Loans to
individuals, 50 loans totaling $110,525, high $10,800,
low $200.
Employer Identification Number: 356024561
Applications: Applications accepted throughout the
year; Interviews required; Applicants must apply in
person.

36
Bagby Foundation for the Musical Arts, The
501 Fifth Avenue
New York, NY 10017   (212) 986-6094
Contact: Eleanor C. Mark, Executive Director

Limitations: Musical study grants based on talent and
need.
Financial data: Year ended 12/31/85. Assets,
$1,070,812 (M); Total giving, $26,690; Grants to
individuals, 12 grants totaling $19,190; Subtotal for
musical study grants, 4 grants totaling $6,540, high
$2,840, low $400.
Employer Identification Number: 131873289
Applications: Applications accepted throughout the
year; Submit written application, setting forth reasons
why assistance is required.

37★
Bailey Foundation, The
c/o State Street Bank & Trust Company
P.O. Box 351
Boston, MA 02101
Contact: Edwin Bailey, 414 Main Street, Amesbury, MA 01913

Limitations: Scholarships to residents of Amesbury, MA.
Financial data: Year ended 6/30/86. Assets, $194,322; Total giving, $7,500 (M); Grants to individuals, 8 grants totaling $7,500, high $1,500, low $500.
Employer Identification Number: 046095808
Applications: Deadline April 15th; Completion of formal application required.
Program description:
The scholarship is awarded to one new individual each year who is a graduate of Amesbury High School or a resident of Amesbury, MA. The scholarship is to be used for tuition, books and supplies, and laboratory expenses for a student pursuing a B.S. or B.A. degree, and is usually renewable for a four-year period. Selection is based on a combination of financial need and scholastic record.

38
Bair (Charles M.) Memorial Trust
c/o First Trust Company of Montana
P.O. Box 30678
Billings, MT 59115   (406) 657-8122
Contact: Alberta M. Bair, Trustee

Limitations: Scholarships to two graduates of Harlowton High School, MT, two graduates of White Sulphur Springs High School, MT, and four graduates of high schools located in Meagher and Wheatland counties, MT.
Financial data: Year ended 1/31/87. Assets, $18,600,242 (M); Total giving, $741,225; Grants to individuals, 38 grants totaling $114,225, high $6,908, low $10.
Employer Identification Number: 810370774
Applications: Deadline April 20th; Completion of formal application required; Financial Assistance Questionnaire signed by parent or guardian required.
Program description:
The basis for selection is achievement in high school, good citizenship, moral character, financial need, and apparent ability to benefit by a college education or vocational training. Scholarships are for a period of four years, and are intended to cover tuition, room and board, and incidental expenses subject to the sole discretion of the trustee as to amounts and continuance.

39
Baker (Clark and Ruby) Foundation
c/o Bank South, Personal Trust Department
P.O. Box 4956
Atlanta, GA 30302   (404) 529-4627
Contact: Odette Capell, Secretary, or Tom Murphy

Limitations: Scholarships based on financial need to Georgia residents for study at a college or university operated by or affiliated with the Methodist Church.
Financial data: Year ended 12/31/86. Assets, $1,440,913 (M); Total giving, $67,500; Grants to individuals, 9 grants totaling, $13,000, high $2,000, low $500.
Employer Identification Number: 581429097
Applications: Applications in letter form, stating educational plans, resumes, expenses and the anticipated amount required, accepted throughout the year; Interviews required.

40
Baker (Jessie H.) Education Fund
c/o Marine Midland Bank-Trust Operation Center
P.O. Box 4203
Buffalo, NY 14240

Limitations: Scholarships for undergraduate education.
Financial data: Year ended 8/31/86. Assets, $1,385,668 (M); Total giving, $71,355; Grants to individuals, 154 grants totaling $71,355, high $1,000, low $50.
Employer Identification Number: 222478098

41
Baker (J.H.) Trust
c/o Farmers and Merchants State Bank
Box 280
La Crosse, KS 67548   (913) 222-2537
Contact: Tom Dechant, Trustee

Limitations: Student loans for postsecondary education only to graduates of high schools in Rush, Barton, Ellis, Ness, and Pawnee counties, KS, who are also under 25 years of age.
Financial data: Year ended 12/31/86. Assets, $1,057,778 (M); Expenditures, $9,275; Loans to individuals, 65 loans totaling $44,174, high $1,400, low $200.
Employer Identification Number: 510210925
Applications: Applications accepted throughout the year; Completion of formal application required.

42★

Balso Foundation, The
c/o The Ball & Socket Manufacturing Company
493 West Main Street
Cheshire, CT 06410   (203) 272-5361
Contact: Neil Longobardi, Trustee

Limitations: Scholarships for Cheshire High School
seniors and college undergraduates in towns which
surround Cheshire, CT.
Financial data: Year ended 12/31/87. Assets, $300,000
(M); Grants to individuals, 20 grants totaling $14,000,
high $1,500, low $500, general range $500-1,500,
average grant $700.
Employer Identification Number: 237159876
Applications: Deadline April 10th; Completion of
formal application required; Contact the principal of
Cheshire High School, South Main Street, Cheshire,
CT 06410; Tel.: (203) 272-5361.
Publications: Application guidelines, financial
statement.
Program description:
Scholarships are available for undergraduate study and
may be renewed. High school seniors and college
undergraduates in Cheshire and surrounding towns
may apply.

43

**Bamberger (Ruth Eleanor) and John Ernest
    Bamberger Memorial Foundation**
1201 Walker Center
Salt Lake City, UT 84111   (801) 364-2045
Contact: William H. Olwell, Secretary-Treasurer

Limitations: Undergraduate scholarships to Utah
residents, with preference given to student nurses.
Occasional loans awarded for medical education.
Financial data: Year ended 12/31/86. Assets,
$7,281,272 (M); Total giving, $278,665; Grants to
individuals, 66 grants totaling $39,686, high $1,887,
low $75.
Employer Identification Number: 876116540
Applications: Applications accepted throughout the
year; Initial approach by letter; Interviews required.
Program description:
Undergraduate scholarship grant payments are made
through local institutions with special emphasis on
student nurses.

44

Bank of America-Giannini Foundation
Bank of America Center, Department 3246
Box 37000
San Francisco, CA 94137   (415) 953-0932
Contact: Caroline O. Boitano, Administrator

Limitations: Fellowships to individuals for postdoctoral
research done at one of the eight medical schools in
California.

Financial data: Year ended 12/31/86. Assets,
$7,500,000 (M); Total giving, $385,000; Grants to
individuals, 15 grants totaling $255,000.
Employer Identification Number: 946089512
Applications: Deadline December 1st; Initial approach
by letter or telephone; Completion of formal
application required.
Publications: Annual report.

45

Barber (George and Hazel) Scholarship Trust
P.O. Box 938
Hannibal, MO 63401
Contact: Guidance counselor of eligible high schools.

Limitations: Scholarships only to graduating seniors in
Marion County, MO, and Pike County, IL.
Financial data: Year ended 12/31/86. Assets, $167,728
(M); Total giving, $10,000; Grants to individuals, 18
grants totaling $10,000, high $1,000, low $50, general
range $350-1,000.
Employer Identification Number: 237214882
Applications: Deadline April 1st; Completion of
formal application required; Interviews required;
Application must be notarized; Completed application
should be returned to local school official who will
forward it to the foundation.
Program description:
The scholarship award must be used in the academic
year immediately following the student's high school
graduation. Two equal payments will be made directly
to the student annually after verification of enrollment
is confirmed by the college to the scholarship
committee's chairman. The award is renewable if the
recipient maintains a cummulative grade point average
of at least 2.0 and continues to be recognized as a
citizen of the college or university community.

46

Barker Foundation, Inc., The
P.O. Box 328
Nashua, NH 03061   (603) 889-1763
Contact: Allan M. Barker, President

Limitations: Scholarships primarily to residents of New
Hampshire.
Financial data: Year ended 12/31/85. Assets,
$2,573,734 (M); Total giving, $115,352; Grants to
individuals totaling $34,988.
Employer Identification Number: 026005885
Applications: Submissions must allow sufficient lead
time for review by the trustees; Interviews sometimes
required.
Program description:
Grants for scholarships are based on financial need,
academic performance, and recommendations. Funds
available for scholarships are limited, so few new
awards are made.

47★
Barnes (Fay T.) Scholarship Trust
P.O. Box 550
Austin, TX 78789-0001

Limitations: Scholarships for deserving students of Williamson and Travis counties, TX.
Financial data: Year ended 12/31/86. Assets, $2,488,334 (M); Total giving, $221,250; Grants to individuals, 110 grants totaling $221,250, high $3,750, low $1,250, general range $1,250-2,500.
Employer Identification Number: 742256469
Applications: Deadline January 15th; Completion of formal application required; Contact high school principal or counselor for complete application information.
Publications: Application guidelines, financial statement, informational brochure, 990-PF printed copy available upon request.
Program description:
Students are required to submit applications to their high school principal or counselor where a committee of three to five faculty administrators select eligible candidates. Each high school in Travis and Williamson counties may submit to the foundation trustee, Texas Commerce Bank - Austin, one application for every 100 students, or part thereof, in the graduating senior class. The trustee administers the fund and selects approximately fifteen to twenty award recipients from the eligible candidates submitted by each high school. Recipients are chosen on the basis of the following criteria:
1. Scholarship - overall "B" (85) average at graduation, minimum
2. Citizenship character - activities, accomplishments and recommendations
3. Demonstrable need - may be considered.

48
Barnes (Otis A.) and Margaret T. Barnes Trust
First National Bank - Trust Department
P.O. Box 1699
Colorado Springs, CO 80942

Limitations: Scholarships only to students planning to major in chemistry at Colorado College, CO.
Financial data: Year ended 6/30/87. Assets, $2,000,000 (M) approximate; Total giving, $129,977; Grants to individuals, 10 grants totaling $90,200, high $8,840, low $1,800.
Employer Identification Number: 846023466
Applications: Deadline Spring semester prior to matriculation; Initial approach by submitting admission application with a letter requesting consideration to Colorado College, Chemistry Department, Colorado Springs, CO 80903.

49
Barrington (Richard and Jessie) Educational Fund
c/o Wells Fargo Bank
343 Sausane Street, Third Floor
San Francisco, CA 94163
Contact: Washoe Tribe of Nevada and California Education Department, 919 Highway 395 South, Gardnerville, NV 89410; Tel.: (702) 265-4191

Limitations: Scholarships only to enrolled members of the Washoe Tribe for use at colleges (undergraduate and graduate) or vocational schools.
Financial data: Year ended 5/31/87. Assets, $65,122 (M); Total giving, $5,000; Grants to individuals totaling $5,000.
Employer Identification Number: 946448099
Applications: Applications accepted throughout the year; Initial approach by letter; Completion of formal application required.

50
Barrows (Augustus and Kathleen) Memorial and Trust Fund
271 South Union Street
Burlington, VT 05401   (802) 863-4531
Contact: Maureen T. McNeil

Limitations: Scholarships for women residing in Vermont who are under the age of 25.
Financial data: Year ended 12/31/85. Assets, $125,792 (M); Total giving, $8,750; Grants to individuals, 27 grants totaling $8,750, high $400, low $200, average grant $300.
Employer Identification Number: 036010364
Applications: Deadline July prior to the next school year; Completion of formal application required, including two reference letters and college transcript if applicable.

51
Barth (The Theodore H.) Foundation, Inc.
1211 Avenue of the Americas
New York, NY 10036   (212) 840-6000
Contact: Irving P. Berelson, Vice-President

Limitations: Scholarships only to high school graduates of the Wareham, MA, School District.
Financial data: Year ended 12/31/85. Assets, $9,800,814 (M); Total giving, $539,724; Grants to individuals, 21 grants totaling $62,024, high $25,000, low $375.
Employer Identification Number: 136103401
Applications: Applications accepted throughout the year; Initial approach by letter.

52
Bartlett (W.P.) Trust Fund
c/o Burford & Moran
141 East Mill Avenue
Porterville, CA 93257   (209) 784-6642
Contact: William B. Richardson, Secretary, 27349
Avenue 138, Porterville, CA 93257

Limitations: Scholarships to current students of the
Porterville, CA, High School District and the
Porterville College District to attend California colleges
and universities.
Financial data: Year ended 12/31/86. Assets, $458,244
(M); Total giving, $21,250; Grants to individuals, 54
grants totaling $16,650, high $500, low $250.
Employer Identification Number: 946102005
Applications: Deadline February of each school year;
Initial approach by letter stating residence, schools
attended, present school status, and naming
prospective school.
Program description:
The aim of the foundation is to assist needy, qualified
students in meeting school expenses for each quarter
for two years of schooling. Recipients of the
scholarships must have been attending their high
school or college for at least two years prior to
application. Applicants are judged on prior academic
performance, performance on test for ability and
aptitude for college work, recommendations from
instructors, financial need and a personal interview
with the selection committee. Periodic reports on
recipients' progress are required, including a full
disclosure of grades.
 Scholarship awards are determined by scholarship
committees of Porterville College, Porterville High
School, and Monache High School. No application is
required as awards are based on the scholastic rank,
ability, and financial need of each student who is
known to be a college student after graduation and
who is going to attend a public or private accredited
college in California.

53
Batt (Herbert L.) Memorial Foundation Inc.
27 Vista Terrace
New Haven, CT 06515   (203) 389-0213
Contact: Irving Kroopnick, President

Limitations: Grants are for advancement of Hebrew
education for residents of Connecticut and
Massachusetts only.
Financial data: Year ended 12/31/85. Assets, $19,482
(M); Total giving, $2,400; Grants to individuals, 6
grants totaling $2,400, high $500, low $300.
Employer Identification Number: 066068499
Applications: Applications accepted throughout the
year; Initial approach by letter with name of school to
be entered and planned course of study.

54
Baumberger Endowment
7701 Broadway, Suite 206
P.O. Box 6067
San Antonio, TX 78209   (512) 822-8915

Limitations: Scholarships only to Bexar County, TX,
students attending college or university in Texas.
Financial data: Year ended 12/31/86. Assets,
$1,059,158 (M); Total giving, $1,384,564; Grants to
individuals, 346 grants totaling $1,384,564.
Employer Identification Number: 237225925
Applications: Deadlines January 31st for financial aid
forms, February 15th for application and high school
transcript; Applications available from high school
counselor or foundation office.
Publications: Program information, application
guidelines.

55
Beatty (Cordelia Lunceford) Trust
Security Bank Building, Second Floor
101 North Main
Blackwell, OK 74631   (405) 363-3684
Contact: James R. Rodgers, Trustee

Limitations: Scholarships only to permanent residents
of Blackwell, OK, who are under the age of 19.
Financial data: Year ended 12/31/86. Assets,
$1,456,423 (M); Total giving, $42,005; Grants to
individuals, 15 grants totaling $5,224, high $1,000,
low $12.
Employer Identification Number: 736094952
Applications: Deadline prior to start of school year;
Initial approach by letter requesting application;
Completion of formal application required.

56
Bee (Anna H. & Albert W.) Scholarship Fund
c/o Crocker National Bank - Trust Department
P.O. Drawer H-H
Santa Barbara, CA 93102   (805) 963-0811

Limitations: Non-interest-bearing student loans to
long-term residents of Santa Barbara County, CA.
Financial data: Year ended 12/31/86. Assets, $279,076
(M); Expenditures, $26,504; Loans to individuals, 46
loans totaling $21,875, high $750, low $125, general
range $500-1,000, average loan $500.
Employer Identification Number: 956063281
Applications: Deadline June 1st; Applications
accepted January 1st-June 1st; Completion of formal
application accompanied by letters of reference and
official school transcript, required.
Program description:
Two years of non-college residence in the country is
the minimum residence requirement. Loan may be
used at any accredited school of the recipient's
choice. Loans are renewable for subsequent years if a

renewal application is submitted, the need continues to exist, and acceptable grades have been maintained. Loans must be repaid after completion of education.

The fund's trust instrument specifies that the non-interest bearing loans made to students are honorable loans which the recipients are under no obligation to repay. As a result, the loans are in effect grants.

57
Beebe (Charles A.) Scholarship Fund

c/o M. L. Snyder, Trust Tax Office
301 S. W. Adams Street
Peoria, IL 61631
Contact: William Heinhorst, President, Peoples State Bank, Manito, IL 61546; Tel.: (309)968-6689.

Limitations: Scholarships only to graduates of Forman Community High School in Manito, IL.
Financial data: Year ended 12/31/86. Assets, $405,033 (M); Total giving, $28,990; Grants to individuals, 73 grants totaling $29,370, high $460, low $180, general range $240-460, average grant $460.
Employer Identification Number: 376164013
Applications: Deadline May 15th; Completion of formal application required; Applications available from Peoples State Bank.

58
Bend Foundation

416 Northeast Greenwood
Bend, OR 97701   (503) 382-1662
Contact: Michael P. Hollern, Trustee

Limitations: Scholarships to residents of Bend and Deschutes County, OR, who are graduates of Bend and Mountain View high schools.
Financial data: Year ended 12/31/85. Assets, $2,025,305 (M); Total giving, $105,705; Grants to individuals, 18 grants totaling $25,500.
Employer Identification Number: 416019901
Applications: Deadline April; Initial approach by letter; Application guidelines available from Administrative School District No. 1, Bend, OR.
Publications: Application guidelines.

59
Bendheim (Charles and Els) Foundation

Ten Columbus Circle
New York, NY 10019

Limitations: Grants to Jewish individuals for religious study.
Financial data: Year ended 1/31/86. Assets, $304,304 (M); Total giving, $182,942; Grants to individuals amount not specified.
Employer Identification Number: 136103769

60
Benjamin Trust Fund

c/o West Chicago State Bank
600 East Washington Street
West Chicago, IL 60185
Contact: Superintendent of Schools, 326 Joliet Street, West Chicago, IL 60185

Limitations: Scholarships only to graduates of West Chicago Community High School District No. 94, IL.
Financial data: Year ended 2/28/87. Assets, $323,557 (M); Total giving, $8,035; Grants to individuals, 5 grants totaling $8,035, high $3,000, low $350, general range $500-2,500.
Employer Identification Number: 366552295
Applications: Deadline April 15th of year preceeding school year; Completion of formal application required; Applications available from superintendent.

61
Bennett (The James Gordon) Memorial Corporation

200 Park Avenue, Room 2023
New York, NY 10166   (212) 755-8310
Contact: Eleanor H. Keil, New York University, P.O. Box 908, Madison Square Station, New York, NY 10159; Tel.: (212) 481-5905

Limitations: Scholarships to children of journalists who have worked in New York City on a daily newspaper for ten years or more.
Financial data: Year ended 12/31/84. Assets, $2,777,989 (M); Total giving, $145,550; Grants to individuals, 95 grants totaling $145,550; Subtotal for scholarships, 80 grants totaling $88,950, high $2,000, low $250, general range $800-1,000.
Employer Identification Number: 136150414
Applications: Deadline March 1st; Initial approach by letter; Completion of formal application required.
Publications: Program information, application guidelines.
Program description:
Amounts available for scholarships vary each year because the foundation's priority is to supply aid to needy journalists who have worked in New York City ten or more years. With the surplus funds after aiding these journalists, the foundation dispenses the funds among "the issue of members of the immediate families of persons employed for ten years or more on any daily newspaper published in New York or to such persons themselves."

62
Bentley (Frank F.) Trust

c/o Ameritrust Company
P.O. Box 5937
Cleveland, OH 44101
Contact: Joyce A. May, c/o Turner & May, 800 Second National Bank Building, Warren, OH 44481;

Tel.: (216) 399-8801

Limitations: Scholarships only to graduates of high schools in Trumbull County, OH.
Financial data: Year ended 9/30/86. Assets, $417,778 (M); Total giving, $22,436; Grants to individuals totaling $22,436.
Employer Identification Number: 346508762
Applications: Deadline mid-summer; Initial approach by letter requesting application; Completion of formal application required.

63★
Bergen (Frank and Lydia) Foundation
c/o First Fidelity Bank
55 Madison Avenue
Morristown, NJ 07960   (201) 829-7111
Contact: Jane Donnelly, Executive Director

Limitations: Educational support to aid worthy music students in New Jersey in securing a complete and adequate musical education.
Financial data: Year ended 12/31/85. Assets, $4,678,614 (M); Total giving, $200,775; Grants to individuals amount not specified.
Employer Identification Number: 226359304
Applications: Initial approach by letter or telephone.
Publications: Annual report.
Program description:
Grant payments are made directly to the institutions on behalf of the individual recipients.

64
Berry (Charles H.) Trust Fund
c/o George Findell, Jr.
P.O. Box 2036
Rochester, NH 03867   (603) 332-1670

Limitations: Scholarships to male students from New Durham, Farmington, or Rochester, NH, who will be attending college in Strafford County, NH.
Financial data: Year ended 3/31/87. Assets, $52,267 (M); Total giving, $2,600; Grants to individuals, 4 grants totaling $2,600, high $800, low $500.
Employer Identification Number: 026005363
Applications: Applications accepted throughout the year; Completion of formal application required; Submit high school transcript with application.

65
Beta Theta Pi Fraternity Founders Fund
208 East High Street
P.O. Box 111
Oxford, OH 45056   (513) 523-7591
Contact: Thomas A. Beyer, Administrative Secretary

Limitations: Scholarships only to members of Beta Theta Pi fraternities around the country.
Financial data: Year ended 6/30/85. Assets,

$1,140,347 (M); Total giving, $55,000; Grants to individuals, 47 grants totaling $55,000, high $2,000, low $500, general range $1,000-1,500.
Employer Identification Number: 316050515
Applications: Deadline April 15th; Initial approach by letter requesting application; Completion of formal application required.

66
BF Foundation
114 North San Francisco Street, Suite 100
Flagstaff, AZ 86001   (602) 774-2547
Contact: David Chase, Secretary-Treasurer

Limitations: Scholarships and student loans to undergraduates attending colleges and universities in the U.S.
Financial data: Year ended 12/31/86. Assets, $887,726 (M); Total giving, $157,113; Grants to individuals, 194 grants totaling $157,113, high $23,200, low $33; Loans to individuals totaling $36,865.
Employer Identification Number: 366141070
Applications: Deadlines May 31st for first-time applicants and March 31st for continuations; Initial approach by letter requesting application form between February 1st and May 1st; Completion of formal application required; Submit copy of official grade transcript.

67
Biglane (D.A.) Foundation
P.O. Box 966
Natchez, MS 39120

Limitations: Scholarships only to residents of the Natchez, MS, area.
Financial data: Year ended 12/31/86. Assets, $118,435 (M); Total giving, $21,260; Grants to individuals, 9 grants totaling $16,260, high $4,000, low $500, general range $650-2,000.
Employer Identification Number: 646028044

68
Bishop (E.K. and Lillian F.) Foundation
c/o Rainier National Bank, Capital Management Division
P.O. Box 3966
Seattle, WA 98124   (206) 621-4445
Contact: Bishop Scholarship Committee, c/o Rainier National Bank, Grays Harbor Branch, P.O. Box 149, Aberdeen, WA 99520

Limitations: Scholarships limited to students who have resided in Grays Harbor County, WA, at least one year immediately prior to date of application.
Financial data: Year ended 4/30/87. Assets, $15,988,877 (M); Total giving, $1,140,582; Grants to individuals, 60 grants totaling $100,000, high $3,500, low $500.

Employer Identification Number: 916116724
Applications: Deadline June 1st; Initial approach by letter; Completion of formal application required.
Program description:
Scholarship applicants must be in need of financial assistance. Funds are provided to assist students who are enrolled in either their third or fourth year of an approved four-year school of higher education, or their first two years at an approved graduate school. Applicants must have maintained a grade point average of 3.0 or the equivalent.

69
Bivins (Mary E.) Foundation
414 Polk Street
P.O. Box 708
Amarillo, TX 79105
Contact: Mr. Lindy Ward, Director

Limitations: Scholarships for postsecondary education to residents of Texas whose field and institution are religious.
Financial data: Year ended 8/31/86. Assets, $49,225,089 (M); Total giving, $472,967; Grants to individuals totaling $67,113, general range $1,000-3,000.
Employer Identification Number: 750842370
Applications: Deadline October 31st; Initial approach by letter.

70
Black (Albert B. and Evelyn H.) Scholarship Fund
c/o Bank of New England, N.A.
28 State Street
Boston, MA 02107
Contact: George S. Ames, Trust Officer

Limitations: Scholarships to students who are attending or have attended Concord, MA, public schools.
Financial data: Year ended 12/31/85. Assets, $575,856 (M); Total giving, $28,816; Grants to individuals, 42 grants totaling $28,816, high $2,500, low $250, general range $500-850.
Employer Identification Number: 046141425
Applications: Deadline April 1st; Completion of formal application and letter establishing applicant's academic standing required.
Publications: Program information, application guidelines.
Program description:
The fund was established to provide scholarships for needy, worthy, and able high school students. To qualify, the recipient must have maintained a scholastic standing above the average of his class during the preceding year. The applicant must also wish to pursue studies or develop a talent in areas where no instruction or additional instruction is

available in the Concord public schools. Study provided for by such assistance is not limited to that available in a college or university, and it may include advanced training in any one of the fine arts, practical arts, or vocations.
Qualified applicants to the Black Fund will also be considered for several other funds also administered by the Bank of New England.

71
Blackwelder Foundation, Inc.
P.O. Box 1431
Lenoir, NC 28645   (704) 754-3452
Contact: Lloyd M. Rash, President

Limitations: Scholarships to students residing in North Carolina, with preference to residents of Caldwell County, NC, and especially those whose parents work in an unspecified hospital.
Financial data: Year ended 10/31/86. Assets, $852,984 (M); Total giving, $41,000; Grants to individuals, 10 grants totaling $6,500, high $1,000, low $500.
Employer Identification Number: 566060615
Applications: Deadline July; Completion of formal application required.

72★
Blanchard Foundation, The, and The Luke and Jerusha Blanchard Scholarship Fund
c/o Boston Safe Deposit & Trust Company
One Boston Place
Boston, MA 02106   (617) 722-7340
Contact: Sylvia Salas, Trust Officer

Limitations: Scholarships for residents of Boxborough, MA, who graduated from Blanchard Memorial High School.
Financial data: Year ended 12/31/87. Assets, $10,855,820 (M); Total giving, $590,723; Grants to individuals, 22 grants totaling $11,300, high $800, low $400, general range $400-500.
Employer Identification Number: 046093374
Applications: Deadline April 1st; Contact principal of Blanchard Memorial High School for all application inquiries and submissions; Applications available only from Blanchard Memorial High School; Completion of formal application required.

73★
Blandin (Charles K.) Foundation
100 Pokegama Avenue North
Grand Rapids, MN 55744   (218) 326-0523
Contact: Paul Olson, President

Limitations: Scholarships for undergraduate and vocational study are limited to recent graduates under the age of 22 of an Itasca County, Hill City, or Remer, MN, high school.

Financial data: Year ended 12/31/87. Assets, $24,376,362 (M); Total giving, $6,100,751; Grants to individuals, 474 grants totaling $266,182, high $2,800, low $500, average grant $562.
Employer Identification Number: 416038619
Applications: Applications accepted throughout the year; Contact foundation for current application deadline; Initial approach by telephone or letter of inquiry to the Executive Director.
Publications: Annual report, application guidelines, informational brochure, program information.
Program description:
The **Blandin Educational Awards Program** does not make scholarship awards for graduate study or for individuals over the age of 22 for any course of study.

74
Blazek (Joseph) Foundation
Eight South Michigan Avenue, No. 801
Chicago, IL 60603   (312) 372-3880
Contact: Samuel S. Brown, Executive Director

Limitations: Scholarships for high school seniors in public or private secondary schools in Cook County, IL, planning to major in engineering, mathematics, chemistry, physics or related scientific fields.
Financial data: Year ended 6/30/86. Assets, $1,750 (M); Total giving, $24,000; Grants to individuals, 46 grants totaling $24,000, average grant $500.
Employer Identification Number: 237015800
Applications: Deadline February 1st of high school senior year; Completion of formal application required.
Publications: Application guidelines.
Program description:
All grants are automatically renewed for each succeeding undergraduate year for a maximum of four years, dependent upon the grantee's continued enrollment. Grants are made directly to the school.

75★
Bloch-Selinger Educational Trust Fund
c/o Commonwealth Bank & Trust Company, N.A.
P.O. Box 308
Williamsport, PA 17703
Contact: Superintendent of Schools, Danville Area School District, P.O. Box 139, Danville, PA 17821; Tel.: (717) 275-7573

Limitations: Scholarships only to honor students graduating from Danville High School, Danville, PA.
Financial data: Year ended 12/31/86. Assets, $302,590 (M); Total giving, $19,600; Grants to individuals, 9 grants totaling $19,600, high $2,600, low $1,200.
Employer Identification Number: 236558579
Applications: Applications accepted throughout the year; Initial approach by letter requesting application; Completion of formal application required.

76
Bloomer (James J.) Charitable Trust
c/o Chemung Canal Trust Company
P.O. Box 1522
Elmira, NY 14902
Contact: Trustees of St. Patrick's Roman Catholic Church Society of Elmira, NY 14901

Limitations: Scholarships to residents of Elmira, NY, who are members of the Catholic Church, for attendance at Catholic colleges or universities in the U.S.
Financial data: Year ended 12/31/85. Assets, $117,535 (M); Total giving, $8,500; Grants to individuals, 11 grants totaling $8,500, high $1,000, low $500.
Employer Identification Number: 166022129

77★
Blue Mountain Area Foundation
12 East Main Street
P.O. Box 603
Walla Walla, WA 99362   (509) 529-4371
Contact: Eleanor S. Kane, Administrator

Limitations: Scholarships to graduates of high schools in the Blue Mountain area, including Walla Walla, Columbia, Garfield, Benton, and Franklin counties in southeastern WA and Umatilla County in northeastern OR.
Financial data: Year ended 5/31/87. Assets, $995,442 (M); Total giving, $64,466; Grants to individuals, 21 grants totaling $13,201.
Employer Identification Number: 911250104
Applications: Deadlines vary between April 15th and June 1st; Completion of formal application required.
Publications: Annual report.
Program description:
The foundation manages six scholarship funds:
1. **Ralph R. Bennett and Mary Ellen Bennett Scholarship Fund** assists graduates of high schools in Walla Walla County, WA. Applications are available at the foundation office.
2. **Benton City Wranglers Educational Trust** makes annual awards to graduates of Kiona-Benton City High School, WA. Applications are available at the high school.
3. **Howard and Pearl Burgess Scholarship Fund** benefits young men and women active in 4-H Clubs in Walla Walla County, WA. Applications are available at County Extension Office.
4. **Ward and Vera Hoskins Memorial Scholarship Fund** awards scholarships to graduates of Dayton High School. Applications are available at the high school.
5. **Lawrence Slater Scholarship Fund** awards scholarships to graduates of Pomeroy High School, WA. Applications are available at the high school.
6. **Dayl and Doris Graves Scholarship Fund** assists graduates of high schools in Walla Walla

County, WA, with priority to students in auto body and repair courses at Walla Walla Community College. Applications are available at the foundation office.

78★
Boehmer (Arthur C.) and Florence Schubert Boehmer Scholarship Fund
228 West Pine Street
Lodi, CA 95240 (209) 369-2781
Contact: Robert K. Elliott, Co-Trustee

Limitations: Graduate and undergraduate scholarships only to students who have graduated from high school in the Lodi Unified School District, Lodi, CA (including Lodi High School, Tokay High School, Liberty High School, and Lodi Academy) who plan to attend a CA college or university. Preference given to those studying medicine.
Financial data: Year ended 6/30/86. Assets, $570,814 (M); Total giving, $32,600; Grants to individuals, 53 grants totaling $32,600, high $4,500, low $200, general range $500-700, average grant $500.
Employer Identification Number: 942683571
Applications: Deadline June 15th; Completion of formal application required.

79★
Bogardus (Katherine) Trust
c/o The John Warner Bank
301 South Side Square
Clinton, IL 61727 (217) 935-3144
Contact: Ceail L. Nunnery, Trust Officer

Limitations: Educational grants and loans to graduates of high schools in DeWitt County, IL, and to descendants of the first cousins of the creator of this trust.
Financial data: Year ended 12/31/87. Assets, $273,000 (M); Total giving, $34,105; Grants to individuals, 10 grants totaling $34,105, high $6,000, low $1,500; Loans to individuals amount not specified.
Employer Identification Number: 376062479
Applications: Contact foundation for current deadline; Completion of formal application required; Interviews required.
Program description:
Grants and loans may be used for nursing school, law school, and both junior and four-year college, and are payable after graduation on a single term basis only. Applicants must submit course programs, transcripts of grades, and budgets prior to the beginning of the term. Renewal of loans depends on maintenance of academic standards.

80
Bohnett (Vi) Memorial Foundation
315 Uluniu Street, Room 208A
P.O. Box 1361
Kailua, HI 96734

Limitations: Scholarships to individuals.
Financial data: Year ended 12/31/86. Assets, $1,674,294; Total giving, $70,691,; Grants to individuals, 53 grants totaling $44,900, high $3,000, low $200, general range $1,000-1,500.
Employer Identification Number: 956225968
Applications: Initial approach by letter.

81
Bond (Charles H.) Trust
c/o The First National Bank of Boston
P.O. Box 1890
Boston, MA 02105
Contact: Sharon Driscoll, Trust Officer

Limitations: Scholarships to Massachusetts high school seniors who will be attending college the following year.
Financial data: Year ended 9/30/86. Assets, $311,724 (M); Total giving, $5,750; Grants to individuals, 8 grants totaling $5,750, high $750, low $500, average grant $750.
Employer Identification Number: 046007908
Applications: Applications accepted December 15th through April 15th; Completion of formal application required.
Publications: Application guidelines.
Program description:
Scholarship recipients receive a yearly grant provided they notify the trustees by letter of their current academic standing, supported by current transcript.

82
Borden (The Mary Owen) Memorial Foundation
11 Wisteria Drive
Fords, NJ 08863
Contact: Mary L. Miles, Secretary

Limitations: Scholarships only to graduates of Rumson-Fair Haven New Jersey Regional High School, NJ.
Financial data: Year ended 12/31/86. Assets, $6,811,600 (M); Total giving, $336,150; Grants to individuals, 4 grants totaling $24,000.
Employer Identification Number: 136137137
Applications: Applications from individuals who are not graduates of the specified educational institution not accepted.
Publications: Application guidelines.

83★
Borrego Springs Educational Scholarship Committee
P.O. Box 59
Borrego Springs, CA 92004   (619) 767-5314
Contact: David H. West, Chairman

Limitations: Student loans and scholarships to graduating seniors of the Borrego Springs High School, Borrego Springs, CA.
Financial data: Year ended 12/31/86. Assets, $3,270 (M); Total giving, $10,350; Grants to individuals, 9 scholarships totaling $10,350, high $1,500, low $500; Loans to individuals amount not specified.
Employer Identification Number: 956197526
Applications: Contact scholarship committee for current application deadline; Completion of formal application required.
Publications: Application guidelines, 990-PF printed copy available upon request.
Program description:
Loans and grants are made to needy students to further their education.

84
Borton-Ryder Memorial Trust
Bank IV Emporia, N.A.
P.O. Box 1048
Emporia, KS 66801-1048

Limitations: Scholarships only for students in the Emporia, KS, area, for the study of medicine at Newman Hospital.
Financial data: Year ended 6/30/87. Assets, $351,248 (M); Total giving, $17,269; Grants to individuals, 17 grants totaling $17,269; Subtotal for scholarships, 15 grants totaling $17,124, average grant $1,676.
Employer Identification Number: 486110157
Applications: Applications accepted throughout the year; Initial approach by letter.

85★
Bour Memorial Scholarship Fund
P.O. Box 38
Kansas City, MO 64141
Contact: Delores A. Fischer, Boatmen's Bank of Lexington, 1016 Main Street, Lexington, MO 64067; Tel.: (816) 259-4661

Limitations: Scholarships to needy high school graduates residing in Lafayette County, MO, to attend any accredited Missouri college.
Financial data: Year ended 12/31/87. Assets, $434,725 (M); Total giving, $28,000; Grants to individuals, 28 grants totaling $28,000, each grant $1,000.
Employer Identification Number: 436225461
Applications: Deadline April 15th; Completion of formal application required; Application forms available early each year from Boatmen's Bank.

86★
Bowen (Ethel N.) Foundation
First National Bank of Bluefield
500 Federal Street
Bluefield, WV 24701   (304) 325-8181
Contact: R.W. Wilkenson, Secretary-Treasurer

Limitations: Scholarships for students from the coal mining areas of southern West Virginia and southwestern Virginia.
Financial data: Year ended 12/31/87. Assets, $3,576,429 (M); Total giving, $186,540; Grants to individuals, 85 grants totaling $126,771, high $5,000, low $500, average grant $2,000.
Employer Identification Number: 237010740
Applications: Applications accepted from January through April 30th; Deadline April 30th; Initial approach by letter, including a resume and biographical outline; Interviews required.

87
Bowerman Foundation
825 East Park Street
Eugene, OR 97401
Contact: Donald A. Gallagher, Jr., Secretary

Limitations: Scholarships and research grants primarily to residents of Eugene, OR.
Financial data: Year ended 6/30/86. Assets, $1,080,429 (M); Total giving, $23,010; Grants to individuals, 1 grant totaling $2,310.
Employer Identification Number: 930813012
Applications: Applications accepted throughout the year; Initial approach by letter including name, address, transcripts, grades and tuition fees.

88
Bowsher (Nelson P.) Foundation
c/o The First Interstate Bank of Northern Indiana, N.A.
112-114 West Jefferson Boulevard
South Bend, IN 46601   (219) 237-3342
Contact: Principal in local high school

Limitations: Scholarships only to graduates of Saint Joseph County, IN, high schools.
Financial data: Year ended 12/31/86. Assets, $326,914 (M); Total giving, $18,000; Grants to individuals, 15 grants totaling $18,000, each grant $1,200.
Employer Identification Number: 356012966
Applications: Deadline March 31st; Initial approach by letter to local principal; Interviews, three letters of character reference, and high school transcript required; Applicants must file a Financial Aid Form (FAF) prior to March 1st.
Publications: Program information, application guidelines.

89
Boye Scholarship Trust
c/o Wells Fargo Bank
400 Capitol Mall
Sacramento, CA 95814

Limitations: Scholarships to students who are residents of Sacramento County, CA. Preference is given to those pursuing studies in agriculture related fields.
Financial data: Year ended 6/30/87. Assets, $677,433 (M); Total giving, $19,160; Grants to individuals, 3 grants totaling $19,160, high $10,560, low $3,000.
Employer Identification Number: 946067623

90
Boynton Gillespie Memorial Fund
Heritage Federal Building
Sparta, IL 62286   (618) 443-4430
Contact: John Clendenin, Trustee

Limitations: Scholarships for students in the local area.
Financial data: Year ended 12/31/86. Assets, $2,072,039 (M); Total giving, $146,475; Grants to individuals, 104 grants totaling $76,475, high $500, low $475.
Employer Identification Number: 376028930
Applications: Deadline May 1st; Initial approach by letter requesting application; Completion of formal application required.

91
Bradish (Norman C.) Trust
Freedom Savings
P.O. Box 1420
Winter Park, FL 32790
Contact: Decorah High School, Decorah, IA; University of Wisconsin, Department of Philosophy

Limitations: Scholarships to a male graduate of Decorah High School, Decorah, IA, and a male graduate student at the University of Wisconsin who is a major in the Department of Philosophy and selected by the Dean of the Graduate School and Chairman of the Department of Philosophy.
Financial data: Year ended 6/30/86. Assets, $1,530,394 (M); Assets, $145,207; Grants to individuals, 8 grants totaling $22,190, high $5,000, low $200.
Employer Identification Number: 596161559

92
Brandt Scholarship Fund
c/o Wells Fargo Bank, N.A.-Trust Tax Division
343 Sansome Street, Third Floor
San Francisco, CA 94163

Limitations: Scholarships to graduating seniors of high schools in the southern San Joaquin Valley, CA, area.
Financial data: Year ended 7/31/87. Assets, $155,362

(M); Total giving, $9,950; Grants to individuals, 16 grants totaling $9,950, high $1,000, low $250, general range $500-1,000.
Employer Identification Number: 956053020
Applications: Deadline April 15th; Completion of formal application required; Applications available from the chairman of the High School Scholastic Committee at the high school applicant is attending.

93★
Braverman (Joel) Foundation, Inc.
1609 Avenue J
Brooklyn, NY 11230   (718) 377-4466
Contact: Dr. Joel B. Wolowelsky, Administrator

Limitations: Scholarships to graduates of the Yeshiva of Flatbush Joel Braverman High School only.
Financial data: Year ended 7/31/86. Assets, $309,685 (M); Total giving, $14,950; Grants to individuals, 17 grants totaling $14,950, high $1,500, low $450, general range $350-1,500, average grant $1,000.
Employer Identification Number: 116036594
Applications: Contact foundation for current application deadline; Initial approach by letter; Completion of formal application required; Interviews required.
Program description:
All grants are for one year of study at universities or yeshivot in Israel.

94
Brey (Claude) and Ina Brey Memorial Endowment Fund
c/o The Merchants National Bank of Topeka
P.O. Box 178
Topeka, KS 66601
Contact: Ruth Esther Shorthill, 3305 N.E. Kimball Road, Topeka, KS 66617; Tel.: (913) 286-1111

Limitations: Scholarships only to fourth degree Kansas Grange members.
Financial data: Year ended 4/30/87. Assets, $107,607 (M); Total giving, $7,480; Grants to individuals, 11 grants totaling $7,480, each grant $680.
Employer Identification Number: 486187137
Applications: Deadline July 1st; Contact local Grange Chapter for application; Completion of formal application required; Interviews required.

95
Brightwell (A.T.) School, Inc.
254 Oakland Avenue
Athens, GA 30606   (404) 543-6450
Contact: Harold Darden, Executive Secretary

Limitations: Scholarships only to unmarried or divorced (proof of divorce necessary) students under 30 years of age and living within the strictly defined

Maxeys, GA, area for at least six months prior to effective date of scholarship. Parents of student must live and remain in Maxeys area for the duration of the time the scholarship is in effect.

Financial data: Year ended 6/30/85. Assets, $53,794 (M); Total giving, $69,000; Grants to individuals, 18 grants totaling $69,000, high $6,000, low $1,500, general range $2,000-4,000.

Employer Identification Number: 586066256

Applications: Applications accepted throughout the year; Initial approach by letter requesting application; Completion of formal application required; Interviews required.

Publications: Annual report, program information, application guidelines.

Program description:

Scholarships may be used to attend any college, university, vocational, technical, or business school. Scholarships to cover educational courses towards a masters degree will be available only when all needs for undergraduate student scholarships are met.

The boundaries of the Maxeys, GA, area for the purpose of scholarship eligibility shall be a one-mile radius from a marker located at the site of the old home at A.T. Brightwell. Recipients must reside on land within this one-mile radius.

96
Brill (Marion) Scholarship Foundation, Inc.
97 West Street
P.O. Box 420
Ilion, NY 13357
Contact: Ilion Central School District High School Guidance Office

Limitations: Scholarships only to residents of the village of Ilion, NY.

Financial data: Year ended 6/30/86. Assets, $543,228 (M); Total giving $30,785; Grants to individuals, 81 grants totaling $30,785, high $1,000, low $100, general range $100-600.

Employer Identification Number: 222373170

Applications: Deadline April 15th; Completion of formal application required.

Program description:

The foundation's selection committee receives the applications from the Ilion Central School District High School Guidance Office. In addition to the formal application, applicants must submit a financial aid form. High school seniors must submit a copy of their high school transcript and a college letter of acceptance. College students must submit their most recent semester transcript.

97
Brinker (Maureen Connolly) Girls' Tennis Foundation, Inc.
(Formerly Brinker (Maureen Connolly) Tennis Foundation)
5419 Wateka Drive
Dallas, TX 75209   (214) 357-1604
Contact: Mrs. Frank Jeffett, President

Limitations: Grants to young female tennis players, 21 years of age and under.

Financial data: Year ended 4/30/87. Assets, $1,792,767 (M); Total giving, $134,508; Grants to individuals, 7 grants totaling $9,197, high $3,871, low $300.

Employer Identification Number: 237040481

Applications: Applications accepted throughout the year; Initial approach by letter; Interviews required.

Publications: Annual report, program information, application guidelines.

98★
Brown (The Dora Maclellan) Charitable Trust
1101 Maclellan Building
Chattanooga, TN 37402   (615) 266-4574
Contact: Henry A. Henegar, President

Limitations: Scholarships only to evangelical Christian students and to those students studying for the ministry, primarily in Tennessee.

Financial data: Year ended 12/31/87. Assets, $9,387,024 (M); Total giving, $768,201; Grants to individuals, 45 grants totaling $107,083.

Employer Identification Number: 510200174

Applications: Applications accepted throughout the year; Initial approach by letter requesting application; Completion of formal application required; Interviews required.

99
Brown (The Eva H.) Foundation, Inc.
405 Lexington Avenue
New York, NY 10017

Limitations: Scholarships only to residents of upstate New York.

Financial data: Year ended 5/31/86. Assets, $61,422 (M); Total giving, $51,000; Grants to individuals, 35 grants totaling $43,750, each grant $1,250.

Employer Identification Number: 510203745

100★
Brown (Gabriel J.) Trust
112 Avenue E West
Bismarck, ND 58501   (701) 223-5916

Limitations: Student loans to residents of North Dakota.

Financial data: Year ended 3/31/87. Assets,

$1,025,604 (M); Expenditures, $7,774; Loans to individuals totaling $79,200.
Employer Identification Number: 237086880
Applications: Deadline June 15th; Completion of formal application, including current educational grade level, grade point averages, current financial position of the applicant or the applicant's parents, and financial needs, expected income, and other loans for the next school period, required.
Program description:
There are no restrictions placed on location of the educational institution a student wishes to attend.

101
Brown (Joe W. & Dorothy Dorsett) Foundation
1801 Pere Marquette Building
New Orleans, LA 70112   (504) 522-4233
Contact: D. P. Spencer, Vice-President

Limitations: Scholarships primarily to Louisiana and Mississippi residents.
Financial data: Year ended 12/31/86. Assets, $3,464,187 (M); Total giving, $140,521; Grants to individuals, 8 grants totaling $46,142, high $11,097, low $945.
Employer Identification Number: 726027232
Applications: Applications accepted throughout the year.

102★
Brown (Lucille R.) Foundation, Inc.
5770 West Milan Place
Denver, CO 80235   (303) 986-3797
Contact: Cecilia A. Wells, Secretary-Treasurer

Limitations: Scholarships only to Colorado residents doing undergraduate work at Colorado schools.
Financial data: Year ended 12/31/86. Assets, $273,110 (M); Total giving, $32,690; Grants to individuals, 6 grants totaling $9,000, high $2,000, low $500, general range $1,000-2,000.
Employer Identification Number: 846025298
Applications: Applications accepted throughout the year; Apply by letter, giving name, address, telephone number, and brief description of purpose for which grant will be used.

103
Bryan (Dodd and Dorothy L.) Foundation
P.O. Box 6287
Sheridan, WY 82801   (307) 672-3535
Contact: J. E. Goar, Manager

Limitations: Educational loans primarily for students from Sheridan, Campbell, and Johnson counties, WY, and from Powder River, Rosebud, and Big Horn counties, MT.
Financial data: Year ended 12/31/86. Assets, $3,268,800 (M); Expenditures, $59,479; Loans to

individuals, 105 loans totaling $186,175, high $4,000, low $400; average loan $1,500.
Employer Identification Number: 836006533
Applications: Submit application preferably in May or June; Deadline July 15th; Initial approach by letter; Completion of formal application required; Interview desired.
Publications: Application guidelines.
Program description:
Loans are made toward higher education expenses of recipients selected on the basis of need and academic achievement.

104
Bryan (Fred A.) Collegiate Students Fund, Inc.
c/o First Interstate Bank of Northern Indiana, N.A.
112-114 West Jefferson Boulevard
South Bend, IN 46601   (219) 237-3342
Contact: High school counselors

Limitations: Scholarships only to male graduates of high schools in South Bend, IN, with preference given to Boy Scouts in good standing for a period of two years at some time prior to application for scholarship.
Financial data: Year ended 12/31/86. Assets, $180,063 (M); Total giving, $8,400; Grants to individuals, 6 grants totaling $8,400, each grant $1,400.
Employer Identification Number: 356012911
Applications: Deadline March 31st; Initial approach through high school counselor; Completion of formal application required; Interviews, three letters of character reference, and high school transcript required; Applicant must file a Financial Aid Form (FAF) prior to March 1st and, if a Boy Scout, include a copy of Scout Record.
Program description:
Scholarship awards are determined by a committee composed of the principals of the South Bend high schools, the superintendent of the school district, and a representative of the fund's trustee.

105
Bryan (James E. & Mary Z.) Foundation, Inc.
First Citizens Bank and Trust Company
P.O. Box 151
Raleigh, NC 27602   (919) 755-7101
Contact: Bryon E. Bryan, President

Limitations: Scholarships to needy and worthy students who are legal residents of North Carolina attending specified educational institutions, including trade schools, colleges, or universities.
Financial data: Year ended 6/30/86. Assets, $3,570,701 (M); Total giving, $284,113; Grants to individuals, 21 grants totaling $31,500, each grant $1,500.
Employer Identification Number: 560686194
Applications: Deadline January 31st; Initial approach by proposal; Completion of formal application

required; Foundation does not issue application guidelines or procedures, and does not acknowledge receipt of proposals.

106★
Buffalo Foundation, The
237 Main Street
Buffalo, NY 14203   (716) 852-2857
Contact: W.L. Van Schoonhoven, Director

Limitations: Scholarships only to residents of Buffalo and Erie County, NY, on the basis of need.
Financial data: Year ended 12/31/87. Assets, $23,973,370 (M); Total giving, $1,425,788; Grants to individuals, 429 grants totaling $258,026.
Employer Identification Number: 160743935
Applications: Request application forms between March 1st and May 10th; Deadline May 25th; Completion of formal application required; Interviews required.
Publications: Annual report.

107
Buhrman (F.W.) Educational and Scholarship Trust
1002 South Third Street
Mount Vernon, WA 98273   (206) 336-9515
Contact: Warren Gilbert, Jr.

Limitations: Scholarships to students from Skagit County, WA, who are pursuing or plan to pursue a course of education or vocational training.
Financial data: Year ended 12/31/85. Assets, $86,440 (M); Total giving, $4,633; Grants to individuals, 10 grants totaling $4,633, high $800, low $400.
Employer Identification Number: 237083165
Applications: Deadline December 31st; Initial approach by letter; Completion of formal application required.
Program description:
Most grants are made to graduating high school seniors.

108★
Bulkeley School (Trustees of The)
c/o Richard Woodworth
Crocker Street
New London, CT 06320

Limitations: Scholarships only to residents of New London, CT.
Financial data: Year ended 4/30/87. Assets, $1,016,893 (M); Total giving, $80,925; Grants to individuals, 95 grants totaling $80,925, high $1,050, low $350.
Employer Identification Number: 066040926
Applications: Deadline April 1st; Initial approach by March 15th; Completion of formal application

required; Interviews and a copy of financial aid statement required; Additional application address: P.O. Box 1426, New London, CT 06320.
Publications: 990-PF printed copy available upon request.

109
Bunn (Henry) Memorial Fund
c/o Marine Bank of Springfield
One Old State Capitol Plaza
Springfield, IL 62701

Limitations: Scholarships only to graduating seniors of Sangamon County, IL.
Financial data: Year ended 12/31/86. Assets, $503,913 (M); Total giving, $31,639; Grants to individuals totaling $31,639, general range $150-500.
Employer Identification Number: 376041599
Applications: Deadline March 1st; Applications accepted through local high school counselors.
Program description:
Scholarship recipients must exhibit high moral character, industry and good study habits. Their high school record and qualifications must be superior, indicating the potential for successful college work. They also must demonstrate a need for financial assistance beyond reasonable levels of parent and self-help. The scholarship may be renewed annually for a maximum of three years, provided the student remains in financial need and good academic standing.

110
Burgess (The William, Agnes & Elizabeth) Memorial Scholarship Fund
c/o First National Bank
1515 Charleston
Mattoon, IL 61938   (217) 234-7454
Contact: Clark W. Brogan, Vice-President and Senior Trust Officer, First National Bank

Limitations: Scholarships only to graduating seniors of Mattoon Community High School in Mattoon, IL, for use at institution of recipient's choice.
Financial data: Year ended 3/31/87. Assets, $1,226,998 (M); Total giving, $51,900; Grants to individuals, 90 grants totaling $51,900, high $600, low $300.
Employer Identification Number: 376024599
Applications: Deadline March 15th; Completion of formal application required; Application forms are available at Mattoon Community High School.

111
Burkett (George W.) Trust
c/o First National Bank of Monterey
Six East Main Street
Monterey, IN 46960
Contact: See program description below

Limitations: Scholarships only to graduating seniors from the following high schools in Starke County, IN: Culver Community High School, Knox Community High School, North Judson-San Pierre High School, and Oregon-Davis High School.
Financial data: Year ended 11/30/86. Assets, $105,670 (M); Total giving, $8,750; Grants to individuals, 14 grants totaling $8,400, each grant $600.
Employer Identification Number: 356338505
Applications: Deadline Spring; Initial approach by letter; Completion of formal application required.
Publications: Annual report.
Program description:
Applicants should contact the following school superintendents for scholarship application information:
  1. For Knox Community High School students, contact Dr. Harold Huff, 306 South Pearl Street, Knox, IN 36534; Tel.: (219) 772-3712.
  2. For North Judson-San Pierre High School students, contact Dr. Steven Timler, Highway 10 West, North Judson, IN 46366; Tel.: (219) 896-2155.
  3. For Oregon-Davis High School students, contact John Slusher, P.O. Box 65, Hamlet, IN 46532; Tel.: (219) 867-2111.
  4. For Culver Community High School students, contact William F. Mills, 222 North Ohio Street, Culver, IN 46511; Tel.: (219) 842-3364.

112
Burton (The William T. and Ethel Lewis)
  Foundation
101 North Huntington Street
Sulphur, LA 70663   (318) 527-5221
Contact: William B. Lawton, Chairman

Limitations: Scholarships for southwest Louisiana high school seniors.
Financial data: Year ended 5/31/87. Assets, $3,148,868 (M); Total giving, $111,187; Grants to individuals amount not specified; 1986, Grants to individuals, 76 grants totaling $70,398, high $1,500, low $333.
Employer Identification Number: 726027957
Applications: Initial approach by letter; Completion of formal application required.
Program description:
A scholarship committee of three education administrators and three members of the business community receives the applications and makes the final selection of the recipients. After notification by

the committee, the foundation makes the scholarship payments directly to the college or university in the name of the individual recipient.

113★
Bush Foundation, The
East 900 First National Bank Building
St. Paul, MN 55101   (612) 227-0891

Limitations: Fellowships to residents of Minnesota, North Dakota, and South Dakota, and specified counties of Wisconsin for career advancement; and fellowships to Minnesota residents who are physicians currently practicing in rural Minnesota, North Dakota, South Dakota, and western Wisconsin.
Financial data: Year ended 11/30/87. Assets, $332,263,000 (M); Total giving, $13,889,666; Grants to individuals, 146 grants totaling $1,570,179; Subtotal amounts for programs not specified; 1986, Grants to individuals totaling $1,435,852; Subtotal for Leadership Program, 42 fellowships totaling $873,368; Subtotal for Clinical Program, 11 fellowships totaling $249,540.
Employer Identification Number: 416017815
Applications: Deadline January 1st for Bush Leadership Fellowships, March 1st for Bush Summer Fellowships; Applications available in the fall; Initial approach by letter; Completion of formal application required; Interviews may be required.
Publications: Annual report, program information, application guidelines, financial statement.
Program description:
Bush Leadership Fellowships for Midcareer Development: Awards under this program (particularly administrative ones) are usually made to persons in midcareer likely to advance to top positions in a variety of professional fields including: architecture, business, engineering, farming, forestry, government, journalism, law, law enforcement, social work, theology, trade unionism, and administration of arts, education, and health or scientific (related to public policy) organizations.
  Applicants must be current residents of Minnesota, North or South Dakota, or the 26 western counties of Wisconsin that fall within the Ninth Federal Reserve District and have been there for at least one continuous year. The individual must also be a U.S. citizen or permanent resident, 28 through 54 years of age, have five years work experience, and should already have substantial standing in his/her field. Persons already enrolled full-time in a graduate study program are ineligible.
  Each grant consists of a $2,800 monthly stipend and $2,000 moving allowance, plus the payment of 50 percent of tuition and fees ($15,000 maximum). The fellowship period ranges from 4 to 18 months and may include internship.
  Also part of this program is the **Bush Summer Fellowships Programs** which has basically the same purposes and requirements as Leadership Fellowships.

Each grant consists of a $600 weekly stipend and $500 travel allowance, as well as the payment of 50 percent of tuition and fees ($8,000 maximum). Preference is given to individuals who participate in administrative training with an appropriate peer group.

Inquiries concerning the Leadership Program should be directed to Donald Peddie, Program Director, P.O. Box 24140, Minneapolis, MN 55424.

Bush Clinical Fellows Program: Through this program, the foundation seeks to improve the quality of health care in individual communities, to develop individual rural physicians' potential for leadership in clinical medicine, administration, and education, and to improve the linkages between rural communities and health training institutions by providing fellowships for clinical and supportive study. Applicants must be physicians currently in primary care settings in non-metropolitan areas of Minnesota, North Dakota, South Dakota, and western Wisconsin. They should have seven or more years of clinical practice experience, be at least 35 years old, and present a plan of study suitable both to their own career needs and to the health care needs of the communities they serve.

Since 1986, the program has also been available to a limited number of metropolitan area physicians seeking training for major administration or policy development positions. Two program options are available:

● Primary care physicians practicing in non-metropolitan areas are eligible for clinical programs and programs in medical administration, management, or policy development.

● Physicians practicing in metropolitan areas (the Twin Cities, Rochester, Duluth, Sioux Falls, and Rapid City) are eligible only for programs in medical administration, management, and policy development.

Fellowship awards provide $3,000 per month for up to 12 months of full-time study plus tuition and travel allowances totaling $4,000 over the term of their fellowships. Inquiries about the program should be addressed to Jon D. Wempner, Program Director, Box 206, Waconia, MN 55387.

114★
Bushee (Florence Evans) Foundation, Inc.
Palmer & Dodge
One Beacon Street, Room 2000
Boston, MA 02108   (617) 227-4400
Contact: Ann Reidy, Secretary

Limitations: Scholarships only to college students who are residents of Newburyport, MA.
Financial data: Year ended 12/31/87. Assets, $2,458,369 (M); Total giving, $121,050; Grants to individuals, 118 grants totaling $110,050.
Employer Identification Number: 046035327

Applications: Deadline May 1st. Initial approach by letter or telephone; Completion of formal application required.
Publications: Informational brochure.

115★
Byrnes (James F.) Foundation
P.O. Box 9596
Columbia, SC 29290   (803) 776-1211
Contact: Margaret Courtney, Executive Secretary

Limitations: Scholarships to South Carolina residents who have lost one or both parents by death.
Financial data: Year ended 6/30/85. Assets, $1,956,545 (M); Total giving, $163,638; Grants to individuals totaling $146,372.
Employer Identification Number: 576024756
Applications: Deadline March 1st; Submit application form preferably in January or February; Initial approach by letter or telephone; Completion of formal application required; Interviews for semifinalists required.
Publications: Application guidelines, program information.
Program description:
College scholarships are awarded to students planning to pursue a B.A. or B.S. degree (scholarships are not available for technical education). Recipients may attend colleges or universities within or outside of South Carolina.

Applicants must demonstrate financial need, a satisfactory scholastic record, and qualities of character, ability, and enterprise which indicate a worthwhile contribution to society.

The scholarships are in the amount of approximately $1,500 each and are renewable for a maximum of four years, contingent upon maintenance of adequate academic standing, personal involvement in the Byrnes Scholarship program, and continuing need for financial aid.

116
Cady (George A.) Educational Trust
c/o First Interstate Bank of Washington
P.O. Box 21927
Seattle, WA 98111

Limitations: Scholarships to graduating seniors from Valley High School, Menlo, WA.
Financial data: Year ended 12/31/86. Assets, $74,706 (M); Total giving, $3,098; Grants to individuals, 7 grants totaling $3,098, high $750, low $112.
Employer Identification Number: 916088092
Applications: Deadline first Friday in May; Completion of formal application required, including applicant's GPA, name of college or university to be attended, and future plans; Application information available from Valley High School guidance counselor; Tel.: (206) 942-5855.

117
Cady (May and Wallace) Memorial Trust
c/o Commerce Bank of St. Louis, N.A.
8000 Forsyth Boulevard
Clayton, MO 63105 (314) 726-2255
Contact: Gerald L. Wedemeier, Assistant
Vice-President

Limitations: Scholarships only to graduates of United Presbyterian Homes of Synod, TX, for use at Washington University in St. Louis, MO.
Financial data: Year ended 12/31/86. Assets, $143,784 (M); Total giving, $4,100; Grants to individuals, 1 grant totaling $4,100.
Employer Identification Number: 436054036
Applications: Applications accepted throughout the year; Initial approach by letter.

118
Caestecker (The Charles and Marie) Foundation
c/o Frank Karaba
111 West Monroe Street, Suite 2200E
Chicago, IL 60603
Contact: Guidance Counselor, c/o Green Lake Public High School, Green Lake, WI 54941

Limitations: Scholarships to individuals who have attended Green Lake Public High School, Green Lake, WI, for at least two years and who plan to attend a four-year college or university for study leading to a traditional baccalaureate degree.
Financial data: Year ended 4/30/87. Assets, $4,705,128 (M); Total giving, $196,932; Grants to individuals, 5 grants totaling $20,832, high $5,000, low $2,100.
Employer Identification Number: 363154453
Applications: Deadline February 1st of graduation year; Completion of formal application required.
Program description:
Applicants must show academic promise as indicated by past academic performance, college entrance examination scores and recommendations. Extracurricular involvement is considered along with financial need.

The winner must enter a fully accredited college or university as a full-time day student in the fall term following selection and must pursue a course of study leading to one of the traditional baccalaureate degrees. The winner is expected to remain in good academic and disciplinary standing at the college attended.

119★
Caldwell (Charles W.) Scholarship Fund
c/o State Street Bank & Trust Company
P.O. Box 351
Boston, MA 02101 (617) 654-3361
Contact: Sharon Doherty-Clancy

Limitations: Scholarships only to male seniors at Princeton University for obtaining postgraduate degrees.
Financial data: Year ended 12/31/85. Assets, $128,000 (M); Total giving, $6,000; Grants to individuals, 2 grants totaling $6,000, each grant $3,000.
Employer Identification Number: 046452445

120
Caldwell-Pitts Scholarship Fund
c/o Bank of America Trust Department
233 North Fair Oaks Avenue
Pasadena, CA 91103
Contact: Biggs Unified School District, P.O. Box 379, Biggs, CA 95917

Limitations: Scholarships only to graduates of Biggs High School, Biggs, CA.
Financial data: Year ended 9/30/86. Assets, $184,214 (M); Total giving, $13,325; Grants to individuals totaling $13,325.
Employer Identification Number: 946069672
Applications: Deadline April 1st to file completed application with high school principal; Completion of formal application required.
Program description:
Applicants must have resided within the boundaries of the Biggs Unified School District while attending four years (8 semesters) at Biggs High School.

121
California Junior Miss Scholarship Foundation
c/o Burningham
8854 Golf Drive
Spring Valley, CA 92077
Contact: Don Landes, 233 A Street, San Diego, CA 92101; Tel.: (619) 232-4955

Limitations: Educational scholarships only to contestants and former contestants of California's Junior Miss Pageant. Contestant must apply within five years of having been in pageant.
Financial data: Year ended 6/30/87. Assets, $46,941 (M); Total giving, $29,310; Grants to individuals, 28 grants totaling $29,310, high $4,300, low $97.
Employer Identification Number: 956145279
Publications: Annual report.
Program description:
Recipient as a condition to continued receipt of grant monies must submit progress reports at the end of each academic term to the foundation, either personally or through the educational institution attended, as evidence that the funds were used for the purpose of the grant. Failure to comply with the foundation's rules and regulations may be cause for forfeiture of the remaining scholarship balances.

122
California Masonic Foundation
1111 California Street
San Francisco, CA 94108   (415) 776-7000

Limitations: Scholarships for full-time undergraduate
students in California or Hawaii who are U.S. citizens.
Financial data: Year ended 6/30/87. Assets,
$1,483,769 (M); Total giving, $81,500; Grants to
individuals totaling $81,500, average grant $500.
Employer Identification Number: 237013074
Applications: Applications accepted throughout the
year; Initial approach by personal letter requesting a
scholarship; Completion of formal application
required, including transcripts, name of college where
accepted, evidence of financial need, information
about other scholarships received, and letters of
recommendations; Interviews not granted.

123
Callaway (Fuller E.) Foundation
209 Broome Street, P.O. Box 790
La Grange, GA 30241   (404) 884-7348
Contact: J.T. Gresham, General Manager

Limitations: Scholarships only to residents of Troup
County, GA.
Financial data: Year ended 12/31/86. Assets,
$24,703,210 (M); Total giving, $855,875; Grants to
individuals, 67 grants totaling $205,430, high
$15,000, low $800, average grant $2,401.
Employer Identification Number: 580566148
Applications: Deadlines February 15th for college
scholarships, July 15th for law school scholarships;
Initial approach by letter; Completion of formal
application required; Interviews granted at the
discretion of the Scholarship Committee.
Program description:
The **Hatton Lovejoy Scholarships** are awarded to
worthy graduating high school students who are
residents of Troup County, GA, to aid them in
obtaining an undergraduate degree. Ten new
scholarships are awarded each year.

124★
Callejo-Botello Foundation Charitable Trust
4314 North Central Expressway
Dallas, TX 75206   (214) 741-6710
Contact: William F. Callejo

Limitations: Scholarships primarily to students
planning to attend educational institutions in TX.
Financial data: Year ended 12/31/86. Assets, $732,743
(M); Total giving, $498,061; Grants to individuals, 5
grants totaling $14,095, high $7,600, low $1,000.
Employer Identification Number: 751678195
Applications: Deadline April 23rd; Initial approach by
letter requesting application; Completion of formal
application required.
Publications: Annual report.

Program description:
Scholarship payments are made directly to the
educational institution on the individual recipient's
behalf.

125
Cameron (The Dave) Educational Foundation
P.O. Box 181
York, SC 29745   (803) 684-4968
Contact: Margaret S. Adkins

Limitations: Educational grants are limited to
undergraduate students within the York, SC, area who
maintain a minimum of a 2.0 grade point average.
Financial data: Year ended 3/31/87. Assets, $341,520
(M); Total giving, $29,075; Grants to individuals, 25
grants totaling $29,075, high $2,000, low $500,
average grant $1,000.
Employer Identification Number: 237080657
Applications: Applications accepted throughout the
year; Completion of formal application required.

126
Camp Foundation
P.O. Box 813
Franklin, VA 23851   (804) 562-3439
Contact: Harold S. Atkinson, Executive Director

Limitations: Scholarships to graduates of high schools
in Southampton and Isle of Wight counties, and
Franklin, and Tidewater, VA, and northeastern North
Carolina only. Applicants must file with their high
school principal who then files with the foundation.
Financial data: Year ended 12/31/86. Assets,
$9,690,000 (M); Total giving, $527,000; Grants to
individuals, 27 grants totaling $60,000.
Employer Identification Number: 546052488
Applications: Deadlines February 26th for filing with
high school principals and March 15th for principals
to file with foundation.
Publications: Informational brochure.

127★
Cantrall (Ruth A.) Trust
c/o Bank IV Olathe
P.O. Box 400
Olathe, KS 66061   (913) 782-3010

Limitations: Financial assistance only for needy
students attending the Kansas State School for the
Deaf.
Financial data: Year ended 9/30/87. Assets, $93,969
(M); Total giving, $8,659 Grants to individuals, 48
grants totaling $8,659, high $625, low $15.
Employer Identification Number: 486208276
Applications: Applications accepted throughout the
year.
Publications: Annual report.

128
Cape Foundation, Inc.

550 Pharr Road, N.E., Suite 605
Atlanta, GA 30305   (404) 231-3865
Contact: S. G. Armstrong, Trustee

Limitations: Scholarship grants to undergraduate students attending colleges and universities in the Atlanta, GA, area.
Financial data: Year ended 10/31/86. Assets, $173,656 (M); Total giving, $5,970; Grants to individuals, 2 grants totaling $4,510, high $2,300, low $2,210.
Employer Identification Number: 136160904
Applications: Applications are supplied between March 1st and September 10th; Application form must be submitted along with a copy of the final response and/or proposal from the college's financial aid office to the applicant's request for financial aid for the same term or year for which aid is to be requested from the foundation; Completion of formal application required.
Program description:
Partial scholarships to needy and deserving undergraduate students.

In addition to exhibiting real need, merit and constructive potential, a student's present or prior activities must reflect humane concerns. Applicants must make a substantial contribution to their education, including personal borrowing.

The application form will require listing of all assets and every source of funds including grants, scholarships, gifts from friends and family, loans outstanding and applied for.

129★
Carlsbad Foundation, Inc.

116 South Canyon Street
Carlsbad, NM 88220   (505) 887-1131
Contact: John Mills, Executive Director

Limitations: Student loans to medical and paramedical students in the South Eddy County and Carlsbad, NM, area. Also various scholarships to local scholars planning on teaching careers attending local and out-of-town institutions.
Financial data: Year ended 6/30/87. Assets, $3,655,688 (M); Total giving, $738,069; Grants to individuals totaling $2,000; Loans to individuals, 18 loans totaling $18,000, each loan $1,000.
Employer Identification Number: 850206474
Publications: Annual report (including application guidelines), newsletter, informational brochure.
Program description:
The medical education loans are converted to grants if the recipient completes his/her training and practices those skills in the South Eddy County, NM, area.

130
Carman (Nellie Martin) Scholarship Trust

c/o Seattle Trust & Savings Bank
P.O. Box 12907
Seattle, WA 98111   (206) 223-2220
Contact: Mrs. Warren E. Kraft, Jr., Secretary, Scholarship Committee

Limitations: Scholarships for students graduating from public high schools in King, Snohomish, and Pierce counties, WA, and planning to attend colleges or universities in Washington State.
Financial data: Year ended 5/31/87. Assets, $1,775,863 (M); Total giving, $40,300; Grants to individuals, 81 grants totaling $40,000, high $500, low $250.
Employer Identification Number: 910668186
Applications: Deadlines March 15th for first-time applicants, April 2nd for renewal requests; Completion of formal application required.

131
Carnegie Corporation of New York

437 Madison Avenue
New York, NY 10022   (212) 371-3200
Contact: Dorothy Knapp, Secretary

Limitations: The foundation does not operate any program of scholarships, fellowships educational loans, assistance to needy individuals, travel grants or dissertation fellowships. It occasionally supports research by an individual who is not affiliated with a charitable organization in an announced program area.
Financial data: Year ended 9/30/86. Assets, $715,333,222 (M); Total giving, $26,714,591; Grants to individuals, 6 grants totaling $159,324.
Employer Identification Number: 131628151
Applications: Applications accepted throughout the year; Initial approach by letter or telephone.
Publications: Annual report.
Program description:
In 1986, grants to individuals were made among the following program areas:

1. **Education: Science, Technology and the Economy** - including support for writing or improving education through the application of cognitive science and information technology, and toward the completion of a report on a study of centers of technological innovation.
2. **Toward Healthy Child Development: The Prevention of Damage to Children** - for a project to reformulate approaches to the prevention of a range of adolescent problems, which will result in a book entitled "Adolescents at Risk: Who is at Risk of What?"
3. **Avoiding Nuclear War** - support for research and writing on American and European views about military policy.

132
Carter (Arthur H.) Scholarship Fund
c/o Cummings and Lockwood
P.O. Box 120
Stamford, CT 06904

Limitations: Scholarships for students who have
completed two years of accounting courses and wish
to pursue the accounting field in college or graduate
school.
Financial data: Year ended 8/31/86. Assets,
$1,223,136 (M); Total giving, $100,000; Grants to
individuals totaling $100,000.
Employer Identification Number: 066177169
Applications: Deadline April 1st; Initial approach by
letter requesting application, c/o American Accounting
Association, Sarasota, FL 33581; Completion of formal
application required, including letters of
recommendation and school transcript.
Publications: Application guidelines.

133★
**Carter (Marjorie Sells) Boy Scout Scholarship
Fund**
c/o Cummings and Lockwood
P.O. Box 120
Stamford, CT 06904
Contact: Joan Shaffer, P.O. Box 527, West Chatham,
MA 02669

Limitations: College scholarships only to former Boy
Scouts who are residents of the New England area.
Financial data: Year ended 8/31/86. Assets,
$1,118,805 (M); Total giving, $110,148; Grants to
individuals totaling $110,148.
Employer Identification Number: 066174937
Applications: Deadline April 1st; Initial approach by
letter requesting application form; Completion of
formal application required.
Program description:
The fund awards four-year college scholarships of
$1,000 per year to Boy Scouts in the New England
area.

134
Cary (Isaac Harris) Educational Fund
c/o Lexington Savings Bank
1776 Massachusetts Avenue
Lexington, MA 02173   (617) 861-0650
Contact: F. David Wells, Jr.

Limitations: Scholarships only to males of New
England parentage, with emphasis on residents of the
Lexington, MA, area.
Financial data: Year ended 4/30/86. Assets, $749,639
(M); Total giving, $30,576; Grants to individuals, 21
grants totaling $26,150, high $2,000, low $500,
general range $1,200-1,500.
Employer Identification Number: 046023807

Applications: Contact foundation for current
application deadline; Completion of formal
application required.
Publications: Annual report.

135
Caston (M.C. & Mattie) Foundation, Inc.
c/o Navarro College
Corsicana, TX 75110   (214) 874-6501
Contact: Ken Walker

Limitations: Graduate and undergraduate scholarships
for residents of Navarro, TX, and surrounding counties
(including Ellis, Limestone, and Freestone) who are
applying for or presently attending Navarro College.
Financial data: Year ended 12/31/86. Assets,
$4,758,980 (M); Total giving, $128,000; Grants to
individuals, 138 grants totaling $128,000, high
$1,695, low $150.
Employer Identification Number: 751844992
Applications: Deadline March 1st; Application
information available in high schools and colleges in
January; See program description below for
application information on specific programs.
Program description:
The **Caston General Scholarship** awards 54
scholarships each year to Navarro County, TX, high
school graduates who demonstrate genuine interest in,
and proven intellectual capacity for, an education at
Navarro College. Each recipient will receive a
two-year scholarship in the amount of $250 per
semester to be used for tuition, fees, and books.
Graduates from Ellis, Freestone, and Limestone
counties, TX, will be considered the next priority
based on the same requirements and qualifications.
No direct payments will be made to students.
Applicants must meet the following criteria:
 • Be a high school graduate with at least a "B"
average, SAT score of at least 800, or ACT score
of at least 18
 • Submit forms for admission to Navarro College
and application for Caston General Scholarship,
along with most current official high school
The **Caston Distinguished Student Scholarship**
awards 12 scholarships each year. Navarro County
high school graduates will be given first consideration;
but graduates from Ellis, Limestone, and Freestone
counties are also eligible to apply. These scholarships,
which are to be used for tuition, fees, books, and
room and board at Navarro College, are intended to
recognize exceptionally able and active student
leaders and scholars. Each recipient will receive up to
$750 per semester. No funds will be distributed
directly to students. Applicants must meet the criteria
indicated for the Caston General Scholarship in
addition to the following:
 • Be a high school graduate with an "A"
average, SAT score of at least 1100, or ACT score
of at least 25

- Show evidence of having received special awards, achievements, and honors as a high school student.

The **Caston Graduate Scholarship** awards five scholarships each year to outstanding Navarro College graduates who present definite plans for continuing their study and preparing for a career at a four-year college or university. Preference will be given to Navarro County graduates with a grade point average of at least 3.5. To apply, prospective recipients must submit a written proposal describing in detail the educational programs they hope to pursue, and include three letters of recommendation from members of the Navarro College faculty. Scholarship recipients will receive up to $2,500 per semester. Recipients must request renewal each semester and must submit transcripts to support request.

136
Cattell (James McKeen) Fund
Department of Psychology, Duke University
Durham, NC 27706
Contact: Dr. Gregory Kimble, Secretary-Treasurer

Limitations: Grants for postdoctoral training to supplement sabbatical allowances of psychologists teaching at universities in North America.
Financial data: Year ended 12/31/86. Assets, $2,271,447 (M); Total giving, $105,849; Grants to individuals totaling $105,849.
Employer Identification Number: 136129600
Applications: Applications accepted throughout the year; Initial approach by letter; Completion of formal application required.
Publications: Annual report, application guidelines.
Program description:
Grants are made to tenured psychology faculty to enable them to take a sabbatical for a full year rather than for only half a year. Selection is based on evidence of scholarly productivity, the recommendation of notable colleagues, and the nature of the research proposed for the sabbatical year.

Depending on the fund's budget, an average of five to six grants are awarded annually in amounts equal to half the individual's regular yearly salary to a maximum of $20,000.

137
Centerre Trust Company Charitable Trust Fund
510 Locust Street
P.O. Box 14737
St. Louis, MO 63178   (314) 436-9228
Contact: Martin E. Galt III

Limitations: Scholarships primarily to residents in the greater St. Louis, MO, area.
Financial data: Year ended 12/31/86. Assets, $502,123 (M); Total giving, $107,145; Grants to individuals amount not specified.

Employer Identification Number: 436023132
Applications: Applications accepted throughout the year; Initial approach by letter.

138
Central Valley High School Scholarship Fund
P.O. Box 4138
Redding, CA 96099

Limitations: Scholarships only to graduates of Central Valley High School in Redding, CA.
Financial data: Year ended 7/31/85. Assets, $64,545 (M); Total giving, $20,000; Grants to individuals, 4 grants totaling $20,000, each grant $5,000.
Employer Identification Number: 946293818
Applications: Deadline before end of school year; Completion of formal application required.

139★
Chapman (William H.) Foundation
P.O. Box 1321
New London, CT 06320   (203) 443-8010
Contact: Caroline Driscoll

Limitations: Undergraduate scholarships only to residents of New London County, CT, for study at an accredited institution.
Financial data: Year ended 3/31/88. Assets, $1,455,722 (M); Total giving, $65,990; Grants to individuals, 95 grants totaling $65,990, high $800, low $150, general range $500-750, average grant $750.
Employer Identification Number: 066034290
Applications: Deadline April 1st; Initial approach by letter before March 20th; Completion of formal application required; Interviews required.
Program description:
Criteria for selection are scholarship and financial need. No awards for graduate study.

140★
Charles Foundation
c/o Steven Charles
1700 North Alpine, Suite 311
Rockford, IL 61107   (815) 394-1700

Limitations: Scholarships only to residents of Rockford, IL.
Financial data: Year ended 5/31/86. Assets, $247,243 (M); Total giving, $20,623; Grants to individuals, $0; 1985, Grants to individuals, 4 grants totaling $2,218, high $1,500, low $134.
Employer Identification Number: 366103364

141
Chattanooga, The Community Foundation of Greater, Inc.
1600 American National Bank Building
Chattanooga, TN 37402   (615) 267-4311
Contact: William A. Walter, Executive Secretary

Limitations: Scholarships to residents of the
Chattanooga, TN, area who will be working in nursing
or advanced social work.
Financial data: Year ended 12/31/86. Assets,
$7,070,581 (M); Total giving, $674,843; Grants to
individuals, 7 grants totaling $14,096.
Employer Identification Number: 626045999

142
Chattanooga Orthopaedic Educational and Research Foundation
979 East Third Street, Suite 1203
Chattanooga, TN 37403   (615) 267-4585
Contact: Dr. Thomas E. Curry

Limitations: Grants only to residents who are in
training in the Residency Program at the University of
Tennessee, Chattanooga Branch, to enable them to
attend the American Academy of Orthopaedic
Surgeons convention and for courses dealing with
orthopaedic training.
Financial data: Year ended 12/31/86. Assets, $4,129
(M); Total giving, $8,385; Grants to individuals, 7
grants totaling $8,385, high $2,140, low $72, average
grant $1,500.
Employer Identification Number: 237091528
Applications: Initial approach by letter; Completion of
formal application required. **Applications from
individuals who are not within the stated recipient
restriction not accepted.**

143★
Chautauqua Region Community Foundation, Inc.
812 Hotel Jamestown Building
Jamestown, NY 14701   (716) 661-3390
Contact: Francis B. Grow, Vice-President and
Manager

Limitations: Scholarships only to residents of 11
school districts in the Chautauqua County, NY, area.
Financial data: Year ended 12/31/87. Assets,
$7,070,572 (L); Total giving, $269,926; Grants to
individuals, 205 grants totaling $170,282, high
$3,000, low $400, general range $700-1,200, average
grant $900.
Employer Identification Number: 161116837
Applications: Deadline February 28th; Initial approach
by letter or telephone before December 1st;
Completion of formal application required;
Applications available from the foundation and
Jamestown banks; No interviews.

Publications: Application guidelines, financial
statement, informational brochure, newsletter.
Program description:
The foundation administers 37 separate scholarship
funds. Almost all awards are for undergraduate college
study, although a few awards are made to graduate
students, primarily for medical education.

144
Chicago Community Trust, The
222 North LaSalle Street, Suite 1400
Chicago, IL 60601   (312) 372-3356
Contact: Ms. Trinita Logue, Assistant Director,
Administration

Limitations: Fellowships to residents of Cook County,
IL, who are involved in community service in Cook
County, for the purpose of enhancing their skills in
their areas of community service.
Financial data: Year ended 9/30/87. Assets,
$278,024,000 (M); Total giving, $48,510,367; Grants
to individuals amount for fellowship program not
specified.
Employer Identification Number: 362167000
Applications: Deadline June 30th; Initial approach by
proposal; Completion of formal application required.
**Applications from individuals who are not within the
stated recipient restriction not accepted.**
Publications: Annual report.
Program description:
The **Community Service Fellowship** is a one-year
personal study program for individuals working in a
leadership position in a community service occupation
in Cook County. Awards of up to $60,000 include a
stipend equal to current salary, tuition, travel, lodging,
and related expenses. Up to three individuals are
selected each year for an individual program of study
and investigation which has been judged to have
significant benefit for the recipient and, ultimately, for
the community. Applicants must earn no more than
$40,000 a year.

Since 1946, The Chicago Community Trust has
provided the funds for the administration and awards
of the **William J. Cook Scholarship Fund**, established
to help needy and worthy males who are graduates of
high schools in Cook County attend the educational
institution of their choice. Recipients of these
scholarships are called William J. Cook Scholars.

The trust allocates the funds required to cover the
costs of the scholarships and administrative expenses
to the George M. Pullman Educational Foundation,
which makes the final selection of recipients on behalf
of the trust. In fiscal 1987, William J. Cook Scholars,
both incoming freshmen and upperclassmen, received
awards totaling $200,000 for the 1987-88 academic
year.

For more information on this program, individuals
must contact Corinne Asher, Director of the Cook
Scholarship Program, c/o George M. Pullman

Educational Foundation, 5020 South Lake Shore Drive, Chicago, IL 60615; Tel.: (312) 363-6191.

145
Children's Foundation of Lake Wales, Florida, Inc., The

c/o Albert E. McCormick
1175 Yarnell Avenue
Lake Wales, FL 33853
Contact: David Rockness, Chairman, Organization Committee, 16 North Third Street, Lake Wales, FL 33853; Tel.: (813) 676-4714

Limitations: Undergraduate scholarships to students of the Lake Wales, FL, high school district.
Financial data: Year ended 5/31/87. Assets, $72,873 (M); Total giving, $5,200; Grants to individuals, 14 grants totaling $5,200, high $400, low $300, average grant $400.
Employer Identification Number: 596137951
Applications: Deadline May 15th; Initial approach by letter.

146
Childs (The Jane Coffin) Memorial Fund for Medical Research

333 Cedar Street
New Haven, CT 06510   (203) 785-4612
Contact: Elizabeth M. Ford, Administrative Director

Limitations: Fellowships for cancer research.
Financial data: Year ended 6/30/86. Assets, $23,754,565 (M); Total giving, $1,179,348; Grants to individuals amount not specified.
Employer Identification Number: 066034840
Applications: Deadline January 1st; Initial approach by letter or telephone; Completion of formal application required.
Publications: Annual report, program information, application guidelines.
Program description:
Fellowships are awarded for research into the causes, origins, and treatment of cancer. In general, applicants should not be more than 30 years old and must hold either a M.D. or Ph.D. degree or the equivalent in experience. U.S. recipients may apply the award to research in the U.S. or any foreign country. Foreign applicants must plan to pursue their research in the U.S.

The initial appointment may be for one to two years. Extension of the fellowship period for a third year will be considered upon request by both the Fellow and the sponsor. The fund recognizes that in some instances there may be valid reasons for changing both laboratory and sponsor for the third year. Applicants who, at the time of initiation of the fellowship, will have completed one year in a position as postdoctoral fellow or equivalent will normally be awarded a maximum of two years of fellowship support from the foundation.

Only under exceptional circumstances will an award be made to an individual who will have had two years or more of postdoctoral research experience. The basic stipend is presently $17,000 the first year and $18,000 the second year, with an additional $750 for each dependent child. There is no dependency allowance for a spouse. An allowance of $1,000 a year toward the cost of the research usually will be made available to the laboratory sponsoring the Fellow.

147
Churches Home Foundation, Inc.

c/o Bank South, N.A. - Personal Trust Department
P.O. Box 4956
Atlanta, GA 30302
Contact: Duncan G. Peek, President, 1100 Spring Street, N.W., Suite 600, Atlanta, GA 30367; Tel.: (404)872-8733

Limitations: Scholarships primarily to Georgia residents with evidence of financial need and satisfactory prior academic performance.
Financial data: Year ended 3/31/87. Assets, $2,734,789 (M); Total giving, $183,475; Grants to individuals totaling $124,086.
Employer Identification Number: 580568689
Applications: Applications accepted throughout the year; Initial approach by letter including a brief resume of academic performances and references from previous instructors; Interviews required.

148
Clapp (Charles I. and Emma J.) Scholarship Fund

First of America Bank-Michigan, N.A.
Kalamazoo, MI 49007
Contact: John Withee, c/o First of America Bank-Michigan, N.A.- Otsego Office, 110 East Allegan Street, Otsego, MI 49078

Limitations: Non-interest-bearing student loans to non-drinkers. Female applicants must, in addition, be non-smokers.
Financial data: Year ended 12/31/86. Assets, $224,973 (M); Expenditures, $16,174, Loans to individuals, 10 student loans totaling $8,500, high $1,000, low $250, general range $500-1,000.
Employer Identification Number: 386041673
Applications: Applications accepted throughout the year; Completion of formal application required.

149★
Clark Foundation, The
30 Wall Street
New York, NY 10005   (212) 269-1833
Contact: Edward W. Stack, Secretary

Limitations: Undergraduate scholarships to students
residing in the Cooperstown, NY, area.
Financial data: Year ended 6/30/87. Assets,
$210,106,662 (M); Total giving, $7,164,612; Grants to
individuals, 672 grants totaling $1,769,779; Subtotal
for scholarships, 648 grants totaling $1,655,376,
general range $500-3,000.
Employer Identification Number: 135616528
Applications: Applications accepted throughout the
year; Initial approach by letter; Completion of formal
application required; Interviews required.
Publications: Program information, application
guidelines.
Program description:
Most scholarship applicants are referred to the
program by their high schools during their senior year.

150★
Clark (Morris J.) Medical Education Foundation
c/o Mellon Bank, N.A.
Mellon Bank Center
Pittsburgh, PA 15258-0001

Limitations: Scholarships and fellowships to students
attending the University of Pittsburgh School of
Medicine.
Financial data: Year ended 12/31/86. Assets, $541,979
(M); Total giving, $21,600; Grants to individuals
totaling $21,600.
Employer Identification Number: 256018886
Applications: Contact foundation for current
application information through the School of
Medicine.
Program description:
Payments are made directly to the institution on the
recipient's behalf.

151
Clarke-Aff League Memorial Fund
c/o Mary Clarke League
Mellon Bank (East) N.A., P.O. Box 7236
Philadelphia, PA 19101
Contact: Local medical school financial aid office

Limitations: Scholarships to students attending medical
school in Philadelphia, PA, including the School of
Podiatric Medicine.
Financial data: Year ended 6/30/87. Assets, $243,549
(M); Total giving, $11,734; Grants to individuals
totaling $11,734.
Employer Identification Number: 236225542
Applications: Contact local medical school financial
aid office for applications and current deadline;
Completion of formal application required.

152
Clemens Foundation, The
P.O. Box 427
Philomath, OR 97370   (503) 929-3541
Contact: Leon Stratton

Limitations: Scholarships and some loans to graduates
of high schools in the Alsea, Crane, Eddyville, and
Philomath, OR, school districts.
Financial data: Year ended 12/31/86. Assets,
$4,733,576 (M); Total giving, $414,451; Grants to
individuals, 359 grants totaling $414,451, high
$2,426, low $368.
Employer Identification Number: 936023941
Applications: No set deadline, however, application
should be submitted before the school term begins;
Initial approach by letter or telephone; Completion of
formal application required.
Program description:
Scholarships are awarded to students for education at
a college level, recognized institution or accredited
vocational school on a full-time basis. Tuition grants
equal the amount of tuition charged by Oregon State
University to resident students.
   In addition, two grants of slightly higher amounts
are awarded to the first- and second-place swimmers
at Philomath (Oregon) High School.

153★
Clements (H. Loren) Scholarship Fund
c/o Third National Bank
130 Wyoming Avenue
Scranton, PA 18501

Limitations: Scholarships to graduates of North
Pocono High School in Moscow, PA.
Financial data: Year ended 12/31/87. Assets, $256,500
(M); Total giving, $9,000; Grants to individuals, 18
grants totaling $9,000, each grant $500.
Employer Identification Number: 236410082
Applications: Deadline April 15th.
Publications: Financial statement, 990-PF printed copy
available upon request.

154
Close Foundation, Inc.
(Formerly Springs (Frances Ley) Foundation, Inc.)
P.O. Drawer 460
Lancaster, SC 29720   (803) 286-2196
Contact: Charles A. Bundy, President

Limitations: Student loans generally limited to North
Carolina and Lancaster County, Chester Township of
Chester County and Fort Mill Township, South
Carolina.
Financial data: Year ended 12/31/86. Assets,
$8,725,274 (M); Expenditures, $606,004; Loans to
individuals, 3 loans totaling $3,300.
Employer Identification Number: 237013986

Applications: Completion of formal application required.
Publications: Annual report, program information, application guidelines.

155★
Cobb (Ty) Educational Fund
P.O. Box 725
Forest Park, GA 30051
Contact: Rosie Atkins, Secretary

Limitations: Scholarships limited to Georgia needy and deserving residents who have completed one year in an accredited institution of higher learning; graduate school scholarships available to law, medical, or dental students.
Financial data: Year ended 12/31/86. Assets, $4,645,567 (M); Total giving, $234,694; Grants to individuals, 605 grants totaling $234,694.
Employer Identification Number: 586026003
Applications: Deadlines June 15th for applications, July 1st for college transcripts which must include grades of most recent term of attendance; Initial approach by letter; Completion of formal application required.
Publications: Program information.
Program description:
Scholarships are awarded to students who have demonstrated financial need and completed at least one academic year of B quality or higher work. Ordinarily, scholarships are awarded for undergraduate study, but awards may also be made for professional study in law, medicine, and dentistry.
  Scholarships are paid directly to the institution for a full academic year of nine months and are renewable.

156
Coffey Foundation, Inc.
P.O. Box 1170
Lenoir, NC 28645
Contact: Hope Huffstetler, Trustee, 406 Norwood Street Southwest, Lenoir, NC 28645; Tel.: (704) 754-6594

Limitations: Scholarships and student loans limited to residents of Caldwell County, NC.
Financial data: Year ended 11/30/86. Assets, $2,857,245 (M); Total giving, $200,000; Grants to individuals totaling $91,800; Loans to individuals, 1 loan totaling $1,000.
Employer Identification Number: 566047501
Applications: Deadline April 15th; Application forms available at high schools in Caldwell County, NC; Completion of formal application, including photograph, essay explaining chosen course of study and future work, letter of recommendation (principal, guidance counselor, pastor, or community leader), high school transcript, and results of any supplemental tests (SAT, ACT), required; Deadline April 15th;

Application forms available at high schools in Caldwell County, NC.

157★
Cogan (George T.) Trust
P.O. Box 418
Portsmouth, NH 03801   (603) 436-4010
Contact: Wyman P. Boynton, Trustee, 82 Court Street, Portsmouth, NH 03801; Tel.: (603) 436-4101

Limitations: Scholarships to students who have resided in Portsmouth, NH, for at least four years prior to graduation from either Portsmouth High School or St. Thomas Aquinas High School.
Financial data: Year ended 12/31/86. Assets, $319,466 (M); Total giving, $12,800; Grants to individuals, 26 grants totaling $12,800, high $1,500, low $100, general range $500-800, average grant $600.
Employer Identification Number: 026019789
Applications: Deadline May 5th; Completion of formal application with at least two letters of recommendation, copy of transcript and SER required.

158
Cohen (Sarah) Scholarship Fund
c/o Sovran Bank, N.A.
P.O. Box 3000
Norfolk, VA 23514
Contact: Rabbi, Ohef Sholon Temple, Stockley Gradens, Raleigh Avenue, Norfolk, VA.

Limitations: Scholarships to residents of Norfolk, VA.
Financial data: Year ended 12/31/86. Assets, $160,281 (M); Total giving, $5,050; Grants to individuals, 9 grants totaling $5,050, high $1,100, low $350, general range $350-750.
Employer Identification Number: 546033744
Applications: Deadline August 1st; Initial approach by letter.

159
Cole (Olive B.) Foundation, Inc.
3242 Mallard Cove Lane
Fort Wayne, IN 46804   (219) 436-2182
Contact: John E. Hogan, Jr., Executive Vice-President

Limitations: Scholarships to graduates of Noble County, IN, high schools.
Financial data: Year ended 3/31/87. Assets, $17,097,669 (M); Total giving, $518,336; Grants to individuals, 197 grants totaling $113,931.
Employer Identification Number: 356040491
Applications: Deadline March 15th; Initial approach by letter; Completion of formal application required; Interviews granted upon request.
Publications: Program information.

160
Coleman (William S. and Lillian R.) Scholarship Trust

c/o Bank One, Indianapolis, NA
101 Monument Circle
Indianapolis, IN 46277   (317) 639-7544
Contact: Jackie Weitz, Assistant Vice-President, Bank One, Indianapolis NA

Limitations: Scholarships for postsecondary education to residents of Rush County, IN.
Financial data: Year ended 6/30/87. Assets, $1,726,255 (M); Total giving, $91,000; Grants to individuals, 183 grants totaling, $91,000, high $950, low $100.
Employer Identification Number: 356279390
Applications: Deadline April 1st or 60 days prior to beginning of a school term; Completion of formal application required.

161
Colgan (The James W.) Fund

c/o Bank of New England-West, Trust Department
1391 Main Street, P.O. Box 9003
Springfield, MA 01101   (413) 787-8700
Contact: Suzanne N. Renault-Morgan, Trust Officer

Limitations: Undergraduate loans only to residents of Massachusetts.
Financial data: Year ended 12/31/85. Assets, $2,000,947 (M); Expenditures, $176,932; Loans to individuals, 189 loans totaling $158,075, high $2,000, low $250, average loan $1,000.
Employer Identification Number: 046032781
Applications: Deadline May 31st; Initial approach by letter or telephone; Completion of formal application required; Interviews granted upon request.

162
Collins (Joseph) Foundation

One Citicorp Center
153 East 53rd Street
New York, NY 10022
Contact: Mrs. Augusta L. Packer, Secretary-Treasurer

Limitations: Scholarships to needy students attending accredited medical schools in pursuit of the M.D. degree.
Financial data: Year ended 6/30/86. Assets, $8,087,513 (M); Total giving, $269,938; Grants to individuals, 147 grants totaling $269,938, high $2,200, low $900, average grant $1,900.
Employer Identification Number: 136404527
Applications: Deadline March 1st; Applications accepted between January 1st and March 1st; Initial approach by proposal; Application forms are required and are available only through the medical school authorities, to whom completed forms should also be returned for forwarding to the foundation with a

supporting letter from dean of medical school.
Publications: Annual report, program information, application guidelines.
Program description:
Scholarships to a maximum of $2,500 each are awarded to needy and outstanding M.D. students. The majority of awards are made to second-, third-, and fourth-year students. The individual must demonstrate interest in arts and letters or other cultural pursuits outside the field of medicine, and indicate an intention to specialize in neurology or psychiatry or to become a general practitioner. Additional factors considered are: evidence of good moral character of the applicant; age (applicants commencing their medical education before attaining the age of 30 are preferred); marital status; geographical proximity (applicants residing within 200 miles of the medical school are preferred); and financial need. Awards are not made for the benefit of pre-medical or postgraduate medical students.

163
Collins (Paul and Mary) Trust, No. 2

c/o Lyon County State Bank
Rock Rapids, IA 51246   (712) 472-2581

Limitations: Scholarships to individuals to pursue college education.
Financial data: Year ended 5/31/87. Assets, $212,662 (M); Total giving, $14,450; Grants to individuals, 68 grants totaling $14,450, high $300, low $150, general range $200-300.
Employer Identification Number: 426120024
Applications: Deadline June 1st; Completion of formal application required.
Program description:
Relatives of Paul and Mary Collins are not eligible to apply.

164
Collins-McDonald Trust Fund

620 North First Street
Lakeview, OR 97630   (503) 947-2196
Contact: James C. Lynch, Trustee

Limitations: Scholarships for higher education limited to graduates of Lake County, OR, high schools.
Financial data: Year ended 12/31/86. Assets, $2,403,269 (M); Total giving, $86,307; Grants to individuals, 26 grants totaling $38,940, high $2,520, low $610, general range $1,000-1,800.
Employer Identification Number: 936021894
Applications: Deadline May 14th; Completion of formal application required; Interviews required.
Publications: Application guidelines.

165★
Colorado Masons Benevolent Fund Association

1770 Sherman Street
Denver, CO 80203   (303) 837-0367
Contact: See program description below for contact information.

Limitations: Scholarships only to graduates of high schools in Colorado planning to attend institutions of higher learning in Colorado; Educational loans only to children of Master Masons of Colorado Lodges, who are either juniors or seniors in colleges.
Financial data: Year ended 10/31/87. Assets, $7,344,346 (M); Total giving, $748,056; Grants to individuals, 164 grants totaling $731,906; Subtotal for scholarships, 77 grants totaling $400,600, high $7,500, low $1,950, general range $3,000-6,000; Loans to individuals amount not specified.
Employer Identification Number: 840406813
Applications: Deadline February 15th for scholarships; Initial approach by letter; Completion of formal application required including picture of applicant, personal letter outlining goals, objectives, and explanation of need, high school transcript, college letter of acceptance, and letters of recommendation (see application guidelines for complete details).
Publications: Application guidelines.
Program description:
Masonic affiliation is not required for eligibility to receive these scholarships; neither is race nor creed a factor. Masonic affiliation is required for educational loans.

Scholarship recipients cannot be married during their freshman or sophomore years. Marriage in either year will forfeit scholarship. Any recipient, if need continues, is eligible to renew his/her assistance for the second, third and fourth years. Renewals are made prior to the following year.

Scholarships are made payable to the director of financial aid at the educational institution for the account of the individual recipient.

Applications for scholarships are mailed each year in mid-October to all public schools in Colorado and to all Masonic lodges in Colorado, and may also be obtained by writing to Scholarship Correspondent, P.O. Box 7729, Colorado Springs, CO 80904.

The **Jacobson Memorial Educational Fund** assists sons and daughters of Master Mason of Colorado Lodges who need to obtain loans to complete their college education while in their junior or senior year. Requests for consideration should be directed to the association's Denver offices.

166
Community Welfare Association of Colquitt County

P.O. Box 460
Moultrie, GA 31776

Limitations: Scholarships for higher education.
Financial data: Year ended 12/31/86. Assets, $1,956,534 (M); Total giving, $92,002; Grants to individuals, 4 grants totaling $3,333, high $1,333, low $333.
Employer Identification Number: 586032259

167
Continental Grain Foundation

277 Park Avenue
New York, NY 10172
Contact: Dwight C. Coffin, Secretary

Limitations: Grants to students for exchange programs between the U.S. and other countries.
Financial data: Year ended 1/31/86. Assets, $25,645 (M); Total giving, $76,220; Grants to individuals, 5 grants totaling $3,750, high $1,000, low $500.
Employer Identification Number: 136160912
Applications: Applications accepted throughout the year; Initial approach by letter.

168
Cook (Loring) Foundation

P.O. Box 1060
McAllen, TX 78502
Contact: Counselor, McAllen Memorial High School, McAllen, TX 78502

Limitations: Scholarships limited to graduating seniors of Memorial High School, McAllen, TX.
Financial data: Year ended 3/31/87. Assets, $1,764,020 (M); Total giving, $60,395; Grants to individuals totaling $6,250.
Employer Identification Number: 746050063
Applications: Deadline March 1st; Submit application to counselor of Memorial High School; Completion of formal application required; Interviews required.
Program description:
Scholarships are awarded to recipients seeking to continue their academic education or to obtain vocational training. Recipients must be "well-rounded" students who are highly involved in scholastic studies (maintaining at least a B average), extracurricular school activities, and possess a high moral character and religious beliefs. Applicants must be able to demonstrate these qualities in addition to a financial need for scholarship support.

The foundation's selection committee includes a representative of the foundation, a faculty member, a student leader not applying for aid, and a member of the school's administration (counselor, principal, or other administrator).

169★
Corbett (Laura R. & William M.) Trust
c/o University of South Carolina
School of Medicine
Columbia, SC 29208   (803) 733-3151

Limitations: Low-interest loans only to worthy medical
students attending the University of South Carolina
School of Medicine.
Financial data: Year ended 12/31/86. Assets,
$1,370,606 (M); Expenditures, $138,472; Loans to
individuals, 60 loans totaling $121,700, high $3,500,
low $300.
Employer Identification Number: 570685862
Applications: Contact foundation for current
application deadline; Applications available at the
Office of Student Affairs at the School of Medicine;
Completion of formal application required; Submit
completed application to Office of Student Affairs.
Program description:
The **Corbett Trust Loan Program** has been designed to
provide financial assistance only, to USC medical
students. The primary program is for long-term loans
to cover costs associated with medical education and
provides for extended repayment. The secondary
program is for short-term loans designed to meet
emergency needs and to be repaid within one
calendar year, or upon leaving school, whichever
occurs first.
    The Office of Student Affairs at the School of
Medicine forwards all completed applications to the
Scholarship and Loan Committee for review, which
submits the applications with recommendations to the
Citizen and Southern Trust Company (South Carolina),
N.A.
    A student borrower's indebtedness under the trust's
long-term program will not exceed $3,500 per year
with a cumulative indebtedness of $14,000 per
individual. The repayment period may extend for up
to ten years from graduation, dismissal, or withdrawal.
There is no interest charged or accrued while the
student is enrolled in good standing. A borrower may
apply for a deferment of scheduled payments on the
principal of a long-term loan for the lesser of five
years or the period of postgraduate medical training.
    Under the short-term program, qualified students
may borrow up to $1,000 for a period not to exceed
one year. This program is to be used as an emergency
fund and must be repaid within one year. There will
be no interest charged on the portion of the loan
repaid within 60 days; thereafter, interest will be
charged from the date of the note on the balance.

170★
Cornerhouse Fund, Inc.
1270 Avenue of the Americas, Room 2300
New York, NY 10020-1702   (212) 315-8300
Contact: Dorothy D. Eweson, Vice-President

Limitations: Grants to faculty and students in the
social sciences.
Financial data: Year ended 6/30/86. Assets, $639,406
(M); Total giving, $61,370; Grants to individuals, 3
grants totaling $61,370, high $43,370, low $8,000.
Employer Identification Number: 237046553
Applications: Applications accepted throughout the
year.
Program description:
The grants are made payable to the educational
institution with which the individual recipient is
affiliated.

171
**Corpina (Joseph B.), Jr. Memorial Foundation,
Inc.**
46 Candlewood Road
Scarsdale, NY 10583-6041
Contact: Joseph B. Corpina, Director

Limitations: Scholarships, awards, and grants to
students of Iona Grammar School, NY.
Financial data: Year ended 12/31/85. Assets, $41,912
(M); Total giving, $5,130; Grants to individuals, 6
grants totaling $5,130, high $1,515, low $100.
Employer Identification Number: 133188830
Applications: Applications accepted throughout the
year; Initial approach by letter.

172★
Corti Family Agricultural Fund
c/o Wells Fargo Bank, Trust Department
618 East Shaw Avenue
Fresno, CA 93710   (209) 442-6232
Contact: William F. Richey, Assistant Vice-President -
Trust, Wells Fargo Bank

Limitations: Scholarships only to graduates of Kern
County, CA, high schools who are pursuing an
agricultural education in a college or university.
Financial data: Year ended 3/31/87. Assets, $875,139
(M); Total giving, $24,605; Grants to individuals, 133
grants totaling $24,605, high $366, low $100.
Employer Identification Number: 956053041
Applications: Deadline February 28th; Completion of
formal application required; Reference letters (one
from academic source, one from personal source),
financial statement, transcript of grades, and letter
stating goals and plans should accompany formal
application; Interviews granted upon request.
Program description:
The following is an additional application address to
use when requesting or submitting an application: c/o

Theresa Corti Scholarship Committee, Kern County Superintendent of Schools, 5801 Sundale Avenue, Bakersfield, CA 93309; Tel.: (805) 398-3600.

Recipients are selected by a committee composed of a senior trust officer of the Bank of America, the superintendent of schools for Kern County, and the chairman of the Kern County Board of Supervisors.

173
Coshocton Foundation

P.O. Box 15
Coshocton, OH 43812
Contact: Orville Fuller, Treasurer, or Sam C. Clow, Chairman, Distribution Committee

Limitations: Scholarships limited to residents of Coshocton County, OH.
Financial data: Year ended 9/30/86. Assets, $1,872,912 (M); Total giving, $219,033; Grants to individuals, 5 grants totaling $7,600.
Employer Identification Number: 316064567
Applications: Initial approach by letter.
Publications: Annual report.

174
Coulter (Viola Vestal) Foundation, Inc.

c/o United Bank of Denver
1700 Broadway
Denver, CO 80274   (303) 863-6023
Contact: Charles H. Myers, Vice-President

Limitations: Scholarships to students at specifically designated colleges and universities in the western United States for graduate and undergraduate degree programs.
Financial data: Year ended 12/31/86. Assets, $1,050,926 (M); Total giving, $62,500; Grants to individuals amount not specified.
Employer Identification Number: 846029641
Applications: Applications accepted throughout the year; Initial approach by personal letter with biographical sketch.
Program description:
The foundation awards grants directly to the educational institution in the names of the individual recipients.

175★
Council on Library Resources, Inc.

1785 Massachusetts Avenue, N.W.
Washington, DC 20036   (202) 483-7474
Contact: Warren J. Haas, President

Limitations: Grants are generally limited to librarians for research grants, and the Academic Library Management Intern Program.
Financial data: Year ended 6/30/87. Assets, $8,552,741 (M); Total giving, $443,643; Grants to individuals, 3 grants totaling $11,347, high $10,000, low $347, average grant $3,782.
Employer Identification Number: 530232831
Applications: Applications accepted throughout the year for general grants; Contact foundation for current application deadline for Intern Program; Initial approach by letter; Completion of formal application required for Intern Program.
Publications: Annual report, application guidelines, program information, informational brochure, newsletter.
Program description:
The **Academic Library Management Intern Program** enables potential library leaders to develop administrative and managerial abilities through a planned program centered on practical experience with the director of a large academic library recognized for its administrative excellence. Individuals interested in the Intern Program should contact the Council to find out if the program will be offered in the future.

176★
Cox (Opal G.) Charitable Trust

Interfirst Bank Austin
P.O. Box 908
Austin, TX 78781

Limitations: Scholarships to students attending Southwestern Baptist Theological Seminary, TX, or Baylor University, TX, with preference given to students in the top 25 percent of the class, studying as missionaries, or foreign students.
Financial data: Year ended 8/31/86. Assets, $1,832,629 (M); Total giving, $165,000; Grants to individuals, 64 grants totaling $165,000, high $5,000, low $1,500.
Employer Identification Number: 746307500
Applications: Deadlines March 18th for Baylor University and April 1st for Southwestern Baptist Theological Seminary; Completion of formal application, accompanied by transcript of grades required; See program description below for application addresses.
Program description:
Baylor University students should contact William J. Dube III, Assistant Vice-President for Baylor Academic Scholarship and Financial Aid, Baylor University, Box 6237, Waco, TX 76706. Applicants must have a GPA of 3.2 or above and, if selected, enroll in a minimum of 12 semester hours of undergraduate studies per semester. The final selection is based on merit and need as revealed in the application provided by the trustees. Faculty recommendations should be forwarded directly to the student Financial Aid Office by the faculty.

Southwestern Baptist Theological Seminary students should contact David McQuitty, Director of Student Aid, P.O. Box 22000, Fort Worth, TX 76122 for application information and forms.

177★
Crary (Bruce L.) Foundation, Inc.
Hand House, River Street
P.O. Box 396
Elizabethtown, NY 12932   (518) 873-6496
Contact: Richard W. Lawrence, Jr., President

Limitations: Postsecondary scholarships limited to
residents of Clinton, Essex, Franklin, Hamilton, and
Warren counties, NY.
Financial data: Year ended 6/30/87. Assets,
$5,276,381 (M); Total giving, $175,687; Grants to
individuals, 313 grants totaling $152,833, high $800,
low $250, average grant $500.
Employer Identification Number: 237366844
Applications: Deadline March 31st; Initial approach
made through local schools to foundation; Completion
of formal application required; Scholarships awarded
in early July.
Program description:
There are approximately 125 new awards available
each year. There are no scholastic requirements other
than ability to complete the education requirements of
the attending institution.

Although there is no obligation to repay the award,
recipients are encouraged to do so.

178
Croston (Elaine R.) Scholarship Fund
c/o Bank of Boston
P.O. Box 1861
Boston, MA 02105
Contact: Arthur Veasey III, c/o Bank of Boston, P.O.
Box 1891, Boston, MA 02105; Tel.: (617) 434-4016

Limitations: Scholarships to graduates of Haverhill
High School, Haverhill, MA, for college education.
Financial data: Year ended 12/31/85. Assets, $217,237
(M); Total giving, $13,800; Grants to individuals, 53
grants totaling $13,800, high $700, low $300.
Employer Identification Number: 046079522
Applications: Applications accepted throughout the
year; Initial approach by letter of inquiry.

179
Cultural Society, Inc., The
P.O. Box 1374
Bridgeview, IL 60455   (312) 371-6429
Contact: Mohammad Nasr, M.D., Treasurer

Limitations: Scholarships to Muslim students.
Financial data: Year ended 6/30/86. Assets, $143,301
(M); Total giving, $126,053; Grants to individuals, 13
grants totaling $69,203; Subtotal for scholarships, 5
grants totaling $28,969, high $13,000, low $1,451.
Employer Identification Number: 510183515
Applications: Applications accepted throughout the
year; Initial approach by letter.

180
Curran (Gertrude D.) Trust FBO Curran Music School
(Also known as Curran Music Scholarship Fund)
c/o Marine Midland Bank
P.O. Box 4203
Buffalo, NY 14240

Limitations: Music scholarships to residents of Utica,
NY.
Financial data: Year ended 12/31/85. Assets, $216,320
(M); Total giving, $9,000; Grants to individuals
amount not specified.
Employer Identification Number: 156015514

181
Daly (Bernard) Educational Fund
P.O. Box 309
Lakeview, OR 97630   (503) 947-2196
Contact: James C. Lynch, Secretary

Limitations: Scholarships only to students in Lake
County, OR, for study at Oregon state-supported
universities, colleges, and technical schools.
Financial data: Year ended 5/31/87. Assets,
$1,757,801 (M); Total giving, $93,440; Grants to
individuals, 49 grants totaling $93,440.
Employer Identification Number: 936025466
Applications: Deadline April 1st; Initial approach by
telephone; Completion of two copies of formal
applications required; Interviews required.
Program description:
Grants are given for a single year of study. Students
meeting grades and hours requirements are eligible for
reappointment up to a maximum of four years (12
terms).

182★
Daly (Nathan and Harry) Scholarship
Mellon Bank N.A.
One Mellon Bank Center - 3845
Pittsburgh, PA 15258   (412) 234-5712
Contact: Marilyn King, Assistant Trust Officer

Limitations: Scholarships only to deserving persons
from Butler County, PA, attending Duquesne
University.
Financial data: Year ended 12/31/87. Assets, $60,000
(M); Total giving, $2,200; Grants to individuals
totaling $2,200.
Employer Identification Number: 256082584
Applications: Contact trust for current application
deadline; Completion of formal application required.

183★
Daso (Edith M.) Scholarship Trust
c/o Bar Harbor Banking & Trust Company
82 Main Street
Bar Harbor, ME 04609-0400   (207) 288-3314
Contact: Trust Department

Limitations: Scholarships only to graduates of Mount Desert Island Regional High School, Mt. Desert, ME.
Financial data: Year ended 10/31/87. Assets, $52,808 (M); Total giving, $2,750, Grants to individuals, 6 grants totaling $2,750, high $800, low $300, general range $300-800, average grant $300.
Employer Identification Number: 016057578
Applications: Deadlines April 15th and May 15th; Completion of formal application required.

184★
Daughters of the Cincinnati
122 East 58th Street
New York, NY 10022   (212) 319-6915
Contact: Scholarship Administrator

Limitations: Scholarships only to high school seniors who are daughters of regular commissioned officers (on active duty or retired) in the Army, Navy, Air Force, Coast Guard, or Marines.
Financial data: Year ended 12/31/85. Assets, $882,478 (M); Total giving, $37,600; Grants to individuals, 80 grants totaling $37,600, high $750, low $250.
Employer Identification Number: 136096069
Applications: Deadline April 15th; Completion of formal application required.
Publications: Application guidelines.
Program description:
Undergraduate scholarships, awarded to high school seniors, are available in amounts up to $1,500 annually for 4 years, subject to a review each year of the candidates academic record.

     The foundation requires copies of the applicant's SAT or ACT test scores in addition to her completion of the Biographical Questionnaire and a letter of recommendation from a member of the community other than family or school. Applicant's school must complete the Secondary School Questionnaire and submit an official transcript. The applicant's parents must complete the Financial Aid Form; it should be filed with The College Scholarship Service and should indicate that a copy is to be sent to the foundation, code number 0174. The applicant must enclose two dollars for postage and handling.

     The foundation also provides two scholarships for one year of postgraduate study in American history at Teachers College (contact the Director of Student Aid, Teachers College, Columbia University, New York, NY); undergraduate Pruden Scholarships are available to daughters of Episcopal ministers at Duke University (contact the Office of Undergraduate Financial Aid, Duke University).

185★
Davenport (George P.) Trust Fund
55 Front Street
Bath, ME 04530   (207) 443-3431

Limitations: Scholarships only to Bath, ME, area high school graduates.
Financial data: Year ended 12/31/87. Assets, $4,526,050 (M); Total giving, $290,320; Grants to individuals, 61 grants totaling $80,300, high $3,000, low $500, general range $1,000-1,500, average grant $1,000.
Employer Identification Number: 016009246
Applications: Applications accepted throughout the year; Completion of formal application required.
Publications: Application guidelines, 990-PF printed copy available upon request.

186
Davi (Vincent A.) Memorial
c/o Horace A. Enea
1155 Pine Street
Pittsburg, CA 94565
Contact: Pittsburg Unified School District, 2000 Railroad Avenue, Pittsburg, CA 94565

Limitations: Scholarships only to students of the Pittsburg Unified School District, Pittsburg, CA, for college attendance.
Financial data: Year ended 12/31/86. Assets, $48,713 (M); Total giving, $3,000; Grants to individuals, 4 grants totaling $3,000, high $1,000, low $500.
Employer Identification Number: 946138193
Applications: Deadline beginning of semester; Completion of formal application and school district administered test required.
Program description:
Consideration for the scholarship awards include scholastic achievement (determined by an exam administered in May by the Pittsburg Unified School District) and financial ability of the parents to contribute to applicant's education. The scholarship is for one year only, is not renewable, and is awarded only to students who will be attending a four-year college. Additional consideration is given to the type of school selected and the subjects to be studied.

187
Davis (James A. and Juliet L.) Foundation, Inc.
802 First National Center
P.O. Box 2027
Hutchinson, KS 67504-2027   (316) 663-5021
Contact: William Y. Chalfant, Secretary

Limitations: Scholarships only to students graduating from Hutchinson High School, KS who will attend college in Kansas or Missouri.
Financial data: Year ended 12/31/86. Assets, $2,205,385 (M); Total giving, $85,705; Grants to

individuals, 29 grants totaling $35,250, high $2,000, low $750.
Employer Identification Number: 486105748
Applications: Deadline March 15th.

188
Davis (William G.) Charitable Trust
c/o Pittsburgh National Bank
Department 970
Pittsburgh, PA 15265
Contact: David L. Wylie, 409 Chestnut Road, Sewickely, PA 15143

Limitations: Scholarships to children of Master Members of Doric Lodge No. 630.
Financial data: Year ended 12/31/86. Assets, $320,437 (M); Total giving, $14,495; Grants to individuals, 14 grants totaling $14,095, high $1,997, low $373.
Employer Identification Number: 251289600
Applications: Deadline December 1st; Completion of formal application required.
Program description:
Scholarships are for undergraduate school and to cover tuition only.

189★
Davis-Roberts Scholarship Fund, Inc.
116 Lummis Court
Cheyenne, WY 82007   (307) 632-2948
Contact: Charles H. Moore, Secretary-Treasurer

Limitations: Scholarships only to members or former members of the Order of DeMolay or Jobs Daughters Bethel in Wyoming, for full-time study in any college or university.
Financial data: Year ended 12/31/86. Assets, $52,150 (M); Total giving, $3,850; Grants to individuals, 11 grants totaling $3,850, each grant $350.
Employer Identification Number: 836011403
Applications: Deadline June 15th; Completion of formal application required.
Program description:
Scholarship amounts are determined by financial need and are renewable. Applicants must be of good moral character.

190
Day (Carl and Virginia Johnson) Trust
108 West Madison Street
Yazoo City, MS 39194   (601) 746-4901
Contact: J. C. Lamkin, Manager

Limitations: Interest-free student loans only for residents of Mississippi attending Mississippi schools.
Financial data: Year ended 12/31/86. Assets, $2,514,743 (M); Expenditures, $226,846; Loans to individuals, 124 loans totaling $203,224, high $3,000, low $300.
Employer Identification Number: 640386095

Applications: Deadlines December 15th and August 15th; Initial approach by letter.
Program description:
Approximately 100 students are assisted annually. Loans are repaid at the rate of $50 per month, $100 per month by medical students.

191
DeKalb County Producers' Supply and Farm Bureau Scholarship Trust Fund
315 North Sixth Street
DeKalb, IL 60115

Limitations: Scholarships to Illinois residents obtaining a medical education (including veterinary medicine, nursing, and pharmacology) whose parents have been members of the DeKalb County Farm Bureau in good standing for two years.
Financial data: Year ended 9/30/86. Assets, $103,942 (M); Total giving, $10,160; Grants to individuals, 4 grants totaling $10,160, high $4,166, low $1,829.
Employer Identification Number: 237136011
Applications: Applications accepted throughout the year.

192
Deke Foundation
16 East 64th Street
New York, NY 10021-7291   (212) 759-0660

Limitations: Scholarships to undergraduate members of the Delta Kappa Epsilon Fraternity.
Financial data: Year ended 12/31/85. Assets, $115,623 (M); Total giving, $3,020; Grants to individuals, 5 grants totaling $3,020, high $1,020, low $500.
Employer Identification Number: 136112657
Applications: Initial approach by letter, including transcript, recommendations, verification of financial need, and statement of qualifications and goals.

193★
Delmas (The Gladys Krieble) Foundation
c/o Reid and Priest
40 West 57th Street
New York, NY 10019   (212) 603-2302
Contact: Joseph C. Mitchell, Trustee

Limitations: Predoctoral or postdoctoral grants for research in Venice, Italy.
Financial data: Year ended 12/31/85. Assets, $1,342,624 (M); Total giving, $255,912; Grants to individuals, 32 grants totaling $80,912, high $8,000, low $577, general range $1,000-4,000.
Employer Identification Number: 510193884
Applications: Deadline December 15th; Submit proposal preferably in October or November; Initial approach by proposal.
Publications: Application guidelines, program information.

Program description:
Predoctoral and postdoctoral fellowships are awarded for travel and research in Venice. Support will be considered for research in the following areas: the history of Venice and the former Venetian empire in its various aspects including art, architecture, archaeology, theatre, music, literature, natural science, political science, economics, and law; and studies related to the contemporary Venetian environment such as ecology, oceanography, urban planning and rehabilitation.

Applicants must be U.S. citizens or permanent residents and have had some experience in advanced research. Graduate students must have completed all doctoral requirements except for the dissertation. Applications will be considered for grants from $500 to a maximum of $10,000 for a full academic year. Eventually, funds will be available for aid in the publication of studies resulting from research made possible by these grants at the discretion of the trustees and advisory board.

194
Deloitte Haskins & Sells Foundation
1114 Avenue of the Americas
New York, NY 10036   (212) 790-0588
Contact: Gerald A. Sena, President

Limitations: Fellowships and research grants to doctoral and graduate accounting students.
Financial data: Year ended 8/31/85. Assets, $4,875,136 (M); Total giving, $794,018; Grants to individuals, 45 grants totaling $213,750, Subtotal amounts not specified.
Employer Identification Number: 136400341
Applications: Deadline for Doctoral Fellowship Program October 15th; Initial approach by letter; Contact foundation for current application deadline for Graduate Research Assistant Program; Completion of formal application required for Doctoral Fellowship Program.
Publications: Informational brochure.
Program description:
The foundation gives grants in two categories: The **Doctoral Fellowship Program**, to provide support for doctoral accounting candidates in the last two years of their doctoral program; and The **Graduate Research Assistant Program**, to provide support for graduate accounting students other than doctoral candidates to serve as Graduate Research Assistants to full-time accounting faculty members engaged in research projects approved by the foundation.

195
Delta Tau Delta Educational Fund
8250 Haverstick Road, Suite 150
Indianapolis, IN 46240   (317) 259-1187
Contact: Gale Wilkerson

Limitations: Scholarships and student loans to undergraduate members of Delta Tau Delta.
Financial data: Year ended 7/31/87. Assets, $1,497,938 (M); Expenditures, $98,419; Grants to individuals, 43 grants totaling $14,414, high $1,500, low $50; Loans to individuals, 33 loans totaling $49,000.
Employer Identification Number: 237405401
Applications: Applications accepted throughout the year; Completion of formal application required; Some grants are restricted to a specific chapter or curriculum.

196
Deseranno Educational Foundation, Inc.
4600 Bellevue
Detroit, MI 48207
Contact: The Right Reverend Ferdinand DeCheudt, Father Taillieu Senior Citizen Home, Inc; 18760 East Thirteen Mile Road, Roseville, MI 48066.

Limitations: Scholarships to students attending Madonna College, MI.
Financial data: Year ended 12/31/86. Assets, $1,984,549 (M); Total giving, $54,100; Grants to individuals, 12 grants totaling $10,600, high $1,000, low $600.
Employer Identification Number: 237005737
Applications: Applications accepted throughout the year; Initial approach by letter.

197
Dolan (E. John) Foundation
c/o Herbert Susser
370 Seventh Avenue
New York, NY 10001

Limitations: Grants only for study for the Roman Catholic priesthood.
Financial data: Year ended 12/31/85. Assets, $69,941 (M); Total giving, $4,000; Grants to individuals, 2 grants totaling $4,000, each grant $2,000.
Employer Identification Number: 136271587
Applications: Deadline April 1st; Interviews required.

198
Dougherty Foundation, Inc.
3336 North 32nd Street, Suite 115
Phoenix, AZ 85018   (602) 956-3980
Contact: Mary J. Maffeo, Secretary

Limitations: Scholarships and loans based on financial need only to Arizona residents who are U.S. citizens

and enrolled in an accredited college-degree program.
Financial data: Year ended 12/31/86. Assets,
$6,913,079 (M); Expenditures, $583,187; Grants to
individuals totaling $225,674, average grant $1,000;
Loans to individuals totaling $202,665, average loan
$2,000.
Employer Identification Number: 866051637
Applications: Applications accepted between January
and April; Initial approach by letter or telephone;
Completion of formal application required.
Publications: Program information, application
guidelines.
Program description:
The number of scholarships and loans to students
going outside of Arizona for undergraduate or
graduate studies is limited. Loans are awarded only for
graduate program. Scholarships are awarded only for
community college education.

199★
Dow Jones Newspaper Fund, Inc., The
P.O. Box 300
Princeton, NJ 08543-0300   (609) 452-2820
Contact: Thomas E. Engelman, Executive Director

Limitations: Three internship programs for journalism
students: one for minority college sophomores, one for
undergraduates in their junior year, and one for
minority candidates who are college seniors. There is
also a fellowship program for high school journalism
teachers and newspaper advisers.
Financial data: Year ended 12/31/87. Assets, $379,067
(M); Total giving, $327,277; Grants to individuals, 141
grants totaling $91,035; Subtotal for internships not
specified, high $1,500, low $350.
Employer Identification Number: 136021439
Applications: Deadlines January 31st for reporting
internship program, November 15th for editing
internship programs, and March 1st for fellowship
program; Initial approach by letter; Completion of
formal application required.
Publications: Annual report, application guidelines.
Program description:
The fund operates one reporting internship program
and two editing internship programs which offer
students the opportunity to earn scholarships after
successfully completing a summer of paid employment
as a reporter or copy editor on a daily newspaper.

The **Minority Reporting Internship Program for
College Sophomores** provides grants to identify and
attract talented minorities to newspaper careers.
Interns receive two weeks of training before being
placed at daily newspapers as reporters. Interns
receive regular wages and a $1,000 undergraduate
scholarship at the end of the summer.

The **Minority Editing Intern Program for College
Seniors** provides grants to aid and attract talented
minority students interested in newspaper work to
journalism careers by participating in the program.
Interns will receive two weeks of intensive training

before being assigned to copy desks at daily
newspapers for 12 weeks during the summer. At the
conclusion of their internships a scholarship grant of
$1,500 will be awarded to each intern who will attend
graduate school or $1,000 to pay outstanding
undergraduate student loans.

The **Newspaper Editing Intern Program for College
Juniors** provides grants to aid in attracting talented
young journalists to editing and newspaper
management. Interns receive two weeks of intensive
training before being placed on copy desks of daily
newspapers. Interns receive a $1,000 scholarship to
complete undergraduate studies.

The **High School Teacher Fellowship Program**
awards up to $350 each to inexperienced high school
journalism teachers and high school publications
advisors to cover the cost of a workshop at a
journalism school or institute offering special summer
workshops/programs in order to enhance their ability
to teach students to write and edit more effectively.

200
**Doyle (Dr. Edgar Clay) and Mary Cherry Doyle
Memorial Fund**
c/o South Carolina National Bank, Trust Department
101 Greystone Boulevard, Unit 9344
Columbia, SC 29226
Contact: South Carolina Foundation of Independent
Colleges, Scholarship Committee, P.O. Box 6998,
Greenville, SC 29606; Tel.: (803) 23-6894

Limitations: Scholarships only to residents and
graduates of high schools in Oconee County, SC, for
undergraduate work at a South Carolina college.
Financial data: Year ended 1/31/87. Assets, $917,610
(M); Total giving, $67,240; Grants to individuals
totaling $64,240.
Employer Identification Number: 576019447
Applications: Deadline March 1st; Completion of
formal application required.
Program description:
One-year partial scholarships are renewable if grade
requirements are met. About 30 new awards are
available annually.

201
Dozzi (Eugene) Charitable Foundation
2000 Lincoln Road
Pittsburgh, PA 15235

Limitations: Scholarships to Pennsylvania residents,
primarily those living in Pittsburgh.
Financial data: Year ended 4/30/87. Assets, $171,980
(M); Total giving, $15,293; Grants to individuals, 5
grants totaling $13,643, high $5,897, low $1,198.
Employer Identification Number: 237023479
Applications: Completion of formal application
required.

202★
Dunbar (The Saidie Orr) Nursing Education Fund

c/o American Lung Association of Oregon
1776 S.W. Madison
Portland, OR 97205   (503) 224-5145
Contact: Evelyn Schindler, Chairman

Limitations: Scholarships to individuals accepted in a master's or doctoral nursing degree program in Oregon which emphasizes the education of community health nurses. Applicants must practice in Oregon upon graduation.
Financial data: Year ended 12/31/86. Assets, $73,156 (M); Total giving, $7,415; Grants to individuals, 3 grants totaling $7,000, high $3,000, low $2,000.
Employer Identification Number: 936017534
Applications: Applications accepted between December 1st and March 30th; Initial approach by telephone or letter; Completion of formal application required; Interviews required of finalists.

203
Dutchess County, The Area Fund of

Nine Vassar Street
Poughkeepsie, NY 12601   (914) 452-3077

Limitations: Grants to teachers in Dutchess County, NY, for special projects and professional development.
Financial data: Year ended 12/31/86. Assets, $749,691 (M); Total giving, $57,777; Grants to individuals, 20 grants totaling $14,988, high $1,800, low $95.
Employer Identification Number: 237026859
Applications: Applications accepted throughout the year; Initial approach by letter or telephone.
Publications: Annual report.
Program description:
The **Area Fund Partnership in Education Grants** program supports efforts contributing to enhancing the quality of education in Dutchess County, NY. The program is open to classroom teachers of prekindergarten through twelfth grade in public, private and parochial schools. Grants are given directly to teachers to be used for professional development and/or special projects with their classes.

204
Duxbury Yacht Club Charitable Foundation

c/o State Street Bank & Trust Company
P.O. Box 351
Boston, MA 02101

Limitations: Scholarships only to Duxbury, MA, high school graduates.
Financial data: Year ended 12/31/84. Assets, $38,974 (M); Total giving, $4,500; Grants to individuals, 9 grants totaling $4,500, each grant $500.
Employer Identification Number: 046115247

205★
Dyett (Herbert T.) Foundation, Inc.

218 North Washington Street
Rome, NY 13440
Contact: Principals, Rome Free Academy and Rome Catholic High Schools

Limitations: Scholarships for the first two years of college only to members of the graduating classes of Rome Free Academy and Rome Catholic High School in Rome, NY, who have attended the schools for two years prior to graduation and who rank in the top one-third of their class.
Financial data: Year ended 12/31/84. Assets, $690,300 (M); Total giving, $43,150; Grants to individuals amount not specified.
Employer Identification Number: 166041857
Applications: Deadline May 11th; Completion of formal application required; Interviews required.
Program description:
The scholarship recipients are selected on the basis of financial need, personality, character, leadership, citizenship, and health.

206
Eagles Memorial Foundation, Inc.

4710 14th Street West
Bradenton, FL 33507

Limitations: Scholarships to the children of deceased Eagle servicemen and women, law officers, or firefighters, and to graduates of Home on the Range for Boys in Sentinel Butte, ND, High Sky Girls Ranch in Midland, TX, and Bob Hope High School in Port Arthur, TX.
Financial data: Year ended 5/31/87. Assets, $8,962,061 (M); Total giving, $949,318; Grants to individuals totaling $61,518; Subtotal for scholarships, 76 grants totaling $47,330, high $1,500, low $1.
Employer Identification Number: 396126176
Program description:
To be eligible for scholarship assistance, individuals must be graduates of the aforementioned institutions, or the children of members of the Fraternal Order of Eagles and the Ladies Auxiliary to it who die from injuries or diseases incurred or aggravated while serving:
- In the armed forces
- As a law enforcement officer
- As a full-time or volunteer firefighter.

Educational assistance is available to eligible individuals to the age of 25, unless married or self-supporting before the age of 25. The re-marriage of either parent does not change an individual's eligibility.

Educational grants shall not exceed $3,000 per school year, or a total of $15,000 for all years per recipient. Grants may be used to help defray the cost of college education or vocational school training after high school.

The term "vocational school" includes any continuous trade training schools, such as business, beauty, nursing, or other technical schools.

207
Eagleton War Memorial Scholarship Fund, Inc.
c/o Bridgehampton National Bank
Bridgehampton, NY 11932
Contact: William Skretch, President

Limitations: Scholarships to graduates of Bridgehampton High School, Bridgehampton, NY.
Financial data: Year ended 12/31/85. Assets, $133,372 (M); Total giving, $8,750; Grants to individuals, 8 grants totaling $8,750, high $1,750, low $500, general range $500-1,500.
Employer Identification Number: 237149864

208
Earhart Foundation
Plymouth Building, Suite 204
2929 Plymouth Road
Ann Arbor, MI 48105   (313) 761-8592
Contact: David B. Kennedy, President

Limitations: Fellowship research grants are also awarded to individuals who have distinguished themselves professionally.
Financial data: Year ended 12/31/86. Assets, $39,352,411 (M); Total giving, $1,573,714; Grants to individuals, 212 grants totaling $895,498, high $50,000, low $500; Subtotal for fellowship research grants not specified.
Employer Identification Number: 386008273
Applications: Deadline three to four months before requested effective date for fellowship research grants; Initial approach by letter; Interviews granted upon request.
Publications: Annual report, program information.
Program description:
Applicants for fellowship research grants should be associated with educational and research institutions, and the effort supported should lead to the advancement of knowledge through teaching, lecturing, and publication. The applications evaluated must include (1) a personal history statement, (2) a full description of the proposed research, (3) the intended end use or publication, (4) an abstract of approximately 250 words, (5) a budget and time schedule, (6) a list of references, and (7) a statement about applications pending elsewhere. Each award is for a specific purpose and progress is monitored.

209★
Ebell of Los Angeles Scholarship Endowment Fund; and the Ebell of Los Angeles Mr. & Mrs. Charles N. Flint Scholarship Endowment Fund
743 South Lucerne Boulevard
Los Angeles, CA 90005
Contact: Ebell Scholarship Chairman

Limitations: Undergraduate scholarships to unmarried, no older than 27 years of age, full-time undergraduate students who are U.S. citizens and residents of Los Angeles County, CA, attending colleges and universities in Los Angeles County. Students must be of at least sophomore standing, in financial need, and with a GPA of at least 3.25.
Financial data: Year ended 6/30/86. Assets, $2,425,783 (Combined); Total giving, $105,301 (Combined); Grants to individuals totaling 105,301.
Employer Identification Number: 237049580
Applications: Deadline July 1st for fall semester; Applications accepted throughout the year; Completion of formal application and interviews required; Contact financial aid office of the institution student is attending for further details and scholarship application.
Publications: Application guidelines.
Program description:
The financial data represents the combined assets of the Ebell of Los Angeles Scholarship Endowment Fund (assets $1,523,548) and the Ebell of Los Angeles Mr. & and Mrs. Charles N. Flint Scholarship Endowment Fund (assets $902,235).

Grades, moral character, financial need and leadership are carefully weighed in considering scholarships. A grade point average of 3.25 is essential.

Approximately 20 new scholarships are awarded each year, for a total of about 60 recipients. Students are automatically carried for three years, or until graduation, whichever comes first, providing original qualifications remain the same. The scholarship award is $200 per month for ten months.

210
Eddy (C.K.) Family Memorial Fund
c/o Second National Bank of Saginaw
101 North Washington Avenue
Saginaw, MI 48607
Contact: Marsha Sieggreen

Limitations: Student loans to individuals who have been residents of Saginaw County, MI, for at least one year prior to application deadline.
Financial data: Year ended 6/30/87. Assets, $8,740,075 (M); Expenditures, $574,526; Loans to individuals totaling $196,372.
Employer Identification Number: 386040506
Applications: Deadline May 1st; Completion of formal application required.

Program description:
The need for economic assistance in the form of a student loan must be proven. If the applicant has not attained his/her 23rd birthday as of the application deadline, the financial need will be based upon the financial status of the parents. If the applicant reaches his/her 23rd birthday prior to the deadline, financial need will be based upon the applicant's financial status.

A loan recipient may attend any institution he/she wishes, however, there are limited funds available for non-Michigan schools. Grade point average requirement for the loan is at least 2.0 cumulative during high school and college.

The maximum amount of the loan will depend upon the school the recipient plans to attend. The recipient will be advised of the amount of the loan at the time he/she receives notice of loan approval. The interest rate of the loan will be five percent while attending school as a full-time student. Interest will begin to accrue upon receipt of the loan. It will be to the recipient's advantage to request the actual payment no sooner than the funds are needed. As long as the recipient is a full-time student annual payment of only the interest is required.

The recipient must notify the fund once his/her schooling is completed. Monthly payments of the principal and interest will begin no later than nine months after completion of education. The terms of the loan will be up to ten years with payments of no less than $30 and no more than $125 per month, at seven percent per annum. Deferment on loan payment may be requested if the student pursues graduate studies.

211★
Eddy (Edwin H.) Family Foundation
(Formerly Eddy Foundation)
c/o Norwest Bank Duluth
Capital Management and Trust Department
Duluth, MN 55802   (218) 723-2773
Contact: Murray George, Trustee

Limitations: Scholarships to Duluth, MN, area residents who are college seniors or graduate students in communication disorders, attending the University of Minnesota-Duluth or other accredited institutions, and to non-residents attending the University of Minnesota-Duluth.
Financial data: Year ended 6/30/88. Assets, $2,298,000 (M); Total giving, $119,962; Grants to individuals, 15 grants totaling $28,000, high $1,500, low $333, average grant $1,200.
Employer Identification Number: 416242226
Applications: Deadline March 31st; Initial approach by letter; Completion of formal application, including certified copy of most recent transcript(s) from present or previous institution(s) attended, required; Interviews required.

Program description:
Applicants must have a minimum grade point average of 3.0 to qualify. Priorities for granting scholarships shall be made in the following order:
1. Duluth area residents attending the University of Minnesota, Duluth
2. Duluth area residents attending other accredited institutions
3. Non-Duluth area residents attending the University of Minnesota, Duluth.

Interviews must be arranged by the applicant at the Office of Communicative Disorders Department at the University of Minnesota, Duluth.

Graduate level students will receive awards of $3,000, on the basis of $500 per quarter, not to exceed six quarters, even though enrolled in a college with a two-year graduate level program. Senior level students will receive awards of $1,000 for the regular school year. Scholarship payments are made in quarterly installments directly to the applicant upon evidence of enrollment each quarter. To receive continued payments, the applicant must provide the foundation with a G.P.A. report at the end of each quarter.

212
Eddy (Royal A. and Mildred D.) Student Loan Trust Fund
P.O. Box 209, Trust Department
Gary, IN 46401
Contact: Joseph N. Thomas, Attorney at Law, 2999 McCool Road, Portage, IN 46368

Limitations: Loans to students throughout the U.S. who have completed at least two years of college and are within two years of graduation.
Financial data: Year ended 2/28/87. Assets, $108,919 (M); Expenditures, $12,206; Loans to individuals, 1 loan totaling $2,000.
Employer Identification Number: 356020912
Applications: Applications accepted throughout the year; Completion of formal application required.
Publications: Program information.
Program description:
Loans are limited to $2,000 per year with a maximum total of $4,000. Interest of ten percent is charged from the date the loan commences. Two co-signers are required for the loan.

213★
Edmonds (James H. & Minnie M.) Educational Foundation
c/o First Republic Bank Houston, Trust Department
P.O. Box 18
Houston, TX 77252-2518   (713) 652-6533
Contact: Elizabeth A. Calvert, Assistant Vice-President and Trust Officer

Limitations: Scholarships primarily for needy college

or university students residing in Texas with preference given to those residing in Houston. Applicants must be U.S. citizens.
Financial data: Year ended 6/30/87. Assets, $12,730,770 (M); Total giving, $772,820; Grants to individuals, 477 grants totaling $772,820, high $2,000, low $1,000.
Employer Identification Number: 742167363
Applications: Deadline March 1st; Completion of formal application required.
Program description:
Scholarship payments are made directly to the educational institution on behalf of the individual recipients.

214★
Educational Communications Scholarship Foundation
721 North McKinley Road
Lake Forest, IL 60045   (312) 295-6650
Contact: Ms. J. E. McGuinn

Limitations: Scholarships to high school students throughout the U.S.
Financial data: Year ended 3/31/87. Assets, $73,588 (M); Total giving, $91,901; Grants to individuals, 65 grants totaling $65,000, each grant $1,000.
Employer Identification Number: 237032032
Applications: Deadline June 1st; Initial approach by written request from student; Completion of formal application required; Applications may be obtained from high school guidance offices or the foundation.
Program description:
The objective of the award is to recognize mature students who have demonstrated ability and effort. Ability and performance are the major criteria for selection with some consideration also given to financial need.

Semi-finalists will be selected on the basis of aptitude test scores, leadership qualifications, student interests, and work experience. Finalists will be asked to provide financial information and to respond to essay questions. Winners are notified by August 1st each year.

The scholarships of $1,000 each are paid directly through the educational institutions on behalf of individual recipients.

215★
Educational Foundation of the National Restaurant Association
20 North Wacker Drive
Chicago, IL 60606   (312) 782-1703

Limitations: Scholarships and fellowships to individuals studying in the food service area, as well as work-study grants to teachers and administrators.
Financial data: Year ended 12/31/86. Assets, $2,836,601 (M); Total giving, $222,400; Grants to

individuals, 191 grants totaling $222,400.
Employer Identification Number: 366103388
Applications: Deadline April 1st for scholarships and fellowships, December 31st for work-study grants; Completion of formal application required.
Publications: Application guidelines, program information.
Program description:
In 1988, the National Institute for the Food Service Industry merged with the association.

216
Edwards Scholarship Fund
One Federal Street
Boston, MA 02110   (617) 426-4434

Limitations: Scholarship loans to young men and women, under the age of 25, whose families live in the city of Boston.
Financial data: Year ended 7/31/86. Assets, $4,489,144 (M); Expenditures, $255,012; Loans to individuals, 160 loans totaling $193,600, high $2,000, low $300, general range $500-800.
Employer Identification Number: 046002496
Applications: Deadline March 1st; Completion of formal application required.
Program description:
Scholarship loans to students, with preference to undergraduates enrolled in a program leading to a bachelor's or advanced degree at an accredited college or university, for not more than six years. No grants to individuals attending junior colleges, community colleges, or hospital schools of nursing. Students to repay grant when financially able.

217
El Paso Community Foundation
Texas Commerce Bank Building, Suite 1616
El Paso, TX 79901   (915) 533-4020
Contact: Janice W. Windle, Executive Director

Limitations: Scholarships only to students in the El Paso, TX, area to attend the University of Texas at El Paso.
Financial data: Year ended 12/31/86. Assets, $5,067,219 (M); Total giving, $850,265; Grants to individuals amount not specified.
Employer Identification Number: 741839536
Publications: Annual report.

218
Eldred (Ruby Marsh) Scholarship Trust
c/o Marine Bank Trust Division
P.O. Box 8480
Erie, PA 16553
Contact: Honorable Robert Walker, Crawford County Courthouse, Meadville, PA 16335

Limitations: Scholarships to students from the

Meadville, PA, area and western Crawford County, PA.
Financial data: Year ended 12/31/86. Assets, $205,782 (M); Total giving, $10,100; Grants to individuals, 53 grants totaling $10,100, high $600, low $50.
Employer Identification Number: 256114997
Applications: Deadline March 1st.
Program description:
Scholarships are awarded to students who have completed secondary school studies and plan to continue study in an accredited four-year college or university or in an associate degree program in an accredited two-year junior or community college.

219
Elenberg (Charles and Anna) Foundation, Inc.
c/o Jack Scharf
P.O. Box 630193, Spuyten Duyvil Station
Bronx, NY 10463
Contact: Rabbi David B. Hollander, 3133 Brighton Seventh Street, Brooklyn, NY 11235; Tel.: (718) 769-8728

Limitations: Scholarships to needy students of Hebrew faith who are attending high school or college, with preference given to orphans. No grants to married students.
Financial data: Year ended 6/30/86. Assets, $826,552 (M); Total giving, $51,450; Grants to individuals, 341 grants totaling $51,450, high 500, low $100, general range $150-300.
Employer Identification Number: 116042334
Applications: Deadline November 15th; Completion of formal application required.

220
Elizabeth City Foundation
P.O. Box 574
Elizabeth City, NC 27909
Contact: Ray S. Jones, Jr., Executive Director

Limitations: Scholarships only to students in Camden County, NC.
Financial data: Year ended 7/31/85. Assets, $1,586,128 (M); Total giving, $126,300; Grants to individuals totaling $27,500.
Employer Identification Number: 237076018
Applications: Deadline April 1st; Application forms available at Wachovia Bank and Trust Company and Camden High School; Completion of formal application required.

221★
Ellis (Charles E.) Grant and Scholarship Fund
c/o Provident National Bank
1632 Chestnut Street
Philadelphia, PA 19103
Contact: Trust Administration Department

Limitations: Scholarships to functionally orphaned female students who reside in Philadelphia County, PA, for high school level education. Scholarships not available for college level education.
Financial data: Year ended 2/29/88. Assets, $20,000,000 (M); Total giving, $1,200,000; Grants to individuals, 1,200 grants totaling $1,200,000, high $2,600, low $500, average grant $1,000.
Employer Identification Number: 236725618
Applications: Applications accepted throughout the year; Applications should be mailed to EASI, 1101 Market Street, Philadelphia, PA 19107; Tel.: (215) 928-0900.
Publications: Application guidelines, informational brochure, program information.
Program description:
The scholarship grants are awarded to individual named recipients; however, all funds are paid directly to the educational institution the individual attends.

The fund's use of the term "functionally orphaned" includes girls from single-parent families.

222
Emery Air Freight Educational Foundation, Inc.
Old Danbury Road
Wilton, CT 06897   (203) 762-8601
Contact: John C. Emery, Jr., President, c/o Coleman Association, P.O. Box 1283, New Canaan, CT 06840

Limitations: Scholarships only to children of employees of Emery Air Freight Corporation.
Financial data: Year ended 12/31/85. Assets, $2,035,641 (M); Total giving, $109,850; Grants to individuals, 42 grants totaling $109,850, high $5,000, low $500.
Employer Identification Number: 066071565
Applications: Submit application by January testing date for Scholastic Aptitude Test; Parents must apply to their Regional Manager or Department Head; Completion of formal application required.
Publications: Informational brochure, application guidelines.
Program description:
Children of employees who have had three or more full years of full-time service with the company are eligible to apply for scholarship aid. Applications may be made for both undergraduate and graduate study. Company scholarships may not be combined with another outside source of financial assistance.

223
English Foundation - Trust, The
1522 Main Street
Altavista, VA 24517   (804) 369-4771
Contact: E. R. English, Trustee

Limitations: Scholarships for residents in the Campbell County, VA, area.
Financial data: Year ended 12/31/85. Assets, $1,310,915 (M); Total giving, $71,208; Grants to individuals totaling $8,375.
Employer Identification Number: 546036409
Applications: Initial approach by letter requesting application form from manager; Completion of formal application required.

224★
Eppley Foundation for Research, Inc.
c/o Turk, Marsh, Kelly & Hoare
575 Lexington Avenue
New York, NY 10022   (212) 371-1660
Contact: Huyler C. Held, Secretary

Limitations: Grants primarily for postdoctoral research in advanced scientific subjects through recognized educational and charitable organizations.
Financial data: Year ended 12/31/86. Assets, $740,000 (M); Total giving, $97,648; Grants to individuals, 7 grants totaling 97,648, high $25,300, low $1,150.
Employer Identification Number: 050258857
Applications: Applications accepted throughout the year; Initial approach by letter, including short statement of qualifications, proposed research and an estimate of funding required; Completion of formal application not required.

225
Erie Community Foundation, The
419 G. Daniel Baldwin Building
P.O. Box 1818
Erie, PA 16507   (814) 454-0843
Contact: Edward C. Doll, Chairman

Limitations: Scholarships for higher education limited to students attending the four public high schools of Erie County, PA.
Financial data: Year ended 12/31/86. Assets, $8,406,932 (M); Total giving, $1,005,153; Grants to individuals, 5 grants totaling $4,500.
Employer Identification Number: 256032032
Applications: Completion of formal application required.
Publications: Annual report.

226★
Ernst & Whinney Foundation, The
2000 National City Center
Cleveland, OH 44114   (216) 861-5000
Contact: J. S. DiStasio, Chairman

Limitations: Grants to doctoral candidates in accounting for work on dissertations; for students in the U.S. and Canada only.
Financial data: Year ended 12/31/86. Assets, $8,426,109 (M); Total giving, $1,272,150; Grants to individuals, 10 grants totaling $99,675.
Employer Identification Number: 346524211
Applications: Deadline June 1st; Completion of formal application required.
Publications: Program information.
Program description:
Grants are awarded to doctoral candidates to enable them to complete their dissertation work in the field of accounting.
A maximum of $18,000 per grant may be awarded for a maximum period of one year.

227
Ewald (H.T.) Foundation
15175 East Jefferson Avenue
Grosse Pointe, MI 48230   (313) 821-2000
Contact: Henry T. Ewald, President

Limitations: Undergraduate scholarships to high school seniors who are residents of the metropolitan Detroit area.
Financial data: Year ended 12/31/86. Assets, $1,680,820 (M); Total giving, $80,481; Grants to individuals, 58 grants totaling $70,481, high $1,900, low $200, average grant $1,400.
Employer Identification Number: 386007837
Applications: Deadline May 1st; Completion of formal application required; Interview required.
Publications: Program information.
Program description:
Financial need is one of the most important considerations. Scholastic record, extracurricular activities, honors or awards, and character are also used as criteria for selection.
The amount of the scholarship varies with the need of the applicant. The awards are renewable for up to four years during pursuit of the B.A. degree, contingent upon maintenance of a satisfactory grade point average. Approximately 10-15 new awards are available each year.

228★
Fahrney Education Foundation
c/o Union Bank-Trust Department
123 East Third Street
Ottumwa, IA 52501   (515) 683-1641
Contact: Scholarship Committee

Limitations: Scholarships only to residents of Wapello County, IA.
Financial data: Year ended 2/29/87. Assets, $2,432,413 (M); Total giving, $104,000; Grants to individuals totaling $104,000.
Employer Identification Number: 426295370
Applications: Deadline February 15th; Completion of formal application required.
Publications: Application guidelines.
Program description:
Scholarships will be awarded in the amount of $1,500 each. Scholarships will be transferred directly to student's account in the business office of the college or university for use for any school-related expenses. Should the student fail or drop out or drop below full-time status, the scholarship will immediately terminate and funds will be returned to the foundation.

Applicants must reapply annually. Scholarships will be granted on a yearly basis. No applicant will be eligible to receive more than four scholarship awards. Applicants must be enrolled in a full-time course of study in one of the following:
    1. A four-year accredited Iowa college or university program leading toward a bachelor degree
    2. A two-year Iowa college associate arts or science program leading to a four-year course of study and bachelor degree
    3. A postgraduate program at an accredited college or university.

229
Fairey (Kittie M.) Educational Fund
c/o The South Carolina National Bank
101 Greystone Boulevard, No. 9344
Columbia, SC 29226

Limitations: Scholarships to residents of South Carolina attending a college or university within the state.
Financial data: Year ended 9/30/86. Assets, $1,809,268 (M); Total giving, $140,501; Grants to individuals totaling $140,501.
Employer Identification Number: 576037140
Applications: Deadline March 31st; Initial approach by letter.

230
Fairfield (Freeman E.) - Meeker Charitable Trust
First Interstate Bank of Denver
Terminal Annex, P.O. Box 5825
Denver, CO 80217   (303) 893-2211
Contact: Randall C. Rieck, Senior Trust Officer

Limitations: Scholarships only to graduates of Meeker High School, Meeker, CO.
Financial data: Year ended 11/30/86. Assets, $2,416,143 (M); Total giving, $135,148; Grants to individuals, 47 grants totaling $21,747.
Employer Identification Number: 846068906
Applications: Applications accepted throughout the year; Initial approach by letter; Interviews granted upon request.
Program description:
The trust is for the benefit of people residing in the town of Meeker and its immediate environs, Rio Blanco County, CO.

231★
Fargo-Moorhead Area Foundation
315 North Eighth Street
P.O. Box 1609
Fargo, ND 58107   (701) 234-0756
Contact: Susan M. Hunke, Executive Director

Limitations: Scholarships primarily to students in the Fargo-Moorhead area.
Financial data: Year ended 12/31/86. Assets, $2,976,718 (M); Total giving, $422,463; Grants to individuals, 29 grants totaling $90,159, high $9,385, low $80, general range $100-1,000, average grant $250.
Employer Identification Number: 456010377
Applications: Deadline April 15th; Submit application between December 31st and April 15th; Initial approach by letter or telephone; Completion of formal application required.
Publications: Annual report, application guidelines, informational brochure, 990-PF printed copy available upon request.
Program description:
The foundation's scholarship funds include:
    1. Amy Andrews Scholarship Fund - Provides scholarships to students attending Moorhead State University.
    2. George Comstock Fund - Provides scholarships to students attending Moorhead State University.
    3. Comstock Memorial Fund - Provides scholarships to students attending Moorhead State University.
    4. Arthur and Clara Cupler Fund - Provides scholarships to area students attending North Dakota State University, Moorhead State University, Concordia College, North Dakota State College of Science, Hamline University and Jamestown College.
    5. Willard Grager Scholarship Fund - Provides scholarships to students attending North Dakota State College of Science in Wahpeton.
    6. Spencer and Fern Jones Charitable Trust - Provides college scholarship to a graduating senior interested in athletics from Moorhead High School, who will be attending Moorhead State University, Concordia College or North Dakota State University.
    7. Joseph Kise Scholarship Fund - Provides scholarships to students attending Moorhead State University.

8. M.S.U. Alumni Fund - Provides scholarships to students attending Moorhead State University.
9. Retail Credit Association Scholarship Fund - Provides scholarships to area students attending North Dakota State University, Moorhead State University and Concordia College.
10. Stern Charitable Fund - Provides scholarships to area students attending Jamestown College and Valley City State College.
11. C. Edmund Strinden Scholarship Fund - Supports scholarships for Pelican Rapids High School graduates attending post-high school education institutions.
12. Tex Scholarship Fund - Provides college scholarships to seniors graduating from Moorhead High School.
13. Tharalson Scholarship Fund - Provides scholarships to athletes attending North Dakota State University.

Scholarship payments are made directly to the educational institutions on behalf of individual recipients.

232
Faught Memorial Scholarship Trust
Bellows Falls Trust Company
P.O. Box 399
Bellows Falls, VT 05101   (802) 463-4524
Contact: Joyce H. Miller, Trust Officer

Limitations: Scholarships only to graduates of Bellows Falls Union High School, District 27, VT.
Financial data: Year ended 9/30/86. Assets, $92,371 (M); Total giving, $3,000; Grants to individuals, 5 grants totaling $3,000, high $1,000, low $500, average grant $500.
Employer Identification Number: 036036458
Applications: Deadline June 1st; Initial approach by letter stating educational goals and financial situation, including a transcript of school record; Completion of formal application required.
Program description:
Scholarships are granted to worthy students who have a good scholastic record, who qualify for an advanced education at an accredited college or university and are in need of financial assistance.

Awards are limited to students who have a good scholastic record in Bellows Falls Union High School or in an institution of higher learning during the academic year preceeding the year for which the award is made.

233
Fed-Mart Foundation
P.O. Box 81667
San Diego, CA 92138   (714) 282-0690
Contact: Joseph N. Forror, Secretary-Treasurer

Limitations: Scholarships only to graduating seniors of high schools in San Diego County, CA.
Financial data: Year ended 11/30/86. Assets, $738,874 (M); Total giving, $43,500; Grants to individuals, 145 grants totaling $43,500, each grant $300.
Employer Identification Number: 956034800
Applications: Deadline March 15th; Completion of formal application required; Application will not be considered if not accompanied by high school transcript, including the first semester of senior year; Applications available in January from San Diego County high schools.
Program description:
Academic achievement is the primary criterion for selection, and individuals should have a minimum grade point average of 3.5 to apply.

234
Feild Co-Operative Association, Inc.
P.O. Box 5054
Jackson, MS 39216   (601) 939-9295
Contact: Ann Stephenson

Limitations: Educational loans only to Mississippi residents.
Financial data: Year ended 12/31/86. Assets, $6,638,027 (M); Expenditures, $753,256; Loans to individuals totaling $262,766.
Employer Identification Number: 640155700
Applications: Deadline six to eight weeks before semester begins; Initial approach by letter; Completion of formal application required; Interviews required.
Publications: Informational brochure, application guidelines.
Program description:
Interest-bearing student loans to Mississippi residents who are juniors or seniors in college, graduate and professional students, or students in special fields (unspecified).

235
Fellows (J. Hugh and Earl W.) Memorial Fund
c/o Beggs and Lane
P.O. Box 12950
Pensacola, FL 32576-2950   (904) 432-2451
Contact: The President, Pensacola Junior College, 1000 College Boulevard, Pensacola, FL 32504; Tel.: (904) 476-5410

Limitations: Low-interest loans to students of nursing, medicine, medical technology, and theology who reside in Escambia, Santa Rosa, Okaloosa, or Walton counties, FL, and who agree to pursue their professions in this area for five years after graduation.

Financial data: Year ended 4/30/87. Assets, $2,460,101 (M); Expenditures, $19,933; Loans to individuals totaling $176,825.
Employer Identification Number: 596132238
Applications: Applications accepted throughout the year; Initial approach by letter; Interviews occasionally required and also granted upon request.
Publications: Program information.
Program description:
Applicants must be of good moral character, qualified scholastically and intellectually for the education desired, an accepted by, or successfully pursuing training in an accredited school in the appropriate field. Loans to ministerial students are limited to those whose religious beliefs are not in substantial conflict with Episcopal doctrines. Ordinarily interest is not charged until one year after graduation. Approximately ten new applicants are awarded loans each year.

236
Ferebee (Percy B.) Endowment
c/o Wachovia Bank and Trust Company
P.O. Box 3099
Winston-Salem, NC 27150   (919) 748-5269
Contact: E. Ray Cope, Vice-President, Wachovia Bank and Trust Company

Limitations: Scholarships to residents of the North Carolina counties of Cherokee, Clay, Graham, Jackson, Macon, and Swain, and the Cherokee Indian Reservation, for study only at North Carolina colleges and universities.
Financial data: Year ended 12/31/86. Assets, $1,888,856 (M); Total giving, $98,148; Grants to individuals, 105 grants totaling $51,686, high $1,000, low $500.
Employer Identification Number: 566118992
Applications: Deadline February 15th; Application forms available from high school guidance counselors, the Cherokee Indian Reservation, and school superintendents; Completion of formal application required; Submit completed forms to scholarship committee of the high schools; Interviews required.
Publications: Program information.
Program description:
Scholarships are granted annually to worthy young men and women and will not exceed the cost of tuition, books, fees, and reasonable living and travel expenses.
   Applications of the candidates recommended by the high schools are forwarded to the superintendents of each school system, who will recommend candidates to the trustee.
   The committee takes into consideration the respective abilities, educational goals, career ambitions, and financial needs of the applicants. The amount of each scholarship and the manner in which it will be paid is determined by the awards committee. A scholarship may be renewed annually if the student is making satisfactory academic progress.

237★
Ferree Educational & Welfare Fund
101 Sunset Avenue
P.O. Box 2207
Asheboro, NC 27204-2207   (919) 629-2960
Contact: Claire C. Sprouse, Administrative Director

Limitations: Student loans and scholarships for higher education limited to residents of Randolph County, NC.
Financial data: Year ended 12/31/87. Assets, $1,343,194 (M); Expenditures, $19,824; Grants to individuals, 25 grants totaling $26,500, high $1,500, low $1,000; Loans to individuals, 68 loans totaling $56,900, high $1,000, low $400, average loan $1,000.
Employer Identification Number: 566062560
Applications: Deadline June 15th; Initial approach by May 1st; Completion of formal application, including financial statements, required; Interviews required.
Publications: Application guidelines, financial statement, informational brochure, program information.
Program description:
Consideration for student loans is based on requirements similar to those of the federal government loans. Loans are granted only to students attending institutions of higher learning and are limited to $1,000 per student per academic year.

238★
Fields (Laura) Trust
P.O. Box 2394
Lawton, OK 73502   (405) 355-3733
Contact: Jay Dee Fountain, Executive Secretary

Limitations: Student loans only to residents of Comanche County, OK.
Financial data: Year ended 6/30/87. Assets, $1,608,587 (M); Expenditures, $132,066; Loans to individuals, 40 loans totaling $76,290.
Employer Identification Number: 736095854
Applications: Applications accepted throughout the year; Initial approach by letter requesting application; Completion of formal application required.

239★
First Mississippi Corporation Foundation, Inc.
700 North Street
P.O. Box 1249
Jackson, MS 39215-1249   (601) 948-7550
Contact: Bonnie H. Kelley, Administrative Assistant

Limitations: Scholarships only to valedictorians of local high schools.
Financial data: Year ended 6/30/87. Assets, $725,609 (M); Grants to individuals, 24 grants totaling $12,000, each grant $500.
Employer Identification Number: 510152783
Applications: Initial approach by letter.

Program description:
Scholarship payments are made directly to the college the graduating valedictorian will be attending.

240
Fitzgerald (Father James M.) Scholarship Trust
c/o Commercial National Bank of Peoria
301 Southwest Adams Street
Peoria, IL 61631   (309) 655-5322

Limitations: Scholarships to priesthood students attending a Catholic university or college, and to the highest ranking boy and girl at St. Mark's Catholic School, Peoria, IL, enrolling in any Roman Catholic high school.
Financial data: Year ended 12/31/83. Assets, $1,400,000 (M); Total giving, $80,000; Grants to individuals totaling $80,000.
Employer Identification Number: 376050189
Applications: Applications accepted throughout the year; Initial approach by letter.

241
Flatirons Foundation, The
P.O. Box 2088
Aspen, CO 81611   (303) 925-2094
Contact: Sue W. Hall

Limitations: Undergraduate scholarships to students who have attended Aspen High School, Aspen, CO, for higher education.
Financial data: Year ended 12/31/86. Assets, $189,697 (M); Total giving, $7,000; Grants to individuals, 5 grants totaling $4,000, high $1,000, low $500.
Employer Identification Number: 840563062
Applications: Deadline April 15th; Completion of formal application required.

242
Flickinger Memorial Trust, Inc., The
115 West North Street
P.O. Box 1255
Lima, OH 45802   (419) 227-6506
Contact: F. Miles Flickinger, M.D., Chairman

Limitations: Student loans primarily for residents of Ohio.
Financial data: Year ended 12/31/86. Assets, $1,844,239 (M); Expenditures, $201,318; Loans to individuals, 50 loans totaling $98,776, high $2,000, low $100, general range $400-1,000.
Employer Identification Number: 346527156
Applications: Applications accepted throughout the year; Initial approach by letter; Interviews required.
Program description:
Applications for student loans should be submitted in letter form and include: high school transcript, three letters of recommendation (including one from a school representative), an itemized budget showing

income and expenses for the first school year, and a recent photograph of the applicant. The applicant's future plans should be outlined. The application is followed up with an oral conference.

243★
Folsom (Maud Glover) Foundation, Inc.
P.O. Box 151
Harwinton, CT 06791   (203) 485-0405
Contact: Leon A. Francisco, President

Limitations: Scholarships to men of American ancestry and of Anglo-Saxon or German descent to the age of thirty-five. Initial grants limited to males between the ages of fourteen and twenty.
Financial data: Year ended 7/31/87. Assets, $2,465,345 (M); Total giving $150,000; Grants to individuals, 60 grants totaling $150,000, each grant $2,500.
Employer Identification Number: 111965890
Applications: Applications accepted throughout the year; Contact foundation for current application deadline; Initial approach by letter; Completion of formal application required; Interviews required in Connecticut at applicant's expense.
Publications: Informational brochure (including application guidelines).
Program description:
Grants of $2,500 annually are made for preparatory school, high school, college, professional and graduate school, or any advanced school the individual selects to advance his education. First-time applicants must be between the ages of 14 and 20, but support may be continued to the age of 35.

244
Ford Foundation, The
320 East 43rd Street
New York, NY 10017   (212) 573-5000
Contact: Barron M. Tenny, Secretary

Limitations: Fellowships for professorships and internships, advanced research, training, and other activities related to urban poverty, human rights, rural poverty, education and culture, public policy, and international affairs.
Financial data: Year ended 9/30/86. Assets, $4,758,862,000 (M); Total giving, $169,718,877; Grants to individuals, 457 grants totaling $4,189,104, high $85,000, low $118, general range $6,600-$12,000.
Employer Identification Number: 131684331
Publications: Annual report, program information, newsletter.
Program description:
Grants to individuals are few in number relative to demand, and are limited to research, training, and other activities related to the foundation's program interests which generally focus on enhancing the

quality of life of disadvantanged groups in the U.S. and the Third World. These are, in descending order of budget allocation, urban poverty, rural poverty and resources, education and culture, human rights and social justice, international affairs and governance and public policy. Grants are generally awarded either through publicly announced competitions or on the basis of nominations from universities and other nonprofit institutions. The foundation generally makes awards to persons with advanced qualifications. Candidates from the U.S. and all over the world are eligible to apply.

The following description of program areas is based on the foundation's published "Current Interests, 1986 and 1987."

Program Areas. The foundation places strong emphasis on the needs of people who suffer the brunt of economic, social, and cultural deprivation. It is equally concerned with the consequences of such deprivation for the larger society. In the U.S., the foundation has a long-standing commitment to action on problems confronting blacks, Hispanics, Native Americans, poor women, and other disadvantaged groups. Strategies to advance these commitments largely depend upon community self-help initiatives and link these local efforts to public and private resources in the greater society. The foundation's other interests span a range of domestic, international, and multinational issues, including the reduction of poverty and dependency, the quality of education, the vitality of cultural pursuits, world peace, and the rights of individuals in free and closed societies.

Urban Poverty: The foundation concentrates on low-income neighborhoods of U.S. cities. Programs are aimed at new ways of revitalizing depressed communities, improving the health and intellectual development of children, preventing welfare dependency and teen pregnancy, strengthening secondary schools, reducing school dropout, and training and employing poor youth.

Although most grants fund projects in the United States, an increasing number of initiatives address the problems of the urban poor in developing countries.

Rural Poverty and Resources: The foundation is concerned with agricultural development, the welfare of the poor, and natural resource management in the Third World. Such projects involve efforts to expand agricultural production, improve the management of deteriorating land and water resources, and enhance economic opportunites for small farmers and the landless poor. The foundation supports a limited set of activities to address similar problems in the U.S.

Education and Culture: In higher education, the foundation has three principal aims: to broaden access to colleges and universities and enhance the quality of education available to members of disadvantaged groups; to strengthen the intellectual and professional engagement of faculty in their teaching and scholarship; and to improve undergraduate curricula in selected fields. Advancing social science research and training in developing countries is also a longstanding concern.

In the arts, the foundation aims to encourage the development of new work and innovative forms of expression in the performing arts; to further cultural diversity by strengthening art and art institutions outside the mainstream; to preserve performances through film, tape, or notation; and to document the lives of major American artists through oral or audio-visual histories. In developing countries, the foundation supports efforts to preserve and interpret traditional cultures and to enhance their contribution to contemporary society.

Human Rights and Social Justice: In the U.S. and abroad the foundation is concerned with the struggle to protect human rights and promote political and civil liberty. Substantial support has gone to international human rights organizations and their legal support centers, projects that educate people about their rights as well as those that provide legal services, research on societal factors that lead to human rights violations--for example--governmental misuse of its own authority, and on the cultural bases for human rights in non-Western traditions. The foundation is also interested in projects that enhance understanding of the rights of asylum, exchange or information, the promotion of rights of racial minorities in the U.S. and the improvement of the status and opportunites of women in the areas of occupational segregation, sex discrimination in employment, and reproductive rights.

International Affairs: The foundation encourages informed analysis and public debate on seven complex international issues: the maintenance of peace, security, and arms control; the changing world economy; the increasing flow of migrants and refugees around the world; conduct of U.S. foreign policy; international relations in developing countries; international organizations and law; and neglected fields of foreign area studies. Grants have gone to individuals in the U.S. and abroad for research, training and conferences and publications on these concerns. A major goal is the development of networks of analysts in industrialized and developing countries who can view international issues from a mix of global, regional, national and disciplinary perspectives.

Government and Public Policy: Grants made in the field of governance are aimed at strengthening democratic processes and institutions, improving the design and delivery of state and local government services, and clarifing fiscal and economic policy options. Public policy grants are made for studies of the effects of public policys on minorities and the disadvantage, for efforts to increase minority participation in the policy-making process, and for research and public education on the future of social insurance and welfare programs in the U.S.

245
Ford (Guy Stanton) Educational Foundation, Inc.
P.O. Box 1664
Madison, WI 53701
Contact: Jack D. Walker, Treasurer, 119 Martin Luther King, Jr. Boulevard, Madison, WI 53703; Tel.: (608) 257-4812

Limitations: Scholarships only to active or pledged members of the Sigma Deuteron Charge of Theta Delta Chi Fraternity attending the University of Wisconsin at Madison.
Financial data: Year ended 12/31/86. Assets, $33,741 (M); Total giving, $2,096; Grants to individuals, 16 grants totaling $2,096, high $491, low $37.
Employer Identification Number: 396101946
Program description:
An eligibility list comprised of all active members and all persons then pledged to become active members of the Sigma Deuteron Charge of Theta Delta Chi Fraternity is compared to the university's all-men undergraduate grade average for the semester immediately preceding the semester then concluded. Scholarships are awarded in equal shares to those on the eligibility list whose grade average exceeds the applicable all-men's average. Additional awards are made to recipients on the list with the three highest grade averages.

Scholarships are paid directly to the individual recipients. Recipients must be able to show that they are still students of the University of Wisconsin at the time of payment; however, recipients need not be an active member or pledged to become an active member of Sigma Deuteron Charge of Theta Delta Chi Fraternity at the time of distribution.

246
Ford (The S.N.) and Ada Ford Fund
P.O. Box 849
Mansfield, OH 440901   (419) 526-3493
Contact: Ralph H. LeMunyon, Distribution Committee, 35 North Park Street, Mansfield, OH 44901

Limitations: Scholarships only to qualified residents of Richland County, Oh.
Financial data: Year ended 12/31/86. Assets, $6,137,779 (M); Total giving, $331,551; Grants to individuals, 357 grants totaling $294,251; Subtotal amount for scholarships not specified.
Employer Identification Number: 340842282
Publications: Annual report.

247
Forman (Hamilton M. & Blanche C.) Christian Foundation
3600 North Federal Highway
Fort Lauderdale, FL 33308

Limitations: Grants for education.
Financial data: Year ended 10/31/86. Assets, $1,134,752 (M); Total giving, $40,435; Grants to individuals, 1 grants totaling $11,500.
Employer Identification Number: 596131560

248★
Forsyth (Fred) Educational Trust Fund
Merrill/Norstar Bank
Exchange Street
Bangor, ME 04401
Contact: Bucksport High School, Bucksport, ME 04416

Limitations: Scholarships only to graduates of Bucksport High School, ME.
Financial data: Year ended 7/31/86. Assets, $401,479 (M); Total giving, $21,100; Grants to individuals, 37 grants totaling $21,100, high $800, low $300.
Employer Identification Number: 016059631
Program description:
Most of the scholarship recipients attend colleges and vocational schools in Maine, Vermont, and New Hampshire.

249
Fort Howard Paper Foundation, Inc.
1919 South Broadway
P.O. Box 11325
Green Bay, WI 54307-1325   (414) 435-8821
Contact: Scholarship Selection Committee

Limitations: Scholarships only to graduating high school seniors in Brown County, WI.
Financial data: Year ended 9/30/86. Assets, $13,956,541 (M); Total giving, $373,695; Grants to individuals totaling $18,337; Subtotal for scholarships, 3 grants totaling $12,337, high $5,000, low $2,500.
Employer Identification Number: 362761910
Applications: Deadline November 1st; Completion of formal application including two letters of recommendation and high school transcript required; Interviews required.
Program description:
The **Fort Howard Paper Foundation Annual College Scholarship** is a $20,000 award intended to cover 75 percent of the cost to tuition, room and board, and books, in the amount of up to $5,000 per year, and is renewable for three consective years provided recipient remains in good academic standing.

Recipients must:

    1. be graduating seniors attending a high school in Brown County, WI

2. rank in the upper one-third of their graduating class as of the end of junior year spring semester
3. have demonstrated achievements in one or more extracurricular activities
4. be recommended by two instructors, high school administrators, or other individuals not related to the student
5. demonstrate financial need
6. be or good character
7. be available for an interview with the selection committee.

250
Fort Pierce Memorial Hospital Scholarship Foundation
c/o Lawnwood Medical Center, P.O. Box 188
1700 South 23rd Street
Fort Pierce, FL 33450   (305) 461-4000

Limitations: Scholarships limited to bona fide residents of St. Lucie County, FL, who are following a course of study leading to a career in the health field. Undergraduate students only must be unmarried.
Financial data: Year ended 9/30/86. Assets, $3,650,141 (M); Total giving, $155,026, high $15,000, low $2,500.
Employer Identification Number: 590651084
Applications: Deadline April 15th; Completion of formal application required; Submit high school and/or college transcript; Declaration of domicile and citizenship completed by Clerk of the Circuit Court required.
Program description:
Applicants must already have been accepted at an accredited medical or dental school at the time of application. Recipients are selected by the foundation's scholarship committee.

251
Foundation for Biblical Research and Preservation of Primitive Christianity
144 Main Street
Box 373
Charlestown, NH 03603
Contact: Jan L. Kater, President

Limitations: Scholarships only to graduating students of Fall Mountain Regional High School, Alstead, NH, who are at the freshman and sophomore levels attending an accredited institution for religious education.
Financial data: Year ended 4/30/86. Assets, $1,865,260 (M); Total giving, $2,994; Grants to individuals totaling $2,000.
Employer Identification Number: 020243633
Applications: Deadline April 1st; Completion of formal application required.

Program description:
Grants are not to exceed $500 per school year and are to be used for tuition only at an accredited institution. The amount is divided equally over the terms of the school year and unused amounts are to be returned.
    The grants are based on excellent character, good scholarship, and definite financial need as assessed by the foundation scholarship committee.

252★
Foundation for Nutritional Advancement
600 New Hampshire Avenue, N.W., No. 700
Washington, DC 20037   (202) 337-4442
Contact: Curtis Cutter, Executive Director

Limitations: Grants primarily for research on micronutrition and health and nutrition in the treatment and prevention of diseases.
Financial data: Year ended 12/31/86. Assets, $689,796 (M); Total giving, $162,740; Grants to individuals, 10 grants totaling $162,740, high $79,000, low $2,000.
Employer Identification Number: 521075437
Applications: Applications accepted throughout the year; Initial approach by proposal.
Publications: Informational brochure.

253★
Foundation for the Carolinas
301 South Brevard Street
Charlotte, NC 28202   (704) 376-9541
Contact: Barbara T. Hautau, Vice-President

Limitations: Limited scholarships and student loans only to students residing in NC or SC.
Financial data: Year ended 12/31/87. Assets, $32,141,601 (M); Total giving, $7,842,200; Grants to individuals, 40 grants totaling $34,545.
Employer Identification Number: 566047886
Applications: Contact foundation for current application deadline; Initial approach by letter; Completion of formal application required.
Publications: Annual report.
Program description:
The foundation administers the following programs:
    1. **Charlotte Housing Authority Scholarships** are need-based undergraduate scholarships awarded to residents of Charlotte public housing.
    2. **William Tasse Alexander Scholarships** are undergraduate merit scholarships, primarily in the field of education.
    3. **Rotary Scholarship** provides assistance to graduates of Central Piedmont Community College who seek a bachelor's degree at a four-year college in Mecklenburg County, NC.
    4. **Washburn Graphics Scholarships** are awarded annually to high school seniors displaying excellence in art, scholarship, character, and community service.

5. **The Crowder Scholarship Fund** provides assistance to children of employees of construction companies located in Mecklenburg, NC.

254

Frautschy (John Cowles) Scholarship Trust Fund

c/o First National Bank of Monroe
1625 Tenth Street
Monroe, WI 53566

Limitations: Scholarships to male Protestant graduating seniors of Monroe High School, Monroe, WI.
Financial data: Year ended 5/31/87. Assets, $199,011 (M); Total giving, $13,500; Grants to individuals, 24 grants totaling $13,500, high $1,500, low $200, general range $300-800.
Employer Identification Number: 930799642
Applications: Applications available from guidance counselors of Monroe High School; Completion of formal application required.
Program description:
Selected guidance counselors submit the application forms to the Scholarship Selection Group. If requested, the counselors will also present additional information about the applicants, including class rank, aptitude test scores, and an appraisal of financial need. Primary emphasis is given to financial need of the applicants and their record of scholastic accomplishment. Emphasis is also placed on attitude and aptitude.

Grants are made for college scholarships or for other training and are awarded to adults as well as to high school seniors.

255

Friendship Fund, Inc.

c/o Boston Safe Deposit & Trust Company
One Boston Place, OBP-2
Boston, MA 02106　　　　　　　(617) 722-7538

Limitations: Virtually all funds for scholarship grants are committed in advance by the trustees.
Financial data: Year ended 6/30/86. Assets, $2,722,814 (M); Total giving, $138,850; Grants to individuals, 1 grant totaling $3,000.
Employer Identification Number: 136089220
Applications: Submit cover letter during May only; Additional information will be requested if trustees' interest so warrants.
Program description:
A very small number of scholarship grants are awarded each year to institutions on behalf of individuals whose needs are known to the trustees. Grants are not normally made to graduate students. Awards do not exceed $3,000 each and are usually renewable contingent upon academic progress.

256

Fromm (Walter and Mabel) Scholarship Trust

c/o First Wisconsin Trust Company
P.O. Box 2054
Milwaukee, WI 53201
Contact: G. Lindermann

Limitations: College and nursing school scholarships to graduates of the Mable Grove (elementary) School in Hamburg, WI and/or Merrill Senior Public High School in Merrill, WI.
Financial data: Year ended 2/28/87. Assets, $1,908,012 (M); Total giving, $97,620; Grants to individuals, 27 grants totaling $97,620, high $3,700, low $1,050, average grant $3,700.
Employer Identification Number: 396250027
Publications: Application guidelines.
Program description:
Scholarship grants are distributed to three recipients in the Merrill, WI, area, with preference to applicants in Class I. Consideration is then given to Classes II and III, respectively. The classes include students enrolled in four-year degree programs and three-year nursing schools who meet the following requirements:
　Class I:
　1. attended grades 1-6 at and graduated from Maple Grove School, Hamburg, WI;
　2. attended grades 7-12 in City of Merrill, WI, Public School System and graduated from Merrill Public High School.
　3. maintained a 2.5 or better grade point average in grades 9-12.
　Class II:
　1. attended grade 6 and graduated from Maple Grove School, Hamburg, WI;
　2. and 3. same as Class I
　Class III:
　1. attended grades 9-12 and graduated from Merrill Public High School;
　2. maintained a 2.5 or better grade point average in grades 9-12.

257★

Fukunaga Scholarship Foundation

900 Fort Street Mall, Suite 500
Honolulu, HI 96813　　　　　　(808) 521-6511
Contact: Scholarship Selection Committee, P.O. Box 2788, Honolulu, HI 96803

Limitations: Scholarships to residents of Hawaii for a minimum of one year to study business administration at the University of Hawaii or other accredited universities.
Financial data: Year ended 11/30/86. Assets, $647,428 (M); Total giving, $17,937; Grants to individuals, 41 grants totaling $17,937, high $750, low $250, average grant $500.
Employer Identification Number: 990600370
Applications: Deadline March 15th; Completion of formal application, accompanied by school transcript,

SAT scores, and at least two letters of reference (one from high school principal, teacher, or counselor, one from business or professional person in the community), required; Interviews required for semi-finalists.

Program description:
Applicants must demonstrate academic ability, leadership qualities, interest in business in the Pacific Basin Area, and financial need. Applicants must be in the top 25 percent of their classes, with a high school cumulative grade point average of at least 3.0.

258
Fuller (C.G.) Foundation
c/o NCNB South Carolina
P.O. Box 2307
Columbia, SC 29202   (803) 771-2990
Contact: Thomas W. Duke, Jr.

Limitations: Scholarships to residents of South Carolina, attending South Carolina colleges or universities.
Financial data: Year ended 12/31/86. Assets, $1,702,233 (M); Total giving, $143,000; Grants to individuals, 41 grants totaling $80,750, high $2,000, low $750.
Employer Identification Number: 576050492
Applications: Deadlines March 31st; Initial approach by letter; Completion of formal application required.

259
Furnas Foundation, Inc.
1000 McKee Street
Batavia, IL 60510   (312) 879-6000
Contact: Jo Ann Hogan

Limitations: Undergraduate scholarships only to students residing within twelve miles of the Batavia Government Center, Batavia, IL, or in Clarke County, IA.
Financial data: Year ended 12/31/86. Assets, $619,351 (M); Total giving, $299,453; Grants to individuals, 77 grants totaling $76,538, high, $5,126, low $300.
Employer Identification Number: 366049894
Applications: Deadline March 1st; Initial approach by letter requesting application from Scholarship Committee; Completion of formal application required.
Publications: Program information, application guidelines, informational brochure.
Program description:
A full tuition scholarship is awarded yearly to the University of Purdue; otherwise maximum scholarship amount is $1,500.

260
Gardner Foundation, The
P.O. Box 126
Middletown, OH 45042   (513) 423-1795
Contact: Calvin F. Lloyd, Secretary

Limitations: Scholarships limited to graduating seniors of Middletown and Hamilton County, OH. Students must attend a non tax-supported college.
Financial data: Year ended 5/31/87. Assets, $3,393,461 (M); Total giving, $110,000; Grants to individuals, 24 grants totaling $84,000, each grant $3,500.
Employer Identification Number: 316050604
Applications: Deadline April 1st; Completion of formal application required.

261
General Educational Fund, Inc.
c/o The Merchants Trust Company
P.O. Box 1009, 123 Church Street
Burlington, VT 05402
Contact: David W. Webster, President

Limitations: Undergraduate scholarships only to residents of Vermont.
Financial data: Year ended 7/31/86. Assets, $18,003,221 (M); Total giving, $339,400; Grants to individuals, 382 grants totaling $339,400, high $1,000, low $300, general range $100-500.
Employer Identification Number: 036009912
Applications: Initial approach by letter; Completion of formal application required.

262
Geneseo Foundation
c/o Central Trust & Savings Bank
P.O. Box 89
Geneseo, IL 61254   (309) 944-5601
Contact: Jack K. Austin, c/o Central Trust & Savings Bank, 101-North State Street, Geneseo, IL 61254

Limitations: Scholarships only to graduates of Geneseo High School, IL.
Financial data: Year ended 3/31/87. Assets, $2,500,937 (M); Total giving, $64,839; Grants to individuals amount not specified.
Employer Identification Number: 366079604
Applications: Deadline first week of the month; Completion of formal application required.

263★
German Marshall Fund of the United States
11 Dupont Circle, N.W., Suite 750
Washington, DC 20036   (202) 745-3950
Contact: Frank E. Loy, President

Limitations: Postdoctoral fellowship program for U.S. scholars for research concerned with contemporary problems of industrial societies; also provides professional fellowships to U.S. and European environmentalists as well as short-term travel awards, for participation at conferences only, as a discussant or presenter of papers.

Financial data: Year ended 5/31/87. Assets, $60,860,823 (M); Total giving, $3,818,746; Grants to individuals, 220 grants totaling $1,021,432; Subtotal for fellowships to U.S. scholars not specified.

Employer Identification Number: 520954751

Applications: Deadline November 15th for Research Fellowship Program; Deadlines for other programs vary from year to year; Applications accepted throughout the year for travel awards, however, applications must be received no less than six weeks before the conference date; Completion of formal application required for all other fellowship programs.

Publications: Multi-year report, program information.

Program description:

The **Research Fellowship Program** provides support to scholars whose proposed research projects promise to contribute to a better understanding of significant contemporary problems of industrial societies. Comparative political, economic, and social aspects of both domestic and international issues will receive careful consideration. Each project must have U.S. and European (Western or Eastern) components.

The fund is particularly interested in identifying promising younger scholars (two to seven years beyond the Ph.D.) who are seeking to expand dissertation research in new directions or to launch a new research project. However, senior scholars may also apply.

Applicants must plan to devote full-time to their projects during the period of the fellowship, which may extend from an academic term to a year. Fellows are selected on the basis of scholarly qualifications, promise, and achievements; importance and originality of the proposed work, and its contemporary relevance; and the likelihood of completing the project within the scheduled time. Research leading to an advanced degree is not supported.

The amount of the fellowship will help meet, but not exceed, the recipient's current income and will also cover limited travel expenses.

Environmental Fellowships are awarded to up to twelve professional American and European environmentalists to spend two months on the other side of the Atlantic gaining firsthand knowledge of selected environmental policies and institutions. The American fellows pursue their inquiries under the guidance of the Institute for European Environmental Policy, based in Bonn, London, and Paris.

Short-Term Grants for Transatlantic Travel aim to encourage interaction between the world of scholarly analysis and the world of practical action. Awards of up to $1,000 each are made solely to assist participation at conferences on the opposite side of the Atlantic. For purposes of this award "participation" means either presentation of a paper or a scheduled role as discussant.

Grants are for transatlantic travel; conferences may take place in either North America or Europe and must fit within one of the fund's program areas. Currently these are:

(1) U.S.-European economic issues, including problems of competition and adjustment within sectors and industries and public policies which affect this competition

(2) U.S.-European relations, particularly the establishment and continuation of a dialogue among people who can influence these relations

(3) employment, focusing on labor market policies; the employability of youth, women, dislocated workers, and the long-term unemployed;

(4) public and private action, and policy relevant to the environment, energy conservation, and immigration.

Eligible applicants are from Europe or North America and may be scholars from universities or research institutions, or officials, professionals, and practitioners in government, business, trade unions, public interest groups, and international organizations. Applicants apply by letter enclosing an official invitation from the conference organizers.

264
GFF Educational Foundation, Inc.

P.O. Box 826
Norcross, GA 30091   (404) 447-4488
Contact: F. Roy Nelson, Secretary

Limitations: Scholarships primarily for residents of Georgia.

Financial data: Year ended 5/31/86. Assets, $46,000 (M); Total giving, $120,510; Grants to individuals, 19 grants totaling $41,604; Subtotal for scholarships, 11 grants totaling $40,069, high $6,444, low $1,513.

Employer Identification Number: 581477023

265
Ghidotti (William & Marian) Foundation

P.O. Box 925
Nevada City, CA 95959   (916) 265-2708
Contact: Erica Erickson, Trustee

Limitations: Scholarships only to residents of Nevada County, CA.

Financial data: Year ended 12/31/86. Assets, $5,770,360 (M); Total giving, $263,238; Grants to individuals, 124 grants totaling $168,834, high $2,000, low $500.

Employer Identification Number: 946181833

Applications: Deadlines February for new scholarships, August for renewals; Completion of formal application including transcript of grades, student and family income, and personal resume required.

266
Gibson (Addison H.) Foundation

Two PPG Place, Suite 310
Pittsburgh, PA 15222   (412) 261-1611
Contact: Charlotte G. Kisseleff, Secretary

Limitations: Loans to male students residing in western
Pennsylvania after at least one year's self-maintenance
in an undergraduate or graduate degree program.
Financial data: Year ended 12/31/86. Assets,
$14,377,661 (M); Expenditures, $1,803,967; Loans to
individuals, 87 loans totaling $514,735, high $10,000,
low $1,000, general range $2,000-6,000.
Employer Identification Number: 250965379
Applications: Contact foundation for current
application guidelines; Initial approach by letter or
telephone to schedule personal interview; Completion
of formal application required; Interviews required.
Program description:
Interest at the rate of two percent per annum will be
charged on loans, from date of issue, increasing to five
percent per annum one year after the student
completes his education, at which time he will be
required to begin repayment of the principal.
Endorsement of notes will be required in every case.
The endorser shall be a person owning real estate in
Pennsylvania. Students are required to show the
disposition of the funds borrowed and to submit their
academic reports to the foundation at regular intervals.

267★
Gibson (E.L.) Foundation

201 South Edwards
Enterprise, AL 36330   (205) 393-4553
Contact: J. B. Brunson, Manager

Limitations: Scholarships for health-related study to
residents of Coffee County, AL, and bordering
counties.
Financial data: Year ended 12/31/86. Assets,
$1,959,187 (M); Total giving, $97,479; Grants to
individuals, 32 grants totaling $8,891, high $1,000,
low $46.
Employer Identification Number: 630383929
Applications: Applications accepted throughout the
year; Initial approach by letter.

268
Gilman Paper Co. Foundation, Inc.

111 West 50th Street
New York, NY 10020

Limitations: Scholarships for higher education.
Financial data: Year ended 12/31/85. Assets, $519
(M); Total giving, $133,524; Grants to individuals, 18
grants totaling $69,800, high $4,000, low $3,000,
average grant $4,000.
Employer Identification Number: 133134047

269
Gimbel (Jake) Scholarship Fund

c/o Bank of America, N.T. & S.A., Trust Department
No. 8250
200 East Delmar Boulevard, Third Floor
Pasadena, CA 91101
Contact: Ms. Minh Lee, Wells Fargo Bank, 555 South
Flower, Sixth Floor, Los Angeles, CA 90071; Tel.:
(213) 253-7216

Limitations: Loans to male students studying for
graduate degrees in selected colleges and universities
in California.
Financial data: Year ended 5/31/87. Assets, $299,809
(M); Expenditures, $32,590; Loans to individuals, 22
loans totaling $22,000, each loan $1,000.
Employer Identification Number: 956024827
Applications: Deadline May 15th; Completion of
formal application, accompanied by undergraduate
transcripts, and two letters of reference from persons
engaged in the field applicant proposes to study,
required.
Publications: Program information.
Program description:
Annual awards are for ten-year interest-free
scholarship loans. Submit completed application to
Lydia D'Antonio, Trust Administrator, Bank of
America, Private Testamentary Trust No. 8250, P.O.
Box 54721, Los Angeles, CA 90054.

270
Glenn (Paul F.) Foundation for Medical
Research, Inc.

72 Virginia Drive
Manhasset, NY 11030
Contact: Barbara Boyd, Vice-President

Limitations: Grants for research on the biology of
aging.
Financial data: Year ended 9/30/85. Assets,
$1,704,214 (M); Total giving, $47,928; Grants to
individuals totaling $15,000.
Employer Identification Number: 136191732
Applications: Contact foundation for current
application deadline; Initial approach by proposal.
Program description:
The foundation makes grants to 1) encourage and
accelerate research on the biology of aging; 2) assist
those engaged in research on causes of the aging
process; 3) increase the stature of the field of
gerontology; 4) broaden public understanding of
aging; and 5) educate the public on ways to delay or
prevent senility and prolong the human life span. The
foundation is particularly interested in the investigation
of proper nutrition as a factor in the aging process.

271
Goldman (William) Foundation
1700 Walnut Street, Suite 800
Philadelphia, PA 19103   (215) 546-2779
Contact: Marilyn Klein, Executive Director

Limitations: Scholarships to residents of the
metropolitan Philadelphia, PA, area for full-time
graduate or medical study at specific Philadelphia
institutions.
Financial data: Year ended 12/31/86. Assets,
$2,549,761; Total giving, $108,250; Grants to
individuals, 53 grants totaling $39,750, average grant
$1,000.
Employer Identification Number: 236266261
Applications: Deadline March 15th; Initial approach
by letter; Completion of formal application required;
Interviews required for finalists.
Publications: Program information.
Program description:
Scholarships are for the benefit of students attending
the following nine graduate or medical schools: Bryn
Mawr College, Drexel University, Hahnemann
Medical College and Hospital, Medical College of
Pennsylvania, Philadelphia College of Osteopathic
Medicine, Temple University, Thomas Jefferson
University and Medical College, University of
Pennsylvania, and Villanova University.

   Grants only cover tuition and are renewable.
However, first-year students must be accepted for
admittance at one of the above schools in order to
apply. Applicants must normally be in top third of
their class.

272
Goldstein Scottish Rite Trust
P.O. Box 1194
Juneau, AK 99802
Contact: James H. Taylor, 4365 North Douglas Road,
Juneau, AK 99801; Tel.: (907) 586-2849

Limitations: Scholarships to needy graduates of local
Juneau, AK, schools.
Financial data: Year ended 12/31/86. Assets, $65,066
(M); Total giving, $12,440; Grants to individuals, 11
grants totaling $12,440, high $2,000, low $440,
general range $900-2,000.
Employer Identification Number: 916031605
Applications: Deadline May 1st; Initial approach by
letter stating educational plans, finances available, and
assistance required.

273★
Gooding (George L.) Trust
c/o State Street Bank & Trust Company
P.O. Box 351
Boston, MA 02101

Limitations: Scholarships for graduating seniors of the
Plymouth Regional High School, Plymouth, MA.

Financial data: Year ended 12/31/87. Assets, $367,219
(M); Total giving, $18,000; Grants to individuals
totaling $18,000.
Employer Identification Number: 046095797

274
Goodwin (Howard D. and Rose E.) Scholarship Fund
Meridian Trust Company
P.O. Box 1102
Reading, PA 19603-1102   (215) 320-3115
Contact: R. Kemp

Limitations: Scholarships only to students who reside
in the Antietam School District, Berks County, PA,
who have graduated from Mt. Penn High School and
are in need of financial assistance.
Financial data: Year ended 12/31/86. Assets, $73,727
(M); Total giving, $7,000; Grants to individuals, 14
grants totaling $7,000, each grant $500.
Employer Identification Number: 236476039
Applications: Applications accepted throughout the
year; Completion of formal application required;
Applications available from Mt. Penn High School;
Interviews required.

275
Gore Family Memorial Foundation
c/o Sun Bank
P.O. Box 14728
Fort Lauderdale, FL 33302

Limitations: Graduate and undergraduate scholarships
for the handicapped; undergraduate scholarships for
Broward County, FL, residents.
Financial data: Year ended 1/31/87. Assets,
$14,623,583 (M); Total giving, $627,434; Grants to
individuals, 506 grants totaling $359,850; Subtotal for
scholarships, 158 grants totaling $104,099.
Employer Identification Number: 596497544
Applications: Applications accepted throughout the
year; Initial approach by letter to the foundation, 501
East Las Olas Boulevard, Fort Lauderdale, FL 33302.
Publications: Informational brochure.
Program description:
Scholarships are granted to Florida residents and to the
handicapped. Most scholarships are for college
education, but there are some for secondary
education. No scholarships for graduate studies,
except to the handicapped.

276
Grable (Dr. Harry G.) Memorial Fund
215 East Sycamore Street
P.O. Box 626
Kokomo, IN 46903-0626   (317) 459-8063
Contact: Thomas J. Simmons, Trustee

Limitations: Scholarships only to students who have graduated from high schools in Howard County, IN, and will be studying nursing or medicine.
Financial data: Year ended 5/31/87. Assets, $7,348 (M); Total giving, $2,500; Grants to individuals, 5 grants totaling $2,500, each grant $500.
Employer Identification Number: 237138131
Applications: Deadline between April 15th and May 1st; Applications available from the high schools.
Program description:
The foundation only grants scholarships to college students. The number of scholarships and the amounts awarded vary from year to year, but average from seven to ten scholarships of $500 each per year. Applicants must have SAT (or equivalent) scores of 1000 and must graduate in upper ten percent of their class.

277
Graham (Florence B.) - Clemma B. Fancher Scholarship Fund
149 Josephine Street, Suite A
Santa Cruz, CA 95060   (408) 423-3640
Contact: Robert H. Darrow, Trustee

Limitations: Scholarships to graduating seniors from high schools in northern Santa Cruz County, CA.
Financial data: Year ended 4/30/87. Assets, $281,950 (M); Total giving, $44,518; Grants to individuals, 47 grants totaling $44,518, high $1,800, low $167, general range $600-1,200, average grant $900.
Employer Identification Number: 946233118
Applications: Deadline May 31st; Completion of formal application required; Application forms available through eligible high schools.
Program description:
Scholarships are awarded primarily on the basis of need, but academic standing and high school achievements are also considered.

278★
Graham Foundation For Advanced Studies in the Fine Arts
Four West Burton Place
Chicago, IL 60610   (312) 787-4071
Contact: Carter H. Manny, Jr., Executive Director

Limitations: Fellowships for advanced research in contemporary architecture, design, and the study of urban planning, principally to Americans working within the U.S. who have demonstrated mature, creative talent and have specific work objectives.
Financial data: Year ended 12/31/86. Assets, $18,016,767 (M); Total giving, $227,002; Grants to individuals, 7 grants totaling $24,700, high $9,000, low $1,050.
Employer Identification Number: 362356089
Applications: Deadlines June 1st and December 1st; Initial approach by letter describing and supporting the objectives of the grant request, including curriculum vitae for participants, specific amount being requested; Applicants are advised to request three qualified references candidly assessing worthiness of the individual and the project to be submitted in confidence to the foundation directly.
Publications: Annual report (including application guidelines).
Program description:
Recent support has included architectural research, including student-involved projects; publications, including biographies, manuscripts, and photography; films; and independent study and travel.

279
Graham Memorial Fund
P.O. Box 533
Bennettsville, SC 29512

Limitations: Scholarships for postsecondary education only to residents of Bennettsville, SC.
Financial data: Year ended 9/30/85. Assets, $137,059 (M); Total giving, $13,918; Grants to individuals, 32 grants totaling $13,918; Subtotal for scholarships, 22 grants totaling $10,858, high $800, low $250, general range $250-600.
Employer Identification Number: 576026184
Applications: Deadline June 1st; Completion of formal application required.
Program description:
Scholarship payments are made directly to the institution of higher learning on the behalf of the named recipient.

280
Grand Haven Area Community Foundation, Inc.
One South Harbor, Suite 3
Grand Haven, MI 49417   (616) 842-6378
Contact: Gerald Retzlaff, Chairman, Distribution Committee

Limitations: Student loans to residents in the Tri-City and northwest Ottawa County, MI, areas.
Financial data: Year ended 4/30/86. Assets, $2,130,964 (M); Expenditures, $179,286; Loans to individuals, 59 loans totaling $118,491.
Employer Identification Number: 237108776
Applications: Completion of formal application required.
Publications: Annual report.

281
Grand Rapids Foundation
300-E Waters Building
161 Ottawa, N.W.
Grand Rapids, MI 49503   (616) 454-1751
Contact: Diana R. Sieger, Executive Director

Limitations: Scholarships and loans only to residents of Kent County (Greater Grand Rapids), MI.
Financial data: Year ended 6/30/87. Assets, $38,334,470 (M); Total giving, $1,721,581; Grants to individuals totaling $50,750, Loans to individuals amount not specified; 1986, Loans to individuals, 21 loans totaling $80,090.
Employer Identification Number: 386032912
Applications: Student loan applications accepted between January 1st and April 1st; Initial approach by letter or telephone; Completion of formal application required.
Publications: Annual report, informational brochure (including application guidelines).
Program description:
The foundation administers several programs for scholarships to local high school graduates:
 a. Doyle Trust for graduates of Lowell High School.
 b. Grand Rapids Foundation annual undergraduate grants of up to $500 for attendance at Aquinas College, Calvin College, Davenport College, Grand Rapids Baptist College, Grand Rapids Junior College, Grand Valley State Colleges, or Kendall College.
 c. Meijer Trust for children of Meijer Store employees.
 d. Snauble Trust for graduates of Cedar Springs High School.

282★
Grass Foundation, The
77 Reservoir Road
Quincy, MA 02170   (617) 773-0002
Contact: Mary G. Grass, Secretary

Limitations: Fellowships to M.D.'s and Ph.D.'s, predoctoral and postdoctoral researchers in neurophysiology and allied fields of science and medicine.
Financial data: Year ended 12/31/85. Assets, $4,302,155 (M); Total giving, $426,813; Grants to individuals amount not specified.
Employer Identification Number: 046049529
Applications: See program description below for application information.
Publications: Application guidelines.
Program description:
Grass Fellowships in Neurophysiology are to conduct a research project at the Marine Biological Laboratories in Woods Hole, MA. It covers traveling

and reasonable living expenses for the fellow and family, and certain laboratory costs, for a 10- to 14-week summer residency at MBL.
 Candidates should have had no more than three years of postdoctoral experience and no prior research experience at MBL. The deadline for application is December 1st for consideration for the following summer. The application requires presentation of a research proposal, and a budget itemizing travel expenses, equipment shipping expenses, and living accomodations required. A letter of recommendation from a senior investigator familiar with the candidate's work is required and can be sent with the application or separately. Successful candidates will be notified by March 1st. In 1987, 12 fellowships were provided.
 The Robert S. Morison Fellowships are for advanced research training to prepare for an academic career as a clinical investigator in mammalian neurophysiology. Applicant must be an M.D. who has been accepted into or just completed a residency in neurology or neurosurgery. The research may be combined as part of the residency program or be designated as intensive supplemental years.
 The fellowship program is offered only in odd-numbered years and last two years. The awards carry a stipend of $25,000 per year, with $700 each for the fellow's dependent spouse and children. Up to $3,000 is available to cover research costs, and/or travel to one scientific meeting.
 The deadline for application is November 1st of even-numbered years in anticipation of an award to commence between the following July 1st and December 31st. Applications are to come jointly from the candidate and the sponsoring laboratory program director. The foundation provides a suggested outline upon request. Both applicant and supervisor should carefully outline the proposed program of research and clinical duties anticipated, supplemental studies to be accomplished (if any), as well as career and program goals.

283
Griffin (Abbie M.) Educational Fund
111 Concord Street
Nashua, NH 03060   (603) 882-5157
Contact: S. Robert Winer, Trustee

Limitations: Scholarships to residents of Merrimack, NH.
Financial data: Year ended 12/31/85. Assets, $189,123 (M); Total giving, $11,350; Grants to individuals, 10 grants totaling $11,350, high $2,000, low $300, general range $1,000-1,650.
Employer Identification Number: 026021466
Applications: Written applications accepted throughout the year; Interviews required.

284

Grim (Clifford D.) and Virginia S. Grim Educational Fund

c/o First National Bank Trust Department
P.O. Box 1301
McLean, VA 22101-1340
Contact: Donald R. Grubbs, c/o First American Bank
of Virginia, P.O. Box 1000, Winchester, VA 22601;
Tel.: (703) 667-2000

Limitations: Educational loans to students primarily in
the Winchester, VA, area.
Financial data: Year ended 7/31/87. Assets, $687,583
(M); Expenditures, $77,334; Loans to individuals, 27
loans totaling $74,269, high $8,250, low $1,000,
general range $1,000-3,000.
Employer Identification Number: 546046865
Applications: Deadline May 1st for following fall and
spring semesters; Completion of formal application
required; Interviews required.
Program description:
The first repayment on the fund's student loan is due
no later than six months after graduation or
immediately if recipient leaves school for any reason.

285

Grotefend (George) Scholarship Fund

c/o Wells Fargo Bank Trust Department
400 Capital Mall
Sacramento, CA 95814   (916) 244-4600
Contact: Grotefend Scholarship Board, 1644 Magnolia
Avenue, Redding, CA 96001

Limitations: Graduate and undergraduate scholarships
to students who have received their entire high school
education in Shasta County, CA, and who demonstrate
need.
Financial data: Year ended 4/30/87. Assets, $801,629
(M); Total giving, $63,475; Grants to individuals, 476
grants totaling $62,550, high $400, low $150.
Employer Identification Number: 946969687
Applications: Deadline May 1st; Completion of formal
application required.

286

Grubb (James B.) Oakland Scottish Rite Scholarship Foundation

Oakland Scottish Rite Temple
1547 Lakeside Drive
Oakland, CA 94612   (415) 451-1906
Contact: John Oliver Rothi, Executive Secretary, 141
St. James Drive, Piedmont, CA 94611; Tel.: (415)
547-5464

Limitations: Scholarships to African and American
students for graduate study at colleges and universities
situated between Bakersfield in the central part of
California and the northern part of the state.
Financial data: Year ended 12/31/86. Assets, $469,433

(M); Total giving, $35,950; Grants to individuals, 29
grants totaling $35,950; high $1,800, low $300.
Employer Identification Number: 946175561
Applications: Deadline March 31st; Completion of
formal application required; Interview required.
Program description:
All candidates, whether native or naturalized
Americans, or foreign-born students in the U.S. on
visa, must agree to the following conditions if selected
by the foundation:
   1. To be aware of one's status as a university
   student, to conduct oneself in accordance with
   the laws of the U.S.
   2. To display high moral and ethical conduct,
   recognizing that the responsibilities of freedom
   and democracy are the most important ingredients
   of the American way of life.
   3. In consideration of the direct conflict of
   political views between American and those new
   and emerging African countries which have
   adopted and implemented Marxism, all recipients
   are obligated to assure the foundation's board that
   they themselves do not espouse the Marxist
   theory of government, and that, on the contrary,
   they favor in thought and practice the principles
   of freedom for the individual man as contained in
   the basic concepts of democracy throughout the
   world.
   4. Candidates must plan to return to their home
   countries for several years upon completion of
   their education to help improve conditions in
   Africa. For this reason, the foundation has placed
   some emphasis on studies in the areas of
   education, political science, and agriculture.
   In connection with this application, it is understood
that candidates authorized anyone appointed by the
foundation to secure full information as to character,
general reputation, and such other information as may
be necessary. All grants are paid in monthly
installments of $150.
   In the event that the candidate does not return to
his/her country of origin within five years from the
date of the award, the award will be considered a
loan payable to the foundation without interest five
years from the date thereof.

287

Grupe (William F.) Foundation, Inc.

22 Old Short Hills Road
Livingston, NJ 07039   (201) 740-1919
Contact: Abdol H. Islami, M.D., President

Limitations: Medical, nursing, and paramedical
scholarships only to residents of Bergen, Essex, and
Hudson counties, NJ, planning to practice within the
state.
Financial data: Year ended 12/31/85. Assets, $986,126
(M); Total giving, $119,000; Grants to individuals, 110
grants totaling $119,000, high $1,500, low $500.
Employer Identification Number: 226094704

Applications: Deadline March 1st; Initial approach by letter requesting application; Completion of formal application required; Interviews and two letters of recommendation required.
Publications: Application guidelines.

288★
Guggenheim (The Harry Frank) Foundation
527 Madison Avenue, 15th Floor
New York, NY 10022-4301   (212) 644-4907
Contact: Karen Colvard, Program Officer

Limitations: Grants for postdoctoral research in behavioral, social, and biological sciences.
Financial data: Year ended 6/30/87. Assets, $51,705,000 (M); Total giving, $1,556,949; Grants to individuals, 20 grants totaling $469,253, high $35,000, low $5,900, average grant $23,000; Subtotal for research grants not specified.
Employer Identification Number: 136043471
Applications: Deadlines August 1st and February 1st; Initial approach by telephone or letter; Completion of formal application required; Contact foundation for application guidelines.
Publications: Multi-year report, application guidelines, program information, newsletter, informational brochure, 990-PF printed copy available upon request.
Program description:
The foundation sponsors an international program of scientific research and scholarly study concerning the causes and consequences of dominance, aggression, and violence. Awards will be made only for projects with well-defined aims clearly germane to the human case. The foundation will consider projects designed to reveal basic physiological mechanisms, to elucidate fundamental psychological processes, to analyze critical social interrelations, or otherwise advance knowledge from any discipline that will further the foundation's intellectual and practical objectives. Whatever the discipline and whatever the method, the principal criteria for support of a project proposed to the foundation are the same: excellence and relevance.

While the average grant has been approximately $25,000 yearly, applications for greater or lesser sums will be judged on their merits. Proposals may be submitted for one-, two-, or three-year projects. All awards, however, are of one-year terms initially. Funding for second and third years of projects tentatively approved for more than one year will require annual applications for continuation and will depend upon evidence of satisfactory progress and an account of expenditures during the previous year. The principal objective of these short-term grants is to provide seed money to get new projects started rather then to lend continuing support to already well established endeavors.

Applications must include

1. a title page, abstract and statement of relevance to the foundation's program

2. curricula vitae for the principal investigator and all professional personnel
3. detailed budget and budget justification
4. a descriptive research plan
5. information about sources of other support
6. steps taken for protection of human or animal subjects
7. the tax exempt status of the home institution.

Six copies of an application must be submitted, and comments from two referees chosen by the applicant are to be sent directly to the foundation.

289★
Guggenheim (John Simon) Memorial Foundation
90 Park Avenue
New York, NY 10016   (212) 687-4470
Contact: Joel Conarroe, President

Limitations: Fellowships to published authors, exhibited artists, and others in the fine arts. Guggenheim fellowships may not be held concurrently with other fellowships.
Financial data: Year ended 12/31/87. Assets, $116,595,296 (M); Total giving, $7,041,000; Grants to individuals, 303 grants totaling $7,041,000, high $26,000, low $9,000, average grant $23,000.
Employer Identification Number: 135673173
Applications: Deadlines: October 1st for U.S. and Canada, December 1st for Western Hemisphere and the Philippines; Initial approach by letter; Completion of formal application required.
Publications: Annual report, informational brochure (including application guidelines).
Program description:
Fellowships to Assist Research and Artistic Creations are awarded to citizens of the U.S. and Canada who have high intellectual and personal qualifications and have already demonstrated unusual capacity for productive scholarship or unusual creative ability in the fine arts. Applicants are asked to show evidence of achievement through publication or exhibition and, if applying in the arts, submit examples of work. Individuals in all branches of the sciences and mathematics, all areas of the humanities, social sciences, and the creative arts may apply.

The usual term of the fellowship is one year, but periods of a minimum of six months will be considered. Amounts of the grants vary according to the needs of the individuals and their projects. The same requirements and guidelines apply to a program of fellowships to citizens of all other countries and territories of the Western Hemisphere and of the Philippines.

A list of the members of the Committee of Selection and Educational Advisory Board (which rotates about every four years) is available in the foundation's annual report, as are the biographies of the recipients of grants for each year. Numerous authorities and experts in each field serve as consultants.

290
Guslander (A.B.)-Masonic Lodge Scholarship Fund

P.O. Box 67
Willits, CA 95490 (707) 459-2307
Contact: Secretary, Masonic Lodge

Limitations: Scholarships only to graduates of Willits High School, Willits, CA, in their junior or senior year of college or in graduate school.
Financial data: Year ended 8/31/85. Assets, $86,925 (M); Total giving, $4,500; Grants to individuals, 10 grants totaling $4,500, high $800, low $300.
Employer Identification Number: 237323314
Applications: Deadline May 1st; Initial approach by letter which should include education completed, where applicant is enrolled for ensuing year and references.

291★
Haas (Paul and Mary) Foundation

P.O. Box 2928
Corpus Christi, TX 78403 (512) 888-9301
Contact: Nancy Wise Somers, Director

Limitations: Undergraduate scholarships to needy college and vocational school students exclusively in the Corpus Christi, TX, area.
Financial data: Year ended 12/31/87. Assets, $1,140,366 (M); Total giving, $515,591; Grants to individuals, 70 grants totaling $57,361, high $800, low $111, average grant $750.
Employer Identification Number: 746031614
Applications: Deadline preferably three months prior to each semester; Applications accepted throughout the year; Initial approach should be made four months prior to each semester; Completion of written application required; Interviews required.
Publications: Annual report (including application guidelines), application guidelines, program information, 990-PF printed copy available upon request.
Program description:
The objectives of the **Student Scholarship Grant Program** are to promote the enrichment of the community of free men through education, to aid persons from financially limited backgrounds to become economically self-sufficient by acquiring employment skills, and to provide the Coastal Bend of Texas with men and women who have the knowledge and skills to contribute to the area's economic growth.

High school graudates and college undergraduates seeking college or vocational education but lacking the financial means to do so may apply. Candidates must have demonstrated above average academic or vocational motivation through high school grade point, standardized test scores, or in the opinion of counselors, will develop sufficiently to overcome existing grade deficiencies.

Awards are made on the basis of financial need and academic or vocational motivation and ability.

292★
Hachar (D.D.) Charitable Trust Fund

c/o Laredo National Bank
P.O. Box 59
Laredo, TX 78044 (512) 723-1151
Contact: Margie H. Weatherford, Administrator

Limitations: Scholarships and loans primarily to residents of Laredo and Webb County, TX, for higher education.
Financial data: Year ended 4/30/87. Assets, $7,164,959 (M); Expenditures, $673,258; Grants to individuals, 183 grants totaling $182,500, high $3,000, low $500; Loans to individuals, 31 loans totaling $56,500.
Employer Identification Number: 742093680
Applications: Deadlines last Friday in April and October; Initial approach by telephone or letter; Completion of formal application required; Interviews required.
Publications: Application guidelines, informational brochure, program information, annual report (including application guidelines).

293★
Hamilton Community Foundation, Inc.

P.O. Box 283
Aurora, NE 68818

Limitations: Scholarships for residents of Hamilton County, NE.
Financial data: Year ended 12/31/85. Assets, $332,551 (M); Total giving, $48,383; Grants to individuals, 24 grants totaling $7,000, each grant $350.
Employer Identification Number: 476038289
Publications: Annual report.

294
Hamilton (Esther) Alias Santa Claus Club Scholarship Fund

c/o Dollar Savings & Trust Company
P.O. Box 450
Youngstown, OH 44501 (216) 744-9000
Contact: Herbert H. Pridham, Sr., Vice-President, Dollar Savings & Trust Company

Limitations: Scholarships to graduating seniors in the top 25 percent of their class of all city, county, or parochial high schools in Mahoning County, OH, to attend Youngstown State University.
Financial data: Year ended 12/31/86. Assets, $75,728 (M); Total giving, $3,000; Grants to individuals, 2 grants totaling $3,000, each grant $1,500.
Employer Identification Number: 346575611
Applications: Deadline June of graduation year from

high school; Completion of formal application required; Interviews required; Applications available from high school principals.

295★
Hamman (George and Mary Josephine) Foundation
1000 Louisiana, Suite 820
Houston, TX 77002   (713) 658-8345
Contact: Thomas P. Stone, Operating Manager

Limitations: Undergraduate scholarships only to graduating high school seniors residing in the Houston, TX, area.
Financial data: Year ended 4/30/87. Assets, $23,938,228 (M); Total giving, $817,500; Grants to individuals, 97 grants totaling $168,750, high $2,500, low $1,250, general range $1,250-2,500, average grant $1,875.
Employer Identification Number: 746061447
Applications: Deadline March 15th; Initial approach before November by letter including name, address, and name of high school applicant is attending; Completion of formal application required; Interviews required.
Publications: Application guidelines, financial statement, program information.
Program description:
Scholarship recipients receive $10,000 for a four-year term, issued in semester increments.

296
Hancock (Sumner O.) Scholarship Fund
Casco, ME 04015   (207) 627-4354
Contact: Elizabeth Hancock, President

Limitations: Scholarships only to students of the Casco, ME, area.
Financial data: Year ended 12/31/85. Assets, $68,312 (M); Total giving, $4,400; Grants to individuals, 16 grants totaling $4,400, high $600, low $100, general range $100-300.
Employer Identification Number: 016028898
Applications: Deadline May 15th; Completion of formal application required.
Program description:
Scholarships are paid directly to colleges and universities for the benefit of deserving students.

297
Hansen (Dane G.) Foundation
P.O. Box 187
Logan, KS 67646   (913) 689-4832
Contact: Dane G. Bales, Vice-President

Limitations: Scholarships to graduates of high schools in central or northwest Kansas; postgraduate scholarships for theology, medical, and dental students

from other areas.
Financial data: Year ended 9/30/86. Assets, $25,523,638 (M); Total giving, $771,873; Grants to individuals, 104 grants totaling $154,000, high $3,500, low $250, general range $500-3,000.
Employer Identification Number: 486121156
Applications: Deadlines September and October; Initial approach by letter or telephone for information about eligibility requirements, application forms, and interviews.
Program description:
Scholarships are awarded to local students, primarily in Logan and Phillips County, KS, for a number of study programs. Local high school and junior college applicants may apply for grants to continue their education in colleges, universities, vocational, and technical schools. The program also grants postgraduate scholarships for medical, dental, and theological studies.

298★
Hardin (Phil) Foundation
c/o Citizens National Bank
P.O. Box 911
Meridian, MS 39302   (601) 483-4282
Contact: C. Thompson Wacaster, Vice-President, P.O. Box 3429, Meridian, MS 39301

Limitations: Limited student loans only to residents of Mississippi.
Financial data: Year ended 12/31/85. Assets, $17,975,444 (M); Expenditures, $847,157; Loans to individuals totaling $24,239.
Employer Identification Number: 646025706
Applications: Applications accepted throughout the year; Initial approach by letter or telephone; Completion of formal application required.

299★
Harding Foundation, The
Harding Foundation Building
P.O. Box 130 - Fifth and Hidalgo
Raymondville, TX 78580   (512) 689-2706
Contact: Glenn W. Harding, President

Limitations: Scholarships primarily to pre-seminary students residing in Texas after the student is enrolled in the seminary school.
Financial data: Year ended 12/31/86. Assets, $1,582,704 (M); Total giving, $47,147; Grants to individuals, 10 grants totaling $17,147, each grant $1,200.
Employer Identification Number: 746025883
Applications: Applications accepted throughout the year; Initial approach by letter.

300
Harless (James) Foundation, Incorporated
Drawer D
Gilbert, WV 25621   (304) 664-3227
Contact: Ruth Phipps, Secretary

Limitations: Scholarship loans only to residents of the Gilbert, WV, area.
Financial data: Year ended 12/31/86. Assets, $1,546,955 (M); Expenditures, $157,469; Loans to individuals, 7 loans totaling $4,425.
Employer Identification Number: 237093387
Applications: Applications accepted thoughout the year; Initial approach by letter; Completion of formal application required.

301
Harrison (Fred G.) Foundation
101 South Park Avenue
Herrin, IL 62948

Limitations: Scholarships primarily for seniors of Herrin High School, IL.
Financial data: Year ended 12/31/86. Assets, $1,812,349 (M); Total giving, $49,287; Grants to individuals, 4 grants totaling $2,000, each grant $500.
Employer Identification Number: 375608520

302
Harvey Foundation, Inc.
First Federal Building, Suite 507
1519 Ponce de Leon Avenue
Santurce, PR 00909

Limitations: Scholarships only to residents of Puerto Rico.
Financial data: Year ended 12/31/86. Assets, $1,464,901 (M); Total giving, $73,235; Grants to individuals, 5 grants totaling $13,035, high $3,000, low $2,000.
Employer Identification Number: 660271454

303
Hassel Foundation, The
1845 Walnut Street, Suite 1409
Philadelphia, PA 19103   (215) 561-6400
Contact: Herman H. Krekstein, Secretary

Limitations: Scholarships to graduating seniors of Reading Senior High School, Reading, PA, and Exeter Township Senior High School, Exeter Township, PA.
Financial data: Year ended 12/31/86. Assets, $3,973,224 (M); Total giving, $111,400; Grants to individuals, 8 grants totaling $13,000, high $2,500, low $1,000.
Employer Identification Number: 236251862
Applications: Applications accepted throughout the year; Applications available at office of high school principal.

Program description:
Two four-year college scholarships are awarded annually, one each to a student of the specified high school. Students are eligible to apply for the scholarship if they are in the top five percent of their class and have been accepted for enrollment as candidate for a degree at a college or university.

Recipients are chosen by a selection committee composed of the principal, vice-principal, guidance counselor head, the heads of two major education departments, and a foundation trustee. In making its selection the committee will consider the academic competence and achievements, leadership qualities, and diversity of interests, and activities of the eligible applicants.

The amount of the scholarship award will be paid directly to the educational institution on the recipient's behalf, and will be applied and used toward payment of tuition and related expenses. The amount of the award will be $2,500 for the first year, $1,500 for the second and third years, and $1,000 for the fourth year.

304★
Hatterscheidt Foundation, Inc., The
c/o First Bank-Aberdeen
320 South First Street
Aberdeen, SD 57401   (605) 225-9400
Contact: Markyn S. Hearnen, Trust Officer, First Bank-Aberdeen

Limitations: Scholarships for the first year of college to graduating high school seniors in the top 25 percent of the class in South Dakota and a 100-mile radius of Jamestown, North Dakota.
Financial data: Year ended 12/31/87. Assets $3,546,175 (M); Total giving, $158,400; Grants to individuals, 39 grants totaling $100,500.
Employer Identification Number: 466012543
Applications: Submit proposal preferably in February; Initial approach by letter; Completion of formal application required.

305
Hauss-Helms Foundation, Inc., The
People's National Bank Building
P.O. Box 25
Wapakoneta, OH 45895   (419) 738-4911
Contact: James E. Weger, President

Limitations: Scholarships to needy graduating high school students who are residents of Auglaize or Allen counties, OH, who wish to continue their education through college, university or technical school.
Financial data: Year ended 12/31/86. Assets, $5,517,129 (M); Total giving, $269,156; Grants to individuals, 262 grants totaling $269,156, high $4,000, low $97.
Employer Identification Number: 340975903
Applications: Deadline January 15th; Initial approach

by letter; Completion of formal application required;
Interviews granted upon request.
Publications: Program information, application
guidelines.
Program description:
Candidates must be of good moral character, in the
top half of their classes, unable to fund college on
their own, and recommended for the grant by the
principal, guidance counselor or faculty member in
their school.

306★
Hayes (Cecil M.) Scholarship Fund
c/o Marine Midland Bank
Rochester, NY 14639

Limitations: Scholarships to medical students attending
the University of Rochester Medical Center.
Financial data: Year ended 6/30/86. Assets, $364,980
(M); Total giving, $24,500; Grants to individuals
totaling $24,500.
Employer Identification Number: 166152521
Applications: Contact the Office of Financial Aid at
the University of Rochester Medical Center for
application information.

307
Heath Educational Fund, The
c/o First Florida Bank, N.A.
P.O. Box 11311
St. Petersburg, FL 33713   (813) 892-3746

Limitations: Scholarships only to male high school
graduates from schools within the southeastern U.S.
who wish to study for the ministry, missionary
activities, or social work.
Financial data: Year ended 9/30/86. Assets, $125,420
(M): Total giving, $11,970; Grants to individuals, 5
grants totaling $11,970, high $3,500, low $1,000.
Employer Identification Number: 596218458
Applications: Applications accepted throughout the
year; Initial approach by letter with brief background
of applicant, field of study, and reason for request.

308
Heed Ophthalmic Foundation
303 East Chicago Avenue
Chicago, IL 60670-0111   (312) 908-8673
Contact: David Shoch, M.D., Executive Secretary

Limitations: Fellowships to men and women of
exceptional ability who desire to further their
education in the field of diseases of the eye and
surgery, or to conduct research in ophthalmology.
Financial data: Year ended 10/31/86. Assets,
$3,183,692 (M); Total giving, $168,800; Grants to
individuals, 39 grants totaling $168,800, high $4,800,
low $1,600, average grant $10,000.
Employer Identification Number: 366012426

Applications: Deadline November 30th for fellowships
starting the following academic year; Completion of
formal application required.
Publications: Application guidelines, program
information.
Program description:
The applicant must be an American citizen, a graduate
of a medical school accredited by the A.M.A., and
must agree to pursue education or research in the U.S.
   Preference is given to candidates who have
completed the training requirements of the American
Board of Ophthalmology and who wish additional
training in a particular phase of the specialty. Special
consideration is also given to candidates who plan to
devote full- or part-time to teaching ophthalmology or
to conducting research in ophthalmology within a
medical school.
   The fellowship is in the amount of $800 per month
for up to six months of any one calendar year.

309★
Helvering (R.L. and Elsa) Trust
307 South 13th Street
Marysville, KS 66508   (913) 562-3437
Contact: Ira O. Shrock, Trustee

Limitations: Scholarships only to high school seniors
in Marshall County, KS.
Financial data: Year ended 3/31/87. Assets,
$1,484,452 (M); Total giving, $104,450; Grants to
individuals, 5 grants totaling $3,750, each grant $750.
Employer Identification Number: 480924200
Applications: Deadline May 1st; Completion of formal
application required.
Program description:
One four-year scholarship is awarded annually for
attendance at a Kansas college or university. Selection
criteria used by the trustee includes:
   1. The recipient must have been recommended
   by his/her high school principal
   2. The recipient must have a high scholastic
   average during his/her high school career
   3. The recipient must be deserving and show
   financial need
   4. The recipient's parents have a financial
   condition, such that they are reasonably unable to
   pay for their child's college education.

310
Hemenway (Charles R.) Scholarship Trust
c/o Hawaiian Trust Company, Ltd.
Box 3170
Honolulu, HI 96802

Limitations: Undergraduate scholarships to residents of
Hawaii attending the University of Hawaii who are
committed to Hawaii and its people.
Financial data: Year ended 11/30/86. Assets,
$2,065,376 (M); Total giving, $105,490; Grants to

individuals totaling $105,490.
Employer Identification Number: 996003089
Applications: Deadline April 1st; Applications
available from the Financial Aid Offices of the
following University of Hawaii campuses: Manoa
Campus, 2442 Campus Road, Honolulu, HI; Tel.:
(808) 961-9311, and Hilo Campus, Box 1357, Hilo,
HI; Tel.: (808) 961-9323; Completion of formal
application required; Interviews required.
Program description:
Selection of recipients, scholarship amounts, and
manner of paying the scholarships are determined
jointly by the trust scholarship committee and the
University of Hawaii. Eligible applicants are selected
upon the following criteria:
1. Financial need as determined from F.A.F.
2. Academic promise or performance at the
University of Hawaii
3. Evidence of good character and citizenship.

311
Heritage Fund of Bartholomew County, Inc.
P.O. Box 1547
Columbus, IN 47202   (812) 376-7772
Contact: Edward F. Sullivan, Executive Director

Limitations: Scholarships only to residents of
Bartholomew County, IN.
Financial data: Year ended 12/31/86. Assets,
$3,527,402 (M); Total giving, $106,889; Grants to
individuals totaling $6,061.
Employer Identification Number: 351343903
Applications: Initial approach by letter.
Publications: Annual report.

312
Hershey (Andrew J.) Memorial Scholarship
Fund
c/o York Bank & Trust Company
21 East Market Street
York, PA 17401   (717) 843-8651
Contact: Helen G. Markle

Limitations: Scholarships primarily to graduates of
Spring Grove, PA, area high schools. Second
preference to other York County high school
graduates.
Financial data: Year ended 9/30/86. Assets, $27,629
(M); Total giving, $3,000; Grants to individuals, 3
grants totaling $3,000, high $2,000, low $500.
Employer Identification Number: 236285862
Applications: Deadline April 1st; Completion of
formal application required.

313★
Hertz (Fannie and John) Foundation
P.O. Box 2230
Livermore, CA 94550-0130   (415) 449-0855
Contact: Dr. Wilson K. Talley, President

Limitations: Graduate fellowships for students in
engineering, applied science, the physical sciences
and all other fields of science at specified nationwide
institutions; also provides scholarships to high school
graduates from the San Francisco Bay area.
Financial data: Year ended 6/30/87. Assets,
$22,000,000 (M) (approximate); Total giving,
$2,700,000; Grants to individuals, 130 fellowships
totaling $2,700,000, average grant $23,000.
Employer Identification Number: 362411723
Applications: Submit application form in September or
October; Deadline November 1st; Completion of
formal application required; Interviews required.
Publications: Program information, informational
brochure (including application guidelines).
Program description:
Graduate Fellowships in Applied Physical Sciences are
awarded to worthy students of engineering and other
applied physical sciences whose education may be of
value to the defense of the U.S. Awards are made to
outstanding students who seem likely to have an
impact on scientific and technological advancement or
to become exemplars of teaching skills in the applied
sciences. Awards are made to enable such candidates
to complete an advanced degree at one of the
following selected universities: California Institute of
Technology, University of California, Carnegie-Mellon
University, University of Chicago, Cornell University,
Courant Institute (NY), Massachusetts Institute of
Technology, Princeton University, Rensselaer
Polytechnic Institute (NY), Rice University, University
of Rochester, Stanford University, University of Texas
at Austin, Vanderbilt University, University of
Wisconsin, University of Illinois, Yale University.

Fellowships are $15,000 per nine months plus
tuition and fees, up to $8,000, and are subject to
renewal for the same individuals. Renewals are
normally for a total fellowship tenure of three
academic years.

No professional programs or joint Ph.D. professional
degree programs are supported.

Approximately 25 scholarships are awarded each
year and are renewable for up to three years. A
cost-of-education allowance of up to $8,000 is
provided. In addition, a living stipend is awarded in
the amount of $15,000 per year based on a
nine-month study year.

314★
Hickman (Leona M.) Trust
U.S. Bank of Washington
P.O. Box 720, Trust Division
Seattle, WA 98111   (206) 344-3687
Contact: Jean V. Tennant, Trust Officer

Limitations: Student loans to male residents of King
County, WA, under age 26, for advanced education.
Financial data: Year ended 12/31/87. Assets, $792,552
(M); Loans to individuals, 15 loans totaling $37,000.
Employer Identification Number: 916022912
Applications: Applications accepted throughout the
year; Completion of formal application required;
Interviews are preferred.
Program description:
Applicants must be in school on a full-time basis as
defined by the institution they attend. Loans may be
extended for the duration of a program of study upon
reapplication by the recipient each year. The average
undergraduate loan is $2,000, and the average
graduate loan is $3,000.

315
Hiebler (Thomas and Jennie) Memorial
    Scholarship Fund Trust
c/o California First Bank
P.O. Box 109
San Diego, CA 92112
Contact: Scholarship Committee, Montrose High
School, Montrose, CO 81401 or Scholarship
Committee, Mancos High School, Mancos, CO 81320

Limitations: Scholarships to needy and deserving
graduates of the Mancos and Montrose high school
districts in Colorado who plan to attend colleges or
universities in the state of Colorado.
Financial data: Year ended 6/30/87. Assets, $212,561
(M); Total giving, $10,875; Grants to individuals, 10
grants totaling $10,875, high $1,500, low $775,
general range $850-1,500.
Employer Identification Number: 956111386
Applications: Submit application prior to high school
graduation.
Program description:
The scholarship committees of the school districts
have been provided with the qualifications set forth in
the Hieblers' will. Each year, based on these
qualifications, the committees recommend graduating
seniors. A trust committee then acts upon their
recommendations.

316
High (Charles F.) Foundation
1520 Melody Lane
Bucyrus, OH 44820   (419) 562-2074
Contact: John R. Clime, Secretary-Treasurer

Limitations: Scholarships only to male residents of
Ohio to attend Ohio State University.
Financial data: Year ended 12/31/86. Assets,
$2,144,334 (M); Total giving, $66,409; Grants to
individuals totaling $66,409.
Employer Identification Number: 346527860
Applications: Deadline June 1st; Initial approach by
letter; Completion of formal application required.

317
Hirsch (Harold) Scholarship Fund
c/o Kilpatrick & Cody
100 Peachtree Street, Suite 3100
Atlanta, GA 30043   (404) 572-6500
Contact: Anne J. Rivers

Limitations: Scholarships to local individuals for
higher and secondary education. All funds available
have been committed for some time to come.
Financial data: Year ended 6/30/86. Assets,
$1,590,315 (M); Total giving, $48,810; Grants to
individuals, 4 grants totaling $11,060.
Employer Identification Number: 586036125
Applications: Deadline at least six months prior to the
date of the beginning of the period for which
assistance is requested; Initial approach by letter.

318
Historical Research Foundation
c/o Arthur Anderson
700 South Fourth Street
Harrison, NJ 07029

Limitations: Grants for scholarly research and studies
in social sciences.
Financial data: Year ended 12/31/85. Assets, $170,325
(M); Total giving, $18,500; Grants to individuals, 4
grants totaling $13,500, high $5,000, low $2,000.
Employer Identification Number: 136059836

319
Hobbs Foundation
131 South Barstow Street, Room 309
Eau Claire, WI 54701   (715) 832-6645
Contact: Francis J. Wilcox, Trustee

Limitations: Scholarships to residents of the Eau
Claire, WI, area. Scholarship program for special
purposes only, and not presently open to any new
applicants.
Financial data: Year ended 12/31/85. Assets,
$1,450,230 (M); Total giving, $937,370; Grants to
individuals, 12 grants totaling $24,000.

Employer Identification Number: 396068746
Applications: New applications not invited.

320
Hodges (Mary E.) Fund
2115 Broad Street
Cranston, RI 02905 (401) 467-2970
Contact: Arthur Medley, Secretary

Limitations: Student aid for individuals who have a masonic affiliation or who have been residents of Rhode Island for five years or more.
Financial data: Year ended 10/31/86. Assets, $2,666,513 (M); Total giving, $121,324; Grants to individuals totaling $26,200.
Employer Identification Number: 056049444
Applications: Deadline June 1st.

321
Hoffman (James M.) Scholarship Trust
c/o SouthTrust Bank of Calhoun County, N.A.
P.O. Box 1000
Anniston, AL 36202 (205) 238-1000

Limitations: Scholarships only to high school or preparatory school graduates from Calhoun County, AL.
Financial data: Year ended 9/30/85. Assets, $167,027 (M); Total giving, $16,000; Grants to individuals, 32 grants totaling $16,000, each grant $500.
Employer Identification Number: 636077959
Applications: Deadline March; Completion of formal application required. **Applications from individuals residing outside of stated geographic restriction not accepted.**

322★
Hope (Blanche and Thomas) Memorial Fund
c/o Third National Bank
P.O. Box 1270
Ashland, KY 41105

Limitations: Scholarships limited to students graduating from high schools in Boyd and Greenup counties, KY, and Lawrence County, OH.
Financial data: Year ended 12/31/87. Assets, $1,829,000 (M); Total giving, $120,000; Grants to individuals, 100 grants totaling $120,000, high $2,900, low $90.
Employer Identification Number: 616067105
Applications: Deadline March 1st; Completion of formal application required; Interviews required.
Program description:
Scholarship grants are based primarily on need, although character, grades, and inclination are also important.

323★
Hopedale Foundation, The
43 Hope Street
Hopedale, MA 01747 (617) 473-0820
Contact: Thad R. Jackson, Treasurer

Limitations: Student loans primarily for local high school graduates.
Financial data: Year ended 10/31/87. Assets, $3,651,052 (M); Expenditures, $203,052; Loans to individuals, 51 loans totaling $59,350.
Employer Identification Number: 046044779
Applications: Initial approach by letter.

324
HOR Foundation
Route 4, Box 88
Richmond, TX 77469 (713) 342-7150
Contact: Joseph A. Imparato, Director

Limitations: Direct research grants only to Ph.D.'s and physicians who have five or fewer years of active experience in medical research and who are members of the teaching or research faculties or staffs of, or otherwise affiliated with, publicly supported medical schools or research hospitals.
Financial data: Year ended 11/30/86. Assets, $139,548 (M); Total giving, $129,500; Grants to individuals, 2 grants totaling $129,500, high $70,000, low $59,500.
Employer Identification Number: 742171639
Applications: Deadline March 31st; Initial approach by proposal, which may be submitted from September to March; Completion of formal application required; Notification on or about May 15th.
Program description:
Grants are for one year, renewable annually as long as recipient appears to be making reasonable progress toward his or her stated objective. Research is expected to culminate in the issuance and publication of a research report, and the purpose of grants will be the advancement of medical science for the benefit of the general public.

325
Horbach Fund, The
c/o National Community Bank of New Jersey
113 West Essex Street
Maywood, NJ 07607

Limitations: Scholarships to needy, gifted, young people under the age of 20, residing in Connecticut, Massachusetts, New Jersey, New York, or Rhode Island.
Financial data: Year ended 12/31/85. Assets, $83,117 (M); Total giving, $7,500; Grants to individuals amount not specified.
Employer Identification Number: 237171692
Applications: Deadline August 1st.

Program description:
Grants are awarded to gifted young people who would otherwise be unable to develop their talents in a variety of fields including arts, sports, journalism, agriculture, environmental issues, and the professions.

326
Horne (Dick) Foundation
P.O. Box 306
Orangeburg, SC 29116   (803) 534-2096
Contact: Andrew Berry, Manager, 360 Russell Street, S.E., Orangeburg, SC 29115; Lenora R. Player, 595 Calhoun Drive, Orangeburg, SC; or John F. Shuler, 250 Keitt Street, N.E., Orangeburg, SC

Limitations: Scholarships only to residents of the trading area served by Horne Motors of Orangeburg, SC.
Financial data: Year ended 12/31/86. Assets, $1,659,952 (M); Total giving, $72,086; Grants to individuals, 133 grants totaling $64,275; Subtotal for scholarships, 131 grants totaling $63,605, high $1,206, low $63, general range $200-500.
Employer Identification Number: 237015996
Applications: Applications accepted throughout the year; Initial approach by letter requesting application, including information relating to income and resources available, educational background, and purpose for which grant is sought; Completion of formal application and interviews required.
Program description:
Scholarships are awarded on the basis of need, character or ability.
  In 1986, a number of scholarships were awarded for studies leading towards undergraduate degrees, technical education, and nursing education.

327
Hosler (Dr. R.S.) Memorial Educational Fund
50 Bortz Street
P.O. Box 5
Ashville, OH 43103
Contact: Vaundell White, Trustee, 154 East Main Street, Ashville, OH 43103

Limitations: Scholarships to high school graduates of Teays Valley and Amanda Clearcreek, OH, school systems.
Financial data: Year ended 12/31/86. Assets, $3,306,962 (M); Total giving, $189,252; Grants to individuals, 5 grants totaling $44,252, high $22,112, low $2,500.
Employer Identification Number: 311073939
Applications: Applications accepted throughout the year; Completion of formal application required.

328★
House (Susan Cook) Educational Trust
Marine Bank of Springfield
One East Old Capital Plaza
Springfield, IL 62701   (217) 525-9600

Limitations: Scholarships only to residents of Sangamon County, IL.
Financial data: Year ended 11/30/86. Assets, $1,754,962 (M); Total giving, $123,500; Grants to individuals, 19 grants totaling $13,500, high $1,000, low $500, general range $500-750.
Employer Identification Number: 376087675
Applications: Applications accepted throughout the year; Initial approach by letter.

329
Howard Memorial Fund
500 East 62nd Street
New York, NY 10021
Contact: Gayle F. Robinson, Chairman, Scholarship Committee

Limitations: Scholarships only to residents of the greater metropolitan New York area who are at least 14 years of age.
Financial data: Year ended 6/30/86. Assets, $382,459 (M); Total giving, $15,594; Grants to individuals, 41 grants totaling $15,375, high $500, low $150, general range $300-450.
Employer Identification Number: 136161770
Applications: Deadline May 30th; Completion of formal application required.
Publications: Program information.
Program description:
Scholarships are awarded to disadvantaged students whose academic averages may not qualify them for other scholarships, but who have the potential to pursue a bona fide course of study, either academic or vocational, at a high school, college, or professional institution. Applicants must be accepted by a school of their choice and demonstrate financial need. The grants may be used for tuition or living expenses.

330
Howell (Robert L.) Foundation
P.O. Box 1071
Greenwood, MS 38930
Contact: R.C. Wingate, Trustee

Limitations: Educational support through student loans.
Financial data: Year ended 12/31/86. Assets, $2,532,875 (M); Expenditures, $308,722; Loans to individuals, 72 loans totaling $97,623, high $3,000, low $500, average loan $1,000.
Employer Identification Number: 646024550
Applications: Applications accepted throughout the year; Completion of formal application required.

331
Hoyt Foundation, The
c/o First National Bank Building
P.O. Box 1488
New Castle, PA 16103   (412) 652-5511
Contact: Dorothy A. Patton

Limitations: Scholarships primarily to individuals in Lawrence County, PA.
Financial data: Year ended 10/31/86. Assets, $8,146,319 (M); Total giving, $481,597; Grants to individuals, 122 grants totaling $115,484, high $4,400, low $100.
Employer Identification Number: 256064468
Applications: Deadlines July 15th and December 15th.
Program description:
Scholarships are awarded based on need. Recipients are selected by an independent committee.

332
Huffman Cornwell Foundation
c/o Wachovia Bank & Trust Co.
P.O. Box 3099
Winston-Salem, NC 27150
Contact: Graham S. DeVane, Secretary, P.O. Box 98, Morgantown, NC 28655; Tel.: (919) 437-4874

Limitations: Scholarships only to high school students of Burke County, NC.
Financial data: Year ended 12/31/86. Assets, $1,295,816 (M); Total giving, $54,990; Grants to individuals, 14 grants totaling $10,000, high $1,000, low $500.
Employer Identification Number: 566065286
Applications: Applications accepted throughout the year; Initial approach by letter; Completion of formal application required.

333
Hugg (Leola W. and Charles H.) Trust
c/o Carroll Sunseri, First City National Bank
P.O. Box 809
Houston, TX 77001

Limitations: Scholarships for students from Williamson County to attend colleges and universities in Texas.
Financial data: Year ended 12/31/86. Assets, $2,098,930 (M); Total giving, $107,625; Grants to individuals totaling $107,625.
Employer Identification Number: 741907673
Applications: Deadline May 1st; Application forms and guidelines are available upon request from participating high schools, or from the director of the Texas Baptist Children's Home in Round Rock, TX, or the Office of Student Financial Aid at Southwestern University in Georgetown, TX; Completion of formal application required.
Publications: Application guidelines.

334
Hughes (James E.) Scholarship Fund
c/o Indiana National Bank
1 Indiana Square, No. 733
Indianapolis, IN 46266
Contact: Financial aid offices of educational institutions specified below.

Limitations: Scholarships to residents of Marian County, IN, attending Butler University, University of Indianapolis, or Marian College in Indianapolis, IN.
Financial data: Year ended 5/31/87. Assets, $490,051 (M); Total giving, $29,750; Grants to individuals totaling $29,750.
Employer Identification Number: 356009013
Applications: Contact schools for current application deadlines; Applications are made through the scholarship office of each school.
Program description:
Applicants must be in the upper one-half of their class. Scholarships are awarded on the basis of financial need; payments are made directly to the educational institution on behalf of individual recipient.

335
Humane Society of the Commonwealth of Massachusetts
177 Milk Street
Boston, MA 02109

Limitations: Fellowships primarily to residents of MA for medical education and research.
Financial data: Year ended 3/31/86. Assets, $2,073,184 (M); Total giving, $77,250; Grants to individuals, 29 grants totaling $8,750, high $750, low $100.
Employer Identification Number: 042104291
Applications: Applications accepted throughout the year.

336★
Humane Studies Foundation
P.O. Box 2256
Wichita, KS 67201
Contact: Walter Grinder, President, c/o George Mason University, 4400 University Drive, Fairfax, VA 22030; Tel.: (703) 323-1055

Limitations: Research grants and fellowships in any area of knowledge, with emphasis on the social sciences.
Financial data: Year ended 12/31/87. Assets, $1,099,454 (M); Total giving, $24,400; Grants to individuals, 15 grants totaling $24,400, high $11,667, low $500, general range $2,000-2,500, average grant $2,000.
Employer Identification Number: 480891418
Applications: Applications accepted throughout the year; Initial approach by proposal; See program

description below for detailed application information.
Program description:
The foundation awards research grants to qualified
scholars to research and prepare reports, papers, or
other products of research on topics which require
scholarly research and study in any area of
knowledge. The social sciences is of primary interest
to the foundation.

Individual applicants should submit a brief resume
of academic qualifications, and an outline as to:

1. Topic
2. Procedures and research methods which such
   individual proposes to follow
3. The anticipated timetable which such
   individual contemplates will be involved to
   complete the project and the various stages
   thereof
5. The amount of grant required to finance the
   project.

In 1987, the foundation conducted two week-long
conferences and seminars to promote further study
and increase understanding in the related subject areas
of free-market economics and philosophy. In addition
to the conferences, a summer resident research and
writing fellowship program was conducted for nine
weeks, in which twelve fellows participated. Three
additional research fellowships were awarded in 1987.

337★
Humbolt Area Foundation, The
P.O. Box 632
Eureka, CA 95502   (707) 442-7993
Contact: Ellen A. Dusick, Executive Director

Limitations: Scholarships primarily to residents of
Humboldt County, CA.
Financial data: Year ended 12/31/87. Assets,
$8,400,000 (M); Total giving, $460,000; Grants to
individuals, 12 grants totaling $9,300.
Employer Identification Number: 237310660
Applications: Completion of formal application
required.
Publications: Annual report.
Program description:
The foundation sponsors various funds that were
established specifically to provide scholarships for
individuals. The funds are the following:

The Bancroft Scholarship Fund - available to local
students majoring in business administration or music
at Humboldt State University.

The Ralph Bryant Scholarship Fund - established for
Eureka High School graduates preparing for teaching
careers who plan to attend College of the Redwoods
or Humboldt State University.

The Dr. Sam Burke Historical Award Fund -
provides awards to local high school students for
historical essays.

The Gust Dalianes Memorial Scholarship Fund -
provides scholarships for students of Greek or
Greek-American heritage attending Humboldt State

University or College of the Redwooods to pursue an
education in the field of business.

The Hun Kwan Goh Memorial Scholarship Fund
provides a $1,000 scholarship for a Humboldt County
high school graduate of Asian or part-Asian descent
for study at an accredited four-year college or
university.

An annual $1,000 fellowship to a Humboldt State
University student for postgraduate study is provided
for through the Donald Morris Hegy Memorial
Scholarship Fund.

The Humboldt-Del Norte Life Underwriters
Scholarship Fund was established to provide
scholarships to students planning to enter the
insurance field.

Annual scholarships to graduates of Hoopa Valley
High School are provided through the Kathryn E.
Jackson Memorial Scholarship Fund.

An annual $1,000 two-year scholarship is awarded
to Fortuna/Ferdale school district students after their
graduation from College of the Redwoods to continue
their education through the James and Rebecca
Jensen-Loleta IOOF Scholarships Fund.

The Charlotte Niskey Scholarship Fund provides
piano scholarships to young children.

The Steven Clark Smith Memorial Fund provides a
yearly scholarship to a student of junior standing at St.
Bernard High School.

The Bud H. Wheat Scholarship Fund provides for an
annual scholarship to a graduate of St. Bernard High
School.

Scholarships to music majors at College of the
Redwoods are made available through the Catherine
Wilson-Lewis Memorial Fund.

The O.H. Bass Memorial Fund provides scholarships
for Eureka High School graduates attending College of
the Redwoods.

The Ralph E. Bumpus Memorial Scholarship Fund
furnishes scholarships for Eureka High School
graduates attending College of the Redwoods studying
automotive technology.

The Alice Nelson Franks Scholarship Fund provides
an annual scholarship to a Humboldt County high
school graduate to attend any California college or
university. Each recipient must have at least one
parent or grandparent who graduated from a
Humboldt County high school.

The Arthur Hilfiker Scholarship Fund benefits Utah
State University geo-technical engineering graduate
students.

Nursing scholarships are provided for through the
John L. Ledgerwood Memorial Fund.

The Col. Mathew Santino Memorial Scholarship
Fund is a general scholarship fund.

338
Hurley (Ed E. and Gladys) Foundation
c/o The First National Bank of Shreveport
P.O. Box 2116
Shreveport, LA 71154   (318) 226-2110

Limitations: Scholarships to students attending Scarritt College for Christian Workers, TN; educational loans to residents of Arkansas, Louisiana, and Texas to attend the institution of their choice.
Financial data: Year ended 12/31/86. Assets, $2,605,097 (M); Expenditures, $69,012; Grants to individuals totaling $25,495; Loans to individuals totaling $$85,733.
Employer Identification Number: 726018854
Applications: Deadline May 31st; Completion of formal application required.

339
Hurley (Ed E. and Gladys) Foundation
c/o InterFirst Bank Dallas
P.O. Box 83776
Dallas, TX 45283
Contact: Alice Gayle

Limitations: Scholarships to theological students who are residents of Arkansas, Louisiana, and Texas to attend the institution of their choice.
Financial data: Year ended 8/31/86. Assets, $1,371,754 (M); Total giving, $63,485; Grants to individuals totaling $57,125.
Employer Identification Number: 756006961
Applications: Deadline April 15th; Initial approach by letter; Completion of formal application required.

340
Ilgenfritz (May H.) Testamentary Trust
108 West Pacific
Sedalia, MO 65301   (816) 826-3310
Contact: John Pelham, Trustee

Limitations: Scholarships only to residents of the Sedalia, MO, area.
Financial data: Year ended 12/31/86. Assets, $2,219,596 (M); Total giving, $73,175; Grants to individuals, 63 grants totaling $43,175, high $1,300, low $300.
Employer Identification Number: 440663403
Applications: Applications accepted throughout the year; Completion of formal application required.

341
Ingram (Joe) Trust
c/o Centerre Bank of Kansas City
1130 Walnut, P.O. Box 419666
Kansas City, MO 64141
Contact: C. E. Griswold, Joe W. Ingram Trust "B" Committee, 111 West Third Steet,, Salisbury, MO

65281, Tel.: (816) 388-5555.

Limitations: Student loans to individuals in the Chariton County, MO, area, and awards to valedictorians of graduating classes of Chariton County high schools.
Financial data: Year ended 12/31/86. Assets, $7,121,087 (M); Expenditures, $409,794; Grants to individuals, 4 grants totaling $4,000 for valedictorian awards, each grant $1,000; Loans to individuals totaling $302,484.
Employer Identification Number: 446006475
Applications: Deadlines for loan applications March 1st to July 1st for fall term, August 1st to December 1st for spring term, and January 1st to April 1st for summer term; Initial approach by letter; Completion of formal loan application required.

342
Institute for Aegean Prehistory
c/o The Millburn Corporation
1211 Avenue of the Americas
New York, NY 10036
Contact: Malcolm H. Wiener

Limitations: Research grants to study Aegean prehistory with the expectation of research publication under the direct supervision and control of the institute.
Financial data: Year ended 6/30/86. Assets, $4,115,586 (M); Total giving, $192,189; Grants to individuals, 24 grants totaling $70,009, high $17,500, low $100.
Employer Identification Number: 133137391
Applications: Applications accepted throughout the year; Initial approach by letter including resume, project description and budget, and references.

343★
Institute of Current World Affairs, Inc.
(Also known as Crane-Rogers Foundation, The)
Four West Wheelock Street
Hanover, NH 03755   (603) 643-5548
Contact: Peter Bird Martin, Executive Director

Limitations: Fellowships to persons 35 years or younger (preferably without children) for minimum two-year fellowships outside the U.S.
Financial data: Year ended 2/28/87. Assets, $1,776,056 (M); Total giving, $154,271; Grants to individuals, 12 grants totaling $149,271, high $46,009, low $168.
Employer Identification Number: 131621044
Applications: Applications accepted throughout the year; Initial approach by letter; Write for brochure listing current areas of interest.
Publications: Application guidelines, informational brochure.

Program description:
The purpose of the foundation is to identify areas or issues of the world in need of in-depth understanding, and then to select young persons of outstanding character to study and write about those areas or issues for fellowship periods ranging from two to four years.

Fellowships have been given--normally one or two a year--to men and women of varied academic and professional backgrounds. In keeping with its generalist and interdisciplinary approach, the institute's fellowships are not awarded to support work toward academic degrees, nor to underwrite specific studies or programs of research as such.

Full support, including living and travel expenses, is provided. In return, Fellows are required to write periodic reports to the Executive Director, which are circulated to persons in education, business, government, and the professions who are interested in the subject of the Fellow's inquiry.

The foundation currently recognizes four major Fellowship areas: Relations between East and West Europe; Hungary; Canada; and Mexico.

Applicants are invited to write to the Executive Director, explaining briefly the personal background and professional experience that would qualify them for the fellowship areas under consideration. If the candidates wish to have material returned, they should enclose a stamped, self-addressed envelope.

344
Irwin (Agnes and Sophie Dallas) Memorial Fund
Provident National Bank
1632 Chestnut Street
Philadelphia, PA 19103   (215) 585-5695
Contact: Ms. Kafes

Limitations: Grants to teachers in private girls' schools who have earned the right to retire and to provide opportunities for travel, study, and research.
Financial data: Year ended 12/31/86. Assets, $598,030 (M); Total giving $25,225; Grants to individuals, 6 grants totaling $16,850, high $4,200, low $750.
Employer Identification Number: 236207350
Applications: Applications accepted throughout the year; Applications should be submitted in written form.

345
Jackson (Corwill and Margie) Foundation
c/o Detroit Bank and Trust Company
Comerica Bank - Detroit
Detroit, MI 48275

Limitations: Scholarships only to first year university students from Ludington, MI.
Financial data: Year ended 12/31/86. Assets, $471,501 (M); Total giving $25,000; Grants to individuals, 36 grants totaling $25,000, high $5,250, low $250.

Employer Identification Number: 386064502

346★
Jackson (Maria C.)-General George A. White Student Aid Fund
c/o U.S. National Bank of Oregon, Trust Group
P.O. Box 3168
Portland, OR 97208   (503) 275-4456

Limitations: Scholarships and student loans only to U.S. Armed Forces veterans or children of veterans who are high school graduates or long time residents of Oregon and are studying at institutions of higher learning in Oregon.
Financial data: Year ended 6/30/87. Assets, $617,234 (M); Expenditures, $35,442; Grants to individuals totaling $19,500; Loans to individuals totaling $2,363.
Employer Identification Number: 936020316
Applications: Initial approach by letter; Completion of formal application required; Interviews required for scholarship finalists.
Publications: Program information.
Program description:
All loans and scholarships must be approved by a committee of three persons who are residents of Oregon and appointed by the foundation trustee.

Both scholastic ability and financial need of the applicant will be taken into consideration. Scholarship applicants who are unsuccessful may apply for loans.

Generally, $750 is the maximum loan amount awarded to any one applicant for each school year, although successive loans up to this amount may be made available during a full college course. Payments will be scheduled to begin three months following graduation. The interest rate is eight percent and begins to accrue the day the promissory note is drawn.

The repayment terms for a typical loan obtained at the start of the first year of a four-year academic program are as follows:
- Amount financed: $750
- Schedule of payments: 22 payments consisting of 21 consecutive monthly payments of $50 plus one final monthly payment of $5.74
- Total of payments: $1,055.74.

347
Janesville Foundation, Inc.
121 North Parker Drive
P.O. Box 1492
Janesville, WI 53547   (608) 752-1032
Contact: Alan W. Dunwiddie, Jr., Executive Director

Limitations: Scholarships limited to Janesville, WI, high school graduates.
Financial data: Year ended 12/31/86. Assets, $7,877,697 (M); Total giving, $360,190; Grants to individuals, 34 grants totaling $33,925.
Employer Identification Number: 396034645
Applications: Deadline May 1st; Completion of formal

application required; Applications obtained from principals of Janesville high schools.
Publications: Program information, application guidelines.
Program description:
Scholarships are based on scholastic rank in the graduating class and recommendation by the principal. Written application is made through the principal of each high school. Four scholarships of $6,000 are given each year, payable in four annual installments of $1,500.

Eight scholarships of $750 are paid in single playments as are three or four scholarships of $150-500. All payments are made upon presentation of evidence of satisfactory completion of the first semester's work at an accredited higher educational institution.

348
Jaunich (Clem) Education Trust
5353 Gamble Drive, Suite 110
Minneapolis, MN 55416   (612) 546-1555
Contact: Joseph L. Abrahamson, Trustee

Limitations: Scholarships only to students who have attended public or parochial schools in, or reside within seven miles of, Delano, MN, and are attending accredited medical, pre-medical, seminary, or pre-seminary schools.
Financial data: Year ended 6/30/87. Assets, $108,529 (M); Total giving, $5,000; Grants to individuals, 4 grants totaling $5,000, high $2,000, low $750.
Employer Identification Number: 416118376
Applications: Deadline August 1st; Initial approach by letter with statement of residence and scholastic eligibility, estimate of current year's expenses, schedule of funds available to meet year's needs, statement of amount of aid requested, and copy of prior years' transcripts.
Publications: Annual report.

349
Jay (George S. & Grace A.) Memorial Trust
c/o Pauline Morton
612 1/2 Sheridan Avenue
Shenandoah, IA 51601   (712) 246-3399
Contact: Pauline Morton

Limitations: Student loans only to graduates of Shenandoah, Essex, and Farragut, IA, high schools for use at an accredited college, university or trade school.
Financial data: Year ended 3/31/87. Assets, $1,421,781 (M); Expenditures, $159,356; Loans to individuals, 106 loans totaling $108,686, high $1,350, low $350.
Employer Identification Number: 426061515
Applications: Deadline May 31st; Contact foundation for application information; Telephone inquiries

accepted on Tuesdays only during regular business hours; Completion of formal application required.
Program description:
Loans to individual students shall not exceed the amount of $600 per semester or $400 per quarter. Loans for summer school session are made in amounts not to exceed $350. Loans will be repayable bearing an interest rate of three percent.

350★
Jeffers (Michael) Memorial Foundation
c/o Second National Bank of Saginaw
101 North Washington Avenue
Saginaw, MI 48607   (517) 776-7353
Contact: Marcia Sieggreen, Student Loan Administrator

Limitations: Educational loans only for residents of Saginaw County, MI.
Financial data: Year ended 12/31/86. Assets, $3,204,616 (M); Expenditures, $283,496; Loans to individuals totaling $247,065, general range $1,000-2,000.
Employer Identification Number: 237059762
Applications: Deadlines June 1st for new applications and renewals; Completion of formal application required.
Program description:
Applicants for student loans must 1) have a cumulative grade point average of 2.00 or better; 2) show financial need, and 3) be between 15 and 30 years old.

351
Jehovah Jireh, Inc.
P.O. Box 795
Clifton Park, NY 12065   (518) 383-0782
Contact: Larry Deason, Director

Limitations: Scholarships to theological students.
Financial data: Year ended 3/31/86. Assets, $664,400 (M); Total giving, $95,516; Grants to individuals, 9 grants totaling $13,976, high $6,216, low $200.
Employer Identification Number: 222239206
Applications: Applications accepted throughout the year.

352
Jenkins (Ruth) Scholarship Fund
c/o Wells Fargo Bank, N.A.
233 North Fair Oaks
Pasadena, CA 91103   (619) 230-5871
Contact: Doris Towne, Wells Fargo Bank, N.A., San Diego, CA

Limitations: Scholarships to black students from the San Diego, CA, area.
Financial data: Year ended 2/28/87. Assets, $68,294 (M); Total giving, $4,550, Grants to individuals, 8

grants totaling $4,550, high $1,550, low $400.
Employer Identification Number: 956154849
Applications: Deadline May 31st; Initial approach by
letter; Completion of formal application required;
Interviews required.
Program description:
Scholarship awards are made to the educational
institution on behalf of the individual recipients.

353★
Jenkins Student Loan Fund
c/o U.S. Bank of Oregon - Trust Group
321 S.W. Sixth Avenue, P.O. Box 3168
Portland, OR 97208   (503) 275-4456

Limitations: Student loans only to Oregon residents for
enrolled college and university students with a
cumulative grade point average of 3.0 or better.
Financial data: Year ended 6/30/87. Assets,
$1,288,740 (M); Expenditures, $172,018; Loans to
individuals totaling $138,120.
Employer Identification Number: 936020672
Applications: Applications accepted from February
15th to May 1st for ensuing academic year; Initial
approach by letter; Completion of formal application
required; Applications must be supplemented by two
letters of personal reference and a transcript of grades.
Publications: Program information, application
guidelines.
Program description:
Student loans are available to high school graduates
who have shown a desire and ability to help educate
themselves.

354★
Jewish Foundation for Education of Women
330 West 58th Street, Suite 5J
New York, NY 10019   (212) 265-2565
Contact: Florence Wallach, Executive Director

Limitations: Scholarships and loans to women who
are legal residents of the greater New York City
metropolitan area (a 50-mile radius which includes
Long Island and New Jersey but not Connecticut).
Financial data: Year ended 6/30/86. Assets,
$14,312,200 (M); Total giving, $644,140; Grants to
individuals, 515 grants totaling $644,140, high
$3,300, low $250, general range $500-2,000,; Loans
to individuals, 12 loans totaling $22,500.
Employer Identification Number: 131860415
Applications: Deadline January 31st; Submit proposal
preferably between October and January; Initial
approach by letter; Completion of formal application
required; Interviews required.
Publications: Application guidelines, program
information.
Program description:
Financial aid is given in the form of undergraduate
and graduate scholarships and interest-free loans to

females on a non-sectarian basis. In selected cases, aid
is given for vocational and professional studies (i.e.,
medicine). Scholarships and loans are awarded for one
year and are renewable subject to academic
performance and continuing financial need.

355
Johnson (Barbara Piasecka) Foundation
c/o Shearman and Sterling, Citicorp Center
153 East 53rd Street
New York, NY 10022

Limitations: Grants to defray expenses of scientific or
artistic endeavors, including costs of equipment,
supplies, tuition, basic living expenses, and related
costs.
Financial data: Year ended 12/31/85. Assets, $1,699
(M); Total giving, $74,150; Grants to individuals, 1
grant totaling $7,150.
Employer Identification Number: 510201795
Applications: Applications accepted throughout the
year; Completion of formal application required.

356
Johnson (Dexter G.) Educational and
Benevolent Trust
900 First City Place
Oklahoma City, OK 73102
Contact: Phil E. Daugherty, Trustee

Limitations: Educational loans limited to residents of
Oklahoma.
Financial data: Year ended 12/31/86. Assets,
$5,170,433 (M); Total giving $285,575; Loans to
individuals, 20 loans totaling $94,600, high $11,200,
low $500, average loan $5,000.
Employer Identification Number: 237389204
Applications: Applications accepted throughout the
year; Completion of formal application required,
including financial information, family history,
physical condition, age, education goals, and other
data necessary to show need.
Program description:
Loans are made to deserving students who do not
possess and cannot obtain funds elsewhere to
complete their education in: Oklahoma high schools,
Oklahoma A and M College, Oklahoma City
University, or the University of Oklahoma. Preference
is given to:
  ● Physically handicapped students
  ● Students who, by a misfortune or calamity,
  cannot complete their education.

357★
Johnson (The S.S.) Foundation
P.O. Box 356
Redmond, OR 97756 (503) 548-8104
Contact: Elizabeth Hill Johnson, President

Limitations: Non-recurring emergency grants and loans to students primarily residing in Oregon and northern California.
Financial data: Year ended 5/31/86. Assets, $3,414,252 (M); Total giving, $104,434; Grants to individuals, 13 grants totaling $7,383; Loans to individuals, 1 loan totaling $500.
Employer Identification Number: 946062478
Applications: Applications accepted throughout the year; Initial approach by letter; Completion of formal application required for scholarships.
Publications: Program information.
Program description:
Grants are made jointly to the individual and to the institution or agency involved. Grants and loans are restricted to students currently in their junior, senior, or graduate years of college or an accredited institution.

358
Jones (Clinton O. & Lura Curtis) Memorial Trust
184 North Street
Pittsfield, MA 01201
Contact: F. M. Meyers, Trustee

Limitations: Scholarships only.
Financial data: Year ended 12/31/84. Assets, $1,069,257 (M); Total giving, $71,650; Grants to individuals, 57 grants totaling $71,650, high $8,050, low $250.
Employer Identification Number: 046173271
Applications: Deadline May 30th; Initial approach by letter with school transcripts.

359★
Jones (The Harvey and Bernice) Foundation
P.O. Box 233
Springdale, AR 72765 (501) 756-0611
Contact: Bernice Jones, Co-Chairman

Limitations: Scholarships to needy students whose principal place of resdience is Springdale, AR, pursuing further education in the fields of health care, including medicine and nursing, and religion.
Financial data: Year ended 11/30/87. Assets, $7,445,353 (M); Total giving, $1,286,820; Grants to individuals, 36 grants totaling $24,850, high $1,200, low $400, general range $400-800.
Employer Identification Number: 716057141
Applications: Applications accepted throughout the year; Initial approach by letter; Completion of formal application required.

360
Jones (Walter S. and Evan C.) Foundation
527 Commercial Street, Room 515
Emporia, KS 66801 (316) 342-1714
Contact: Dorothy E. Melander, General Manager

Limitations: Scholarships to persons who have been continuous residents of Lyon, Coffey or Osage counties, KS, for at least one year, and who are under the age of 21.
Financial data: Year ended 3/31/87. Assets, $3,779 (M); Total giving, $705,174; Grants to individuals, 1,997 grants totaling $705,174; Subtotal for scholarships, 297 grants totaling $144,154, high $1,500, low $75, general range $150-568.
Employer Identification Number: 237384087
Applications: Submit application preferably in May; Initial approach by letter; Completion of formal application required.
Publications: Program information.
Program description:
Educational grants for training beyond the high school level are awarded on the basis of financial need. Parents of applicant must complete a comprehensive financial statement and furnish any additional information requested.
In addition to college scholarships, grants for special education are available.

361★
Jordaan Foundation Trust
c/o First State Bank and Trust Company
111 East Eighth Street, P.O. Box 360
Larned, KS 67550 (316) 285-3127
Contact: Glee S. Smith, Chairman

Limitations: Undergraduate scholarships only to college-bound graduates of Pawnee County, KS, high schools.
Financial data: Year ended 12/31/87. Assets $1,682,784 (M); Total giving, $100,000; Grants to individuals 20 grants totaling $30,000, each grant $1,500.
Employer Identification Number: 486155003
Applications: Deadline April 15th; Completion of formal application required; Interviews required.
Publications: Program information.
Program description:
Initial awards are made to high school seniors and are renewable for all four years of undergraduate college.

362
Juhl (George W. & Sadie Marie) Scholarship Fund
c/o Southern Michigan National Bank
51 West Pearl Street
Coldwater, MI 49036   (517) 279-7511

Limitations: Scholarships for students residing in Branch County, MI, to attend schools of higher education in MI.
Financial data: Year ended 3/31/86. Assets, $1,226,969 (M); Total giving, $60,450; Grants to individuals, 40 grants totaling $60,450.
Employer Identification Number: 382571129
Applications: Completion of formal application required.

363
Kaiulani Home for Girls Trust
c/o Hawaiian Trust Company, Ltd.
P.O. Box 3170
Honolulu, HI 96802   (808) 525-8511

Limitations: Undergraduate scholarships to girls who are legal residents of Hawaii, with preference given to those of Hawaiian or part Hawaiian ancestry, to attend colleges and universities in the United States, with emphasis on Hawaiian institutions.
Financial data: Year ended 3/31/87. Assets, $1,462,478 (M); Total giving, $42,400; Grants to individuals, 134 grants totaling $42,400, high $550, low $50, general range $150-400.
Employer Identification Number: 996003331
Applications: Deadline March 1st; Completion of formal application required; Applicants must reapply each year.
Publications: Application guidelines.

364★
Kaltenborn Foundation, The
349 Seaview Avenue
Palm Beach, FL 33480
Contact: Rolf Kaltenborn, Trustee

Limitations: Research fellowships only to individuals conducting scholarly written research in the theory and practice of communication ideas.
Financial data: Year ended 12/31/86. Assets, $280,960 (M); Total giving, $25,860; Grants to individuals, 21 grants totaling $24,300, high $1,500, low $50.
Employer Identification Number: 136122557
Applications: Applications in the form of a brief letter outlining project proposal accepted throughout the year.
Program description:
Grants are not awarded for tuition assistance or as loans.

365
Kanawha Valley Foundation, The Greater
P.O. Box 3041
Charleston, WV 25331   (304) 346-3620
Contact: Betsy B. VonBlond, Executive Director

Limitations: Scholarships primarily to residents of West Virginia for undergraduate, graduate, vocational, and technical education.
Financial data: Year ended 12/31/85. Assets, $17,615,914 (M); Total giving, $989,745; Grants to individuals, 314 grants totaling $392,034.
Employer Identification Number: 556024430
Publications: Annual report (including application guidelines).

366★
Kaplan (Lazare and Charlotte) Foundation, Inc.
P.O. Box 216
Livingston Manor, NY 12758   (914) 439-4544
Contact: Irving Avery, Treasurer

Limitations: Scholarships for higher education primarily to students from Livingston Manor, Roscoe, Liberty and Jeffersonville in Sullivan County, NY.
Financial data: Year ended 12/31/87. Assets, $1,390,000 (M); Total giving, $107,000; Grants to individuals, 93 grants totaling $87,000, high $2,000, low $400, average grant $850.
Employer Identification Number: 136193153
Applications: Deadline May 1st; Initial approach by school guidance; Completion of formal application and F.A.F. form required.
Program description:
Scholarship payments are made directly to the college on behalf of the recipients.

367
Karnes Memorial Fund
c/o Harvey S. Traub
P.O. Box 8
Fairbury, IL 61739
Contact: Board of Governors, P.O. Box 2, Fairbury, IL 61739

Limitations: Scholarships primarily to college students who are residents of Fairbury, Forrest and Chatsworth, IL.
Financial data: Year ended 12/31/86. Assets, $1,075,663 (M); Total giving, $17,000; Grants to individuals, 10 grants totaling $17,000.
Employer Identification Number: 376243213
Applications: Deadline March 1st; Completion of formal application required.

368
Kawabe Memorial Fund
(Also known as Kawabe (Harry S.) Trust)
c/o Seattle First National Bank, Charitable Trust
Administration
P.O. Box 3586
Seattle, WA 98124 (206) 442-3388
Contact: Rod K. Kohnson, Vice-President, Seattle First
National Bank

Limitations: Scholarships to residents of Alaska.
Financial data: Year ended 12/31/86. Assets,
$1,643,842 (M); Total giving, $68,000; Grants to
individuals, 2 grants totaling $4,000, each grant
$2,000.
Employer Identification Number: 916165549
Applications: Applications accepted throughout the
year; Initial approach by letter requesting application
guidelines.
Publications: Application guidelines.

369
Kelley (Edward Bangs) and Elza Kelley
Foundation, Inc.
243 South Street
P.O. Drawer M
Hyannis, MA 02601 (617) 775-3117
Contact: Henry L. Murphy, Jr., Administrative
Manager

Limitations: Scholarships to residents of Barnstable
County, MA, only. Preference is given to those
entering medical and paramedical fields.
Financial data: Year ended 12/31/86. Assets,
$2,670,000 (M); Total giving, $105,000; Grants to
individuals amount not specified.
Employer Identification Number: 046039660
Applications: Deadline April 30th; Initial approach by
letter; Completion of formal application required.
Publications: Annual report (including application
guidelines).
Program description:
Scholarships are awarded to individuals who, by
acquisition of their acquired skills, will benefit the
health and welfare of the inhabitants of Barnstable
County, MA.

370★
Kempner (Harris and Eliza) Fund
P.O. Box 19
Galveston, TX 77553 (409) 765-6671
Contact: Leonora K. Thompson, Chairman

Limitations: Interest-free student loans only to
residents of Texas; no scholarship grants. Limit per
student of $10,000 over the three- or four-year
program.
Financial data: Year ended 12/31/86. Assets,
$17,564,871 (M); Expenditures, $760,552; Loans to

individuals totaling $633,900.
Employer Identification Number: 746042458
Applications: Deadlines July 1st and October 1st;
Informal applications accepted throughout the year;
Initial approach by letter; Co-signers required.
Publications: Annual report, program information,
application guidelines.
Program description:
Monthly repayments required after completion of
academic program. Loan must be repaid within five
years of termination of schooling.
 The fund's loan program is limited in scope and
dependent on the rate of repayments received from
prior recipients.

371★
Kennedy (Francis Nathaniel and Katheryn
Padgett) Foundation
P.O. Box 1178
Greenwood, SC 29646 (803) 942-1400
Contact: Sam M. Smith, Trustee

Limitations: Scholarships to young men and women
primarily in South Carolina studying at an accredited
college for the ministry in the Southern Baptist Church
and for foreign mission work or Christian education in
their local church.
Financial data: Year ended 12/31/87. Assets,
$1,210,894 (M); Total giving, $102,500 (approximate);
Grants to individuals, 48 grants totaling $25,000, high
$1,000, low $400, average grant $521.
Employer Identification Number: 237347655
Applications: Deadline May 15th; Applications
accepted throughout the year; Completion of formal
application required; Interviews required.
Publications: Application guidelines, financial
statement.
Program description:
Scholarships are awarded to young men and women
who are studying at an accredited college for the
ministry in the Southern Baptist Church and for foreign
mission work or Christian education in their local
church. The grants are based upon the needs of the
student, verified by financial statements of the parents
and the students. No grants are awarded for graduate
training except to those attending accredited
seminaries.

372
Kennedy (The Joseph P.), Jr. Foundation
1350 New York Avenue, N.W., Suite 500
Washington, DC 20005 (202) 393-1250
Contact: Eunice Kennedy Shriver, Executive
Vice-President

Limitations: Fellowships for research in the study of
mental retardation.
Financial data: Year ended 12/31/86. Assets,
$24,095,025 (M); Total giving, $1,812,697; Grants to

individuals, 8 grants totaling $96,374.
Employer Identification Number: 136083407
Publications: Program information.
Program description:
The **Joseph P. Kennedy, Jr. Post-Residency Fellowships in Medical Ethics** are awarded to physicians for research involving the ethical, religious, philosophical, and legal implications of medical decision-making, with emphasis on problems related to mental retardation. Fellows may work toward an advanced degree or pursue a program of independent interdisciplinary study in preparation for a career in research and teaching in medical ethics. Awards are usually in amounts up to $18,000 per year.

Applicants should submit a description of the proposed project, including specific goals and methodology, information concerning their academic and professional background, future plans, detailed budget requirements, and evidence of institutional acceptance of the program.

The **Joseph P. Kennedy, Jr. Fellowships in Medical Ethics for Nursing Faculty** are awarded to enable fellows to augment a career in nursing education by pursuing an advanced degree or interdisciplinary program of study involving the ethical and legal implications of medical decision-making.

As in the Post-Residency Fellowship program, problems relating to mental retardation are stressed. Grant amounts and application guidelines are the same as for the Post-Residency Fellowships.

373★
Kent Medical Foundation
1155 Front Avenue, NW
Grand Rapids, MI 49504   (616) 458-4157
Contact: William G. McClimans, Executive Director

Limitations: Scholarships and loans to residents of Kent, MI, and bordering counties pursuing education in medicine, nursing, or related health fields.
Financial data: Year ended 12/31/87. Assets, $280,125 (M); Total giving, $9,000; Grants to individuals, 14 grants totaling $9,000, high $900, low $500, general range $500-800; Loans to individuals amount not specified.
Employer Identification Number: 386089794
Applications: Applications accepted throughout the year; Scholarship applications are made through the financial aid office at the student's school; Completion of formal application required; Interviews and at least three letters of recommendation required.
Program description:
The **Kent Medical Foundation Tuition Grant Program** provides aid for tuition and fees to residents of Kent and bordering counties in Michigan who are pursuing a career in medicine or an allied health field and studying at a local college or hospital nursing school. Payments are made to the school on behalf of the students for one school year at a time. Students must reapply for aid in subsequent years.

The foundation also makes student loans to medical students who are residents of Kent County or bordering counties. Applicants must be regularly registered students, and have successfully completed the freshman year, in any Class A medical school within the U.S. Loans are interest-free until completion of first year postgraduate medical education, then are low-interest-bearing until paid.

374
Kent (Senah C. and C.A.) Foundation
c/o Wachovia Bank & Trust Company
P.O. Box 3099
Winston-Salem, NC 27102
Contact: See program description below for contact information.

Limitations: Scholarships limited to students attending Wake Forest University, North Carolina School of the Arts, or Salem College.
Financial data: Year ended 12/31/86. Assets, $1,274,488 (M); Total giving, $48,716; Grants to individuals amount not specified.
Employer Identification Number: 566037248
Applications: Deadline July 1st; Contact individual schools for current application information; Completion of formal application required.
Program description:
Scholarship recommendations are made to the foundation by the specified educational institutions. Submit applications to:
● G. William Joyner, Jr., Vice-President for Development, Wake Forest University, 7227 Reynolds Station, Winston-Salem, NC 27109; Tel.: (919) 761-5265;
● Patsy Braxton, Director of Financial Aid, North Carolina School of the Arts, Box 12189, Winston-Salem, NC 27107; Tel.: (919) 784-7170; or
● Ms. Len Brinkley, Director of Financial Aid, Salem College, Winston-Salem, NC 27108.

375
Keyes (Bernice A.B.) Trust
c/o Puget Sound National Bank
P.O. Box 1150
Tacoma, WA 98411-5052   (206) 593-3832
Contact: John A. Cunningham, Trust Officer, Puget Sound National Bank

Limitations: Scholarships to individuals in the Tacoma, WA, area.
Financial data: Year ended 12/31/86. Assets, $1,562,855 (M); Total giving, $87,000; Grants to individuals, 35 grants totaling $52,500, each grant $1,500.
Employer Identification Number: 916111944
Applications: Applications accepted throughout the year; Completion of formal application required;

Application forms available through college counselors at local high schools.

376
Kibble Foundation
P.O. Box 723
Pomeroy, OH 45769

Limitations: Scholarships only to graduates of Meigs County, OH, high schools pursuing four-year degrees or lesser technical degrees on a full-time basis.
Financial data: Year ended 12/31/86. Assets, $3,107,651 (M); Total giving, $180,569; Grants to individuals totaling $180,569.
Employer Identification Number: 316175971

377★
Kiewit (Peter) Foundation
Woodmen Tower, Suite 900
Farnam at Seventeenth
Omaha, NE 68102   (402) 344-7890
Contact: Lyn Wallin Ziegenbein, Executive Director

Limitations: Undergraduate scholarships only for high school students in the Omaha, NE-Council Bluffs, IA, area.
Financial data: Year ended 6/30/87. Assets, $196,132,258 (M); Total giving, $6,731,892; Grants to individuals, 92 grants totaling $363,226, high $4,000, low $1,750.
Employer Identification Number: 476098282
Applications: Deadline March 1st; Initial approach by letter or telephone; Request application form from high school principal; Completion of formal application required; Interviews required.
Publications: Annual report.
Program description:
The applicant's high school principal makes the scholarship selection. Scholarships are awarded annually. Financial need is a principal criterion. First consideration will be given to students interested in engineering or related fields. Scholarship aid is to continue for four years, given satisfactory achievement. The high school principal makes the scholar selection for his or her school on behalf of the foundation.

378
Kilbourne (E.H.) Residuary Charitable Trust
c/o Lincoln National Bank, Trust Department
P.O. Box 960
Fort Wayne, IN 46801   (219) 461-6451
Contact: Alice Kopfer, Assistant Vice-President

Limitations: Scholarships only to graduating seniors in Allen County, IN.
Financial data: Year ended 1/31/86. Assets, $6,012,166 (M); Total giving, $483,410; Grants to individuals, 287 grants totaling $221,703, high

$1,500, low $100.
Employer Identification Number: 356332820
Applications: Deadline April 15th; Initial approach by letter; Completion of formal application required.

379
Kilburger (Charles) Scholarship Fund
Equitable Building
Lancaster, OH 43130   (614) 653-0461
Contact: Kermit Sitterley

Limitations: Scholarships limited to residents of Fairfield County, OH, who are recommended by guidance counselors at high schools and colleges.
Financial data: Year ended 5/31/87. Assets, $3,180,680 (M); Total giving, $187,455; Grants to individuals, 83 grants totaling $187,455, high $6,000, low $470.
Employer Identification Number: 316086870
Applications: Individual applications without guidance counselor recommendations not accepted; Interviews required.

380★
King (Carl B. & Florence E.) Foundation
One Preston Centre
8222 Douglas Avenue, Suite 370
Dallas, TX 75225   (214) 750-1884
Contact: Carl Yeckel, Vice-President

Limitations: Scholarships and student loans limited to Texas high school students.
Financial data: Year ended 12/31/86. Assets, $27,357,367 (M); Total giving, $911,595; Grants to individuals, 69 grants totaling $73,600, high $4,000, low $1,000, average grant $1,000; Loans to individuals, 56 loans totaling $110,000, average loan $2,000.
Employer Identification Number: 756052203
Applications: Contact Texas Interscholastic League for current application deadline; Initial approach by letter; Applications available from foundation and Texas Interscholastic League; Completion of formal application and high school transcript required.
Program description:
Scholarships are limited to $1,000 per year, per student.

381
King (Charles A.) Trust
c/o Bank of New England
28 State Street
Boston, MA 02109   (617) 973-1793
Contact: John M. Dolan, Senior Trust Officer, Bank of New England

Limitations: Postdoctoral fellowships for research in medicine and surgery in institutions within the Commonwealth of Massachusetts.

Financial data: Year ended 12/31/85. Assets, $8,208,237 (M); Total giving, $383,374; Grants to individuals, 19 grants totaling $383,374, high $30,000, low $1,417.
Employer Identification Number: 046012742
Applications: Deadline October 15th for projects to start on or after February 1st of the following year; Initial approach by telephone; Completion of formal application required.
Publications: Application guidelines.
Program description:
Grants are made for research in medicine or surgery as they are connected with the investigation of diseases of human beings and the alleviation of human suffering through improved methods of treatment. Funds are disbursed to the sponsoring institution.

382
King's Daughters Of Wisconsin Foundation, Inc., The
P.O. Box 1917
Appleton, WI 54913   (414) 739-6311
Contact: Scholarship Committee

Limitations: Scholarships and grants only to students in the current graduating class from high schools in the following communities: Appleton, Kaukauna, Lake Mills, Menasha, Neenah, Sheboygan, Sheboygan Falls, for use in an accredited college or university within the state of Wisconsin.
Financial data: Year ended 8/31/87. Assets, $174,905 (M); Total giving, $9,577; Grants to individuals, 9 grants totaling $8,000, high $1,500, low $500.
Employer Identification Number: 510160730
Applications: Deadline March 1st; Completion of formal application required, including information on applicant's academic record and standing, leadership characteristics, and financial need; Interviews required.
Program description:
Scholarships are renewable, depending on the student's scholastic performance.

383★
Kittredge (John Anson) Educational Fund
c/o Key Trust Company of Maine
P.O. Box 1054
Augusta, ME 04330
Contact: Kittredge Fund, P.O. Box 2883, Cambridge, MA 02238

Limitations: Grants awarded to artists and scholars in very special circumstances.
Financial data: Year ended 4/30/86. Assets, $1,029,439 (M); Total giving, $56,435; Grants to individuals, 21 grants totaling $56,435, high $10,000, low $1,000, general range $1,000-2,000.
Employer Identification Number: 016007180

Applications: Initial approach by letter, stating purpose, amount requested, period of funding, and supporting letters.
Program description:
No student scholarships are awarded.

384★
Klemstine (G. William) Foundation
c/o Pittsburgh National Bank C. & I. Trust Dept.
One Oliver Plaza
Pittsburgh, PA 15265   (412) 762-3706
Contact: Patricia Laird

Limitations: Educational loans only to residents of Cambria and Somerset counties in western Pennsylvania.
Financial data: Year ended 9/30/86. Assets, $37,037 (M); Expenditures, $826; Loans to individuals, 34 student loans totaling $25,866, high $1,500, low 125, general range $400-500.
Employer Identification Number: 256058872
Applications: Applications accepted throughout the year; Initial approach by letter of introduction requesting aid.

385
Klicka (Jessie) Foundation
c/o Wells Fargo Trust Department
450 B Street, Suite 1000
San Diego, CA 92101
Contact: Thelma M. Dewar, Secretary, 3550 Third Avenue, Suite 2A, San Diego, CA 92103

Limitations: Scholarships only to graduates of San Diego City or County, CA, high schools.
Financial data: Year ended 12/31/86. Assets, $929,063 (M); Total giving, $46,500; Grants to individuals, 25 grants totaling $36,500, high $2,500, low $500, average grant $2,000.
Employer Identification Number: 956093455
Applications: Deadline April 15th; Completion of formal application required.
Program description:
The foundation prefers to award scholarships in special situations where the need is not adequately met by other sources. There has to be proven financial need and students must have the necessary scholastic requirements to be admitted to the school of their choice. The award is renewable for four years of undergraduate study.

386
Klingelhoefer (August W.) Needy Student Assistance Fund

c/o Texas American Bank
154 East Main Street
Fredericksburg, TX 78624   (512) 997-7551
Contact: John Clawson, Principal, Fredericksburg High School, Fredericksburg, TX 78624; Tel.: (512) 987-7551

Limitations: Scholarships to residents of Fredericksburg, TX.
Financial data: Year ended 12/31/86. Assets, $42,055 (M); Total giving, $4,800; Grants to individuals, 12 grants totaling $4,800, each grant $400.
Employer Identification Number: 746070540
Applications: Deadline May 1st; Completion of formal application required along with a student financial assistance form including information regarding need, ambition, merit, scholastic ability, and financial data.
Program description:
Funds granted must be used by recipient for tuition, fees, room/board at an institution of higher learning in either the summer or fall semester of the same year the grant is awarded.

387
Klingenstein (The Esther A. and Joseph) Fund, Inc.

200 Park Avenue
New York, NY 10166-0090   (212) 578-0285
Contact: John Klingenstein, President

Limitations: Fellowship awards for research in the neurosciences for individual investigators endorsed by their institutions.
Financial data: Year ended 9/30/86. Assets, $50,683,782 (M); Total giving, $2,665,500; Grants to individuals amount not specified.
Employer Identification Number: 136028788
Applications: Deadline November 1st; Awards will be announced in February to commence July 1st; Selections will be made by an Advisory Committee of distinguished neuroscientists; Initial approach by letter or telephone; Completion of formal application required.
Publications: Informational brochure.
Program description:
Up to 12 **Joseph Klingenstein Fellowship Awards in the Neurosciences** will be awarded in 1987 (awards are made biennially). The purpose of the fund is to encourage both clinical and basic science investigators to engage in research which may lead to a better understanding of the etiology, treatment, and prevention of epilepsy. Recognizing that fundamental research in the field of neurobiology and related fields may elucidate mechanisms relevant to the clinical study of epilepsy, the fund proposes to support investigators in basic science departments of neurobiology as well as clinical scientists.

Candidates must have completed all research training, including postdoctoral training. Investigators at all career levels are eligible for the awards, as well as young clinicians who have completed their clinical training and who wish to have research training in the neurosciences. Clinicians who wish to use the award for research training must have completed clinical training by June 30, 1987. U.S. citizenship is not a requirement, but it is expected that candidates will be permanent residents of the U.S. Although there are no departmental restrictions, candidates must present plans for research or research training in biomedical fields or disciplines. Holding other fellowships concurrently with a Klingenstein Award requires the approval of the Advisory Committee.

Fellows receive an award of $100,000 payable over three years. Individuals may apply with the endorsement of their university, medical school, or research institute. Fellowships are paid through the various institutions where the research is conducted and may be used for salary support, research activities, or any other purpose which promotes the scientific activities of the Fellows.

388
Knezevich (Steven) Trust

161 West Wisconsin Avenue
Milwaukee, WI 53203-2644   (414) 271-6364
Contact: Stanley F. Hack

Limitations: College scholarships to persons of Serbian descent.
Financial data: Year ended 12/31/86. Assets, $46,914 (M); Total giving, $1,600; Grants to individuals, 10 grants totaling $1,600, high $200, low $100; 1985, Grants to individuals, 11 grants totaling $2,000, high $350, low $100.
Employer Identification Number: 396150899
Applications: Deadline September 1st; Completion of formal application required with copy of Serbian map showing family location.

389★
Knott (Marion Burk) Scholarship Fund

St. Mary's Seminary Building
5400 Roland Avenue
Baltimore, MD 21210   (301) 323-4300
Contact: Marie Lehnert, Consultant/Director

Limitations: Scholarships for Catholic students residing in the Archdiocese of Baltimore to attend Catholic elementary or high schools in Baltimore City, Anne Arundel, Baltimore, Carroll, Frederick, Harford, or Howard counties, MD, or to attend Loyola College or College of Notre Dame of Maryland or Mount Saint Mary's College in Emmitsburg, MD.
Financial data: Year ended 12/31/87. Assets, $12,070 (M); Total giving, $772,939; Grants to individuals, 68 grants totaling $772,939, 12 college scholarships, 17

secondary school scholarships, and 39 elementary school scholarships. (See program description below for average award at each level.).
Employer Identification Number: 526212483
Applications: Deadlines February 15th for Elementary School Scholarships, March 1st for High School Scholarships, and after acceptance by college for College Scholarships; Contact fund office for current application guidelines; Application forms available January 1st; Completion of formal application required; Interviews for college sholarships required; Notification of award in early April or May.
Publications: Application guidelines, informational brochure, program information.
Program description:
The fund was given to the Archbishop of Baltimore and his successors by Mr. Henry J. Knott, Sr., to provide Catholic students with a quality education, and began making awards in 1981. It is administered by an independent committee of private citizens chaired by the Archbishop. Four-year, full-tuition awards are made to students for college, high school, or grades 5-8. Of the total funds awarded each year, 45 percent is allocated at the college level, 30 percent at the high school level, and 25 percent at the elementary school level.

Awards are made on a competitive basis, however, additional points are added to scores in cases of demonstrated family financial need. Of the total number of students receiving scholarships in 1987, the financial need benefit applied to 69 percent at the college level, 42 percent at the high school level, and 13 percent at the elementary school level.

Eligibility and the amount of each award varies according to the educational level:

College Scholarships - High school seniors apply for awards directly to the Catholic college of their choice in the Baltimore Archdiocese. After students have been accepted, colleges evaluate and make selections based on SAT scores (generally must be above 1200), grades, rank in high school, letters of reference, motivation, and an interview. The average award in 1987 was approximately $29,000 for four years.

High School Scholarships - All students entering Catholic high schools in the Baltimore area (see Limitations) are eligible. Students are ranked based on national standardized test scores for Grade 8 with additional points added for financial need benefit. An additional test is administered to the top 130 students and students are reranked. The average award in 1987 was $13,000 for four years.

Elementary School Scholarships - Students entering fifth grade of any Catholic parochial (not private) school in the Baltimore area (see Limitations) are eligible. Students are ranked by national standardized test scores for Grade 4, report cards, and principals' reports; extra points are added for financial need. The average award in 1987 was $5,000 for four years.

390★
Kohler Foundation
104 Orchard Road
Kohler, WI 53044   (414) 458-1972
Contact: Eleanor A. Jung, Executive Director

Limitations: College scholarships only to Sheboygan County, WI, graduating high school seniors recommended by their schools.
Financial data: Year ended 12/31/86. Assets, $21,419,657 (M); Total giving, $801,677; Grants to individuals, 81 grants totaling $77,601, high 7,603, low $500.
Employer Identification Number: 390810536
Applications: Deadline April 15th; Completion of formal application required; Interviews sometimes required; Candidates must be recommended by their schools.
Program description:
The foundation's program includes scholarship awards, awards in the humanities, and awards in mathematics and science. Scholarships may be used to attend any accredited college or university in the U.S.

391
Kosciuszko Foundation, Inc.
15 East 65th Street
New York, NY 10021

Limitations: Scholarships for Polish scholars desiring to study in the U.S., and for American scholars desiring to study in Poland, and for American students to attend summer courses at Polish universities.
Financial data: Year ended 6/30/86. Assets, $5,285,140 (M); Total giving, $447,556; Grants to individuals, 169 grants totaling $434,453, high $13,514, low $100, general range $1,000-5,000.
Employer Identification Number: 131628179

392★
Krause (Charles A.) Foundation
c/o Krause Consultants, Ltd.
330 East Kilbourne Avenue, Two Plaza East 570
Milwaukee, WI 53202   (414) 273-2733
Contact: Charles A. Krause, Secretary-Treasurer

Limitations: Undergraduate scholarships primarily to residents of Wisconsin.
Financial data: Year ended 12/31/87. Assets, $2,565,906 (M); Total giving, $175,950; Grants to individuals, 7 grants totaling $19,500, high $3,000, low $1,500.
Employer Identification Number: 396044820
Applications: Deadline November 30th; Completion of formal application required; Completion of recommendation from high school administration required; Submit parents' financial statement.
Publications: 990-PF printed copy available upon request.

393★
Kress (Samuel H.) Foundation
174 East 80th Stret
New York, NY 10021   (212) 861-4993
Contact: Dr. Marilyn Perry, President

Limitations: Grants to doctoral candidates for dissertation research in art history and archaeology and to graduate students in art conservation. Fellowships in art history must have support of department chairman.
Financial data: Year ended 8/31/87. Assets, $63,967,746 (M); Total giving, $1,656,491; Grants to individuals, 111 grants totaling $310,489, high $17,000, low $1,000, general range $1,000-10,000, average grant $6,000.
Employer Identification Number: 131624176
Applications: Deadline November 30th for art history research fellowships, January 31st for art conservation fellowships; Initial approach by proposal; Completion of formal application required.
Publications: Annual report (including application guidelines), financial statement, informational brochure, program information, 990-PF printed copy available upon request.
Program description:
The foundation's programs of grants to individuals are designed not only to support scholarship in the field of art history, but also to encourage young scholars to pursue museum careers, to aid in the development of faculty members for college and university programs in art history, and to increase the national competence in the conservation and restoration of works of art.

To these ends, the foundation awards stipends to American doctoral candidates for dissertation research in art history and archaeology and to postgraduate students in art conservation. Fellowship candidates must be nominated by the chairman of their university's graduate department of art history from whose office application forms may be obtained.

Applicants should send a statement on the project and the country or countries to be visited, including the total amount of money requested and the period of time in which the sum is to be used. Particular care should be given to the accuracy of language, both of foreign languages and references to literature. Each individual should have sent a transcript of credits and letters of endorsement from the chairman of the art history department and two other faculty members or qualified individuals familiar with the applicant's project.

The foundation also sponsors fellowship programs for research at the American Academy in Rome, American Schools of Oriental Research, American School of Classical Studies at Athens, and ICCROM, Rome. The institutions should be contacted directly for further information. These grants are cooperative with the foundation.

An additional fellowship program, administered through the National Gallery of Art, Washington, DC, makes funds available for four fellows and is intended to encourage exceptional young people in the art history field to consider a museum career. It includes a doctoral dissertation program abroad and residence for a stipulated time at the National Gallery in Washington. Similar programs for scholars in the history of art are administered at The Institute for Advanced Study, Princeton, and the Villa I Tatti of Harvard University.

394
Kutz (Milton and Hattie) Foundation
101 Garden of Eden Road
Wilmington, DE 19803   (302) 478-6200
Contact: Robert N. Kerbel, Executive Secretary

Limitations: Scholarships only to Delaware residents. First time applications for freshmen only.
Financial data: Year ended 6/30/86. Assets, $1,741,685 (M); Total giving, $100,550; Grants to individuals, 40 grants totaling $50,000.
Employer Identification Number: 510187055
Applications: Deadline March 15th; Completion of formal application required.

395
La Crosse Foundation
P.O. Box 489
La Crosse, WI 54602-0489   (608) 782-1148
Contact: Carol B. Popelka, Program Director

Limitations: Scholarships limited to residents of La Crosse, WI.
Financial data: Year ended 12/31/86. Assets, $3,874,186 (M); Total giving, $235,245; Grants to individuals, 71 grants totaling $40,112.
Employer Identification Number: 396037996
Applications: Initial approach by letter.
Publications: Annual report.
Program description:
General and music scholarships are awarded through the foundation's general fund, in addition to the following component funds:

The Ella F. Ambrosius Fund for the support of music awards and scholarships.

The Mary Jane Bice Fund provides the **Mary Lousia and Frederick T. Whitbeck Scholarship** and the **Alfred W. Rice Scholarship**, for La Crosse and Onalaska public high school students to study journalism or environmental studies.

The Nellie L. Case Fund provides scholarships for the education of needy students who desire to study chemistry at higher than the high school level. The awards are made directly to the educational institutions.

The Josephine Hintgen Fund provides scholarships for La Crosse public high school students.

The Louis I. Rehfuss Fund provides scholarships to La Crosse area students.

The Burton C. Smith Fund provides scholarships for La Crosse Logan High School students who attend the University of Wisconsin-Stout in Menomonie.

396
Laboratories for Therapeutic Research, Inc.
425 West 59th Street
New York, NY 10019

Limitations: Grants primarily for medical research and for student aid.
Financial data: Year ended 9/30/85. Assets, $91,726 (M); Total giving, $260,000; Grants to individuals, 1 grant totaling $10,000.
Employer Identification Number: 116038959

397
Ladies Branch of The New Bedford Port Society
One Johnny Cake Hill
New Bedford, MA 02740
Contact: Chairperson, Educational Grants Committee

Limitations: Scholarships only to needy students from the New Bedford, MA, area.
Financial data: Year ended 12/31/85. Assets, $179,388 (M); Total giving, $7,653; Grants to individuals, 8 grants totaling $4,000.
Employer Identification Number: 046079892
Applications: Deadline May 1st; Initial approach by letter explaining educational plans and financial situation. **Applications from individuals residing outside of stated geographic restriction not accepted.**

398
Laerdal (Asmund S.) Foundation, Inc.
c/o Geller & Geller
600 Third Avenue, 8th Floor
New York, NY 10016-1938

Limitations: Grants for medical research.
Financial data: Year ended 12/31/85. Assets, $3,103,339 (M); Total giving, $83,000; Grants to individuals, 1 grant totaling $3,000.
Employer Identification Number: 132885659
Applications: Applications accepted throughout the year.

399
Lancaster County Foundation, The
29 East King Street
Lancaster, PA 17602   (717) 397-1629
Contact: Nancy L. Neff, Executive Secretary

Limitations: Limited number of scholarships for residents of Lancaster County, PA.
Financial data: Year ended 4/30/86. Assets, $4,271,973 (M); Total giving, $265,084; Grants to individuals, 3 grants totaling $1,257.

Employer Identification Number: 236419120
Applications: Deadline October 15th; Completion of formal application required.
Publications: Annual report.

400
Landis (John W.) Scholarship Trust
c/o D. Williams Evans, Jr.
1670 Christmas Run
Wooster, OH 44691

Limitations: Scholarships to residents of Wayne County, OH, who are high school graduates and desire further education, not necessarily leading to a degree, in agriculture, horticulture, home economics, farm economics, animal husbandry, soil and water conservation, and forestry.
Financial data: Year ended 6/30/87. Assets, $49,779 (L); Total giving, $3,500; Grants to individuals, 9 grants totaling $3,500, high $500, low $300.
Employer Identification Number: 237396151
Applications: Deadline March 15th; Completion of formal application required; Interviews granted upon request; Applications available from, and to be returned to, Wayne County Superintendent of Schools, 2534 Burbank Road, Wooster, OH 44691.

401
Lane (Winthrop and Frances) Foundation
c/o FirsTier Bank
17th & Farnam Street
Omaha, NE 68102   (402) 348-6350

Limitations: Scholarships only to students at Creighton University School of Law or the University of Nebraska College of Law.
Financial data: Year ended 12/31/86. Assets, $2,032,517 (M); Total giving, $105,835; Grants to individuals, 59 grants totaling $85,335, high $4,500, low $300, general range $530-3,500, average grant $1,000.
Employer Identification Number: 470581778
Applications: Applications accepted throughout the year; Completion of formal application required.

402
Lasker (Albert and Mary) Foundation, Inc.
865 First Avenue, Apt. 14A
New York, NY 10017   (212) 421-9010
Contact: Mary W. Lasker, President

Limitations: Awards to medical researchers.
Financial data: Year ended 12/31/85. Assets, $4,377,406 (M); Total giving, $325,594; Awards to individuals totaling $226,484.
Employer Identification Number: 131680062
Applications: Applications accepted throughout the year; Interviews required.

Program description:
The **Albert Lasker Medical Research Awards** are given annually to honor and encourage medical research and medical journalism, in recognition of work by an investigator or group which contributes information, techniques, or concepts which may result in the prolongation of the prime of life, or lead to elimination or alleviation of major disease-related causes of death.

403
Lauffer (Charles A.) Trust
c/o Landmark Union Trust Bank
P.O. Box 11388
St. Petersburg, FL 33733   (813) 821-1111
Contact: Dorothy Williams, Trust Department

Limitations: Student loans only to medical students studying for a M.D. degree.
Financial data: Year ended 8/31/85. Assets, $1,752,208 (M); Expenditures, $40,093; Loans to individuals, 44 loans totaling $66,000, each loan $1,500.
Employer Identification Number: 596121126
Applications: Initial approach by letter.
Program description:
The trust makes loans to a maximum of $1,500 per year. Interest at the rate of two percent per year is due and payable one year from date of ceasing to attend or graduation from medical school. The principal balance is due in full ten years from date of graduation or ceasing to attend medical school.

404★
Leavenworth (Elisha) Foundation, Inc.
35 Park Place
Waterbury, CT 06702
Contact: Mrs. E. Donald Rogers, Three Mile Hill, Middlebury, CT 06702; Tel.: (203) 758-1042

Limitations: Scholarships to college women who are residents of the Waterbury, CT, area.
Financial data: Year ended 12/31/84. Assets, $907,368 (M); Total giving, $59,448; Grants to individuals, 10 grants totaling $10,000.
Employer Identification Number: 066035206
Applications: Applications accepted throughout the year; Initial approach by letter, including copy of transcripts, personal information, and explanation of why help is needed.

405
Lee Endowment Foundation
c/o First Trust Company of Montana
P.O. Box 30678
Billings, MT 59115
Contact: Dr. David L. Buettner, Chairman, Nominating Committee, North Iowa Area Community

College, 500 College Drive, Mason City, IA 50401; Tel.: (515) 421-4399

Limitations: Scholarships primarily to residents of Mason City and Cerro Gordo County, IA.
Financial data: Year ended 12/31/86. Assets, $11,076,332 (M); Total giving, $390,014; Grants to individuals, 57 grants totaling $68,500, high $1,200, low $100.
Employer Identification Number: 421074052
Applications: Deadline February 24th; Completion of formal application required.
Program description:
The **Will F. Muse Scholarship Fund** awards students on the basis of scholarship, financial need, and good moral character for any course of study or education beyond the high school level, including, but not limited to trade schools, craft schools, college courses leading to degrees, and college postgraduate courses of every kind and nature. Scholarships may be renewed if recipient remains eligible through the years of a planned course of study.

406
Leidy-Rhoads Foundation Trust
Mellon Bank (East) N.A.
P.O. Box 7236
Philadelphia, PA 19101

Limitations: Scholarships to residents of Boyertown, PA, for all types of education but usually limited to higher education at a college, university or trade school.
Financial data: Year ended 12/31/85. Assets, $609,038 (M); Total giving, $39,200; Grants to individuals, 52 grants totaling $38,700, high $1,200, low $150, general range $600-900.
Employer Identification Number: 236227398
Applications: Deadline February for initial contact; Completion of formal application required; Applications are available from Jean Butt, Boyertown Area School District, 911 Montgomery Avenue, Boyertown, PA 19512.

407
Lesher (Margaret and Irvin) Foundation
P.O. Box 374
Oil City, PA 16301   (814) 677-5085
Contact: Stephen P. Kosak, Consultant

Limitations: Scholarships to graduates of Union High School, Clarion County, PA.
Financial data: Year ended 12/31/86. Assets, $1,521,646 (M); Total giving, $79,272; Grants to individuals, 51 grants totaling $79,272, high $2,150, low $100, general range $100-2,000.
Employer Identification Number: 256067843
Applications: Submit proposal preferably in April, August, or November; Initial approach by letter; Completion of formal application required.

Program description:
Scholarships are granted on the basis of financial need; students may attend the college, trade school, business school, or technical school of their choice.

408
Leu Foundation, Inc.
2409 Abbott Martin Road
Nashville, TN 37315
Contact: Frank Leu

Limitations: Grants for scholarship with preference given to students in the North Platte, NE, area.
Financial data: Year ended 12/31/86. Assets, $1,454,276 (M); Total giving, $55,500; Grants to individuals totaling $28,500.
Employer Identification Number: 470576937
Applications: Applications accepted throughout the year; Completion of formal application required including an essay stating interest in higher education, goals for the future, and need for the scholarship.

409
Levie (Marcus and Theresa) Educational Fund
c/o Jewish Federation of Metropolitan Chicago
One South Franklin Street
Chicago, IL 60606   (312) 346-6700
Contact: Ruth Elbaum, Secretary

Limitations: Scholarships awarded to Jewish students who are residents of Cook County, IL, and who have demonstrated career promise and have financial need to complete their professional or vocational training in the helping professions.
Financial data: Year ended 7/31/86. Assets, $2,693,811 (M); Total giving, $137,000; Grants to individuals, 32 grants totaling $137,000, average grant $5,200.
Employer Identification Number: 366010074
Applications: Deadline March 1st; Applications accepted between November and February; Initial approach by letter or telephone; Requests for applications preferably taken by phone; Completion of formal application required; Interviews required.
Publications: Application guidelines, program information.

410
Lewis (Mabelle McLeod) Memorial Fund
P.O. Box 3730
Stanford, CA 94305
Contact: Ms. Shirleyann Shyne, Executive Secretary

Limitations: Grants to advanced doctoral candidates affiliated with northern California universities.
Financial data: Year ended 3/31/87. Assets, $2,574,775 (M); Total giving, $101,750; Grants to individuals, 12 grants totaling $101,750, high $10,900, low $3,000.

Employer Identification Number: 237079585
Applications: Deadline January 15th; Submit application preferably in November or December; Initial approach by letter; Completion of two copies of formal application, including copy of resume, required.
Publications: Program information, application guidelines.
Program description:
Grants are awarded for the last year of study and research in the humanistic disciplines (e.g., literature, history, philosophy). The awards are made for a maximum of one year and are intended to allow completion of a scholarly dissertation project upon which significant work has already been accomplished; however, grants will not be made for the purpose of publishing dissertation research.

Grants may cover academic fees, living expenses, and travel as required by the project, but not stipends for research assistants.

Applicants must demonstrate financial need and arrange for recommendations from three recognized scholars.

411
Li Foundation, Inc., The
66 Herbhill Road
Glen Cove, NY 11542
Contact: E. Leong Way, President

Limitations: Scholarships only to graduate students from China.
Financial data: Year ended 12/31/85. Assets, $5,126,754 (M); Total giving, $237,025; Grants to individuals, 38 grants totaling $237,025, high $14,689, low $833.
Employer Identification Number: 136098783
Applications: Applications accepted throughout the year; Completion of formal application required.

412
Lincoln National Life Foundation, Inc., The
P.O. Box 1110
1300 South Clinton Street
Fort Wayne, IN 46801   (219) 427-3271
Contact: Wilburn Smith, Tel.:(219) 427-2064; or Melvin McFall, Tel.:(219) 427-3057

Limitations: Scholarships to students of actuarial science, and to minority students pursuing business-related studies.
Financial data: Year ended 12/31/86. Assets, $2,916,177 (M); Total giving, $50,396; Grants to individuals totaling $46,196.
Employer Identification Number: 356042099
Applications: Applications accepted throughout the year; Initial approach by letter; Completion of formal application required.

Publications: Application guidelines.
Program description:
The Thomas A. Watson Scholarship: This scholarship program is designed to promote career mobility through higher education for black, Hispanic, and other ethnic minority students. Applicants must:

1. Be a graduate of an Allen County high school, in Fort Wayne, IN
2. Pursue a business-related curriculum such as accounting, finance, insurance, computer science, mathematics, etc.
3. Be a candidate for a four-year degree in an accredited college or university
4. Be in the upper fourth of his/her graduating class with a minimum SAT score of 850, or equivalent ACT score
5. Have a financial need as revealed in parents'/guardians' W-2 Federal Income Tax Return
6. Have filed a Financial Aid Form (FAF) with the college or university he/she will attend.
7. Submit at least three letters of recommendation from high school instructors/officials, in addition to the scholarship application, official high school transcript, and copy of parents'/guardians' W-2 form.

The amount of the scholarship shall not exceed $8,000 per student per academic year. The scholarship is not transferable from one student to another. All scholarships will be awarded at the beginning of the academic school year. Recipients are chosen by a selection committee composed of local minority representatives.

Dependent children of employees of Lincoln National Corporation and/or its subsidiaries are not eligible.

The McAndless Scholarship: Under this program, the foundation makes awards to students majoring in actuarial science. McAndless Scholars may attend the school of their choice. Candidates planning to attend a university with an established actuarial science program will receive some preference in the selection process. Such universities include Ball State University, IN, The University of Illinois, The University of Iowa, The University of Michigan, The University of Nebraska, and the University of Wisconsin. Students attending schools that do not have actuarial science programs will be expected to pursue a curriculum consistent with a career in actuarial science; this will generally mean a mathematics major with supporting course work in business and computer science.

Applicants must:

1. Apply for admission to the college or university of their choice, preferably prior to February 1st
2. Submit financial data to the college or university
3. File a Financial Aid Form
4. Submit the Applicant's and Principal's Statement forms and copies of their high school transcripts to Lincoln National by February 1st.

413★
Lincoln-Lane Foundation, The
One Main Plaza East, Suite 1102
Norfolk, VA 23510   (804) 622-2557
Contact: Margaret B. Belvin, Secretary

Limitations: Scholarships only to college students who are permanent residents of the Norfolk-Virginia Beach, VA, area.
Financial data: Year ended 7/31/87. Assets, $6,121,186 (M); Total giving, $207,500; Grants to individuals, 127 grants totaling $207,500, high $2,500, low $500, general range $1,000-1,500, average grant $1,500.
Employer Identification Number: 540601700
Applications: Applications available after October 1st; Applications accepted throughout the year; Initial approach by letter or telephone; Completion of formal application and interviews required; Recipients notified in April.
Publications: Application guidelines, program information, 990-PF printed copy available upon request.
Program description:
About 30 new scholarships are awarded annually to college students for full-time study at accredited postsecondary schools, colleges and universities in the U.S. Applicants are selected on the basis of academic achievement and financial need; community service and extracurricular activities are also considered.

414
Lindsay (Franklin) Student Aid Fund
Texas Commerce Bank of Austin
P.O. Box 550
Austin, TX 78789-0001   (512) 476-6611
Contact: Rebecca Gassenmayer, Administrative Officer

Limitations: Undergraduate and graduate loans to students attending Texas colleges or universities.
Financial data: Year ended 12/31/86. Assets, $9,289,658 (M); Expenditures, $1,103,511; Loans to individuals, 385 student loans totaling $922,224, high $4,000, low $500.
Employer Identification Number: 746031753
Applications: Deadline varies according to each committee member; Completion of formal application required; Applications available from any one of 16 loan committee members whose names and addresses are listed in a brochure available from the fund.
Publications: Program information, application guidelines, informational brochure.
Program description:
Loans are not to exceed a maximum of $5,000 for the student's total school career. Loans are noninterest-bearing while the student is in school and carry interest of six percent once the studies are terminated. Must have completed one year of college when loan is approved. Apply in spring of freshman year.

415
Lippoldt (Arthur H.) Trust
4123 North Spencer Road
Spencer, OK 73084   (405) 771-3786
Contact: Ed J. Poole, Trustee

Limitations: Scholarships to students at the University of Oklahoma who meet academic requirements.
Financial data: Year ended 7/31/87. Assets, $145,270 (L); Total giving, $7,500; Grants to individuals, 3 grants totaling $7,500, each grant $2,500.
Employer Identification Number: 736159069
Applications: Submit application in reasonable time to be considered prior to beginning of each semester; Completion of formal application required.

416★
Loats Foundation, Inc.
P.O. Box 240
Frederick City, MD 21701   (301) 662-2191

Limitations: Scholarships only to residents of Frederick County, MD.
Financial data: Year ended 5/31/87. Assets, $2,038,435 (M); Total giving, $99,729; Grants to individuals, 81 grants totaling $92,727, high $2,500, low $500.
Employer Identification Number: 520610535
Applications: For application deadline information, contact Glenn E. Biehl, Treasurer, c/o Evangelical Lutheran Church, 35 East Church Street, Frederick, MD 21701; Tel.: (301) 663-6361; Completion of formal application required; Applications available at Frederick County high schools; Interviews required.
Publications: Program information, application guidelines.
Program description:
The purpose of this program is to encourage young people, particularly orphans or those from broken homes, to continue their education so that they will be better able to take their place in and make a commendable contribution to society. The foundation especially seeks applications from young women who are interested in the secretarial or service professions though no exclusion is made of any person who desires to prepare for any profession or occupation.

Scholarship recipients shall be required to furnish to the board of trustees a copy of their grades and a brief summary of their extracurricular activities at the end of each semester or term.

417★
Lorain County, The Community Foundation of Greater
1865 North Ridge Road East, Suite A
Lorain, OH 44055   (216) 277-0142
Contact: Carol G. Simonetti, Executive Director

Limitations: Scholarships to residents of Lorain County, OH.
Financial data: Year ended 12/31/87. Assets, $8,394,651 (M); Total giving, $327,984; Grants to individuals, 32 grants totaling $30,800.
Employer Identification Number: 341322781
Applications: Deadline April 15th for Lake Erie Electric Scholarships, April 21st for Elyria Chronicle-Telegram Scholarships and Nord Scholarships; Initial approach by letter or telephone; Completion of formal application required; Application forms for Nord Scholarships may be obtained from any Lorain County high school counselor; Application forms for Chronicle-Telegram Scholarships available from the newspaper's offices in Elyria; Application forms for other scholarship programs are available from the foundation.
Publications: Annual report, program information.
Program description:
The **Walter and Virginia Nord Scholarship Fund** awards undergraduate scholarships to Lorain County residents who are seniors in Lorain County high schools. Applicants must be in the upper one-third of their graduating class and show financial need. Scholarships in the amount of $500 each are awarded for one year and may be renewed for four years contingent upon maintenance of satisfactory grades.

The **Mary J. and Paul J. Kopsch Fund** awards medical scholarships to Lorain County residents who are entering or presently enrolled in a U.S. medical school as candidates for a medical degree, either allopathic or osteopathic. Scholarships in the amount of $2,500 each are granted for a one-year period and may be renewed upon re-application at the discretion of the foundation. Grants are awarded on or about June 30th, and payments are made directly to the medical school on or about August 1st.

The **Lake Erie Electric Scholarship Fund** awards undergraduate scholarships to Lorain County residents in financial need who are planning to seek a career in the electrical industry. Applicants must be enrolled or planning to enroll in a college, graduate school, or vocational or technical school of a post high school nature. Scholarships in the amount of $500 each are granted for a one-year period and may be renewed upon re-application at the discretion of the foundation. Grants are awarded on or about June 30th and are normally paid directly to the school around September 1st. Selection criteria include evidence of academic ability, work habits, personal qualities and degree of financial need.

Elyria Chronicle-Telegram Scholarship Fund awards undergraduate scholarships to residents of Lorain County.

The **Jonathan Klein Memorial Fund** provides scholarships for senior students at Vermilion High School who will study theatre following graduation. This fund will also privide summer camp scholarships for children of the Agudath B'nai Israel Synagogue.

The **Roy E. Hayes, M.D. Memorial Fund** provides scholarships to Lorain County students enrolled in U.S. medical schools.

418
Lord (Henry C.) Scholarship Fund Trust

c/o Amoskeag Bank
P.O. Box 150
Manchester, NH 03105   (603) 624-3614
Contact: Pamela D. Mallett, Trust Officer

Limitations: Scholarships to needy residents of Petersborough, NH, and contiguous towns.
Financial data: Year ended 6/30/86. Assets, $4,634,842 (M); Total giving, $276,350; Grants to individuals, 210 grants totaling $276,350.
Employer Identification Number: 026051741
Applications: Deadline April 30th for first-time applicants and June 15th each year thereafter; Initial approach by letter; Completion of formal application required.

419
Lotta Agricultural Fund

c/o Trustees under the Will of Lotta M. Crabtree
294 Washington Street, Room 636
Boston, MA 02108   (617) 451-0698
Contact: Claire M. McCarthy, Trust Manager

Limitations: Farm loans to students and/or graduates of University of Massachusetts College of Natural Resources or of the Stockbridge School of Agriculture at the University.
Financial data: Year ended 12/31/85. Assets, $2,908,742 (M); Expenditures, $187,821; Loans to individuals, 4 loans totaling $70,000, high $25,000, low $10,000.
Employer Identification Number: 042610674
Applications: Applications accepted throughout the year; Initial approach by letter; Completion of formal application required; Interviews required.

420
Louisville Community Foundation, Inc., The

Meidinger Tower, Suite 101
Louisville, KY 40202   (502) 585-4649
Contact: Darrell L. Murphy, Executive Director

Limitations: Scholarships and student loans, as well as a teacher awards program for professional development. Giving is in the greater Louisville, KY, area.
Financial data: Year ended 6/30/85. Assets, $1,380,395 (M); Total giving, $90,219; Grants to

individuals amount not specified.
Employer Identification Number: 616019497
Publications: Annual report.

421★
Luling Foundation, The

523 South Mulberry Avenue
P.O. Drawer 31
Luling, TX 78648   (512) 875-2438
Contact: Archie Abrameit, Manager

Limitations: Scholarships to residents of Caldwell, Gonzales, and Guadalupe counties, TX, who are working toward an agricultural degree.
Financial data: Year ended 12/31/86. Assets, $5,551,229 (M); Total giving, $12,175; Grants to individuals, 3 grants totaling $3,000, each grant $1,000.
Employer Identification Number: 741143102
Applications: Deadline May 15th; Completion of formal application required.
Publications: 990-PF printed copy available upon request, application guidelines.

422
Lundquist (Walter E.) Scholarship Testamentary Trust

c/o First Interstate Bank of Oregon, N.A.
P.O. Box 2971
Portland, OR 97208
Contact: Superintendent, Kalama School District, P.O. Box 1097, Kalama, WA 98625

Limitations: Scholarships to graduates of Kalama High School, WA, who have resided in the state of Washington for at least one year.
Financial data: Year ended 3/31/87. Assets, $1,037,492 (M); Total giving, $75,786; Grants to individuals, 120 grants totaling $68,586, high $3,200, low $46, general range $250-750.
Employer Identification Number: 936145913
Applications: Deadline April 1st; Completion of formal application required.

423
Lurcy (Georges) Charitable and Educational Trust

c/o LeBoeuf, Laub, Leiby & Macrae
520 Madison Avenue
New York, NY 10022
Contact: Seth Frank, Trustee

Limitations: Fellowships for students of American colleges or universities to study in France and students of French colleges or universities to study in the U.S.
Financial data: Year ended 6/30/86. Assets, $12,224,550 (M); Total giving, $336,399; Grants to individuals amount not specified.

Employer Identification Number: 136372044
Applications: Fellowship applicants from America must be recommended by their universities; Applicants from France must apply to the Franco-American Commission for Educational Exchange. **Applicants cannot apply directly to the foundation.**

424
Lynch (John B.) Scholarship Foundation
P.O. Box 4248
Wilmington, DE 19807-0248   (302) 654-3444
Contact: Miss Eleanor L. Clemo, Secretary

Limitations: Scholarships to residents of the Wilmington, DE, area, of no more than 30 years of age, for undergraduate education.
Financial data: Year ended 12/31/86. Assets, $3,540,588 (M); Total giving, $165,706; Grants to individuals totaling $165,706.
Employer Identification Number: 516017041
Applications: Deadline March 15th; Completion of formal application required including transcript of academic records, three personal references, and a handwritten letter describing academic goals, summer employment, other efforts to finance education, something about self; Interviews granted upon request.
Publications: Program information, application guidelines.
Program description:
Undergraduate scholarships are awarded to needy and deserving students in the local area; applicants must be no more than 30 years of age. In addition to academic proficiency and financial need, selection criteria include capacity for leadership at home, at school, and in the community; demonstrated self-reliance; and a willingness to assume responsibility. It is assumed that applicants will have exhausted opportunities for assistance in their local community and school before approaching the foundation. No scholarships awarded for studies beyond the baccalaureate level.

Grants are given directly to the school on behalf of the recipient. A grant is generally made out right and repayment is not required. But it was the hope of the founder that persons who benefit from grants will recognize a moral commitment to reimburse the foundation if able to do so in later life. In this way, benefits received by present-day recipients will extend to needy and deserving students in the future.

Aid is given for only one academic year and may be renewed when justified. A recipient must reapply for each grant and should keep trustees informed of his/her academic and personal progress.

425
Lynch (William A.) Trust
Naumkeag Trust Company
217 Essex Street
Salem, MA 01970
Contact: Principal, Beverly High School, Beverly, MA 01915

Limitations: Scholarships to deservng Catholic graduates of public high schools in Beverly, MA, and nearby Catholic schools.
Financial data: Year ended 8/31/85. Assets, $52,131 (M); Total giving, $3,800; Grants to individuals, 15 grants totaling $3,800, high $700, low $10.
Employer Identification Number: 046016042
Applications: Deadline on or about June 1st; Initial approach by letter; Completion of formal application required.

426
Lyon Foundation, Inc.
65th and Scott Hamilton Drive
Little Rock, AR 72204
Contact: Ralph Cotham, Secretary-Treasurer, P.O. Box 4408, Little Rock, AR 72214

Limitations: Scholarships to residents of Arkansas.
Financial data: Year ended 12/31/86. Assets, $1,214,649 (M); Total giving, $378,883; Grants to individuals totaling $20,163; Subtotal for scholarships not specified.
Employer Identification Number: 716052168
Applications: Applications accepted throughout the year; Initial approach by letter or proposal, giving all pertinent information.

427
Lyons (Charles) Memorial Foundation, Inc.
2420 Pershing Road, Suite 400
Kansas City, MO 64108
Contact: Honorable H. Townsend Hader, President, P.O. Box 236, Lexington, MO 64067

Limitations: Scholarships only to graduates of Lafayette County, MO, high schools who are residents of Lafayette County at the time the application is made.
Financial data: Year ended 12/31/86. Assets, $815,964 (M); Total giving, $45,596; Grants to individuals, 83 grants totaling $45,596, high $800, low $200, average grant $500.
Employer Identification Number: 436056850
Applications: Deadline April 1st; Completion of formal application required.
Program description:
The foundation's scholarship program is not available to a parent, spouse, lineal descendent or spouse thereof of individuals who are substantial contributors, foundation managers, or members of the selection committee at the time the scholarship is granted.

428
MacCurdy-Salisbury Educational Foundation, Inc., The
Old Lyme, CT 06371   (203) 434-7983
Contact: Willis H. Umberger, Secrertary-Treasurer

Limitations: Scholarships only to residents of Lyme and Old Lyme, CT.
Financial data: Year ended 5/31/86. Assets, $2,454,531 (M); Total giving, $78,000; Grants to individuals, 158 grants totaling $78,000, high $1,250, low $125, general range $250-750.
Employer Identification Number: 066044250
Applications: Deadlines April 30th for first semester, November 15th for second semester; Completion of formal application required.

429
Mack Industrial School
c/o Fiduciary Trust Company
175 Federal Street
Boston, MA 02110
Contact: Mrs. William F. Cass, 92 Columbus Avenue, Salem, MA 01970; Tel.: (617) 744-7640; or Mrs. Robert F. Prentiss, 24 Dearborn Street, Salem, MA 01970; Tel.: (617) 745-0268

Limitations: Scholarships to women residents of Salem, MA, who are students primarily at various New England institutions.
Financial data: Year ended 8/31/86. Assets, $422,588 (M); Total giving, $24,700; Grants to individuals, 54 grants totaling $24,700, high $650, low $200.
Employer Identification Number: 046032773
Applications: Deadline May 1st; Completion of formal application required.

430
Maddox (J.F.) Foundation
P.O. Box 5410
Hobbs, NM 88241   (505) 393-6338
Contact: Robert Socolofsky, Executive Director

Limitations: Student loans primarily for residents of New Mexico and Western Texas.
Financial data: Year ended 6/30/86. Assets, $42,174,061 (M); Expenditures, $1,426,962; Loans to individuals, 45 loans totaling $62,165.
Employer Identification Number: 756023767
Applications: Applications accepted throughout the year; Initial approach by letter requesting application; Completion of formal application required.
Program description:
Student loans cover educational and living expenses and carry an interest rate of 6 percent per annum. Repayment begins one year from the date of completion of studies as determined by the foundation.

431★
Madison Scholarship Committee
3 Wilson Lane
Madison, NJ 07940
Contact: Mrs. Willard Thatcher, Applications Chairman

Limitations: Scholarships only to graduates of Madison, NJ, high schools.
Financial data: Year ended 6/30/85. Assets, $22,911 (M); Total giving, $18,150; Grants to individuals, 43 grants totaling $18,150, high $900, low $200, general range $300-500.
Employer Identification Number: 226100079
Applications: Deadline February 15th; Completion of formal application required; Interviews required.

432
Maffett (Minnie L.) Scholarship Trust
c/o RepublicBank Dallas
P.O. Box 241
Dallas, TX 75221
Contact: Margaret Gregory, Director of Financial Aid, Southern Methodist University, Dallas, TX 75275; Tel.: (214) 692-3417

Limitations: Scholarships to Texas students attending colleges and universities in Texas, majoring in pre-med, nursing or medical-related undergraduate studies, with preference to students from Limestone County, TX.
Financial data: Year ended 4/30/87. Assets, $809,839 (M); Total giving, $68,075; Grants to individuals, 106 grants totaling $68,075, high $2,000, low $100, general range $200-2,000, average grant $1,000.
Employer Identification Number: 756037885
Applications: Deadline April 1st; Completion of formal application and an official transcript required.

433
Magale Foundation, Inc., The
First National Bank of Shreveport
P.O. Box 21116
Shreveport, LA 71154   (318) 226-2382
Contact: Mary J. Fain, Treasurer

Limitations: Student loans only to residents of Arkansas, Louisiana, and Texas.
Financial data: Year ended 11/30/85. Assets, $1,467,715 (M); Expenditures, $145,120; Loans to individuals, 13 loans totaling $10,875, high $1,250, low $375.
Employer Identification Number: 726025096
Applications: Deadline April 1st; Initial approach by letter requesting application; Completion of formal application required.

434★
Maine Community Foundation, Inc., The
210 Main Street
P.O. Box 148
Ellsworth, ME 04605   (207) 667-9735
Contact: Marion Kane, Associate Director

Limitations: Scholarships to residents of Maine.
Financial data: Year ended 12/31/87. Assets,
$2,127,164 (M); Grants to individuals, 8 grants
totaling $7,100, high $1,000, low $100, average grant
$500.
Employer Identification Number: 010391479
Applications: Deadlines February 1st, April 1st, August
1st, October 1st and December 1st; Initial approach
by letter or telephone; Completion of formal
application required.
Publications: Annual report, application guidelines,
financial statement, informational brochure, 990-PF
printed copy available upon request.
Program description:
The foundation's scholarship program is comprised of
five funds:
    1. Maine Vietnam Veterans Scholarship Fund - To
    provide scholarship support to veterans of the
    United States Armed Forces who served in the
    Vietnam Theater and to their descendants and, as
    a second priority, to children of veterans of the
    armed services.
    2. Point Harbor Scholarship Fund - To provide
    scholarships to outstanding seniors of Sumner
    High School attending private liberal arts colleges
    or universities of national stature, and to support
    them during their undergraduate study.
    3. Marion and Irving Spurling Scholarship Fund -
    To provide scholarships to students and adults
    from Mt. Desert Island, the Cranberry Islands,
    Frenchboro and Swans Island seeking to pursue
    vocational training or education.
    4. Clifton K. and Martha A. Hale Scholarship
    Fund - To provide scholarships to residents of
    Sorrento, ME, and Sullivan, ME, who are
    graduating seniors or recent graduates and
    enrolled in an accredited college, university or
    technical school.
    5. Carl and Gwendolyn Hammar Scholarship
    Fund - To provide scholarship support to residents
    of Islesboro, ME, who are graduating seniors or
    recent graduates and who are enrolled in an
    accredited technical school or have been
    valedictorian of their high school graduating class
    and are enrolled in an accredited college,
    university or technical school.

435★
Mallinckrodt (Edward), Jr. Foundation
611 Olive, Suite 1400
St. Louis, MO 63101
Contact: Charles C. Allen, Jr., Secretary

Limitations: Research grants to individuals in
biomedical areas. Must by connected with a U.S.
university.
Financial data: Year ended 9/30/87. Assets,
$17,380,565 (M); Total giving, $681,382; Grants to
individuals, 6 grants totaling $416,308, high
$110,000, low $45,000.
Employer Identification Number: 436030295
Applications: Applications accepted throughout the
year; Initial approach by letter.
Publications: Annual report, 990-PF printed copy
available upon request.

436
Maloney (William E.) Foundation
157 Emerson Road
P.O. Box 515
Lexington, MA 02173   (617) 862-9200
Contact: 275 Massachusetts Avenue, Lexington, MA
02173; Tel.: (617) 862-3400.

Limitations: Scholarships primarily to residents of
Massachusetts.
Financial data: Year ended 12/31/85. Assets,
$1,055,963 (M); Total giving, $88,000; Grants to
individuals, 3 grants totaling $15,500.
Employer Identification Number: 046131998
Applications: Applications accepted throughout the
year; Completion of formal application required.

437
Marshall & Ilsley Bank Foundation, Inc.
770 North Water Street
Milwaukee, WI 53202

Limitations: Scholarships only to residents of the
greater Milwaukee, WI, area.
Financial data: Year ended 12/31/86. Assets,
$2,785,531 (M); Total giving, $799,525; Grants to
individuals, 11 grants totaling $16,000, high $2,000,
low $1,000.
Employer Identification Number: 396043185

438
Marymount (Mother Joseph Rogan) Foundation
2217 Clayville Court
Chesterfield, MO 63017   (314) 533-0400
Contact: Joseph E. Lynch, Treasurer

Limitations: Scholarships to high school students and
loans to college and university students. Preference
given to residents of the greater St. Louis, MO, area.
Financial data: Year ended 6/30/87. Assets, $571,306

(M); Total giving, $9,785; Grants to individuals, 7 grants totaling $7,535, high $1,200, low $1,000, average grant $1,000.

Employer Identification Number: 237418805

Applications: Applications accepted throughout the year; Initial approach by letter stating financial situation.

Program description:

The purpose of the scholarship program is to aid students entering or attending high school and colleges or universities through the provision of financial grants or loans.

College students receive loans which are repayable at a later date.

439
Mason (Fanny Peabody) Music Foundation, Inc.

c/o Fiduciary Trust Co.
175 Federal Street
Boston, MA 02110

Limitations: Scholarships to pianists to further their musical studies.

Financial data: Year ended 3/31/86. Assets, $182,162 (M); Total giving, $10,000; Grants to individuals, 1 grant totaling $10,000.

Employer Identification Number: 042319266

Applications: Deadline October 31st; Completion of formal application required; Submit applications to the foundation at 192 Commonwealth Avenue, Suite 4, Boston, MA 02116.

Publications: Application guidelines.

440
Masonic Educational Foundation, Inc.

1300 Masonic Temple Building
333 St. Charles Street
New Orleans, LA 70130
Contact: Jack Crouch, Grand Secretary

Limitations: Scholarships to residents of Louisiana.

Financial data: Year ended 12/31/86. Assets, $254,528 (M); Total giving, $27,001; Grants to individuals, 46 grants totaling $27,001, high $1,000, low $400.

Employer Identification Number: 237423947

Applications: Funds severely limited; Completion of formal application including family financial statement required. **Applications from individuals residing outside of stated geographic restriction not accepted.**

441
McCallay (Edwin L. and Louis B.) Educational Trust Fund

c/o First National Bank of Southwestern Ohio, Trust Division
P.O. Box 476
Hamilton, OH 45012
Contact: Trust Officer, First National Bank of

Southwestern Ohio, P.O. Box 220, Monroe, OH 45050

Limitations: Scholarships to graduates of high schools in the Middletown, OH, city school district, including Fenwick High School, to attend colleges, universities or other institutions of higher learning.

Financial data: Year ended 2/28/87. Assets, $285,415 (M); Total giving, $7,300; Grants to individuals, 20 grants totaling $7,300, high $800, low $100, general range $300-700.

Employer Identification Number: 316111939

Applications: Applications can be obtained at high schools in the Middletown, OH, city school district.

Program description:

Students must show ability and financial need. Scholarship grants are paid to the institution for the benefit of the student to cover the expense of tuition, school fees, room and board, transportation, and related incidentals.

442★
McClure (James G.K.) Educational and Development Fund, Inc.

Hickory Nut Gap Farm
Route 6, Box 100
Fairview, NC 28730   (704) 628-3105
Contact: John Curtis Ager, Executive Director

Limitations: Scholarships limited to residents of western North Carolina, including the following counties: Alleghany, Ashe, Avery, Buncombe, Burke, Caldwell, Cherokee, Clay, Graham, Haywood, Henderson, Jackson, Macon, Madison, McDowell, Mitchell, Polk, Rutherford, Swain, Transylvania, Watauga, and Yancey.

Financial data: Year ended 12/31/87. Assets, $1,706,021 (M); Total giving, $68,877; Grants to individuals totaling $51,107.

Employer Identification Number: 560690982

Applications: Initial approach by letter; Completion of formal application required.

Publications: Biennial report.

Program description:

Scholarship payments are made directly to specific colleges on behalf of the recipients, and all applications must be submitted to these colleges, which include Asheville-Buncombe Technical College, Appalachian State University, Berea College, Blue Ridge Community College, Brevard College, Gardner-Webb College, Haywood Technical College, Isothermal Community College, Lees-McRae College, Mars Hill College, Mayland Technical College, McDowell Technical College, Montreat-Anderson College, North Carolina School of the Arts, North Carolina State University, Southwestern Technical College, Tri-County Technical College, University of North Carolina-Asheville, University of North Carolina-Greensboro, Warren Wilson College,

Western Carolina University, Western Piedmont Community College, Wilkes Community College, and Young Harris College.

The following factors will be considered:
- High school record for both scholarship and leadership
- Evidence of Christian character
- Financial need
- Intellectual promise and demonstrated ambition.

A special effort is made to offer scholarships to minority students from the region, and students entering into nursing and other health career related fields. Students facing a sudden and catastrophic financial problem may apply for a hardship grant to finish their course of study.

The **Dumont Clarke Scholarship Fund** is available for active ministers in the region who would like to attend a course of study to enhance some aspect of their work. Application forms are available from the fund office.

The **Edward deZulueta Greenebaum Fund** is a special scholarship fund reserved for promising students from the Canada Township of Jackson County.

443
McCormick (Anne O'Hare) Memorial Fund, Inc.
c/o Newswomens Club of NY
15 Gramercy Park
New York, NY 10003   (212) 777-1612
Contact: Foundation Trustees

Limitations: Scholarships limited to women accepted by the Columbia University School of Journalism, NY.
Financial data: Year ended 12/31/85. Assets, $84,052 (M); Total giving, $14,600; Grants to individuals, 7 grants totaling $14,600, high $3,100, low $1,500.
Employer Identification Number: 136144221
Applications: Applications accepted throughout the year; Completion of formal application stating need for scholarship award required.
Program description:
The **Anne O'Hare McCormick Scholarship** and the **Mary E. Watts Award** are awarded to women who have been accepted by the Graduate School of Journalism at Columbia University. Selection is based on financial need and academic background, but primarily on the fund's assessment of the individual's potential for contributing to journalism in either broadcast or print media. Prior experience in the field is not necessary.

444
McCurdy Memorial Scholarship Foundation
134 West Van Buren Street
Battle Creek, MI 49017   (616) 962-9591
Contact: Michael C. Jordan

Limitations: Undergraduate scholarships to residents of Calhoun County, MI.
Financial data: Year ended 12/31/86. Assets, $437,432 (M); Total giving, $23,750; Grants to individuals, 26 grants totaling $23,750, general range $500-1,000, average grant $1,000.
Employer Identification Number: 381687120
Applications: Deadline April 1st; Completion of formal application required; Interviews required.
Program description:
Awards are made on the basis of excellence in scholastic and other activities and are renewable contingent upon the continuance of above-average work in college. Approximately six to eight new awards are available each year.

445
McDavid (G.N. and Edna) Dental Education Trust
c/o Mercantile Bank, N.A.
P.O. Box 387, Main Post Office
St. Louis, MO 63166   (314) 425-2672
Contact: Ms. Jill Fivecoat, Assistant Vice-President

Limitations: Student loans to residents of Missouri attending an accredited dental school in Missouri. Preference given to residents of Madison County, MO.
Financial data: Year ended 12/31/86. Assets, $1,481,607 (M); Expenditures, $15,434, Loans to individuals, 32 loans totaling $96,182, high $5,800, low 1,500, average loan, $2,500.
Employer Identification Number: 436192984
Applications: Contact Financial Aid office of dental school for application information.

446
McDonald Memorial Fund Trust
c/o First National Bank of Warsaw
P.O. Box 1447
Warsaw, IN 46580

Limitations: Loans for high school, college, or professional studies.
Financial data: Year ended 12/31/86. Assets, $1,349,751 (M); Expenditures, $174,044; Loans to individuals, 198 loans totaling $150,591, high $3,000, low $500.
Employer Identification Number: 356018326
Applications: For application information, contact the Superintendent of Warsaw Community Schools, Warsaw, IN 46580.
Publications: Informational brochure.

Program description:
Students applying for loans must be enrolled and in good standing or have been accepted for enrollment at an eligible school (most public and private institutions meet these requirements).

Loans are interest free while the recipient is in school and four months thereafter. However, all loans are interest-bearing during the repayment period, which begins five months after the recipient completes his course of study or leaves school, and is normally scheduled from five-to-ten years.

447
McDowell (Verne Catt) Corporation
P.O. Box 128
Albany, OR 97321   (503) 928-5955
Contact: Katherine Buike

Limitations: Scholarships to members of the Christian Church (Disciples of Christ) for graduate theological studies.
Financial data: Year ended 12/31/86. Assets, $331,510 (M); Total giving, $24,575; Grants to individuals, 9 grants totaling $20,476, high $3,298, low $1,458.
Employer Identification Number: 936022991
Applications: Completion of formal application required; Interviews required.
Program description:
Applicants for scholarships must have baccalaureate degrees from accredited liberal arts colleges or universities, and be accepted at graduate institutions of theological education accredited by the Association of Theological Schools. Approximately two new awards are available each year.

448
McFarland Charitable Foundation
c/o Havana National Bank
112 South Orange Street
Havana, IL 62644
Contact: Kathy Tarvin, Director of Nursing Service, Mason District Hospital, 520 East Franklin Street, Havana, IL 62644; Tel.: (309) 543-4431

Limitations: Scholarships to student nurses from Mason County, IL.
Financial data: Year ended 12/31/86. Assets, $1,500,000 (L); Total giving, $80,000; Grants to individuals, 10 grants totaling $80,000, high $8,048, low $1,549.
Employer Identification Number: 376022376
Applications: Deadline May 1st; Completion of formal application and interviews required.
Publications: Application guidelines, program information.
Program description:
Students may apply during their senior year of high school. Grants normally cover three years of study.

449
McIntire (John) Educational Fund
c/o First National Bank, Trust Department
P.O. Box 2668, 422 Main Street
Zanesville, OH 43701   (614) 432-8444
Contact: R. L. Hecker, Senior Trust Officer

Limitations: College scholarships to residents of Zanesville, OH, who are single and under 21 years of age.
Financial data: Year ended 6/30/87. Assets, $4,441,759 (M); Total giving, $144,075; Grants to individuals, 140 grants totaling $144,075, high $1,600, low $250.
Employer Identification Number: 316021239
Applications: Deadline May 1st; Completion of formal application required.

450
McKaig (Lalitta Nash) Foundation
c/o Pittsburgh National Bank
Trust Department 966
Pittsburgh, PA 15265
Contact: Henry C. Flood, Vice-President, Pittsburgh National Bank

Limitations: Scholarships to residents of Bedford and Somerset counties, PA, Mineral and Hamshir counties, WV, and Allegany and Garrett counties, MD, for undergraduate, graduate, or professional education at any accredited college or university located in the U.S.
Financial data: Year ended 9/30/86. Assets, $5,008,161 (M); Total giving, $194,627; Grants to individuals, 283 grants totaling $194,627, high $3,000, low $50.
Employer Identification Number: 256071908
Applications: Deadline May 31st; Application forms available from Cumberland, MD, area high school guidance offices, Frostburg State College and Allegany Community College financial aid offices, the Pittsburgh National Bank, or the foundation's Cumberland office, P.O. Box 1360, Cumberland, MD 21502; Tel.: (301) 777-1533; Completion of formal application required; Submit Financial Aid Form (F.A.F.) and Supplement directly to College Scholarship Service; Interviews required.
Program description:
Scholarship recipients are selected primarily on the basis of their financial need as computed by the College Scholarship Service from information contained on the Financial Aid Form (F.A.F.) and Supplement. The foundation will not normally base any selection of a recipient on his/her past academic performance. Persons applying for a renewal grant, however, will also be evaluated on their scholarship performance during all prior periods of college level education.

All persons are eligible to apply for renewal grants provided they resubmit their application and F.A.F.

and Supplement for the applicable year and continue to meet the residency requirement. A renewal applicant is not automatically guaranteed a renewal grant.

451
McKee (Ella G.) Foundation
c/o First National Bank
First National Bank Building
Vandalia, IL 62471   (618) 283-1141

Limitations: Scholarships to individuals who are current residents of Fagette County, IL, for at least four years.
Financial data: Year ended 12/31/86. Assets, $760,600 (M); Total giving, $64,028; Grants to individuals, 63 grants totaling $64,028, high $1,800, low $140, general range $600-1,600.
Employer Identification Number: 376099863

452★
McKnight Foundation, The
410 Peavey Building
Minneapolis, MN 55402   (612) 333-4220
Contact: Russell V. Ewald, Executive Vice-President

Limitations: Grants only to researchers in neuroscience or plant biology.
Financial data: Year ended 12/31/86. Assets, $711,287,900 (M); Total giving, $31,648,302; Grants to individuals, 68 grants totaling $3,541,462; Subtotal for Neuroscience, 42 grants totaling $1,641,462, high $100,000, low $30,000; Subtotal for Plant Biology, 16 grants totaling $1,850,000, high $300,000, low $35,000.
Employer Identification Number: 410754835
Applications: See program description below for application information on specific programs.
Publications: Annual report (including application guidelines).
Program description:
Neuroscience Research Awards Programs: In late 1986, the foundation established The McKnight Endowment Fund for Neuroscience which will now administer the neuroscience awards previously managed by the foundation. All inquiries should be directed to the fund in care of Fred Plum, M.D., President, Box 117, 525 East 68th Street, New York, NY 10021; Tel.: (212) 472-4665.

The **McKnight Scholars Awards** are granted to support M.D. and/or Ph.D. candidates who have completed two to five years of meritorious postdoctoral research in neuroscience, and who are embarking on an independent career in research. Applicants (and institutions) must reside in the U.S. and be U.S. citizens or hold Visa 1-151 status. The sponsoring institution receives the award, which may be used at the discretion of the awardee. Funds may be used for salary and direct costs but not for indirect

costs. Five new awards are made each year in the amount of $105,000 disbursed evenly over a three-year period or $35,000 per annum subject to annual review of the research progress.

The **McKnight Awards for Research Projects** are granted to support investigative programs of outstanding quality involving established neuroscientists and their associates. The awards are few in number and highly selective. The purpose of the award is to encourage experienced and gifted investigators to direct more of their eforts to develop new approaches to the understanding of the basic mechanisms of memory and diseases affecting memory.

Applications are solicited only by invitation following an extensive nominating process. Applications are evaluated by an outside Review Committee of expert advisors which recommends potential recipients to the foundation's directors. Awards are for a minimum of three years in the amount of $50,000 per year.

The **McKnight Neuroscience Development Awards** were initiated in 1981, to encourage experienced investigators to direct more of their efforts to the basic mechanisms of memory and diseases affecting memory. Applications solicited only by invitation following an extensive nominating process. Awards are available every three years.

Plant Biology Research Awards Program: The **McKnight Awards for Individual Research Projects in Plant Biology** are awarded to outstanding individual scientists who are conducting basic research in plant biology as it relates to agriculture. The primary purpose is to make research support available to gifted individuals who have conducted independent research for a period of more than two years but less than six years following completion of postdoctoral studies. A second purpose is to support investigators who desire to undertake new initiatives in plant biology which may be beyond the scope of their previous endeavors. Awards are 10 in number in the amount of $35,000 per year for a three-year period. Use of funds is flexible to permit approaches to research and training that are not presently possible through the usual funding channels. Funds may be used for salary and direct costs but not indirect costs.

In 1986, six recipients were awarded substantial grants (ranging form $200,000 to $300,000) through the foundation's Interdisciplinary Awards in Plant Biology 1986-1989.

Information about the plant biology per research program is available from the foundation office.

453
McMannis (William J.) and A. Haskell McMannis Educational Fund

6170 Central Avenue, Suite F
St. Petersburg, FL 33707   (813) 345-8689
Contact: Fred B. Sieber, Executive Director

Limitations: Scholarships for higher education only to students who are U.S. citizens.
Financial data: Year ended 8/31/87. Assets, $2,678,848 (M); Total giving, $102,750; Grants to individuals, 102 grants totaling $102,750, high $2,000, low $250, average grant, $1,000.
Employer Identification Number: 256191302
Applications: Deadline May 1st; Completion of formal application including additional three copies required.
Publications: Informational brochure (including application guidelines).
Program description:
Grants are paid directly to the institution for the benefit of the recipient who is "enrolled and in good standing."

454★
McMillan (Bruce), Jr., Foundation, Inc.

P.O. Box 9
Overton, TX 75684   (214) 834-3148
Contact: Ralph Ward, President

Limitations: Scholarships to graduates of eight high schools in the immediate Overton, TX, area.
Financial data: Year ended 6/30/85. Assets, $11,801,779 (M); Total giving, $719,399; Grants to individuals, 129 grants totaling $78,999, high $1,500, low $125.
Employer Identification Number: 750945924
Applications: Deadline May 31st for scholarship interviews, June 15th for scholarship applications; Initial approach by letter; Completion of formal application required; Interviews required.
Program description:
The foundation provides scholarship support to high school seniors attending the following high schools within an approximate 15-mile radius of Overton, TX: West Rusk High School, Overton High School, Henderson High School, Leverett Chapel High School, Kilgore High School, Troup High School, Arp High School, and Carlisle High School.

455
Mellen Foundation, The

3200 National City Center
Cleveland, OH 44114
Contact: Lillie R. Marquis, 9519 Arban Drive, St. Louis, MO 63126

Limitations: Fellowships for registered nurses in states east of the Mississippi River, or in metropolitan Minneapolis, MN, St. Louis, MO, or New Orleans, LA.

Financial data: Year ended 12/31/85. Assets, $12,756,812 (M); Total giving, $936,858; Grants to individuals, 19 grants totaling $105,858, high $8,600, low $1,694.
Employer Identification Number: 346560874
Applications: Deadline January 15th for requesting applications; Completion of formal application required.
Program description:
The foundation grants graduate fellowships in critical care nursing to registered nurses licensed to practice in the U.S. who are seeking an MSN specializing in critical care nursing. All applicants must be U.S. citizens or permanent residents and meet the following additional requirements:
  1. Be legal residents of or employed in a state east of the Mississippi River, or Minneapolis, MN, St. Louis, MO, or New Orleans, LA.
  2. Hold a BSN degree from an accredited program.
  3. Have three years experience in nursing, including at least one year in a critical care capacity.
  4. Must take the Miller Analogies Test (if unavailable in applicant's state, Graduate Record Exam scores must be substituted).
Fellowships will provide payment for tuition and fees up to a maximum annual as determined by the foundation's board of trustees. The fellowships shall be awarded for a one-year period although they may be continued for a second year upon satisfactory progress toward the MSN degree.
The applicants for fellowships will be screened by a committee of consultants selected by the president of the foundation. The principal standards to be applied in screening and selecting the applicants for fellowships are as follows:
  1. Evidence of personal qualities which assist acute/critical patient care;
  2. Evidence of outstanding intellectual and academic abilities;
  3. Evidence of the ability to impart to other nurses the specialized knowledge acquired in the graduate program;
  4. Indication of personal and professional leadership and qualities which will serve as role models for nurses;
  5. Evidence of interest in nursing practice research and of commitment to employing this research practice;
  6. A sense of nursing as a profession and of a responsibility to that profession;
  7. Evidence of concern with the ethical, normal and social implications of the nursing profession;
  8. A clear philosophy of patient care and a commitment to being an agent of change; and
  9. Indication of a career committed to the practice of critical care nursing.

456★
Mellinger (Edward Arthur) Educational
Foundation, Inc.

1025 East Broadway
P.O. Box 278
Monmouth, IL 61462   (309) 734-2419
Contact: Scholarship Committee

Limitations: Scholarships to undergraduate and student loans primarily to graduate students residing in or attending institutions in the Midwest.
Financial data: Year ended 12/31/86. Assets, $12,423,446 (M); Expenditures, $975,759; Grants to individuals totaling $391,697; Loans to individuals totaling $338,624.
Employer Identification Number: 362428421
Applications: Deadline June 1st for completed applications; Submit application February through May; Initial approach by letter; Completion of formal application required.
Publications: Program information, application guidelines.
Program description:
The foundation awards scholarships to undergraduate students and loans to graduate and fifth-year students who are scholastically qualified full-time students in need of financial assistance to attend accredited institutions in the U.S.

Geographic limitations for the foundation's scholarship and student loan program are as follows:

● Priority is given to those residing and attending schools in Illinois and Iowa.

● Second consideration is given to applicants residing in states contiguous to Illinois and Iowa, including Indiana, Kansas, Kentucky, Michigan, Minnesota, Missouri, Nebraska, South Dakota and Wisconsin.

● Third consideration is given to students who attend institutions in the above named states.
Students not in these categories do not normally receive consideration.

Scholarships can be renewed annually up to a maximum of four years (including the original grant) for students enrolled in programs leading to a bachelor's degree. For students enrolled in other programs, scholarships can be renewed annually up to the completion of the prescribed course of study.

Loans may be granted on a renewal basis to graduate students to complete the degree program applied for.

In all cases, renewals are contingent upon the student's maintaining normal progress toward completion of the prescribed course of study.

457
Menasha Corporation Foundation

P.O. Box 367
Neenah, WI 54956   (414) 729-0326
Contact: Oliver C. Smith, President

Limitations: Scholarships only to children of employees of Menasha Corporation.
Financial data: Year ended 12/31/86. Assets, $579,898 (M); Total giving, $140,518; Grants to individuals, 57 grants totaling $43,150, high $1,500, low $500, average grant $750.
Employer Identification Number: 396047384
Applications: Applications accepted throughout the year; Initial approach by letter.

458★
Menn (Gregory) Foundation

c/o The Marine Trust Co., N.A.
P.O. Box 1308
Milwaukee, WI 53201   (414) 735-1382
Contact: Claude Radtke, Appleton High School-East, Guidance Office, Appleton, WI 54911

Limitations: Scholarships to students and graduates of Appleton High School-East, Appleton, WI.
Financial data: Year ended 6/30/87. Assets, $411,968 (M); Total giving, $12,807; Grants to individuals totaling $12,807.
Employer Identification Number: 396143254
Applications: Deadline May 1st.
Program description:
Selection criteria include academic excellence and school participation.

459
Meriden Foundation, The

Meriden Trust & Safe Deposit Company
P.O. Box 951
Meriden, CT 06450
Contact: Jeffrey F. Otis, Secretary, Distribution Committee

Limitations: Scholarships primarily to residents of the Meriden-Wallingford, CT, area.
Financial data: Year ended 12/31/85. Assets, $2,536,364 (M); Total giving, $117,029; Grants to individuals, 55 grants totaling $45,613, high $2,438, low $225.
Employer Identification Number: 066037849
Applications: Applications accepted throughout the year; Initial approach by letter.

460
Meyer (Roy E. and Merle) Foundation
408 Main Street, Suite M-101
Red Wing, MN 55066   (612) 388-4788
Contact: Guidance Office, Red Wing Central High
School, Red Wing, MN 55066

Limitations: Scholarships to Red Wing Central High
School, MN, seniors who intend to pursue a career in
engineering or the sciences.
Financial data: Year ended 12/31/86. Assets, $72,820
(M); Total giving, $4,200; Grants to individuals, 5
grants totaling $4,200, high $900, low $600, average
grant $900.
Employer Identification Number: 416078887
Applications: Contact Red Wing Central High School
for current application deadline.
Program description:
The foundation considers past scholastic achievements
including grade point average, financial need, and
college entrance exam results of applicants.

461★
Meyers (Allen H.) Foundation
P.O. Box 100
Tecumseh, MI 49286   (517) 423-7629

Limitations: Scholarships only to seniors in Lenawee
County, MI, planning studies in the sciences and allied
fields.
Financial data: Year ended 4/30/87. Assets, $196,790
(M); Total giving, $6,000; Grants to individuals, 20
grants totaling $6,000, each grant $300.
Employer Identification Number: 386143278
Applications: Deadline March 15th; Initial approach
by letter requesting application form and including
information about intended field of study; Interviews
required.
Publications: Program information.
Program description:
The foundation was established to encourage, support,
and stimulate scientific education, teaching, research
and related efforts such as in engineering and
aerospace study and design.

High school graduates and college students
planning studies in the sciences and allied fields (e.g.
natural sciences, physical sciences, medicine,
chemistry, engineering, computer science,
mathematics, aeronautics, space science) may apply
for scholarships. Selection is based on character,
academic purpose, financial need, and leadership
qualities. Awards are made only once to any
individual and are only renewable under exceptional
circumstances.

462
Middlesex County Medical Society Foundation, Inc.
P.O. Box 674
Franklin Park, NJ 08823   (201) 257-6800
Contact: Mary Alice Bruno

Limitations: Scholarships only to residents of at least
five years of Middlesex County, NJ, for the study of
medicine, nursing or pharmacy.
Financial data: Year ended 9/30/86. Assets, $154,303
(M); Total giving, $7,750; Grants to individuals, 17
grants totaling $7,750, high $1,625, low $150, general
range $150-500, average grant $250.
Employer Identification Number: 221767843
Applications: Deadline February 1st; Completion of
formal application required.

463
Midland Foundation
212 West Main Street
P.O. Box 289
Midland, MI 48640   (517) 839-9661
Contact: M. Gene Arnold, Executive Director

Limitations: Loans only to residents of the Midland
County, MI, area.
Financial data: Year ended 12/31/86. Assets,
$7,684,668 (L); Expenditures, $343,842; Loans to
individuals totaling $40,703.
Employer Identification Number: 382023395
Applications: Applications accepted throughout the
year; Initial approach by telephone.
Publications: Annual report.

464★
Miles Foundation
(Formerly Miles Laboratories Foundation)
1127 Myrtle Street
P.O. Box 40
Elkhart, IN 46515   (219) 264-8225
Contact: Lehman F. Beardsley, Chairman

Limitations: Scholarships to students attending the
Goshen College School of Nursing in Goshen, IN, and
to high school students from Indiana.
Financial data: Year ended 12/31/87. Assets,
$2,944,908 (M); Total giving, $494,849, Grants to
individuals, 25 grants totaling $20,400, high $1,000,
low $200, general range $400-1,000, average grant
$800.
Employer Identification Number: 356026510
Applications: Applications accepted throughout the
year; Contact foundation for current application
deadline; Initial approach by letter; Interviews
required by high school administrator.
Publications: Financial statement.

465
Milford Educational Foundation
P.O. Box 483
Milford, NH 03055
Contact: Allen G. White, Treasurer

Limitations: Student loans only to residents of Milford, NH.
Financial data: Year ended 12/31/85. Assets, $193,714 (M); Expenditures, $12,310 (M); Loans to individuals, 12 loans totaling $11,500, high $1,500, low $500, average loan $1,000.
Employer Identification Number: 237147469
Applications: Deadlines May 25th for fall term and November 15th for spring term.
Program description:
The student loan is interest-free until recipient graduates or leaves school. Repayment must begin 60 days after the earlier event.

466★
Millar Scholarship Fund
c/o Oregon Bank
P.O. Box 2808
Portland, OR 97208
Contact: Reynolds High School, 1200 NE 201st, Troutdale, OR 97060; Tel.: (503) 667-3178

Limitations: Scholarships to high school graduates of Reynolds High School and Columbia High School, OR, for study at Oregon postsecondary institutions.
Financial data: Year ended 12/31/86. Assets, $365,000 (M); Total giving, $18,567; Grants to individuals, 54 grants totaling $18,567, high $800, low $67, general range $200-400.
Employer Identification Number: 936054074
Applications: Deadline March 30th; Completion of formal application required.
Program description:
Initial selection of academically able but financially needy students is made by a committee consisting of counselors from Reynolds High School and Columbia High School, and the trustees of Smith Memorial Church, Fairview, OR. Scholarships are renewable after the first year to provide up to a maximum of four years of postsecondary education.

Recipients may attend a college, university, community college, nursing school, business college, and any other institution offering a course of study leading to a degree or certificate in the State of Oregon. The student must show satisfactory progress in his/her studies during the initial year.

467
Millhollon (Nettie) Educational Trust
P.O. Box 32
Stanton, TX 79782
Contact: Ed Lawson, Chairman

Limitations: Educational loans to needy residents of Texas.
Financial data: Year ended 6/30/87. Assets, $2,081,492 (M); Total giving, $78,688; Loans to individuals totaling $114,350.
Employer Identification Number: 756024639
Program description:
Student loans are interest-free until the student completes his/her education. Thereafter the loans bear eight percent interest per annum.

The criteria for approval of the loan application are, financial need, good character, evidence of ability and desire to learn and further one's education, and unavailability of financial assistance from any other source.

468★
Milwaukee Music Scholarship Foundation
c/o First Wisconsin Trust Company
P.O. Box 2054
Milwaukee, WI 53201   (414) 765-5908
Contact: M. Gregis

Limitations: Financial assistance to residents of Wisconsin who are needy, worthy, and talented, and wish to pursue training and education in the field of music.
Financial data: Year ended 5/31/87. Assets, $48,381 (M); Total giving, $2,700; Grants to individuals, 4 grants totaling $2,700, high $1,000, low $500, general range $500-1,000, average grant $675.
Employer Identification Number: 396036838
Applications: Deadline February 1st for spring audition; Initial approach by letter requesting application; Completion of formal application required; Auditions required. Those applicants selected are granted an audition before the selection committee to determine grantees.
Program description:
Successful applicants are only eligible to receive awards from the foundation once. Previous winners may not reapply.

469
Minear (Ruth M.) Educational Trust
c/o First National Bank in Wabash
202 South Wabash Street
Wabash, IN 46992   (219) 563-1116
Contact: Allen P. Spring, Senior Vice-President, P.O. Box 397, Wabash, IN 46992

Limitations: Scholarships only to graduates of Wabash High School, Wabash, IN, for study at an accredited post-secondary school in Indiana. Must apply annually.

Financial data: Year ended 2/28/86. Assets, $1,413,585 (M); Total giving, $122,250; Grants to individuals totaling $122,250.

Employer Identification Number: 356335021

Applications: Deadline middle of February; Completion of formal application required along with State of Indiana financial aid forms and certification of acceptance at accredited college.

470★
Minnesota Foundation
1120 Norwest Center
St. Paul, MN 55101   (612) 224-5463
Contact: Judith K. Healey, President

Limitations: Scholarships to residents of Minnesota. Grants are limited by fund agreements.

Financial data: Year ended 12/31/87. Assets, $8,025,244 (M); Total giving, $570,525; Grants to individuals, 7 grants totaling $10,093, high $5,990, low $500, general range $500-6,000; average grant $1,400.

Employer Identification Number: 410832480

Applications: Deadline varies.

Publications: Annual report.

Program description:
In recent years, grants to individuals have included scholarships and travel grants to attend conferences in the areas of business and library science.

471
Minor (The Berkeley) and Susan Fontaine Minor Foundation
c/o John L. Ray
1210 One Valley Square
Charleston, WV 25301

Limitations: Scholarships only to residents of West Virginia.

Financial data: Year ended 12/31/86. Assets, $1,600,785 (M); Total giving, $71,800; Grants to individuals, 20 grants totaling $71,800, high $6,800, low $1,000.

Employer Identification Number: 556014946

Applications: Deadline August 1st; Initial approach by letter; Only students attending West Virginia University or Marshall University should apply directly to the foundation. Applicants must be admitted to and recommended for financial aid by the University of Charleston, the University of Virginia, or the Protestant Episcopal Theological Seminary of Virginia.

Program description:
Scholarships are awarded for a four-year period to regular, full-time students attending the University of Charleston (formerly Morris Harvey College), Marshall University or the University of Virginia; for a three-year period to students attending the Protestant Episcopal Theological Seminary of Virginia; for a two-year period to nursing students attending the University of Charleston; and for a one-year period to students at the College of Law of West Virginia University. The scholarships are paid to the institutions on behalf of the individuals.

472
Miskoff (John) Foundation
665 North East 58th Street
Miami, FL 33137   (305) 754-5169

Limitations: Scholarship loans for students who have completed their sophomore year of college.

Financial data: Year ended 6/30/86. Assets, $1,789,434 (M); Expenditures, $97,646; Loans to individuals, 13 loans totaling $52,000, high $5,000, low $2,500.

Employer Identification Number: 592193608

Publications: Program information.

Program description:
Preliminary screening is done by the college. Applicants are then interviewed by the foundation.

473
Mocquereau (The Dom) Foundation, Inc.
c/o Davis Polk & Wardwell
499 Park Avenue
New York, NY 10020   (212) 759-3076
Contact: James F. Dolan, President

Limitations: Grants to teachers of Gregorian chants.

Financial data: Year ended 9/30/86. Assets, $1,156,398 (M); Total giving, $134,950; Grants to individuals, 4 grants totaling $52,950, high $18,000, low $9,950.

Employer Identification Number: 237118643

Applications: Funds fully committed.

Program description:
The foundation's support for the teaching of Gregorian chants is represented by providing direct payment of salary of teachers of Gregorian chants.

474
Monterey County, Community Foundation for
P.O. Box 1384
Monterey, CA 93942   (408) 375-9712
Contact: Todd Lueders, Executive Director

Limitations: Scholarships primarily to residents of Monterey County, CA.

Financial data: Year ended 12/31/86. Assets, $4,300,000 (M); Total giving, $267,000; Grants to individuals, 2 grants totaling $2,000.

Employer Identification Number: 941615897

Applications: Initial approach by telephone or letter.

Applications from individuals residing outside of stated geographic restriction not accepted.

Publications: Annual report.

475
Moody Foundation, The
704 Moody National Bank Building
Galveston, TX 77550   (409) 763-5333
Contact: Peter M. Moore, Grants Officer

Limitations: Scholarships only for graduates of high schools of Galveston County, TX.
Financial data: Year ended 12/31/86. Assets, $221,694,669 (M); Total giving, $12,106,057; Grants to individuals totaling $185,411.
Employer Identification Number: 741403105
Applications: Contact foundation for current application information.
Publications: Annual report, program information.
Program description:
Grants are made to colleges and universities on behalf of individuals under a scholarship program funded by the foundation.

476
Moore (Alfred) Foundation
c/o C.L. Page Enterprises, Inc.
P.O. Box 18426
Spartanburg, SC 29318   (803) 582-6844
Contact: Cary L. Page, Jr., Chairman

Limitations: Scholarships and loans to residents of Spartanburg and Anderson counties, SC.
Financial data: Year ended 12/31/86. Assets, $1,923,691 (M); Total giving, $65,550; Grants to individuals, 16 grants totaling $19,750; Loans to individuals amount not specified.
Employer Identification Number: 576018424
Applications: Deadline March 29th for scholarships; Contact foundation for loan application deadline; Initial approach by letter.

477
Moore (Harry W. and Margaret) Foundation, Inc.
5051 Kitridge Road
Dayton, OH 45424   (513) 233-0233
Contact: A. C. Reiger, Jr., Secretary-Treasurer

Limitations: Low-interest loans only to undergraduate students from the Dayton, OH, area who plan to attend local public, non-sectarian universities.
Financial data: Year ended 8/31/85. Assets, $1,006,000 (M); Expenditures, $45,250; Loans to individuals, 15 loans totaling $27,500, high $3,000, low $1,000, average loan $2,000.
Employer Identification Number: 316040186
Applications: Applications accepted throughout the year; Initial approach by telephone or letter.

478
Moorman (James) Orphans Home
526 West North Street
Winchester, IN 47394   (317) 584-4944
Contact: James M. Mock, Secretary-Treasurer

Limitations: Scholarships only to graduating seniors of Randolph County, IN, high schools.
Financial data: Year ended 9/30/86. Assets, $79,456 (M); Total giving, $4,500; Grants to individuals, 5 grants totaling $4,500, each grant $900.
Employer Identification Number: 350883508
Applications: Deadline usually late April or early May; Contact foundation for current application deadlines; Completion of formal application required; Application forms available through Randolph County, IN, high schools.
Publications: Application guidelines.
Program description:
To be eligible for a scholarship, applicants must meet the following criteria:
- A graduate of a Randolph County high school who attended the school for at least two years prior to graduation
- Recommendation by the school's principal or guidance director
- Applicant has made application to, or been accepted at, an accredited college, university, technical school, trade or business school
- The recipient shall have received no other major scholarship award.

Scholarship awards are considered in relation to the applicant's probability of succeeding in his/her chosen field. Each scholarship will be a single grant awarded for a one-year period applied directly to the cost of tuition and/or regularly assessed fees for a school year or equivalent term to a maximum of $1,500. Special grants may be awarded at the discretion of the governing board.

The scholarship award is made on a competitive basis. A single application will be accepted, upon proper recommendation, from each Randolph County high school for each school year.

479
Morrison (Ollege and Minnie) Foundation
c/o Texas Commerce Bank
P.O. Box 2558
Houston, TX 77252

Limitations: Scholarships only to graduating seniors of the Livingston Intermediate School District, Livingston, TX, area.
Financial data: Year ended 12/31/86. Assets, $945,033 (M); Total giving, $40,000; Grants to individuals, 23 grants totaling $36,500, high $2,000, low $500.
Employer Identification Number: 237073336

480
Mountain Protective Association Scholarship Fund

c/o Colorado National Bank of Denver
Terminal Annex, P.O. Box 5168, 1A
Denver, CO 80217   (303) 893-1862
Contact: P.O. Box 669, Evergreen, CO 80439

Limitations: Scholarships only to graduates of the following Colorado high schools: Evergreen High School, Idaho Springs High School, Platte Canyon High School, and Open Living High School (the Evergreen School District).
Financial data: Year ended 12/31/86. Assets, $119,530 (M); Total giving, $5,250; Grants to individuals, 5 grants totaling $5,250, high $1,500, low $750.
Employer Identification Number: 237457169
Applications: Deadline April 15th; Completion of formal application required; Interviews required; Initial approach through one of the four high schools.
Program description:
Scholarships are awarded for a two- to four-year period, as funds are available.

481
Murphy College Fund Trust

c/o First National Bank of Warsaw, Trust Department
P.O. Box 1447
Warsaw, IN 46580

Limitations: Scholarships only to residents of Kosciusko County, IN, or graduates of Kosciusko County School.
Financial data: Year ended 12/31/86. Assets, $61,754 (M); Total giving, $3,750; Grants to individuals, 7 grants totaling $3,750, high $750, low $375; Loans to individuals, 1 loan totaling $750.
Fmployer Identification Number: 356018330
Applications: Deadline April 15th; Completion of formal application required.
Program description:
Awards are made to individuals in the fields of music education, church ministries, physical therapy, secondary education, computer programming, nursing, Spanish language education, and engineering. Selection is based on financial need as well as academic criteria. Some preference is given to students entering a medical field of any kind.

Scholarships are renewed for the second year for one-half of the original grant amount, and are not renewed thereafter.

482
Murphy Foundation, The

Murphy Building
El Dorado, AR 71730   (501) 862-6411
Contact: Lucy A. Ring, Secretary

Limitations: Scholarships to students from southern Arkansas.
Financial data: Year ended 4/30/86. Assets, $7,031,925 (M); Total giving, $467,506; Grants to individuals, 16 grants totaling $27,351, high $3,500, low $661.
Employer Identification Number: 716049826
Applications: Deadline August 1st; Initial approach by letter; Completion of formal application required.
Program description:
Scholarships are awarded primarily for college level study. In the past, recipients have largely been local residents and received aid for personal expenses related to their education as well as tuition.

483★
Muskegon County Community Foundation, Inc.

Frauenthal Building, Suite 304
425 West Western Avenue
Muskegon, MI 49440   (616) 722-4538
Contact: Patricia B. Johnson, Executive Director

Limitations: Scholarships only to students in Muskegon County, MI.
Financial data: Year ended 3/31/87. Assets, $13,777,967 (M); Total giving, $930,625; Grants to individuals, 227 grants totaling $148,404, high $1,500, low $200, general range $500-1,000, average grant $750.
Employer Identification Number: 386114135
Applications: Deadline April 16th; Initial approach by telephone or letter; Completion of formal application including $5.00 application fee required; Interviews required for high school seniors.
Publications: Annual report (including application guidelines), newsletter, program information.
Program description:
The foundation's scholarship funds include:
1. J. Fred and Helen Barnard Boyd Scholarship Fund - for students interested in health careers.
2. Bill Boyden Rotary - YFCA Scholarship Fund - one scholarship annually to a deserving individual who has served as a counselor at Camp Pendalouan.
3. Bonnie, Kenneth and Charles Buitendorp Fund - for students demonstrating scholastic ability and financial need.
4. Robert Busch Academic Athletic Memorial Fund - one scholarship annually to a graduating senior from Holton High School who has been outstanding in academic and athletic areas.
5. Cotie Scholarship Fund - provides a scholarship for a member of a local track team.

6. Louise M. Cryderman Scholarship Fund - scholarships to worthy students.

7. Lewis G. and Margaret R. Curtis Scholarship Fund - for students interested in nursing or health-related careers, and those pursuing a vocational, technical, or trade career.

8. J. Paul Dunworth Scholarship Fund - aid to students graduating from Muskegon Catholic Central High School to attend colleges or institutions providing seminarian training.

9. Julie Herrick Easterly Memorial Fund - to students pursuing careers in journalism.

10. Effah Elizabeth Ferris Revolving Fund - to students graduating from Whitehall District Schools.

11. Charles and Jessie Goodnow Fund - scholarships to area students.

12. George H. Hartman Scholarship Fund - one scholarship annually to a student from Whitehall High School who is a member of the golf team and has done well academically.

13. Don Harwood Nursing Scholarship Fund - aid to worthy individuals pursuing nursing careers.

14. Marianne Jewell Scholarship Fund - scholarships to worthy students attending Muskegon Business College.

15. V.S. and Pearl Laurin Fund - one scholarship annually to a graduate of Mona Shores High School entering the legal field.

16. Maureen Linck Scholarship Fund - to students in the Ravenna, MI, area.

17. Frederick G. Mesyar, "Laddie" Memorial Scholarship Fund - one scholarship annually to a Fennville High School graduate pursuing a degree in math or science.

18. Ernest D. Moylan Scholarship Fund - four-year scholarships for students to attend Muskegon Community College and thereafter complete their education at a four-year school.

19. James Mullally Scholarship Fund - for students residing in the Laketon Township area.

20. Muskegon City Council PTA Scholarship Fund - one scholarship annually to a deserving youth within Muskegon County.

21. Muskegon County Medical Society Auxiliary Scholarship and Loan Fund - for students in the health field.

22. Muskegon Eagles Monsignor Kehren Scholarship Fund - for Muskegon area students.

23. Trevor Nichols Scholarship Fund - to graduates of Fennville High School, in Allegar County, for a degree in horticulture or music.

24. Henrik Olving Fund for the Gifted - provides an award to give public recognition to extraordinary talent in a high school senior in Muskegon or Ottawa County.

25. People Allied for Community College Education Fund - for students with outstanding academic records to attend Muskegon Community College.

26. Leigh T. Prettyman Scholarship Fund - for students to attend a four-year college.

27. Schrier Scholarship Fund - to enable students to attend Hope College in Holland, Michigan.

484
Myrick (William E.) Scholarship Trust

c/o Valley Bank & Trust Company
80 West Broadway, Suite 210
Salt Lake City, UT 84101
Contact: University of Utah, College of Business, 202 Park Building, Salt Lake City, UT 84112

Limitations: Scholarships primarily to senior students attending the University of Utah or a successor institution, and majoring in banking and finance.
Financial data: Year ended 11/30/86. Assets, $22,897 (M); Total giving, $2,500; 2 grants to individuals, 2 grants totaling $2,500, each grant $1,250.
Employer Identification Number: 876164360
Applications: Deadline April 1st; Initial approach by letter, including a brief resume of academic qualifications and other information as required by the University of Utah.

485★
Nation Foundation

2532 Irving Boulevard
Dallas, TX 75207

Limitations: Scholarships awarded to residents of Texas.
Financial data: Year ended 1/31/88. Assets, $4,139,079 (M); Total giving, $155,400; Grants to individuals, $0; 1986, Grants to individuals, 2 grants totaling $4,000, high $3,000, low $1,000.
Employer Identification Number: 756036339

486
Naurison (James Z.) Scholarship Fund

c/o Bank of New England-West
P.O. Box 9006
Springfield, MA 01102-9006　　　　　(413) 787-8745
Contact: Phyllis J. Farrell, Administrator

Limitations: Scholarships to college-bound students who are residents of Hampden, Hampshire, Franklin or Berkshire counties, MA, or residents of Enfield or Suffield counties, CT, for at least one year.
Financial data: Year ended 7/31/86. Assets, $5,237,404 (M); Total giving, $277,800; Grants to individuals, 450 grants totaling $277,800, high $800, low $400, general range $500-700.
Employer Identification Number: 046329627
Applications: Deadline May 1st; Applications accepted between December and April; Initial approach by letter; Completion of formal application required; No interviews.
Publications: Application guidelines.

Program description:

The applicant must by accepted by a college before applying to the foundation. However, the foundation does consider applications from students still in high school and may award scholarships to students who are already attending college.

The applicant must be of such a financial condition that he could not obtain the desired education without the assistance of the scholarship.

Students are judged according to need, academic record, and extra-curricular activities, including work.

487
Nesbitt Medical Student Foundation

c/o The National Bank & Trust Company of Sycamore
230 West State Street
Sycamore, IL 60178   (815) 895-2125
Contact: James M. Kirby, Assistant Vice-President

Limitations: Scholarships to students attending medical school who are in need of financial assistance. Preference given to women, persons who are residents of DeKalb County, IL, and students already attending an approved medical college in Illinois.
Financial data: Year ended 12/31/86. Assets, $549,760 (M); Total giving, $30,000; Grants to individuals, 11 grants totaling $30,000, high $3,000, low $2,500.
Employer Identification Number: 510171682
Applications: Deadline April 1st for application materials including letters of recommendation; Initial approach by letter requesting application; Completion of formal application required; Applications are also available in the appropriate office of applicant's medical college; Previous recipients must submit renewal application for each succeeding year.
Publications: Program information.
Program description:
Individual awards will generally not exceed $3,000 for any single academic year. The need of each applicant will be determined on an individual basis as a matter of judgment by the NMSF Scholarship Committee. The committee will base its judgment on the financial information submitted by the applicant and by such information as may be available. The financial information must clearly show the inability of the student to meet his educational expenses without assistance. Academic qualifications, letters of recommendation, and personal interviews will also be considered in evaluating the scholarship applications.

488
Nestor (Mary Margaret) Foundation

Reiff and West Streets
Lykens, PA 17048   (717) 453-7113
Contact: Robert E. Nestor

Limitations: Scholarships to residents of Lykens, PA, and the surrounding areas.
Financial data: Year ended 6/30/86. Assets, $401,985

(M); Total giving, $60,506; Grants to individuals, 76 grants totaling $55,925; Subtotal for scholarships, 74 grants totaling $55,605, high $1,305, low $400.
Employer Identification Number: 236277570
Applications: Applications accepted throughout the year; Initial approach by letter.

489
New England Education Society

c/o James F. Farr, Treasurer
One Boston Place
Boston, MA 02108   (617) 723-2920
Contact: Dr. Robert L. Treese, Boston University School of Theology, 745 Commonwealth Avenue, Boston, MA

Limitations: Loans to graduate students for theological education in Christian ministry in New England theological schools or seminaries.
Financial data: Year ended 4/30/86. Assets, $612,546 (M); Expenditures, $17,279; Loans to individuals, 30 totaling $13,650, average loan $450, high $900, low $150.
Employer Identification Number: 046067431
Applications: Applications accepted throughout the year; Interviews required.

490★
New Hampshire Charitable Fund, The

One South Street
P.O. Box 1335
Concord, NH 03302-1335   (603) 225-6641
Contact: Judith Burrows, Director, Student Aid

Limitations: Scholarships and loans to New Hampshire residents pursuing undergraduate or graduate study at an accredited college, university or vocational school.
Financial data: Year ended 12/31/87. Assets, $33,829,000 (M); Total giving, $5,358,000; Grants to individuals totaling $460,805; Loans to individuals totaling $221,145, average award (grant or loan) $1,100.
Employer Identification Number: 026005625
Applications: Deadline early May for upcoming academic year; Contact foundation for current application deadline; Applications available in April and May for assistance during the following academic year; Initial approach by telephone; Completion of formal application required.
Publications: Annual report (including application guidelines), financial statement, informational brochure, program information.
Program description:
The fund has a particular interest in assisting adults entering or returning to school, or studying part-time while maintaining family or other work responsibilities.

491
New Orphan Asylum Scholarship Foundation
2340 Victory Parkway, Suite One
Cincinnati, OH 45206   (513) 961-6626
Contact: Norma Lane

Limitations: Scholarships for college education limited to residents of, or graduates of high schools in the greater Cincinnati, OH, area.
Financial data: Year ended 12/31/86. Assets, $1,294,892 (L); Total giving, $46,435; Grants to individuals totaling $46,435.
Employer Identification Number: 310536683
Applications: Deadline July 31st; Completion of formal application required.
Program description:
Student aid payments are made directly to the educational institutions on behalf of individual recipients. **Scholarship applications for postgraduate study are not accepted.**

492★
Niccum Educational Trust Foundation
c/o Midwest Commerce Banking Company
P.O. Box 27
Goshen, IN 46526   (219) 533-2175
Contact: Rod Diller or JoAnne Pickens

Limitations: Scholarships to graduates of public schools in the Goshen, IN, area.
Financial data: Year ended 12/31/87. Assets, $111,800 (M); Total giving, $4,800; Grants to individuals, 4 grants totaling $4,800, high $1,500, low $800.
Employer Identification Number: 356017515
Applications: Deadline March 1st; Applications available from Midwest Commerce Bank; Completion of formal applications with student transcripts, high school recommendation, and three references, required.

493
Nicholl (James R.) Memorial Foundation
c/o The Central Trust Company of Northern Ohio, Trust Department
1949 Broadway
Lorain, OH 44052   (216) 244-1965
Contact: David E. Nocjar, Trust Officer

Limitations: Medical school scholarships to needy students who have been residents of Lorain County, OH, for at least two years and intend to return to Lorain County to practice.
Financial data: Year ended 12/31/86. Assets, $782,713 (M); Total giving, $33,758; Grants to individuals, 78 grants totaling $33,758; Subtotal for scholarships, 14 grants totaling $23,764, high $2,000, low $558.
Employer Identification Number: 346574742
Applications: Applications accepted throughout the year; Completion of formal application required.

Publications: Annual report, program information, application guidelines.

494★
Norfolk Foundation, The
1410 Sovran Center
Norfolk, VA 23510   (804) 622-7951
Contact: Lee C. Kitchin, Executive Director

Limitations: Scholarships primarily to residents of Norfolk, VA, and the area within fifty miles of its boundaries.
Financial data: Year ended 12/31/87. Assets, $26,061,409 (M); Total giving, $1,309,766; Grants to individuals, 203 grants totaling $247,844.
Employer Identification Number: 540722169
Applications: Deadline December 1st to March 1st; Initial approach by letter or telephone; Completion of formal application required.
Publications: Annual report.
Program description:
The scholarships are designated by donors. An applicant must qualify as to residence, school attended, or course of study chosen. Payments are made directly to the educational institution on behalf of the individual recipients.

495★
North Dakota Community Foundation
1002 East Central Avenue
Bismarck, ND 58501   (701) 222-8349
Contact: Richard H. Timmins, President

Limitations: Scholarships to individuals, primarily in North Dakota, for the study of medicine, dentistry, agriculture, or agriculturally related activities.
Financial data: Year ended 12/31/87. Assets, $2,243,938 (M); Total giving, $116,682; Grants to individuals, 32 grants totaling $13,399.
Employer Identification Number: 450336015
Applications: Contact foundation for current application deadline; Initial approach by letter; Completion of formal application and interviews required.
Publications: Annual report, program information, application guidelines.
Program description:
Some grants are based on need.

496
Northrup Educational Foundation, Inc.
RD 1, Box 38
Watkins Glen, NY 14891   (607) 535-4732
Contact: Jane H. Isley, Secretary-Treasurer

Limitations: Educational loans and awards to students who have been residents of Schuyler County, NY, for ten years preceding high school graduation.
Financial data: Year ended 8/31/85. Assets, $213,572

(M); Expenditures, $18,648; Grants to individuals, 2 awards totaling $1,000; Loans to individuals, 25 loans totaling $12,500, each loan $500.
Employer Identification Number: 156020359
Applications: Deadline June 15th; Interviews granted upon request or letter of explanation may be attached to application.
Publications: Annual report.
Program description:
Loans are made to students for expenses of any kind incurred in the pursuit of higher education. If a student remains in school and maintains satisfactory educational progress, the loan does not become due until graduation.

Northrup Awards for college expenses are given annually to Schuyler County, NY, residents who receive high SAT/ACT scores.

497
Nucor Foundation, Inc.
4425 Randolph Road
Charlotte, NC 28211   (704) 366-7000
Contact: James M. Coblin

Limitations: Scholarships for children of employees of Nucor Foundation, Inc.
Financial data: Year ended 12/31/86. Assets, $234,399 (M); Total giving, $166,080; Grants to individuals, 129 grants totaling $166,080, high $3,000, low $104.
Employer Identification Number: 237318064
Applications: Deadline March 1st; Completion of formal application required.

498
Oakland Scottish Rite Scaife, Oakland Scottish Rite Scholarship, and Helen Parmelee Educational Foundations
(Formerly Oakland Scottish Rite Scaife and Oakland Scottish Rite Scholarship Foundations)
1547 Lakeside Drive
Oakland, CA 94612   (415) 451-1906
Contact: Merv Weiner, Secretary

Limitations: Scholarships to graduates of public high schools in northern California recommended by principals or counselors.
Financial data: Year ended 5/31/87. Assets, $5,410,562 (M); Total giving, $233,420; Grants to individuals, 133 grants totaling $233,420, high $1,800, low $360, average grant $1,800.
Employer Identification Number: 941540333
Applications: Deadline March 31st; Initial approach by letter; Completion of formal application required.
Publications: Application guidelines, program information, informational brochure.
Program description:
Scholarships for undergraduate study are awarded to qualified individuals. Applicants must be recommended to the foundation by a principal or

senior counselor before an application form is mailed and must be in good health, be of excellent moral character, and show high scholastic achivement. Candidates must be unable to meet the expenses of a higher education without financial help, and be willing to earn a portion of their expenses while in college. Scaife scholarship candidates must be sons of American-born parents and must have a clear idea of what they intend to adopt for their life work and must exclude medicine and the ministry as professional goals.

Scholarships are renewable for up to four years of undergraduate study contingent upon maintenance of a "B" average.

499
Ochoco Scholarship Fund
P.O. Box 668
Prineville, OR 97754
Contact: David Doty, Trustee, Crook County High School, East First Street, Prineville, OR 97754; Tel.: (503) 447-5661

Limitations: Scholarships only to residents of the Prineville (Crook County), OR, area.
Financial data: Year ended 12/31/86. Assets, $199,983 (M); Total giving, $19,680; Grants to individuals totaling $19,680.
Employer Identification Number: 936024017
Applications: Applications accepted throughout the year; Completion of formal application required.
Program description:
Grantees selected on the basis of academic standing, financial need, character, personality, and social adjustment. Grants not usually given for first college semester; exceptions are made in cases where the applicant has shown marked ability in high school and is financially unable to enter college without a grant.

500
Ogden College Fund, The
P.O. Box 930
Bowling Green, KY 42101   (502) 781-2121
Contact: c/o Cooper R. Smith, Jr., 520 Hillwood Drive, Bowling Green, KY 42101

Limitations: Scholarships to graduates of Kentucky public and private high schools who have a grade average of "B" or better and who intend to pursue a major or minor in the Ogden College of Science, Technolgy and Health at Western Kentucky University.
Financial data: Year ended 10/31/86. Assets, $2,204,239 (M); Total giving, $78,467; Grants to individuals, 222 grants totaling $57,967, high $1,500, low $250.
Employer Identification Number: 237078715
Applications: Applications accepted throughout the year, however scholarships are awarded on a first-come, first-served basis, so that submission by at

least January 1st is encouraged; Completion of formal application required; Interviews required.

Program description:
Scholarships in the amount of $250 per semester, renewable for up to eight semesters ($2,000) are currently being awarded. About 60 new grants for freshmen are available each year.

501
Olliff (Matred Carlton) Foundation
P.O. Box 385
Wauchula, FL 33873
Contact: Mr. Doyle E. Carlton, Jr., Trustee

Limitations: Grants for scholarships primarily in Florida.
Financial data: Year ended 8/31/86. Assets, $4,110,399 (M); Total giving, $230,585; Grants to individuals, 31 grants totaling $16,728, high $1,750, low $50.
Employer Identification Number: 592241303
Applications: Deadline July 1st; Initial approach by letter.

502
Oppenheim Students' Fund, Inc.
Anne Lascelle, Board of Education
607 Walnut Avenue
Niagara Falls, NY 14303

Limitations: Loans to male students who are current residents of Niagara County, NY.
Financial data: Year ended 12/31/85. Assets, $91,639 (M); Expenditures, $36; Loans to individuals totaling $74,360, general range $250-500.
Employer Identification Number: 166040269
Applications: Deadline as early as possible before start of semester; Completion of formal application, including three letters of recommendation and transcript of grades, required.

Program description:
Interest-free loans are granted to qualified students in the amount of $500 per year, $250 per semester. Repayment must begin upon graduation from college or termination of full-time studies. In 1985, nine new loans were awarded.

Although residence in Niagara County is required for loan eligibility, students may attend colleges elsewhere.

503
Orange Scholarship Foundation
25 Pleasant Street
Orange, MA 01364
Contact: Robert P. Collen, Chairman

Limitations: Scholarships only to graduates of Ralph C. Mahar Regional High School, Orange, MA.
Financial data: Year ended 12/31/85. Assets, $28,571

(M); Total giving, $4,900; Grants to individuals, 17 grants totaling $4,900, average grant $300.
Employer Identification Number: 046138742
Applications: Deadline June 1st; Completion of formal application required.

504
Orscheln Industries Foundation, Inc.
c/o Boatman's First National Bank of Kansas City
P.O. Box 38
Kansas City, MO 64183
Contact: William E. Clark, Orscheln Industries Foundation Scholarship Committee, P.O. Box 266, Moberly, Mo 65270; Tel.: (816) 263-6693

Limitations: Scholarships only to graduates of Cairo, Higbee, Moberly, and Westran high schools, in Randolph County, MO.
Financial data: Year ended 9/30/86. Assets, $6,829,807 (M); Total giving, $243,741; Grants to individuals, 21 grants totaling $9,750, high $500, low $150.
Employer Identification Number: 237115623
Applications: Deadline April 1st; Completion of formal application required.
Publications: Informational brochure.

505
Osceola Foundation, Inc.
51 East 42nd Street, Suite 1601
New York, NY 10017
Contact: Walter Beinecke, Jr., President and Treasurer

Limitations: Scholarships for higher education.
Financial data: Year ended 12/31/86. Assets, $4,295,789 (M); Total giving, $581,576; Grants to individuals, 4 grants totaling $18,715, high $7,600, low $500.
Employer Identification Number: 136094234
Applications: Deadline prior to tuition due dates; Initial approach by letter indicating reason for request.
Program description:
In recent years scholarships were awarded to individuals attending college in Massachusetts or New York.

506
Oshkosh Foundation
c/o First Wisconsin National Bank of Oshkosh
P.O. Box 2448
Oshkosh, WI 54903   (414) 424-4283
Contact: Sandra A. Noe, Trust Officer

Limitations: Scholarships only for Oshkosh, WI graduating high school seniors for a four-year term.
Financial data: Year ended 2/28/86. Assets, $5,227,792 (M); Total giving, $335,781; Grants to individuals amount not specified.
Employer Identification Number: 396041638

Applications: Applications accepted throughout the year.
Publications: Annual report.

507★
Pack (Beulah) Scholarship Fund
c/o Casco Northern Bank, N.A.; Trust Department
P.O. Box 678
Portland, ME 04104   (207) 774-8221
Contact: Dianne L. Nason

Limitations: Scholarships to residents of Union, ME.
Financial data: Year ended 12/31/85. Assets, $46,267 (M); Total giving, $4,600; Grants to individuals, 7 grants totaling $4,600; Grants to individuals, 7 grants totaling $4,600, high $795, low $475, average grant $650.
Employer Identification Number: 016036292
Applications: Applications accepted throughout the year; Completion of formal application required.

508
Packer (Horace B.) Foundation, Inc.
P.O. Box 35
Wellsboro, PA 16901
Contact: Charles G. Webb, President

Limitations: Scholarships to students attending medical institutions who intend to work in Tioga County, PA.
Financial data: Year ended 12/31/86. Assets, $1,146,898 (M); Total giving, $186,114; Grants to individuals, 50 grants totaling $29,700; high $1,900, low $100.
Employer Identification Number: 236390932
Applications: Applications accepted throughout the year; Initial approach by letter.

509
Paine Webber Foundation
1285 Avenue of the Americas
New York, NY 10019
Contact: Gerald P. Linnane, 120 Broadway, Tax Department, New York, NY 10271

Limitations: Research grants to individuals for studies on economics.
Financial data: Year ended 12/31/85. Assets, $1,775,850 (M); Total giving, $30,000; Grants to individuals, 1 grant totaling $30,000.
Employer Identification Number: 046032804
Applications: Deadline December 1st; Initial approach by letter.

510
Palen-Klar (Countess Frances Thorley) Scholarship Fund
c/o The Connecticut Bank and Trust Company
P.O. Box 3334
Hartford, CT 06103

Limitations: Scholarships to students attending colleges and universities in New England.
Financial data: Year ended 12/31/85. Assets, $243,304 (M); Total giving, $15,300; Grants to individuals, 25 grants totaling $15,300, general range $500-700.
Employer Identification Number: 066033692

511
Palm Beach County Community Foundation
324 Datura Street, Suite 340
West Palm Beach, FL 33401-9938   (305) 659-6800

Limitations: Scholarships to residents of Palm Beach County, FL, and surrounding regions.
Financial data: Year ended 6/30/87. Assets, $3,309,261 (M); Total giving, $284,402; Grants to individuals totaling $22,000.
Employer Identification Number: 597181875
Publications: Annual report.
Program description:
The foundation's scholarship funds include:
1. The Barnett Banks of Palm Beach County Minority Student Scholarship Fund is designed to help minority students obtain higher education to successfully enter the business world. Priority is given to economically disadvantaged individuals in good academic standing who intend to major in business.
2. The Maura & William Benjamin Scholarship Fund is awarded annually to worthy students residing in Palm Beach County. In addition to scholastic excellence the students should reflect qualities of potential leadership and an inclination toward service to their community.
3. The Don Dahlberg Memorial Scholarship Fund is given to graduating students at Jupiter High School who display loyalty to school, interest in people and sports, and a desire to attend college.
4. The Ellen Beth Eddleman Memorial Scholarship Fund is awarded to a John I. Leonard High School student who exhibits strong artistic talent and leadership ability.
5. The Palm Beach Newspapers Scholarship Fund presents an annual award and considers factors such as overall scholastic excellence, community involvement, and financial need.
6. The Theodore Satter Memorial Scholarship Fund is given to a Palm Beach County student majoring in the field of business.
7. The Ann E. Stewart Memorial Scholarship Fund is given to a student graduating from Forest Hill Community High School who has demonstrated an interest in music.

512★
Palmer (Arthur C. and Lucia S.) Foundation, Inc.

471 Pennsylvania Avenue
Waverly, NY 14892   (607) 565-4603
Contact: H. Slade Palmer, President

Limitations: Scholarships limited to residents of
Waverly, NY, and Sayre and Athens, PA, and vicinity.
Financial data: Year ended 12/31/87. Assets, $192,674
(M); Total giving, $28,756; Grants to individuals, 25
grants totaling, $21,250, high $2,000, low $250,
general range $500-1,000, average grant $850.
Employer Identification Number: 156021397
Applications: Deadline June 1st; Interviews required.
Program description:
Scholarships for college tuition and expenses are
awarded to highly motivated students who may have
poor scholastic records or be considered "late
bloomers." Three to six new awards are available
each year.

513
Panwy Foundation

Greenwich Office Park
P.O. Box 1800
Greenwich, CT 06836   (203) 661-6616
Contact: Ralph M. Wyman, Vice-President

Limitations: Scholarships for higher education.
Financial data: Year ended 12/31/86. Assets, $604,921
(M); Total giving, $320,945; Grants to individuals
amount not specified.
Employer Identification Number: 136130759
Applications: Applications accepted throughout the
year; Initial approach by letter.

514
Parapsychology Foundation, Inc.

228 East 71st Street
New York, NY 10021   (212) 628-1550
Contact: Mrs. Eileen Coly, President

Limitations: Research grants for study in
parapsychology.
Financial data: Year ended 12/31/86. Assets,
$3,935,703 (M); Total giving, $20,000; Grants to
individuals, 7 grants totaling $15,500, high $4,000,
low $1,000.
Employer Identification Number: 131677742
Applications: Applications accepted throughout the
year, however, two copies of the proposal should be
submitted between January and March; Initial
approach by letter; Completion of formal application
required; Interviews granted upon request.
Publications: Annual report, program information.

Program description:
Grants to scientists and others engaged in study,
research, and experiments on original projects
pertaining to parapsychology and parapsychological
phenomena.
   Applicants should submit a prospectus outlining the
nature and objectives of the project, biographical and
professional data and estimated expenditures. Grants
are approved for one year only.
   No grants for travel, graduate and undergraduate
studies, or for writing and publishing projects.

515★
Parkhurst (Cora B.) Scholarship Trust

c/o Old Kent Bank - Southwest
210 East Main Street
Niles, MI 49120
Contact: Bruce Taiclet, Committee Chairman, Berrien
Springs High School, Berrien Springs, MI 49102; Tel.:
(616) 471-2891

Limitations: Scholarships only to graduates of Berrien
Springs High School, Berrien Springs, MI.
Financial data: Year ended 12/31/86. Assets, $114,653
(M); Total giving, $3,375; Grants to individuals, 8
grants totaling $3,375, high $750, low $250, general
range $250-750.
Employer Identification Number: 386148571
Applications: Deadline April 1st; Completion of
formal application and interviews required.
Program description:
The Cora B. Parkhurst Scholarships were created to
provide graduates of Berrien Springs High School, MI,
a scholarship to any degree-awarding college or
university in the U.S. The scholarships may be
awarded for one year or may be continuing in that
they are re-awarded each year if they are warranted
and earned.

516★
Parrett (Arthur and Doreen) Scholarship Trust Fund

c/o U.S. Bank of Washington, N.A.
P.O. Box 720, Trust Division
Seattle, WA 98111   (206) 344-3685
Contact: George H. Carpenter, Trust Officer

Limitations: Scholarships only to Washington residents
for study in schools of engineering, science, medicine
and dentistry.
Financial data: Year ended 11/30/86. Assets, $114,387
(M); Total giving, $9,000; Grants to individuals, 15
grants totaling $9,000, high $1,000, low $300.
Employer Identification Number: 916228230
Applications: Deadline July 31st; Initial approach by
letter requesting application; Completion of formal
application required.

517
Patterson (Alicia) Foundation
655 Fifteenth Street, NW, Suite 320
Washington, DC 20005
Contact: Helen McMaster Coulson, Executive Director

Limitations: Fellowships to U.S. citizens who are
working professionally as print journalist. Must have at
least five years experience as a print journalist.
Financial data: Year ended 12/31/85. Assets,
$2,723,563 (M); Total giving, $187,897; Grants to
individuals, 7 grants totaling $187,897, average grant
$25,000.
Employer Identification Number: 136092124
Applications: Deadline October 1st; Submit proposal
between June and September; Initial approach by
letter, telephone, or proposal; Completion of formal
application required; Interviews of finalists.
Publications: Annual report, application guidelines,
informational brochure, newsletter.
Program description:
The Alicia Patterson Foundation Fellowship Program
awards three to seven new fellowships each year to
newspaper, magazine, wire service, and freelance
journalists or editors for a year of travel and inquiry
into significant foreign or domestic issues.

Fellows write articles on their chosen subject for the
APF Reporter, a quarterly magazine published by the
foundation. The Reporter is circulated to newspaper
and magazine editors and other interested people in
business, government and the professions throughout
the U.S. All articles appearing in the magazine may be
reprinted freely with proper credit.

Fellowships include reimbursement for travel
expenses and a living stipend to allow the Fellow and
family, if any, to live in reasonable comfort.

518
Peckitt (Leonard Carlton) Scholarship Fund
c/o Catasauqua High School
850 Pine Street
Catasauqua, PA 18032   (215) 264-0506

Limitations: Scholarships only to graduates of
Catasauqua High School, PA.
Financial data: Year ended 12/31/86. Assets, $14,812
(M); Total giving, $10,700; Grants to individuals, 60
grants totaling $10,700, high $300, low $100, average
grant $200.
Employer Identification Number: 236298745
Applications: Deadline May 15th.
Program description:
Recipients primarily attend colleges in Pennsylvania.

519
Peeples (Marion D. & Eva S.) Foundation
c/o Union Bank and Trust Company
P.O. Box 369
Franklin, IN 46131   (317) 736-7191
Contact: Ed Teets, Vice-President, Union Bank & Trust
Co.

Limitations: Scholarships primarily to graduates of
Indiana high schools to pursue studies in nursing or
dietetics, or to obtain training in teaching industrial
arts.
Financial data: Year ended 6/30/87. Assets,
$1,224,736 (M); Total giving, $81,550; Grants to
individuals, 58 grants totaling $81,550, high $2,500,
low $750.
Employer Identification Number: 356306320
Applications: Deadline March 20th; Completion of
formal application required; Interviews required;
Submit completed application to the foundation's
Scholarship Committee, c/o Union Bank and Trust
Company, 34 West Jefferson Street, Franklin, IN
46131.
Program description:
In the awarding of scholarships, preference is given
first to graduates of Franklin Community High School,
IN, attending Franklin College, IN. Funds are available
to graduates of other Indiana high schools studying in
the specified fields and attending other educational
institutions if there are insufficient applicants from
Franklin Community High School and/or the courses
are not offered at Franklin College.

All grants are for one year only but in the discretion
of the scholarship committee, grants may be awarded
for up to four years. The amount of the grant is
determined by the scholarship committee.

The criteria used by the scholarship committee
include:
  1. Prior academic performance
  2. Performance on tests designed to measure
  ability and aptitude for college work
  3. Recommendation from instructors and other
  responsible persons
  4. Financial needs
  5. Conclusions drawn from a personal interview
  as to the potential recipient's motivation,
  character, ability, and potential.

520
Pellerin (Willis & Mildred) Foundation
6514 Pratt Drive
New Orleans, LA 70122
Contact: A.A. Harman and Company, 311 Baronne
Street, First Floor, New Orleans, LA 70122

Limitations: Scholarships for residents of Louisiana
who are enrolled in a college or university in that
state.
Financial data: Year ended 5/31/86. Assets,
$1,200,232 (M); Total giving, $44,747; Grants to

individuals, 114 grants totaling $44,747, high $570, low $200.
Employer Identification Number: 510166877
Applications: Deadline six months preceding beginning of school term; Initial approach by letter; Completion of formal application required.
Program description:
Applicants are required to repay one-half of the grant.

521
Pemco Foundation
325 Eastlake Avenue
Seattle, WA 98109   (206) 628-4000
Contact: Stanley O. McNaughton, Secretary-Treasurer

Limitations: Scholarships only to students who, at the time of acceptance, are residents of Washington State.
Financial data: Year ended 6/30/87. Assets, $98,066 (M); Total giving, $163,050; Grants to individuals, 94 grants totaling $43,950, high $900, low $150, general range $300-600.
Employer Identification Number: 916072723
Applications: Applications accepted throughout the year; Initial approach by letter from principal stating academic qualifications of student.

522★
Peninsula Community Foundation
1204 Burlingame Avenue
P.O. Box 627
Burlingame, CA 94011-0627   (415) 342-2477
Contact: Bill Somerville, Executive Director

Limitations: Educational grants to residents of San Mateo County and northern Santa Clara County, CA.
Financial data: Year ended 12/31/07. Assets, $14,119,000 (M); Total giving, $1,384,000; Grants to individuals amount not specified.
Employer Identification Number: 942746687
Publications: Annual report.
Program description:
The foundation provides educational support through the following:
The **McNair Scholars Project** is a new initiative the foundation is supporting to encourage middle school students to finish high school. In 1987, 230 scholars were chosen to receive this award.
The **Ralph Hale and Lenore Martha Ruppert Education Grants** awards scholarships for college education to graduating high school seniors. In 1987, 19 grants were made of $789 each.
The **Eleanor Curry Fund** provides scholarships to women and young girls.
The **R. Carter & Mildred E. Crain Educational Program** gives grants up to $5,000 for persons who graduated from high school in San Mateo or Santa Clara counties.

523
Perkins (B.F. & Rose H.) Foundation
P.O Box 1064
Sheridan, WY 82801   (307) 674-8871

Limitations: Scholarships and student loans to graduates of Sheridan County High School, WY. First time applicants must be under 20 years of age.
Financial data: Year ended 12/31/86. Assets, $5,461,464 (M); Expenditures, $107,264 (M); Grants to individuals, 156 grants totaling $46,921; Subtotal for scholarships, 5 grants totaling $900, high $200, low $100; Loans to individuals, 137 loans totaling $230,991, high $3,150, low $500.
Employer Identification Number: 830138740
Applications: Deadline June 1st for receipt of application and transcripts for Fall admissions and the first of each month for awards for all other months; Completion of formal application required.

524★
Permanent Endowment Fund for Martha's Vineyard
c/o Martha's Vineyard National Bank
Main Street
Vineyard Haven, MA 02568   (617) 693-9400
Contact: John H. Ware, Jr., Chairman, RFD Box 149, Vineyard Haven, MA 02568; Tel.: (617) 693-0721

Limitations: Scholarships only to graduates of Martha's Vineyard Regional High School, MA.
Financial data: Year ended 12/31/87. Assets, $538,868 (M); Total giving, $10,000; Grants to individuals, 5 grants totaling $3,250, high $1,000, low $325.
Publications: Annual report, informational brochure.
Program description:
The **Alfred F. Ferro and Arthur T. Silva Scholarship Fund** provides scholarships to the two highest ranking Martha's Vineyard Regional High School seniors who have spent all four years at the school, with preference to those who have not received any other sizable award. **The Dr. David Rappaport Memorial Scholarship Fund** provides scholarships in medical or health care for graduating seniors or former graduates of the Martha's Vineyard Regional High School.

525
Petersburg Methodist Home for Girls
c/o John G. Sayers
20 Franklin Street, P.O. Box 270
Petersburg, VA 23804
Contact: Hilde T. Atkinson, Secretary, 910 Northampton Road, Petersburg, VA 23805

Limitations: Scholarships primarily to residents of Southside, VA.
Financial data: Year ended 12/31/86. Assets, $1,734,681 (M); Total giving, $66,200; Grants to individuals, 28 grants totaling $22,000, high $2,250,

low $400, average grant $750.
Employer Identification Number: 540542500
Applications: Deadlines July and February;
Completion of formal application required.

526
Petersen (Esper A.) Foundation
1300 Skokie Highway
Gurnee, IL 60031   (312) 677-0049

Limitations: Scholarships to students attending
colleges in Illinois and the surrounding area.
Financial data: Year ended 12/31/86. Assets,
$5,770,763 (M); Total giving, $201,657; Grants to
individuals totaling $21,222.
Employer Identification Number: 366125570
Applications: Deadline January 1st; Initial approach
by letter; Completion of formal application required.
Publications: Program information.
Program description:
Scholarships of up to $1,000 per year are available for
study at colleges, junior colleges, universities, trade
schools, technical schools and nurses training. Grants
are renewable.

527
Phi Kappa Psi Fraternity, Inc., The Endowment
Fund of
510 Lockerbie Street
Indianapolis, IN 46202   (317) 632-5647

Limitations: Student loans, fellowships, grants, and
awards to students enrolled in colleges and
universities in the U.S.
Financial data: Year ended 5/31/86. Assets,
$1,195,658 (M); Total giving, $153,097; Grants to
individuals amount not specified.
Employer Identification Number: 366130655
Applications: Applications accepted throughout the
year.
Program description:
The average award for the **Shockley Founders
Fellowships** is $2,000. **Outstanding Summerfield
Scholars** receive awards ranging from $500-3,000.
Summerfield Scholars receive awards of $100.

528
Phi Kappa Sigma Educational Foundation of
Orono
Merrill Trust Company
Trustee Exchange Street
Bangor, ME 04401
Contact: Peter Averill, Phi Kappa Sigma House,
Orono, ME

Limitations: Scholarships restricted to members of
Alpha Delta Chapter of Phi Kappa Sigma.
Financial data: Year ended 4/30/87. Assets, $119,264

(M); Total giving, $7,420; Grants to individuals, 13
grants totaling $7,420, high 1,500, low $120.
Employer Identification Number: 016011407
Applications: Applications accepted throughout the
year.

529★
Phi Kappa Theta National Foundation
c/o Greg Stein
111-55 77th Avenue
Forest Hills, NY 11375   (718) 793-2193

Limitations: Scholarships only to members of Phi
Kappa Theta Fraternity.
Financial data: Year ended 9/30/87. Assets, $365,000
(M); Total giving, $32,500; Grants to individuals, 8
grants totaling $4,000, each grant $500.
Employer Identification Number: 237209653
Applications: Deadline April 30th; Applications forms
available at fraternity's undergraduate chapters in
March; Completion of formal application, copy of
applicant's Form 1040, college transcripts, and
certification from college in which student is enrolled.
Publications: Application guidelines, financial
statement, 990-PF printed copy available upon
request.
Program description:
Grants are awarded on the basis of leadership,
scholarship, moral qualities, and need.

530
Philippe Foundation, Inc.
122 East 42nd Street
New York, NY 10168   (212) 687-3290
Contact: Merton Holman, Treasurer

Limitations: Research grants to French and American
physicians and scientists.
Financial data: Year ended 12/31/86. Assets,
$2,279,882 (M); Total giving, $138,631; Grants to
individuals, 74 grants totaling $138,631, high $6.750,
low $250, general range, $1,000-6,000.
Employer Identification Number: 136087157
Applications: Deadlines March 1st, June 1st,
September 1st, and December 1st; Initial approach by
letter.
Publications: Application guidelines, program
information.
Program description:
The foundation is primarily concerned with the
exchange of physicians and scientists between the
U.S. and France and for advanced study and scientific
research.
   Except for the most unusual circumstances, grants
are not intended to provide the principle source of
support.

531★
Phillips (The Dr. P.) Foundation
60 West Robinson Street
P.O. Box 3753
Orlando, FL 32802   (305) 422-6105
Contact: J. A. Hinson, President

Limitations: Student loans to residents of Orange
County, FL, for study of medicine, engineering or
accounting.
Financial data: Year ended 5/31/87. Assets,
$18,468,587 (M); Expenditures, $451,139; Loans to
individuals, 1 loan totaling $7,000.
Employer Identification Number: 596135403

532★
Pickett & Hatcher Educational Fund, Inc.
1800 Buena Vista Road
P.O. Box 8169
Columbus, GA 31908   (404) 327-6586
Contact: Robert E. Bennett, Executive Vice-President

Limitations: Undergraduate student loans limited to
residents of the southeastern U.S., including AL, FL,
GA, KY, MS, NC, SC, TN, and VA. No support for
students planning to enter fields of medicine, law, or
the ministry.
Financial data: Year ended 9/30/87. Assets,
$15,511,738 (M); Expenditures, $444,413; Loans to
individuals, 608 loans totaling $1,302,746, general
range $800-3,200, average loan $2,143.
Employer Identification Number: 580566216
Applications: Deadline May 15th; Initial approach by
letter or telephone; First-time applicants may request
application form after October 1st; Completion of
formal application required.
Publications: Informational brochure (including
application guidelines).
Program description:
Applicants must be U.S. citizens and should be of
good character, have a good academic record, and
demonstrate need. Giving limited to Alabama, Florida,
Georgia, Kentucky, Mississippi, North Carolina, South
Carolina, Tennessee, and Virginia.
    Loans are made to undergraduates. However,
exceptions may be made for graduate students who
received fund assistance as undergraduates in order
that they will not be forced to borrow from two or
more sources. The trustees consider such requests
individually.
    Students pursuing courses in colleges and
universities offering broad liberal education and
degrees are eligible for assistance, but students
enrolled in vocational or business schools are not
eligible. Loans carry a two percent interest rate while
in college, and six percent after college. Interest is
payable quarterly while in college and monthly
thereafter; repayment of the principal begins six
months after leaving college.

Consideration is given to applications for the
amount required for fees, tuition, room and board up
to a maximum of $2,400 per academic year or $3,200
per calendar year. The total amount which may be
borrowed is $9,600.
    **No loans for students planning to enter the
professions of law, medicine, or the ministry.**

533
Pilgrim Foundation, The
478 Torrey Street
Brockton, MA 02401-4654   (617) 586-6100
Contact: Sherry Yuskaitis, Executive Director

Limitations: Scholarships for higher education to
residents of Brockton, MA.
Financial data: Year ended 12/31/86. Assets,
$2,310,246 (M); Total giving, $49,604; Grants to
individuals totaling $49,604; Subtotal for scholarships,
102 grants totaling $34,800, high $500, low $200.
Employer Identification Number: 042104834
Applications: Deadlines April 1st for graduating high
school seniors and May 1st for returning college
students; Completion of formal application and
interviews required.

534★
Pillsbury (Mary K. and Edith) Foundation
c/o Santa Barbara Foundation
15 East Carrillo Street
Santa Barbara, CA 93101   (805) 963-1873
Contact: Isabel H. Bartolome, Student Aid Director

Limitations: Scholarships to U.S. citizens who reside
or have resided in Santa Barbara County, CA, and are
pursuing an education in music.
Financial data: Year ended 7/31/87. Assets, $870,000
(M); Total giving, $42,000; Grants to individuals, 35
grants totaling $42,000, high $2,500, low $400,
general range $1,000-1,500.
Employer Identification Number: 956063292
Applications: Interviews and auditions required.
Program description:
Assistance is given to students who demonstrate
unusual aptitude or potential in the field of music. In
determining the amount of assistance, the committee
will be influenced by the financial circumstances of
each individual or family and the cost of the program
involved.

535
Pinellas County Community Foundation
1253 Park Street
Clearwater, FL 33516   (813) 443-3281
Contact: Thomas R. Bruckman, Executive Director

Limitations: Scholarships only to residents of Pinellas
County, FL.
Financial data: Year ended 12/31/86. Assets,

$3,353,479 (M); Total giving, $245,621; Grants to individuals, 25 grants totaling $23,900.
Employer Identification Number: 237113194
Program description:
The foundation's educational support includes a fund which provides an annual scholarship of $500 to a student at St. Petersburg Junior College, FL, and a fund which provides 18 scholarships annually to students who are children of active or retired postal workers attending St. Petersburg Junior College or state universities in Florida.

536
Piper (Minnie Stevens) Foundation
GPM South Tower, Suite 530
800 NW Loop 410
San Antonio, TX 78216-5699   (512) 227-8119
Contact: Michael J. Balint, Executive Director

Limitations: Student loans for undergraduate juniors or seniors, or graduate students who are residents of Texas attending Texas colleges, universities, or graduate schools.
Financial data: Year ended 12/31/86. Assets, $17,253,000 (M); Expenditures $1,110,000, Loans to individuals, 355 loans totaling $338,981.
Employer Identification Number: 741292695
Applications: Loan applications must be made through recipient's college or university; Completion of formal application required; Application should be accompanied by transcript of grades and letter of recommendation regarding character and ability from head of department of student's major or dean of students.
Publications: Multi-year report, program information.
Program description:
The Student Loan Program makes about $350,000 available yearly for loans to Texas students attending Texas colleges or universities at the rate of six percent interest per year. The loans are available to juniors, seniors, and graduate students. A maximum of $5,000 will be loaned to any student, which may be repaid over a period of four years after graduation. Monthly payments begin one year after graduation.
Loans to undergraduate students will not exceed $750 per full semester or $375 per summer semester. Loans to graduate students will not exceed $1,000 per full semester or $500 per summer semester.
Loan applications will not be considered for students seeking an additional similar degree, i.e., obtaining a second Bachelor's degree.

537★
Pipp Foundation, The
c/o First of America Bank-Michigan
Kalamazoo, MI 49007
Contact: Dr. Robert J. Tisch, 235 North Sunset, Plainwell, MI 49080; Tel.: (616) 685-8940

Limitations: Scholarships only to seniors of Plainwell High School, MI, who rank in the top 20 percent of their class.
Financial data: Year ended 7/31/87. Assets, $756,453 (M); Total giving, $32,789; Grants to individuals, 8 grants totaling $18,000, high $2,500, low $2,000.
Employer Identification Number: 386041733
Applications: Deadline June 30th; Completion of formal application, including high school record, required; Applications available from Plainwell High School, Plainwell, MI.
Program description:
Scholarships are determined by need, scholastic achievement, and satisfactory progress and may be used at any institution of higher learning, including four and two-year college degree programs, non-degree programs, and trade schools.

538
Piton Foundation, The
511 Sixteenth Street, Suite 700
Denver, CO 80202   (303) 825-6246
Contact: Mary Gittings or Phyllis Buchete

Limitations: Scholarships and student loans to residents of Colorado, with emphasis on Denver.
Financial data: Year ended 11/30/85. Assets, $5,018,512 (M); Total giving, $1,975,435; Grants to individuals, 59 grants totaling $14,642.
Employer Identification Number: 840719486
Applications: Applications accepted throughout the year; Initial approach by letter.
Publications: Annual report.
Program description:
A limited number of educational scholarships and loans are available to residents of the Rocky Mountain States pursuing undergraduate, graduate, vocational, or professional studies at an accredited institution within the continental U.S.
Selection criteria include assessment of financial need, prior academic performance, and performance on educational or vocational aptitude tests, recommendations from the applicant's instructor, and personal traits including character, motivation, and potential, as assessed by members of the Grant Selection Committee during interviews.

539
Plym Foundation
Star Building
Niles, MI 49120   (616) 683-8300
Contact: Murry C. Campbell, Secretary

Limitations: Scholarships primarily for residents of the Niles, MI, area.
Financial data: Year ended 9/30/86. Assets $3,512,634 (M); Total giving, $152,194; Grants to individuals, 2 grants totaling $4,244, high $3,500, low $744.
Employer Identification Number: 386069680
Applications: Applications accepted throughout the year; Initial approach by letter, including achievement goals, resources, and scholarship amount required.

540
Poncin Scholarship Fund
c/o Seattle-First National Bank, Charitable Trust Administration
P.O. Box 3586
Seattle, WA 98124   (206) 442-3388
Contact: Rod Johnson, Vice-President

Limitations: Grants awarded to individuals engaged in medical research in a recognized institution of learning within the state of Washington.
Financial data: Year ended 12/31/86. Assets, $1,838,983 (M); Total giving, $92,400; Grants to individuals, 31 grants totaling $92,400, high $3,600, low $300, average grant $3,600.
Employer Identification Number: 916069573
Applications: Applications accepted throughout the year; Initial approach by proposal.
Program description:
The fund awards annual grants of $3,600, payable in increments of $300 per month, which are renewable twice. Approval of application by medical school dean or other head of medical department of institution is required.

541
Pope (Ida M.) Memorial Scholarship Fund
c/o Hawaiian Trust Company, Ltd.
P.O. Box 3170
Honolulu, HI 96802
Contact: Mrs. G. Johansen, c/o The Kamehameha Schools, Counseling Office, Kapalama Heights, Honolulu, HI 96817; Tel.: (808) 842-8612

Limitations: Scholarships to female residents of Hawaii who are of Hawaiian or part-Hawaiian ancestry for undergraduate or graduate education.
Financial data: Year ended 6/30/87. Assets, $623,429 (M); Total giving, $27,500; Grants to individuals, 108 grants totaling $27,500, high $1,000, low $150, general range $400-800.
Employer Identification Number: 996003339
Applications: Deadline May 1st; Completion of formal application and Financial Aid Form (FAF) required.

542
Porter Art Foundation
19 North Broadway
P.O. Box 370
Peru, IN 46970
Contact: James O. Cole, Box 536, Peru, IN 46970; Tel.: (317) 472-2723

Limitations: Scholarships only to graduating seniors in Miami County, IN, high schools for higher education in fine arts, music, and performing arts.
Financial data: Year ended 12/31/86. Assets, $13,653 (M); Total giving, $5,000; Grants to individuals, 4 grants totaling $5,000, each grant $1,250.
Employer Identification Number: 356067146
Applications: Contact foundation for current application deadline; Completion of formal application required; Interviews required.

543
Porter (Laura E.) Trust
Drawer H
Pratt, KS 67124   (316) 672-5533
Contact: B. V. Hampton, Bill Hampton, Jr., E. M. Baker, Trustees

Limitations: Educational loans and grants to men graduating from Pratt County Community College, KS, to further their education at a university approved by the trustees.
Financial data: Year ended 12/31/86. Assets, $507,170 (M); Expenditures, $48,563; Grants to individuals, 19 grants totaling $8,750, high $500, low $400, average grant $450; Loans to individuals, 41 loans totaling $31,946, high $2,230, low $250, average loan $750.
Employer Identification Number: 486105318
Applications: Applications accepted throughout the year; Completion of formal application required; Interviews granted upon request.

544
Potter (Philip E.) Foundation
Six Ford Avenue
Oneonta, NY 13820   (607) 432-6720
Contact: Henry L. Hulbert, Secretary

Limitations: Scholarships to residents of Otsego and Delaware counties, NY.
Financial data: Year ended 10/31/84. Assets, $485,067 (M); Total giving, $32,200; Grants to individuals, 112 grants totaling $32,200, high $750, low $150, general range $200-350.
Employer Identification Number: 166169167
Applications: Applications accepted throughout the year; Completion of formal application required; Application forms available from local high schools or foundation office; High school evaluation form required.

545
Poynter Fund, The
490 First Avenue South
P.O. Box 1121
St. Petersburg, FL 33731   (813) 893-8111
Contact: Catherine Heron, Secretary

Limitations: Undergraduate scholarships and graduate fellowships in journalism.
Financial data: Year ended 11/30/86. Assets, $2,147,544 (M); Total giving, $128,099; Grants to individuals, 41 scholarships totaling $51,099, high $5,000, low $250, and 3 fellowships totaling $11,000, high $9,000, low $1,000.
Employer Identification Number: 596142547
Applications: Contact foundation for current application deadline; Completion of formal application required.
Publications: Program information.
Program description:
The **Poynter Fund Scholarship Fellowship Program** is aimed at the development of better qualified staff in all areas of newspaper and communications media. The fund is particularly concerned with the improvement of reporting and objective interpretation of the news of domestic governments--national, state and local--foreign governments, and international governmental organizations. It encourages the linking of the academic study of political science with the practice of journalism and government.

Scholarships in amounts up to $2,000 per year are awarded to individuals of merit who demonstrate dedication and outstanding aptitude for publishing and broadcasting careers, regardless of financial need. Graduate fellowships of $1,000 or more are also awarded and may be used for study or travel which will further a newspaper or broadcasting career. These awards are open to applicants within five years of graduation from college.

Recipients must make a commitment to pursue careers in the field of journalism for at least three years following completion of their education. Selected applicants who cannot make this commitment or who do not enter the journalism field will be required to repay the scholarship as a loan within five years of graduation. All awards are on a one-year basis and may be renewed only upon re-application each year.

546★
Pratt (Annie Swift) Memorial Foundation
820 Senior Way
Sacramento, CA 95831   (916) 422-7198
Contact: Herschel Beauchamp, Trustee

Limitations: Scholarships only to residents of the Sacramento, CA, area.
Financial data: Year ended 12/31/86. Assets, $86,345 (M); Total giving, $7,000; Grants to individuals, 5 grants totaling $7,000, high $1,500, low $1,000.

Employer Identification Number: 946136964
Applications: Applications accepted throughout the year; Initial approach by letter; Completion of formal application required; Interviews required.

547
Pratt-Northam Foundation, The
c/o Hunt & Hunt
5564 Woodlawn Avenue
Lowville, NY 13367
Contact: Donald Exford, P.O. Box 104, Lowville, NY 13367

Limitations: Scholarships to individuals in the Black River Valley region of northern New York.
Financial data: Year ended 12/31/84. Assets, $1,656,505 (M); Total giving, $158,159; Grants to individuals, 1 grant totaling $5,700.
Employer Identification Number: 166088207
Applications: Applications accepted throughout the year; Completion of formal application required.

548
Preston (Elmer O. & Ida) Educational Trust
Des Moines Building, 11th Floor
Des Moines, IA 50309   (515) 243-4191
Contact: Nancy Dickey, Administrative Assistant

Limitations: Scholarships and student loans limited to worthy and needy young Protestant men residing in Iowa pursuing collegiate or professional studies in Iowa in preparation of a career in Christian service.
Financial data: Year ended 12/31/86. Assets, $1,369,680 (M); Total giving, $52,500; Grants to individuals, 35 grants totaling $52,500, high $2,300, low $500.
Employer Identification Number: 426053621
Applications: Applications accepted throughout the year; Completion of formal application required; Interviews required.

549
Price (Herschel C.) Educational Foundation
P.O. Box 412
Huntington, WV 25708-0412   (304) 529-3852
Contact: E. Joann Price, Trustee

Limitations: Scholarships primarily to undergraduates residing in West Virginia and/or attending West Virginia colleges and universities.
Financial data: Year ended 4/30/87. Assets, $2,668,832 (M), Total giving, $127,750; Grants to individuals, 190 grants totaling $127,750, high $1,500, low $250, general range $500-750.
Employer Identification Number: 556076719
Applications: Deadlines April 1st for fall semester awards and October 1st for spring semester awards; Submit application from February to March, or from August to September; Initial approach by letter;

Completion of formal application and interview required.

Program description:

There are no absolute geographical requirements for recipients; however, approximately 93 percent of the foundation's disbursed funds are granted to West Virginia residents and/or students attending West Virginia colleges and universities. Specifically, program policy is based upon the following statement: "Scholarships are given directly to deserving students for attendance at accredited educational institutions with preference given to undergraduates residing in West Virginia and attending West Virginia institutions. Interviews are generally required with selection based on financial need as well as scholastic standing."

Prospective grantees are notified of final action regarding their application by May 15th and December 15th respectively. Grants may range anywhere from $75 to a maximum of $1,500 per semester. Each applicant and recipient may re-apply each subsequent semester by updating his/her file for any change in financial status and submitting continuously current transcripts, other required data, and updated additional pertinent information.

The trustees of the foundation feel that it is an improper expenditure of foundation funds to answer all requests and inquiries from students residing in areas outside this foundation's main focus of attention and/or those requests and inquiries from students that obviously do not fit the basic guidelines and policies of the foundation.

550

Price (Joseph and Florence A.) Scholarship Fund

c/o First National Bank of Boston

P.O. Box 1861

Boston, MA 02105

Contact: Michael Donato, Headmaster, Hyde Park High School, Hyde Park, MA 02126

Limitations: Scholarships only to seniors of Hyde Park High School, MA.

Financial data: Year ended 12/31/85. Assets, $170,872 (M); Total giving, $9,750; Grants to individuals, 17 grants totaling $9,750, high $1,285, low $250.

Employer Identification Number: 046031925

Applications: Applications accepted throughout the year.

551

Pritchard Educational Fund

c/o Cherokee State Bank

212 West Willow Street

Cherokee, IA 51012   (712) 225-5131

Contact: Dennis Gano, Foundation Manager

Limitations: Student loans for residents of Cherokee County, IA, for high school or college education expenses.

Financial data: Year ended 12/31/86. Assets, $2,406,345 (M); Expenditures, $126,984; Loans to individuals totaling $91,288.

Employer Identification Number: 426051872

Applications: Applications accepted throughout the year; Completion of formal application required.

552

Professional Engineers Scholarship Fund, Inc.

c/o Bexar Chapter Texas Society of Professional Engineers

7073 San Pedro

San Antonio, TX 78216

Contact: Mr. Michael Couch, Secretary, 6735 Carters Bluff, San Antonio, TX 78239

Limitations: Scholarships to residents within the geographic boundaries of the Bexar Chapter Texas Society of Professional Engineers to attend accredited engineering colleges.

Financial data: Year ended 8/31/86. Assets, $12,627 (M); Total giving, $7,657; Grants to individuals, 11 grants totaling $7,657, high $875, low $383, average grant $875.

Employer Identification Number: 741671143

Applications: Deadline November 1st; Completion of formal application required using current NSPE Educational Foundation Scholarship application form; Interviews required.

553

Psychophysical Research Laboratories

1034 Smith Brentwood Boulevard, Suite 1620

St. Louis, MO 63117

Contact: M. Witunski, President

Limitations: Grants for research in areas related to psychology.

Financial data: Year ended 10/31/86. Assets, $519,954 (M); Total giving, $193,388; Grants to individuals, 3 grants totaling $193,388, high $90,000, low $16,000.

Employer Identification Number: 431153734

Applications: Initial approach by proposal; See program description below for complete application information.

Program description:

Submitted proposals should set forth, as a minimum, the following information:

    1. Description of the work to be undertaken

    2. Significance of the work proposed in relation to the field and to comparable work that may be in progress elsewhere

    3. Bibliography of pertinent literature citations

    4. Full and complete biography of the applicant including a list of the applicant's important achievements and publications

    5. Description of the facilities available for performing the work proposed

6. Estimate, with appropriate description, of the total cost of the program including salaries, materials, travel, equipment and facilities

7. Desired starting date and length of time for which support is being requested.

The decision to accept or reject a proposal will be based solely on an objective and nondiscriminatory evaluation as to the significance of the study or research proposed, and the ability of the applicant to execute the work and achieve the goals proposed, and not on any consideration as to sex, color, religion, age or ethnic background.

Grants are to achieve a specific educational objective or to produce a report or other similar product recording the research results obtained by the grantee during the period of the grant. A grant will be awarded on the condition that the grantee agrees, as part of the approved plan of work, to submit the following reports:

1. A final report, on the completion of the study, which will contain a comprehensive review of the grantee's accomplishments with respect to the grant, and a chronological bibliography of all publications, books, monographs, articles in professional and popular magazines and journals, resulting from the work performed.

2. Interim reports, at least quarterly but monthly in some instances during the course of the study or research, containing a summary of progress, difficulties encountered, if any, and a list of publications resulting to date.

3. An annual report on the use of funds and the progress made toward achieving the purposes of the grant. In many instances the fourth quarterly report may serve as the annual report.

4. A financial report accounting for all funds received under the grant upon completion of the undertaking for which the grant was made.

554
Pullman (George M.) Educational Foundation

5020 South Lake Shore Drive, Suite 307
Chicago, IL 60615   ·   (312) 363-6191
Contact: John H. Munger, Executive Director

Limitations: College scholarships to residents of Cook County, IL, or to children or grandchildren of graduates of Pullman Free School of Manual Training.
Financial data: Year ended 7/31/87. Assets, $16,155,125 (M); Total giving, $597,391; Grants to individuals, 530 grants totaling $597,391, high $3,000, low $300, average $1,000.
Employer Identification Number: 362216174
Applications: Deadlines April 1st for vocational students, May 1st for new upperclassmen, June 1st for renewal college students, and December 1st for freshmen; Completion of formal application and interviews required.
Publications: Biennial report, program information.

Program description:
About 200 new scholarships for undergraduate study at an accredited college or university are awarded annually.

555★
Racine Environmental Committee Educational Fund

310 Fifth Street, Room 101
Racine, WI 53403   (414) 631-5600
Contact: Mary Day, Executive Director

Limitations: College or vocational scholarships and tuition payments only for students residing in the Racine area who have been accepted by an institution.
Financial data: Year ended 12/31/86. Assets, $13,884 (M); Total giving, $66,570; Grants to individuals, 63 grants totaling $66,570, high $1,200, low $50, average grant $1,080.
Employer Identification Number: 396123892
Applications: Deadline June 30th; Initial approach by telephone; Completion of formal application required; Interviews required.
Publications: Annual report, application guidelines.
Program description:
The **Educational Assistance Program** provides counseling and financial assistance to high school graduates who are aspiring to obtain an undergraduate degree. Recipients must maintain a 2.0 grade point average per semester and must reapply each year. Financial assistance is in the form of grants to reduce a student's self-help (loan and/or work-study) offered by the financial aid office. Tuition payments are made directly to the institution for the benefit of individual grantees.

556
Ramona's Mexican Food Products Scholarship Foundation

c/o David L. Scarbrough
2001 East Fourth Street, Suite 125
Santa Ana, CA 92705
Contact: Alejandro Banuelos, President

Limitations: Scholarships to Hispanic residents of California.
Financial data: Year ended 9/30/86. Assets, $169,987 (M); Total giving, $24,430; Grants to individuals, 10 grants totaling $24,430, high $9,400, low $582.
Employer Identification Number: 237425268
Applications: Applications accepted throughout the year; Completion of formal application required.
Program description:
Scholarships are awarded to needy students for tuition, books, and fees.

557★
Rangeley Educational Trust
c/o Crestar Bank
P.O. Box 4911
Martinsville, VA 24115   (703) 632-6361
Contact: Paul J. Turner, Vice-President, Personal
Financial Services

Limitations: Loans to students primarily in the city of
Martinsville and Henry County, VA.
Financial data: Year ended 10/31/85. Assets,
$1,257,211 (M); Expenditures, $113,141; Loans to
individuals, 52 loans totaling $96,125, high $4,600,
low $500.
Employer Identification Number: 546077906
Applications: Deadline May 1st; Completion of formal
application required; Interviews usually required.
Program description:
Loans will be based on grades and scholastic ability,
and family financial need. Loan repayments must
begin within one year after completion of course of
study and must be paid in full within five to seven
years from the time repayment commences. Simple
interest is charged at the rate of 6 percent per annum.

558★
Raskob (The Bill) Foundation, Inc.
P.O. Box 4019
Wilmington, DE 19807   (302) 655-4440
Contact: Patricia M. Garey, 1st Vice-President

Limitations: Student loans to American citizens
currently enrolled at accredited institutions as full-time
upperclassmen for the upcoming school year.
Financial data: Year ended 12/31/87. Assets,
$2,205,688 (M); Expenditures, $333,395; Loans to
individuals, 69 loans totaling $198,800, high $5,000,
low $500, general range $1,000-2,000.
Employer Identification Number: 510110185
Applications: Deadline May 1st; Request application
forms from January 1st to April 1st; Initial approach by
letter and self-addressed, stamped size ten envelope
between December and March; Completion of formal
application required; Interviews may be requested,
depending upon geographical location.
Publications: Program information, application
guidelines.
Program description:
Interest-free loans are made to students to finance their
education. The foundation requires that all applicants
first apply for government loans or grants. If funds are
not available, or only a portion of the amount needed
can be granted, then application can be made to the
foundation.
   At present, the foundation is not accepting
applications from law students, incoming students on
any level (undergraduate, medical, dental, nursing,
veterinary, etc.), foreign students, or American students
studying abroad. It is not the policy of the foundation
to fund a student through more than one degree.

559
Ratner, Miller, Shafran Foundation, The
10800 Brookpark Road
Cleveland, OH 44130   (216) 267-1200
Contact: Nathan Shafran

Limitations: Scholarships for residents of Cuyahoga
County, OH.
Financial data: Year ended 11/30/86. Assets, $435,931
(M); Total giving, $207,959; Grants to individuals, 96
grants totaling $31,400, high $1,500, low $150.
Employer Identification Number: 346521216
Applications: Deadline May 1st; Completion of formal
application required.

560
Realty Foundation of New York
551 Fifth Avenue
New York, NY 10017
Contact: Scholarship Aid Committee, 531 Fifth
Avenue, Suite 921, New York, NY 10017

Limitations: Scholarships for higher education.
Financial data: Year ended 6/30/85. Assets, $978,130
(M); Total giving, $147,800; Grants to individuals, 47
grants totaling $80,300, high $5,000, low $300.
Employer Identification Number: 136016622
Applications: Completion of formal application
required.

561
Record (George J.) School Foundation
P.O. Box 581
Conneaut, OH 44030   (216) 599-8283
Contact: Charles N. Lafferty, President and Executive
Director

Limitations: Scholarships to legal residents of
Ashtabula County, OH, for tuition and fees at
approved private colleges and universities.
Financial data: Year ended 12/31/86. Assets,
$2,685,770 (L); Total giving $170,462; Grants to
individuals totaling $170,462, average grant $2,000.
Employer Identification Number: 340830818
Applications: Deadline May 20th for freshmen, June
20th for upperclassmen; Completion of formal
application and interviews required.
Publications: Program information, application
guidelines.
Program description:
Applicants must attend an approved private college
and complete the equivalent of six quarters of
religious study.

562★
Reese (Spence) Foundation
c/o Security Pacific National Bank
P.O. Box 3189, Terminal Annex
Los Angeles, CA 90051
Contact: John W. Treiber, Executive Director, Boys
Club of San Diego, 3760 4th Avenue, No. 1, San
Diego, CA 92103; Tel.: (619) 232-3061

Limitations: Scholarships only to male high school
students majoring in medicine, law, engineering, or
political science.
Financial data: Year ended 4/30/86. Assets, $559,236
(M); Total giving, $41,787; Grants to individuals, 36
grants totaling $36,000, each grant $1,000.
Employer Identification Number: 956206264
Applications: Deadline May 15th; Initial approach by
letter requesting application, including statement of
academic achievements, and educational goals;
Completion of formal application required.
Program description:
Scholarships are generally renewable for up to four
years. Four new scholarships are awarded each year.

563
Reifel-Ellwood Education Trust
323 Reed Street
P.O. Box 378
Red Oak, IA 51566   (712) 623-4828
Contact: Kenneth Rech, Trustee

Limitations: Scholarships to high school seniors who
are residents of Montgomery County, IA.
Financial data: Year ended 1/31/87. Assets, $83,050
(M); Total giving, $5,600; Grants to individuals, 28
grants totaling $5,600, each grant $200.
Employer Identification Number: 426149714
Applications: Deadline April 21st; Completion of
formal application required.
Program description:
Scholarships are granted to students attending any
accredited school of their choice in the U.S. Payments
are made directly to the university and the individual
recipient.

564
Research Corporation
6840 East Broadway Boulevard
Tucson, AZ 85710-2815   (602) 296-6771
Contact: John P. Schaefer, President; or Brian H.
Andreen, Grants Coordinator

Limitations: Grants and awards for research in the
physical and natural sciences at colleges and
universities in the U.S. and Canada.
Financial data: Year ended 10/31/86. Assets,
$69,632,722 (M); Total giving, $6,035,203; Grants to
individuals $2,461,709.
Employer Identification Number: 131963407
Applications: Completion of formal application

required if preliminary description of project indicates
that it is within program guidelines. See program
description below for application information on
specific programs.
Publications: Annual report, application guidelines,
program information.
Program description:
The foundation supports grants to educational
institutions where basic research is an accepted part of
a faculty member's work. Grants will be awarded to
institutions for the work of individual investigators.
  1. **Cottrell College Science Program** provides
  grants to help academic scientists at private,
  predominantly undergraduate institutions conduct
  basic research of orginality and importance in the
  natural sciences. There are no restrictions with
  regard to age or rank. Applications are judged
  primarily on scientific originality and significance.
  Other factors include the degree of student
  participation, the suitability of the problem, and
  the contribution the research effort may make
  toward strengthening the college's science
  program. Grants are made for items of direct
  expense, including student and faculty summer
  research stipends, equipment and supplies, travel
  to use special facilities and certain unusual
  expenses. Grants may be made for periods of up
  to three years with installment payments
  contingent on satisfactory progress. Applications
  are accepted throughout the year. Published
  guidelines for the Cottrell College Science
  Program are available from the foundation's
  Tucson office. An application packet is available
  to prospective applicants whose projects conform
  to the guidelines.
  2. **Research Opportunity Awards**: For mid-career
  and senior scientists of demonstrated productivity
  who are seeking to explore new areas of
  experimental research. One nomination annually
  is invited from the chair of each Ph.D. granting
  physics and chemistry department in the United
  States. A candidate's statement should include a
  description of proposed research, which will be
  evaluated for significance and originality. Typical
  grants will be in the range of $10,000-25,000.
  3. Other initiatives and programs will be
  launched from time to time to address areas of
  special opportunity. One such initiative is the
  High School-College Research Partnerships,
  available on an experimental basis in Arizona,
  California and New Mexico. The Partnerships are
  designed to create summer research opportunites
  for high school science teachers by teaming them
  up with university scientists who will serve as
  mentors. To apply, the college mentor must: be
  former or current Research Corporation grantees;
  have active research programs; hold appoinments
  in chemistry or physics departments at institutions
  in AZ, CA, or NM granting at least four-year
  baccalaureate degrees; and make arrangements
  with appropriate high school teachers who should

possess academic qualifications in the appropriate disciplines.

Each award will be in the amount of $5,000 per summer (proposals for two summers of support will be considered). Up to $3,500 may be used as a stipend for the high school teacher with the balance available for supplies, minor items of equipment and miscellaneous expenses.

Grant application guidelines and application packets for certain programs are available from the foundation by writing to the Grants Program Coordinator. Although the grants are administered by institutions, they support individual researchers. Application forms will be furnished if it appears that the proposal meets applicable criteria.

Interim progress reports are due annually and a terminal report (co-signed by the appropriate administrative official) is required when funds are fully expended. Installment payments of multi-year grants are contingent upon receipt of satisfactory progress reports. The foundation requests that publication of results in professional journals include acknowledgement of Research Corporation support.

In 1986, the major portion of funds was disbursed through the **Cottrell Research Program**, now terminated.

565
Reynolds (Edith Grace) Estate Residuary Trust
c/o Key Trust Company
60 State Street, P.O. Box 1965
Albany, NY 12207
Contact: Micheline Cardillo, Trust Officer, Key Trust Company

Limitations: Scholarships to individuals in School District #1, Rensselaer County, N.Y.
Financial data: Year ended 3/31/86. Assets, $1,193,432 (M); Total giving, $137,050; Grants to individuals totaling $137,050.
Employer Identification Number: 237170056
Applications: Deadline February 15th; Completion of formal application required; Include high school transcript and a copy of parents' 1040 tax form with application.

566
Richards (Anita H.) Trust
353 Chicago Avenue
Savanna, IL 61074   (815) 273-2028
Contact: Donald S. Wolf, Jr.

Limitations: Scholarships only to residents of Carroll County, IL.
Financial data: Year ended 12/31/86. Assets, $44,111 (L); Total giving, $1,980; Grants to individuals, 1 grant totaling $1,836; 1985, Grants to individuals, 1 grant totaling $3,550.
Employer Identification Number: 366504644

Applications: Deadline April 15th; Completion of formal application required; Interviews granted upon request.
Program description:
The **David Carlyle III Scholarships** are granted to one high school senior on the basis of financial need. Scholarships are renewable for four years of undergraduate work; for this reason, new awards are made only once every four years.

567★
Richards (The Mabel Wilson) Scholarship Fund
Trustees
3333 Glendale Boulevard, Suite One
Los Angeles, CA 90039   (213) 661-1396

Limitations: Scholarships to girls residing in the city of Los Angeles, CA, or one of about 140 adjacent communities in California as specified by the fund, and attending a specific California college or university.
Financial data: Year ended 3/31/87. Assets, $7,847,828 (M); Total giving, $413,924; Grants to individuals, 61 grants totaling $413,924, high $45,898, low $150, average grant $500.
Employer Identification Number: 956021322
Applications: Deadlines October 15th and February 15th; Initial approach by letter; Completion of formal application required.
Publications: Application guidelines, program information.
Program description:
Scholarships are awarded to provide financial assistance for the education of worthy and needy girls. Applications are accepted only through the financial aid office of one of about 40 California colleges (list provided by the fund). The financial aid offices make recommendations to the fund's trustees, who make the final selection of recipients. Scholarship payments are paid directly to the educational institution on behalf of the individual recipient. All grants are made on a competitive basis, consideration being given to scholastic achievement, financial need, high moral character and good citizenship.

568
Richland County Foundation of Mansfield, Ohio, The
34 1/2 South Park Street, Room 202
Mansfield, OH 44902   (419) 525-3020
Contact: Betty J. Crawford, Executive Director

Limitations: Scholarships for full-time undergraduate students who are residents of Richland County, OH.
Financial data: Year ended 12/31/86. Assets, $15,245,105 (M); Total giving, $1,085,173; Grants to individuals, 180 grants totaling $141,037.
Employer Identification Number: 340872883
Applications: Applications are available from the

foundation after January 1st for the following academic year; Applications accepted throughout the year; Completion of formal application, including grade transcripts required; Student must also file a Financial Aid Form (FAF) with College Scholarship Service using the foundation's code number (which appears on the application form).
Publications: Annual report (including application guidelines).
Program description:
Scholarships are based primarily on need and a grade point average of at least 2.0 must be maintained. Payments are made directly to the educational institution.

569
Rinker Companies Foundation, Inc.
1501 Belvedere Road
West Palm Beach, FL 33406   (305) 833-5555
Contact: Jack L. Osteen, Assistant Secretary

Limitations: Scholarships to Florida residents with business or construction industry-related majors.
Financial data: Year ended 3/30/87. Assets, $6,145,489 (M); Total giving, $763,308; Grants to individuals, 120 grants totaling $209,558, high $4,500, low $103, general range $1,000-2,000.
Employer Identification Number: 596139266
Applications: Deadline April; Completion of formal application required.

570
Riverside County Physicians Memorial Foundation
3993 Jurupa Avenue
Riverside, CA 92506   (714) 686-3342
Contact: C. P. Rowlands, Executive Director

Limitations: Student loans for medical education only to residents of Riverside County, CA.
Financial data: Year ended 8/31/86. Assets, $35,461 (M); Expenditures, $82; Loans to individuals, 1 loan totaling $2,500.
Employer Identification Number: 956080778
Applications: Applications accepted throughout the year; Initial approach by letter; Completion of formal application required.
Program description:
Loans have been awarded to assist residents of Riverside County, CA, with medical school tuition. Scholars have attended medical schools both within and outside California.

571
Robertson (Lois and Edward) Foundation
691 Lake Sue Avenue
Winter Park, FL 32789
Contact: Edward H. Robertson, Vice-President

Limitations: Scholarships to graduates of Winter Park High School, Winter Park, FL.
Financial data: Year ended 3/31/87. Assets, $62,768 (L); Total giving, $5,100; Grants to individuals, 2 grants totaling $2,000, each grant $1,000.
Employer Identification Number: 366146685
Program description:
From time to time, the foundation's officers may decide to make a scholarship grant. When such a grant is to be made, the foundation will notify the head of the appropriate academic department at Winter Park High School.

572
Robin Scholarship Foundation
1333 North Wells Street
Chicago, IL 60610   (312) 642-6301

Limitations: Scholarships only to Illinois high school seniors of low income families showing high promise, with emphasis on Chicago, IL, residents.
Financial data: Year ended 12/31/86. Assets, $1,240,962 (M); Total giving, $160,454; Grants to individuals, 88 grants totaling $160,454, high $3,750, low $130, average grant $1,250.
Employer Identification Number: 363204864
Applications: Deadline January 15th; Applications available through high schools; Completion of formal application required.

573★
Robinson (John W.) Welfare Trust
Gardiner Public Library
Gardiner, ME 04345
Contact: Maxine Lamb, 12 Spruce Street, Gardiner, ME; Tel.: (207) 582-2488

Limitations: Scholarships for residents of Gardiner, ME.
Financial data: Year ended 12/31/86. Assets, $587,860 (M); Total giving, $26,088; Grants to individuals, 110 grants totaling $8,100, high $100, low $50, average grant $75.
Employer Identification Number: 016009329
Applications: Deadline June 15th; Completion of formal application required; Interviews required.

574
Rocco (August Michael) Scholarship Foundation
c/o AmeriTrust Company
P.O. Box 5937
Cleveland, OH 44101
Contact: Christine E. Sutton-Kruman, AmeriTrust
Company, 237 Tuscarawas Street West, Canton, OH
44702

Limitations: Grants and loans to graduates of Central
Catholic High School or St. Thomas Aquinas in Stark
County, OH, to attend Notre Dame University in
Indiana.
Financial data: Year ended 12/31/86. Assets, $313,160
(M); Total giving, $23,200; Grants to individuals
totaling $23,200; Subtotals for grants and loans not
specified.
Employer Identification Number: 346500558
Applications: Applications accepted throughout the
year; Initial approach by letter.

575★
Rochester Area Foundation
335 Main Street East, Suite 402
Rochester, NY 14604   (716) 325-4353
Contact: Linda S. Weinstein, President

Limitations: Scholarships and fellowships to residents
of Genesee, Livingston, Monroe, Ontario, Orleans,
and Wayne counties, NY. Recipients are chosen by
specified educational institutions.
Financial data: Year ended 2/28/88. Assets,
$11,351,291 (M); Total giving, $940,979; Grants to
individuals totaling $50,375.
Employer Identification Number: 237250641
Publications: Annual report.
Program description:
The foundation administers the following scholarship
funds:
   The **Dr. Abraham R. Bullis Memorial Fund** provides
a scholarship grant of $1,000-3,000 to a graduate of
Palmyra-Macedon High School who is studying
medicine.
   The **Bullis Family Scholarship Fund** provides
scholarships, $100 minimum per grant, to any
graduate of Palmyra-Macedon High School who has
lived in the district for a minimum of eight years and
maintains a "C" average in an institution of higher
education.
   The **Ronald and Marilyn Furman Fund** awards
fellowships of $500-750 for teachers in the City
School District and Pittsford School Districts.
   The **Heidi Hoenig Memorial Scholarship Fund**
provides a scholarship grant of $1,000 to a graduate of
Irondequoit High School majoring in architecture or
art.
   The **Lawrence R. Klepper Fund** provides a
scholarship grant of $500-750 to a scholar-athlete of
the City School District of Rochester who has

maintained an A average for four years and is a
member of a varsity athletic team.
   The **Natalie K. Meyer Memorial Scholarship Fund**
awards a scholarship grant of $200 to a graduate of
Pittsford-Mendon High School.
   The **Barbara Wheeler Schneider Memorial
Scholarship Fund** provides a grant of $500-700 to a
graduate of Arkport Central School District.
   The **Reineman Family Scholarship Fund** awards
scholarship grants to a Monroe County student.
   The **Maxine Tillotson Fund** awards scholarship
grants to a graduate of Webster Central Schools who
studies at the Eastman School of Music.

576
Rockefeller Foundation, The
1133 Avenue of the Americas
New York, NY 10036   (212) 869-8500
Contact: Lynda Mullen, Secretary

Limitations: See program description below for
specific limitations for various programs.
Financial data: Year ended 12/31/86. Assets,
$1,605,602,953 (M); Total giving, $45,438,683;
Grants to individuals, 276 grants totaling $3,562,163,
high $50,000, low $382, general range
$5,000-20,000.
Employer Identification Number: 131659629
Applications: Applications accepted throughout the
year. See program description below for application
information on specific programs.
Publications: Annual report, application guidelines,
program information.
Program description:
I. Arts and Humanities: The major objectives of this
program are:
      1. Support for the creative person.
      2. Strengthening secondary school education for
      the arts and humanities.
      3. Enhancing the American public's understanding
      of international affairs through the arts and
      humanities.
      4. Forging connections between artists, humanists,
      and society.
   **Rockefeller Foundation Fellowship Program for
Playwrights** includes two categories of annual awards:
   Playwright Awards are made to eight individuals a
year to enable them to concentrate on their work
relatively free from outside pressures. The stipends of
$12,000 each are administered by a producing theatre
which the playwright selects and at which a residency
of a minimum of six weeks is spent. An additional
$6,000 is available to the theatre for costs related to
the playwright's work. A significant proportion of
recipients have consistently been women and
members of minority groups.
   Regional Theatre Awards are made to about ten
small companies each year which then select
playwrights to serve in residence and receive $2,500
stipends. An additional $1,000 is awarded to the

theatres for related costs. The emphasis of this part of the program is on the discovery and encouragement of new writers outside the New York area.

Recipients of both the playwright and regional theatre awards are selected by an independent committee of theatre professionals. **No direct applications from individuals are accepted.**

Rockefeller Foundation Humanities Fellowships are awarded to writers and scholars in the traditional humanistic disciplines (such as literature, history, and philosophy) whose projects contribute to the analysis and evaluation of contemporary issues or values. Similar proposals in fields not usually defined as humanistic (such as political science, law, and anthropology) are encouraged if their humanistic implications are clear and substantial.

For 1988-89, the fellowships will be offered as residencies at host institutions selected for their potential to promote individual scholarship in the humanities. In accord with guidelines recently approved by the foundation's trustees, the sites selected to sustain such scholarship increasingly will be concentrated on international studies and foreign languages, on the cultures of non-Western nations, and on American cultural pluralism. Host institutions include academic departments, area studies and other interdisciplinary programs, museums, and arts and cultural organizations. These institutions select scholars to receive Rockefeller Foundation Fellowship stipends. They encourage interaction between their permanent experts and the visiting scholars, and they make libraries, special collections, and other facilities available in their specialized areas of research. By providing resident fellowships, the foundation seeks to make outstanding resources accessible to individual scholars, to stimulate exchange within and between disciplines, and to strengthen emerging areas of inquiry in the humanities.

The fellowships are meant to serve scholars who are testing disciplinary boundaries or moving into newer fields of inquiry within the humanities. Although the majority of the scholar's time will be spent pursuing his or her own research toward publication, the residency may involve participation in seminars, conferences, or other responsibilities within the program. Complete information about eligibility, stipends and procedures for application are available directly from the current 21 host institutions. For a list of host institutions, write to: Rockefeller Residency Program in Humanities, The Rockefeller Foundation, Division of Arts and Humanities.

II. Agricultural Sciences: Four objectives have been established within this program:

    1. To increase food production by strengthening the international and national agricultural research and development systems.

    2. To strengthen agricultural research, with specific reference to the food legumes, hemoparasitic diseases of animals, aquatic species, and new dimensions of plant breeding, physiology, and resistance to disease and insects.

    3. To encourage and support effective utilization of fragile environments and marginal lands, such as tropical rain forests, arid lands, and hill areas.

    4. To support work on food and agricultural policy, with specific reference to production, distribution, and nutrition in the developing countries.

III. Equal Opportunity: This program seeks to further the establishment of equal opportunity for all Americans, concentrating on four areas:

    1. Expanding economic opportunity--the identification of effective strategies for improving the employment and income status of minority groups.

    2. Broadening career opportunities to help increase educational opportunities--for minorities in fields such as the natural sciences, mathematics, and economics, especially at the graduate level.

    3. Support and protection of basic rights--assistance to selected individuals and to national and regional organizations involved in activities that help secure the basic rights of all citizens and seek to overcome the effects of past racial discrimination.

The Research Fellowship Program for Minority-Group Scholars supports research designed to influence the understanding and resolution of minority-group issues. Under this program, approximately 15 to 20 minority-group fellows will be selected through a national competition. The program will enable outstanding men and women to undertake policy-oriented social science and humanistic research on problems of high priority in areas such as education, employment, housing, and civil rights.

There are no rigid criteria for eligibility. Previous experience in an appropriate field or demonstrated research ability may be considered minimally necessary qualifications. A Ph.D. may be an important credential in some fields.

Fellowships are usually awarded for a one-year period. Each grant will vary in amount, depending on individual circumstances, although the ordinary grant will be in the range of $20,000 to $23,000 and no grant will exceed $25,000. The grant may cover maintenance, travel, and other approved costs. It is anticipated that, in some cases, fellows will work on special projects while continuing their existing institutional relationships, but no award will be made for less than six months of full-time work on an approved project. If the applicant is associated with a tax-exempt institution, the grant ordinarily will be made through that institution; successful applicants will be asked to provide a letter from the appropriate administrative officer of such an institution indicating its willingness to administer the grant without overhead charges.

Proposals should be typed, double-spaced, with five copies, and include:

    1. The scope, purpose, and methodology of the proposed abstract.

2. A covering sheet showing:
- the applicant's full name, address, telephone number, and social security number
- the title of the project
- the amount of funds required
- the duration of the project.

3. A budget outlining basic minimum requirements, not to exceed $25,000.

4. A curent curriculum vitae.

5. The names and addresses of three persons familiar with the applicant's work who will be asked to serve as references.

The foundation will write directly to the references requesting that confidential statements about the project and the applicant's qualifications be sent directly to the foundation.

A more detailed description of application requirements is given in foundation literature on the program.

IV. International Relations: In this program the foundation has set the following goals:

1. Within the U.S., to strengthen the contribution of nongovernmental international relations research to U.S. foreign policy.

2. In countries other than U.S., to strengthen the analytical capacity of international relations research institutions that can operate substantially without government constraint and have the potential to increase the intellectual underpinnings of these countries' foreign policies.

3. To provide more effective opportunities for public and private experts from different countries to analyze problems jointly and develop practical solutions that can command wide public support.

4. Through its fellowship program and other mechanisms, to identify outstanding young people trained in international relations and increase their opportunities for career development.

International Relations Fellowships are to help the career development of individuals who have demonstrated the ability to conduct scholarly research and who seek to broaden these skills in ways relevant to improving the formulation of foreign policies. To this end, the foundation will award approximately ten fellowships to enable young scholars and professionals to conduct full-time research outside their own country, for a period not to exceed two years.

The competition is open to men and women, anywhere in the world, who have completed their academic or professional training and have had several years of work experience in the international field. Scholars and practitioners from the areas of political science and government, economics, history, sociology, law, business, journalism, and the sciences are encouraged to apply. Research should center on public policy issues of vital concern to relations among states, a specific region, or to the world at large.

The fellowship competition is aimed primarily at young people between the ages of 25 and 35, although unusual circumstances may warrant

awarding a fellowship to a recipient up to age 40. The foundation is especially interested in attracting qualified women and applicants from developing countries.

Applications must be received by January 15th and should include the following: a proposal (3,000-5,000 words, typed and double-spaced) defining the research issue of the study, methods by which the applicant plans to pursue the research, and a half-page abstract of the above. Applicants should also include a curriculum vitae, postgraduate academic transcripts, an abstract of the candidate's master's or doctoral thesis, when applicable, and a budget listing living, travel, and research costs.

Applicants should also list the names, titles, and addresses of six individuals who are familiar with their work and fellowship proposal. Applicants should ask only three of the six to write recommendations in support of the proposals, and should send the foundation these three names. The foundation will request further information from the additional three references if necessary. Those providing references should indicate the extent of personal knowledge about the applicant; rate the applicant in his or her field and discipline; describe the applicant's strengths and weaknesses as a scholar and professional; and evaluate the project's feasibility and importance.

More details on program objectives and application procedures are given in foundation literature on the program.

V. Population and Health: The current objectives of the **Population** program are as follows:

1. Research in reproductive biology--strengthening research both by supporting individuals presently engaged in significant work and by drawing new people of excellence into the field.

2. Research on new contraceptive technology--maintaining strong research efforts to develop safer, more effective, and inexpensive methods of fertility regulation.

3. Policy studies--helping to shape national policy formulation through research and training to improve understanding of the determinants of fertility and of the socio-economic factors affecting population dynamics and acceptance of contraceptive technology.

Fellowships in Population Sciences are awarded for advanced training in reproductive biology/medicine and in population studies in demography, or for studies of population in combination with a social science discipline.

Selections will be based on the recommendation of a fellowship committee composed of distinguished scholars and researchers in the field of population. Selection criteria will stress academic excellence and potential contributions to the population field. Preference will be given to persons from developing countries who have a firm committment to return to their home countries upon completion of training.

Awards may be made for two types of study programs:

1. **Postdoctoral Study Awards** are open to persons 35 years of age or under having a Ph.D. degree or equivalent who wish to undertake postdoctoral training and/or research with population specialization.

2. **Graduate Study Awards** are restricted to persons 35 years of age or under who have completed all work, except dissertation, towards the Ph.D. degree (or equivalent) in one of the social sciences with a specialization in population.

Awards are made for up to one year (not less than six months). Renewals for up to one additional year will be considered in competition with first-time applicants.

Awards consist of a monthly stipend (based on type of fellowship and place of study), tuition payments and related fees, transportation expenses, and health insurance. A family allowance may be granted to appointees who have dependents in their immediate families--limited to spouse and children--for whom they are financially responsible.

Information concerning application procedures can be obtained by writing to: "Population Sciences/Fellowships" at the above address.

The **Health Sciences** program is currently focusing on:

1. Great neglected diseases--to increase both our knowledge and means of control of the great neglected diseases of the developing world by attracting outstanding biomedical scientists to these problems through the formation of an international network of investigative units, and to apply the results of this work through operational studies in the less-developed countries.

2. Health of populations--to foster quantitative approaches in clinical medicine and the provision of health care through the use of population-based disciplines (biometry, demography, epidemiology, health statistics, and survey methods) as integral parts of medical education, clinical practice, and the organization and administration of health services and as a means of extending the vision and understanding of physicians and others beyond the individual patient.

3. Coping with biomedical information--to assist producers, librarians, and users of the scientific literatures and statistical data in identifying and utilizing the small proportion of information that is significant and relevant to particualr needs through the design of practical, rational health information and communication systems.

VI. The Bellagio Study and Conference Center: The Center is located at Lake Como, Bellagio, Italy, and hosts both a residential program for scholars and a program of international conferences.

Each year about 80 scholars and artists are invited to spend approximately four weeks at the center to enable them to work on a book, monograph, major article, musical composition, or other creative undertaking. Because the library facilities are limited, it is suggested that scholars not plan to conduct research there and that the center can best be used at the beginning or final stages of a project. Seven scholars and their spouses can be accomodated at any one time. No monetary assistance is provided to scholars-in-residence, nor are travel funds ordinarily supplied. Exceptions may be made in the case of scholars from developing countries in Africa, Asia, and Latin America, for whom assistance with travel expenses may be available.

In addition, the foundation invites about 35 groups to the center each year to hold small conferences concerned with problems or topics of international significance.

For both programs, preference is given to projects or conferences that address issues of concern to the foundation as enumerated above.

577
Rooke Foundation, Inc.
P.O. Box 7
Woodsboro, TX 78393   (512) 543-4533
Contact: Frank J. Scanio, Jr.

Limitations: Scholarships only to graduates of Refugio County High School, TX.
Financial data: Year ended 12/31/86. Assets, $196,157 (M); Total giving, $32,695; Grants to individuals, 6 grants totaling $4,500, high $1,000, low $500.
Employer Identification Number: 746003460
Applications: Deadline April 1st; Completion of formal application, available from Refugio County High School, required; Interviews required.

578★
Roothbert Fund, Inc., The
475 Riverside Drive, Room 565
New York, NY 10115   (212) 870-3116
Contact: Jacob Van Rossum, Administrative Secretary

Limitations: Scholarships to students who are primarily motivated by spiritual values, with preference to those considering teaching as a profession; Applicants must by available for an interview in New York City.
Financial data: Year ended 12/31/86. Assets, $2,238,634 (M); Total giving, $81,200; Grants to individuals, 70 grants totaling $81,200, high $5,000, low $400, average grant $1,000.
Employer Identification Number: 136162570
Applications: Deadline March 1st; Submit Fund form in January or February; Initial approach by letter; Completion of formal application required; Interviews in New York City required.
Publications: Annual report, application guidelines.
Program description:
The fund assists college or university students who are primarily motivated by spiritual values, with preference to those who are considering teaching as a vocation.

The term "spiritual" is intended to reflect a personal commitment or direct awareness of a spiritual Force or Being in the universe to which the individual feels responsive rather than affiliation with a particular established religious dogma or group. Grants are awarded annually in April.

579
Rosenkrans (Fred A.) Trust
c/o First Interstate Bank of Oregon, N.A.
P.O. Box 2971
Portland, OR 97208
Contact: Charles K. Woodcock, Trust Officer

Limitations: Student loans only to undergraduates attending Oregon State University.
Financial data: Year ended 12/31/86. Assets, $334,549 (M); Expenditures, $14,615; Loans to individuals, 6 loans totaling $8,732, high $2,000, low $600, average loan $2,000.
Employer Identification Number: 936017353
Applications: Applications accepted throughout the year; Completion of formal application required; Financial budget, transcript of grades, verification of enrollment, and general background information required.
Program description:
Loans repayable at an interest rate of five percent are awarded.

580
Ross (Charles M.) Trust
P.O. Box 160
Fairbury, IL 61739   (815) 692-4336
Contact: Henry W. Phillips, Director

Limitations: Primarily graduate scholarships in the fields of religion, sociology, medicine, and teaching.
Financial data: Year ended 6/30/87. Assets, $320,469 (M); Total giving, $14,000; Grants to individuals, 13 grants totaling $14,000, high $2,000, low $500, general range $500-1,000.
Employer Identification Number: 376075511
Applications: Applications accepted between April 1st and August 1st; Completion of formal application required.
Program description:
Graduate scholarships are awarded to gifted students committed to world service and embarked on a course of training in a field that is designed to develop leadership qualities in areas devoted to the welfare of mankind.

581
Ross (John M.) Foundation
c/o Bishop Trust Company, Ltd., Hilo Branch
Box 397
Hilo, HI 96720

Limitations: Scholarships only to residents of the Island of Hawaii (Big Island).
Financial data: Year ended 6/30/87. Assets, $514,718 (M); Total giving, $14,100; Grants to individuals, 40 grants totaling $10,000, each grant $250.
Employer Identification Number: 996007327
Applications: Applications accepted throughout the year; Completion of formal application required.

582
Rotch Travelling Scholarship, Inc.
c/o Fiduciary Trust Company
175 Federal Street
Boston, MA 02110   (617) 868-4200
Contact: Norman C. Fletcher, Secretary, 46 Brattle Street, Cambridge, MA 02138

Limitations: Grants to architects under thirty-five years of age, with educational or professional experience from Massachusetts for foreign travel and study in architecture.
Financial data: Year ended 12/31/86. Assets, $668,637 (M); Total giving, $24,500; Grants to individuals, 5 grants totaling $24,500, high $10,500, low $200.
Employer Identification Number: 046062249
Applications: Deadline January 22nd; Initial approach by letter to request application should be submitted by January 2nd; Completion of formal application required.
Publications: Program information.
Program description:
The Rotch Travelling Scholarship for the Advancement of Education in Architecture is awarded annually to provide for eight months of foreign travel and study in the field of architecture. The award is in the amount of $13,000, with an additional $1,500 to be paid after acceptance of the scholar's final report by the Committee.
   Applicants must be U.S. citizens who have either:
      1. received a degree in architecture from an accredited school of architecture plus one full year of professional experience in a Massachusetts architectural office;
      2. received a degree from an accredited Massachusetts school of architecture and at least one full year of professional experience in an architectural office not necessarily in Massachusetts;
      3. received a certificate from the Boston Architectural Center signifying completion of its former five-year program or, for those applicants who have graduated from the center since its degree-granting program, a degree and one year

of professional experience in an architectural office.

A detailed statement of eligibility requirements is sent out with the application form which may be obtained by writing to the secretary of the foundation.

583
Roth Foundation
410 Vernon Road
Jenkintown, PA 19046   (215) 576-1191
Contact: Linda Schwartz, Trustee

Limitations: Scholarships primarily to students attending Pennsylvania institutions for nursing education.
Financial data: Year ended 10/31/86. Assets, $1,865,606 (M); Total giving, $46,000; Grants to individuals totaling $46,000.
Employer Identification Number: 236271428
Applications: Applications accepted throughout the year; Initial approach by letter.
Program description:
Applicants must have completed one year of attendance in a recognized school of nursing prior to application. Scholarship payments are made directly to the institution on the named recipient's behalf.

584
Rouch (A.P. and Louise) Boys Foundation
c/o Twin Falls Bank & Trust, Trust Department
P.O. Box 7
Twin Falls, ID 83303-0007

Limitations: Scholarships only to needy students attending college in the Magic Valley area of Idaho.
Financial data: Year ended 12/31/85. Assets, $202,906 (M); Total giving, $17,144; Grants to individuals, 94 grants totaling $17,144; Subtotal for scholarships, 13 grants totaling $3,732, high $375, low $59, average grant $300.
Employer Identification Number: 826005152

585
Rounds (George) Trust
c/o Ethel B. Pierce, Trustee
P.O. Box 123
West Columbia, TX 77486   (409) 345-3863

Limitations: Scholarships only to residents of West Columbia, TX, and vicinity.
Financial data: Year ended 12/31/86. Assets, $189,554 (M); Total giving, $2,498; Grants to individuals, 5 grants totaling $2,498, high $1,000, low $126.
Employer Identification Number: 746062601
Applications: Completion of formal application required; Applications to be submitted to District Judge, Angleton, TX.

586
Rowan (C.L.) Charitable & Educational Fund, Inc.
1918 Commerce Building
Fort Worth, TX 76102   (817) 332-2327
Contact: Elton Hyder, Jr.

Limitations: Grants primarily to Texas residents attending Texas universities.
Financial data: Year ended 10/31/86. Assets, $939,075 (M); Total giving, $117,433, Grants to individuals, 4 grants totaling $30,354, high $14,275, low $79.
Employer Identification Number: 756009661
Applications: Applications accepted throughout the year; Initial approach by letter.

587★
Royston (The Rachel) Permanent Scholarship Foundation of Alpha Sigma State of the Delta Kappa Gamma Society International
2600 Century Square
1501 Fourth Avenue
Seattle, WA 98101-1688
Contact: Gwen Page, 14607 S.E. 267th Street, Kent, WA 98042

Limitations: Scholarships only for graduate study to women educators who are bona fide residents of the state of Washington.
Financial data: Year ended 6/30/87. Assets, $533,891 (M); Total giving, $22,000; Grants to individuals, 8 grants totaling $22,000, high $4,670, low $1,500.
Employer Identification Number: 916060790
Applications: Deadline January 1st; Initial approach by letter requesting application and award regulations; Completion of formal application and interviews required, including:
  ● a list of names from who board will directly receive recommendations
  ● official transcripts of all undergraduate and graduate work
  ● full statement of proposed program of study
  ● letter of acceptance by the institution if working in a field of special interest, or from graduate school if working towards a graduate degree
  ● an offical statement indicating the stage of doctoral progress, if applicable, usually from the advisor.
Publications: Program information (including application guidelines).
Program description:
The purpose of this scholarship is to assist selected women in pursuing study beyond the bachelor degree level. Recipients may pursue work toward a Master's or Doctor's degree, or work in a field of special interest. Awards may only be made for one year or a portion thereof; however, additional applications may be requested and submitted in later years. Competition for the awards is keen, and importance is attached to

the project on which the candidate wishes to work, its significance to the field of education, and the evidence of the candidate's ability to pursue it.

Applicants must be bona fide residents of the state of Washington, and must be doing graduate work in an approved institution of higher learning which has been accredited by a regional and/or national accrediting association and ranks high in the applicant's field.

588
Rubenstein (David) Memorial Scholarship Foundation
c/o Michael Rubenstein
60 Green Street
San Francisco, CA 94111   (415) 781-5348
Contact: Cecilia Metz, c/o Golden Gate Restaurant Association, 291 Geary Street, San Francisco, CA 94102; Tel.: (415) 781-5348

Limitations: Scholarships by recommendation only to northern California students graduating from hotel and restaurant high school and junior college programs who are planning to continue their training full-time on the college level.
Financial data: Year ended 12/31/86. Assets, $103,727 (M); Total giving, $5,250; Grants to individuals, 10 grants totaling $5,250, high $1,000, low $250.
Employer Identification Number: 237012819
Applications: Deadline April 30th; Completion of formal application required; Interviews required; Applications are to be submitted by teachers and administrators of high school and junior college food preparation and service programs on behalf of qualified students; **Individual applications not accepted.**
Program description:
Grants are dependent on maintainence of grade point average, student's needs and degree of seriousness and interest.

589★
Rubinow (Mary B. and William) Scholarship Fund Trust
49 Pitkin Street
Manchester, CT 06040   (203) 643-5632
Contact: Jay E. Rubinow, Secretary

Limitations: Interest-free loans only to residents of Manchester, CT, for undergraduate or graduate education.
Financial data: Year ended 12/31/84. Assets, $52,185 (M); Expenditures, $8,567; Loans to individuals, 5 loans totaling $8,500, high $2,000, low $1,500.
Employer Identification Number: 066034723
Applications: Applications accepted throughout the year; Applications available only through the guidance office of Manchester High School, 134 Middle Turnpike East, Manchester, CT 06040; Completion of

formal application required.
Program description:
Notes for loans are payable within five years and must be signed by one parent of student and by student.

590★
Rudel (Julius) Award Trust Fund
1800 West Magnolia Boulevard
Burbank, CA 91506

Limitations: Scholarships for the study of opera.
Financial data: Year ended 2/28/87. Assets, $105,331 (M); Total giving, $6,500; Grants to individuals, 1 grant totaling $6,500.
Employer Identification Number: 956240600
Applications: Initial approach by letter to General Director, New York City Opera, State Theatre, Lincoln Center, New York, NY 10023.

591
Rutledge (Edward) Charity
P.O. Box 758
404 North Bridge Street
Chippewa Falls, WI 54729   (715) 723-6618
Contact: John Frampton, President

Limitations: Scholarships primarily to high school graduates who are residents of Chippewa County, WI.
Financial data: Year ended 5/31/87. Assets, $2,409,780 (M); Total giving, $76,136; Grants to individuals, 222 grants totaling $57,036; Subtotal for scholarships, 30 grants totaling $41,108, high $1,901, low $535, average loan $1,447.
Employer Identification Number: 390806178
Applications: Deadline July 1st; Initial approach by telephone; Completion of formal application required.

592★
Saak (Charles E.) Trust
c/o Wells Fargo Bank - Trust Department
618 East Shaw Avenue
Fresno, CA 93710   (209) 442-6232

Limitations: Undergraduate scholarships to underprivileged students under 21 years of age residing in the Porterville/Poplar area of Tulare County, CA.
Financial data: Year ended 1/31/87. Assets, $1,070,433 (M); Total giving, $41,894; Grants to individuals, 343 grants totaling $37,192; Subtotal for scholarships, 111 grants totaling $15,307, high $500, low $9, general range $100-200.
Employer Identification Number: 946076213
Applications: Deadline March 31st; Completion of formal application required; Application must be submitted with educational statement, financial statements of student and parents, latest income tax return, and transcripts of high school and (if applicable) college grades; Additional telephone

number is (805) 395-0920.
Program description:
Scholarships will be awarded for one year of full-time study; successful applicants may reapply each year scholarship support is sought. Recipients must achieve at least a 2.0 GPA each sememster/quarter and 12 units.

The majority of the scholarship recipients attend Porterville College; others attend colleges in California and neighboring states.

593★
Sachs Foundation
101 North Cascade Avenue, Suite 430
Colorado Springs, CO 80903   (719) 633-2353
Contact: Morris A. Esmiol, Jr., President

Limitations: Graduate and undergraduate scholarships, and medical research grants to black residents of Colorado.
Financial data: Year ended 12/31/86. Assets, $1,045,607 (M); Total giving, $438,358; Grants to individuals, 217 grants totaling $438,358, high $5,000, low $318, average grant $2,250.
Employer Identification Number: 840500835
Applications: Deadline March 15th; Initial approach by letter; Completion of two copies of application required; Interviews required.
Publications: Program information, application guidelines.
Program description:
Scholarships are awarded to black residents of Colorado desiring to obtain undergraduate or graduate degrees. Recipients must maintain a 2.5 GPA average or better without incompletes or failures and be enrolled a minimum of 12 hours. Awards are made for a maximum of four years or until graduation. Graduate scholarships are considered on a case-by-case basis. Recipients can attend educational institutions in any state.

594★
Sage (Russell) Foundation
112 East 64th Street
New York, NY 10021   (212) 750-6000
Contact: Mr. Peter de Janosi

Limitations: Grants to individuals and research teams affiliated with colleges, universities and institutes for social science research that will improve the social and living conditions in the United States.
Financial data: Year ended 8/31/87. Assets, $103,022,217 (M); Total giving, $3,252,753; Grants to individuals, 20 grants totaling $850,000, high $114,611, low $2,000.
Employer Identification Number: 131635303
Applications: Contact foundation for specific information.
Publications: Biennial report, application guidelines.

Program description:
Through its **External Projects Program** the foundation makes grants to individuals and research teams for social and public policy research projects. Major areas of interest include:
- **The Social Analysis of Poverty Program** - To foster new analytic strategies that offer insights into the nature of poverty and the reasons for its persistence.
- **The Behavioral Economics Program** - To examine the possibility of reconstructing economic science on the basis of more realistic assumptions about human nature and economic institutions.
- **The Research Synthesis Program** - To provide financial support and technical assistance designed to encourage more effective use of statistical methods for summarizing the significant generalizations that can be derived from multiple studies of the same social problem or program.
- **New York City**.

The foundation conducts a **Visiting Scholar Program** in which scholars working in areas of interest to the foundation are invited, usually as part of a collaborative group, to pursue research and writing in residence for periods of up to a year.

595
Saint Paul Foundation, The
1120 Norwest Center
St. Paul, MN 55101   (612) 224-5463
Contact: Paul A. Verret, President

Limitations: Scholarships to residents of St. Paul and Minneapolis, MN, and to children of employees of 3M Company.
Financial data: Year ended 12/31/86. Assets, $100,007,539 (M); Total giving, $4,664,281; Grants to individuals, 145 grants totaling $108,991; Subtotal for scholarships amount not specified.
Employer Identification Number: 416031510
Publications: Annual report.

596
Salem Lutheran Foundation
c/o Clark A. Harmon, Trustee
760 Northlawn Drive
Columbus, OH 43214
Contact: Rev. Marc Schroder, Prince of Peace Lutheran Church, 6470 Centennial Drive, Reynoldsburg, OH 43088, Tel.: (614) 863-3124

Limitations: Scholarships only to men studying to become Lutheran ministers in the Wisconsin Evangelical Lutheran Synod.
Financial data: Year ended 12/31/86. Assets, $1,300,365 (M); Total giving, $93,100; Grants to individuals, 154 grants totaling $52,400, high $750, low $350.

Employer Identification Number: 316084166
Applications: Deadline July 1st; Completion of formal application including pastor interview sheet, transcript and resume required.
Publications: Annual report, program information.

597★
Sample (Adrian M.) Trust No. 2
c/o Sun Bank/Treasure Coast, N.A.
P.O. Box 8
Fort Pierce, FL 34954   (305) 461-6300
Contact: Charles W. Sample, 5311 Burningtree Drive, Orlando, FL 32811; Tel.: (305) 423-0314

Limitations: Scholarships to Protestant residents of St. Lucie or Okeechobee counties, FL.
Financial data: Year ended 12/31/86. Assets, $1,420,238 (M); Total giving, $102,950; Grants to individuals, 94 grants totaling $102,950, high $4,500, low $200.
Employer Identification Number: 596490788
Applications: Deadline April 15th; Application forms available only through churches in St. Lucie or Okeechobee counties; Initial approach by letter; Completion of formal application with one additional copy required.
Publications: Program information, application guidelines.
Program description:
Applicants must be active church members and unmarried. Funds are allocated directly to students.

598★
San Antonio Area Foundation
808 Travis Building
405 North Saint Mary's
San Antonio, TX 78205   (512) 225-2243
Contact: Katherine Netting Folbre, Executive Director

Limitations: Scholarships primarily to high school seniors in Bexar County, TX; one fund limited to San Antonio residents in religious education.
Financial data: Year ended 12/31/87. Assets, $13,471,331 (M); Total giving, $1,478,940; Grants to individuals, 94 grants totaling $87,156, high $3,000, low $200, general range $1,000-1,500, average grant $1,000.
Employer Identification Number: 746065414
Publications: Annual report.
Program description:
Approximately 14 scholarship funds with the majority administered with Bexar County Scholarship Clearing House and the Minnie Stevens Piper Foundation.

599
Santa Barbara Foundation
15 East Carrillo Street
Santa Barbara, CA 93101   (805) 963-1873
Contact: Edward R. Spaulding, Executive Director

Limitations: Student loans to residents who are also graduates of a Santa Barbara County, CA, high school, who have attended that school for three years and who are pursuing undergraduate studies. Loans for graduate education are available only in the fields of family practice or internal medicine.
Financial data: Year ended 12/31/86. Assets, $30,180,472 (M) Expenditures, $2,053,171; Loans to individuals, 201 loans totaling $424,501.
Employer Identification Number: 951866094
Applications: Deadline mid-February; Applications accepted October 1st to mid-February; Initial approach by letter or telephone; Completion of formal application required.

600
Sapelo Island Research Foundation, Inc.
1425 21st Street, N.W.
Washington, DC 20036   (202) 822-9193
Contact: Margery Tabankin, Excutive Director

Limitations: Scholarships only to Georgia residents for study in marine biology and marine research.
Financial data: Year ended 6/30/86. Assets, $13,297,552 (M); Total giving, $540,961; Grants to individuals, 18 grants totaling $23,841.
Employer Identification Number: 580827472
Applications: Deadlines March 15th and September 15th; Initial approach by letter.
Publications: Annual report.

601
Scadron (Irene Haas) Memorial Educational
Foundation
c/o Quincy State Bank, Trust Department
P.O. Box 898
Qunicy, FL 32351

Limitations: Educational loans to needy young white male students graduated from Florida high schools, especially Gadsden County.
Financial data: Year ended 6/30/86. Assets, $85,438 (M); Expenditures, $1,222; Loans to individuals, 2 loans totaling $1,500; 1985, Loans to individuals, 2 loans totaling $2,000, each loan $1,000.
Employer Identification Number: 596215956
Applications: Applications accepted throughout the year; Completion of formal application required.

602
Scalp and Blade Scholarship Trust
c/o Manufacturers & Traders Bank Trust Department
One Manufacturers and Traders Plaza
Buffalo, NY 14240   (716) 842-5547
Contact: Erie County High School guidance
counselors or principals

Limitations: Scholarships only to graduating males
from high schools in Erie County, NY, who plan to
attend schools outside Erie and Niagara counties.
Financial data: Year ended 12/31/85. Assets, $89,018
(M); Total giving, $4,750, Grants to individuals, 12
grants totaling $4,750, high $500, low $250.
Employer Identification Number: 166020842
Applications: Deadline May; Interviews granted upon
request.
Program description:
Scholarship awards up to $500 annually for eligible
applicants.

603
Scarborough Foundation
P.O. Box 1536
Midland, TX 79702   (915) 682-8960
Contact: Evelyn Linebery, President

Limitations: Scholarships primarily to residents of
Texas.
Financial data: Year ended 6/30/87. Assets, $751,834
(M); Total giving, $128,928; Grants to individuals, 18
grants totaling $25,228, high $4,275, low $35.
Employer Identification Number: 752056704
Applications: Applications accepted throughout the
year; Initial approach by letter describing the need for
a grant.
Program description:
Scholarship payments are made directly to the
individual recipient.

604
Scarlett (Andrew J.) Scholarship Fund
74 Prospect Street
Lebanon, NH 03766
Contact: Clark A. Griffiths, Trustee

Limitations: Student loans only to undergraduate
members of the Sigma Alpha Epsilon Fraternity at
Dartmouth College, NH.
Financial data: Year ended 6/30/86. Assets, $174,011
(M); Expenditures, $7,562; Loans to individuals
totaling $5,200.
Employer Identification Number: 026012571
Program description:
The fund serves to motivate high academic excellence
for members of the Sigma Alpha Epsilon Fraternity at
Dartmouth College.

605
Scheehl (Frank H.) Trust
(Also known as Scheehl (Emeline H.) College
Scholastic Fund)
c/o Connecticut Bank & Trust Company
P.O. Box 3334
Hartford, CT 06103
Contact: Robert Satter, Trustee

Limitations: Scholarships to seniors of Conard High
School, West Hartford, CT.
Financial data: Year ended 6/30/86. Assets, $107,485
(M); Total giving, $5,490; Grants to individuals, 6
grants totaling $5,490, high $1,000, low $830.
Employer Identification Number: 066177823
Program description:
The scholarship awards are paid directly to the
educational institution on behalf of the individual
recipients.

606★
Schepp (Leopold) Foundation
15 East 26th Street, Suite 1900
New York, NY 10010-1505   (212) 889-9737
Contact: Mrs. Edythe Bobrow, Executive Director

Limitations: Scholarships to students who are U.S.
citizens enrolled on a full-time basis at an accredited
college or university. Only one member of a family
may apply at the same time. Undergraduate
scholarships to individuals under 30, graduate
scholarships to individuals under 40, and a limited
number of postdoctoral fellowships to individuals in
the arts and literature, medicine, and oceanography.
Financial data: Year ended 2/28/86. Assets,
$8,000,000 (M); Total giving, $355,500; Grants to
individuals totaling $355,500.
Employer Identification Number: 135562353
Applications: Deadline December 31st; Initial
inquiries may be made between June 1st and
December 31st by letter; Completion of formal
application required; Applications distributed to
eligible students and lists close when a sufficient
number of applications have been completed and
received for committee decision.
Publications: Program information, application
guidelines.
Program description:
Scholarships are awarded to U.S. citizens of character
and ability who have insufficient means to obtain or
complete their formal education. Preference is given to
those with goals that show promise of future
usefulness to society. Only a limited number of high
school seniors may be considered. Those who have
only the doctoral dissertation to complete may not
apply.
   A limited number of grants are made for
independent study and research beyond the doctoral
level to individuals in the fields of literature, the arts,
oceanography, and medicine (including public health)

upon the recommendation of a recognized institution. Research likely to improve the general welfare of mankind is particularly favored and encouraged.

607
Schiff (Helen Martha) Foundation
c/o Bank of California, N.A.
P.O. Box 3095
Seattle, WA 98114

Limitations: Scholarships primarily for residents of Washington.
Financial data: Year ended 12/31/86. Assets, $836,197 (M); Total giving, $36,628; Grants to individuals, 5 grants totaling $6,628, high $1,670, low $668.
Employer Identification Number: 237120813
Applications: Applications accepted throughout the year; Initial approach by letter.

608
Scholarship Fund, Inc.
c/o Dean Ernest Weaver, Jr., Secretary
University of Toledo, 2801 West Bancroft Street
Toledo, OH 43606   (419) 537-4632

Limitations: Scholarships based on need and academic record to students residing in the northwest Ohio area, with emphasis on those pursuing baccalaureate degrees. Preference is given to upper class, highly ranked students who are commuting.
Financial data: Year ended 12/31/86. Assets, $579,688 (M); Total giving, $24,033; Grants to individuals, 24 grants totaling $24,033, high $1,600, low $400, average grant $800.
Employer Identification Number: 346533380
Applications: Applications accepted throughout the year; Completion of formal application and interviews required.
Publications: Program information.

609
Scholarships Foundation, Inc., The
P.O. Box 170
Canal Street Station
New York, NY 10013

Limitations: Scholarships to undergraduate and graduate students with priority given to those who do not fit into defined scholarship categories.
Financial data: Year ended 6/30/86. Assets, $711,980 (M); Total giving, $45,700; Grants to individuals totaling $45,700.
Employer Identification Number: 066043809
Applications: Applications accepted throughout the year; however, letters received after May 1st cannot be considered in time for September grants; Initial approach by letter, no longer than one typewritten page, including a stamped, self-addressed envelope.

Program description:
Awards are based on merit and need. Approximately 35 awards are given each year. Foundation is unable to reply to form letters or to those from computer/search companies. Grants rarely made to high school students, foreign students or for study abroad.

610
Schramm Foundation
P.O. Box 625
West Chester, PA 19381-0625   (215) 696-2500
Contact: Norman Greet, Personnel Officer

Limitations: Scholarships only to graduates of high schools in the vicinity of West Chester, PA, for business and engineering degrees.
Financial data: Year ended 12/31/86. Assets, $144,648 (M); Total giving, $10,250; Grants to individuals, 12 grants totaling $3,600, each grant $300.
Employer Identification Number: 236291235
Applications: Recipients are recommended by their high schools in March of each year; Foundation notifies the schools as to submission dates; Interviews required.
Program description:
The foundation awards scholarships for degree programs at trade schools, junior colleges, and four-year colleges. The scholarship committee reviews the information submitted by the local high schools on each applicant and makes a final selection based on the following factors:
• The likelihood of the student completing the degree program.
• The degree of financial need.
• The overall ability of the student in nonacademic areas.
Recipient's performance at the postsecondary institution is monitored on a semester basis by grade transcripts sent from the school.
Scholarship payments are made directly to the school each fall for each recipient. Scholarships are renewable.

611
Schreck (Robert) Memorial Educational Fund
Texas Commerce Bank-El Paso
P.O. Drawer 140
El Paso, TX 79980
Contact: Terry Crenshaw, Charitable Services Officer

Limitations: Scholarships only to individuals who are residents of El Paso County, TX, and are studying for the Episcopal clergy in the Diocese of southwest Texas and New Mexico (now the Diocese of the Rio Grande), the medical profession, including veterinary medicine, physics, chemistry, engineering, or architecture.
Financial data: Year ended 12/31/86. Assets, $122,549 (M); Total giving $5,500; Grants to individuals, 8

grants totaling $5,500, low $1,300, low $300.

Employer Identification Number: 237034361

Applications: Applications accepted throughout the year; Completion of formal application and interview required.

Publications: Program information (including application guidelines).

Program description:

Applicants must meet the following standards to qualify for consideration as a recipient of the Robert Schreck Memorial Educational Fund:

- The applicant must be a United States citizen
- High scholastic standing must be shown
- The applicant must have completed two full years of college courses
- The applicant must have been a bona fide resident of El Paso County, TX, for not less than two consecutive years prior to the time the distribution is made.

Scholarship awards will be made based on the following factors:

- Prior academic performance
- Recommendations from instructors
- Financial need
- Results of a personal interview at which time the applicant's motivation, character, ability, and potential are evaluated
- Prior funding status. Unless there has been a material change in circumstances, a renewal of funding shall be given preference over a new application.

612

Schwab Foundation

c/o Wright and Sawyer
P.O. Box 3247
Enid, OK 73702 (405) 233-4455
Contact: L. T. Sawyer, Vice-President

Limitations: Scholarships only to residents of Joplin, MO, and Enid, OK.

Financial data: Year ended 12/31/86. Assets, $4,062 (M); Total giving, $34,252; Grants to individuals, 6 grants totaling $25,465, high $11,035, low $384.

Employer Identification Number: 730739942

Applications: Applications accepted throughout the year; Initial approach by letter containing personal information and need and intended use of grant.

613

Schweppe Foundation, The

c/o John E. McGovern, Jr.
135 South LaSalle Street, Room 2300
Chicago, IL 60603
Contact: The Schweppe Foundation, 845 North Michigan Avenue, Room 949 W, Chicago, IL 60611

Limitations: Medical research fellowships for training at Chicago area medical schools or university-affiliated

hospitals.

Financial data: Year ended 12/31/86. Assets, $201,805 (M); Total giving, $105,000; Grants to individuals, 7 grants totaling $105,000, each grant $15,000.

Employer Identification Number: 366014667

Applications: Deadline September 1st; Completion of formal application required.

Publications: Informational brochure.

Program description:

All fellowships are granted to institutions on behalf of individuals. Grants are to support a medical research project carried on by an individual of junior rank (not above that of Assistant Professor) who holds a faculty or fellowship appointment in the university or hospital, and who has been assured the use of the physical facilities of the sponsoring institution.

Grants last for three years, subject to annual approval.

614

Scott (Olin) Fund, Inc.

100 South Street
P.O. Box 1208
Bennington, VT 05201 (802) 447-1096
Contact: Melvin A. Dyson, Treasurer

Limitations: Student loans limited to young men in Bennington County, VT.

Financial data: Year ended 6/30/87. Assets, $2,496,558 (M); Expenditures, $118,033; Loans to individuals, 45 loans totaling $66,200, high $1,500, low $600.

Employer Identification Number: 036005697

Applications: Applications accepted throughout the year; Initial approach by letter or telephone; Completion of formal application required.

615

Scottish Rite Educational and Fellowship Program of Texas

P.O. Box 3080
Waco, TX 76707
Contact: N. Lee Dunham, Chairman, Awards Committee, 2632 Lake Oaks Road, Waco, TX 76710; Tel.: (817) 754-3942

Limitations: Fellowships to Texas residents for doctoral degree studies at universities in Texas having accredited curricula in public school administration. Special consideration will be given to individuals with family Masonic connections.

Financial data: Year ended 12/31/86. Assets, $496,563 (M); Total giving, $16,900; Grants to individuals, 16 grants totaling $16,900, high $3,700, low $200.

Employer Identification Number: 742177244

Applications: Applications accepted throughout the year; Completion of formal application required.

Publications: Program information, application guidelines.

Program description:
The program encourages award recipients to enroll in a two-year course of study under the full-time grant to complete their doctoral degree at the earliest possible date. It is strongly recommended that the degree be completed within a 42-month period for those who elect to become part-time students. All recipients must profess a belief in a supreme being.

The part-time student is granted $6,000 maximum ($100 per semester hour) plus $500 for dissertation typing and printing costs, provided one copy of the dissertation is deposited in the Texas Scottish Rite Library in Waco, TX. The full-time student is granted $9,000 maximum ($150 per semester hour) plus $500 for dissertation typing and printing costs, provided one copy of the dissertation is deposited in the Texas Scottish Rite Library in Waco.

The following accredited Texas universities offer approved doctoral degree programs in public school administration: Baylor University, Waco; East Texas State University, Commerce; North Texas State University, Denton; Texas A & M University, College Station; Texas Tech University, Lubbock; University of Houston; and University of Texas, Austin.

616
Scottish Rite Foundation in Kentucky
200 East Gray Street
Louisville, KY 40202   (502) 584-6185
Contact: George R. Effinger, Chairman

Limitations: Fellowships for undergraduate studies.
Financial data: Year ended 6/30/87. Assets, $423,568 (M); Total giving, $21,299; Grants to individuals, 4 grants totaling $21,299, high $6,098, low $4,066.
Employer Identification Number: 616036090

617★
Scripps Howard Foundation
P.O. Box 5380
Cincinnati, OH 45201   (513) 977-3035
Contact: Albert J. Schottelkotte, President

Limitations: Scholarships to professional print and broadcast journalists or students pursuing careers in same.
Financial data: Year ended 12/31/87. Assets, $9,361,148 (M); Total giving, $778,148; Grants to individuals, 236 grants totaling $238,050; Subtotal for scholarships, 222 scholarships totaling $279,050, high $2,000, low $500, general range $1,000-1,500.
Employer Identification Number: 316025114
Applications: Deadline December 20th for initial submission consisting of a self-addressed typewritten mailing label with the words "Scholarship Application," only; Application packets will be mailed by the foundation in late December, and must be completed and returned by February 25th.
Publications: Annual report, program information,

application guidelines.
Program description:
The foundation awards scholarships to encourage deserving young persons to prepare for careers in the communications industry as well as scholarship grants for working journalists. These grants embrace print and broadcast media, and editorial or business operations of newspapers, magazines, radio, or television. Full-time undergraduate or graduate students who are U.S. citizens or hold a valid U.S. visa, with a good scholastic standing and evidence of journalism work on school papers, magazines, radio or television stations, or work in private industry may apply. Preference is given to junior, senior, or graduate students, to prior recipients, and to students residing in, or attending schools located in areas of company operations. Consideration is also given to minority applicants.

In addition, the foundation sponsors two special scholarship programs: **The Robert P. Scripps Graphic Arts Grants** for students majoring in graphic arts as applied to the newspaper industry, whom, in the opinion of the college authorities, have the potential of becoming administrators in newspaper production; and the **Ellen B. Scripps Fellowships** which enable professional journalists to pursue graduate studies in any field, for example, business, science, or law, which will enhance their proficiency in their journalism speciality.

Grants are not automatically renewed and must be re-applied for annually.

618★
Searls (William) Scholarship Foundation
c/o First National Bank of Bar Harbor
102 Main Street
Bar Harbor, ME 04609
Contact: Margo Stanley, Secretary

Limitations: Scholarships limited to residents of Southwest Harbor, ME.
Financial data: Year ended 12/31/85. Assets, $138,671 (M); Total giving, $4,650; Grants to individuals, 36 grants totaling $4,650, high $200, low $50, general range $100-200.
Employer Identification Number: 016009698

619
Seibel (The Abe and Annie) Foundation
c/o United States National Bank
P.O. Box 179
Galveston, TX 77553   (409) 763-1151
Contact: Judith T. Whelton, Trust Director, United States National Bank

Limitations: Interest-free student loans to graduates of Texas high schools attending Texas colleges and universities.
Financial data: Year ended 7/31/87. Assets,

$14,962,730 (M); Expenditures, $1,401,327; Loans to individuals, 608 loans totaling $1,111,600, high $3,000, low $250, general range $1,000-1,500.
Employer Identification Number: 746035556
Applications: Deadline February 28th; Initial approach by letter or telephone; Completion of formal application required; Interviews required.

620
Selling (Ben) Scholarship
c/o First Interstate Bank of Oregon
P.O. Box 2971
Portland, OR 97208
Contact: Charles K. Woodcock, Trust Officer

Limitations: Low-interest student loans to Oregon residents attending Oregon schools.
Financial data: Year ended 9/30/86. Assets, $378,069 (M); Expenditures, $48,131; Loans to individuals, 20 loans totaling $39,500, high $2,000, low $1,500, average loan $2,000.
Employer Identification Number: 936017158
Applications: Deadline August 15th; Applications accepted June 1st to August 15th; Completion of formal application, including school transcript and proof of enrollment, required; Interviews granted upon request.

621
Seneker (James S.) Trust for Religious Education
c/o First Republic Bank Dallas, N.A.
P.O. Box 83776
Dallas, TX 75283
Contact: See program description below for application addresses

Limitations: Graduate scholarships awarded to students preparing for careers as professional Christian educators in the local church. Scholarships also for students in the Master of Religious Education program in Perkins School of Theology at Southern Methodist University.
Financial data: Year ended 5/31/87. Assets, $1,487,217 (M); Total giving, $95,503; Grants to individuals totaling $95,503.
Employer Identification Number: 756318275
Applications: Deadline February 1st for Schisler Awards; Completion of formal application required; Completion of pastor's confidential evaluation form, college transcripts, official verification of acceptance in graduate school, and five letters of recommendation required for Schisler Awards. See program description below for application information of Senecker Awards.
Program description:
The **John Q. Schisler Graduate Awards** are for outstanding students who 1) are studying in a professional accredited graduate school; 2) have been a member of The United Methodist Church for at least three years; 3) is a citizen of the U.S.

Awards, which are based on academic standing, leadership ability, character, need, and vocational goals in Christian education, are granted for one year only and are not renewable. Awards vary in value from $500 to $2,000 as determined by the scholarship committee. Applications are available from the Board of Higher Education and Ministry, The United Methodist Church, Office of Loans and Scholarships, P.O. Box 871, Nashville, TN 37202-0871; Tel.: (615) 327-2700.
The **Seneker Scholarship Awards** give three types of scholarships:
Full or Merit Scholarship awards:
* This program is available to first-year students in the Master of Religious Education program with a G.P.A. of at least 3.4 on a 4.0 scale.
* Applicants must submit an application for admission to Perkins School of Theology, an application for the Merit Scholarship and a 500-to-750 word essay on "Why I would like to meet_____" (a biblical, historical or contemporary religious figure of their choosing).
* Scholarships will be granted on the basis of academic excellence, vocational clarity, and qualities of character and of leadership reflected by personal recommendations and by extracurricular accomplishments and the quality of the essay.
* All materials must be returned to the Perkins Admissions Office by March 15th.
Regular Scholarship Awards:
* This program provides aid to students enrolled in the Master of Religious Education program on the basis of demonstrated need.
* The award varies from zero to full tuition and fees and are made once a year for the complete academic year.
* As long as admission requirments have been fulfilled, students may complete formal application for financial aid up to the day classes begin. The award selection and notification is the responsibility of the Perkins' Director of Financial Aid.
Intern/Practicum Scholarship Awards:
* This program is available to students who are doing their internship in the Master of Religious Education program as required by their degree.
* Scholarship awards provide up to $4,000 for a seven-month internship.
* The awards are made by the Perkin Religious Education faculty in areas where the sponsoring church can provide conditions conducive to professional growth in religious education and where the church does not have the full financial resources for the scholarship.
* No formal deadline nor application are required for these scholarships. The placement process will take place each fall before the spring sememster that the internships begin.

For information or application for any of the Seneker Scholarships, contact the Perkins School of Theology, Southern Methodist University, Dallas, TX 75275.

622
Seran (Chester A. and Ethel J.) Scholarship Foundation
c/o AmeriTrust Company, N.A.
P.O. Box 5937
Cleveland, OH 44101-0937
Contact: Christine Sutton-Kruman, AmeriTrust Company National Association, 237 Tuscarawas Street West, Canton, OH 44702

Limitations: Scholarships to undergraduate students who are members of Westbrook Park United Methodist Church, enrolled at Otterbein or Malone Colleges, or from the Stark County, OH, area.
Financial data: Year ended 9/30/86. Assets, $256,846 (M); Total giving, $18,950; Grants to individuals totaling $18,950.
Employer Identification Number: 237440777
Applications: Applications accepted throughout the year; Initial approach by letter requesting application; Completion of formal application required.

623
Shanor (The M.L.) Foundation
P.O. Box 7522
Wichita Falls, TX 76307   (817) 761-2401
Contact: J. B. Jarratt, President

Limitations: Student loans primarily to residents of Cherokee, Midland, Wichita, and Wilbarger counties, TX.
Financial data: Year ended 12/31/86. Assets, $1,924,782 (M); Expenditures $155,099; Loans to individuals, 63 loans totaling $95,025, high $2,500, low $275, general range $1,000-2,000, average loan $2,000.
Employer Identification Number: 756012834
Applications: Deadline August 1st; Completion of formal application required.

624
Shaull (Clyde L. and Mary C.) Education Trust Fund
c/o Robert C. Bricker
1519 Fisher Road
Mechanicsburg, PA 17055
Contact: Guidance counselors at Mechanicsburg High School

Limitations: Scholarships only to graduates of Mechanicsburg High School, PA.
Financial data: Year ended 12/31/86. Assets, $587,433 (M); Total giving, $45,050; Grants to individuals,

approximately 52 grants totaling $45,050, average grant $880.
Employer Identification Number: 237101845
Applications: Applications accepted March 15th to April 15th; Completion of formal application required; Applications to be obtained from Mechanicsburg High School.
Program description:
Grants are paid directly to the educational institution on behalf of individual recipients.

625★
Shepard (Leon and Josephine Wade) Scholarship Fund Foundation, Inc.
c/o First of America Bank of Michigan
108 East Michigan Avenue
Kalamazoo, MI 49007
Contact: Alexander Galligan, Superintendent Fennville Public Schools, Fennville, MI 49408, Tel.: (616) 561-5045.

Limitations: Scholarships only to needy, qualified graduates of Fennville High School, enrolled in institutions of higher learning approved by the Michigan Department of Public Instruction.
Financial data: Year ended 3/31/87. Assets, $598,033 (M); Total giving, $28,405; Grants to individuals, 32 grants totaling $28,405, high $1,000, low $500.
Employer Identification Number: 386101349
Applications: Deadline May 1st; Completion of formal application required; Applications available in Fennville High School office.
Program description:
Students must be enrolled in twelve or more credit hours. Grants are awarded for two years, not to exceed $1,000 per year.

626
Shinnick (William M.) Educational Fund
534 Market Street
Zanesville, OH 43701   (614) 452-2273

Limitations: Scholarships and student loans to residents of Muskingum, OH.
Financial data: Year ended 6/30/87. Assets, $2,384,005 (M); Expenditures, $2,238,343; Grants to individuals, 1 grant totaling $528; Loans to individuals, 190 loans totaling $141,305, high $1,500, low $200.
Employer Identification Number: 314394168
Applications: Deadline June 30th.

627

Showler (Isabelle G.) Scholarship Fund

c/o Torrance Teachers Association
1619 Cravens Avenue
Torrance, CA 90501   (213) 320-8200
Contact: Mrs. E. Kenny de Groot

Limitations: Scholarships only to graduates of
Torrance High School, Torrance, CA.
Financial data: Year ended 12/31/86. Assets, $9,357
(L); Total giving, $3,000; Grants to individuals, 6
grants totaling $3,000, each grant $500.
Employer Identification Number: 930670970
Applications: Deadline May 15th; Completion of
formal application, including name of college student
will be attending, need for scholarship, transcript of
grades, and letter of recommendation, required.

628

**Shreve (William A. and Mary A.) Foundation,
Inc.**

c/o Robert M. Wood, Esquire
200 Atlantic Avenue
Manasquan, NJ 08736
Contact: Dr. Clifford G. Pollock, Route 1, Box 408,
Wallingford, VT 05773; Tel.: (802) 446-2513

Limitations: Scholarships primarily to students in New
Jersey, Pennsylvania, and Vermont.
Financial data: Year ended 12/31/85. Assets,
$1,008,167 (M); Total giving, $97,610; Grants to
individuals, 34 grants totaling $52,010, high $3,500,
low $250, general range $500-2,000.
Employer Identification Number: 226054057
Applications: Applications accepted throughout the
year; Completion of formal application required.
Program description:
The foundation monitors grants by periodically
obtaining grades and reports from the institutions that
recipients attend.

629

Shumaker (Paul and Adelyn C.) Foundation, The

c/o Bank One, Trust
28 Park Avenue West
Mansfield, OH 44902   (419) 522-2011
Contact: R.J. Sutter, Senior Vice-President

Limitations: Loans only to residents of Richland
County, OH, who are graduate students studying for
the medical profession.
Financial data: Year ended 12/31/85. Assets, $306,004
(M); Expenditures, $29,436; Loans to individuals, 22
grants totaling $24,330, high $4,249, low $75.
Employer Identification Number: 346621245
Applications: Applications accepted throughout the
year; Completion of formal application required.

630

Shunk (John Q.) Association

P.O. Box 625
Bucyrus, OH 44820
Contact: Jane C. Peppard, 1201 Timber Lane, Marion,
OH 43302; Tel.: (614) 389-3132

Limitations: Scholarships only to graduates of four
specified high schools in Crawford County, OH.
Financial data: Year ended 12/31/86. Assets,
$1,378,917 (M); Total giving, $76,500; Grants to
individuals totaling $75,500.
Employer Identification Number: 340896477
Applications: Deadline February 15th; Initial approach
by letter; Completion of formal application required;
Annual interviews required; Scholarships must be
renewed each year; Applications may be obtained
from guidance offices of the specified high schools.
Program description:
The **John Q. Shunk Scholarship Program** is available
to graduates of the following Crawford County, OH,
schools: Bucyrus High School, Colonel Crawford High
School, Wynford High School, and Buckeye Central
High School.
   Scholarships are awarded on the basis of need,
attitude, and worthiness. There are no stipulations
concerning a required grade point average. The
scholarship is automatically terminated and will not be
reinstated if recipient is suspended for any reason,
including grades. Scholarship checks are given directly
to the individual recipient; however, the check is
made payable to the educational institution.

631

Sigma Nu Educational Foundation, Inc.

P.O. Box 1869
Lexington, VA 24450   (703) 463-2164
Contact: Maurice E. Littlefield, Executive
Vice-President

Limitations: Graduate scholarships, academic awards,
and emergency educational aid grants only to Sigma
Nu Fraternity members.
Financial data: Year ended 12/31/85. Assets, $744,079
(M); Total giving, $132,497; Grants to individuals, 22
grants totaling $7,000, high $1,000, low $50.
Employer Identification Number: 546035735
Applications: Applications accepted throughout the
academic year.
Publications: Annual report, program information.
Program description:
Emergency Aid Grants are available to members of
Sigma Nu Fraternity who are academically qualified
but who may have to leave college for financial
reasons unless such support is forthcoming.
   Academic Encouragement Awards are given to that
member of each of 20 Sigma Nu Fraternity chapters
per year who has contributed most to the chapter's
academic status, either through his own scholarship
achievements or through his encouragement of others

to achieve. Candidates are nominated by their chapters.

Graduate Scholarships are open to Sigma Nu Fraternity members who have been admitted to a graduate or professional school of an institution where a chapter of Sigma Nu is located, and who have expressed their willingness to give academic counsel to the members of that chapter. Awards are made annually, on the basis of direct application to the foundation.

632
Silberman (The Lois and Samuel) Fund, Inc.
133 East 79th Street
New York, NY 10021   (212) 737-8500
Contact: Mrs. Lois V. Silberman, Vice-President

Limitations: Grants and awards to students and professionals in the field of social work education and practice.
Financial data: Year ended 7/31/86. Assets, $3,164,000 (M); Total giving, $198,205; Grants to individuals, 5 grants totaling $72,657, high $57,339, low $1,165.
Employer Identification Number: 136097931
Publications: Multi-year report, program information.
Program description:
The fund's commitment to the support and promotion of the field of social work is expressed by grants for various research studies and projects on the subject.

In addition to its general grantmaking process, the fund presents the **Hexter Award** annually to honor an alumna of the Hunter College School of Social Work for the individual's outstanding contributions to social work education and practice. Each recipient of the award receives an honorariun and a medal encased with the citation.

The fund also promotes the publication of scholarly work in the field of social work by the faculty, students, and graduates of the Hunter College School of Social Work through the **Saul Horowitz, Jr. Memorial Series.**

633
Simmons Charitable Trust, The
c/o Miners and Mechanics Savings & Trust Co.
124 North Fourth Street
Steubenville, OH 43952

Limitations: Music scholarships to students of Steubenville High School, OH.
Financial data: Year ended 5/31/86. Assets, $1,753,302 (M); Total giving, $50,053; Grants to individuals, 1 grant totaling $6,853.
Employer Identification Number: 346743541
Applications: Initial approach by letter.

634
Simpson Foundation, The
c/o First Alabama Bank
P.O. Box 511
Montgomery, AL 36134

Limitations: Scholarships limited to residents of Wilcox County, AL.
Financial data: Year ended 4/30/87. Assets, $2,697,018 (M); Total giving, $8,000; Grants to individuals, 4 grants totaling $8,000, each grant $2,000.
Employer Identification Number: 630925496
Applications: Applications accepted from January 1st to March 31st; Completion of formal application including school transcripts, photograph and letters of recommendation, required.

635
Sinek (Joseph J.) Scholarship Trust
Commercial State Bank
Pocahontas, IA 50574

Limitations: Undergraduate scholarships only to graduates of Pocahontas Community School, Pocahontas, IA.
Financial data: Year ended 12/31/86. Assets, $1,197,837 (M); Total giving, $71,992; Grants to individuals, 139 grants totaling $71,992, high $972, low $186.
Employer Identification Number: 426336481
Applications: Deadline March 31st; Completion of formal application required; For application information contact Martin Jacobemier, Guidance Counselor, Pocahontas Community School, Pocahontas, IA 50574; Tel.: (712) 335-4848.

636★
Singleton (M.E.) Scholarship Trust
P.O. Box 717
Waxahachie, TX 75165   (214) 937-2411
Contact: George H. Singleton, President

Limitations: Scholarships only to students who graduate from high schools in Ellis County, TX, and are unable to enter college without financial assistance.
Financial data: Year ended 7/31/86. Assets, $550,344 (M); Total giving, $24,375; Grants to individuals, 20 grants totaling $24,375, high $1,250, low $625, average grant $1,250.
Employer Identification Number: 756037399
Applications: Applications accepted throughout the year; Initial approach by letter requesting application; Completion of formal application required.
Program description:
Students are recommended for scholarship assistance by the principals of Ellis County high schools. The board chooses the most needy persons.

637
Skidmore, Owings & Merrill Foundation
33 West Monroe Street
Chicago, IL 60603
Contact: Sonia Cooke, Administrative Director

Limitations: Fellowships, scholarships and awards for research, education or publication relating to architecture and/or architectural engineering.
Financial data: Year ended 8/31/86. Assets $3,303,758 (M); Total giving, $63,377; Grants to individuals, 8 grants totaling $63,377, high $18,000, low $800, average grant $7,200.
Employer Identification Number: 362969068
Applications: Applications accepted throughout the year; Initial approach by letter with proposal.

638
Slemp Foundation, The
c/o The First National Bank of Cincinnati
P.O. Box 1118
Cincinnati, OH 45201   (513) 632-4585

Limitations: Undergraduate scholarships limited to Lee and Wise counties, VA.
Financial data: Year ended 6/30/87. Assets, $7,618,752 (M); Total giving, $383,350; Grants to individuals, 257 grants totaling $209,600, average grant $800.
Employer Identification Number: 316025080
Applications: Deadline October 1st; Initial approach by letter; Completion of formal application required.
Program description:
Approximately 25 new college scholarships are granted each year to qualified individuals. Applications should be made during student's senior year in high school.

639
Slocum-Lunz Foundation, Inc.
Grice Marine Biological Laboratory
205 Fort Johnson
Charleston, SC 29412   (803) 795-3716
Contact: Dr. Charles K. Biernbaum, Chairman, Scholarship Committee

Limitations: Scholarships, fellowships, and research grants only to students of marine biology and closely related natural science.
Financial data: Year ended 12/31/86. Assets, $218,645 (M); Total giving, $22,000; Grants to individuals, 15 grants totaling $22,000, high $2,500, low $500, general range $1,000-2,000.
Employer Identification Number: 570371213
Applications: Deadline April 1st for subsequent twelve-month period; Initial approach by letter; Completion of formal application required.
Publications: Application guidelines.

Program description:
Priority is given to candidates for the doctoral degree who plan to work in South Carolina at the completion of their education. Applications from beginning graduate students and advanced undergraduates will also be considered. Academic work does not have to be performed in South Carolina.

640★
Smith (Belle) Scholarship Fund
c/o Greater Tacoma Community Foundation
Washington Building, Suite 620, P.O. Box 1121
Tacoma, WA 98401-1121   (206) 383-5622
Contact: Margy McGroarty

Limitations: Scholarships only to graduates of high schools in Peninsula Consolidated School District 401, located in Gig Harbor, WA.
Financial data: Year ended 12/31/87. Assets, $524,841 (M); Total giving, $30,000; Grants to individuals, 12 grants totaling $30,000, each grant $2,500.
Employer Identification Number: 916064697
Program description:
Approximately four new scholarships are available each year.

641★
Smith (Horace) Fund
1441 Main Street
Box 3034
Springfield, MA 01101   (413) 739-4222
Contact: Philip T. Hart, Executive Secretary

Limitations: Scholarships, fellowships and loans to residents and secondary school graduates of Hampden County, MA.
Financial data: Year ended 3/31/87. Assets, $5,550,197 (M); Total giving, $268,287; Grants and loans to individuals totaling $268,287; Subtotals for loans and grants not specified.
Employer Identification Number: 042235130
Applications: Deadlines before June 15th for loan applications for college students and before July 1st for high school seniors; December 31st for scholarships; February 1st for fellowships; Applications available after April 1st for loans, after September 1st for fellowships; Scholarship applications are available in the guidance offices of schools specified below; Completion of formal application required; Interviews required.
Publications: Program information.
Program description:
Horace Smith Fund Loans are made for full-time undergraduate education to graduates of secondary schools in Hampden County, MA. No interest is charged for the first year after the student completes his/her education, but begins to accrue after that period.

Walter S. Barr Scholarships are awarded to seniors in secondary schools in Agawam, Chicopee, East Longmeadow, Longmeadow, Ludlow, Springfield, West Springfield, and Wilbraham, MA, for undergraduate education. Awards are granted on the basis of school records, college entrance exams, general attainment, and financial need, and are renewable for up to four years.

Walter S. Barr Fellowships are awarded to Hampden County residents for full-time graduate study and are determined on the basis of scholastic record and financial need.

642
Snayberger (Harry E. and Florence W.) Memorial Foundation

c/o Pennsylvania National Bank and Trust Company
One South Centre Street
Pottsville, PA 17901-3003   (717) 622-4200
Contact: Paul J. Hanna, II, Senior Vice-President and Trust Officer, Pennsylvania National Bank and Trust Company

Limitations: Scholarships to residents of Schuylkill County, PA.
Financial data: Year ended 3/31/86. Assets, $3,652,570 (M); Total giving, $253,125; Grants to individuals, 571 grants totaling $212,700, high $700, low $250.
Employer Identification Number: 232056361
Applications: Deadline February 28th; Initial approach by letter; Completion of formal application required; Recipients notified the middle of October.

643★
Snyder (Burt) Educational Foundation

620 North First Street
Lakeview, OR 97630   (503) 947-2196
Contact: Jim Lynch

Limitations: Scholarships only to students graduating from Lake County, OR, area high schools.
Financial data: Year ended 6/30/87. Assets, $194,661 (M); Total giving, $9,240; Grants to individuals, 4 grants totaling $9,240, high $2,520, low $1,680.
Employer Identification Number: 936033286
Applications: Applications accepted throughout the year; Contact foundation for current application information.

644★
Society for the Increase of the Ministry, The

120 Sigourney Street
Hartford, CT 06105
Contact: Rev. Canon J.S. Zimmerman, Executive Director

Limitations: Scholarships only to persons preparing for ordination in the Episcopal Church and studying in an accredited Episcopal theological seminary.
Financial data: Year ended 8/31/86. Assets, $1,859,114 (M); Total giving, $98,555; Grants to individuals, 158 grants totaling $98,555, general range $500-750.
Employer Identification Number: 066053077
Applications: Deadline March 1st; Contact foundation for current application deadline; Completion of formal application required.
Publications: Application guidelines, informational brochure.

645
Sorey (Vincent) Music Foundation, Inc.

1039 18th Street
Miami Beach, FL 33139

Limitations: Grants to needy students for music lessons and education.
Financial data: Year ended 12/31/85. Assets, $331,972 (M); Total giving, $2,615; Grants to individuals totaling $2,615.
Employer Identification Number: 237069577

646
Southwest Florida Community Foundation, Inc., The

Drawer LL
Fort Meyers, FL 33902   (813) 332-3315
Contact: Christine M. Roberts, Executive Director

Limitations: Scholarships only to students from Lee County high schools with a B average or better.
Financial data: Year ended 9/30/86. Assets, $3,344,280 (M); Total giving, $195,625; Grants to individuals amount not specified.
Employer Identification Number: 596580974
Applications: Deadlines February 1st and May 1st; Initial approach by telephone or letter; Completion of formal application required.
Publications: Annual report.

647
Spain (The E. Leo and Louise F.) Scholarship Foundation

c/o Robert J. O'Brien
83 Bay Street, Box 785
Glen Falls, NY 12801   (518) 793-5173

Limitations: Scholarships to worthy or needy students of St. Mary's Academy, Glen Falls, NY, or to a student from some other school in the same locality.
Financial data: Year ended 9/30/85. Assets, $58,142 (M); Total giving, $3,000; Grants to individuals, 6 grants totaling $3,000, each grant $500.
Employer Identification Number: 510238536
Applications: Applications accepted throughout the

year; Initial approach by letter requesting a scholarship, including reasons why applicant should be considered.

Program description:
The scholarship is a gift to the student to be used each year for tuition and other educational expenses. The following criteria are used in making the selection of recipients:

1. Recommendation of school authorities
2. Scholastic standing
3. Participation in school activities
4. Personality
5. Desire for higher education.

Each year the principal of St. Mary's Academy is contacted by the foundation to discuss the applicants for that year's scholarship awards.

648★
Speas (Victor E.) Foundation
c/o Boatmen's First National Bank of Kansas City
14 West Tenth Street
Kansas City, MO 64183   (816) 234-7481
Contact: David P. Ross, Senior Vice-President, Boatmen's First National Bank of Kansas City

Limitations: Scholarships and student loans for medical students attending the University of Missouri at Kansas City.
Financial data: Year ended 12/31/87. Assets, $18,466,272 (M); Total giving, $1,018,522; Grants and loans to individuals amounts not specified.
Employer Identification Number: 446008340
Applications: Applications accepted throughout the year; Initial approach by telephone; Interviews required.
Publications: Program information, application guidelines.

649
Spencer Foundation, The
875 North Michigan Avenue
Chicago, IL 60611   (312) 337-7000
Contact: Marion M. Faldet, Vice-President

Limitations: Research grants to individuals with advanced qualifications in the behavioral sciences, working under the auspices of an institution. No loans, scholarships or fellowships.
Financial data: Year ended 3/31/87. Assets, $219,558,357 (M); Total giving, $4,698,296; Grants to individuals totaling $3,297,973, general range $15,000-75,000.
Employer Identification Number: 366078558
Applications: Deadline March 1st, July 1st or November 1st; Initial approach by letter or preliminary brief proposal, including a curriculum vitae of the principal investigator, preliminary cost estimate for the proposed research, and an indication of how long it will take to complete; Interviews granted upon request.
Publications: Annual report, application guidelines, program information.
Program description:
Grants are awarded to individuals or teams of investigators to do research in the behavioral sciences aimed at expanding the knowledge, understanding, and practice of education. Research is to be conducted under the auspices of an educational institution. Amounts and devotion of the grants may vary depending on the individual projects, ranging from three months to several years.

The foundation supports studies in three principal categories:

Education as a Social Institution - Studies in the humanities and social sciences that contribute to a deeper understanding of the aims of education, of the the situations and institutions in which education proceeds in various societies, and of the inextricable ties between educative institutions and the societies that sustain them and are in turn affected by them.

Human Development and the Educative Process - Studies in the humanities and in the social and behavioral sciences that contribute to a deeper understanding of human developement over the entire life span and of the ways in which development bears on education and education influences development.

Teaching and Learning - Studies in the humanities and the behavioral sciences, as well as in pedagogy, that contribute to a deeper understanding of the theory and practice of teaching and learning.

In 1986, the foundation established a **Small Grants Program** to increase the number of able scholars working on problems in education. The program is intended to facilitate investigators in pursuing exploratory research, problem-finding research, pilot research, modest research projects, and the initial phases of larger investigations. Grants made under this program range from $1,000-7,500. Inquiries about this program may be directed to Coralie Novotny, Small Grants Administrator, at the foundation address.

650★
Spencer (George and Marie G.) Education Foundation and Trust
c/o Citizens National Bank
102 North Main Street
Tipton, IN 46072   (317) 675-7431
Contact: Tipton Community High School, Tipton, IN 46072 or Tri-Central High School, R.R. No. 2, Sharpsville, IN 46072

Limitations: Scholarships only to residents of Tipton County, IN.
Financial data: Year ended 12/31/86. Assets, $1,415,305 (M); Total giving, $72,000; Grants to individuals, 72 grants totaling $72,000, each grant

148   EDUCATIONAL SUPPORT

$1,000.
Employer Identification Number: 356072759
Applications: Deadline September 1st; Completion of formal application required; Interviews required.

651★
Spokane Inland Northwest Community Foundation
(Formerly Spokane Inland Empire Foundation)
400 Paulsen Center
West 421 Riverside
Spokane, WA 99201-0403   (509) 624-2606
Contact: Jeanne L. Ager, Executive Director

Limitations: Scholarships for students living in western Spokane and Lincoln counties, WA, or Bonner County, ID.
Financial data: Year ended 6/30/87. Assets, $3,559,356 (M); Total giving, $709,531; Grants to individuals, 53 grants totaling $34,175.
Employer Identification Number: 910941053
Applications: Deadline April 1st; Initial approach by letter; Completion of formal application required.
Publications: Annual report.
Program description:
The scholarship funds include:
1. The Dale Wilson Educational Trust for residents of Spokane and Lincoln counties, WA, who are majoring in agriculture, business, or psychology
2. The Rev. H. Rice Educational Trust for handicapped and orphaned Spokane, WA, youth for higher education within the state of Washington
3. The Doris L. Kenney Memorial Scholarship Fund for residents of Bonner County, ID, for higher education
4. The Carrow Memorial Scholarship Fund for graduating seniors of University High School, Spokane, WA, who are active in the band program.

652
Springs Foundation, Inc.
P.O. Drawer 460
Lancaster, SC 29720   (803) 286-2196
Contact: Charles A. Bundy, President

Limitations: Scholarships to medical students who make a commitment to practice in Lancaster County and Fort Mill and Chester townships, SC. Awards are not made each year. A decision on awards is made in January of each year. Student loans only to residents of Lancaster County, and Fort Mill and Chester townships, SC.
Financial data: Year ended 12/31/86. Assets, $20,230,332 (M); Total giving, $1,220,307; Grants to individuals amount not specified; Loans to individuals, 114 loans totaling $150,924.
Employer Identification Number: 570426344

Applications: Applications accepted throughout the year; Initial approach by telephone or brief letter; Completion of formal application required for student loans.
Publications: Annual report, program information.
Program description:
The **Springs Medical Scholarship Program** was established to attract doctors to the area in South Carolina which is its concern, namely Lancaster County and the townships of Fort Mill and Chester. For this purpose scholarships are awarded to medical students who have been accepted at an accredited medical school in one of the original 48 states and who make a commitment to practice in the communities mentioned above for one year for every year of scholarship aid accepted. If the recipient does not practice in those areas for the full period, he or she must repay the funds awarded at an eight percent rate of interest.
Awards of $5,000 per year are made for a period of four years. Approximately three new awards are made each year.
In addition, scholarship loans of up to $6,000 over four years are made on the basis of need to individuals attending four-year, accredited colleges and nursing schools in South Carolina. Loans are generally made only for undergraduate education; however, graduate loans, which may not exceed $8,000 after a four-year period, are made to local students in dental or medical programs.

653★
Stark County Foundation, The
c/o United Bank Building
220 Market Avenue South, Suite 1180
Canton, OH 44702   (216) 454-3426
Contact: Deannakay Skolfield, Program Director

Limitations: Student aid and loans only to students who are residents of Stark County, OH.
Financial data: Year ended 12/31/87. Assets, $23,345,400 (L); Expenditures, $971,000; Grants to individuals, 22 grants totaling $16,757; Loans to individuals, 61 loans totaling $71,000.
Employer Identification Number: 340943665
Applications: Deadline March 1st; Completion of formal application required; Applications not reviewed by foundation; Separate board reviews and interviews applicants; Contact foundation for individuals who are on the board; Interviews, references, and grade records required.
Publications: Annual report.
Program description:
Student aid and loans made on basis of necessity and ability to complete college. No restrictions on race, religion, or creed.

654
Stark (Donald A. and Jane C.) Charitable Trust
c/o B. Wade White, Trustee
5036 Willow Leaf Way
Sarasota, FL 33583

Limitations: Grants for student scholarships.
Financial data: Year ended 12/31/86. Assets,
$1,094,618 (M); Total giving, $387,500; Grants to
individuals amount not specified.
Employer Identification Number: 346522476

655
Stark (Nelda C. and H.J. Lutcher) Foundation
602 West Main Street
P.O. Box 909
Orange, TX 77631-0909   (713) 883-3351
Contact: Clyde V. McKee, Jr., Secretary-Treasurer

Limitations: Scholarships limited to residents of Texas
and southwest Louisiana.
Financial data: Year ended 2/28/87. Assets,
$73,149,446 (M); Total giving, $217,050; Grants to
individuals, 5 grants totaling $2,250, high $750, low
$250.
Employer Identification Number: 746047440
Applications: Applications accepted throughout the
year; Initial approach by letter.
Program description:
Scholarship awards are made through the **Miriam
Lutcher Stark Reading and Declamation Contest**.

656★
Starr Foundation, The
70 Pine Street
New York, NY 10270   (212) 770-6882
Contact: Mr. Ta Chun Hsu, President

Limitations: Support for four scholarship programs: to
children of employees of American International, in
the U.S.; to children of employees of American
International overseas companies; to graduates of high
schools in the Brewster, NY, School District; and to
students of three specific schools in the lower
Manhattan area.
Financial data: Year ended 12/31/86. Assets,
$460,546,892 (M); Total giving, $16,333,449; Grants
to individuals, 310 grants totaling $660,788, high
$6,000, low $100.
Employer Identification Number: 136151545
Applications: Applications accepted throughout the
year; Initial approach by letter. See program
description below for further information.
Program description:
The foundation supports the following scholarship
programs:
　　1. **Scholarship Program for "American
International" Children--U.S.** - provides aid to
children of permanent, full-time employees of
American International companies anywhere in

the world and to dependent children of full-time
agents who sell insurance exclusively for
American International companies. Aid is for
degree studies in U.S. colleges. Recipients are
selected on basis of academic ability and
financial need by College Scholarship Service of
Princeton, NJ, an independent nonprofit
educational organization which administers the
program.
　　2. **Scholarship Program for "American
International" Children--Overseas** - program for
degree studies at local institutions of higher
learning overseas, for children of permanent,
full-time employees of American International
companies anywhere in the world and to
dependent children of full-time agents who sell
insurance exclusively for American International
companies. Program is administered by the
International Institute of Education, an
independent nonprofit educational organization,
headquartered in New York City.
　　3. **Brewster Starr Scholarship Program** - available
to all high school students who reside in the
Brewster, NY, area or who graduate from
secondary schools in the Brewster area. Aid is for
schooling beyond the secondary level. Program is
administered and recipients selected by a special
committee of professional educators from the
Brewster area chosen and headed by the
superintendent of the Brewster Central School
District.
　　4. **Lower Manhattan Starr Scholarship Program** -
provides aid for postsecondary education to
deserving students going to school in the lower
Manhattan area as defined in the program. Three
schools participate in the program, namely
Murray Bergtraum High School for Business
Careers, Lower Eastside Preparatory School, and
Seward Park High School. Administration of the
program, including selection of recipients, rests
completely with a joint committee consisting of
representatives of the participating schools.

657★
Statler Foundation, The
Statler Towers, Suite 508
Buffalo, NY 14202   (716) 852-1104
Contact: Peter J. Crotty, Chairman

Limitations: Scholarships to students of hotel or food
service management.
Financial data: Year ended 12/31/87. Assets,
$22,000,000 (M) (approximate); Total giving, $725,00;
Grants to individuals amount not specified.
Employer Identification Number: 131889077
Applications: Deadline April 15th; Initial approach by
letter; Completion of formal application required.
Applications are available from the Western New York
Scholarship Awards Committee and hotel and motel
associations, which are funded by the foundation.

658★
Steele-Reese Foundation, The
c/o Messrs. Davidson, Dawson and Clark
330 Madison Avenue
New York, NY 10017
Contact: Lydia Schofield, Scholarship Director, Box 922, Salmon, ID 83467

Limitations: Scholarships only to residents of Lemhi and Custer counties, ID.
Financial data: Year ended 8/31/87. Assets, $25,938,641 (M); Total giving, $684,500; Grants to individuals, 52 grants totaling $60,000.
Employer Identification Number: 136034763
Applications: Applications accepted throughout the year; Initial approach by letter; High school seniors can apply for scholarships through their schools.
Publications: Annual report (including application guidelines).
Program description:
Scholarship candidates recommended by their principals are interviewed and a committee considers the applications on the basis of financial need and academic potential. The committee recommends a list of recipients and amounts to the foundation trustees who are charged with making the final decisions.

The scholarship awards are restricted to tuition, course-related fees, books, supplies, and equipment. They may not be applied to room, board, travel, or personal expenses. Scholarship payments are made directly to the educational institution on behalf of the individual recipients.

659
Steinman (John Frederick) Foundation
Eight West King Street
Lancaster, PA 17603
Contact: Jay H. Wenrich, Fellowship Program Secretary

Limitations: Fellowships primarily to residents of Lancaster, PA, for graduate study in mental health and related fields.
Financial data: Year ended 12/31/86. Assets, $9,377,857 (M); Total giving, $569,610; Grants to individuals totaling $30,000.
Employer Identification Number: 236266378
Applications: Deadline February 1st; Completion of formal application required.

660
Stephenson Scholarship Foundation
Five Hillside Lane
Vacaville, CA 95688   (707) 448-2128
Contact: Helen E. Stephenson, at above address and telephone, or Donald Stephenson, 500 Main Street, Vacaville, CA 95688; Tel.: (707) 448-6894

Limitations: Scholarships only to graduating seniors in the Vacaville, CA, Unified School District or college

undergraduates who resided in the school district at the time they graduated from a public high school and were involved in athletics. Applicants must be planning to major in professions outlined in guidelines.
Financial data: Year ended 6/30/86. Assets, $131,603 (M); Total giving, $11,700; Grants to individuals, 13 grants totaling $11,700 for scholarships, each grant $900.
Employer Identification Number: 237412597
Applications: Deadline early August; Completion of formal application required; Interviews required.
Publications: Application guidelines.
Program description:
Applicants must have supported their high school athletic program for two years as a player, manager, or in some other capacity and have been in the top ten percent of their high school graduating class or be a "B" student in college; also, must have shown financial responsibility by having saved money they earned or, in the view of the selection committee, spent it wisely, i.e., helped family or for their own expenses.

661★
Sternberger (Emanuel) Educational Fund
P.O. Box 1735
Greensboro, NC 27402   (919) 275-6316
Contact: Ms. Brenda Henley, Executive Director

Limitations: Educational loans only for legal residents of North Carolina, for use by juniors, seniors, and graduate school students.
Financial data: Year ended 7/31/86. Assets, $291,954 (M); Expenditures, $9,478; Loans to individuals, 18 loans totaling $19,500, high $1,750, low $750.
Employer Identification Number: 560571222
Applications: Deadline April 30th; Applications available beginning of February; Initial approach by letter requesting application form; Completion of formal application, including four references, transcript of college grades, and photograph, required; Interviews required.
Program description:
Recipients of loans may attend any college, beginning with their junior year and extending through graduate school. The loans must be repaid in monthly payments within a reasonable time.

662★
Sternberger (Sigmund) Foundation, Inc.
P.O. Box 3111
Greensboro, NC 27402   (919) 373-1500
Contact: Robert O. Klepfer, Jr., Executive Director

Limitations: Scholarships only to residents of Guilford County, NC, who are pursuing undergraduate studies at a college or university in North Carolina, and to children of members of the Revolution Masonic

Lodge.
Financial data: Year ended 3/31/87. Assets, $9,223,412 (M); Total giving, $421,400; Grants to individuals, 18 grants totaling $16,450, high $1,400, low $500.
Employer Identification Number: 566045483
Applications: Applications accepted throughout the year; Initial approach by letter; Completion of formal application required.

663★
Stevens (Harley and Mertie) Memorial Fund
c/o United States National Bank of Oregon
P.O. Box 3168
Portland, OR 97208   (503) 225-4884

Limitations: Scholarships and student loans only to graduates of Clackamas County, OR, high schools attending college or university supported by Oregon state or owned and operated by any Protestant church organization.
Financial data: Year ended 6/30/87. Assets, $1,097,296 (M); Expenditures, $89,820; Grants to individuals totaling $35,033; Loans to individuals totaling $32,590.
Employer Identification Number: 936053655
Applications: Deadlines May 1st for scholarships and between June 1st and June 15th for loans; Completion of formal application required; Interviews for scholarship finalists required. Additional information may be obtained from the foundation.
Publications: Program information.
Program description:
The fund was established to give financial assistance to worthy students without regard to race, creed, color or origin who have graduated from a Clackamas County, OR, high school. Students are eligible for scholarship grants for their first and fourth years of undergraduate schooling, and eligible to apply for a loan for their second and third years. Scholarships are based upon GPA and financial need and may include the cost of room and board and books or any one or more of said items.
   All loans bear interest and are repayable in monthly installments beginning 90 days after completion of academic training.

664
Stewart (J.C.) Memorial Trust
8901 Annapolis Road
Lanham, MD 20706   (301) 459-4200
Contact: Robert S. Hoyert, Trustee

Limitations: Scholarships and student loans to Maryland residents.
Financial data: Year ended 11/30/86. Assets, $4,696,322 (M); Total giving, $47,500; Grants to individuals, 2 grants totaling $2,500, high $1,500, low $1,000; Loans to individuals amount not specified.

Employer Identification Number: 237357104

665★
Stifel (George E.) Scholarship Fund
c/o Security National Bank & Trust Company
1114 Market Street
Wheeling, WV 26003   (304) 233-0600
Contact: Endowment Trustee

Limitations: Scholarships only to needy residents, aged 17 to 25, of Ohio County, WV, who are graduates of the Wheeling, WV, public high school.
Financial data: Year ended 4/30/87. Assets, $951,514 (M); Total giving, $43,230; Grants to individuals, 32 grants totaling $33,230, high $2,000, low $280, average grant $1,000.
Employer Identification Number: 556018248
Applications: Deadline spring for the following academic year; Completion of formal application required; Interviews required.
Program description:
While scholastic attainments will be given considerable weight, the selection of recipients will not be restricted only to those who have received high grades, but the scholarship trustees will consider the personality of each applicant, his or her extracurricular activities, deportment, spirit of cooperation with school authorities, and the general promise which that applicant shows of becoming a better citizen if given the opportunity of a college education.
   In general, a scholarship will be awarded for one academic year, usually September through June. A scholarship will not be awarded to one person for more than four years. A scholarship, once awarded, may be discontinued if, in the discretion of the trustees, the recipient does not prove worthy thereof.

666
Stillman (Chauncey) Benevolent Fund
c/o Kelley, Drye & Warren
101 Park Avenue
New York, NY 10178
Contact: Louis B. Warren, Trustee

Limitations: Scholarships for qualifying students. All funds presently committed.
Financial data: Year ended 1/31/86. Assets, $48,482 (M); Total giving, $31,702; Grants to individuals, 9 grants totaling $31,702; Subtotal for scholarships, 3 grants totaling $22,000, high $11,000, low $5,000.
Employer Identification Number: 136113811
Applications: All funds presently committed.
Program description:
Grants are made for educational assistance including tuition, fees, and expenses, on the basis of the applicant's scholastic aptitude, financial need, indications of good character, and desire for

educational improvement. Applications are reviewed annually. Whenever possible, scholarships are paid directly to the school the applicant attends.

667
Stock (Paul) Foundation
1130 Rumsey Avenue
P.O. Box 2020
Cody, WY 82414   (307) 587-5275
Contact: Kenneth S. Bailey, Secretary-Treasurer

Limitations: Educational grants and scholarships to Wyoming residents of at least one year, usually from the Cody area.
Financial data: Year ended 12/31/86. Assets, $8,135,510 (M); Total giving, $817,221; Grants to individuals, 92 grants totaling $112,380, high $2,750, low $400.
Employer Identification Number: 830185157
Applications: Deadline June 30th and November 30th; Initial approach by letter; Completion of formal application required.

668
Stockwitz (Anna & Charles) Fund for Education of Jewish Children
c/o Wells Fargo Bank
343 Sansome Street, Third Floor
San Francisco, CA 94163
Contact: Shirley Scott, c/o Anna and Charles Stockwitz Fund, 1600 Scott Street, San Francisco, CA 94115

Limitations: Scholarships only to Jewish children of San Francisco, CA, who are attending area high schools.
Financial data: Year ended 12/31/86. Assets, $441,630 (M); Total giving, $44,706; Grants to individuals, 15 grants totaling $12,233, high $1,500, low $300, general range $400-750, average grant $1,000.
Employer Identification Number: 941267565
Applications: Applications accepted throughout the year; Initial approach by letter.
Publications: Program information.

669★
Stokes (Ann Bradshaw) Foundation
3204 Beverly Drive
Dallas, TX 75205   (214) 528-1924

Limitations: Scholarships to students majoring in theatre and drama at colleges and universities in Texas.
Financial data: Year ended 12/31/86. Assets, $1,817,405 (M); Total giving, $94,592; Grants to individuals amount not specified.
Employer Identification Number: 751866981
Applications: Completion of formal application

required; Institutional recommendation of applicant's potential required.

670
Stone (Albert H. & Reuben S.) Fund
232 Logan Street
Gardner, MA 01440   (617) 632-2770
Contact: Carlton E. Nichols or Carlton E. Nicols, Jr., Trustees

Limitations: Scholarships only to residents of Gardner, MA, who are full-time day students.
Financial data: Year ended 12/31/85. Assets, $2,543,381 (M); Total giving, $94,725; Grants to individuals totaling $94,725.
Employer Identification Number: 046050419
Applications: Deadline end of June; Initial approval by letter; Applications may be obtained personally through group appointments set with guidance department of high school; Completion of formal application required; Interviews required. Past recipients of grants receive applications automatically each spring.

671
Stonecutter Foundation, Inc.
300 Dallas Street
Spindale, NC 28160   (704) 286-2341
Contact: J. T. Strickland, Treasurer

Limitations: Undergraduate student loans only to residents of the Rutherford and Polk County, NC, areas.
Financial data: Year ended 8/31/86. Assets, $4,826,222 (M); Expenditures, $204,025; Loans to individuals, 25 loans totaling $21,150, high $2,000, low $500.
Employer Identification Number: 566044820
Applications: Applications accepted throughout the year; Completion of formal application required.

672★
Stony Wold-Herbert Fund, Inc.
136 East 57th Street, Room 1705
New York, NY 10022   (212) 753-6565
Contact: Mrs. Cheryl S. Friedman, Executive Director

Limitations: Support for three programs: research grants to doctors within the greater New York area involved in studying respiratory diseases; pulmonary fellowships to doctors in the greater New York area training in the respiratory field; and supplementary scholarships for college or vocational school students, 16 years or older, living in the greater New York area only, with respiratory illnesses.
Financial data: Year ended 12/31/85. Assets, $3,681,159 (M); Total giving, $178,001; Grants to individuals, 18 grants totaling $47,932.
Employer Identification Number: 132784124

Applications: Deadline October 15th for research and fellowship grants; Applications for scholarships accepted throughout the year; Initial approach by letter or telephone; Completion of formal application required; Interviews granted upon request.
Program description:
Direct Service Grants award supplemental scholarships to eligible students to help them meet the peripheral expenses involved in attending school, in addition to tuition assistance. The grants average $200 monthly during the educational or vocational training period of selected students, who suffer from a documented pulmonary problem. The grants are based on the financial need of the recipient, as well as his/her educational goals.

673
Straub (Gertrude S.) Trust Estate
c/o Hawaiian Trust Company, Ltd.
P.O. Box 3170
Honolulu, HI 96802   (808) 525-6512
Contact: Janis A. Reischman, Administrator

Limitations: Scholarships to Hawaiian high school graduates to attend mainland U.S. colleges or universities, with a major relating to international understanding and cooperation, and world peace.
Financial data: Year ended 9/30/87. Assets, $3,829,214 (M); Total giving, $72,150; Grants to individuals, 64 grants totaling $72,150, high $2,150, low $100, average grant $600.
Employer Identification Number: 996003243
Applications: Submit application between January 1st and March 1st; Deadline March 1st; Initial approach by telephone or letter; Completion of formal application required.
Publications: Application guidelines, program information.
Program description:
Scholarships are awarded annually and are renewable for up to four years.

674★
Strong (Hattie M.) Foundation
Cafritz Building, Suite 409
1625 Eye Street, N.W.
Washington, DC 20006   (202) 331-1619
Contact: Thelma L. Eichman, Secretary

Limitations: Non-interest-bearing college loans to American students who are within one year of completing their studies in a degree program from an accredited four-year college or graduate school, and to residents of the metropolitan Washington, DC, area who are enrolled in vocational schools in the Washington, DC area.
Financial data: Year ended 8/31/87. Assets, $16,949,818 (M); Expenditures, $718,709; Loans to individuals, 246 loans totaling $496,575, high $2,500,

low $700, general range $1,500-2,500.
Employer Identification Number: 520237223
Applications: Deadline March 31st; Initial approach by letter; Completion of formal application required; Interviews are not conducted.
Publications: Annual report.
Program description:
Applicants should send letter between January 1st and March 31st for following scholastic year, giving brief history and date expected to complete studies. Applications forms are then sent to eligible students. The maximum loan amount available is $2,500. The terms of repayment are based upon monthly income after graduation and are arranged individually to avoid hardship. **Foreign students temporarily in this country do not qualify for loans.**

675
Student Aid Foundation
c/o First National Bank of Atlanta, Trust Tax Dept.
P.O. Box 4148, MC701
Atlanta, GA 30302
Contact: Marjorie S. Ware, Executive Secretary, 788 Reckle Drive, Decatur, GA

Limitations: Student loans to women and girls who are legal residents of Georgia.
Financial data: Year ended 3/31/87. Assets, $556,065 (M); Expenditures, $13,370; Loans to individuals, 143 loans totaling $87,380, high $1,500, low $300, general range $300-750.
Employer Identification Number: 580612611
Applications: Applications accepted throughout the year; Initial approach by letter requesting application; Completion of formal application required, including school transcript.
Publications: Program information.
Program description:
Funds are loaned for regular college work and for most specialized training programs. Loans are for one academic year and must be re-applied for each year. Loans are limited to $1,000 a year for undergraduates and $1,500 a year for graduate students. Medical students are not eligible for loans until the junior year. All notes must be co-signed. Loans are interest free while the student is still in college or training. Interest at five percent begins three months after the student completes her courses or leaves school for any cause. If the loan is not repaid within three years of completion of studies, interest at eight percent is charged on the remaining unpaid balance.

676
Student Aid Foundation Enterprises
800 Commerce Street
Houston, TX 77002
Contact: Frank T. Abraham, President

Limitations: Scholarships only to younger students, particularly underprivileged youth, who are residents of Houston, TX. Funds presently committed.
Financial data: Year ended 6/30/86. Assets, $2,233,094 (M); Total giving, $21,753; Grants to individuals, 4 grants totaling $5,441, high $1,973, low $250.
Employer Identification Number: 746060745
Applications: Applications currently not accepted.

677★
Stump (Jacob), Jr. and Clara Stump Memorial Scholarship Fund
c/o Central National Bank of Mattoon
Broadway and Charleston at 14th Street
Mattoon, IL 61938   (217) 234-6434
Contact: Malcolm O'Neill, Trust Officer

Limitations: Scholarships to high school graduates from Coles, Cumberland, Douglas or Moultrie counties, IL, to attend any state-supported college or university in Illinois.
Financial data: Year ended 7/31/87. Assets, $1,315,381 (M); Total giving, $49,350; Grants to individuals, 132 grants totaling $49,350, high $400, low $150, average grant $400.
Employer Identification Number: 376064295
Applications: Deadline April 1st; Completion of formal application required; Applications available at high schools and at Central National Bank.

678
Sudbury Foundation
c/o Mechanics Bank Trust Department
P.O. Box 987
Worcester, MA 01613   (617) 798-6467
Contact: John E. Arsenault, Vice-President and Trust Officer

Limitations: Scholarships and student loans to residents of Sudbury, MA, or persons who have matriculated from the Sudbury Regional School District.
Financial data: Year ended 12/31/85. Assets, $4,844,556 (M); Expenditures, $261,055; Grants to individuals, 10 grants totaling $6,350, high $1,350, low $500, average grant $500; Loans to individuals, 85 loans totaling $197,611, high $5,400, low $650, average loan $2,500.
Employer Identification Number: 046037026
Applications: Deadline April 1st; Initial approach by letter; Completion of formal application required.

Program description:
In recent years loans have only been made to students at the undergraduate level.

679
Suder-Pick Foundation, Inc.
c/o Foley & Lardner
777 East Wisconsin Avenue
Milwaukee, WI 53202   (414) 289-3528
Contact: Harrold J. McComas

Limitations: Scholarships only to graduating seniors of West Bend High School, WI.
Financial data: Year ended 12/31/86. Assets, $20,896 (M); Total giving, $35,100; Grants to individuals, 37 grants totaling $17,400, high $500, low $300.
Employer Identification Number: 396048255
Applications: Applications accepted throughout the year; Initial approach by letter.
Program description:
All applications are reviewed by the administration and faculty of the school. Recommendations are made to the foundation's board of directors, who selects the recipients.

680
Sullivan (Ray H. & Pauline) Foundation
c/o Connecticut National Bank
777 Main Street
Hartford, CT 06115
Contact: John J. Curtin, c/o Connecticut National Bank, 250 Captain's Walk, New London, CT 06320; Tel.: (203) 447-6132

Limitations: Scholarships and student loans to graduates of St. Bernard's High School, CT, "to acquire educational advantages that might otherwise not be available to them.".
Financial data: Year ended 7/31/86. Assets, $6,912,883 (M); Total giving, $178,600; Grants to individuals, 5 grants totaling $4,500, high $2,500, low $500; Loans to individuals, 124 loans totaling $58,000, each loan $500.
Employer Identification Number: 066141242
Applications: Deadline May 1st; Completion of formal application required.

681
Sunnyside, Inc.
8609 N.W. Plaza Drive, Suite 201
Dallas, TX 75225   (214) 692-5686
Contact: Mary Rothenflue, Executive Director

Limitations: Educational aid to underprivileged children residing in Texas to provide for their intellectual needs.
Financial data: Year ended 12/31/86. Assets, $1,303,662 (M); Total giving, $179,731; Grants to individuals, 83 grants totaling $99,731; Subtotal for

education, 18 grants totaling $29,900, high $3,750, low $500.
Employer Identification Number: 756037004
Applications: Applications accepted throughout the year; Completion of formal application required.

682
Sussman (Otto) Trust
c/o Sullivan and Cromwell
125 Broad Street, 28th Floor
New York, NY 10004
Contact: Nancy Beagan

Limitations: Education expenses to residents of New York, New Jersey, Oklahoma, and Pennsylvania who are in need due to illness or death in their immediate family or some other unusual or unfortunate circumstance.
Financial data: Year ended 12/31/85. Assets, $2,136,281 (M); Total giving, $103,318; Grants to individuals, 43 grants totaling $103,318; Subtotal for education, 18 grants totaling $44,026.
Employer Identification Number: 136075849
Applications: Applications accepted throughout the year; Initial contact by letter requesting application and setting forth circumstances giving rise to need; Completion of formal application required.
Publications: Application guidelines.
Program description:
The trust is not a scholarship fund and applications for scholarship grants are considered only if all other kinds of aid available to students, including student loans, have been explored and proven fruitless.

683
Suttell Foundation, The
c/o St. Paul's Church
50 Park Place
Pawtucket, RI 02860
Contact: T. Earl Haworth, President

Limitations: Undergraduate educational grants or loans only to residents of Rhode Island. Preference will be given to grants for medical studies or work with youth.
Financial data: Year ended 12/31/86. Assets, $87,619 (M); Total giving, $4,100; Grants to individuals, 8 grants totaling $4,000 for educational grants or loans, each grant $500.
Employer Identification Number: 056015551
Applications: Deadline September 1st; Initial approach by letter requesting application; Completion of formal application required including brief resume of academic qualifications and course of study and expense involved; Individuals should submit name of college and address.
Program description:
A determination is made on the basis of information in the application as to whether a grant or loan will be

awarded and whether or not the loan is interest-free. Grants are made for one year and are subject to renewal. Grants usually do not exceed $500.

684
Swann Foundation for Caricature and Cartoon, The
655 Madison Avenue
New York, NY 10021   (212) 838-2424
Contact: Henry J. Goldschmidt, President

Limitations: Fellowships for Ph.D. candidates in the U.S. or Canada working in the field of cartoon and caricature, with a preference for research into American satiric art. Limited number of grants in aid to individuals doing work consistent with the foundation's purposes.
Financial data: Year ended 9/30/86. Assets, $672,165 (M); Total giving, $45,333; Grants to individuals, 11 grants totaling $38,230; Subtotal for fellowship awards, 2 grants totaling $10,000, each grant $5,000; Subtotal for grants-in-aid, 9 grants totaling $28,230, high $5,000, low $1,000.
Employer Identification Number: 136274647
Applications: Deadline February 15th for fellowship applications; Contact foundation for current deadline for grants-in-aid. Applications should include detailed proposal and budget; Three letters of recommendation are required for fellowship applications.
Publications: Informational brochure, application guidelines.
Program description:
The foundation's purpose is to support the study and public understanding of original works of humorous and satiric art in all media by artists of all nations. It encourages exploration of the development of caricature and cartoon in relation to other visual arts and to social history. Grants-in-aid are awarded to support various projects. They do no cover living expenses or the costs of enterprises that are expected to be commercially viable.

The doctoral fellowship to support a Ph.D. dissertation was awarded for the first time in 1980 to cover a period of uninterrupted study from September until the following June. The fellowship carries a stipend of $10,000. Applicants must have completed all requirements except the dissertation.

685
Swiss Benevolent Society of Chicago
P.O. Box 2137
Chicago, IL 60690
Contact: Professor Jean Devaud, Chairman of S.B.S. Scholarship Committee, 629 South Humphrey Avenue, Oak Park, IL 60304.

Limitations: Undergraduate scholarships for full-time students of Swiss descent residing in IL, IN, IA, MI, or WI.

Financial data: Year ended 12/31/86. Assets, $1,311,558 (M); Total giving, $58,482; Grants to individuals totaling $58,482.
Employer Identification Number: 366076395
Applications: Deadline March 1st; Completion of formal application required.
Publications: Program information.
Program description:
Awards totaling $35,000 will be distributed to the respective institutions of higher learning where the top qualifying applicants have indicated they will attend. There will be full ($1,650), two-thirds ($1,100), half ($800), and one-third ($550) awards depending on the applicants' overall rating and tuition charged.

In addition, the **Ralph Wyseling Scholar Award** in the amount of $2,500 may be awarded to a prospective college senior who has been a previous winner of an S.B.S. award for three consecutive years and ranks highest among eligible candidates. Financial need is not a requirement; all candidates will be judged on academic merit.

The follwing criteria is required:
1. Applicants must be a Swiss national or of documentarily proven Swiss descent.
2. Applicants must have a GPA of at least 3.4 (for high school grades if a prospective college freshman, or for college studies if currently a college student).
3. Students who have completed any kind of a bachelor's degree are not eligible for S.B.S. scholarships.
4. Applicants must submit an official, signed transcript of high school grades, including GPA, official copy of ACT, SAT, PSAT, etc., and statement regarding applicant's rank in class.
5. Current college student applicants must submit a complete, official signed college transcript from each institution of higher learning attended.

All award applications are examined, analyzed, and rated by a neutral, outside agency. Decisions of the scholarship committee are final.

686
Tai (J.T.) & Company Foundation, Inc.
18 East 67th Street
New York, NY 10021
Contact: J. T. Tai, President

Limitations: Grants for medical education expenses.
Financial data: Year ended 12/31/85. Assets, $3,971,363 (M); Total giving, $100,560; Grants to individuals, 2 grants totaling $13,480.
Employer Identification Number: 133157279
Applications: Applications accepted throughout the year; Initial approach by letter.

687
Thatcher Foundation, The
P.O. Box 1401
Pueblo, CO 81002
Contact: Charlene Burkhard, The Thatcher Foundation, c/o Minnequa Bank of Pueblo County, CO, 81004 Tel.: (303)544-3565

Limitations: Scholarships only to residents of Pueblo County, CO, for undergraduate study.
Financial data: Year ended 12/31/86. Assets, $3,090,589 (M); Total giving, $207,562; Grants to individuals, 18 grants totaling $24,850, high $5,150, low $500.
Employer Identification Number: 840581724
Applications: Deadline prior to beginning of school year in which assistance is requested; Completion of formal application required.

688★
Thomson (The John Edgar) Foundation
The Rittenhouse Claridge, Suite 318
Philadelphia, PA 19103   (215) 545-6083
Contact: Gilda Verstein, Director

Limitations: Scholarships for daughters of deceased railroad employees.
Financial data: Year ended 12/31/87. Assets, $4,551,901 (M); Total giving, $226,335; Grants to individuals, 144 grants totaling $226,335, average grant $2,167.
Employer Identification Number: 231382746
Applications: Applications accepted throughout the year; Completion of formal application required; Interviews required.
Publications: Newsletter, informational brochure, application guidelines.

689★
Thorn (Columbus W.), Jr. Foundation
109 East Main Street
Elkton, MD 21921   (301) 398-0611

Limitations: Educational loans to worthy and needy high school graduates of Cecil County, MD.
Financial data: Year ended 12/31/87. Assets, $4,507,364 (M); Expenditures, $177,878; Loans to individuals, 85 loans totaling $160,600, high $4,400, low $500, average grant $1,900.
Employer Identification Number: 237153983
Applications: Applications accepted throughout the year; Completion of formal application required; Submit completed loan application to Doris P. Scott and Charles L. Scott at foundation address.
Program description:
Repayment of the loan is required within four years after completion or discontinuation of student's advanced education. Repayment is guaranteed by student's parents. Interest rate on the loan is five percent.

690★
Thrasher Research Fund
50 East North Temple Street, Seventh Floor
Salt Lake City, UT 84150   (801) 531-3386
Contact: Robert M. Briem, Associate Director

Limitations: Grants for child health research and demonstration projects by individuals affiliated with nonprofit academic and research institutions.
Financial data: Year ended 12/31/87. Assets, $24,028,159 (M); Total giving, $1,117,885; Grants to individuals, 18 grants totaling $1,117,885, high $134,712, low $28,483, general range $75,000-150,000.
Applications: Prospectus submissions accepted throughout the year; Telephone consultation before submission is encouraged; If proposed study is of interest, full proposal and completion of formal application required.
Publications: Annual report, application guidelines, financial statement, informational brochure.
Program description:
The principal objective of the fund is to promote both national and international child health research. The fund currently emphasizes practical and applied interventions that have the potential to improve the health of children throughout the world.

There is no restriction on the types of diseases or child health problems considered for funding as long as the research is directed to solving the problems or improving the health of children. Because infectious diseases and nutrition are of such importance in determining the health of children, the fund places some emphasis on work in these fields. However, innovative projects in any area of child health will be given serious consideration.

691★
Tibbetts Industries Foundation
P.O. Box 1096
Camden, ME 04843   (207) 236-3301
Contact: W. Kent Stanley

Limitations: Scholarships only to graduates of specified high schools or colleges in Maine.
Financial data: Year ended 12/31/84. Assets, $63,182 (M); Total giving, $6,400; Grants to individuals, 7 grants totaling $6,250, high $1,500, low $250, general range $700-1,000.
Employer Identification Number: 016019029
Applications: Applications accepted throughout the year; Initial approach by letter including a written request detailing projected income for the next school year, most recent transcript of grades, and any other scholastic information; Written requests should be submitted by mid-July for consideration for the next school year.

Program description:
A grant or other form of aid may be made to an applicant who satisfies at least one of the following criteria:
- graduate of a public high school in the school administrative district of which the Town of Camden, ME, is a member
- graduate of a recognized public or private high school located within the County of Knox, ME
- holder of a bachelor's degree conferred by the University of Maine, the Maine Maritime Academy, a state (of Maine) teachers college, or their successors
- and additionally a graduate of a secondary school, public or private, located within the state of Maine.

692
Tilles (Rosalie) Nonsectarian Charity Fund
705 Olive Street, Suite 906
St. Louis, MO 63101   (314) 231-1721
Contact: Susan Shrago, Secretary-Investigator

Limitations: Scholarships to high school graduates who are residents of the city or county of St. Louis, MO.
Financial data: Year ended 6/30/87. Assets, $2,161,166 (M); Total giving, $65,498; Grants to individuals, 76 grants totaling $64,498, high $3,500, low $119.
Employer Identification Number: 436020833
Applications: Deadline March 1st; Applications accepted from January 1st through March 1st; Applicant should apply for financial aid based on need at the college he or she wishes to attend; Recommendations by the high school principal or counselor should be sent with application to the financial aid director at the college the applicant wishes to attend.
Publications: Application guidelines.
Program description:
Scholarships are awarded to residents of the city or county of St. Louis to attend any of five participating higher education institutions: St. Louis University, University of Missouri (Columbia, Rolla, and St. Louis campuses), and Washington University. Scholarships are renewable for four years, contingent on satisfactory academic progress and pay one-third of the tuition fee charged by each university, including room and board at the Columbia and Rolla campuses of the University of Missouri.

Recipients are chosen on the basis of their secondary school academic record, test scores, financial need, and other information available to the universities. Each applicant must be in the upper ten percent of his or her graduating class and must be recommended by the high school principal or counselor. Awards are made early in the Spring, and payment is made directly to the college.

693
Todd (The Vera H. and William R.) Foundation
c/o Connecticut National Bank
777 Main Street
Hartford, CT 06115
Contact: Sandra Porr, Connecticut National Bank;
Tel.: (203) 579-3534

Limitations: Scholarships for students of Derby-Shelton
School System, CT.
Financial data: Year ended 12/31/86. Assets, $177,703
(M); Total giving, $11,300; Grants to individuals, 13
grants totaling $11,300, high $1,000, low, $300.
Employer Identification Number: 066031931
Applications: Deadline March 15th; Completion of
formal application required, including two letters of
recommendation: for high school seniors, one letter
must be from a high school teacher or administrative
personnel; for college students, one letter must be
from current college, preferably an assistant to or a
department head (neither letter can be from high
school personnel).

694★
Tozer Foundation, Inc.
c/o First Trust N.A.
SPFS0200 First National Bank Building, P.O. Box
64704
St. Paul, MN 55164   (612) 291-5134
Contact: Grant T. Waldref, President

Limitations: Scholarships to graduating high school
students in three counties in Minnesota.
Financial data: Year ended 10/31/87. Assets,
$14,408,166 (M); Total giving, $723,360; Grants to
individuals, 578 grants totaling $481,200, high
$1,200, low $600.
Employer Identification Number: 416011518
Applications: Applications accepted throughout the
year; Initial approach by letter; Candidates must apply
for scholarships through selected high schools.

695
Tracy (Perry S. and Stella H.) Scholarship Fund
c/o Wells Fargo Bank
400 Capitol Mall
Sacramento, CA 95814   (916) 622-3634

Limitations: Scholarships only to graduates of high
schools of El Dorado County, CA.
Financial data: Year ended 5/31/87. Assets, $973,716
(M); Total giving, $48,311; Grants to individuals, 118
grants totaling $48,311, high $1,500, low $300,
average grant $400.
Employer Identification Number: 946203372
Applications: Deadline April 30th; Applications
available through area high schools; Completion of
formal application required.

Program description:
The completed application should be submitted to the
principal of applicant's high school, who will then
forward it to the scholarship selection committee. Each
recipient of a scholarship is advised of the
requirements for making a renewal application. The
selection committee consists of the principals of El
Dorado County high schools, mayors of the towns
within the county, and the managers of the Bank of
America branches in the county.
    In order to qualify for a scholarship award, the
recipient must be enrolled as a full-time student before
funds will be disbursed.

696★
Treacy Company
Box 1700
Helena, MT 59624   (406) 442-3632
Contact: James O'Connell

Limitations: Scholarships for undergraduate study only
to residents of, or students attending institutions of
higher education in, the northwest, including ID, MT,
ND, SD, and WA.
Financial data: Year ended 12/31/86. Assets,
$1,122,945 (M); Total giving, $46,687; Grants to
individuals, 80 grants totaling $22,500, average grant
$300.
Employer Identification Number: 810270257
Applications: Deadline June 15th; Completion of
formal application required.
Program description:
Recipients are chosen by the Scholarship Selection
Committee on the basis of personal motivation and
financial need. The scholarships are renewable up to a
limit of four years; graduate students are not eligible.
Grants are paid directly to the institution to be applied
to the student's account; some scholarships are
awarded to institutions to be given out as they see the
need. The company awards approximately 60
scholarships each year, the number of new awards
depending on the number of renewals.

697
Trinity Foundation
P.O. Box 7008
Pine Bluff, AR 71611   (501) 534-7120
Contact: W. K. Atkinson, Secretary-Treasurer

Limitations: Scholarships for higher education to
residents of Arkansas.
Financial data: Year ended 9/30/86. Assets,
$6,899,312 (M); Total giving, $225,900; Grants to
individuals, 21 grants totaling $2,600, high $1,500,
low $750.
Employer Identification Number: 716050288
Applications: Deadline April 10th of senior year in
high school; Completion of formal application
required; Application information available only at

high school guidance office.

698★
Trust Funds Incorporated
100 Broadway, 3rd Floor
San Francisco, CA 94111   (415) 434-3323
Contact: Albert J. Steiss, President

Limitations: Scholarships to residents of the San
Francisco Bay Area, CA, only under extraordinary
circumstances.
Financial data: Year ended 12/31/86. Assets,
$3,622,253 (M); Total giving, $184,477; Grants to
individuals, 4 grants totaling $17,537.
Employer Identification Number: 946062952
Applications: Initial approach by letter; Interviews
granted upon request.
Publications: Program information.
Program description:
Grants are made directly to individuals for educational
purposes only on rare occasions and generally require
the sponsorship of a responsible local person who
knows the applicant well. The fund has a Catholic
orientation and mainly supports local projects.

699
Tuckerman (Elizabeth) Foundation
Bank of America, NT & SA
233 North Fair Oaks Avenue
Pasadena, CA 91103

Limitations: Scholarships for students who
demonstrate scholastic ability and financial need.
Financial data: Year ended 11/30/86. Assets,
$1,017,344 (M); Total giving, $41,130; Grants to
individuals, 11 grants totaling $41,130, high $10,650,
low $500.
Employer Identification Number: 956601661

700
Turner (Tommy C.) Memorial Foundation
P.O. Box 89
Wetumpka, AL 36092   (205) 567-5141
Contact: Bobby Barrett

Limitations: Scholarships only for students of
Wetumpka High School, AL, to attend the University
of Alabama.
Financial data: Year ended 4/30/87. Assets, $42,209
(M); Total giving, $3,277; Grants to individuals, 1
grant totaling $3,277.
Employer Identification Number: 636067289
Applications: Deadline April 30th; Initial approach by
letter.

701
Tweed (Ethel H. and George W.) Scholarship
Endowment Trust
c/o First Florida Bank, N.A.
7500 Gulf Boulevard
St. Petersburg, FL 33706   (813) 367-2786
Contact: Robert L. Baker, Vice-President

Limitations: Scholarships only to graduating seniors of
high schools located within the corporate confines of
St. Petersburg, FL.
Financial data: Year ended 10/31/86. Assets, $143,648
(M); Total giving, $7,375; Grants to individuals, 9
grants totaling $7,375, high $1,250, low $375.
Employer Identification Number: 596145533
Applications: Deadline April 30th; Initial approach by
letter.
Program description:
Grants to qualified undergraduate students of $125 per
month on a nine-month school year basis.
Scholarships extend over four successive years of
attendance.

702
Tyson Foundation, Inc.
P.O. Drawer E
Springdale, AR 72764
Contact: Cleta Selman

Limitations: Scholarships to students attending
accredited colleges and universities.
Financial data: Year ended 12/31/86. Assets,
$7,348,790 (M); Total giving, $246,322; Grants to
individuals, 136 grants totaling $85,122.
Employer Identification Number: 237087948
Applications: Applications accepted throughout the
year; Completion of formal application required.

703
Ullery Charitable Trust
c/o First National Bank and Trust Company of Tulsa
P.O. Box 1
Tulsa, OK 74193   (918) 586-5845
Contact: Marilyn Pierce, Trust Officer

Limitations: Scholarships awarded primarily for study
at Presbyterian theological seminaries.
Financial data: Year ended 1/31/87. Assets, $300,400
(M); Total giving, $16,100; Grants to individuals, 13
grants totaling $16,100, high $2,600, low $100,
general range $500-2,500.
Employer Identification Number: 736142334
Applications: Applications accepted throughout the
year.
Program description:
Grants are awarded to individuals who are
contemplating entering full-time Christian service.

704
University Students Club, Inc.
1414 South Weller Street
Seattle, WA 98144
Contact: Ken Sato, President

Limitations: Scholarships primarily for students of
Japanese ancestry who attend the University of
Washington at Seattle on a full-time basis.
Financial data: Year ended 6/30/87. Assets, $114,556
(M); Total giving, $6,400; Grants to individuals, 8
grants totaling $6,400, each grant $800.
Employer Identification Number: 916035190
Applications: Deadline March 15th for following or
next school year; Completion of formal application
required; Application form available at the University
of Washington; Completed application should be sent
to Scholarship Chairman, University Students Club,
Inc., c/o 400 Boylston Avenue East No. 106, Seattle,
WA 98102.
Program description:
In addition to customary awards offered to students on
the basis of their financial need, academic
achievement, and community service, one or more
scholarships will be granted to individuals who have
the potential for college success, but who have not
distinguished themselves academically.

705★
Upjohn (W.E.) Unemployment Trustee
Corporation
300 South Westnedge Avenue
Kalamazoo, MI 49007   (616) 343-5541
Contact: Robert G. Spiegelman, Executive Director

Limitations: Research grants for studies on the causes,
effects, prevention, and alleviation of unemployment.
Financial data: Year ended 12/31/87. Assets,
$12,585,685 (M); Grants to individuals, 9 grants
totaling $202,724, high $35,000, low $2,000.
Employer Identification Number: 381360419
Applications: Applications accepted twice a year by
response to formal application request.
Publications: Program information, application
guidelines.
Program description:
A private operating foundation, the W.E. Upjohn
Unemployment Trustee Corporation supports research
into the causes, effects, prevention, and alleviation of
unemployment through the W.E. Upjohn Institute for
Employment Research.

The grant program is aimed at supporting
policy-relevant research expected to result in
publication of a monograph by the institute. In
keeping with its charter, the institute conducts
"research into the causes and effects of unemployment
and measures for the alleviation of unemployment," at
the national, state, and local level. The grant program
is intended to extend and complement the internal
research program at the institute. Areas of interest are:

1. Income Replacement and Social Insurance
Programs
2. Worker Adjustment
3. Labor-Management Relations
4. Demographic Change and Labor Market
Dynamics
5. Regional Economic Growth and Development
Policy.
   Application submissions should include the
following:
● Statement of the problem or hypothesis to be
investigated
● Methodology in sufficient detail to make it
possible to judge the workability of the proposal
● Timetable
● Budget
● Vita of the principal investigators
● Statement of research currently underway or
proposed to other institutions in the subject areas
of application.
   The application, excluding items four through six,
should not exceed 20 double-spaced pages. Three
copies of the application should be submitted.
Prospective applicants are encouraged to submit brief
descriptions of their ideas prior to writing a full
proposal to determine the institute's interest.

Applications are evaluated by an institute grant
committee on the basis of four equally weighted
evaluation criteria: policy significance, technical merit,
feasibility, and professional qualifications. The review
cycles in 1988 have application deadlines of March
25th and September 23rd.

The grant program does not fund dissertation
research, international travel, multi-year projects, or
conferences not initiated by the Upjohn Institute.

706▲
Urann Foundation
P.O. Box 1788
Brockton, MA 02403   (508) 588-7744
Contact: Howard Whelan, Administrator

Limitations: Scholarships to members of families
located in Massachusetts engaged in the production of
cranberries.
Financial data: Year ended 12/31/87. Assets,
$1,864,605 (M); Total giving, $88,843; Grants to
individuals, 30 grants totaling $41,843; Subtotal for
scholarships, 19 grants totaling $39,400, high $2,500,
low $1,250, general range $1,600-2,500.
Employer Identification Number: 046115599
Applications: Deadline April 15th; Initial approach by
telephone or letter; Completion of formal application
required. Applications also available at guidance
departments of high schools.
Program description:
The foundation makes scholarship grants to provide
assistance for postsecondary education. Additional

grants may be made on a yearly basis for continuation in undergraduate or graduate school. Applicants must show financial need.

707
Van Buren Foundation, Inc., The
c/o Farmers State Bank
Keosauqua, IA 52565 (319) 293-3794
Contact: Arthur P. Ovrum, Treasurer

Limitations: Scholarships and student loans limited to graduating seniors living in and attending a Van Buren County, IA, high school.
Financial data: Year ended 12/31/86. Assets, $2,404,755 (M); Total giving, $82,786; Grants to individuals totaling $14,333; Subtotals for scholarships and student loans not specified.
Employer Identification Number: 426062589
Applications: Applications accepted throughout the year; Application forms available from the foundation or high school counselors in Van Buren County; Completion of formal application required.
Program description:
The foundation's student loan program is primarily for the benefit of medical and health care students.

708
Van Wert County Foundation, The
101-1/2 East Main Street
Van Wert, OH 45891 (419) 238-1743
Contact: Robert W. Games, Executive Secretary

Limitations: Scholarships only to residents of Van Wert County, OH.
Financial data: Year ended 12/31/86. Assets, $5,175,598 (M); Total giving, $226,997; Grants to individuals, 104 grants totaling $56,686, high $1,425, low $100.
Employer Identification Number: 340907558
Applications: Deadlines May 25th and November 25th; Initial approach by letter; Completion of formal application required; Interviews required.
Publications: Application guidelines.
Program description:
Approximately 15 new grants are made annually for study leading to an undergraduate degree. Giving emphasizes scholarships for study in art, music, agriculture, and home economics.

709★
Vance (Esther) Music Scholarship Fund
c/o First National Bank of Colorado Springs, Trust Department
P.O. Box 1699
Colorado Springs, CO 80942 (303) 471-5125
Contact: Trustees

Limitations: Music scholarships only to graduating high school seniors in the Colorado Springs, CO, area.

Financial data: Year ended 12/31/86. Assets, $58,319 (M); Total giving, $3,400; Grants to individuals, 3 grants totaling $3,400, high $1,700, low $850.
Employer Identification Number: 237066945
Applications: Deadline May 15th; Completion of formal application, including outline of student's reason for pursuing musical education, and letters of recommendation from student's teacher required; Interviews granted upon request.
Program description:
Scholarships are awarded to three students per year who are majoring in music.

710
Vatra's Educational Foundation, The
c/o Bank of Boston
P.O. Box 1861
Boston, MA 021015
Contact: Peter D. Peterson, Chairman, 517 East Avenue, New York, NY 10017

Limitations: Scholarships only to students of Albanian lineage or descent.
Financial data: Year ended 12/31/85. Assets, $61,176 (M); Total giving, $2,300; Grants to individuals, 51 grants totaling $2,300.
Employer Identification Number: 046011128

711
Vaughn (James M.) Jr. Foundation Fund
c/o MBank - Austin, Trust Department
P.O. Box 2266
Austin, TX 78780

Limitations: Fellowships only to scholars pursuing research or publishing work in the field of mathematical research format conjecture.
Financial data: Year ended 12/31/86. Assets, $3,074,912 (M); Total giving, $386,737; Grants to individuals, 9 grants totaling $87,960 for fellowships, high $15,000, low $1,250.
Employer Identification Number: 237166546
Applications: Applications accepted throughout the year; Completion of formal application through the American Mathematical Association required; Interviews required.

712
Veen (Jan) Educational Trust
c/o Peter B. Seamans, Trustee
Seamans, Peabody and Arnold, One Beacon Street
Boston, MA 02108
Contact: Ruth S. Ambrose, Director, Department of Dance, Boston Conservatory of Music, 8 The Fenway, Boston, MA 02110

Limitations: Scholarships to students studying the Laban Method in the dance department of the Boston Conservatory of Music.

EDUCATIONAL SUPPORT

Financial data: Year ended 12/31/84. Assets, $251,997 (M); Total giving, $16,250; Grants to individuals totaling $16,250.
Employer Identification Number: 046167791
Applications: Applications accepted throughout the year.
Program description:
Scholarship awards are paid directly to the Boston Conservatory of Music on behalf of individual recipients.

713
Viele (Frances S.) Scholarship Trust
626 Wilshire Boulevard, Number 804
Los Angeles, CA 90017   (213) 629-3571
Contact: Stevens Weller, Jr., Manager

Limitations: Scholarships only to members of Sigma Phi Society.
Financial data: Year ended 5/31/87. Assets, $1,818,129 (M); Total giving, $72,000; Grants to individuals, 28 grants totaling $72,000, high $4,000, low $2,500.
Employer Identification Number: 953285561
Applications: Contact foundation for current application deadline; Completion of formal application, including complete financial and academic disclosures, two essays, and transcripts, required.

714
Viles Foundation, Inc.
c/o Sunwest Bank of Albuquerque
P.O. Box 26900
Albuquerque, NM 87125

Limitations: Scholarships limited to needy residents of San Miguel and Mora counties, NM. Funds are very limited.
Financial data: Year ended 12/31/86. Assets, $1,176 (M); Total giving, $48,982; Grants to individuals, 73 grants totaling $48,982, high $1,625, low $83, general range $400-1,000.
Employer Identification Number: 856011506
Applications: Deadline April 1st; Completion of formal application, including references, photograph, and transcripts required; For application information contact the foundation at P.O. Box 1177, Las Vegas, NM 87701. **Applications from individuals residing outside of stated geographic restriction not accepted.**
Program description:
The foundation relies heavily on recommendations received from San Miguel and Mora counties high school guidance counselors for nearly all grants awarded. Grants are made for attendance at colleges, universities, and vocational-technical schools and are renewable. Emphasis is placed on providing benefits to orphaned, fatherless, or motherless girls, although aid is not limited to these groups.

715★
Villa Park Bank Foundation
10 South Villa Avenue
Villa Park, IL 60181   (312) 834-0800
Contact: James R. Volkman, Secretary

Limitations: Scholarships for high school or preparatory school seniors only in foundation's immediate area, with preference given to residents of Villa Park, IL, and the areas juxtaposed to Villa Park.
Financial data: Year ended 12/31/86. Assets, $14,929 (M); Total giving, $12,835; Grants to individuals, 13 grants totaling $7,350, high $800, low $300, average grant $500.
Employer Identification Number: 366198333
Applications: Deadline December 1st; Applications only accepted in September, October, and November each year; Application forms available at Villa Park area high schools or at Villa Park Trust & Savings Bank.
Program description:
The **Carol M. Nelson Scholarship Award Program** awards three new scholarships, designated as the winner, the first alternate, and the second alternate, each year to individuals attending universities and colleges in Illinois and other states. Scholarship money is paid directly to the college or business office. Scholarships are renewable annually, for a maximum of four years, dependent upon recipient maintaining satisfactory grades. The foundation determines the sum received by the winner; the first alternate receives two-thirds of that amount and the second alternate receives one half the sum.

All Scholarship recipients are expected to maintain a satisfactory standing in class; an official report of grades should be sent to the foundation as soon as available. A recipient forced to drop out of school due to illness or for military service may be eligible for re-instatement. Since continuation of the scholarship is at the foundation's discretion, and grades, conduct, and choice of college and curriculum will be considered in the awarding of the scholarship, changes in course of study or in the college attended should be reported to the foundation. The foundation reserves the right to require the forfeiture of this award by a recipient who receives a substantial sum per year as a scholarship award from any other source.

716
Villers Foundation, Inc., The
1334 G Street, N.W.
Washington, DC 20005   (202) 628-3030
Contact: Ronald F. Pollack, Executive Director

Limitations: Grants to individuals for academic research projects concerning areas of importance to the elderly.
Financial data: Year ended 12/31/86. Assets, $16,397,818 (M); Total giving, $1,900,909; Grants to individuals, 4 grants totaling $10,000, each grant

$2,500.
Employer Identification Number: 042730934
Applications: Applications accepted throughout the year.
Publications: Multi-year report.
Program description:
The research reports made possible by the grants awarded will be published as part of the foundation's Health Policy Series on the elderly.

717
Vincent (Anna M.) Trust
c/o Mellon Bank (East)
P.O. Box 7236, Three Mellon Bank Center
Philadelphia, PA 19101-7236   (215) 585-3208
Contact: Pat Kling, Trust Officer, Mellon Bank (East)

Limitations: Scholarships to long-term residents of Delaware Valley, PA, for graduate or undergraduate study at any recognized college, university, or other institution of higher learning.
Financial data: Year ended 6/30/87. Assets, $3,738,177 (M); Total giving, $103,150; Grants to individuals, 90 grants totaling $103,150, high $2,500, low $300, general range $500-1,500.
Employer Identification Number: 236422666
Applications: Deadline March 1st; Initial approach by letter; Completion of formal application required; Application forms available at high schools.
Program description:
Most applicants are seniors in high school. The trust also awards multiple-year grants, renewable for up to five years.

718
Vitramon Foundation, Incorporated
P.O. Box 544
Bridgeport, CT 06601   (203) 268-6261
Contact: Robert Swart, Trustee

Limitations: Scholarships and awards only to high school students in five Connecticut communities: Newtown, Monroe, Trumbull, Shelton, and Easton-Redding.
Financial data: Year ended 12/31/85. Assets, $867,493 (M); Total giving, $26,402; Grants to individuals totaling $16,982; See program description below for subtotal amounts.
Employer Identification Number: 066068987
Applications: Deadline November 1st for project proposal for Barton L. Weller Scholarship Award.
Program description:
The Barton L. Weller Scholarship is available to senior-year students attending one of the following Connecticut high schools: Joel Barlow High School, Masuk High School, Newtown High School, Shelton High School, or Trumbull High School. The award is determined by a regional competition designed to encourage academic excellence in a substantial

independent research or study project of the student's choosing. Sample topics include the fine arts, computer projects, economics, science or engineering, mathematics, or political or environmental factors affecting the immediate geographic area. The scholarship award is for $8,000 ($2,000 in four annual increments). Five finalists are selected by the foundation to become eligible to participate in the project phase, carrying out the proposal submitted. Each finalist receives $100. Awards of $200 each are awarded to four applicants. In 1985, a total of $11,300 was disbursed through the Weller Scholarship.
The **Vincent Voccia Vocational Award** is presented annually to a high school student from Monroe, CT, who has selected a vocational-technical career. In 1985, awards totaled $2,620.
The **Vitramon Senior Science Award** is presented annually in each of the five high schools previously named. The award is presented to honor students in science and business studies and is in the form of shares of stock in Vitramon Inc. The recipients are chosen by the faculties of the named high schools. **Individual applications are not accepted.** In 1985, awards totaled $1,531.
The **Eleanor F. Moore Award** is presented annually in each of the five high schools previously named. The award is presented to honor students in business studies, and is in the form of shares of stock in Vitramon Inc. The recipients are chosen by the faculties of the named high schools. **Individual applications are not accepted.** In 1985, awards totaled $1,531.

719★
Vomberg Foundation, The
1023 Reynolds Road
Charlotte, MI 48813   (517) 543-0430

Limitations: Scholarship program for students who are residents of Eaton County, MI.
Financial data: Year ended 12/31/87. Assets, $558,661 (M); Total giving, $55,858; Grants to individuals, approximately 140 grants totaling $55,858, high $1,000, low $100, general range $100-1,000, average grant $400.
Employer Identification Number: 386072845
Applications: Deadline December 1st of senior year; Completion of formal application required; Interviews required.
Publications: Program information.
Program description:
The scholarship program is open to high school seniors of good academic standing who can demonstrate financial need. Any awards outside the Eaton County, MI, area are made at the foundation's sole discretion.

720
Wacker Foundation
10848 Strait Lane
Dallas, TX 75229   (214) 373-3308
Contact: John A. Wacker

Limitations: Research grants pertaining to the
neurophysiological aspect of learning and behavior
disorders.
Financial data: Year ended 6/30/87. Assets, $519,835
(M); Total giving, $44,000; Grants to individuals, 4
grants totaling $44,000, high $14,500, low $5,000.
Employer Identification Number: 237412635
Applications: Applications accepted throughout the
year; Initial approach by letter, including proposal and
budget.
Publications: Annual report.

721
Wagnalls Memorial, The
150 East Columbus Street
Lithopolis, OH 43136   (614) 837-4765
Contact: Jerry W. Neff, Executive Director

Limitations: Scholarships and fellowships only to
graduates of high schools in Bloom Township, OH.
Financial data: Year ended 8/31/86. Assets,
$11,262,119 (M); Total giving, $265,408; Grants to
individuals, 228 grants totaling $210,215, high
$3,000, low $167.
Employer Identification Number: 314379589
Applications: Deadline June 15th; Initial approach by
letter requesting application; Completion of formal
application required.

722
Wagner (Edward) and George Hosser
  Scholarship Fund Trust
c/o Amoskeag Bank
P.O. Box 150
Manchester, NH 03105   (603) 624-3614
Contact: Pamela D. Mallett, Trust Officer, Amoskeag
Bank

Limitations: Scholarships only to male residents of
Manchester, NH.
Financial data: Year ended 6/30/86. Assets,
$1,960,822 (M); Total giving, $156,000; Grants to
individuals, 168 grants totaling $156,000, high
$2,000, low $500, general range $1,000-1,500.
Employer Identification Number: 026005491
Applications: Deadline April 30th; Completion of
formal application required.

723
Wagner (R.H.) Foundation, Ltd.
441 Milwaukee Avenue
Burlington, WI 53105
Contact: Paul B. Edwards, Trustee

Limitations: Scholarships for individuals interested in
aviation schooling.
Financial data: Year ended 6/30/87. Assets,
$3,107,850 (M); Total giving, $70,392; Grants to
individuals, 4 grants totaling $65,199, high $63,435,
low $400.
Employer Identification Number: 391311452
Applications: Applications accepted throughout the
year; Initial approach by typewritten letter detailing
relationship to aviation.
Program description:
Scholarship payments are made directly to the aviation
school.

724
Walker (W.E.) Foundation
P.O. Box 9407
Jackson, MS 39206   (601) 362-9895
Contact: Mary Morris

Limitations: Scholarships only to local residents
attending graduate school, with a focus on theology
and human service.
Financial data: Year ended 12/31/86. Assets,
$11,136,556 (M); Total giving, $969,768; Grants to
individuals, 9 grants totaling $19,438, high $6,000,
low $500.
Employer Identification Number: 237279902
Applications: Applications accepted throughout the
year; Completion of formal application required.

725
Warman (Marion W.) Irrevocable Scholarship
  Fund
c/o Gordon W.H. Buzza, Jr.
P.O. Box 1029
Presque Isle, ME 04769   (207) 769-2211

Limitations: Scholarships only to graduates of schools
in Aroostook County, ME.
Financial data: Year ended 12/31/84. Assets, $1,536
(M); Total giving, $19,683; Grants to individuals, 28
grants totaling $19,683, high $2,000, low $250,
general range $750-1,625.
Employer Identification Number: 016040382
Applications: Deadline May 10th.

726
Warner (Mary Ellen) Educational Trust
1040 South Orange Grove Boulevard, No. 4
Pasadena, CA 91105
Contact: T. L. Stromberger, Trustee

Limitations: Loans to upper division or graduate students who are residents of and are attending fully accredited colleges or universities in California.
Financial data: Year ended 10/31/87. Assets, $240,966 (M); Expenditures, $21,542; Loans to individuals, 4 loans totaling $13,200, high $5,000, low $1,200.
Employer Identification Number: 956037882
Applications: Applications accepted throughout the year; Initial approach by letter explaining reason for loan request; Completion of formal application required; Interview in southern California required.
Program description:
Loans only to students whom the trustees deem "needy and deserving." Repayment must begin not more than 30 months from date of loan, at approximately five percent of value of loan, per month. The trust makes no awards for scholarships or grants.

727
Warren Benevolent Fund, Inc.
P.O. Box 46
Ashland, MA 01721   (617) 881-2077
Contact: Mrs. Ann Thurston, Treasurer

Limitations: Scholarships and student loans only to graduates of Ashland High School, Ashland, MA.
Financial data: Year ended 12/31/85. Assets, $568,537 (M); Expenditures, $57,353; Grants to individuals, 2 grants totaling $10,000; Loans to individuals totaling $72,275.
Employer Identification Number: 042309470
Applications: Initial approach by letter. **Applications from individuals who are not graduates of the specified educational institution not accepted.**

728
Warren Foundation, The
c/o Warren National Bank
P.O. Drawer 69
Warren, PA 16365
Contact: Holger N. Elmquist, Director

Limitations: Scholarships only to residents of Warren County, PA.
Financial data: Year ended 12/31/84. Assets, $4,394,000 (M); Total giving, $388,789; Grants to individuals amount not specified.
Employer Identification Number: 256020340

729
Washington (George) Foundation
3012 Tieton Drive
Yakima, WA 98902   (509) 457-4827
Contact: Leslie Tripp, Secretary-Treasurer

Limitations: Scholarships for undergraduate study to local high school graduating seniors, primarily to attend community colleges.
Financial data: Year ended 6/30/87. Assets, $1,095,566 (M); Total giving, $90,910; Grants to individuals totaling $90,910.
Employer Identification Number: 916024141
Applications: Deadline April 1st; Completion of formal application required; Interviews required; Applications available from local public high school principals or counselors; See program description below for complete application information.
Program description:
Scholarships are generally paid to community colleges located primarily in Washington on behalf of specific students, and a large percentage of scholarships are awarded for use at Yakima Valley College. However, the foundation places no restrictions on awards as to geographical areas, and scholarships have been awarded to institutions nationwide.
  Applications will consist of:
    1. Student's personal and family data sheet
    2. An unmounted photograph of student
    3. Letter of recommendation from a selected reference, preferably not one of the school staff
    4. Personal letter from the student, covering information not covered elsewhere in the application
    5. Confidential form covering the family's financial information
    6. High school principal's data sheet
    7. Transcript of the student's high school grades.
  The board of trustees of the foundation selects recipients on the basis of need for financial assistance, academic standing, and on those personal qualities such as leadership, emotional stability, use of time and energy, initiative, citizenship, chance of success in college, and primary interests. The student should be in the upper twenty percent of his/her class. However, this last requirement might be waived in case of financial difficulty at home, such as widowed mother, illness of father, or large number of children in the family. This waiver is made for the purpose of improving the student's earning ability through further education, thereby assisting in the well-being of his/her family.

730
Wasserman (The David) Scholarship Fund, Inc.
107 Division Street
Amsterdam, NY 12010   (518) 843-2800
Contact: Norbert J. Sherbunt, President

Limitations: Scholarships only to residents of
Montgomery County, NY.
Financial data: Year ended 4/30/86. Assets, $190 (M);
Total giving, $19,350; Grants to individuals, 124
grants totaling $19,350, high $300, low $150, average
grant $150.
Employer Identification Number: 146030183
Applications: Completion of formal application
required; Requests for applications accepted up to
April 15th.
Program description:
Approximately 15-20 new undergraduate scholarships
of $150 per semester are awarded annually.

731
Watertown Foundation, Inc.
120 Washington Street
P.O. Box 6106
Watertown, NY 13601   (315) 782-7110
Contact: James E. McVean, Executive Director

Limitations: Scholarships only to legal residents of
Watertown and Jefferson County, NY, who are
enrolled as full-time undergraduate students at
accredited institutions located within the continental
U.S.
Financial data: Year ended 2/28/85. Assets,
$1,376,051 (M); Total giving, $588,638; Grants to
individuals totaling $201,367.
Employer Identification Number: 156020989
Applications: Deadline April 1st; Applications may be
obtained after March 1st from the foundation office, at
the guidance offices of Jefferson County high schools
and at the financial aid office of certain colleges in the
region; Initial approach by letter, telephone, or office
visit; Completion of formal application required.
Publications: Annual report.
Program description:
The foundation administers three scholarship
programs: **The Herring College Scholars Program**
provides scholarships to students enrolled in
engineering, technology, certain fields of science and
related fields of study; the **Visiting Nurse Association
Program** provides scholarships to students enrolled in
health science fields; the **Watertown Foundation
Scholarship Program** provides scholarships to students
enrolled in all academic disciplines except theology.

First time recipients are selected at the freshman and
junior class levels only. To be eligible for
consideration a freshman must rank in the top ten
percent of his or her high school class and/or carry an
overall average of at least 90 percent. College juniors
must have a cumulative average of not less than 3.0
on a 4.0 base for their first two years. Selection is

made by the Scholarship Selection Committee on the
basis of a variety of background data in addition to
grades and ranking. For freshman, these include results
of Regents examinations and standardized tests. For all
candidates, the nature of the academic background,
the extent of co-curricular and community activities,
and work record may be factors in the final selection.

While selection is independent of financial need,
the amount of the grant is dependent upon several
factors, including the level of unmet financial need as
confirmed by applicant's college. The foundation must
receive a financial aid summary from the college prior
to the final selection on or about July 1st in order for
an award above the minimum level. Other factors
include the scholarship program for which applicant
has been selected and applicant's class level and
G.P.A.

Scholarships are normally granted through
completion of the program for which it is approved,
providing student maintains academic requirements.
Grants are issued directly to recipient's college.

732
Watson (Clara Stewart) Foundation
c/o InterFirst Bank - Dallas, N.A.
P.O. Box 83791
Dallas, TX 75283   (214) 573-4628
Contact: Jane Wolfe

Limitations: Loans to graduates of high schools in
Dallas and Tarrant counties, TX, for undergraduate
education in colleges and universities in Texas.
Financial data: Year ended 8/31/86. Assets, $755,101
(M); Expenditures, $22,575; Loans to individuals, 11
loans totaling $16,500, each loan $1,500.
Employer Identification Number: 756064730
Applications: Deadline March 31st; Completion of
formal application required.
Program description:
Applicants must be of good moral character, have
above average grades, need financial assistance to
attend college and seriously intend to pursue and
complete an academic or technical education. The
terms of the student loan program are:
    1. The maximum amount for each loan is $1,500
    per academic year
    2. Interest rate is three percent
    3. Loans are to be co-signed by applicant's parent
    or guardian
    4. The term of the loan shall be five years,
    payable in monthly installments beginning ten
    months after graduation.
Successive loans, for a maximum of four years, are
available to recipients who exhibit satisfactory college
performance.

733
Watson (John W. and Rose E.) Foundation
c/o Second National Bank of Saginaw
101 North Washington Avenue
Saginaw, MI 48607
Contact: Rose Watson, 1551 Avalon, Saginaw, MI
48603; Tel.: (517) 792-2301.

Limitations: Scholarships only to Saginaw, MI,
residents graduating from Catholic high schools.
Financial data: Year ended 12/31/86. Assets, $956,114
(M); Total giving, $72,600; Grants to individuals
totaling $60,600.
Employer Identification Number: 386091611
Applications: Deadline one month prior to academic
year; Completion of formal application required;
Interviews requested.

734
Watterson (Grace Margaret) Trust
c/o First Union National Bank of Florida
444 Seabreeze Boulevard
Daytona Beach, FL 32018   (904) 252-5591
Contact: Mrs. June Phelps, Trust Officer, First Union
National Bank of Florida

Limitations: Higher education scholarships for high
school seniors in the U.S. and Canada.
Financial data: Year ended 2/28/87. Assets,
$1,791,122 (M); Total giving, $121,413, high $4,000,
low $82.
Employer Identification Number: 596807104
Applications: Deadline December 31st; Completion of
formal application required.

735
Waverly Community Foundation
State Bank of Waverly
Waverly, IA 50677
Contact: Arnold A. Frederick, Senior Trust Officer

Limitations: Scholarships primarily for residents of
Waverly, IA.
Financial data: Year ended 12/31/86. Assets,
$1,562,603 (M); Total giving, $97,550; Grants to
individuals totaling $46,450.
Employer Identification Number: 426058774

736
Weber (Jacques) Foundation, Inc.
1460 Broadway
New York, NY 10036
Contact: Dr. Martin A. Satz, Chairman, Scholarship
Committee, Jacques Weber Foundation, Inc., P.O. Box
420, Bloomsburg, PA 17815; Tel.: (717) 784-7701

Limitations: Scholarships primarily to residents within
a 70-mile radius of Bloomsburg, PA, for textile studies
only. Scholarships also to residents of Abbeville, SC,
and surrounding communities.
Financial data: Year ended 9/30/86. Assets,
$1,149,281 (M); Total giving, $80,702; Grants to
individuals, 26 grants totaling $72,202, high $9,340,
low $845, general range $1,648-3,926.
Employer Identification Number: 136101161
Applications: Applications accepted from August or
September until November 30th; Completion of formal
application required; Interviews required.
Program description:
Awards of full four-year scholarships are based on
financial need and performance in a textile-related
curriculum. The foundation considers the following
factors: high school record, S.A.T. scores, interest in
textiles, performance in competitive exam conducted
by the foundation, and financial need.
  Scholarship recipients must enter a textile
curriculum at one of the acknowledged textile
schools: Philadelphia College of Textiles and Science,
North Carolina State University, Clemson University,
Georgia Institute of Technology, and others.
Occasionally, if not enough students qualify,
scholarships have been awarded to students
recommended by Deans of the Textile Schools.
Amounts vary according to financial need and income
available. Approximately five new awards are
available each year.

737
Webermeier (William) Scholarship Trust
c/o National Bank of Commerce
13th and "O" Streets
Lincoln, NE 68508
Contact: Superintendent of Schools, Milford, NE

Limitations: Scholarships only to graduates of Milford
High School, Milford, NE.
Financial data: Year ended 9/30/86. Assets, $302,804
(M); Total giving, $18,373; Grants to individuals, 51
grants totaling $18,373, high $398, low $321.
Employer Identification Number: 476062610
Applications: Contact superintendent of Milford
School District for current application deadlines,
requirements, and restrictions.

738
Webster (Eleanor M.) Testamentary Trust
c/o AmeriTrust Company, N.A.
P.O. Box 5937
Cleveland, OH 44101
Contact: Steven N. More, AmeriTrust Company, 237
Tuscarawas Street West, Canton, OH 44702

Limitations: Scholarships and loans only to students
who have completed at least one year of study at an
Ohio college or university. Preference given to
residents of Stark County, OH.
Financial data: Year ended 6/30/87. Assets, $102,655
(M); Expenditures, $6,489; Grants to individuals, 8

grants totaling $2,800, each grant $350; Loans to individuals, 8 loans totaling $2,400, each loan $300.
Employer Identification Number: 346572997
Applications: Applications accepted throughout the year; Initial approach by letter requesting grant and loan applications; Completion of formal application required.

739
Wedum Foundation
4721 Spring Circle
Minnetonka, MN 55345
Contact: P.O. Box 644, Alexandria, MN 56308

Limitations: Student aid primarily to residents of the Alexandria, MN, area.
Financial data: Year ended 12/31/86. Assets, $5,133,495 (M); Total giving, $156,665; Grants to individuals, 55 grants totaling $13,215, high $1,200, low $75.
Employer Identification Number: 416025661
Applications: Applications accepted throughout the year including resume of academic qualifications.

740★
Weill (Kurt) Foundation for Music, Inc.
Seven East 20th Street
New York, NY 10003-1106   (212) 260-1650
Contact: David Farneth, Director

Limitations: Grants to individuals for projects "intended to promote greater understanding of the artistic legacies of Kurt Weill or Lotte Lenya." Support includes publication assistance, dissertation fellowships, and grants for research, travel, performances, and recording projects.
Financial data: Year ended 12/31/85. Assets, $1,442,389 (M); Total giving, $25,950; Grants to individuals, 3 grants totaling $11,100, high $8,000, low $1,100.
Employer Identification Number: 136139518
Applications: Deadline November 1st; Initial approach by letter, before September 15th, describing the project, a resume or a profile of purposes, activities, and past achievements, and a detailed and itemized budget showing entire project expenses, including income, and other projected funding sources; Completion of formal application required.
Publications: Application guidelines, informational brochure, newsletter.
Program description:
The Advisory Panel on Grant Applications, composed of independent, prominent members from the musical, theatrical, and scholarly communities, will base their selection on the following criteria:
  • Relevance and value of the project to the foundation's purposes
  • Quality of the project
  • Evidence of the applicant's potential,

motivation, and ability to carry-out the project successfully
  • Evidence of the applicant's prior record of achievement in the field covered by the project. Applicants will be informed of awards by February 1st.
The foundation will provide support in the following categories:
  1. **Research and Travel Grants** - Applicants must be pursuing a topic directly related to Kurt Weill and/or Lotte Lenya and must submit a detailed outline of the proposed project.
  2. **Publication Assistance** - Funding may be requested to assist in expenses related to preparing manuscripts for publication in a recognized scholarly medium.
  3. **Dissertation Fellowships** - The application must include a copy of the dessertation proposal and two letters of recommendation, one of which is from the faculty advisor.
  4. **Performance Grants** - Proposals should demonstrate that requested funds will be used to improve the musical qualities of the performance. There is no restriction on the amount requested.
  5. **Recording Projects** - Proposals requesting funds for artist and musician fees, rehearsal expenses, and mastertape production expenses will be eligible.

741
Welch (George T.) Testamentary Trust
c/o Baker-Boyer National Bank
P.O. Box 1796
Walla Walla, WA 99362   (509) 252-2000
Contact: Bettie Loiacono, Trust Officer

Limitations: Scholarships for any three undergraduate years to unmarried needy students who are residents of Walla Walla County, WA, and enrolled in four-year colleges.
Financial data: Year ended 9/30/86. Assets, $2,516,675 (M); Total giving, $116,871; Grants to individuals, 265 grants totaling $101,598; Subtotal for scholarships, 95 grants totaling $75,428, high $1,700, low $150.
Employer Identification Number: 916024318
Applications: Deadline May 1st; Completion of formal application required; Forms available by January 1st; Interviews required.

742★
Welch (The Robert A.) Foundation
4605 Post Oak Place, Suite 200
Houston, TX 77027   (713) 961-9884
Contact: Norbert Dittrich, Executive Manager

Limitations: Grants to full-time faculty members of Texas educational institutions to do research in basic chemistry.

Financial data: Year ended 8/31/87. Assets, $259,179,000 (M); Total giving, $11,921,000; Grants to individuals, 376 grants totaling $11,921,000; Subtotal for research grants, $11,696,000, high $60,000, low $25,000, general range $20,000-30,000.
Employer Identification Number: 741216248
Applications: Deadline February 1st; Initial approach by telephone; Completion of formal application required; Interviews required.
Publications: Annual report, application guidelines, newsletter, program information.
Program description:
The general policy of the program is to support long-range fundamental research in the broad domain of basic chemistry within the state of Texas.

Funds may be requested for stipends, postdoctoral fellowships, graduate fellowships, undergraduate scholarships, scientific equipment, services and maintenance, publication expenses, and travel as related to research in chemistry.

743
Weller Foundation, Inc.
East Highway 20
P.O. Box 636
Atkinson, NE 68713   (402) 925-2803

Limitations: Scholarships only to residents of Nebraska attending one of the Technical Community Colleges in Nebraska or other vocational education institutions in fields such as nursing. Primary consideration for residents of Boyd, Brown, Garfield, Holt, Keya Paha, and Rock counties.
Financial data: Year ended 10/31/86. Assets, $3,494,060 (M); Total giving, $171,450; Grants to individuals, 239 grants totaling $171,450, high $1,250, low $250.
Employer Identification Number: 470611350
Applications: Deadlines June 1st for fall semester and November 1st for spring semester; Completion of formal application required.
Publications: Application guidelines.
Program description:
No grants for scholarships for education towards a Bachelor's degree.

744
Wellons Foundation, Inc.
P.O. Box 1254
Dunn, NC 28334   (919) 892-3123
Contact: John H. Wellons, Sr., President

Limitations: Student loans for higher education.
Financial data: Year ended 12/31/86. Assets, $1,780,168 (M); Expenditures, $194,375; Loans to individuals totaling, $35,192.
Employer Identification Number: 566061476

Applications: Applications accepted throughout the year; Completion of formal application required.

745
Wells (Fred W.) Trust Fund
Bank of New England-West, Trust Department
One Federal Street
Greenfield, MA 01301   (413) 772-0281
Contact: Christopher S. Maniatty, Vice-President

Limitations: Scholarships to residents of Greenfield, Deerfield, Shelburne, Ashfield, Montague, Buckland, Charlemont, Heath, Leyden, Gill, Northfield, Conway, Bernardston, Hawley, Rowe, and Monroe, MA.
Financial data: Year ended 6/30/86. Assets, $2,486,637 (M); Total giving, $125,396; Grants to individuals totaling $87,950, high $1,000, low $250.
Employer Identification Number: 046412350
Applications: Deadline May 1st; Initial approach by letter; Completion of formal application required.
Publications: Application guidelines.
Program description:
Scholarships are awarded to residents of towns in Franklin County, MA, for up to $1,000 per year to a $4,000 total.

746
Wenner-Gren Foundation for Anthropological Research, Incorporated
1865 Broadway
New York, NY 10023-7596   (212) 957-8750
Contact: Mrs. Lisa Osmundsen, President

Limitations: Fellowships and research grants to anthropology scholars, anywhere in the world, affiliated with accredited institutions or organizations.
Financial data: Year ended 12/31/85. Assets, $41,331,953 (M); Total giving, $1,065,300; Grants to individuals, 120 grants totaling $499,853.
Employer Identification Number: 131813827
Applications: Contact foundation for current application deadlines; Initial approach by letter; Completion of formal application required.
Publications: Biennial report, program information.
Program description:
Grants-in-aid are awarded in support of projects in all branches of anthropology and related disciplines pertaining to the sciences of man and may use cross-cultural, historical, biological, and linguistic approaches to understanding man's origins, development, and variation. The **Small Grants Program** makes awards in the range of $500-7,000 to accredited scholars and to students enrolled for an advanced degree for basic research expenses. A small percentage of awards is available for feasibility studies, study trips and small conferences or workshops. Small grants are geared to seeding innovative or untried approaches and ideas, and provide material support to encourage aid from other funding agencies. The

foundation generally gives low priority to filmmaking and to publication subvention, unless resulting from research or conferences previously carried out under the auspices of the foundation.

Included in the **Small Grants Program** are the **Regular Grants Program**, the **Richard Carley Hunt Memorial Postdoctoral Fellowships**, and **Student Grants. Regular Grants** are awarded to individual scholars from anywhere in the world who are affiliated with an accredited institution or organization.

Richard Carley Hunt Memorial Postdoctoral Fellowships are non-renewable awards carrying a maximum stipend of $4,000 to aid younger scholars with the completion of specific studies or in the preparation of field materials.

Student Grants are awarded to individuals at the advanced predoctoral level. Application must be made jointly with an involved senior scholar who will undertake complete responsibility for the project's supervision on both substantive and financial levels. Anyone enrolled in a degree program at the time of application must be considered by the foundation to be in the student category. Whenever possible, student applicants from North America, Western Europe and Japan should demonstrate the availability of matching funds. However, any worthy project will be taken under consideration despite lack of such funds, regardless of the citizenship of the applicant.

Postdoctoral Fellowships are awards of up to $15,000 which are available to recent Ph.D.s in the anthropological sciences for the purpose of training in a related field or fields outside anthropology. No more than two fellowships are awarded annually. Formal enrollment or association with a non-anthropological department or research laboratory is required. The program of study must be designed to broaden interdisciplinary skills relevant to a particular problem or project within the candidate's area of specialization. **Postdoctoral Fellowships** are not designed to support fieldwork. Application materials are mailed on request.

Developing Country Fellowships are available to qualified scholars or students from developing countries. No more than three fellowships (up to $12,500 each) are awarded annually. These fellowships are designed primarily to support younger scholars who need training unavailable in their home country and who cannot meet the cost of such training elsewhere. Additional information and application materials are mailed on request. Only students/ scholars from developing countries are eligible for these fellowships. Excluded from consideration are applicants from Abu-Dhabi, Australia, Bahrain, Brunei, Canada, Hong Kong, Israel, Japan, Kuwait, Libya, New Caledonia, New Zealand, Puerto Rico, Qatar, Saudi Arabia, U.S.S.R., United Arab Emirates, U.S.A., and Western Europe.

Senior Scholar Research Stipends of up to $10,000 are available each year to a maximum of three senior scholars who have established records of research and publication. The stipends provide support for writing and study integrating the scholar's past research with his/her current interests. Priority consideration will be given to retired scholars, to those about to retire, or to those who have no facilities at the time of application. Application materials are mailed on request.

Applicants to the **Small Grants Program** are required to submit project description forms, which are available on request. Project description forms will be accepted only in accordance with the current deadline schedule. Applicants in other categories may submit a brief description of the proposed project, including anticipated starting date and required funding.

If a project is considered eligible, a formal application will be invited and the appropriate forms and guidelines supplied. Copies or facsimiles of project description forms or application forms will not be accepted. It is not necessary to present an application by means of a personal interview. Applications will be accepted only in accordance with the current deadline schedule.

747★
West (Merle S. & Emma J.) Scholarship Fund
U.S. National Bank of Oregon
P.O. Box 3168
Portland, OR 97208

Limitations: Scholarships to high school graduates residing in Klamath County, OR.
Financial data: Year ended 12/31/87. Assets, $3,600,000 (M); Grants to individuals, 185 grants totaling $203,518, high $2,207, low $300, general range $500-1,350, average grant $1,100.
Employer Identification Number: 936160221
Applications: Completion of formal application required; Interviews required; For application information contact Francis S. Landrum, Chairman, West Scholarship Committee, 740 Main Street, Klamath Falls, OR 97601; Tel.: (503) 883-4651.
Publications: Application guidelines, informational brochure, 990-PF printed copy available upon request.

748
West (W.F. and Blanche E.) Educational Fund
c/o First Interstate Bank of Washington, Trust Department
473 North Market Boulevard, P.O. Box 180
Chehalis, WA 98532

Limitations: Scholarships to graduates of W.F. West High School, Chehalis, WA, who have lived in Lewis County, WA, at least two years.
Financial data: Year ended 12/31/85. Assets, $1,844,737 (M); Total giving, $121,872; Grants to individuals, 66 grants totaling $121,872.
Employer Identification Number: 916101769
Applications: Deadline April 15th; Completion of formal application required; Interviews required;

Application forms available at school.
Program description:
Grants are paid to the college or institution attended by the grantee.

749
Westend Foundation, Inc.
c/o American National Bank and Trust Company
736 Market Street
Chattanooga, TN 37402   (615) 265-8881
Contact: Raymond B. Witt, Jr., Secretary

Limitations: Scholarships and grants generally to Chattanooga, TN, area residents.
Financial data: Year ended 12/31/86. Assets, $3,014,889 (M); Total giving, $162,966; Grants to individuals, 56 grants totaling $71,000, high $5,000, low $500, general range $1,000-2,500.
Employer Identification Number: 626041060
Applications: Applications accepted throughout the year; Completion of formal application required; Interviews may be required.
Program description:
Scholarships for higher education are awarded for study at colleges, universities, technical schools, and medical schools. Secondary school scholarships are awarded to students attending preparatory schools in Chattanooga, TN. Grants are awarded to educational institutions for designated students.

750
Westlake (James L. & Nellie M.) Scholarship Fund
c/o Mercantile Trust Company
P.O. Box 387
St. Louis, MO 63166   (314) 725-6410
Contact: Local high school counselor or the foundation at 111 South Bemiston, Suite 412, Clayton, MO 63105

Limitations: Scholarships only to high school seniors who are residents of Missouri.
Financial data: Year ended 9/30/85. Assets, $11,114,026 (M); Total giving, $861,400; Grants to individuals, 248 grants totaling $861,400, high $3,000, low $500, average grant $1,150.
Employer Identification Number: 436248269
Applications: Deadline March 1st; Initial approach by letter requesting application; Completion of formal application required.
Publications: Informational brochure (including application guidelines), program information, newsletter.

751★
Westport-Weston Foundation, The
c/o The Westport Bank & Trust Company
P.O. Box 5177
Westport, CT 06881   (203) 222-6938
Contact: Susanne M. Allen, Trust Officer

Limitations: Undergraduate scholarships and limited graduate loans only to needy residents of Westport or Weston, CT.
Financial data: Year ended 12/31/85. Assets, $736,267 (M); Total giving, $52,349; Grants to individuals, 33 grants totaling $19,871; Subtotal for scholarships and educational loans, 15 grants or loans totaling $16,300, high $1,200, low $500.
Employer Identification Number: 066035931
Applications: Applications accepted throughout the year; Initial approach by letter; Completion of formal application required; Interviews sometimes required.

752★
Wetherbee (Harold and Sara) Foundation
c/o First State Bank & Trust Company
P.O. Box 8
Albany, GA 31703
Contact: Joe Powell, Trust Officer

Limitations: Scholarships to residents of Dougherty County, GA.
Financial data: Year ended 11/30/86. Assets, $122,205 (M); Total giving, $7,000; Grants to individuals, 10 grants totaling $7,000, high $1,000, low $500.
Employer Identification Number: 586068645
Applications: Applications accepted throughout the year; Interviews required. Applications for grants are submitted through the superintendent's office of the Dougherty County School System, which obtains the applications from principals and counselors of high schools in the system.
Program description:
Grants are made on the basis of high grades, outstanding extracurricular activities, and demonstrated financial need.

753★
Wheelwright Scientific School
c/o Chase & Lunt
47 State Street
Newburyport, MA 01950   (617) 462-4434
Contact: Josiah H. Welch, President

Limitations: Scholarships to Protestant young men who are residents of Newburyport, MA, and are pursuing education in the sciences.
Financial data: Year ended 6/30/84. Assets, $1,562,985 (M); Total giving, $66,500; Grants to individuals, 19 grants totaling $66,500, high $4,000, low $2,000, general range $2,000-4,000, average grant $4,000.
Employer Identification Number: 046004390

Applications: Deadline date is published in the Newburyport Daily News in February each year; Completion of formal application required; Continuing students must reapply.

754
White (Eleanor) Trust
c/o Richard S. Smith, Trustee
P.O. Box 147
Rutland, VT 05701

Limitations: Scholarships only to residents of Fair Haven, VT.
Financial data: Year ended 12/31/86. Assets, $387,256 (M); Total giving, $45,760; Grants to individuals, 23 grants totaling $45,760, high $4,000, low $250, general range $1,000-2,000.
Employer Identification Number: 036004915
Applications: Deadline July 31st; Completion of formal application required; Interviews granted upon request.
Publications: Annual report.
Program description:
Scholarships have been awarded to cover the expenses of tuition, room and board, and books at colleges and technical and normal schools in the U.S. Payments are made to the institution.

755★
Whitehall Foundation, Inc.
249 Royal Palm Way, Suite 202
Palm Beach, FL 33480   (407) 655-4474
Contact: Laurel T. Baker, Secretary

Limitations: Research grants in the life sciences, with emphasis on behavioral neuroscience, invertebrate neurophysiology, and ethology. Applicants must hold a Ph.D. and be affiliated with an accredited university or research institution. Also, grants-in-aid for young Ph.D. investigators in the life sciences.
Financial data: Year ended 9/30/87. Assets, $34,896,000 (M); Total giving, $1,839,510; Grants to individuals, 70 grants totaling $176,500, high $49,583, low $4,369.
Employer Identification Number: 135637595
Applications: Deadlines March 1st, September 1st and December 1st for research grants, and January 1st, June 1st, and October 1st for grants-in-aid; Initial approach by letter, including a brief description, in lay terms, of project, and a summary budget; Completion of formal application required; Send letter to Whitehall Foundation, Inc., P.O. Box 3225, Palm Beach, FL 33480.
Publications: Program information, application guidelines, informational brochure.
Program description:
Support is provided for the following areas of fundamental biological research:
 ● Invertebrate Neurophysiology

 ● Behavioral Neuroscience
 ● Ethology
Preference will be given to those projects that are innovative and imaginative.
 Research Grants are available to scientists of all ages. Applications will be judged on the scientific merit of the proposal and evidence of the competence of the applicant. A grant will be for a period of three years. One two-year renewal may be allowed but is not automatic. Applications will not be accepted from investigators who already have, or expect to receive, substantial support from other quarters even though the support may be from an unrelated project.
 Research grants will normally be in the range of $10,000 to $40,000 per annum. Funds may not be used for purchase of major items of permanent equipment, travel, unless it is to unique field areas essential to the research, replacement of salary, living expenses while working at home, travel to conferences or for consultation, or secretarial services. All grants are made to the sponsoring institution.
 Grants-in-aid are designed especially for young investigators who have not yet established themselves and who, for this reason, experience difficulty in competing for funds.
 Criteria upon which applications will be judged include an abstract of the doctoral dissertation, published reprints if available, and letters of recommendation from three experts in the specified field.
 Grants-in-aid will also be made to very senior scientists. In addition to scientific merit, the major criterion upon which these applications will be judged will be past performance and evidence of continued productivity.
 Grants-in-aid will be made for a period of one year and are not renewable. The stipend will not exceed $10,000 per annum. Funds are not offered for replacement of salary or summer salary; living expenses while working at home; travel to conferences or for consultation; or secretarial services.

756★
Whiteley (The John and Elizabeth) Foundation
c/o First of America Bank-Central
101 South Washington Square
Lansing, MI 48933   (517) 374-5436
Contact: Joseph A. Caruso

Limitations: Scholarships to needy and deserving students whose parents live in Ingham County, MI, and who are studying business education or Episcopal theology.
Financial data: Year ended 2/31/86. Assets, $1,785,604 (M); Total giving, $87,456; Grants to individuals, 11 grants totaling $10,966.
Employer Identification Number: 381558108
Applications: Applications accepted throughout the year; Completion of formal application required.
Publications: Annual report.

Program description:
Scholarships are primarily to Lansing Community College but not limited to it. At least one theological scholarship is given each year, sometimes more.

757
Whiteside (Robert B. and Sophia) Scholarship Fund

c/o First Bank Duluth
130 West Superior Street
Duluth, MN 55801   (218) 723-2888
Contact: C.F. Baker

Limitations: Scholarships only to graduates of Duluth, MN, high schools.
Financial data: Year ended 12/31/86. Assets, $2,586,045; (M); Total giving, $598,750; Grants to individuals, 234 grants totaling $598,750, high $4,800, low $400.
Employer Identification Number: 411288761
Applications: Applications accepted throughout the year; Completion of formal application required; Forms available from local high school counselors.
Program description:
Scholarships awarded to students in the top ten percent of graduating classes in Duluth. Applicants are interviewed and selected by a scholarship committee in the spring of their senior year.

Students selecting local colleges receive $1,200 annually, out-of-town colleges $3,600 annually. Student must maintain a 3.0 grade point average to be renewed.

758
Whitney Benefits, Inc.

P.O. Box 691
Sheridan, WY 82801   (307) 674-7303
Contact: Jack R. Hufford, Secretary-Treasurer

Limitations: Interest-free student loans only to graduates of Sheridan County, WY, high schools for baccalaureate degrees.
Financial data: Year ended 12/31/86. Assets, $8,039,708 (M); Expenditures, $188,634; Loans to individuals, 46 loans totaling $116,218.
Employer Identification Number: 830168511
Applications: Submit application preferably between March and June; Initial approach by letter or telephone; Completion of formal application required; Interviews required.
Publications: Annual report.

759
Whitney (The Helen Hay) Foundation

450 East 63rd Street
New York, NY 10021   (212) 751-8228
Contact: Barbara M. Hugonnet, Administrative Director

Limitations: Fellowships to scientists under 35 years of age in North America planning a career in biological or medical research and having recently earned an M.D., Ph.D., or equivalent degree. Selection of a commercial or industrial laboratory for the training experience is not acceptable. U.S. citizenship not required, but applications are not accepted from individuals outside the U.S.
Financial data: Year ended 6/30/86. Assets, $26,903,469 (M); Total giving, $1,008,528; Grants to individuals, 71 grants totaling $1,008,528, high $19,930, low $3,837, general range $5,000-18,000.
Employer Identification Number: 131677403
Applications: Deadline August 15th; Initial approach by letter or telephone; Completion of formal application with six additional copies required; Interviews required of finalists.
Publications: Annual report, program information.
Program description:
Postdoctoral research fellowships are given for early postdoctoral research in basic biomedical sciences.

The fellowship is normally awarded for three years and carries a stipend of $16,000 for the first year, $17,000 for the second year, and $18,000 for the third year, plus $1,000 per year, to the university or research laboratory which administers the grant. Emphasis is on broadening training and experience; the foundation will not consider established scientists or those who plan to tenure in the same laboratory in which postdoctoral training was received. The fellowships begin July 1st.

760
Wilcox-Ware Scholarship Trust

c/o Shawmut Trust, Division 6-15
P.O. Box 2032
Worchester, MA 01613-2032   (413) 625-2516
Contact: Mohawk Regional High School, Achfield Star Route, Shelburne Falls, MA 01370

Limitations: Scholarships to graduates of Mohawk Regional High School and to residents of Buckland, Colrain, or Shelburne, MA.
Financial data: Year ended 12/31/85. Assets, $305,299 (M); Total giving $27,703; Grants to individuals, 73 grants totaling $27,703, high $800, low $54.
Employer Identification Number: 046353839
Applications: Initial approach by letter.
Program description:
Scholarships are granted primarily to students attending preparatory schools, colleges, junior colleges and vocational schools in the Northeast.

761
Williams (Arthur Ashley) Foundation
345 Union Avenue
P.O. Box 665
Framingham, MA 01701   (617) 429-1149
Contact: Frederick Cole, Chairman, P.O. Box 397,
Holliston, MA 01746

Limitations: Generally locally oriented giving for
undergraduate scholarships only. Funding is limited.
Financial data: Year ended 12/31/86. Assets,
$3,039,971 (M); Total giving, $238,774; Grants to
individuals, 38 grants totaling $51,274.
Employer Identification Number: 046044714
Applications: Applications accepted throughout the
year; Initial approach by letter; Completion of formal
application and financial questionnaire required.
Publications: Application guidelines.

762★
Wilson (John & Mary) Foundation
c/o First Interstate Bank of Washington
P.O. Box 21927
Seattle, WA 98111

Limitations: Scholarships only to medical students
(freshmen through seniors) attending the University of
Washington.
Financial data: Year ended 12/31/86. Assets,
$3,318,314 (M); Total giving, $147,986; Grants to
individuals totaling $143,486.
Employer Identification Number: 237425273
Applications: Request application and financial aid
form from the University of Washington Medical
School, Seattle, WA 98195; Completion of formal
application required.

763
Winans (Charles A.) Memorial Trust
P.O. Box 1359
Carlsbad, NM 88220

Limitations: Scholarships only to students graduating
from Beaumont High School, Beaumont, CA, for
college education.
Financial data: Year ended 12/31/86. Assets, $43,893
(M); Total giving, $2,300; Grants to individuals, 4
grants totaling $2,300, high $650, low $500.
Employer Identification Number: 836011160
Applications: Deadline January 15th; Completion of
formal application required; Application information
available from Student Counseling Office, Beaumont
High School, 1591 North Cherry, Beaumont, CA
92223.

764
Winchester Foundation, The
100 Meridian Street
Winchester, IN 47394   (317) 584-3501
Contact: Don Welch, Chairman

Limitations: Scholarships primarily to residents of
Indiana.
Financial data: Year ended 12/31/86. Assets,
$1,258,846 (M); Total giving, $49,720; Grants to
individuals, 4 grants totaling $7,720, high $6,000, low
$190.
Employer Identification Number: 237422941
Program description:
The majority of scholarships granted by the foundation
are selected by a scholarship committee from
Winchester High School and then approved by the
foundation.

765★
Windham Foundation, Inc., The
P.O. Box 70
Grafton, VT 05146   (802) 843-2211
Contact: Stephen A. Morse, Executive Director

Limitations: Undergraduate level (including "trade"
school) college scholarships to Windham County, VT,
residents only.
Financial data: Year ended 10/31/87. Assets,
$31,021,354 (M); Total giving, $283,572; Grants to
individuals, 392 grants totaling $140,253.
Employer Identification Number: 136142024
Applications: Contact foundation for current dates and
other information; Initial approach by letter.
Publications: Annual report.

766
Winkleman (Emma) Trust B
State Bank & Trust Company
100 North Minnesota Street
New Ulm, MN 56073   (501) 354-8215
Contact: Trust Department

Limitations: Scholarships only to nursing students who
graduated from high schools in or live within a
30-mile radius of Fairfax, MN.
Financial data: Year ended 12/31/85. Assets, $104,485
(M); Total giving, $9,145; Grants to individuals, 19
grants totaling $9,145, high $770, low $325.
Employer Identification Number: 416180865
Applications: Deadline April 1st; Completion of
formal application required.
Program description:
Eligible students must have graduated from high
schools, or reside within, the school districts in any of
the following communities: Bird Island, Buffalo Lake,
Fairfax, Franklin, Gibbon, Hector, Morgan, Morton,
New Ulm, Redwood Falls, Sleepy Eye, Springfield,
Stewart, or Winthrop.

Approximately 15 to 20 scholarships are awarded each year. Scholarships vary each year, based on fair market value of trust. Each recipient receives the same amount which is designated at year end.

767
Winkler (Mark and Catherine) Foundation
1900 North Beauregard Street
Alexandria, VA 22311   (703) 998-0400
Contact: Harold Winkler, Vice-President

Limitations: Scholarships primarily for residents of Virginia.
Financial data: Year ended 1/31/86. Assets, $1,453,774 (M); Total giving, $422,305; Grants to individuals, 4 grants totaling $5,100, high $2,000, low $600.
Employer Identification Number: 546054383
Applications: Applications accepted throughout the year; Initial approach by letter requesting application; Completion of formal application required.

768★
Winship Memorial Scholarship Foundation
c/o Comerica Bank-Battle Creek, Trust Division
25 West Michigan Mall
Battle Creek, MI 49016   (616) 966-6340
Contact: Frances A. Hanson, Executive Director

Limitations: Scholarships only to graduates of Battle Creek, MI, area public high schools, including those in the school systems of Battle Creek/Springfield, Climax-Scotts, Galesburg-Augusta, Harper Creek, Lakeview, and Pennfield.
Financial data: Year ended 12/31/87. Assets, $2,149,661 (M); Total giving, $117,163; Grants to individuals, 90 grants totaling $117,163, high $1,700, low $200, general range $200-1,700, average grant $1,300.
Employer Identification Number: 386092543
Applications: Deadline March 1st; Completion of formal application required; Interviews required; Applications processed through local high schools.
Publications: Annual report, informational brochure, application guidelines, financial statement, program information, 990-PF printed copy available upon request.
Program description:
Scholarships are awarded for recipient's entire college education, including postgraduate. Applicants must be enrolled full-time in an accredited institution of higher education.

769
Winston-Salem Foundation, The
229 First Union National Bank Building
Winston-Salem, NC 27101   (919) 725-2382
Contact: L. Andrew Bell III, Assistant Director

Limitations: Student loans to residents of North Carolina. Scholarships primarily to residents of Forsyth County, NC.
Financial data: Year ended 12/31/86. Assets, $39,870,652 (M); Total giving, $4,469,708; Grants to individuals, 64 scholarships totaling $64,400; Loans to individuals, 170 loans totaling $228,300.
Employer Identification Number: 566037615
Applications: Deadlines January 1st, April 1st, May 1st, July 1st, and October 1st; Initial approach by telephone; Completion of formal application required for educational aid (loans and/or scholarships), and must be submitted with $20 application fee; Interviews scheduled to review application materials.
Publications: Annual report, program information.
Program description:
Student aid is provided through 25 different foundation funds. Several loans are available to North Carolina residents pursuing degrees in nursing and allied health fields.
Student loans are made for postsecondary education covering up to one-half of an individual's educational expenses. The maximum aid available per student, per year is $2,500. The current interest rate is eight percent.

770★
Wintermann (The David and Eula) Foundation
P.O. Box 337
Eagle Lake, TX 77434
Contact: Daniel Thorton; Tel.: (409) 234-5551 or (713) 228-7273

Limitations: Scholarships to area high school seniors whose intended field of study is in the medical field.
Financial data: Year ended 6/30/86. Assets, $127,238 (M); Total giving, $4,000; Grants to individuals, 3 grants totaling, $4,000, high $2,000, low $1,000.
Employer Identification Number: 760082100
Applications: Deadline April; Initial approach by letter, including high school transcript, statement of financial need, field of intended study, and a character reference, required.

771
Winton (David H.) Foundation, Inc.
c/o Kirlin, Campbell & Keating
14 Wall Street
New York, NY 10005   (212) 732-5520
Contact: Ernesto C. Luzzattto

Limitations: Scholarships based on financial need to students attending colleges and universities throughout the U.S.

Financial data: Year ended 12/31/85. Assets, $1,308 (M); Total giving, $7,400; Grants to individuals, 3 grants totaling $7,400.
Employer Identification Number: 136167269
Applications: Applications accepted throughout the year; Contact foundation for application guidelines.
Program description:
Scholarships are made on a nondiscriminatory basis to promote the education of worthy students.

772
Wolf (Benjamin & Fredora K.) Foundation

Park Towne Place - North Building 1205
Parkway at 22nd Street
Philadelphia, PA 19130   (215) 787-6079
Contact: David A. Horowitz, Administrator

Limitations: Scholarships upon the recommendation of high school principals and counselors to graduates of Philadephia, PA, area high schools for undergraduate matriculation in post high school, educational and/or training institutions.
Financial data: Year ended 5/31/86. Assets, $1,1638,461 (M); Total giving, $91,925; Grants to individuals, 196 grants totaling $81,175, high $625, low $250.
Employer Identification Number: 236207344
Applications: Applications accepted throughout the year; Initial approach by letter; Completion of formal application required.
Program description:
The foundation shall use and employ the net income for the purpose of enabling young men and women, who in the trustees' judgement would be unable to do so, to obtain a higher education either in colleges, trade schools or otherwise.

773
Woltman (B.M.) Foundation

2200 West Loop South, Suite 225
Houston, TX 77027
Contact: Frederick Boden, Executive Director, Luthern Church Synod, 7900 U.S. 290 East, Austin, TX 78724

Limitations: Scholarships to students from Texas or who are studying in Texas, and preparing for the Lutheran ministry or for teaching in Lutheran schools.
Financial data: Year ended 12/31/86. Assets, $4,749,980 (M); Total giving, $156,200; Grants to individuals, 47 grants totaling $53,700, high $2,400, low $500, general range $500-1,500, average grant $1,000.
Employer Identification Number: 741402184
Applications: Applications must be submitted before the school year begins; Completion of formal application required.

774
Womack Foundation

513 Wilson Street
Danville, VA 24541   (804) 791-4179
Contact: Mrs. Lalor Earle, P.O. Box 521, Danville, VA 24543

Limitations: Student loans by recommendation only from local referral agencies for residents of the city of Danville and Pittsylvania County, VA.
Financial data: Year ended 3/31/86. Assets, $192,470 (M); Expenditures, $70,544; Loans to individuals totaling $4,299.
Employer Identification Number: 546053255
Applications: Completion of formal application and interviews required. **Applications without local referral recommendations not accepted.**
Program description:
Last-resort loans to individuals for post-high school training or education; grants to low-income groups or individuals to provide camping and enrichment experience; and to improve skills of non-college-bound students.

775
Woman's Seamen's Friend Society of Connecticut

74 Forbes Avenue
New Haven, CT 06512   (203) 467-3887
Contact: Capt. Jack M. Seymour, USN (Ret), Executive Director

Limitations: Scholarships for the study of marine sciences in Connecticut or by Connecticut residents in schools out-of-state, and for dependents of Connecticut merchant marine seamen pursuing any course of study.
Financial data: Year ended 12/31/85. Assets, $1,925,117 (M); Total giving, $66,873; Grants to individuals totaling $52,230.
Employer Identification Number: 060655133
Applications: Deadline April 1st for summer programs, May 15th for academic year; Initial approach by letter; Completion of formal application required; Interviews granted upon request.
Publications: Program information.
Program description:
Scholarships are awarded to residents of Connecticut who attend State Maritime Academies or major in marine sciences at the college of their choice as well as to out-of-state residents who are majoring in marine sciences at Connecticut colleges. Support is also provided for Connecticut merchant marine seamen and their dependents to attend the college of their choice and pursue any course of study. Seamen must be active or have served at sea within the last ten years.

Selection criteria include career motivation, personal character, academic potential, and financial need. The amounts of individual awards are determined in cooperation with the college financial aid officer. The scholarships are renewable upon reapplication each year.

776
Women's Aid Society of 1844, Inc.
150 East 45th Street
New York, NY 10017
Contact: Dorothy C. Moore, Secretary-Treasurer

Limitations: Student aid to needy school children.
Financial data: Year ended 12/31/85. Assets, $1,175,846 (M); Total giving, $95,251; Grants to individuals totaling $95,251; Subtotal for student aid totaling $17,968.
Employer Identification Number: 136006486
Applications: Applications accepted throughout the year by mail; Requests should be submitted in letter form and addressed to the society.
Program description:
Financial aid is given for educational expenses of needy school children.

777
Wood (A.R.) Educational Trust
P.O. Box 1953
Sioux Falls, SD 57117-1953   (605) 339-7400
Contact: Mary Jo Curtin

Limitations: Scholarships to graduates of Luverne High School, Luverne, MN.
Financial data: Year ended 12/31/86. Assets, $182,708 (M); Total giving, $14,075; Grants to individuals, 26 grants totaling $14,075, high $650, low $325, average grant $650.
Employer Identification Number: 416023357
Applications: Deadline August 3rd; Completion of formal application required.
Program description:
Scholarships to students in the top 20 percent of their class with a 3.0 GPA.

778★
Wood (Cora W.) Scholarship Fund
c/o First National Bank, Trust Department
P.O. Box 1699
Colorado Springs, CO 80942   (303) 471-5125
Contact: Trustees

Limitations: Scholarships only to graduating high school seniors in Pike's Peak region who will attend a state supported college or university in Colorado.
Financial data: Year ended 12/31/86. Assets, $124,534 (M); Total giving, $8,100; Grants to individuals, 6 grants totaling $8,100, high $1,600, low $850.
Employer Identification Number: 237169976
Applications: Deadline April 30th; Resume, photograph, financial statement, and teacher or counselor statement and comments required.

Program description:
Scholarship awards are made directly to the educational institution on behalf of the individual recipient.

779
Wood (Frank and Bea) Foundation
2304 Midwestern Parkway, Suite 204
Wichita Falls, TX 76308   (817) 692-2522
Contact: Martha Kay Hendrickson

Limitations: Undergraduate educational grants.
Financial data: Year ended 12/31/85. Assets, $133,639 (M); Total giving, $44,194; Grants to individuals, 16 grants totaling $13,400, high $1,900, low $500, general range $500-1,000.
Employer Identification Number: 756012941
Applications: Applications accepted throughout the year; Completion of formal application required.

780
Woodward Foundation, The
2101 L Street, N.W., Suite 210
Washington, DC 20037   (202) 293-8200
Contact: Mrs. David C. Acheson, Director, Education Program, 2700 Calvert Street, N.W., Washington, DC 20008; Tel.: (202) 462-8664

Limitations: Educational grants to eleventh and twelfth graders in Washington, DC, public high schools.
Financial data: Year ended 6/30/85. Assets, $407,552 (M); Total giving, $86,885; Grants to individuals, 66 grants totaling $36,885, high $500, low $15, average grant $275.
Employer Identification Number: 526055545
Applications: Contact foundation for current application deadline; Completion of formal application required; Interviews required for finalists.
Publications: Program information.
Program description:
The foundation's educational programs include: 1) awards to high school students who require financial aid to meet expenses, complete studies, and graduate; and 2) purchase of tools for outstanding vocational students so that they may enter their chosen fields.

Awards are made to juniors and seniors in high schools in the District of Columbia who have demonstrated sincerity, ability, and promise by scholastic achievement or by talent in fields such as art, drama, literature, science, or trade. A need for financial assistance outside the family income must also exist.

A selection committee composed of representatives of the public schools and the foundation reviews applications, interviews finalists, and selects recipients. Money awarded must be used for personal expenses related to education and is deposited in the school bank in a special account. No funds may be withdrawn without approval of the principal or counselor. Tools are purchased by the school and become the student's property upon graduation.

Awards for any academic year are limited to $500 for twelfth graders and $250 for eleventh graders.

781
Worthing Scholarship Fund
c/o Interfirst Bank Houston
P.O. Box 2555
Houston, TX 77252
Contact: F. D. Woesley, 119 East Street, Houston, TX 77018

Limitations: Scholarships only to high school graduates in the Houston Independent School District who plan to attend an accredited college in Texas.
Financial data: Year ended 9/30/86. Assets, $3,188,104 (M); Total giving, $131,750; Grants to individuals, 50 grants totaling $131,750, high $1,000, low $500.
Employer Identification Number: 741160916
Applications: Deadline May 1st; Completion of formal application required.
Program description:
To qualify for a scholarship, the applicant must maintain a 'C' average in college, carry a full-time student load, and send grades for each year to the committee.

782
Wyman (Mary Byrd) Memorial Association of Baltimore City
3130 Golf Course Road West
Owings Mills, MD 21117
Contact: A. Rutherford Holmes, President

Limitations: Scholarships for secondary education.
Financial data: Year ended 5/31/85. Assets, $1,023,851 (M); Total giving, $31,600; Grants to individuals, 27 grants totaling $31,600, high $1,600, low $800.
Employer Identification Number: 520781416
Applications: Deadline January 1st.

783
Young (John B. & Brownie) Memorial Fund
c/o Owensboro National Bank, Trust Department
230 Frederica Street
Owensboro, KY 42301

Limitations: Scholarships for students in school districts of Owensboro Daviess, and McClean counties, KY.
Financial data: Year ended 12/31/86. Assets, $2,695,780 (M); Total giving, $155,600; Grants to individuals, 64 grants totaling, $155,600, high $2,500, low $1,250.
Employer Identification Number: 616025137

Applications: Applications accepted throughout the year; Completion of formal application required.

784
Young (Judson) Memorial Educational Foundation, Inc.
101 West Fourth Street
Salem, MO 65560   (314) 729-3137
Contact: Max J. Coffman, Foundation Manager

Limitations: Student loans primarily to graduates of Salem High School, MO.
Financial data: Year ended 12/31/86. Assets, $1,230,822 (M); Expenditures, $50,104; Loans to individuals totaling $44,200.
Employer Identification Number: 436061841
Applications: Deadlines August 15th for fall term, December 15th for winter term, and May 15th for summer term; Completion of formal application required with two copies.

785★
Young (Sarah E.) Trust
c/o BankEast Trust Company
2 Wall Street
Manchester, NH 03105   (603) 335-1524
Contact: Judi Tuttle, BankEast Trust Company, 22 South Main Street, Rochester, NH 03867; Tel.: (603) 332-4242

Limitations: Scholarships to needy residents of Strafford County, NH, who have completed at least one year of college.
Financial data: Year ended 12/31/87. Assets, $310,000 (M); Grants to individuals, 27 grants totaling $19,000, high $1,500, low $250, general range $500-1,000, average loan $500.
Employer Identification Number: 026004261
Applications: Deadline June 30th; Completion of formal application required, including high school and college grades and showing financial status.
Publications: Application guidelines.

786
Youth Foundation, Inc
36 West 44th Street
New York, NY 10036
Contact: Edward F. L. Bruen, Vice-President

Limitations: Scholarships for undergraduate study.
Financial data: Year ended 12/31/84. Assets, $2,889,534 (M); Total giving, 97,400; Grants to individuals, 55 grants totaling $82,500, each grant $1,500.
Employer Identification Number: 136093036
Applications: Deadline April 15th; Initial approach by letter; Completion of formal application required; All

applications must include self-addressed stamped envelope.
Publications: Application guidelines, program information.
Program description:
The **Alexander and Maude Hadden Scholarships** are awarded to students with need as well as ability. The scholarships are paid to the institution as tuition. Requests for application forms must be accompanied by a written recommendation from an administrative or faculty member of an educational institution. Approximately ten new scholarships are awarded each year.

Application for renewal of a scholarship will be considered upon filing a renewal application form no later than April 15th.

No study abroad aid except "Junior Year Abroad," etc., where credit is given toward a degree from an American institution.

787★
Zigler (Fred B. and Ruth B.) Foundation
P.O. Box 986
Jennings, LA 70546   (318) 824-2413
Contact: Margaret Cormier, Secretary-Treasurer

Limitations: Scholarships to graduating seniors of Jefferson Davis Parish, LA, high schools.
Financial data: Year ended 12/31/86. Assets, $3,685,780 (L); Total giving, $269,883; Grants to individuals totaling $97,636.
Employer Identification Number: 726019403
Applications: Deadline March 10th; Initial approach by letter; Completion of formal application required.
Publications: Annual report.
Program description:
Scholarships are awarded on the basis of financial need and the ability to perform college level work. ACT or SAT scores required. Scholarship payments are made to the educational institutions on behalf of individual recipients.

788
Zimmerman (Hans and Clara Davis) Foundation
c/o Hawaiian Trust Company, Ltd.
P.O. Box 3170
Honolulu, HI 96802   (808) 525-6512
Contact: Janis A. Reischmann, Administrator

Limitations: Scholarships to full-time students who are legal residents of Hawaii to complete studies at an accredited two- or four-year college or university; preference to majors in field of medicine, nursing, or a related health field.
Financial data: Year ended 12/31/86. Assets, $6,799,634 (M); Total giving, $295,550; Grants to individuals, 134 grants totaling $295,550, high $6,100, low $500.
Employer Identification Number: 996006669

Applications: Deadline March 1st; Request application form by February 1st; Completion of formal application required.
Publications: Program information, application guidelines.
Program description:
Scholarships are based on financial need and are awarded on an annual basis. Students must re-apply each year.

GENERAL WELFARE

This section lists sources for all types of grants, loans, and in-kind services provided by foundations on an emergency or long-term basis to individuals for personal, living, or medical expenses. Many of these grants are paid to the hospitals, doctors, or agencies that actually render the service rather than to the individuals, although the programs are open to direct application by individuals. Not included in this section are welfare programs which are company-sponsored; such programs may be found in the "Company Employee Grants" section. Welfare programs whose giving is restricted to artists or those involved in cultural endeavors are also not included in this section; such programs may be found in the "Arts and Cultural Support" section.

Entries are arranged alphabetically by foundation name. Access to grants by specific subject areas, types of support, and geographic focus, is provided in the "Subject," "Types of Support" and "Geographic Focus" indexes in the back of the book.

Limitations on giving are indicated when available. The limitations statement should be checked carefully as a foundation will reject any application that does not fall within the foundation's geographic area, recipient type, or field of interest.

REMEMBER: IF YOU DON'T QUALIFY, DON'T APPLY.

789★
Adams (Emma J.) Memorial Fund, Inc.
c/o Lebeouf, Lamb, Lelby and Macrae
520 Madison Avenue
New York, NY 10022   (212) 715-8000
Contact: Edward R. Finch, Jr., President

Limitations: Welfare assistance primarily to the elderly and indigent in the New York, NY, metropolitan area.
Financial data: Year ended 12/31/87. Assets, $2,603,000 (M); Total giving, $88,000 (approximate); Grants to individuals totaling $18,000 (approximate), high $10,000, low $100, general range $100-1,000, average grant $750.
Employer Identification Number: 136116503
Applications: Applications accepted throughout the year; Initial approach by letter detailing specific need for which request is made; Completion of formal application required; Interviews required.
Publications: Multi-year report, informational brochure.
Program description:
Assistance in 1987 was given mainly to geriatric and other institutions for the elderly, poor, and homeless in the form of emergency aid including grants to cover medical expenses, food and clothing, and rent, etc.

790
Association for the Relief of Aged Women of New Bedford
27 South Sixth Street
New Bedford, MA 02740

Limitations: Relief assistance to needy, aged women in New Bedford, MA.
Financial data: Year ended 3/31/87. Assets, $5,895,501 (M); Total giving, $186,550; Grants to individuals, 19 grants totaling $186,550, high $34,783, low $271.
Employer Identification Number: 046056367

791
Avery-Fuller Children's Center
251 Kearney Street
San Francisco, CA 94108   (415) 930-8292
Contact: Bonnie Van Manen Pinkel, Executive Director

Limitations: Financial assistance to handicapped and disabled children primarily in California for the purpose of increasing their self-sufficiency.
Financial data: Year ended 6/30/86. Assets, $2,725,443 (M); Total giving, $161,662; Grants to individuals totaling $161,662, average grant $1,500.
Employer Identification Number: 941243657
Applications: Deadlines February 15th, May 15th, August 15th and November 15th. Completion of formal application required. Rejected applicants will be reconsidered once at the next review date,

provided applicant requests so in writing.
Program description:
Funds are to be used for medical services, physical and occupational therapy, psychotherapy, special school or remedial education, prosthetics, appliances, prescriptions, and related services.

792★
Babcock (William) Memorial Endowment
305 San Anselmo Avenue, Suite 219
San Anselmo, CA 94960   (415) 453-0901
Contact: Alelia Gillin, Executive Director

Limitations: Assistance for medical costs to residents of Marin County, CA.
Financial data: Year ended 2/28/87. Assets, $2,668,851 (M); Total giving, $356,906; Grants to individuals totaling $356,906.
Employer Identification Number: 941367170
Applications: Initial contact by telephone.
Publications: Application guidelines, informational brochure.
Program description:
Grants or loans to individuals and families who lack the financial resources to pay for exceptional medical, surgical, and hospital expenses not covered by insurance or other community agencies.

793
Babson-Webber-Mustard Fund
c/o Hutchins & Wheeler
One Boston Place
Boston, MA 02108

Limitations: Relief assistance to needy individuals primarily in Boston, MA.
Financial data: Year ended 12/31/85. Assets, $2,191,344 (M); Total giving, $89,425; Grants to individuals, 216 grants totaling $88,425, high $1,000, low, $325.
Employer Identification Number: 042307820

794
Baker (Clark and Ruby) Foundation
c/o Bank South, Personal Trust Department
P.O. Box 4956
Atlanta, GA 30302   (404) 529-4627
Contact: Odette Capell, Secretary, or Tom Murphy

Limitations: Primarily to retired Methodist ministers residing in Georgia for pensions and medical assistance.
Financial data: Year ended 12/31/86. Assets, $1,440,913 (M); Total giving, $67,500; Grants to individuals, 13 grants totaling $17,000; Subtotal for pensions, 3 grants totaling $4,000, high $2,000, low $1,000.
Employer Identification Number: 581429097

Applications: Applications accepted throughout the year; Interviews required.

795
Bendheim (Charles and Els) Foundation
Ten Columbus Circle
New York, NY 10019

Limitations: Grants to Jewish individuals for charitable purposes, including assistance to the sick and destitute.
Financial data: Year ended 1/31/86. Assets, $304,304 (M); Total giving, $182,942; Grants to individuals amount not specified.
Employer Identification Number: 136103769

796
Bennett (The James Gordon) Memorial Corporation
200 Park Avenue, Room 2023
New York, NY 10166   (212) 755-8310
Contact: Patrick T. Finnegan, President

Limitations: Welfare assistance to needy journalists who have been employees for ten or more years on a daily New York City newspaper.
Financial data: Year ended 12/31/84. Assets, $2,777,989 (M); Total giving, $145,550; Grants to individuals, 95 grants totaling $145,550; Subtotal for welfare assistance, 15 grants totaling $56,600, high $6,150, low $1,600, general range $3,150-4,350.
Employer Identification Number: 136150414
Applications: Applications accepted throughout the year, Initial approach by letter; Completion of formal application required.
Publications: Program information, application guidelines.
Program description:
The foundation gives first priority to journalists who have worked in the borough of Manhattan. If, after awarding grants to Manhattan journalists who are eligible, funds remain, they are used to assist other journalists who worked in the other boroughs outside of Manhattan but within New York City.

Acceptance is based on need and is to be used for "the physical needs of persons...who, by reason of old age, accident or bodily infirmity, or through lack of means, are unable to care for themselves."

797
Boston Fatherless & Widows Society
c/o Goodwin, Procter & Hoar
Exchange Place, Room 2200
Boston, MA 02109
Contact: George W. Butterworth III

Limitations: Welfare assistance only to indigent widows and orphans who are residents of the Boston,

MA, area.
Financial data: Year ended 11/30/86. Assets, $3,421,832 (M); Total giving, $206,407; Grants to individuals totaling $80,782.
Employer Identification Number: 046006506
Applications: Applications accepted throughout the year; Initial approach by letter.
Publications: Application guidelines.
Program description:
Grants are awarded to needy individuals to assist them in meeting their expenses for food, housing, clothing, and medical treatment.

798
Burke (Thomas C.) Foundation
182 Riley Avenue, No. B
Macon, GA 31204-2345   (912) 745-1442
Contact: Carolyn P. Griggers

Limitations: Medical assistance to needy individuals in Bibb County, GA.
Financial data: Year ended 9/30/85. Assets, $3,021,470 (M); Total giving, $132,962; Grants to individuals totaling $96,138.
Employer Identification Number: 586047627
Applications: Applications accepted throughout the year; Initial contact by telephone or in person.
Program description:
Medical assistance is given in the form of one-time payments for medical expenses such as doctor bills, purchase or rental of medical equipment, and pharmacy bills, and also as weekly grants of up to $60 to assist with medical expenses. Grants also for transportation to treatment facilities.

799★
Calkins (Ina) Board
c/o Boatmen's First National Bank of Kansas City
Kansas City, MO 64183   (816) 234-7481
Contact: David P. Ross, Secretary

Limitations: Welfare assistance to elderly needy residents of Kansas City, MO.
Financial data: Year ended 12/31/87. Assets, $157,000 (M); Total giving, $207,419; Grants to individuals, 76 grants totaling $33,600.
Employer Identification Number: 237377909

800★
Carnegie Foundation for the Advancement of Teaching, The
Five Ivy Lane
Princeton, NJ 08540   (609) 452-1780
Contact: Verne A. Stadtman, Vice-President

Limitations: Retirement allowances and widows' pensions to teachers of universities, colleges, and technical schools in the U.S. and Canada.
Financial data: Year ended 6/30/87. Assets,

$52,534,120 (M); Total giving, $1,385,921; Grants to individuals, 99 grants totaling $153,728.
Employer Identification Number: 131623924
Applications: Applications accepted throughout the year; Initial approach by letter.
Publications: Annual report.

801
Carroll Foundation
70 Enterprise Avenue
Secaucus, NJ 07094
Contact: Carroll Petrie or Milton Petrie

Limitations: Relief assistance to needy individuals.
Financial data: Year ended 12/31/85. Assets, $0 (M); Total giving, $73,305; Grants to individuals, 21 grants totaling $58,000 for assistance, high $11,000, low $1,000.
Employer Identification Number: 222299776

802
Charitable Society in Hartford
c/o Connecticut National Bank
777 Main Street
Hartford, CT 06115
Contact: Raymond S. Andrews, Jr., Robinson and Cole, One Commercial Plaza, Hartford, CT 06103-3597; Tel.: (203) 275-8200

Limitations: Small grants to needy residents of Hartford, CT, to meet emergencies (e.g., food, shelter, clothing, heat).
Financial data: Year ended 8/31/85. Assets, $449,843 (M); Total giving, $37,860; Grants to individuals totaling $37,860.
Employer Identification Number: 066026007
Applications: Applications accepted throughout the year only from recognized social service agencies.
Program description:
Disbursements of funds are made on the basis of recommendations from churches, schools, and local service organizations.

803★
Clark Foundation, The
30 Wall Street
New York, NY 10005   (212) 269-1833
Contact: Edward W. Stack, Secretary

Limitations: Grants for medical and convalescent care to needy individuals in upstate New York and New York City.
Financial data: Year ended 6/30/87. Assets, $210,106,662 (M); Total giving, $7,164,612; Grants to individuals, 672 grants totaling $1,769,779; Subtotal for welfare assistance, 24 grants totaling $114,403, high $19,272, low $450, general range $1,500-10,000.
Employer Identification Number: 135616528

Applications: Applications accepted throughout the year: Initial approach by letter.

804★
Clarke (The Elizabeth Church) Testamentary Trust/Fund Foundation
U.S. National Bank of Oregon
P.O. Box 3168
Portland, OR 97208
Contact: Walter L. Peters, Executive Secretary, Scottish Rite Temple, 709 S.W. 15th Avenue, Portland, OR 97205; Tel.: (503) 228-9405

Limitations: Grants to individuals for medical assistance.
Financial data: Year ended 12/31/86. Assets, $1,241,659 (M); Total giving, $46,103; Grants to individuals amount not specified.
Employer Identification Number: 936024205
Applications: Applications accepted throughout the year; Initial approach by letter giving complete details of needs and costs.
Program description:
Medical assistance payments may be made directly to the individual recipient, or to the doctors and hospitals providing medical services.

805
Cochems (Jane Nugent) Trust
c/o Colorado National Bank of Denver
P.O. Box 5168
Denver, CO 80217

Limitations: Relief assistance to indigent doctors in Colorado.
Financial data: Year ended 12/31/86. Assets, $224,624 (M); Total giving, $9,044; Grants to individuals, 2 grants totaling $9,044, each grant $4,522.
Employer Identification Number: 846018185
Applications: For current application procedures and deadline information, contact President, Colorado State Medical Society, 6061 Willow Drive, Suite 250, Englewood, CO 80111.

806
Coe (Marion Isabele) Fund
c/o Colonial Bank and Trust Company
Waterbury, CT 06720

Limitations: Relief assistance to worthy adult residents of Goshen, Litchfield, Morris, and Warren, CT, for general living and medical expenses.
Financial data: Year ended 12/31/85. Assets, $318,911 (M); Total giving $12,121; Grants to individuals totaling $12,121, average grant $100.
Employer Identification Number: 066040150

Program description:
Grants are awarded to provide continuing assistance to needy men and women to enable them to live in their own homes. Most awards are paid in monthly installments generally ranging from $45 to $140 per month, and renewed annually. Grants are also given to pay for insurance, taxes, car repairs, and to provide domestic companions.

807★
Colorado Masons Benevolent Fund Association
1770 Sherman Street
Denver, CO 80203   (303) 837-0367
Contact: Local lodge

Limitations: Relief assistance only to distressed members of Colorado Masonic lodges, their wives, widows, mothers, or dependent minor children.
Financial data: Year ended 10/31/87. Assets, $7,344,346 (M); Total giving, $748,056; Grants to individuals, 164 grants totaling $731,906; Subtotal for relief assistance, 87 grants totaling $331,306.
Employer Identification Number: 840406813
Applications: Contact lodge of which brother is (was) a member of good standing in Colorado.
Program description:
These funds are allocated for the specific relief of "distressed worthy Brothers, their widows and orphans, mothers and sisters." Lodge officers who are seeking assistance for a distressed member or his widow should submit a completed application form to Arthur J. Carlson, P.M., Executive Secretary at the association's Denver address.

808
Columbus Female Benevolent Society
292 North Drexel Avenue
Columbus, OH 43209

Limitations: Direct aid on a regular, special, or temporary basis to pensioned widows who are residents of Franklin County, OH; also provides aid for baby clothing and needs, and handicapped baby needs.
Financial data: Year ended 12/31/86. Assets, $95,472 (M); Total giving, $46,474; Grants to individuals totaling $41,755.
Employer Identification Number: 316042036
Program description:
All recipients are referred by local people who are familiar with their circumstances.

809
Copley Fund
P.O. Box 696
Morristown, VT 05661
Contact: Richard Sargent, Trustee

Limitations: Housing assistance for elderly residents of Lamoille County, VT.
Financial data: Year ended 12/31/86. Assets, $1,307,615 (M); Total giving, $86,164; Grants to individuals, 134 grants totaling $86,164.
Employer Identification Number: 036006013
Applications: Deadline December 31st; Initial approach by letter.

810
Crane Fund for Widows and Children
222 West Adams Street, Room 849
Chicago, IL 60606
Contact: The Trustees

Limitations: Welfare assistance to needy and indigent people, mainly in Illinois.
Financial data: Year ended 12/31/86. Assets, $8,434,374 (M); Total giving, $247,915; Grants to individuals, 4 grants totaling $14,967, high $10,605, low $564.
Employer Identification Number: 366116543
Applications: Initial approach by letter.

811
Cultural Society, Inc., The
P.O. Box 1374
Bridgeview, IL 60455   (312) 371-6429
Contact: Mohammad Nasr, M.D., Treasurer

Limitations: Welfare assistance to needy Muslims.
Financial data: Year ended 6/30/86. Assets, $143,301 (M); Total giving, $126,053; Grants to individuals, 13 grants totaling $69,203; Subtotal for welfare assistance, 8 grants totaling $40,234, high $13,000, low $500.
Employer Identification Number: 510183515
Applications: Applications accepted throughout the year; Initial approach by letter.

812★
Curtis (Effie H. and Edward H.) Trust Fund
c/o United Bank of Fort Collins, N.A.
P.O. Box 565
Fort Collins, CO 80522   (303) 482-1100
Contact: Maggi Parker, United Bank of Fort Collins, N.A., P.O. Box 2203, Fort Collins, CO 80522

Limitations: Grants limited to Larimer County, CO, permanent residents under 18 years of age for emergency medical and dental expenses only.
Financial data: Year ended 12/31/86. Assets, $519,475 (M); Total giving, $29,549; Grants to individuals, 130

238

grants totaling $29,549, high $1,200, low $6.
Employer Identification Number: 846019933
Applications: Deadline 15th of each month;
Completion of formal application, with input of
attending physician, required; Include copy of tax
return.
Program description:
Grants for medical assistance are paid directly to the
medical organization for the benefit of the individual
recipients.

813★
Cutter (Albert B.) Memorial Trust Fund
Security Pacific National Bank - Trust Dept.
P.O. Box 712
Riverside, CA 92502

Limitations: Limited emergency grants only to persons
who have been permanent residents of Riverside, CA,
for a minimum of one year and have been referred by
local agencies.
Financial data: Year ended 12/31/87. Assets, $743,514
(M); Total giving, $27,777; Grants to individuals, 25
grants totaling $6,650, high $550, low $22.
Employer Identification Number: 956112842
Applications: Applications accepted from local
agencies throughout the year; Completion of formal
application required; Interview or presentation
recommended; Individuals are referred by local
agencies.
Program description:
Limited funds are available to assist permanent
residents of Riverside, CA, who find themselves in
distressing circumstances largely through no fault of
their own, yet are ineligible for the usual sources of
help. Grant payments are made to those providing the
services to the individual. Individuals and agencies
must be from Riverside, CA.

814
Danforth (Josiah H.) Memorial Fund
Eight Fremont Street
Gloversville, NY 12078

Limitations: Grants only to residents of Fulton County,
NY, for medical assistance.
Financial data: Year ended 12/31/85. Assets, $318,310
(M); Total giving, $16,857; Grants to individuals, 119
grants totaling $16,857, high $500, low $8.
Employer Identification Number: 146023489

815
De Kay Foundation, The
c/o Manufacturers Hanover Trust Company
600 Fifth Avenue
New York, NY 10020   (212) 957-1668
Contact: Lloyd Saltus, II, Vice-President,
Manufacturers Hanover Trust Company

Limitations: Financial assistance to needy elderly
individuals in New York, New Jersey, and
Connecticut.
Financial data: Year ended 2/28/85. Assets,
$12,553,449 (M); Total giving, $678,395; Grants to
individuals, 101 grants totaling $234,796, high
$6,600, low $100, general range $1,000-5,000.
Employer Identification Number: 136203234
Applications: Initial approach by letter requesting
application form; Completion of formal application
required.
Program description:
Grants are awarded to promote the well-being of men
and women of culture or refined heritage who are in
real need of financial assistance, particularly those
who are sick, old, or disabled and otherwise lack
proper care.

816★
duPont (Alfred I.) Foundation
1550 Prudential Drive, Suite 400
P.O. Box 1380
Jacksonville, FL 32207   (904) 396-6600
Contact: Rosemary Cusimano, Assistant Secretary

Limitations: Relief assistance to the elderly indigent
who generally reside in the southeastern U.S.
Financial data: Year ended 12/31/86. Assets,
$13,069,843 (M); Total giving, $532,330; Grants to
individuals, 282 grants totaling $367,692, high
$21,297, low $100.
Employer Identification Number: 591297267
Applications: Applications accepted throughout the
year; Completion of formal application required;
Interviews required.
Program description:
Grants are awarded to the needy elderly whose other
sources of income are inadequate. The majority of
those receiving grants are experiencing extreme
hardship and require health, economic, or educational
assistance.
 Grants are primarily distributed on a regular,
monthly basis, and each case is reviewed periodically
throughout the year. The foundation also awards both
temporary grants and special grants.

817
Eagles Memorial Foundation, Inc.
4710 14th Street West
Bradenton, FL 33507

Limitations: Grants to children of deceased Eagle
servicemen and women, law officers, and firefighters
for dental, medical, and hospital expenses.
Financial data: Year ended 5/31/87. Assets,
$8,962,061 (M); Total giving, $949,318; Grants to
individuals totaling $61,518; Subtotal for dental,
medical, and hospital expenses totaling $14,188.
Employer Identification Number: 396126176

Program description:
To be eligible for assistance, individuals must be children of members of the Fraternal Order of Eagles and the Ladies Auxiliary to it who die from injuries or diseases incurred or aggravated while serving:

- In the armed forces
- As a law enforcement officer
- As a full-time or volunteer firefighter.

Assistance is available to eligible individuals until the age of 18, unless married or self-supporting before the age of 18. The re-marriage of either parent does not change an individual's eligibility.

Total payments to any one recipient for psychiatric, hospital, or orthodontic bills shall not exceed $5,000. No benefits shall be available for injuries or illnesses caused by drug or alcohol abuse, or incurred during the commission of a crime, or if self-inflicted.

818
Eaton Fund, Inc., The
c/o Mercantile-Safe Deposit & Trust Company
Two Hopkins Plaza
Baltimore, MD 21201
Contact: Patricia Bentz, Assistant Vice-President

Limitations: Relief assistance to women 60 years of age or older who are residents of Baltimore, MD, or its vicinity.
Financial data: Year ended 12/31/86. Assets, $82,697 (M); Total giving, $15,450; Grants to individuals, 10 grants totaling $15,450, high $2,700, low $150, general range $1,200-2,400.
Employer Identification Number: 526034106
Applications: Applications accepted throughout the year; Initial approach by letter.
Program description:
Grants are awarded to women who are unable to provide themselves with the adequate necessities of life. The duration of grants depends on the particular situation and need of the recipient.

819
Farmer (Edwin S.) Trust
P.O. Box 9614
Boston, MA 02114-9614
Contact: Harold E. Magnuson, Trustee

Limitations: Grants to aged, indigent women and married couples; preference given to residents of Arlington, MA.
Financial data: Year ended 12/31/84. Assets, $173,899 (M); Total giving, $7,910; Grants to individuals, 5 grants totaling $7,910, high $2,840, low $630.
Employer Identification Number: 046257543
Applications: Applications accepted throughout the year; Initial approach by letter stating marital status, sex, and financial circumstances.

820
Female Association of Philadelphia
c/o Provident National Bank
1632 Chestnut Street
Philadelphia, PA 19103

Limitations: Relief assistance to women in reduced circumstances in the Philadelphia, PA, area.
Financial data: Year ended 9/30/86. Assets, $1,556,613 (M); Total giving, $66,435; Grants to individuals totaling $66,435, high $280, low $125.
Employer Identification Number: 236214961
Applications: Deadlines March 31st and September 30th; Applications should be sent to 2185 Paper Mill Road, Huntingdon Valley, PA 19006.
Program description:
Grants are made to alleviate poverty and distress of elderly women.

821
Ford (The S.N.) and Ada Ford Fund
P.O. Box 849
Mansfield, OH 44901   (419) 526-3493
Contact: Ralph H. LeMunyon, Distribution Committee, 35 North Park Street, Mansfield, OH 44901, President

Limitations: Relief assistance primarily to the aged or incurably ill residing in Richland County, OH.
Financial data: Year ended 12/31/86. Assets, $6,137,779 (M); Total giving, $331,551; Grants to individuals, 357 grants totaling $294,251; Subtotal amount for relief assistance not specified.
Employer Identification Number: 340842282
Publications: Annual report.
Program description:
The fund provides grants for the hospitalization and care of deserving aged people and the incurably sick.

822
Frost (Meshech) Testamentary Trust
c/o BancOhio National Bank Trust Division
155 East Broad Street
Columbus, OH 43251
Contact: Kenneth H. Myers, Secretary-Treasurer, 109 South Washington Street, Tiffin, OH 44883

Limitations: Assistance to needy residents of Tiffin, OH.
Financial data: Year ended 12/31/86. Assets, $2,610,810 (M); Total giving, $145,000; Grants to individuals amount not specified.
Employer Identification Number: 316019431
Applications: Applications accepted throughout the year; Initial approach by letter stating reasons for request.

823
Garrison Community Foundation of Gaston County, Inc.
P.O. Box 123
Gastonia, NC 28053   (704) 864-0927
Contact: Harold T. Sumner, Executive Director

Limitations: Grants for medical expenses only to children, 18 years of age or younger, in the state of North Carolina.
Financial data: Year ended 12/31/86. Assets, $2,353,159 (M); Total giving, $289,586; Grants to individuals, 14 grants totaling $6,741, high $5,000, low $160, average grant $500.
Employer Identification Number: 589830716
Applications: Applications accepted throughout the year; Initial approach by letter; Completion of formal application required; Interviews required.
Publications: Annual report.

824
Gay (Virginia) Fund
c/o Marjorie L. Ater, Secretary-Treasurer
751 Grandon Avenue
Columbus, OH 43209

Limitations: Relief assistance to retired elderly female schoolteachers from Ohio.
Financial data: Year ended 12/31/86. Assets, $975,836 (M); Total giving, $48,394; Grants to individuals, 29 grants totaling $47,394, high $3,600, low $300, general range $1,000-3,000.
Employer Identification Number: 314379588
Applications: Completion of formal application required. Applications from individuals who are not within the stated recipient restriction not accepted.
Program description:
Many awards have been paid in monthly installments on a continuing basis to the same individuals. To be eligible, candidates must have a minimum of 20 years of service as an Ohio schoolteacher.

825
Gibson (Addison H.) Foundation
Two PPG Place, Suite 310
Pittsburgh, PA 15222   (412) 261-1611
Contact: Charlotte G. Kisseleff, Secretary

Limitations: Hospital and medical costs for residents of western Pennsylvania, primarily Allegheny County and the surrounding area, who have correctible physical difficulties.
Financial data: Year ended 12/31/86. Assets, $14,377,661 (M); Total giving, $1,038,976; Grants to individuals, 206 grants totaling $288,976, high $12,000, low $17, general range $300-2,000.
Employer Identification Number: 250965379
Applications: Applications accepted throughout the year; Initial approach by letter requesting application form; Completion of formal application required; Interviews required.
Program description:
An applicant must be referred by a professional in the medical community, and a letter from the patient's physician must attest to diagnosis, plan of treatment, and prognosis. Upon receipt of such written referral, the foundation secretary will schedule an interview with the patient (or a representative of the patient) to discuss the details of financial circumstances accounting for the current need. Only a patient having a correctible physical disability may be eligible for assistance. Application forms are not furnished prior to the personal interview.

826
Gilfillan (Charles D.) Memorial, Inc.
W-555 First National Bank Building
St. Paul, MN 55101
Contact: Marie LaPlante, Secretary of the Committee on Beneficiaries, 200 First Street S.W., Rochester, MN 55905, Tel.: (507) 282-2511

Limitations: Medical, surgical, and dental assistance to financially distressed Minnesota residents, with preference given to those in rural communities and towns with less than 3,000 population.
Financial data: Year ended 3/31/87. Assets, $46,650 (M); Total giving, $48,819; Grants to individuals, 105 grants totaling $48,819, high $1,460, low $6, general range $50-500.
Employer Identification Number: 416028756
Applications: Applications accepted throughout the year; Completion of formal application required.

827★
Gilfillan (Fanny) Memorial, Inc.
c/o Lawrence Harder
Route 4
Redwood Falls, MN 56283

Limitations: Financial assistance only to needy residents of Redwood County, MN.
Financial data: Year ended 12/31/86. Assets, $776,136 (M); Total giving, $64,702; Grants to individuals, 136 grants totaling $64,702, high $5,000, low $6, general range $400-2,000.
Employer Identification Number: 410892731
Applications: Applications accepted throughout the year; Completion of formal application required; Interviews required; Application forms available at Redwood County Welfare Department, Box 27, Redwood Falls, MN 56283; Tel.: (507) 637-6741.
Program description:
The foundation is a charitable organization to help needy people who cannot receive aid by other means, frequently not even through the county welfare office, with which the foundation usually works. People who are not eligible for funds through the office can fill out

an application to the foundation at the welfare office. The board reviews the request and then makes a decision.

Financial assistance usually helps with hospitalization, and medical and dental bills. In 1986, the foundation made awards to 72 individuals, many of whom received multiple awards.

828
Gilmore Foundation
c/o Old Kent Bank of Kalamazoo
151 East Michigan Avenue
Kalamazoo, MI 49007   (616) 383-6956
Contact: Floyd L. Parks, Disbursing Committee

Limitations: Welfare assistance to low-income residents of the Kalamazoo, MI, area who are unable to care for themselves due to physical limitations or advanced age.
Financial data: Year ended 12/31/86. Assets, $1,116 (M); Total giving, $196,062; Grants to individuals, 85 grants totaling $188,513, high $5,725, low $399.
Employer Identification Number: 386052803
Applications: Applications accepted throughout the year; Initial approach by telephone; Completion of formal application required.

829
G.M.L. Foundation
c/o Graham Ralston
P.O. Box 848
Port Angeles, WA 98362

Limitations: Relief assistance limited to residents of Clallam County, WA, who need medical help.
Financial data: Year ended 12/31/86. Assets, $476,360 (M); Total giving, $20,278; Grants to individuals totaling $20,278.
Employer Identification Number: 916030844

830★
God's Love, Inc.
533 North Main Street
Helena, MT 59601   (406) 442-7000
Contact: Ann E. Miller, Manager

Limitations: Welfare assistance primarily to needy individuals and families pending in Helena, MT.
Financial data: Year ended 9/30/86. Assets, $736,589 (M); Total giving, $266,421; Grants to individuals, 1,360 grants totaling $155,608.
Employer Identification Number: 810400234
Applications: Applications accepted throughout the year; Initial approach by letter or telephone.

831
Gore Family Memorial Foundation
c/o Sun Bank
P.O. Box 14728
Fort Lauderdale, FL 33302

Limitations: Relief assistance to needy residents of Broward County, FL, and surrounding areas.
Financial data: Year ended 1/31/87. Assets, $14,623,583 (M); Total giving, $627,434; Grants to individuals, 506 grants totaling $359,850; Subtotal for relief assistance, 348 grants totaling $255,751.
Employer Identification Number: 596497544
Applications: Applications accepted throughout the year; Initial approach by letter to the foundation, 501 East Las Olas Boulevard, Fort Lauderdale, FL 33302.
Publications: Informational brochure.
Program description:
Grants are awarded to assist individuals with medical expenses, equipment for the handicapped, and housing and transportation costs. Most grants are in the form of one-time or short-term assistance.

832
Gossens (Grace A.) Testamentary Trust
c/o Ralph S. Boggs
413 Michigan Street
Toledo, OH 43624   (419) 243-5117

Limitations: Relief assistance to elderly women in rest homes in the Maumee, OH, area.
Financial data: Year ended 9/30/85. Assets, $168,001 (M); Total giving, $5,000; Grants to individuals, 1 grant totaling $5,000.
Employer Identification Number: 346526725

833
Graham Memorial Fund
P.O. Box 533
Bennettsville, SC 29512

Limitations: Medical and general welfare assistance only to residents of Bennettsville, SC.
Financial data: Year ended 9/30/85. Assets, $137,059 (M); Total giving, $13,918; Grants to individuals, 32 grants totaling $13,918; Subtotal for welfare assistance, 10 grants totaling $3,060; high $500, low $96.
Employer Identification Number: 576026184
Applications: Deadline June 1st; Completion of formal application required.

834
Griffin (Abbie M.) Hospital Fund
111 Concord Street
Nashua, NH 03060
Contact: S. Robert Winer, Trustee

Limitations: Grants to needy residents of Merrimack, NH, for the payment of hospital bills.
Financial data: Year ended 12/31/85. Assets, $205,722 (M); Total giving, $12,683; Grants to individuals, 12 grants totaling $12,683, high $4,270, low $84.
Employer Identification Number: 026021464
Applications: Written applications accepted throughout the year.

835
Hall (F.V.), Jr. & Marylou Hall Children's Crisis Foundation
c/o InterFirst Bank, N.A.
P.O. Box 83776
Dallas, TX 75283
Contact: Harry Mayer, Trust Officer, InterFirst Bank

Limitations: Assistance to infants and children under 12 years of age residing in Tom Green County, TX, who are in a situation of crisis, critical need, or critical want.
Financial data: Year ended 4/30/86. Assets, $1,217,038 (M); Total giving, $87,924; Grants to individuals totaling $87,924.
Employer Identification Number: 756260350
Applications: Applications accepted throughout the year; Completion of formal application required; Interviews sometimes required.
Program description:
Eligibility for assistance is limited to children either born as residents in Tom Green County, TX, or who have been physically in residence in the county for more than twelve consecutive months, and whose parents, or those persons responsible for them, have no financial sources available to satisfy the particular critical want or need of the child.

836
Hambay (James T.) Foundation
Dauphin Deposit Bank and Trust Company
P.O. Box 2961
Harrisburg, PA 17105   (717) 255-2174
Contact: Joseph A. Marcri

Limitations: Welfare assistance only to blind, crippled, and indigent children in Harrisburg, PA, and vicinity.
Financial data: Year ended 12/31/86. Assets, $2,048,612 (M); Total giving, $149,116; Grants to individuals totaling $104,833.
Employer Identification Number: 236243877
Applications: Applications accepted throughout the year; Initial approach by letter stating medical expenses and current income.

Program description:
Assistance is primarily given for medical expenses. Support also includes camperships, day care expenses, and transportation. Grants are usually paid directly to the individual or organization providing the services to the individual requiring assistance.

837
Harless (James) Foundation, Incorporated
Drawer D
Gilbert, WV 25621   (304) 664-3227
Contact: Ruth Phipps, Secretary

Limitations: Relief assistance only to distressed families in the Gilbert, WV, area.
Financial data: Year ended 12/31/86. Assets, $1,546,455 (M); Total giving, $152,406; Grants to individuals, 18 grants totaling $8,907, high $2,853, low $50.
Employer Identification Number: 237093387
Applications: Applications accepted throughout the year; Initial approach by letter; Completion of formal application required.

838
Harrison & Conrad Memorial Trust
c/o Sovran Bank
3401 Columbia Pike
Arlington, VA 22204

Limitations: Grants only to children of Leesburg or Loudoun County, VA, suffering from polio, muscular dystrophy or any other crippling disease, and whose families cannot afford treatment.
Financial data: Year ended 1/31/87. Assets, $1,916,429 (M); Total giving, $45,781; Grants to Individuals amount not specified.
Employer Identification Number: 521300410
Applications: Deadline April 1st; Initial approach by letter; Interviews required; Submit application inquiries to the trust committee c/o Loudoun Memorial Hospital, Office of the Administrator, 70 West Cornwall Street, Leesburg, VA 22075; Tel.: (703) 777-3300.

839★
Hawaiian Community Foundation, The
111 South King Street
Honolulu, HI 96813   (808) 538-4540
Contact: Mark J. O'Donnell, Trust Officer, P.O. Box 3170, Honolulu, HI 96802

Limitations: Welfare assistance to needy individuals primarily in Hawaii.
Financial data: Year ended 12/31/86. Assets, $8,881,659 (M); Total giving, $386,296; Grants to individuals, 20 grants totaling $66,257, high $5,000, low $200, general range $200-1,000.
Employer Identification Number: 996003328

Applications: Initial approach by telephone; Completion of formal application required.
Publications: Annual report.
Program description:
The **Winifred D. Robertson Fund** provides one-time only assistance to adult residents of Oahu, HI, who demonstrate financial need or to individuals who have incurred extraordinary expenses because of sudden disability.

The **Alice M.G. Soper Fund** provides one-time only grants to adults, 50 years of age or older, who have financial burdens due to illness or disability.

The **Irving L. Singer Funds** provides one-time only assistance to children of Hawaiian ancestry whose families have insufficient means to pay for expenses incurred in relation to extraordinary medical need, special education, social services, or mental health care.

The **Lillian K. Wilder Fund** provides partial tuition support for learning disabled children. Preference is given to Hawaiian and part-Hawaiian children.

The Children's Fund helps children in need statewide.

The Kitaro Watanabe Fund provides individual assistance to children in need.

840
Hightower (Walter) Foundation
c/o Texas Commerce Bank-El Paso
P.O. Drawer 140
El Paso, TX 79980   (915) 546-6515
Contact: Terry Crenshaw, Charitable Services Officer, Texas Commerce Bank-El Paso

Limitations: Welfare assistance to handicapped children under the age of 21. Project or service must be provided in west Texas or southern New Mexico.
Financial data: Year ended 9/30/86. Assets, $6,528,242 (M); Total giving, $270,701, Grants to individuals, 390 grants totaling $100,860, high $4,116, low $10, general range $50-2,000.
Employer Identification Number: 746293379
Applications: Deadline July 1st; Initial approach by letter; Completion of formal application required.
Program description:
The foundation provides health care items such as orthopedic and orthodontic services, medical and dental treatment, orthopedic shoes, glasses, and prescriptions.

841★
Hopper (The May Templeton) Foundation
(Formerly King's Daughters' Foundation)
1412 Whitney Street
Honolulu, HI 96822   (808) 944-2807
Contact: Diana H. Lord, Administrative Assistant

Limitations: Relief assistance grants only for individuals who are 62 years or older and have been

residents of Hawaii for at least five years. Each applicant is considered on an individual basis without regard to sex, religion, or ethnic background.
Financial data: Year ended 12/31/86. Assets, $7,112,462 (M); Total giving, $346,866; Grants to individuals, 480 grants totaling $287,794, high $7,200, low $240, average grant $3,000.
Employer Identification Number: 990073507
Applications: Deadline: applications generally must be submitted by the fifth working day of the month to be considered during that month; Initial approach by telephone; Completion of two copies of formal application required.
Publications: Annual report, program information, application guidelines.
Program description:
The foundation provides payments to or for numerous individuals to assist with the cost of care or boarding homes, day care center attendance, rental payments, transportation, drug bills, chore and respite service, and general assistance.

842
Howard Benevolent Society
14 Beacon Street, Room 507
Boston, MA 02108

Limitations: Welfare assistance to sick and destitute residents of the Boston, MA, area.
Financial data: Year ended 9/30/85. Assets, $1,367,223 (M); Total giving, $76,925; Grants to individuals, 135 grants totaling $76,925, average grant $570.
Employer Identification Number: 042129132

843
Howland Fund for Aged Women
13 North Sixth Street
New Bedford, MA 02740

Limitations: Relief assistance to poor, aged women primarily residing in New Bedford, MA, area.
Financial data: Year ended 2/28/85. Assets, $170,772 (M); Total giving, $12,000; Grants to individuals, 12 grants totaling $12,000, each grant $1,000.
Employer Identification Number: 046050865
Applications: Applications accepted throughout the year; Initial approach by letter.

844
Hunter (A.V.) Trust, Incorporated
633 Seventeenth Street, Suite 1600
Denver, CO 80202   (303) 292-2048
Contact: Sharon Holt, Secretary

Limitations: Welfare assistance to residents of Denver, CO.
Financial data: Year ended 12/31/86. Assets, $18,662,615 (M); Total giving, $700,027; Grants to

individuals totaling $19,218.
Employer Identification Number: 840461332
Applications: Deadlines July 1st and October 1st;
Initial approach by letter; Completion of formal
application required.
Publications: Annual report (including application
guidelines).
Program description:
Distributions are made to provide aid, comfort,
support, or assistance to children, elderly, indigent
adults, or the crippled, maimed or otherwise needy in
the Denver, CO, area.

845★
Hurlbut (Orion L. & Emma B.) Memorial Fund
c/o First Tennessee Bank, N.A.
701 Market Street
Chattanooga, TN 37401

Limitations: Assistance with medical treatment to
indigent cancer patients at Erlanger Hospital, outside
of Hamilton County, TN.
Financial data: Year ended 4/30/87. Assets,
$9,590,395 (M); Total giving, $328,112; Grants to
individuals, 29 grants totaling $80,171, high $10,352,
low $110.
Employer Identification Number: 626034546
Applications: Applications accepted throughout the
year; For application information contact Jo Ann
Clifford, c/o Chattanooga Tumor Clinic, 975 East Third
Street, Chattanooga, TN 37403; Tel.: (615) 266-3029.
Program description:
Payments are made directly to the physicians and
health facilities providing medical treatment to the
individual recipients.

846
Hutchins (Mary J.) Foundation, Inc.
110 William Street
New York, NY 10038   (212) 602-8529
Contact: John F. Hirsch, III, Senior Vice-President

Limitations: Welfare assistance to indigent people,
primarily in the New York metropolitan area.
Financial data: Year ended 21/31/85. Assets,
$16,954,630 (M); Total giving, $743,175; Grants to
individuals, 13 grants totaling $35,675, high $4,800,
low $1,400.
Employer Identification Number: 136083578

847★
Jefferson (John Percival and Mary C.) Endowment Fund
114 East De La Guerra, No. 7
Santa Barbara, CA 93101
Contact: Patricia M. Brouard, Trustee

Limitations: Relief assistance only to Santa Barbara
County, CA, residents of limited means for medical,
dental and living expenses.
Financial data: Year ended 3/31/87. Assets,
$2,795,714 (M); Total giving, 92,648; Grants to
individuals, 31 grants totaling $71,648, high $7,350,
low $174.
Employer Identification Number: 956005231
Applications: Initial approach by letter; Completion of
formal application required.

848
Jockey Club Foundation
380 Madison Avenue
New York, NY 10017   (212) 599-1919
Contact: Nancy Colletti, Secretary to the Treasurer

Limitations: Relief assistance to needy persons
legitimately connected with the turf and racing.
Financial data: Year ended 12/31/85. Assets,
$3,668,234 (M); Total giving, $136,502; Grants to
individuals, 60 grants totaling $136,502, high $5,200,
low $124.
Employer Identification Number: 136124094
Applications: Applications accepted throughout the
year; Requests should be sent to the above address for
investigation and determination.
Publications: Annual report, program information,
application guidelines.

849
Johnson (Dexter G.) Educational and Benevolent Trust
900 First City Place
Oklahoma City, OK 73102   (405) 232-0003
Contact: Phil E. Daugherty, Trustee

Limitations: Welfare assistance to physically
handicapped residents of Oklahoma.
Financial data: Year ended 12/31/86. Assets,
$5,170,433 (M); Total giving, $17,843; Grants to
individuals, 18 grants totaling $17,843, high $3,836,
low $421.
Employer Identification Number: 237389204
Applications: Applications accepted throughout the
year; Completion of formal application required,
including financial information, family history,
physical condition, age, education goals, and other
data necessary to show need.
Program description:
Assistance includes vocational training, speech
therapy, medical equipment (including orthopedic

devices and hearing aids), audiological evaluations, corrective surgery and hospitalization, and the necessities of life during convalescence.

850
Jones (Walter S. and Evan C.) Foundation
527 Commercial Street, Room 515
Emporia, KS 66801   (316) 342-1714
Contact: Dorothy E. Melander, General Manager

Limitations: Assistance with medical expenses for persons who have been continuous residents of Lyon, Coffey or Osage counties, KS, for at least one year, and who are under the age of 21.
Financial data: Year ended 3/31/87. Assets, $3,779 (M); Total giving, $705,174,; Grants to individuals, 1,688 grants totaling $561,020, high $17,855, low $10, general range $100-700.
Employer Identification Number: 237384087
Applications: Deadline prior to the beginning of services; Initial approach by letter; Completion of formal application required; Interviews sometimes required; Interviews granted upon request.
Publications: Program information.
Program description:
Grants for medical assistance are awarded based on financial need. Parents of applicants must complete a comprehensive financial statement and furnish any additional financial information requested.

851
Lake (William B.) Foundation
Fidelity Bank NA
Broad and Walnut Streets
Philadelphia, PA 19109
Contact: Shopia O'Lessker, Foundation Social Worker, Foxcraft Square Apartments, No. 815, Jenkintown, PA 19046

Limitations: Welfare assistance to residents of Pennsylvania, primarily Philadelphia residents, suffering from lung disease.
Financial data: Year ended 5/31/87. Assets, $521,936 (M); Total giving, $29,152; Grants to individuals, 10 grants totaling $29,152, high $6,450, low $300.
Employer Identification Number: 236266137
Applications: Deadlines May 1st and November 1st; Initial approach by letter with full details and supporting documents.

852
Larrabee Fund Association
c/o The Connecticut National Bank
777 Main Street
Hartford, CT 06115   (203) 728-4150

Limitations: Relief assistance to indigent women in the Hartford, CT, area.
Financial data: Year ended 10/31/85. Assets,

$1,590,665 (M); Total giving, $242,340; Grants to individuals, 61 grants totaling $242,340, high $4,550, low $50.
Employer Identification Number: 066038638
Applications: Applications accepted throughout the year.

853
Leader Foundation, The
8182 Maryland Avenue
St. Louis, MO 63105
Contact: Edwin G. Shifrin, Vice-President

Limitations: Welfare assistance primarily in the form of pensions for residents of St. Louis, MO.
Financial data: Year ended 2/1/87. Assets, $2,577,983 (M); Total giving, $70,129; Grants to individuals, 26 grants totaling $70,129, high $6,160, low $250.
Employer Identification Number: 436036864
Applications: Applications accepted throughout the year; Initial approach by letter.

854
Lend A Hand Society
34 1/2 Beacon Street
Boston, MA 02108

Limitations: Relief assistance to needy individuals in the Boston, MA, area.
Financial data: Year ended 12/31/85. Assets, $1,299,373 (M); Total giving, $88,020; Grants to individuals, amount not specified; 1984, Grants to individuals, 506 grants totaling $31,256, high $457, low $10.
Employer Identification Number: 042104384

855★
Levin (Mosette) Charitable Trust
c/o First Citizens Bank, N.A. - Trust Department
P.O. Box 1125
Michigan City, IN 46360

Limitations: Medical assistance to residents of La Porte County, IN, who are suffering from cancer or who are crippled children under the age of 16.
Financial data: Year ended 12/31/87. Assets, $389,579 (M); Total giving, $7,509; Grants to individuals, 20 grants totaling $7,509, high $2,000, low $10, general range $15-200, average grant $100.
Employer Identification Number: 356031456
Applications: Applications accepted throughout the year; Completion of formal application required; Interviews required.
Publications: Financial statement, 990-PF printed copy available upon request.

Program description:
The trust awards grants for all aspects of aiding recipients in receiving medical treatment, including the emergency purchase of medication and payment for transportation to receive treatment.

856
Mainzer (Max) Memorial Foundation, Inc.
300 Park Avenue South
New York, NY 10010   (212) 533-7100
Contact: United Help's Scholarship Fund

Limitations: Relief assistance to needy members or widows of members of the American Jewish K.C. Fraternity.
Financial data: Year ended 3/31/86. Assets, $274,724 (M); Total giving, $31,170; Grants to individuals, 15 grants totaling $31,170, high $9,600, low $300, general range $500-3,500, average grant $2,000.
Employer Identification Number: 116008008
Applications: Contact foundation for current application information.
Program description:
Grants are made to individuals in the U.S. and other countries.

857
Merchants-Oliver Fund
(Formerly Merchants Fund)
Public Ledger Building, Room 1266
Philadelphia, PA 19106
Contact: Reverand Henry W. Kaufman, Secretary-Treasurer

Limitations: Relief assistance only to indigent merchants or their widows and families in the Philadelphia, PA, area.
Financial data: Year ended 12/31/86 Assets, $3,623,871 (M); Total giving, $199,128; Grants to individuals, 48 grants totaling $199,128, high $5,652, low $900.
Employer Identification Number: 231980213
Applications: Applications accepted throughout the year; Completion of formal application required.

858
Middleton (Kate Klinloch) Fund
P.O. Drawer 2527
Mobile, AL 36601
Contact: Joan Sapp

Limitations: Grants or four-percent loans to residents of Mobile County, AL, to help pay the expenses of unexpected serious illness involving hospitalization and medical services.
Financial data: Year ended 1/31/87. Assets, $1,741,363 (M); Total giving, $125,774; Grants to individuals, 65 grants totaling $125,774, high $4,073, low $31; Loans to individuals, 1 loan totaling $4,508.

Employer Identification Number: 636018539
Applications: Initial approach by interview to disclose medical problem and related financial burden.

859
Moore (Cornelia M.) Free Dental Foundation
c/o Wells Fargo Bank
1001 State Street, P.O. Box HH
Santa Barbara, CA 93102
Contact: Janet Reed Koed, Director, Dental Health Services

Limitations: Assistance with dental expenses only to residents of Santa Barbara, CA, who are under the age of 16.
Financial data: Year ended 12/31/86. Assets, $620,473 (M); Total giving, $38,400; Grants to individuals totaling $38,400.
Employer Identification Number: 956297978
Program description:
Funds are paid to dentists on behalf of individuals. Individual grants do not exceed $300 treatment on the foundation's fee schedule. Each family is responsible for a $20 co-payment.

860
Morton (Mark) Memorial Fund
110 North Wacker Drive
Chicago, IL 60606

Limitations: Grants to individuals to assist with hospital, medical, and surgical expenses, as well as assistance to the aged, blind, or disabled.
Financial data: Year ended 12/31/86. Assets, $9,892,856 (M); Total giving, $496,304; Grants to individuals, 242 grants totaling $496,304.
Employer Identification Number: 237181380
Applications: Applications accepted throughout the year.

861
Mulberger (Lorraine) Foundation, Inc.
10214 North Tatum Boulevard
Phoenix, AZ 85028   (602) 483-1613
Contact: Joseph Erlichman

Limitations: Welfare assistance to needy individuals.
Financial data: Year ended 12/31/86. Assets, $304,765 (M); Total giving, $99,910; Grants to individuals, 11 grants totaling $73,010.
Employer Identification Number: 396106007
Applications: Applications accepted throughout the year; Completion of formal application required.

862
National Solar Energy Consortium
666 Baker Street, Suite 405
Costa Mesa, CA 92626   (714) 557-0202
Contact: Barry S. Tabachnick

Limitations: Grant assistance to individuals installing a qualified solar energy domestic hot water system in their home.
Financial data: Year ended 3/31/86. Assets, $132,512 (M); Total giving, $223,750; Grants to individuals, 165 grants totaling $223,750, high $3,264, low $135.
Employer Identification Number: 330102171
Applications: Submit applications to 17330 Brookhurst Street, Suite 350, Fountain Valley, CA; Tel.: (714) 964-0898.
Program description:
The foundation promotes "energy conservation and the use of renewable energy resources and to assist, to the extent possible, energy conservation applications in a manner which renders such applications financially viable." The Solar Energy Conservation Assistance Program (SECAP) helps defray the cost of a qualified solar energy domestic hot water system by providing grants to individuals who purchase and install the system in their home.

863
New Horizons Foundation
700 South Flower Street, Suite 1122
Los Angeles, CA 90017-4160   (213) 626-4160
Contact: G. Grant Gifford, President

Limitations: Financial assistance to needy Christian Scientists who are over 65 years of age and are residents of Los Angeles County, CA.
Financial data: Year ended 5/31/87. Assets, $425,537 (M); Total giving, $35,962; Grants to individuals, 17 grants totaling $35,962, high $6,000, low $165.
Employer Identification Number: 956031571
Applications: Applications accepted throughout the year; Initial approach by letter or telephone; Interviews required.
Program description:
Applicants, members of any Christian Science Church, must have run out of all conventional means of support, public or otherwise prior to seeking assistance from the foundation.

864
New York Society for the Relief of Widows & Orphans of Medical Men
c/o Davies & Davies
50 East 42nd Street
New York, NY 10017
Contact: Walter Wichern

Limitations: Financial assistance in the form of annuities.

Financial data: Year ended 3/31/86. Assets, $1,754,481 (M); Total giving, $70,384; Grants to individuals, 7 grants totaling $70,384, high $20,289, low $4,215.
Employer Identification Number: 237156733
Applications: Deadline November 15th.

865
NFL Alumni Foundation Fund
c/o Sigmund M. Hyman
P.O. Box 248
Stevenson, MD 21153-0248   (301) 486-5454

Limitations: Relief assistance to physically or mentally disabled former National Football League alumni (prior to 1959), including grants for death benefits and medical expenses.
Financial data: Year ended 5/31/86. Assets, $54,636 (M); Total giving, $179,076; Grants to individuals totaling $179,076.
Employer Identification Number: 237087489
Applications: Applications accepted throughout the year; Initial approach by letter including proof of income.

866
Nicholl (James R.) Memorial Foundation
c/o The Central Trust Company of Northern Ohio, Trust Department
1949 Broadway
Lorain, OH 44052   (216) 244-1965
Contact: David E. Nocjar, Trust Officer

Limitations: Medical and surgical assistance to needy children (2 to 21 years of age) who have been residents of Lorain County, OH, for at least two years.
Financial data: Year ended 12/31/86. Assets, $782,713 (M); Total giving, $33,758; Grants to individuals, 78 grants totaling $33,758; Subtotal for medical assistance, 64 grants totaling $9,994, high $1,070, low $6.
Employer Identification Number: 346574742
Applications: Applications accepted throughout the year; Completion of formal application required.
Publications: Annual report, program information, application guidelines.
Program description:
Many 1986 recipients received multiple awards for medical and surgical assistance.

867★
Nurses House, Inc.
Ten Columbus Circle
New York, NY 10019   (212) 582-1022
Contact: Patricia B. Barry, Executive Director

Limitations: Short-term assistance to ill and indigent registered nurses in the U.S. who are in need of financial assistance to help meet basic living expenses.

Costs of medical care and education are not funded.
Financial data: Year ended 12/31/87. Assets, $741,614
(M); Total giving, $51,537; Grants to individuals, 139
grants totaling $51,537, high $4,490, low $560,
general range $879-2,214, average grant $1,515.
Employer Identification Number: 131927913
Applications: Applications accepted throughout the
year; Initial approach by letter; Completion of formal
application required, except in some one-time
emergency situations; Interviews granted upon request.
Publications: Program information, application
guidelines, financial statement, informational
brochure, newsletter, 990-PF printed copy available
upon request.
Program description:
Recipients are professional registered nurses who may
require assistance because of age, illness, disability,
destitution, or other reasons. Guidance, information,
and referrals are also offered as needed. Services are
given without regard to race, creed, color, or sex.

868
Oshkosh Foundation
c/o First Wisconsin National Bank of Oshkosh
P.O. Box 2448
Oshkosh, WI 54903   (414) 424-4283
Contact: Sandra A. Noe, Trust Officer

Limitations: Medical assistance for the indigent of
Oshkosh, WI.
Financial data: Year ended 2/28/86. Assets,
$5,227,792 (M); Total giving, $335,781; Grants to
individuals amount not specified.
Employer Identification Number: 396041638
Applications: Applications accepted throughout the
year; Initial approach by letter.
Publications: Annual report.
Program description:
Funds may be used for any purpose as long as they
are for the benefit of local residents. Emphasis in the
past has been on medical care of the indigent.

869
Perkins (B.F. & Rose H.) Foundation
P.O. Box 1064
Sheridan, WY 82801   (307) 674-8871

Limitations: Medical assistance to individuals who are
from two to 20 years of age and have been residents
of Sheridan County, TX, for the last two consecutive
years.
Financial data: Year ended 12/31/86. Assets,
$5,461,464 (M); Total giving, $46,921; Grants to
individuals, 156 grants totaling $46,921; Subtotal for
medical assistance, 151 grants totaling $46,021, high
$3,845, low $17.
Employer Identification Number: 830138740
Applications: Deadline to submit completed form from
individual and doctor is by the first week of the month

prior to treatment; Completion of formal application
required; Application forms for individual to be
obtained from above address plus form to be sent by
foundation to doctor for estimate of charges prior to
treatment; Interviews required.

870★
Perpetual Benevolent Fund, The
c/o BayBank Middlesex
300 Washington Street
Newton, MA 02158   (617) 894-6500
Contact: Marjorie M. Kelley, Secretary

Limitations: Financial assistance to needy individuals,
with preference to residents of Newton and Waltham,
and adjacent communities in MA.
Financial data: Year ended 8/31/87. Assets,
$1,787,811 (M); Total giving, $102,953; Grants to
individuals totaling $102,953, high $1,000, low $90,
general range $300-500.
Employer Identification Number: 237011723
Applications: Applications accepted throughout the
year; Initial approach by telephone or proposal;
Completion of formal application required.
Publications: Application guidelines.
Program description:
Financial assistance is given to those who have no
other resource and who need emergency aid as
payment of overdue utility bills, overdue rent, heating
oil deliveries, clothing, therapy sessions and numerous
other needs.
   Applications for funds are channeled through local
agencies, schools, the welfare department, hospitals,
and clinics; the staff of the agencies interview
applicants.
   The majority of grants approved are to one-parent
families and individuals in crisis.

871
Pierce (Katherine C.) Trust
c/o State Street Bank & Trust Company
P.O. Box 351
Boston, MA 02101   (617) 654-3321
Contact: William B. Osgood, Vice-President

Limitations: "For the relief of needy and deserving
gentlewomen in reduced circumstances, that their
lives may be made more comfortable.".
Financial data: Year ended 12/31/85. Assets, $615,311
(M); Total giving, $26,490; Grants to individuals, 12
grants totaling $26,490, high $4,000, low $200,
general range $1,000-4,000.
Employer Identification Number: 046095694
Applications: Applications accepted throughout the
year; Initial approach by letter describing self, needs
and financial condition.

872
Pilgrim Foundation, The
478 Torrey Street
Brockton, MA 02401-4654   (617) 586-6100
Contact: Sherry Yuskaitis, Executive Director

Limitations: Welfare assistance to needy families and children who are residents of Brockton, MA.
Financial data: Year ended 12/31/86. Assets, $2,310,246 (M); Total giving, $49,604; Grants to individuals totaling $49,604; Subtotal for welfare assistance totaling $14,804.
Employer Identification Number: 042104834
Applications: Contact foundation for current application deadline.
Program description:
Assistance includes grants providing camping and memberships in character-building facilities.

873
Pine Mountain Benevolent Foundation, Inc.
P.O. Box 2301
Columbus, GA 31902

Limitations: Welfare assistance primarily to worthy and needy individuals residing in GA.
Financial data: Year ended 6/30/86. Assets, $1,460,967 (M); Total giving, $172,300; Grants to individuals, 4 grants totaling $3,150, high $1,800, low $150.
Employer Identification Number: 586033162
Applications: Applications accepted throughout the year.

874
Portland Female Charitable Society
c/o Janet Matty
P.O. Box 5202
Portland, ME 04101

Limitations: Aid limited to needy residents of Portland, ME, for dental care, prescriptions, hearing aids, glasses, or other needs having to do with health, food, or shelter, with emphasis on the needs of children, the elderly, and the ill.
Financial data: Year ended 9/30/86. Assets, $124,627 (M); Total giving, $6,215; Grants to individuals, 45 grants totaling $6,215, high $364, low $20.
Employer Identification Number: 010370961
Applications: Requests accepted throughout the year; Full information required; Requests usually presented by social workers, public health nurses, counselors, etc.; Interviews required. **Applications from individuals residing outside of stated geographic restriction not accepted.**

875
Portland Seaman's Friend Society
14 Lewis Street
Westbrook, ME 04082
Contact: Franklin C. Emery, Executive Director

Limitations: Welfare assistance in the form of a small monthly stipend to indigent seamen.
Financial data: Year ended 12/31/84. Assets, $84,028 (M); Total giving, $21,810; Grants to individuals, 40 grants totaling $21,810.
Employer Identification Number: 010211545

876
Presser Foundation, The
Presser Place
Bryn Mawr, PA 19010   (215) 525-4797
Contact: Henderson Supplee III, President

Limitations: Emergency aid to needy, aged, music teachers.
Financial data: Year ended 6/30/86. Assets, $9,310,419 (M); Total giving, $665,881; Grants to individuals totaling $17,618.
Employer Identification Number: 232164013
Applications: Applications accepted throughout the year; Completion of formal application required.

877
Quarter Century Fund, The
c/o International Paper Company
77 West 45th Street
New York, NY 10036
Contact: John M. Nevin, President

Limitations: Relief assistance to indigent dependents of deceased members of The Quarter-Century Society, Inc.
Financial data: Year ended 12/31/86. Assets, $47,042 (M); Total giving, $600; Grants to individuals, 1 grant totaling $600; 1985, Grants to individuals, 20 grants totaling $4,958.
Employer Identification Number: 136183090
Program description:
Grants are given upon recommendation from clergy, relatives, or others who have knowledge of the individuals' plight.

878★
Rambaud (Lulu Bryan) Charitable Trust
First RepublicBank Houston, N.A.
P.O. Box 2518
Houston, TX 77252-2518

Limitations: Financial and medical assistance only to indigent, elderly women residents of Houston and Harris County, TX.
Financial data: Year ended 12/31/87. Assets, $775,000 (M); Grants to individuals, 4 grants totaling $10,000,

high $3,000, low $1,200, general range $1,000-5,000, average grant $2,500.
Employer Identification Number: 746033114
Applications: Applications accepted throughout the year.
Publications: Program information.
Program description:
Individuals are referred by Sheltering Arms on the basis of need and lack of other resources.

879
Reade Industrial Fund
c/o Harris Trust and Savings Bank
P.O. Box 755 - 111 West Monroe Street
Chicago, IL 60690   (312) 461-2613
Contact: Ellen A. Bechthold, Assistant Vice-President

Limitations: Emergency loans or grants to individuals who are employed or have been employed in industry in Illinois.
Financial data: Year ended 12/31/85. Assets, $2,186,764 (M); Total giving, $159,999; Grants to individuals, 62 grants totaling $159,999, high $5,000, low $50.
Employer Identification Number: 366048673
Applications: Applications accepted throughout the year; Initial approach by letter; Completion of formal application required.
Program description:
Grants of up to $5,000 are given only to "individuals of good moral character, who are or have been employed in industry in the State of Illinois, and who shall by reason of an emergency beyond their control, such as accidental injury, illness of themselves or family members, inability to obtain any employment, or sudden and involuntary cessation of employment, be unable to care for themselves and their spouse and children and be in need of aid."

880
Rixson (Oscar C.) Foundation, Inc.
P.O. Box 963
Hendersonville, NC 28793   (704) 891-5490
Contact: Thomas Elliott, President

Limitations: Financial assistance for needy active retired religious workers.
Financial data: Year ended 12/31/86. Assets, $1,916,053 (M); Total giving, $103,000; Grants to individuals, 94 grants totaling $18,800, each grant $200.
Employer Identification Number: 136129767
Applications: Applications accepted throughout the year; Initial approach by letter.

881★
Robbins (Charlotte M.) Trust
c/o State Street Bank & Trust Company
225 Franklin Street
Boston, MA 02110   (617) 654-3360
Contact: Cheryl D. Curtin, Vice-President

Limitations: Assistance limited to aged couples and/or aged women who are residents of the towns of Groton, Ayer, Harvard, Shirley, and Littleton, MA.
Financial data: Year ended 12/31/85. Assets, $213,070 (M); Total giving, $11,154; Grants to individuals, 5 grants totaling $11,154, high $4,000, low $454, general range $2,000-4,000.
Employer Identification Number: 046096044
Applications: Applications accepted throughout the year; Initial approach by letter including income, expenses, assets, and why money is requested; Interviews required.

882
Rouch (A.P. and Louise) Boys Foundation
c/o Twin Falls Bank & Trust, Trust Department
P.O. Box 7
Twin Falls, ID 83303-0007

Limitations: Relief assistance to needy children in the Magic Valley area of Idaho.
Financial data: Year ended 12/31/85. Assets, $202,906 (M); Total giving, $17,144; Grants to individuals, 94 grants totaling $17,144; Subtotal for relief assistance, 81 grants totaling $13,412, high $500, low $5.
Employer Identification Number: 826005152
Program description:
Assistance is given in the form of clothing, medical care and summer camp fees.

883
Rutledge (Edward) Charity
P.O. Box 758
404 North Bridge Street
Chippewa Falls, WI 54729   (715) 723-6618
Contact: John Frampton, President

Limitations: Charitable gifts and loans to needy residents of Chippewa County, WI.
Financial data: Year ended 5/31/87. Assets, $2,409,780 (M) Total giving, $76,136; Grants to individuals, 222 grants totaling $57,036; Subtotal for relief assistance, 192 grants totaling $15,928, high $500, low $6.
Employer Identification Number: 390806178
Applications: Applications accepted throughout the year; Completion of formal application required.

884★
Saak (Charles E.) Trust
c/o Wells Fargo Bank - Trust Department
618 East Shaw Avenue
Fresno, CA 93710   (209) 442-6232

Limitations: Dental and emergency medical assistance
to children under 21 years of age from low-income
families residing in the Porterville/Poplar area of
Tulare County, CA.
Financial data: Year ended 1/31/87. Assets,
$1,070,433 (M); Total giving, $41,894; Grants to
individuals, 343 grants totaling $37,192; Subtotal for
dental assistance, 232 grants totaling $21,885, high
$835, low $45, general range $50-70.
Employer Identification Number: 946076213
Applications: Deadline March 31st; Completion of
formal application required; Application must be
submitted with purpose and estimate statement,
parents' financial statement and copy of most recent
income tax return; Additional telephone number is
(805) 395-0920.
Program description:
Medical and dental grants are awarded on a one-time
basis only. One award will cover the total cost up to
the total grant award amount of one injury, sickness,
or dental treatment. Additional unpredicted costs
related to the same injury, sickness, or dental
treatment must be pre-approved by the trustee.
    In 1987, all assistance was awarded for dental
treatment.

885
Sailors' Snug Harbor of Boston
111 Devonshire Street, Third Floor
Boston, MA 02109   (617) 426-7320
Contact: Lincoln B. Hansel, President

Limitations: Welfare assistance to aged sailors,
primarily in the Boston, MA, area.
Financial data: Year ended 4/30/86. Assets,
$4,098,319 (M); Total giving, $202,272; Grants to
individuals, 1 grant totaling $3,685.
Employer Identification Number: 042104430

886
Saint Paul Foundation, The
1120 Norwest Center
St. Paul, MN 55101   (612) 224-5463
Contact: Paul A. Verret, President

Limitations: Relief assistance to residents of St. Paul
and Minneapolis, MN, and to employees of 3M
Company.
Financial data: Year ended 12/31/86. Total giving,
$100,007,539 (M); Total giving, $4,664,281; Grants to
individuals, 145 grants totaling $108,991; Subtotal for
relief assistance amount not specified.
Employer Identification Number: 416031510
Publications: Annual report.

887
Scatena (Virginia) Memorial Fund for San
Francisco School Teachers
c/o Bank of America, NT & SA, Trust Tax No. 8009
233 North Fair Oaks Avenue
Pasadena, CA 91103
Contact: Cheri Kraus, Bank of America NT & SA, 720
Third Street, Santa Rosa, CA 95404

Limitations: Assistance to needy, sick or disabled
teachers of the San Francisco Public School
Department in active duty or retired, as selected by an
advisory committee.
Financial data: Year ended 12/31/86. Assets, $118,054
(M); Total giving, $16,900; Grants to individuals, 10
grants totaling $16,900, high $2,600, low $600.
Employer Identification Number: 946073769
Applications: Applications accepted throughout the
year; Completion of formal application required;
Applications are reviewed semi-annually by advisory
committee.
Program description:
Awards are paid as decided by advisory committee.

888
Schoellkopf (J.F.) Mutual Aid Society Silver
Wedding Fund
c/o Manufacturers Traders Trust Company
1 M&T Plaza
Buffalo, NY 14240   (716) 842-5535
Contact: Mr. Arthur Maciejewski, c/o Buffalo Color
Corporation, 340 Elk Street, Buffalo, NY 14240

Limitations: Welfare assistance primarily to indigent
residents of Buffalo, NY, who are members or spouses
or children of members of the Mutual Aid Society.
Financial data: Year ended 12/31/85. Assets, $817,304
(M); Grants to individuals, 24 grants totaling $36,825,
high $1,950, low $375, general range $1,550-1,750.
Employer Identification Number: 166030147
Program description:
Grants are awarded for the most part on an ongoing
basis to indigent families, as well as to individuals as
temporary aid.

889
Scottish Rite Oregon Consistory Almoner Fund,
Inc.
709 Southwest 15th Avenue
Portland, OR 97205   (503) 228-9405
Contact: G.L. Selmyhr

Limitations: Relief assistance only to distressed
Masons, and wives, widows, or children of Masons,
within the state of Oregon.
Financial data: Year ended 9/30/86. Assets, $293,723
(M); Total giving, $13,728; Grants to individuals
totaling $13,728.
Employer Identification Number: 237154746

Applications: Applications accepted throughout the year.
Program description:
Disbursements have been made to assist with medical, hospital, or other pressing bills.

890
Sequoia Trust Fund
555 California Street, 36th Floor
San Francisco, CA 94104   (415) 393-8552
Contact: Walker M. Baird, Secretary

Limitations: Financial assistance primarily in California to needy people who, by their special talents, have given great pleasure to others. This assistance is only for special and unusual medical expenses.
Financial data: Year ended 9/30/86. Assets, $1,334,305 (M); Total giving, $37,100; Grants to individuals, 3 grants totaling $9,100.
Employer Identification Number: 946065506
Applications: Initial approach by letter; Completion of formal application, with complete details, required.

891
Shaw Fund for Mariner's Children
c/o Russell Brier & Company
50 Congress Street, Room 800
Boston, MA 02109
Contact: Olivia Constable

Limitations: Welfare assistance only to mariners, their wives or widows, and their children who are in distress and reside in Massachusetts.
Financial data: Year ended 12/31/85. Assets, $2,340,556 (M); Total giving, $99,628; Grants to individuals totaling $99,628.
Employer Identification Number: 042104861
Applications: Applications accepted throughout the year; Initial approach by letter addressed to 23 Craigie Street, Cambridge, MA 02138.
Publications: Program information.

892
Sheadle (Jasper H.) Trust
c/o The AmeriTrust Corporation
900 Euclid Avenue
Cleveland, OH 44101   (216) 687-5360
Contact: Robert S. Kessler, Vice-President

Limitations: Annuities only to American born aged couples or aged women (60 and over) of good character residing in Cuyahoga or Mahoning counties, OH.
Financial data: Year ended 12/31/86. Assets, $2,172,933 (M); Total giving, $91,885; Grants to individuals, 340 grants totaling $91,885, high $540, low $50, general range $150-450.
Employer Identification Number: 346506457
Applications: Applications accepted throughout the

year; Completion of formal application required; Interviews required.
Program description:
Applicants for pension assistance are usually nominated by institutions through letter to the trust managers. Information required includes current income, expenses, and assets.

893
Smock (Frank L. and Laura L.) Foundation
c/o Lincoln National Bank and Trust Company
P.O. Box 960
Fort Wayne, IN 46801-0960   (219) 461-6451
Contact: Alice Kopfer, Assistant Vice-President

Limitations: Medical and nursing care assistance to ailing, needy, crippled, blind or elderly individuals of the Presbyterian faith throughout Indiana.
Financial data: Year ended 12/31/86. Assets, $6,779,453 (M); Total giving, $317,562; Grants to individuals, 41 grants totaling $188,942, high $43,651, low $12, genral range $1,000-3,000, average grant $924.
Employer Identification Number: 356011335
Applications: Applications accepted throughout the year; Initial approach by letter; Completion of formal application required.
Program description:
Need level usually means an individual with no more than $3,000 in assets.

894
St. Benedict's Charitable Society
1663 Bristol Pike
Bensalem, PA 19020
Contact: Margaret Kuehmatedt, Treasurer

Limitations: Relief assistance to aged, infirm, needy people, for basic living, funeral, and medical expenses. Funds are completely allocated for the foreseeable future. No new applications are being considered.
Financial data: Year ended 12/31/86. Assets, $160,671 (M); Total giving, $9,900; Grants to individuals, 3 grants totaling $3,600, high $1,800, low $600.
Employer Identification Number: 236256990

895
Stearns-Blodgett Trust
c/o First Interstate Bank of Nevada
P.O. Box 30100
Reno, NV 89520   (702) 784-3316

Limitations: Aid limited to indigent persons in need of ophthalmological care who are residents of Nevada and northern California.
Financial data: Year ended 1/31/87. Assets, $1,173,470 (M); Total giving, $91,087; Grants to individuals, 33 grants totaling $91,087, high $9,656,

low $20.
Employer Identification Number: 886033781
Applications: Completion of formal application required; Application must be certified by a sponsor (licensed M.D., state-certified hospital, member of the Knight Templar or the Free and Accepted Masons, or a cooperating organization approved by the committee).
Publications: Application guidelines.
Program description:
Eligible applicants include persons residing within Nevada or California and north of an irregular line extending in straight segments from the intersection of the Nevada-Utah boundary with the 37th parallel north to the community of Bridgeport, CA, to Yuba City, CA, and then to Point Arena, CA. Very deserving cases may be noted at very short distances to the south of this irregular line. However, the medical treatment itself need not be performed within this geographical area.

Excluded from consideration are the following:
  1. Illegal aliens
  2. Payment of glasses, unless needed as part of authorized surgery, or if the first pair for children to prevent severe eye deterioration.
  3. Payment for cosmetic surgery, except for cross eyes (esotropia, strabismus, squint, or muscle surgery) for persons under the age of 50.

896
Steeplechase Fund
P.O. Box 308
Belmont Race Track
Elmont, NY 11003

Limitations: Relief assistance to injured jockeys and needy widows of jockeys.
Financial data: Year ended 12/31/84. Assets, $318,172 (M); Total giving, $12,176; Grants to individuals, 11 grants totaling $12,176, high $3,000, low $138, general range $200-1,000.
Employer Identification Number: 136067724
Program description:
Assistance to former steeplechase riders and their widows and families includes payment of medical expenses, especially for injuries incurred in racing accidents.

897
Stewards Foundation RGH Trust
P.O. Box 98247
Des Moines, WA 98188   (206) 878-5919
Contact: Robert A. Hanson, Administrator

Limitations: Grants to Washington residents needing assistance to pay for health care.
Financial data: Year ended 12/31/86. Assets, $487,808 (M); Total giving, $189,209; Grants to individuals, 163 grants totaling $189,209, high $38,052, low $10.
Employer Identification Number: 363232076

Applications: Applications accepted throughout the year; Completion of formal application required.
Program description:
Assistance with medical expenses is paid directly to the physician or health care facility on behalf of the individual recipient.

898
Stillman (Chauncey) Benevolent Fund
c/o Kelly, Drye & Warren
101 Park Avenue
New York, NY 10178
Contact: Louis B. Warren, Trustee

Limitations: Relief assistance to the needy, aged, sick and disabled. All funds presently committed.
Financial data: Year ended 1/31/86. Assets, $48,482 (M); Total giving, $31,702; Grants to individuals, 9 grants totaling $31,702; Subtotal for relief assistance, 6 grants totaling $9,702, high $3,000, low $600.
Employer Identification Number: 136113811
Applications: All funds presently committed.
Program description:
Grants to the needy are made on the basis of financial need, age, sickness or disability. Also considered is the existence of the applicant's family and the nature of the individual's general living conditions.

899
Sunnyside, Inc.
8609 N.W. Plaza Drive, Suite 201
Dallas, TX 75225   (214) 692-5686
Contact: Mary Rothenflue, Executive Director

Limitations: Assistance to underprivileged children residing in Texas to provide for their physical, moral and spiritual needs.
Financial data: Year ended 12/31/86. Assets, $1,303,662 (M); Total giving, $179,731; Grants to individuals, 83 grants totaling $99,731; Subtotal for welfare assistance, 65 grants totaling $69,831, high $6,659, low $150.
Employer Identification Number: 756037004
Applications: Applications accepted throughout the year; Completion of formal application required.
Program description:
In 1986, over 25 percent of aid to children was in the form of providing camperships.

900
Sussman (Otto) Trust
c/o Sullivan and Cromwell
125 Broad Street, 28th Floor
New York, NY 10004
Contact: Nancy Beagan

Limitations: Assistance to residents of New York, New Jersey, Oklahoma, and Pennsylvania in need due to death or illness in their immediate families or some

other unusual or unfortunate circumstance.
Financial data: Year ended 12/31/85. Assets,
$2,136,281 (M); Total giving, $103,318; Grants to
individuals, 43 grants totaling $103,318; Subtotal for
assistance, 25 grants totaling $59,292.
Employer Identification Number: 136075849
Applications: Applications accepted throughout the
year; Initial contact by letter requesting application
and setting forth circumstances giving rise to need;
Completion of formal application required.
Publications: Application guidelines.
Program description:
Grants to assist with medical bills and caretaking
expenses for people with serious or terminal illness.

901
Swiss Benevolent Society of Chicago
P.O. Box 2137
Chicago, IL 60690
Contact: Admiral Alan Weber, President

Limitations: Relief assistance to needy or elderly
Chicago area residents of Swiss descent or nationality.
Financial data: Year ended 12/31/86. Assets,
$1,311,558 (M); Total giving, $58,482; Grants to
individuals, $58,482; No grants for relief assistance;
1985, Grants to individuals totaling $54,285; Subtotal
for relief assistance, 10 grants totaling $22,900, high
$2,550, low $1,350.
Employer Identification Number: 366076395
Applications: Contact foundation for current
application deadline; Completion of formal
application required.
Publications: Program information.
Program description:
Grants are made to eligible individuals in case of need
or emergency.

902
Tallman Boys Fund Trust
c/o City National Bank, Trust Department
189 East Court Street
Kankakee, IL 60901   (815) 937-3690

Limitations: Relief assistance to Protestant boys under
21 years of age who are residents of Kankakee
County, IL.
Financial data: Year ended 1/31/87. Assets,
$1,238,408 (M); Total giving, $125,945; Grants to
individuals totaling $125,945.
Employer Identification Number: 366024917
Applications: Applications accepted throughout the
year; Completion of formal application required;
Interviews granted upon request.
Publications: Annual report.
Program description:
The foundation provides funds to help boys who are
neglected or homeless or in need of training,
supervision, or other services. The scope of the

foundation is not intended to aid delinquents or boys
with drug or alcohol problems, but those who need
short-term aid of various types to set their lives in
order. There is not a scholarship fund, but educational
or vocational benefits may be requested. All grants are
made to 501(c)(3) organizations to be applied on
behalf of individuals.

903
Thayer (Pauline Revere) Memorial Pension Fund
State Street Bank & Trust Company
P.O. Box 351
Boston, MA 02101   (617) 266-4860
Contact: President, Chilton Club, 92 Mt. Vernon
Street, Boston, MA

Limitations: Pension assistance only to needy and
deserving employees of the Chilton Club of Boston,
MA.
Financial data: Year ended 12/31/85. Assets, $320,162
(M); Total giving, $13,628; Grants to individuals, 7
grants totaling $13,628, high $3,248, low $1,308.
Employer Identification Number: 046096055
Applications: Applications accepted throughout the
year.

904
Townsend Aid for the Aged
c/o Fleet National Bank
100 Westminster Street
Providence, RI 02903

Limitations: Grants to the needy elderly to provide the
necessities of life.
Financial data: Year ended 4/30/87. Assets,
$1,393,374 (M); Total giving, $80,500; Grants to
individuals totaling $80,500.
Employer Identification Number: 056009549
Program description:
Grants are awarded by the foundation to worthy
individuals as directed by an advisory committee,
which initiates the application process. **Individual
applications are not solicited.**

905★
Urann Foundation
P.O. Box 1788
Brockton, MA 02403   (508) 588-7744
Contact: Howard Whelan, Administrator

Limitations: Medical assistance to families located in
Massachusetts engaged in the production of
cranberries.
Financial data: Year ended 12/31/87. Assets,
$1,864,605 (M); Total giving, $88,843; Grants to
individuals, 30 grants totaling $41,843; Subtotal for
medical assistance, 11 grants totaling $2,443, high
$1,128, low $21.
Employer Identification Number: 046115599

Applications: Applications accepted throughout the year; Initial approach by telephone or letter; Completion of formal application required.
Program description:
The foundation makes grants to provide financial assistance in the payment of hospital and medical bills.

906
Vero Beach Foundation for the Elderly
c/o First National Bank
255 South County Road
Palm Beach, FL 33480

Limitations: Relief assistance only to indigent residents of Vero Beach, FL.
Financial data: Year ended 12/31/86. Assets, $997,965 (M); Total giving, $46,364; Grants to individuals, 35 grants totaling $41,505, high $2,835, low $44, general range $200-1,000.
Employer Identification Number: 596214870
Program description:
Grants are made for medical and convalescent care of indigent individuals, as well as for food and general assistance. Direct payments are also made to physicians and medical facilities.

907★
Warfield (Anna Emory) Memorial Fund, Inc.
103 West Monument Street
Baltimore, MD 21201   (301) 547-0612
Contact: Mrs. Thelma K. O'Neal, Secretary

Limitations: Relief assistance to aged and dependent women in the Baltimore, MD, area.
Financial data: Year ended 12/31/87. Assets, $2,309,657 (M); Total giving, $125,530; Grants to individuals, 44 grants totaling $124,930, high $3,250, low $250, average grant $2,835.
Employer Identification Number: 520785672
Applications: Applications accepted throughout the year; Initial approach by letter; Completion of formal application required; Interviews required.
Publications: Application guidelines.

908
Waterman (Richard) Trust
P.O. Box 55
Greene, RI 02827   (203) 376-2228
Contact: Reverand Byron O. Waterman, Trustee

Limitations: Grants to individuals desiring to preach the Calvinist Baptist doctrine within two miles of the late Richard Waterman's house in Greene, RI.
Financial data: Year ended 12/31/86. Assets, $1,574,065 (M); Total giving, $46,200; Grants to individuals, 5 grants totaling $18,200, high $17,900, low $50.
Employer Identification Number: 056040728

Applications: Applications accepted throughout the year.

909
Welch (Carrie) Trust
P.O. Box 244
Walla Walla, WA 99362

Limitations: Financial assistance only to needy or aged persons residing in the state of Washington, with preference to the Walla Walla area. Funds fully committed.
Financial data: Year ended 10/31/86. Assets, $1,149,097 (M); Total giving, $69,497; Grants to individuals, 17 grants totaling $15,215.
Employer Identification Number: 916030361
Applications: Applications presently not accepted. Funds fully committed.

910
Welch (George T.) Testamentary Trust
c/o Baker-Boyer National Bank
P.O. Box 1796
Walla Walla, WA 99362   (509) 525-2000
Contact: Bettie Loiacono, Trust Officer

Limitations: Medical and welfare assistance to needy residents of Walla Walla County, WA.
Financial data: Year ended 9/30/86. Assets, $2,516,675 (M). Total giving, $116,871; Grants to individuals, 265 grants totaling $101,598; Subtotal for welfare assistance, 170 grants totaling $26,170, high $1,600, low $6.
Employer Identification Number: 916024318
Applications: Deadlines February 20th, May 20th, August 20th, and November 20th; Completion of formal application required.

911★
Westport-Weston Foundation, The
c/o The Westport Bank & Trust Company
P.O. Box 5177
Westport, CT 06881   (203) 222-6938
Contact: Susanne M. Allen, Trust Officer

Limitations: Relief assistance only to residents of Westport or Weston, CT.
Financial data: Year ended 12/31/85. Assets, $736,267 (M); Total giving, $52,349; Grants to individuals, 33 grants totaling $19,871; Subtotal for relief assistance, 18 grants totaling $3,571, high $500, low $37, general range $100-200.
Employer Identification Number: 066035931
Applications: Applications accepted throughout the year via town agencies.
Program description:
Grants for assistance with medical and basic living expenses and for Christmas presents to the needy.

912
Widow's Society
c/o Connecticut National Bank
777 Main Street
Hartford, CT 06115
Contact: Endowment Administrator

Limitations: Welfare assistance to needy residents,
especially women and children, of the Hartford, CT,
area.
Financial data: Year ended 8/31/85. Assets,
$1,561,114 (M); Total giving, $99,148; Grants to
individuals totaling $99,148.
Employer Identification Number: 066026060
Applications: Applications are generally referred
through public or private social service agencies.

913
Wilkin (The R.H.) Charitable Trust
P.O. Box 76561
Oklahoma City, OK 73147   (405) 235-7700
Contact: Peggy Pittman, Co-Trustee

Limitations: Assistance to needy, crippled children of
Oklahoma County, OK, for medical care and
treatment.
Financial data: Year ended 12/31/86. Assets, $908,654
(M); Total giving, $43,447; Grants to individuals, 157
grants totaling $43,447, high $700, low $25, general
range $100-500.
Employer Identification Number: 736157614
Applications: Applications accepted throughout the
year. Statement of financial need and professional
recommendation for special care and treatment of
applicant's handicap required.

914
Women's Aid Society of 1844, Inc.
150 East 45th Street
New York, NY 10017
Contact: Dorothy C. Moore, Secretary-Treasurer

Limitations: Relief assistance to the poor, indigent,
aged and sick, including destitute widows, children,
and families.
Financial data: Year ended 12/31/85. Assets,
$1,175,846 (M); Total giving, $95,251; Grants to
individuals totaling $95,251; Subtotal for relief
assistance totaling $77,283.
Employer Identification Number: 136006486
Applications: Applications accepted throughout the
year by mail; Requests should be submitted in letter
form and addressed to the society.
Program description:
Financial aid is given for regular and special relief
assistance.

915
Word Investments, Inc.
3351 Claystone, S.E., Suite G-16
Grand Rapids, MI 49506
Contact: Mr. Clare DeGraaf, President

Limitations: Welfare assistance primarily to Christian
residents of Michigan.
Financial data: Year ended 12/31/86. Assets,
$5,042,663 (M); Total giving, $543,189; Grants to
individuals, 17 grants totaling $74,343, high $24,300,
low $250.
Employer Identification Number: 382470907
Applications: Applications accepted throughout the
year.

ARTS AND CULTURAL SUPPORT

This section lists sources of support for individuals involved in the arts and cultural fields including visual artists, performing artists, and writers. The main types of support available include the following:

- **Fellowships** - includes grants awarded for independent cultural and artistic projects

- **Residencies** - includes awards of studio, work, or living space, equipment, materials, etc. that enable individuals to pursue creative endeavors

- **Welfare assistance and emergency aid** - includes all types of grants provided by foundations on an emergency or long-term basis to artists or those involved in cultural endeavors for personal, living, or medical expenses

Not included in this section are grants for which individuals are ineligible to apply directly; such programs may be found in the "Awards, Prizes, and Grants by Nomination" section.

Entries are arranged alphabetically by foundation name. Access to grants by the above types of support, as well as to specific subject areas and geographic focus, is provided in the "Subject," "Types of Support" and "Geographic Focus" indexes in the back of the book.

Limitations on grantmaking are indicated in the entry when available. The limitations statement should be checked carefully as a foundation will reject any application that does not fall within its stated geographic area, recipient type, or area of interest.

REMEMBER: IF YOU DON'T QUALIFY, DON'T APPLY.

916★
Albee (Edward) Foundation, Inc.
c/o A. Kozak Company
468 Park Avenue South, Suite 1407
New York, NY 10016   (212) 889-6371
Contact: Edward Albee Foundation, William Flanagan
Memorial Center for Creative Persons, 14 Harrison
Street, New York, NY 10013

Limitations: Grants for free room and board only to
artists and writers seeking studio space.
Financial data: Year ended 12/31/86. Assets, $176,378
(M); No cash awards; Grants in the form of studio
space in the artists' colony.
Employer Identification Number: 136168827
Applications: Deadline January 1st through April 1st;
Initial approach by letter requesting application
information.
Program description:
The foundation maintains the William Flanagan
Memorial Center for Creative Persons where talented
sculptors, visual artists and writers may receive a grant
for free room and board for a period of time in order
to allow them to work free from financial pressure.
Applicants for grants of room and board are
recommended by well known persons in the arts as
well as by application. The residency period is from
June to October.
   The foundation expects all those accepted for
residence to work seriously and to cooperate with
other residents in maintaining the condition of the
center as well as an environment conducive to the
endeavors of all residents.

917★
American Society of Journalists And Authors
Charitable Trust, The
1501 Broadway, Suite 1907
New York, NY 10036   (212) 997-0947
Contact: Murray Teigh Bloom

Limitations: Relief assistance to needy, established,
professional freelance writers who are 60 years of age
or older or disabled.
Financial data: Year ended 8/31/87. Assets, $62,100
(M); Total giving, $14,700; Grants to individuals, 6
grants totaling $14,700, high $2,500, low, 1,250,
average grant $2,200.
Employer Identification Number: 136625578
Applications: Applications accepted throughout the
year; Initial approach by letter explaining need;
Completion of formal application required, including
financial records and references.
Publications: Application guidelines, financial
statement, informational brochure.
Program description:
The Llewellyn Miller Fund of the American Society of
Journalists and Authors was established to help writers
who have demonstrated their professionalism over a
sustained period of years, but who have no pension

from a former employer on which to rely. The fund
also makes grants to professional freelance writers
who are caught up in an extraordinary professional
crisis.

918★
Art Matters, Inc.
131 West 24th Street
New York, NY 10011   (212) 929-7190
Contact: Philip Yenawine, Vice-President

Limitations: Grants and fellowships, to individuals in
the arts, including the fine arts, film, and the
performing arts.
Financial data: Year ended 12/31/85. Assets, $215,609
(M); Total giving, $160,900; Grants to individuals, 29
grants totaling, $71,500, high $4,000, low $1,000.
Employer Identification Number: 133271577
Applications: Initial approach by letter requesting
application information.

919
Artists' Fellowship, Inc.
c/o Salmagundi Club
47 Fifth Avenue
New York, NY 10003
Contact: H. L. Smith

Limitations: Emergency aid to American professional
visual artists and their families.
Financial data: Year ended 10/31/85. Assets, $932,917
(M); Total giving, $34,200; Grants to individuals, 13
grants totaling $34,200, high $6,050, low $250,
general range $750-2,000, average grant $1,200.
Employer Identification Number: 136122134
Applications: Applications accepted throughout the
year; Completion of formal application required.
Program description:
Limited funds are available for relief of financial
distress due to disability, age, or bereavement.

920
Bagby Foundation for the Musical Arts, The
501 Fifth Avenue
New York, NY 10017   (212) 986-6094
Contact: Eleanor C. Mark, Executive Director

Limitations: Relief assistance to aged needy
individuals who have aided the world of music.
Financial data: Year ended 12/31/85. Assets,
$1,070,812 (M); Total giving, $26,690; Grants to
individuals, 12 grants totaling $19,190; Subtotal for
relief assistance, 7 grants totaling $10,400 for pensions
and 1 grant totaling $2,250 for emergency aid.
Employer Identification Number: 131873289
Applications: Applications accepted throughout the
year; Submit written applications, setting forth reasons
why assistance is required.

Program description:
Grants provided for pensions and emergency aid for aged musicians.

921★
Bush Foundation, The
East 900 First National Bank Building
St. Paul, MN 55101   (612) 227-0891
Contact: Sally Dixon, Program Director

Limitations: Fellowships to artists who are residents of Minnesota, South Dakota or North Dakota. (See program description for artistic delineation.).
Financial data: Year ended 11/30/87. Assets, $332,263,000 (M); Total giving, $13,889,666; Grants to individuals, 146 grants totaling $1,570,179; Subtotal amounts for programs not specified; 1986, Grants to individuals totaling $1,435,852; Subtotal for art fellowships, 15 grants totaling $453,600.
Employer Identification Number: 416017815
Applications: Initial approach by letter or telephone; Completion of formal application required.
Publications: Annual report, program information, financial statement.
Program description:
The purpose of the **Bush Foundation Fellowships for Artists** is to assist up to 15 selected artists of exceptional talent and demonstrated ability to set aside a significant period of uninterrupted time for work in their chosen art forms. The time may be used to explore new directions or to accelerate work already in progress. The program is limited to the following artistic disciplines:

- Literature - writers of fiction, creative non-fiction, poetry, and playwriting. Application deadline is October 31st.
- Visual arts - painters, sculptors, graphic artists, still photographers, filmmakers, and video artists Application deadline Is November 14th.
- Performing arts - composers of music and choreographers. Deadline is November 7th.

Artists may be at any stage of their career development, from emerging through mature. Support will not be given to students enrolled full-time or part-time in any academic institution. Teachers are eligible if their proposals are for their development as professional artists rather than as teachers.

Applicants must be at least 25 years of age and must have been residents of Minnesota for at least 12 of the 36 months preceding the application deadline. They must present evidence of professional accomplishment through publication or exhibition and submit examples of recent work.

Grants consist of $2,000 per month for 6 to 11 months or a total possible stipend award of $24,000 for a 12 to 18 month period. In addition, $6,240 is available for equipment, materials, production costs, travel, or other expenses directly related to the project.

922
Cabot (Ella Lyman) Trust, Inc.
109 Rockland Street
Holliston, MA 01746   (617) 429-8997

Limitations: Grants for projects involving a departure from one's usual vocation or a creative extension of it, with a promise of good to others.
Financial data: Year ended 12/31/86. Assets, $1,288,268 (M); Total giving, $71,914; Grants to individuals, 10 grants totaling $71,914, high $20,000, low $2,000, general range $4,000-8,000.
Employer Identification Number: 042111393
Applications: Deadlines February 15th and September 15th; Initial approach by letter briefly describing yourself and your project; Completion of formal application required.
Program description:
Awards are usually made on a one-year basis and are not renewed. Approximately 15 new awards are made each year. Support is not given for undergraduate or graduate scholarships, fellowships, or research pursued as a regular part of a profession.

923
Carnegie Fund For Authors
330 Sunrise Highway
Rockville Centre, NY 11570   (516) 764-8899

Limitations: Emergency assistance to needy writers who have commercially published at least one book of reasonable length which has received reader acceptance.
Financial data: Year ended 12/31/85. Assets, $335,572 (M); Total giving, $10,550; Grants to individuals, 21 grants totaling $10,550, high $1,000, low $100, general range $200-500, average grant $500.
Employer Identification Number: 136084244
Applications: Applications accepted throughout the year; Completion of formal application required.
Program description:
Applicants must have suffered a financial emergency as a result of illness or injury to self, spouse, or dependent child, or some other misfortune that has placed the applicant in pressing, substantial, and verifiable need. The fund does not make loans or grants to permit an applicant to complete a projected or unfinished work for publication.

924★
Cintas Foundation, Inc.
c/o William B. Warren
140 Broadway, Room 4500
New York, NY 10005
Contact: Rebecca Abrams, Art Programs Administrator, Cintas Fellowship Program, Institute of International Education, 809 United Nations Plaza, New York, NY 10017, Tel.: (212) 883-8985

Limitations: Fellowships to individuals of Cuban citizenship or lineage for continuing work outside Cuba in the arts, including the fine arts, music, and literature. No fellowhips to students pursuing academic programs.
Financial data: Year ended 8/31/87. Assets, $2,375,500 (M); Total giving, $100,000; Grants to individuals, 10 grants totaling $100,000, each grant $10,000.
Employer Identification Number: 131980389
Applications: Deadline March 1st; Applications accepted preferably December through February; Initial approach by letter; Completion of formal application and submission of examples of work required.
Publications: Application guidelines.

925★
Colman (Blanche E.) Trust
c/o Boston Safe Deposit & Trust Company
One Boston Place
Boston, MA 02106   (617) 722-7341
Contact: Ms. Sylvia Salas, Trust Officer

Limitations: Grants by recommendation to worthy artists residing in New England (including CT, NH, ME, MA, and VT).
Financial data: Year ended 8/31/87. Assets, $290,000 (M); Total giving, $12,000; Grants to individuals, 5 grants totaling $12,000, high $3,000, low $2,000, general range $1,000-3,000.
Employer Identification Number: 046094293
Applications: Deadline March 1st; Submit two letters of recommendation by recognized art professionals; Completion of formal application and financial information required; Work must be shown to a jury; Individual applications not accepted.
Publications: Application guidelines.
Program description:
Artists should have completed their formal education and have exhibited considerable potential in the art world. Recipients are selected solely at the discretion of a jury of professional artists for their creative work and study in the field of art.

926★
Fleishhacker Foundation
(Formerly Fleishhacker (Mortimer) Foundation)
The Alcoa Building
One Maritime Plaza, Suite 1150
San Francisco, CA 94111   (415) 788-2909
Contact: Sarah Lutman, Executive Director

Limitations: Fellowships to assist individual artists, 25 years of age or older, in the San Francisco Bay, CA, area.
Financial data: Year ended 4/30/87. Assets, $3,991,644 (M); Total giving, $205,200; Grants to individuals, 13 grants totaling $88,750, high $15,750,

low $5,000, average grant, $5,000.
Employer Identification Number: 946051048
Applications: Deadline announced March; Contact foundation for current application deadline; Initial approach by letter; Completion of formal application required. See program description below for detailed application information.
Publications: Application guidelines, program information.
Program description:
The **Eureka Fellowship Program** allows artists of exceptional talent to spend uninterrupted time pursuing creative work, which includes the beginning or completing of a specific project, exploring new directions or techniques or continuing the development of work already in progress.
   Applicants must:
      1. Either live or work in San Francisco, Alameda, Contra Costa, Marin, San Mateo or Santa Clara counties, CA
      2. Be at least 25 years old on the date of the application deadline
      3. Not be a full-time student, nor a part-time student pursuing a degree in the theory, practice or history of art
      4. Not be a '86-'87 Eureka Fellowship recipient.
   Each fellowship carries a cash award of $15,000 (paid in equal monthly stipends) and is intended to provide basic living expenses for one year. Each year the fellowship program will be open to artists in a different medium. A maximum of four fellowships will be awarded for 1988 to sculptors.
   The application form should be submitted with:
      ● A current resume, not exceeding four pages
      ● Ten-to-twenty slides, inserted in clear plastic slide sheet, of applicant's work done within the last three years
      ● A sequential listing of slides submitted
      ● A self-addressed stamped envelope for returning the slides.
   All documentation is reviewed by jurors, who are working curators, artists, or similar art professionals from outside the northern California region.

927★
Fund for Investigative Journalism, Inc.
1755 Massachusetts Avenue, N.W., No. 504
Washington, DC 20036   (202) 462-1844
Contact: John Hanrahan, Executive Director

Limitations: Fellowships to journalists doing investigative work who have a statement of intent to publish from a suitable outlet.
Financial data: Year ended 12/31/86. Assets, $73,231 (M); Total giving, $31,081; Grants to individuals, or groups of individuals, 32 grants totaling $31,081, high $2,766, low $75.
Employer Identification Number: 520895081
Applications: Applications accepted throughout the year in the form of a letter outlining the proposed

investigation, its significance, the proof in hand, further evidence needed, and approach that will be used to complete the project; Budget, resume, and samples of published work required.
Publications: Program information.
Program description:
The fund supports investigative articles and books, and aspirants to investigative journalism are encouraged to apply. Book grants, however, are expected to be repaid if the book makes money over the advance.

The subjects of fund grants cover a broad spectrum including environmental hazards, political corruption, invasion of privacy, organized crime, threats to civil rights, press performance, and abuses of corporate and union authority. Applications are treated confidentially.

928
Gladish (Sarah Cora) Endowment Fund
c/o Margaret Lomax, Trustee
Forest Hills Estate, Apt. C-11
Lexington, MO 64067   (816) 259-3643

Limitations: Scholarships to deserving, worthy, and accomplished artists and musicians, including composers and teachers of music and art, who have resided in Lafayette, Johnson, or Jackson counties, MO, for at least three years.
Financial data: Year ended 12/31/86. Assets, $66,233 (M); Total giving, $2,100; Grants to individuals, 6 grants totaling $2,100, each grant $350.
Employer Identification Number: 436045752
Applications: Deadline July 1st; Applications accepted throughout the year; Completion of formal application required.
Program description:
Scholarships are granted to enable young artists and musicians to secure education and training in those arts. Direct grants of financial assistance are awarded to older, worthy, deserving, accomplished and needy artists and musicians in recognition of the contributions which they have made to teaching or other service in the fields, that their useful and creative lives and careers may be extended and that hardships resulting from their devotion to their work may be alleviated.

929★
Gottlieb (Adolph and Esther) Foundation, Inc.
380 West Broadway
New York, NY 10012   (212) 226-0581

Limitations: Grants for painters, sculptors, and printmakers who have at least 20 years in a mature phase of their art. Emergency assistance available for same visual artists who have at least ten years in a mature phase of their art and are in need as a result of an unexpected, catastrophic event.
Financial data: Year ended 6/30/87. Assets,

$2,645,838 (M); Total giving, $140,900; Grants to individuals, 23 grants totaling $140,900, high $10,000, low $1,000, general range $1,000-10,000.
Employer Identification Number: 132853957
Applications: See program description below for application information on specific programs.
Publications: Informational brochure, program information, 990-PF printed copy available upon request.
Program description:
Grants under the individual support program are made to mature visual artists, including painters, sculptors, and printmakers, who are in current need of financial support in order to continue their artwork. The purpose of the award is to provide general support to qualified artists. Selection is based on financial need, quality of work and length of commitment. Grants are awarded for one-year periods. The deadline for application to the individual support program is December 15th. Initial approach should be by a written request for application. Completion of formal application required.

Assistance is also available, on a one-time basis, to artists who have a current financial need in excess of and unrelated to their normal economic situation, and which is the result of a recent emergency occurence such as a fire, flood, or medical emergency. Applications are accepted throughout the year for emergency assistance. Initial approach may be made by telephone. Completion of formal application required.

930★
Jerome Foundation
West 1050 First National Bank Building
332 Minnesota Street
St. Paul, MN 55101   (612) 224-9431
Contact: Cynthia Gehrig, President

Limitations: Grants for film and video projects by artists residing in New York City, and for travel and study for individuals in dance, literature, theater, and the visual arts residing in the Twin Cities metropolitan area.
Financial data: Year ended 4/30/87. Assets, $33,792,271 (M); Total giving, $1,441,576, Grants to individuals, 10 grants totaling $78,120; Subtotal for Film and Video Program, 6 grants totaling $72,000, high $18,000, low $4,000; Subtotal for Travel and Study Program, 4 grants totaling $6,120, high $2,500, low $1,000.
Employer Identification Number: 416035163
Applications: See program description below for application information on specific programs.
Publications: Annual report, program information.
Program description:
Film and Video Program: This program is intended to fulfill four principal objectives:

1. To encourage experimental, innovative, and creative endeavors in the several areas of the arts and humanities;
2. To assist emerging artists and humanists who show promise of making significant contributions to their fields and to the social and intellectual life of America;
3. To support efforts to make the arts and humanities, both classical and innovative, integral parts of American life;
4. To encourage imaginative and appropriate use of new media in delivering quality arts and humanities programs to the American people.

Grants are not normally awarded directly to individuals, but through appropriate institutions or agencies.

Support is not provided for graduate research projects, the crafts, or for the writing and publishing of books or articles for professional journals with the possible exception of publications related to the outcome of a project supported by the foundation.

Funds are allocated to discover and assist emerging American independent and experimental film and video makers. Awards are made to New York City artists who may apply as individuals without the endorsement of a sponsoring non-profit organization. Selection will be made in consultation with a New York-based panel. Applications are accepted throughout the year and should describe the proposed film project, budget, and schedule. In addition to a resume, the application should include:

- American citizenship or legal permanent residency in the U.S. as well as residency in New York City.
- Completion of formal education or its equivalent (i.e., applicant need not hold a degree but must no longer be a student).
- Evidence that the applicant is an artist seriously striving toward professional status.
- Applicants should be able to submit at least two works of at least two minutes and preferably under 25 minutes in length. Student works are acceptable.

Selection will be based on the quality of the work, references, recognition by one's peers, limited exhibition and production records, a statement from the applicant as to his/her training (both academic and vocational), and a statement as to employment or other source of support during the production of the proposed work. In most cases the subject matter of the proposed work is secondary to evidence of emerging talent. Budgets should be reasonable and well-developed, and must be small enough so that the foundation's support covers a significant portion of the need (i.e., total budget should not be more than $50,000).

Travel and Study Grant Program: Initiated in 1986, this program supports significant periods of professional development for Twin Cities individuals working in the nonprofit communities of dance, literature, theater, and the visual arts.

Grants under this program are restricted to individuals residing in the Twin Cities metropolitan region. Deadlines are April 1st and October 3rd. The completion of a formal application is required. The applicant should describe the proposed study and travel project, including a budget and a specific time schedule. A resume and one letter of reference should accompany the application. An independent panel of experts reviews the applications and makes recommendations to the foundation board for final action.

931★
Koussevitzky Music Foundation, Inc., The
415 Madison Avenue
New York, NY 10017   (212) 752-5300
Contact: Ellis J. Freedman, Secretary

Limitations: Provides commissions based on merit to composers of serious music who are over 25 years of age, have completed formal conservatory studies or have a B.A. from a recognized conservatory, college, or university, or demonstrated equivalent, and whose music has been published, recorded and/or performed in public.
Financial data: Year ended 3/31/86. Assets, $1,383,701 (M); Total giving, $28,000; Grants to individuals, 5 grants totaling $28,000, high $7,500, low $3,500.
Employer Identification Number: 046128361
Applications: Deadline November 30th.

932★
Little (The Bascom) Fund
c/o Richard A. Manuel, Treasurer
34750 Cedar Road
Gates Mills, OH 44040   (216) 442-0360
Contact: Mr. Bain Murray, President of the Advisory Board, The Bascom Little Fund, Cleveland State University, Department of Music, Rhodes Tower 910, Cleveland, OH 44115

Limitations: Grants to cover expenses in connection with the promotion, through the media of concerts, publications, recordings, etc., of serious and semi-popular music, newly composed by Ohio composers performed in or near Cleveland, OH.
Financial data: Year ended 6/30/87. Assets, $611,144 (M); Total giving, $26,577; Grants to individuals, 5 grants totaling $3,875, high $1,850, low $25.
Employer Identification Number: 346572279
Applications: Deadline early May; Applications accepted throughout the year; Completion of formal application required.
Publications: Application guidelines.
Program description:
The application for funds should include the stated purpose of the project; the professional qualifications and current activities of the individual(s) involved; an

itemized budget; and the date when the funds would be needed. It should be indicated if the performance or recording includes among its performers any members of the Cleveland Musicians Union.

933
Lotta Theatrical Fund
c/o Trustees under the Will of Lotta M. Crabtree
294 Washington Street, Room 636
Boston, MA 02108   (617) 451-0698
Contact: Claire M. McCarthy, Trust Manager

Limitations: Grants to deserving, needy members of the theatrical profession.
Financial data: Year ended 12/31/85. Assets, $369,542 (M); Total giving, $8,900; Grants to individuals, 6 grants totaling $8,900, high $3,000, low $100.
Employer Identification Number: 042607210
Applications: Applications accepted throughout the year; Contact foundation for current application deadline; Completion of formal application required; Interviews required.
Program description:
The fund provides both direct grants to theater professionals and grants to theatrical schools and cultural institutions for the benefit of named recipients.

934
Matz (Israel) Foundation
14 East Fourth Street, Room 403
New York, NY 10012
Contact: Dr. Milton Arfa, Chairman

Limitations: Relief assistance to indigent Hebrew writers, scholars, public workers and their dependents.
Financial data: Year ended 12/31/85. Assets, $1,740,009 (M); Total giving, $118,710; Grants to individuals, 30 grants totaling $44,065, high $4,000, low $375.
Employer Identification Number: 136121533
Applications: Applications accepted throughout the year; Initial approach by letter; Interviews granted upon request.
Program description:
Qualified individuals may apply directly or through recommendations of distinguished or reputable writers, scholars or public figures in the field of Hebrew literature, scholarship and culture.

935
Merrill (The Ingram) Foundation
104 East 40th Street, Suite 302
New York, NY 10016
Contact: Milton Maurer, Trustee, P.O. Box 202, Village Station, New York, NY 10014

Limitations: Grants and awards for individual projects in the arts with emphasis on writers.
Financial data: Year ended 12/31/84. Assets, $235,003

(M); Total giving, $197,800; Grants to individuals, 30 grants totaling $197,800, high $15,000, low $1,500, general range $2,000-10,000.
Employer Identification Number: 136042498
Applications: Deadline February; Completion of formal application required; No interviews given.
Program description:
Grants are made to further the advancement of the cultural and fine arts by supporting individuals engaged in creative and scholarly pursuits. In the past grants have been made primarily for independent projects by individual artists, poets, novelists, translators, and scholars in literary criticism and art history, with some emphasis on writers rather than visual or performing artists.
The foundation also awards **The Ingram Merrill Foundation Award in Literature.**

936★
Money for Women Fund/Barbara Deming Memorial Fund, Inc.
(Formerly Money for Women Fund, Inc.)
P.O. Box 40-1043
Brooklyn, NY 11240-1043
Contact: Pam McAllister, Administrator

Limitations: Grants to individual feminists for projects which examine, analyze, or otherwise generally shed light upon the condition of women.
Financial data: Year ended 7/31/86. Assets, $57,654 (M); Total giving, $10,250; Grants to individuals, 19 grants totaling $10,250, high $1,000, low $250, average grant $500.
Employer Identification Number: 510176956
Applications: Deadlines February 1st and July 1st; Completion of formal application required.
Program description:
Consideration is given to proposals for projects involving writings, music, visual arts, media, or other artistic expressions consistent with the objectives of the fund. Although some support for self-development is available, the primary focus is on projects which will reach a large number of women. Grants are generally limited to $500. The fund no longer makes grants for scholarships, personal study, or loans.
The fund has, in addition, recently instituted two special grants which emphasize its longstanding commitment to eliminate homophobia and racism. The **Gerty, Gerty, Gerty in the Arts, Arts, Arts Grant** is awarded to a lesbian whose work either accurately portrays the condition of lesbians or whose project combats homophobia. The **Fannie Lou Hamer Grant**, named for the civil rights activist, is awarded to a woman whose work combats racism through an educational project or through a work of art. No special application need be made for either grant, since recipients will be chosen from all proposals received.

937
Musicians Emergency Relief Fund-Local 802
330 West 42nd Street
New York, NY 10036   (212) 239-4802
Contact: Carl Janelli, Secretary

Limitations: Welfare assistance in the form of
interest-free loans to sick, distressed, or indigent
musicians who have been union members for a
minimum of three years and are in good standing
(membership dues paid-up).
Financial data: Year ended 12/31/84. Assets, $393,635
(L); Expenditures, $99,023; Loans to individuals, 67
loans totaling $49,536, high $2,000, low $49; average
loan $700.
Employer Identification Number: 136222619
Applications: Applications accepted throughout the
year; Completion of formal application required.
Publications: Program information, application
guidelines.
Program description:
An interest-free loan to musicians in dire need, subject
to certain guidelines set forth by the trustees of the
fund. Present guidelines acceptable are as follows:
unable to pay rent to the point of eviction; gas,
electric, telephone cut-off notices; payment of partial
medical costs, in some cases; if instruments are stolen
- aid of some sort (rentals, etc.); if musician requires
transportation in order to work - auto repair bills. All
of the above are scrutinized and judged by the
administrator. If he decides the request is valid,
assistance is granted up to $500. Any amount above
$500 requires approval of a quorum of three trustees.
Maximum loan allowed is $2,000 to be paid within
three years with allowable one year grace period
before first payment.

938
Musicians Foundation, Inc.
200 West 55th Street
New York, NY 10019   (212) 247-5332
Contact: Brent Williams, Secretary-Treasurer

Limitations: Emergency financial assistance to
professional musicians and their families.
Financial data: Year ended 4/30/86. Assets,
$1,134,764 (M); Total giving, $66,645; Grants to
individuals, 36 grants totaling $66,645, high $5,700,
low $143, general range $500-2,000, average grant
$1,300.
Employer Identification Number: 131790739
Applications: Applications accepted throughout the
year.

939★
Peninsula Community Foundation
1204 Burlingame Avenue
P.O. Box 627
Burlingame, CA 94011-0627   (415) 342-2477
Contact: Bill Somerville, Executive Director

Limitations: Grants to artists, including painters,
dancers, photographers and poets who are residents of
San Mateo County and northern Santa Clara County,
CA.
Financial data: Year ended 12/31/87. Assets,
$14,119,000 (M); Total giving, $1,384,000; Grants to
individuals amount not specified.
Employer Identification Number: 942746687
Publications: Annual report.
Program description:
In 1987, the third year of the foundation-initiated
program, **Grants to Individual Artists**, provided
recipients with funds with the stipulation that some
form of public presentation take place. Grants are up
to $500 on a monthly basis.

940★
Pollock-Krasner Foundation, Inc., The
725 Park Avenue
New York, NY 10021   (212) 517-5400
Contact: Charles C. Bergman, Executive
Vice-President, P.O. Box 4957, New York, NY 10185

Limitations: Grants based on financial need to
talented visual artists in the U.S. and abroad to further
their careers and their personal well-being. Emergency
aid is also given in cases of serious illness or personal
catastrophe. Only visual artists, those working in
painting, sculpture, graphic and mixed media, will be
considered.
Financial data: Year ended 6/30/87. Assets,
$22,621,627 (M); Total giving, $510,591; Grants to
individuals, 99 grants totaling $510,591, high
$20,000, low $1,000.
Employer Identification Number: 133255693
Applications: Applications accepted throughout the
year; Initial approach by typed or legibly printed cover
letter stating for what specific purpose funds are
required and in what amount; Completion of formal
application required; Applicants must submit a
biographical record and no more than 10 slides or
photographs of their recent work.
Publications: Annual report, application guidelines,
informational brochure.
Program description:
The purpose of the foundation is to provide financial
assistance to individual working artists of established
ability through the generosity of the late Lee Krasner,
one of the leading abstract expressionist painters and
widow of Jackson Pollock. The foundation welcomes
nominations and applications from painters, sculptors,
graphic and mixed media artists of artistic merit. There
is no age or geographic limitation. The foundation

does not give grants to commercial artists or students who are not or have not been working artists. Grants are not awarded as scholarships or for tuition.

941
Preston (Evelyn W.) Trust
One Constitution Plaza
Hartford, CT 06115   (203) 244-4330
Contact: Norman E. Armour, Senior Vice-President

Limitations: Grants to musicians to perform free band and orchestral concerts in Hartford, CT, from June through September.
Financial data: Year ended 12/31/85. Assets, $2,055,022 (M); Total giving, $125,702; Grants to individuals, 17 grants totaling $31,847; high $4,000, low $500.
Employer Identification Number: 060747389
Applications: Completion of formal application required.

942
Shifting Foundation, The
c/o Sonnenschein, Carlin, Nath & Rosenthal
8000 Sears Tower
Chicago, IL 60606
Contact: Daniel R. Swett

Limitations: Grants to artists who have distinguished themselves or shown promise in the fields of contemporary music, literature, and, less frequently, visual or multimedia forms.
Financial data: Year ended 12/31/86. Assets, $1,524,020 (M); Total giving, $61,350; Grants to individuals, 5 grants totaling $33,500, high $10,000, low $5,000.
Employer Identification Number: 366108560
Applications: Applications accepted throughout the year; Initial approach by letter; Completion of formal application required; Interviews required; Proposals and materials submitted without application form will not be considered; Submitted materials will not be returned.
Program description:
The foundation focuses its grant-making program on "emerging" artists: those who are expanding--or show the potential to expand--the vocabulary of the art form or discipline in which they work, but do not receive significant financial rewards for doing so. The foundation does not support artists whose work, however accomplished, is wholly traditional or mainstream. Rather, it is interested in artists who seek new ground--conceptually, thematically, stylistically, formally--or find new ways of surveying old ground, of reinventing traditions or synthesizing disparate elements. It looks for work that is unusual and provocative though it need not be "experimental."

Grants are made for tuition expenses for formal study at an educational institution; for career or project development; or for unsupervised research.

943
Stacey (John F. and Anna Lee) Testamentary Trust
c/o Security Pacific National Bank
P.O. Box 3189, Terminal Annex
Los Angeles, CA 90051
Contact: R. Brownell McGrew, Stacey Award Committee, P.O. Box 448, Sonoita, AZ 85637

Limitations: Fellowships and scholarships to artists between the ages of 18 and 35 who are U.S. citizens and whose work is devoted to the classical or conservative tradition of western culture.
Financial data: Year ended 4/30/86. Assets, $162,878 (M); Total giving, $3,487; Grants to individuals totaling $3,487.
Employer Identification Number: 956017406
Applications: Deadline November 1st; Initial approach by letter; Completion of formal application, including submission of eight-by-ten black and white glossy photographs of work, required; Interviews and letters of reference required.
Publications: Program information.
Program description:
Scholarships are awarded to young American artists to foster a high standard in the study of form, color, drawing, painting, design and technique in affinity with the classical or conservative tradition of western culture. Grants are limited to the fine arts of painting and drawing and hence, work in such related fields as sculpture, collage, fashion design, etc. is inadmissible. Work should underscore realism and naturalism but should also be esthetically satisfying. Recipients should generally be betweeen the ages of 18 and 35, although in exceptional cases the age limit may be extended.

Appointments are normally for one year, and a fixed amount, generally $3,000, is distributed to one or more applicants. Recipients may use the funds in any way they wish to further their art education; however, the selection committee reserves the right to make recommendations.

944
Sullivan (William Matheus) Musical Foundation, Inc.
410 East 57th Street
New York, NY 10022   (212) 755-8158
Contact: Hugh Ross, Executive Director

Limitations: Financial assistance to gifted young singers who have already begun a public singing career. Applicants must have future engagements with a full orchestra.
Financial data: Year ended 12/31/85. Assets,

$2,432,200 (M); Total giving, $86,050; Grants to individuals, 25 grants totaling $4,900, high $500, low $100.
Employer Identification Number: 136069096
Applications: Deadline August 31st for the following fall; Requests for New York auditions should be accompanied by resume and copy of contract for at least one engagement with full orchestra after November; No West Coast auditions at the present time; Initial approach by letter or proposal with details of educational and musical experience; Completion of formal application required; Applications accepted preferably between June and September.
Publications: Application guidelines.
Program description:
Grants are awarded to advance the careers of gifted young singers either by direct assistance or by finding engagements for the singers by means of grants to organizations in connection with staged oratorios and regional opera companies. Candidates should be able to supply the names of important conductors with whom they have sung or famous artists who have recognized their work. Grants are based on financial need.

After initial screenings international auditions are held in the fall in New York City.

945
Turk (Gladys) Foundation
9777 Wilshire Boulevard, Suite 700
Beverly Hills, CA 90212   (213) 273-6760
Contact: Max Fink, President

Limitations: Grants only for voice culture training, primarily to vocalists residing in southern California. Funds extremely limited.
Financial data: Year ended 12/31/86. Assets, $362,053 (M); Total giving, $72,156; Grants to individuals, 10 grants totaling $5,622, high $1,447, low $30.
Employer Identification Number: 956111858
Applications: Applications accepted throughout the year; Application should include resume, photograph and letter of recommendation.
Program description:
Selection of recipients depends on recommendations from persons established in the voice or singing field. No auditions are held in the selection process.

Applications seeking scholarships for college education are not accepted.

946
Vogelstein (Ludwig) Foundation, Inc.
P.O. Box 4924
Brooklyn, NY 11240-4924   (718) 643-0614
Contact: Frances Pishny, Executive Director

Limitations: Grants to individuals in the arts and humanities. No scholarships, student aid, or faculty assistance granted.

Financial data: Year ended 12/31/85. Assets, $966,762 (M); Total giving, $92,544; Grants to individuals, 48 grants totaling $92,544, high $4,000, low $900, average grant $2,000; Loans to individuals, 1 loan totaling $1,200.
Employer Identification Number: 136185761
Applications: Applications accepted throughout the year; Initial approach by letter describing project and financial need.
Publications: Annual report, application guidelines.
Program description:
The foundation is devoted to aiding individuals in the arts and humanities. Merit as well as need are considered.

In 1985, grants were awarded to artists, sculptors, photographers, poets, writers, playwrights, choreographers, and those involved in scholarly studies.

947
Whitelight Foundation, The
703 Hillcrest
Beverly Hills, CA 90210   (213) 271-3993
Contact: Betty Freeman, Trustee

Limitations: Assistance to established classical musicians primarily in southern California in publishing new compositions, copying scores, and performing new compositions. Grants are generally limited to no more than $7,000.
Financial data: Year ended 12/31/85. Assets, $191,020 (M); Total giving, $244,350; Grants to individuals, 2 grants totaling $12,000, high $7,000, low $5,000.
Employer Identification Number: 953513930
Applications: Applications accepted throughout the year; Initial aproach by letter with a brief resume and an outline of the project, including a budget.

948
Wilbur (Marguerite Eyer) Foundation
P.O. Box B-B
Santa Barbara, CA 93102   (805) 962-0011
Contact: Gary Ricks, Chief Executive Officer

Limitations: Resident fellowships, research grants, and support for writing projects to individuals in the areas of humane literature.
Financial data: Year ended 6/30/86. Assets, $2,876,549 (M); Total giving, $194,674; Grants to individuals, 26 grants totaling $97,625, high $7,000, low $825, general range $3,00-5,000.
Employer Identification Number: 510168214
Applications: Applications accepted between September 1st and December 31st. Application must consist of a single typewritten letter which specifically addresses the following points:
    1. Name, address and telephone number

2. Specific purpose of the grant (an attachment
will not suffice for this description, but may be
used to augment the description)

3. Amount of grant requested

4. Other sources of support

5. Qualifications, including education attainment,
awards, prior works and other matters you
consider worthy of consideration

6. Two references that may be contacted by the
foundation.

Publications: Application guidelines.

Program description:
Resident fellowships are provided to writers of
promise, to live and work in Mecosta, MI, with
preference given to writers in the areas of history,
religion, or philosophy.

Grants to individuals are provided to those who
have demonstrated unique accomplishments or
promise in humane literature, particularly in history,
religion and philosophy.

949
Wurlitzer (The Helene) Foundation of New Mexico
P.O. Box 545
Taos, NM 87571   (505) 758-2413
Contact: Henry A. Sauerwein, Jr., President

Limitations: Residence grants to creative (not
interpretive) artists in all media for rent- and
utilities-free housing in Taos, NM.

Financial data: Year ended 3/31/87. Assets,
$4,240,063 (M); Total giving, $40,189; Grants to
individuals, 14 grants totaling $14,208.

Employer Identification Number: 850128634

Applications: Applications accepted throughout the
year; Initial approach by letter requesting application;
Completion of formal application required along with
sample of work and description of project.

Program description:
The foundation was established to encourage and
stimulate creative work in the humanities, arts, and
allied fields through the provision of rent- and
utilities-free housing in Taos, NM.

No grants to high school students.

GRANTS TO FOREIGN INDIVIDUALS

This section is devoted to grants made exclusively to foreign individuals by foundations in the U.S. The grants cover a broad range of subjects and projects and may include funds for travel to the U.S. Included are grants that provide general welfare assistance as well as grants for creative and scholarly endeavors. Grants for which foreign individuals as well as U.S. citizens may apply and those that involve exchange programs between the U.S. and other countries may be found in other sections, notably "Educational Support" and "Awards, Prizes, and Grants by Nomination."

Entries are arranged alphabetically by foundation name. Access to grants by specific subject areas (including recipient nationality) and types of support is provided in the "Subject" and "Types of Support" indexes in the back of the book.

Limitations on grantmaking are indicated in the entry when available. The limitations statement should be checked carefully as a foundation will reject any application that does not fall within its stated recipient type or area of interest.

REMEMBER: IF YOU DON'T QUALIFY, DON'T APPLY.

950★
American-Nepal Education Foundation
2790 Cape Meares Loop Northwest
Tillamook, OR 97141   (503) 842-4024
Contact: Dr. Hugh B. Wood

Limitations: Scholarships based on need to
academically superior Nepalese citizens for study at
all levels of higher education in Nepal, the U.S., or a
third country. Recipients must agree to return to Nepal
with their individual skills to serve their country.
Financial data: Year ended 12/31/86. Assets, $81,626
(M); Total giving, $58,948; Grants to individuals, 52
grants totaling $58,948, high $6,134, low $71, general
range, $500-2,000.
Employer Identification Number: 936025661
Applications: Deadline November 15th; Completion
of formal application required; Interviews and
recommendations required.
Publications: Annual report, program information,
application guidelines.
Program description:
The **Scholarship Program** emphasizes the selection
and placement of Nepalese scholars in institutions of
higher education, and arranging institutional funding
for them. The foundation's grants provide
approximately 20 percent of the total funding
packages.
  Scholarships are awarded in the fields of education,
science, agriculture, homemaking, business
administration, law, engineering, linguistics,
journalism, architecture, and the social sciences.

951
Byas (The Hugh Fulton) Memorial Foundation
916 Shenandoah Drive
Spring Lake Heights, NJ 07782
Contact: William B. Nagle

Limitations: English nationals or permanent residents
of England only (England excludes Scotland, Wales,
Northern Ireland, and all holders of British passports
from other parts of the Commonwealth), to study at
colleges and universities in the Eastern U.S. only.
Financial data: Year ended 12/31/84. Assets, $73,754
(M); Total giving, $22,456; Grants to individuals, 3
grants totaling $22,456, high $15,256, low $3,000.
Employer Identification Number: 226097534
Applications: Applications accepted throughout the
year; Completion of formal application required.
Program description:
Grants are made to particular colleges and universities
on behalf of selected undergraduate and graduate
students from England to enable them to pursue a
degree in the U.S. Applicants must be English
nationals or permanent residents of England, over 21
years of age, and plan to return to England after
completing their studies. Personal references required
with references from clergymen preferred.

Recipients currently study at Cornell University,
Catholic University, Johns Hopkins University, and
Pratt Institute. In the future, Yale University might be
considered for students who can defray part of their
own expenses. The foundation cannot defray family
expenses or the cost of student insurance.
  Prior to completion of the academic program,
students may be asked to submit to the foundation a
copy of a paper, thesis, or dissertation required by
course work. Topics should promote a feeling of
goodwill between the U.S. and the United Kingdom.
No grants for study in politics, race relations, religion,
or any divisive topic.

952★
Commonwealth Fund, The
One East 75th Street
New York, NY 10021-2692   (212) 535-0400
Contact: See program description below.

Limitations: Research grants and fellowships to
undergraduate students from the United Kingdom,
Australia, and New Zealand for study at colleges and
universities in the United States; each country reviews
prospective applicants. Grants also to eminent
scientists to write and publish books about their fields
of research.
Financial data: Year ended 6/30/87. Assets,
$299,156,099 (M); Total authorized giving,
$8,680,987; Authorizations to individuals totaling
$1,350,000; Subtotal for fellowships, $1,000,000;
Subtotal for Book Program, $350,000.
Employer Identification Number: 131635260
Publications: Annual report, program information,
application guidelines.
Program description:
Harkness Fellowships are awarded to young men and
women of character and ability from Australia, New
Zealand, and the United Kingdom who possess
leadership and "ambassadorial" qualities. The purpose
of the program is to help the Fellow become familiar
with America during a period of study and travel in
this country in order to promote understanding,
overcome stereotyped attitudes, and provide for
personal enrichment and growth. A period of two
academic years is recommended, including three
months of required travel within the country in order
to acquaint the Fellows with America and Americans
outside the normal academic or professional context.
  People in all fields of study, professsions, and
occupations are eligible. All proposed programs,
including selection of a base of operations (which may
be an academic or non-academic institution), are
determined by the individual Fellow. In all countries a
national committee initially screens applicants and
makes final selections.
  Fellowship applicants should contact Alfred Leroy
Atherton, Jr., The Harkness Fellowships, The
Commonwealth Fund, One East 75th Street, New
York, NY 10021-2692; Tel.: (212) 535-0400.

The Commonwealth Fund Book Program sponsors the writing of books by working scientists primarily for a literate lay audience. The authors come from all branches of sciences, although the program has a special interest in biomedical sciences and the behavior and social sciences related to human health. It sponsors up to six books a year, and supplies authors with the freedom to work full-time on a manuscript and covers editing and related expenses. The program offers some editorial direction, as well as assistance in arranging a contract with an established publisher.

For information and application guidelines, write to Lewis Thomas, M.D., The Commonwealth Fund Book Program, Memorial Sloan-Kettering Cancer Center, 1275 York Avenue, Room 1302, Schwartz Hall, New York, NY 10021; Tel.: (212) 794-7646.

953
de Hirsch (The Baron) Fund

c/o Federation of Jewish Philanthropies
130 East 59th Street
New York, NY 10022   (212) 980-1000
Contact: Fellowship Committee, Ministry of Agriculture, Tel Aviv, Israel

Limitations: Fellowships and study grants to Israeli agriculturalists.
Financial data: Year ended 8/31/86. Assets, $5,238,642 (M); Total giving, $317,000; Grants to individuals, 16 grants totaling $39,000.
Employer Identification Number: 135562971
Applications: Deadline August 1st; Initial approach by letter.
Program description:
The foundation makes agricultural study grants as a means of promoting the training and technical knowledge of Israeli farmers and agricultural experts.

954★
German Marshall Fund of the United States

11 Dupont Circle, N.W., Suite 750
Washington, DC 20036   (202) 745-3950
Contact: Frank E. Loy, President

Limitations: Professional fellowships to Europeans in the fields of employment, journalism, and equal opportunity for women. Also funds programs which make awards to Europeans by nomination only.
Financial data: Year ended 5/31/87. Assets, $60,860,823 (M); Total giving, $3,818,746; Grants to individuals, 220 grants totaling $1,021,432; Subtotal for fellowships to Europeans not specified.
Employer Identification Number: 520954751
Applications: Deadlines vary from year to year; Contact foundation for current application deadline; Initial approach by letter; Completion of formal application required. **Individual applications not accepted for certain programs;** See program

description below for application information on specific programs, including addresses for the fund's European representatives.
Publications: Multi-year report, program information.
Program description:
Equal Opportunity Fellowships are awarded to thirteen European specialists in the field of equal opportunity for women for four- to six-week placements in American agencies and organizations whose programs correspond to their professional interests. Applicants must be officials or practitioners who are in a position to implement fellowship results in their own organizations, whether private or governmental.

Employment Fellowships are awarded to up to sixteen European practitioners in job training or local economic development to look into ways government agencies or private-sector organizations in the U.S. are working to expand and improve employment opportunities. Applications are accepted from employment professionals in France, Sweden, the Netherlands, the Federal Republic of Germany, and the United Kingdom. The Calouste Gulbenkian Foundation and the government Manpower Services Commission co-sponsor the U.K. program.

Under the **Journalism Fellowships** program, one European journalist is selected to spend nine months pursuing studies of his or her choice in the Nieman Foundation for Journalism program at Harvard University and the Knight Science Journalism Fellowship program at Massachusetts Institute of Technology. The fund also sponsors a German journalist for six-to-nine months of academic work in the Stanford University Professional Journalism Fellowship program. Four European journalists are selected annually to spend two months each in the Duke University Professional Journalism program.

Under other fund programs, awards result from a structured nomination process. **Individual applications are not accepted for these programs.** In general, nominations are sought from prominent persons in western European countries and individuals are selected for awards by independent national committees. Fellowships of this type (that is, not subject to publicly announced completion) include:

• **Marshall Memorial Fellowships** - Fifty young European professionals with promising careers in business, journalism, trade unions, government, or politics are chosen annually from five countries - Denmark, France, the Netherlands, Spain, and the Federal Republic of Germany. During six weeks of programmed travel in the United States, the Europeans have the opportunity to observe regional differences, traditions, and political institutions, as well as to visit their American counterparts on the job.

• **GMF Campus Fellowships** - This fund program brings prominent Europeans to meet with students and teachers during week-long visits to small U.S. liberal arts colleges.

● **German Congressional Fellowships** - Under fund sponsorship, two young scholars from the Federal Republic participate each fall in the Congressional Fellowship Program of the American Political Science Association. Together with American scholars, journalists, and federal executives, and some professionals from other nations, they serve four-month stints as professional staff assistants to members of the U.S. Congress.

● **German-Language Teaching Assistants Program** - A fund grant to the Institute for International Education enables prospective German high-school teachers to expand their knowledge of American life and culture by spending an academic year at an American college. In exchange, they work part-time as German-language teaching assistants.

● **German Teacher-Trainer Program** - Those faculty members in German teacher-training institutions who specialize in English and American studies, social studies, or history are eligible for awards under this fund program. During six weeks of travel, the educators have the opportunity to augment their substantial academic knowledge of the American scene and to observe how social studies are taught in American secondary schools.

● **Ethnic Minority Fellowships** - An experimental program designed to enable European ethnic minority leaders and employment practitioners whose work is specifically targeted to ethnic minorities currently practicing in the fields of employment, education and economic development to visit the U.S. and learn from the American practice.

The fund's European representatives are David Kramer, Kaiserstrasse 1c, 5300 Bonn 1, Federal Republic of Germany; Tel.: 0228-210041, and Mary Fleming, 20 rue Tournefort, 75005 Paris, France; Tel.: 14-331-8172.

955
Harkham Foundation
857 South San Pedro Street
Los Angeles, CA 90014

Limitations: Scholarships awarded primarily to Israeli students pursuing higher education in the U.S. and abroad.
Financial data: Year ended 3/31/87. Assets, $183,665 (M); Total giving, $1,089,649; Grants to individuals amount not specified.
Employer Identification Number: 953532383
Program description:
Scholarships are awarded through applications submitted to an office in Israel based upon recommendations made by school officials. Final selection of recipients is determined by foundation

directors. Scholarship payments are made directly to the educational institution. **Unsolicited applications are not accepted.**

956
Hawthorne (Hugh A.) Foundation
5634 Briar Drive
Houston, TX 77056
Contact: Claudia Hawthorne

Limitations: Educational and relief grants to Irish individuals living in Ireland.
Financial data: Year ended 6/30/86. Assets, $496,215 (M); Total giving, $77,872; Grants to individuals, 39 grants totaling $32,714; Subtotal for educational grants, 9 grants totaling $2,305, high $344, low $137; Subtotal for relief grants, 35 grants totaling $30,409, high $7,987, low $35.
Employer Identification Number: 726027421
Applications: Applications accepted throughout the year; Initial approach by letter.

957
Jerusalem Fund for Education and Community Development
2435 Virginia Avenue, N.W.
Washington, DC 20037

Limitations: Scholarships, fellowships, and travel and research grants for residents of Palestinian communities in Israel.
Financial data: Year ended 5/31/87. Assets, $5,262,843 (M); Total giving, $425,220; Grants to individuals, 800 grants totaling $403,000, high $3,000, low $500.
Employer Identification Number: 521238142
Applications: Deadlines August 31st and December 15th; Initial approach by letter; Completion of formal application required; Submit a biographical record and supporting material, including a report on academic and/or professional careers, and a statement of training plans; See program description below for application information on specific types of support.
Program description:
Scholarships: Applicants must produce official proof of enrollment in an academic or vocational school.
Fellowships: Applicants must submit evidence of enrollment in an organized program occupied by a recognized academic institution in an area conforming to the purpose of the foundation. Letters of reference from academicians may also be required as well as lists of publications, if any.
Travel Grants: Applicants must establish eligibility to attend the workshop, conference or similar program on a subject or topic matter that is consistent with the foundation's exempt purposes.
Research Grants: Applicants must furnish an outline of the research topic and financial budget for undertaking the research. Applicants must also

demonstrate to the committee their ability to conduct and complete the proposed research, and the research topic must be germane to the foundation's exempt purpose.

There is a preliminary screening of all candidates, consisting of the executive director and three program assistants for scholarship applicants, and a committee of the board of directors for applicants for fellowships, travel grants, or research grants.

In fiscal 1987, all grants to individuals were awarded as scholarships for postsecondary study.

958★
Kellogg (W.K.) Foundation
400 North Avenue
Battle Creek, MI 49017-3398   (616) 968-1611

Limitations: Fellowships to foreign individuals to promote international leadership development.
Financial data: Year ended 8/31/87. Assets, $3,581,473,230 (M); Total giving, $88,979,208; Grants to individuals, 159 grants totaling $2,451,056; Subtotal for International Fellowship Program, 43 grants totaling $575,072, high $30,647, low $25.
Employer Identification Number: 381359264
Applications: Future funding for the International Fellowship Program is uncertain. Contact foundation for current application information.
Publications: Annual report.
Program description:
Kellogg International Fellowship Program: This program was initiated in 1986 to further the accomplishments of leaders from other countries. The program, operated by Michigan State University (East Lansing), selects established leaders from two areas:
● Food systems, and
● Primary health care or health services administration.
The professionals currently in the program represent countries on every continent. The fellowship gives them up to $75,000 over three years and establishes released time from their positions over that period to carry out individual projects and to convene for annual symposiums on issues within their fields.

On a competitive basis, the Fellows' sponsoring institutions are eligible for smaller foundation grants to accentuate Fellows' projects, support publications or products, and reinforce multi-country networks critical to the program. The overall goal is to provide these recognized leaders with the chance to improve food systems and health care throughout the world.

959★
Koulaieff (The Trustees of Ivan V.) Education Fund, Inc.
651 11th Avenue
San Francisco, CA 94118
Contact: W. W. Granitow, Secretary

Limitations: Grants, scholarships, and loans to Russian immigrants throughout the world.
Financial data: Year ended 12/31/87. Assets, $7,744,698 (M); Total giving, $351,885; Grants to individuals, 60 grants totaling $156,696, high $27,900, low $400, average grant $2,611; Loans to individuals, 10 loans totaling $21,805, high $5,000, low $500, average loan $2,000.
Employer Identification Number: 946088762
Applications: Applications accepted throughout the year.

960★
Meftah Scholarship Foundation
2777 McCoy Road
Columbus, OH 43220
Contact: Michael Meftah, M.D. or Patricia Meftah

Limitations: Undergraduate and graduate scholarships to recent immigrant and refugee youths in the field of their choice who are planning to attend colleges in Ohio.
Financial data: Year ended 12/31/86. Assets, $1,065,171 (M); Total giving, $9,240; Grants to individuals, 3 grants totaling $9,240, high $6,042, low $832, average grant $700.
Employer Identification Number: 316271327
Applications: Applications accepted throughout the year; Completion of formal application required; Interviews required.
Publications: Application guidelines, informational brochure, program information.
Program description:
To be eligible, each applicant must:
   1. Be a recent young immigrant or refugee to the U.S.
   2. Have completed high school education in the top ten percent of the class, or; if educated abroad, have successfully obtained the G.E.D. with a high grade, or, if in college, have obtained a GPA of 3.0 or higher.
   3. Apply for and receive all federal, state, and other available grants prior to receiving full supplementary assistance from the foundation.
   4. Plan to attend a state university in Ohio. However, if a student has obtained enough grants and scholarships for a private college, to a point in which the cost to the foundation would be less than or equal to the cost of his/her attending a state college, then the supplementary assistance for the private college may be considered.
   Payments will be made in installments equal to the number of terms/semesters that the college or

university has in its school year. Checks will be made payable to the university only. Upon annual reapplication and good academic performance, the full supplementary assistance may be continued until the student's original education goal has been achieved.

961★
Merck Company Foundation, The
P.O. Box 2000
Rahway, NJ 07065-0900   (201) 574-4375
Contact: Charles R. Hogen, Jr., Executive Vice-President

Limitations: Fellowships to non-residents of the United States who hold M.D. degrees or have equivalent education for specialized training at a recognized training center for clinical pharmacology at a U.S. medical school or university.
Financial data: Year ended 12/21/87. Assets, $7,467,000 (M); Total giving, $5,465,000; Grants to individuals, 12 grants totaling $264,700.
Employer Identification Number: 226028476
Applications: Deadline August 31st; Completion of formal application required.
Program description:
Merck, Sharp and Dohme International Fellowships in Clinical Pharmacology are awarded to support training in clinical pharmacology at a recognized center for clinical pharmacology at a U.S. medical school or university for individuals who have completed at least a one-year internship and two years of residency or some combination of training that adds up to three years of postgraduate experience in clinical and basic sciences. Applicants must by fully licensed to practice medicine in their own countries, be able to write and speak English fluently, be accepted at an appropriate U.S. institution, be planning to return to their countries, and be guaranteed a position in clinical pharmacology in their own country after completion of training.
Grants provide a stipend of $27,000 annually and a travel allowance and may be made for up to two years. Usually four new fellowships are awarded annually.

962
Mostazafan Foundation of New York, The
500 Fifth Avenue, 34th Floor
New York, NY 10110   (212) 944-8333
Contact: Ms. Nasrin Rouzati

Limitations: Scholarships, fellowships, and loans to Iranian citizens who are students at, or have been accepted by, a U.S. college or university.
Financial data: Year ended 3/31/86. Assets, $80,847,488 (M); Total giving, $2,420,193; Grants to individuals, 238 grants totaling $577,964, high $6,000, low $317.

Employer Identification Number: 237345978
Applications: Deadline will be announced through universities and colleges; Completion of formal application required; See program description below for application information.
Program description:
Any citizen of Iran who is either a student in good standing at a college or university located within the U.S., or a student who has been accepted as such by a U.S. college or university, whether or not a candidate for a degree, is qualified to apply for a scholarship, fellowship, or student loan irrespective of race, religion, creed or color.
The grants or loans shall be applied to charges incurred in connection with the educational activities of the recipient including, but not limited to, tuition, room and board, books, and other related items. Recipients will be required to submit annually a written account evidencing the proper application of the grant monies. Receipts and other proof will, from time to time, be required. If the recipient fails to render such accounting or to establish to the satisfaction of the managing director that the funds were used properly, no further advances or grants will be made until the default has been cured.
Applicants must submit a written application with the following documents:
- One passport-size photo
- Transcripts from schools attended (undergraduate, graduate)
- An officially approved copy of the research proposal
- A letter of advancement of candidacy from the applicant's university.
The following factors will be considered in the selection of grant recipients:
- Prior academic performance
- Performance in scholastic tests measuring ability and aptitude for college or university-level study
- Recommendation from school or other officials, professors and institutions
- Qualifications demonstrating an interest in the affairs and the development of Iran
- Personal interviews (when desired) to determine applicant's motivation, character, ability, and potential.
Student loan applicants must:
- Be a graduate student
- Be enrolled in a full-time course of study relevant to the current development needs of the Islamic Republic of Iran
- Have above average academic performance (minimum of 3.3 on a scale of 4.0)
- Not receive any other loan or scholarship aid
- Demonstrate financial need
- Demonstrate his/her willingness to return to the Islamic Republic of Iran upon completion of studies
- Apply for exchange allowance status at the Ministry of Higher Education.

Upon acceptance, the student shall be granted a loan for a maximum period of two years which will include tuition and monthly expenses.

963
Shatford (J.D.) Memorial Trust
c/o Chemical Bank
30 Rockefeller Plaza
New York, NY 10112   (212) 621-2148
Contact: Barbara Strohmeier

Limitations: Scholarships and welfare assistance to residents of Hubbards, Nova Scotia, Canada.
Financial data: Year ended 12/31/85. Assets, $2,543,646 (M); Total giving, $163,070; Grants to individuals, 120 grants totaling $162,730, high $7,887, low $20; Subtotals for scholarships and welfare assistance not specified.
Employer Identification Number: 136029993
Applications: Applications accepted throughout the year; Completion of formal application required for scholarship grants.

964
Taraknath Das Foundation
c/o Southern Asian Institute, Columbia University
420 West 118th Street
New York, NY 10027
Contact: Leonard A. Gordon, Vice-President

Limitations: Scholarships and loans only to Indian students, scholars and writers studying in the U.S.
Financial data: Year ended 5/31/86. Assets, $99,682 (M); Total giving, $5,650; Grants to individuals, 4 grants totaling $3,000, each grant $750; Subtotal for loans not specified.
Employer Identification Number: 136161284
Applications: Deadline July 1st; Completion of formal application required.
Publications: Annual report, informational brochure.
Program description:
Under the **Grant and Research Program**, grants-in-aid and loans are made to Indian students, researchers, writers, and scholars, including undergraduates and doctoral candidates.

965★
Wallenberg (Marcus) Foundation
c/o Sullivan & Cromwell
250 Park Avenue
New York, NY 10177

Limitations: Scholarships for students from Scandanavian countries, in particular Sweden, for U.S. graduate studies concentrating in the fields of international enterprise and commerce.
Financial data: Year ended 3/31/86. Assets, $1,827,564 (M); Total giving, $69,000; Grants to individuals, 6 grants totaling $69,000, high $15,000, low $7,000.
Employer Identification Number: 133176307
Applications: Applications accepted throughout the year.

966★
Wemyss Foundation, The
One Black Gates Road
Wilmington, DE 19803   (302) 658-2483
Contact: Mrs. Ruth B. Harden, Secretary-Treasurer

Limitations: Undergraduate scholarships only for Latin American exchange scholars.
Financial data: Year ended 6/30/87. Assets, $637 (M); Total giving, $3,965; Grants to individuals, 2 grants totaling $3,965, general range $3,000-5,000.
Employer Identification Number: 510097818
Applications: Deadline May 1st, grants awarded mid-June; Initial approach by letter; Completion of formal application required; Interviews required in applicant's country.
Program description:
The foundation makes very few grants and these are largely to persons coming from Latin America countries to pursue studies in the U.S. in four-year colleges and who, upon their return, will contribute to the economic soundness of their native country. Both scholarships and special grants to individuals are awarded. The foundation makes on-going commitments to its recipients and therefore only rarely accepts new applicants. The foundation does not make awards for graduate study.

AWARDS, PRIZES, AND GRANTS BY NOMINATION

This section includes two types of grants for which individuals usually may not apply directly:

● **Awards and Prizes -** encompasses grants in recognition of past achievements, either scholarly, cultural, or civic, or to award winners of competitions sponsored by the foundation or an affiliated organization. Many awards and prizes are by nomination only, as specified in the entry. For some of the awards and prizes listed here, an individual may apply directly. Nevertheless, the entry should be read carefully and the foundation should be contacted for detailed application guidelines before a request is made.

● **Grants by Nomination -** Scholarships, fellowships, research grants and others for which application must be made by an institution on behalf of an individual are listed in this section. Generally not included in this category are student aid grants at the undergraduate or graduate level which require only that the individual filing the application be **recommended** by a high school counselor or dean. The latter have been listed under "Educational Support."

Entries are arranged alphabetically by foundation name. Access to grants by the above types of support, as well as to specific subject areas and geographic focus, is provided in the "Subject," "Types of Support" and "Geographic Focus" indexes in the back of the book.

Limitations on grantmaking are indicated in the entry when available. The limitations statement should be checked carefully as a foundation will reject any application that does not fall within its stated geographic area, recipient type, or area of interest.

REMEMBER: IF YOU DON'T QUALIFY, DON'T APPLY

967★
Alaska Conservation Foundation
430 West Seventh Street, Suite 215
Anchorage, AK 99501   (907) 276-1917
Contact: Denny Wilcher, President

Limitations: Awards to environmentalists in Alaska.
Financial data: Year ended 12/31/86. Assets, $365,779
(M); Total giving, $235,808; Awards to individuals, 2
awards totaling $2,000, each award $1,000.
Employer Identification Number: 920061466
Publications: Annual report.
Program description:
The **Celia Hunter Award** is presented annually to
honor Alaska's outstanding environmental volunteer
activist. In 1986, the foundation made its first
presentation of the **Olaus Murie Award** to Alaska's
outstanding environment professional.

968★
**American Academy and Institute of Arts and
   Letters**
633 West 155th Street
New York, NY 10032   (212) 368-5900
Contact: Lydia Kaim, Assistant to the Executive
Director

Limitations: Awards to artists, writers, and composers
who are not members of the Academy-Institute,
nominated by members.
Financial data: Year ended 12/31/87. Assets,
$21,108,310 (M); Total giving, $500,000
(approximate); Grants to individuals, 63 grants totaling
$439,000, high $50,000, low $1,500, average grant
$5,000.
Employer Identification Number: 130429640
Applications: With the exception of the Richard
Rodgers Production Award, **applications for awards or
financial assistance are not accepted.**
Publications: Annual report, informational brochure.
Program description:
Seventeen awards are made annually to artists, writers,
and composers who are not members of the
Academy-Institute to honor them and encourage them
to continue their creative work. In addition to the
awards, the work of recipients in art and literature is
included in an annual spring exhibit of art,
manuscripts, and books and a recording of the work of
music recipients is sponsored by the
Academy-Institute.
   The Academy-Institute also provides assistance
through the Artists' and Writers' fund to professional
artists, writers, and composers with demonstrated
ability who are in financial distress due to emergency
circumstances, and awards a variety of other named
prizes, scholarships, and fellowships in the fields of
creative writing, music, painting, and architecture.
   The **Richard Rodgers Production Award** (and
Development Grants) subsidizes the production,
Off-Broadway, of a musical.

969
Belgian American Educational Foundation, Inc.
195 Church Street
New Haven, CT 06510   (203) 777-5765
Contact: Dr. Emile L. Boulpaep, President

Limitations: Fellowships by nomination only to
American graduate students who are proficient in
Dutch or French, and Belgian graduate students.
Financial data: Year ended 8/31/86. Assets,
$11,356,503 (M); Total giving, $502,987; Grants to
individuals, 36 grants totaling $487,787, high
$20,000, low $8,000.
Employer Identification Number: 131606002
Applications: Deadline December 31st; Submit
proposal preferably in December; Initial approach by
letter, proposal, or telephone; Completion of formal
application required; Candidates must be nominated
by the dean of their graduate school; Only one
candidate may be nominated by each university.
Applications from individuals are not accepted.
Program description:
The Belgian American Educational Foundation
fellowships were established to promote the exchange
of intellectual ideas between the two countries.
   Predoctoral Fellowships are awarded to American
graduate students to enable them to pursue study and
research in Belgium on projects for which Belgium
provides special advantages. The $8,000 awards are
made for nine-month periods.
   Through the nominating dean, candidates must
submit:
      1. a statement of the dissertation or research
      project and its current status;
      2. a proposed program of study to be undertaken
      during the period of the grant;
      3. a curriculum vitae and a short personal
      biography;
      4. official transcripts of both undergraduate and
      graduate courses;
      5. evidence of language proficiency in French
      and/or Dutch;
      6. reasons for choice of university or other
      institutions including the scholars with whom he
      or she plans to study.
   Applicants can expect to receive notification of final
action on their proposals before March 31st.

970
**Boyer (John) First Troop Philadelphia City
   Cavalry Memorial Fund**
Mellon Bank East, N.A.
P.O. Box 7236
Philadelphia, PA 19101

Limitations: Scholarships by nomination only of the
First Troop Philadelphia City Cavalry to residents of
the Philadelphia, PA, area to study abroad for one
year and to foreign students to study in the U.S.
Financial data: Year ended 6/30/87. Assets, $825,226

(M); Total giving, $16,990; Grants to individuals totaling $16,990.
Employer Identification Number: 236227636
Applications: Applicants nominated by member of Cavalry; **Individual applications not accepted.**
Publications: Annual report.

971★
Brice (Helen) Scholarship Fund
Mellon Bank, N.A.
Mellon Bank Center
Pittsburgh, PA 15258-0001

Limitations: Undergraduate scholarships by nomination only awarded to students who have attended Uniontown, PA, area high schools.
Financial data: Year ended 12/31/86. Assets, $108,510 (M); Total giving, $5,000; Grants to individuals, 12 grants totaling $5,000, high $700, low $300.
Employer Identification Number: 256119807
Program description:
Scholarship awards are paid directly to the educational institution on behalf of the individual recipient.

972★
Burroughs Wellcome Fund, The
3030 Cornwallis Road
Research Triangle Park, NC 27709   (919) 248-4136
Contact: Martha G. Peck, Executive Director

Limitations: Funding is provided through competitive award programs to aid medical education and research with particular emphasis on clinical pharmacology, toxicology, molecular parasitology, pharmacoepidemiology, microbiology and other basic life sciences. Grants only to qualifying U.S. institutions (on behalf of individuals) complying with federal regulations.
Financial data: Year ended 4/30/87. Assets, $15,984,239 (M); Total grants authorized, $3,662,025; Awards and grants to individuals, 51 grants authorized totaling $2,668,959, high $250,000, low $1,000, general range $10,000-40,000, average grant $20,000.
Employer Identification Number: 237225395
Applications: Deadlines vary, see program description below; For Wellcome Research Travel Grant applications, British and Irish inquiries write to The Wellcome Trust, One Park Square West, London NW1 4LJ; U.S. inquiries write to the above address.
Publications: Annual report, informational brochure (including application guidelines), newsletter, application guidelines.
Program description:
The Scholar Awards: The cornerstone of the fund's grantmaking activities, the **Scholar Awards** began in 1960 when clinical pharmacology, the study of therapeutic drugs in man, was targeted as a field in need of special support. Since then, five additional

awards have been established to fund research and education in toxicology, molecular parasitology, pharmacoepidemiology, immunopharmacology of allergic diseases, and innovative methods in drug design.

Each award offers five years of support totaling $300,000. The awards are made over a five-year period at the rate of $60,000 per year, of which $50,000 is to cover the salary of the scholar involved in teaching, research, and/or further specialized training in the field, and $10,000 is to cover incidental expenses such as supplies, publication costs, and travel. Awards are nationally competitive. Applicants are reviewed by the funds special advisory committees, and final selections are approved by the board of directors. These annual awards represent the fund's major contribution to medical research and education. In fiscal 1987, they provided over $1.8 million to support eight new and 25 continuing Scholars. The award areas are as follows:

1. The **Clinical Pharmacology Scholar Award** is designed to promote research, strengthen teaching programs and attract and train young men and women for careers in clinical pharmacology. It is the field of medicine that studies the therapeutic effects of drugs, their metabolism in the body, and the risks associated with their use.

The dean or other appropriate official of the medical school or university who sponsors the candidate must specify in his/her application the facilities for research and teaching which will be available; the role of the candidate within the clinical pharmacology program; and whether it is the medical school's purpose to initiate and develop a new section or division under the direction of the candidate or to provide the salary of the candidate as a faculty member in an established division of clinical pharmacology.

Following review of the written applications, the Advisory Committee will interview some of the proposed candidates. Deadline for application is November 1st.

2. The **Burroughs Wellcome Molecular Parasitology Scholar Program's** purpose is to support research that applies the latest developments in biology and chemistry to the study of parasitic diseases and to their control and prevention in the Third World. It is sponsored in the belief that such fundamental knowledge will lead to new and more efficient methods of prevention and treatment of "the great neglected diseases" of mankind: malaria, trypanosomiasis, filariasis, schistosomiasis, hookworm, leishmaniasis, amebiasis, and other parasitic and tropical diseases. Grantees may undertake a period of study abroad.

The award is made to individuals who have demonstrated a clearly defined commitment to bring innovative methods of biochemistry and molecular biology to bear upon the problems of parasitic and tropical diseases and who are nominated by their institutions. Institutions nominating candidates for this award are expected to document the intention to create or expand an interdisciplinary research and training program in molecular parasitology for which the grantee will serve as a focus. The program is primarily intended for individuals who have established reputations as scientists but are in the early phases of their research careers; however, consideration will also be given to senior individuals.

Application in letter form should be initiated jointly by such appropriate officials as the Dean and Head of the Department in which the candidate holds his primary appointment. The deadline for submitting an application is January 15th.

3. The **Burroughs Wellcome Toxicology Scholar Award** program seeks to develop an increased number of toxicologists, well-trained in understanding the effects of drugs and environmental pollutants on human health. Thus, this program seeks to support the career development of toxicologists and to stimulate teaching, training, and research in academic institutions that have a commitment to toxicology as a basic science.

The awards are intended to provide support for expanded programs in toxicology in academic institutions by helping to provide additional faculty positions, to enlarge opportunities for and stimulate the interest of students and faculty members in this field. The individual grantee is expected to serve as the focus for such activities at his institution.

Applications must be initiated by the Dean or other Administrator having jurisdiction over the academic program(s) involved. Examples of likely sources of candidates are schools of pharmacy, medicine, public health, veterinary medicine, science and life sciences, and such departments as pharmacology, chemistry, biochemistry, toxicology, pathology, internal medicine and pediatrics. Only one application will be accepted from each institution; application deadline is December 1st.

4. The **Pharmacoepidemiology Scholar Award** was developed as the result of an increased awareness from the fields of medicine, pharmacy, pharmacology and epidemiology of the need for a more rigorous and systematic method of assessing the relative safety and effectiveness of pharmaceuticals. Large-scale computer systems now make it possible to identify and quantify acute and delayed adverse effects. The award's purpose is to support research that applies epidemiological principles to evaluate therapeutic experience in large populations.

The aims of the award are to stimulate teaching, training and research in pharmacoepidemiology; facilitate capacity building of systems permitting monitoring of experiences with drugs on a broad scale; support career development of individuals in the the field; and further develop scientific methods in epidemiology relating to pharmaceuticals.

This award is offered to all U.S. medical schools or schools of public health. Applications in letter form are due by February 15th and should include a letter from the Dean or other appropriate official of the institution.

5. The **Developing Investigator Award in the Immunopharmacology of Allergic Diseases** support promising clinical investigators who are applying new developments in immunology, biochemistry and pharmacology to studies of the underlying mechanisms of allergic responses. Better understanding of these mechanisms may lead to the prevention or control of allergic diseases. The deadline for submitting applications is April 15th.

6. The **George H. Hitchings Award for Innovative Methods in Drug Design** is the newest in the Scholar Awards Program. More information on this award can be obtained by writing directly to the fund. Application deadline is April 1st.

The Research Fellowships: Research fellowships are competitive awards that enable researchers to pursue postdoctoral training programs. These one-,two- and three-year fellowships support advanced training in seven disciplines, including clinical and veterinary medicine, pharmacy and the basic sciences. The fund sponsors, in conjunction with outside organizations, the following programs:

1. **Anesthesiology Research Fellowship** - A one-year postdoctoral award administered by the American Society of Anesthesiologists.

2. **Clinical Pharmacokinetics Fellowship** - Initiated in fiscal 1983, a one-year award administered by The American Society of Hospital Pharmacists Research and Education Foundation.

3. **Fellowship in Infectious Diseases** - A two-year postdoctoral award administered by The Infectious Diseases Society of America.

4. **Fellowship in Synthetic Organic Chemistry** - Initiated in fiscal 1987, a one-year award to the outstanding second-year graduate student at Duke University, The University of North Carolina at Chapel Hill, and North Carolina State University.

5. **John Hughlings Jackson Clinical Epilepsy Research Fellowship** - Initiated in fiscal 1983, a one-year postdoctoral award administered by the Epilepsy Foundation of America.

6. **Dermatology Research Fellowship in honor Marion B. Sulzberger, M.D.** - A one-year postdoctoral award administered by the Dermatology Foundation.

7. **Research Fellowship in Nephrology** - A one-year postdoctoral award administered by the National Kidney Foundation.

8. **Research Fellowship in Ophthalmology** - Initiated in fiscal 1982, a one-year postdoctoral award administered by the National Society to Prevent Blindness.

9. **Research Fellowship in the Life Sciences** - A three-year postdoctoral award administered by the LifeSciences Research Foundation.

10. **Urology Research Fellowship** - A two-year postdoctoral award administered by the American Urological Association.

Contact the fund for more information on the research fellowships.

The Visiting Professorships: Visiting professorships offer another kind of support for medical education. These grants bring leading researchers in the medical sciences to U.S. colleges and medical schools. Their lectures and tutorials introduce students to the newest ideas in their fields. Each grant is awarded to a host institution in support of its designated Visiting Professor.

The dean of a medical school should send a letter indicating his choice for a Visiting Professor and include a curriculum vitae or information on his position and fields of interest, as well as a tentative program for his visit. Professors may be from the U.S. or abroad. The deadline for submitting an application is May 1st. **Unsolicited applications from individual researchers are not accepted.**

Selection is made with the guidance of an Advisory Committee and is based on the needs of the applying medical school, suitable matching of the nominated professor and medical school based on those needs, and the total number of applications.

1. **William N. Creasy Visiting Professorships in Clinical Pharmacology** are awarded for the purpose of stimulating interest in the discipline of clinical pharmacology and support for its development in the nation's medical schools.

Up to ten Visiting Professorships are offered annually and are available for use for any week, during which the Visiting Professor will teach medical students, faculty, and house staff, as well as deliver a William N. Creasy Memorial Lecture. Each award is $2,500 plus travel expenses (economy air fare) for the professor and accompanying spouse. The host institutions will receive $350 to assist with attendant expenses incurred for visiting professorship.

2. The **Wellcome Visiting Professorships in the Basic Medical Sciences** are collaborative programs with the Federation of American Societies for Experimental Biology (FASEB). FASEB members represent the disciplines of biological chemistry, immunology, nutrition, pathology, pharmacology, physiology and cell biology. Each Professorship awards $1,500 and travel expenses to the professor and $350 to the host institution.

3. The **Wellcome Visiting Professorships in Microbiology** are administered by the American Society for Microbiology. They award $1,500 travel expenses and $350 to the host institution.

4. The **Burroughs Wellcome Fund Visiting Professorships of the Royal Society of Medicine Foundation** enable distinguished physicians to visit key areas of research and clinical practice in the United Kingdom. Awards are administered by the Royal Society of Medicine Foundation in cooperation with the RSM in London.

The Research Travel Grants: The fund's research travel grants represent a program begun in fall 1977 jointly sponsored by The Burroughs Wellcome Fund and The Wellcome Trust (in London). The grants are intended to promote the direct and rapid exchange of information, methods, and technologies related to research in the basic medical sciences among investigators in Britain, Ireland, and the U.S. The grants are for periods of two weeks to three months to study specific therapies and to share ideas with colleagues in another country.

the research grants cover cost of travel and subsistence. The amount of the individual grant varies., depending on length of stay and location. No provision is made for spouses of families.

Research Grants in the Basic Medical Sciences: The **Burroughs Wellcome Young Investigator Award in Virology**, initiated in fiscal 1987, is a $90,000 three-year award administered by the Infectious Diseases Society of America. It is a competitive award given to support physicians doing patient studies, studies of viruses and how drugs act against them.

973★
Carnegie Hero Fund Commission
606 Oliver Building
Pittsburgh, PA 15222   (412) 281-1302
Contact: Robert W. Off, President

Limitations: Medals and grants awarded by nomination only for acts of heroism voluntarily performed by civilians within the U.S. and Canada in saving or attempting to save the lives of others.
Financial data: Year ended 12/31/87. Assets, $15,259,888 (M); Total giving, $552,985; Awards and grants to individuals totaling $552,985; Subtotals: pensions, $236,395; one-time grants, $305,473; medals, $11,117.
Employer Identification Number: 251062730
Applications: Deadline for nominations within two years of the date of the act; Initial approach by letter giving date, time, and place of heroic actions and addresses of hero and witnesses.
Publications: Annual report, program information, application guidelines.
Program description:
Medals are awarded in recognition of acts of selfless heroism. Monetary assistance is given only to persons who have been awarded the Carnegie Medal and who have need for financial aid as a result of an injury incurred or for their education. In addition, grants may be given to the dependents of those who have lost their lives or have been disabled in such heroic manner. Recommendation for awards may be made by any individual having knowledge of an outstanding act of bravery.

974
Chicago Community Trust, The
222 North LaSalle Street, Suite 1400
Chicago, IL 60601   (312) 372-3356
Contact: Cedrick L. Chernick

Limitations: Grants by nomination only to newly
established investigators in academic research in
medicine, chemistry, or biological science.
Financial data: Year ended 9/30/86. Assets,
$237,400,000 (M); Total giving, $23,396,743; Grants
to individuals, 18 grants totaling $3,240,000, each
grant $180,000.
Employer Identification Number: 362167000
Applications: Nominations accepted throughout the
year; Candidates must be nominated by their
university. **Individual applications not accepted.**
Publications: Annual report.
Program description:
The **Searle Scholars Program** awards grants to
individuals who have demonstrated a potential for
doing innovative research in medicine, chemistry, or
biological science and who might be expected to
make significant contributions to their chosen
profession over a period of time. Universities in the
U.S. are invited to submit no more than two
applications each for the support of the research of
outstanding individuals who are just establishing
independent research careers.

The Searle Scholars are chosen on the
recommendations of an advisory committee of
distinguished scientists. Since its inception in 1980,
105 Searle Scholars have been named with awards
totaling over $17 million.

975
Common Wealth Trust, The
c/o Bank of Delaware
300 Delaware Avenue
Wilmington, DE 19899

Limitations: Distinguished service awards to
prominent individuals in literature, the dramatic arts,
and communications, primarily in Delaware.
Financial data: Year ended 12/31/85. Assets,
$5,516,340 (M); Total giving, $278,797; Grants to
individuals, 55 grants totaling $69,300.
Employer Identification Number: 510232187

976
Cox (Una Chapman) Foundation
P.O. Box 749
Corpus Christi, TX 78403   (512) 883-3621
Contact: Harvie Branscomb, Jr., President

Limitations: Awards to members of the United States
Foreign Service.
Financial data: Year ended 11/30/86. Assets,
$10,980,802 (M); Total giving, $138,129; Awards to
individuals totaling $6,875.

Employer Identification Number: 742150104
Applications: Applications accepted throughout the
year; Completion of formal application required.
Program description:
The foundation finances mid-career one-year
sabbaticals for promising Foreign Service officers. In
1986, funding for sabbatical awards was made
payable to the director of the Center for the Study of
Foreign Affairs at the Foreign Service Institute. The
foundation is also open to requests by individual
officers who need assistance in paying for travel to
seminars.

977
Dayton Foundation, The
1895 Kettering Tower
Dayton, OH 45423   (513) 222-0410
Contact: Frederick Bartenstein, III, Director

Limitations: Awards to teachers in the greater Dayton,
OH, area and to City of Dayton employees.
Financial data: Year ended 12/31/86. Assets,
$17,859,979 (M); Total giving, $1,201,366; Awards to
individuals, 104 awards totaling $42,900, average
award $500.
Employer Identification Number: 316027287
Publications: Annual report.
Program description:
The **Teacher Initiative Grant** program honors teachers
for conducting innovative projects in the classroom.

The **Joseph T. Cline Awards Fund** provides cash
awards to City of Dayton employees who exhibit
excellence and dedication in their work.

978★
Demarest (Eben) Trust
Mellon Bank, N.A.
P.O. Box 185
Pittsburgh, PA 15230   (412) 234-4695
Contact: Eileen Wilhem, Assistant Vice-President

Limitations: Grants by nomination only to
exceptionally gifted individuals in archaeology or the
arts.
Financial data: Year ended 12/31/86. Assets, $138,684
(M); Total giving, $7,258; Grants to individuals, 1
grant totaling $7,258, average grant $7,000.
Employer Identification Number: 256108821
Applications: Deadline June 1st; Applications
accepted throughout the year from institutions on
behalf of individual candidates; Completion of formal
application required; **Individual applications without
nominations not accepted.**
Publications: Application guidelines, program
information.
Program description:
Initial contact is by an organization or a member of
the Demarest Council recommending a candidate for

a grant. Grants are awarded to exceptionally gifted individuals in literature, music, visual or performing arts, or in archaeology.

979★
Dow Jones Newspaper Fund, Inc., The
P.O. Box 300
Princeton, NJ 08543-0300   (609) 452-2820
Contact: Thomas E. Engelman, Executive Director

Limitations: Monetary awards by nomination only to high school journalism students; scholarships by nomination only to minority high school seniors who attend an Urban Journalism Workshop.
Financial data: Year ended 12/31/87. Assets, $379,067 (M); Total giving, $327,277; Grants to individuals, 141 grants totaling $91,035; Subtotal for awards not specified.
Employer Identification Number: 136021439
Applications: Deadlines July 15th (Special Awards Program), September 1st (Urban Writing Competition); Initial approach by letter; Completion of formal application required; **Individual applications not accepted.**
Publications: Annual report, application guidelines.
Program description:
The Newspaper Fund awards two categories of grants by nomination.

Special Awards Program is open to high school seniors intending to major in journalism in college and who are nominated by teachers who have received distinction as National Journalism Distinguished Teacher of the Year or Distinguished Advisers (runners-up). Teachers may be nominated by newspapers, press associations or high school principals for their outstanding abilities as journalism teachers by July 15th of each year.

Winning teachers subsequently nominate students from their respective high schools to enter a writing competition. Prizes are awarded to winning students in honor of their teachers, $1,000 for first place, $500 for each of four runners-up.

The Urban Writing Competition gives grants to minority high school seniors who write news and/or feature articles under the direction of professional newspaper reporters, editors and journalism teachers in Urban Journalism Workshops operated by the Dow Jones Newspaper Fund in the summer. Candidates are nominated by workshop directors, and if successful, receive $1,000 college scholarship grants renewable up to four years based on need, continued interest in journalism career, and grades.

980★
Dreyfus (The Camille and Henry) Foundation, Inc.
445 Park Avenue
New York, NY 10022   (212) 753-1760
Contact: L. M. Stephenson, Executive Director

Limitations: Research and teaching grants by nomination only to young faculty members of academic institutions in the U.S. See program description below for limitations on specific programs.
Financial data: Year ended 12/31/87. Assets, $41,717,468 (M); Total giving, $1,985,943; Grants to individuals, 32 grants totaling $1,300,000 (approximate), high $50,000, low $5,000, general range $25,000-50,000; Subtotal for Teacher-Scholar Grant Program totaling $600,000; Subtotal for Young Faculty in Chemistry Program totaling $250,000; Subtotal for Chemistry for Liberal Arts Colleges Program totaling $450,000.
Employer Identification Number: 135570117
Applications: Deadlines April 15th for Teacher-Scholar Grant Program, May 1st for Chemistry for Liberal Arts Colleges Program, and May 15th for Distinguished New Faculty in Chemistry Program; Nomination forms available from the foundation; Candidates must be nominated by applying academic institution; See program description below for application information on specific programs; **Individual applications not accepted.**
Publications: Annual report, informational brochure (including application guidelines).
Program description:
The purpose of the **Dreyfus Teacher-Scholar Grant Program** is to provide funds to the nominating academic institution to be used by young faculty members with freedom to develop their potential both as teachers and scholars in accordance with their plans which are submitted to and approved by the academic institution. Candidates should have completed their academic training for the Ph.D. degree, served as full-time faculty member for not more than five years, and preferably should not be older than 36 years. Only one nomination from an institution will be considered in any one year. The following guidelines are applied:

1. This is a one-time grant to promote the development of a promising career and is not a research grant per se.
2. The grant should foster better contact with students and should not take the young faculty member out of the classroom.
3. The young faculty member should bear in mind that the academic institution and its students should be benefitted by the use put to these funds.

The twelve grants of $50,000 each are awarded annually.

The **Distinguished New Faculty in Chemistry Grant Program** supplements the Teacher-Scholar Grants. It is intended to provide early funds to allow promising new faculty an early start in their research at the beginning of their appointment in the areas of chemistry, biochemistry, or chemical engineering. The candidates (whose ages preferably should not exceed 30 years) are chosen for their potential to make significant contributions from fundamental research in chemistry. Their teaching abilities are also considered. The funds are awarded in time for use by the young faculty member when he or she formally begins the first year of teaching. The grant funds are primarily for research purposes, particularly as seed money for new ideas and concepts and not for salary during the regular academic year. The funds may also be used for student research stipends, for scientific equipment, and for other need related to research. Ten grants of $25,000 each are awarded annually.

Candidates for the New Faculty in Chemistry Program should have gained a Ph.D. degree in one of the stated sciences and may have some postdoctoral experience, but should not have had any prior full-time faculty experience. The nomination form should be submitted by the department chairman and confirmed by an administrative officer.

The **Chemistry for Liberal Arts Colleges Program** places a teaching/research fellow in a liberal arts institution under the guidance of a nominated mentor. The fellow participates in the mentor's research program and takes on some of the mentor's teaching duty. It is a one-year program funded at $45,000, of which $25,000 is allocated as the fellow's salary.

981★
Duke Endowment, The
200 South Tryon Street, Suite 1100
Charlotte, NC 28202   (704) 376-0291
Contact: John F. Day, Executive Director or Billy G. McCall, Deputy Executive Director

Limitations: Pension assistance by nomination only to retired ministers, or their widows and dependent children, from the two North Carolina conferences of the United Methodist Church.
Financial data: Year ended 12/31/87. Assets, $771,871,787 (M); Total giving, $41,417,156; Grants to individuals totaling $566,733.
Employer Identification Number: 560529965
Applications: Individual applications not accepted.
Publications: Annual report.
Program description:
Lists of individuals to be considered for assistance is provided to the endowment by the two North Carolina conferences of the United Methodist Church. No applications are submitted.

982★
Durfee Foundation, The
11444 West Olympic Boulevard
Suite 1015
Los Angeles, CA 90064   (213) 312-9543
Contact: Robert S. Macfarlane, Jr., Managing Director

Limitations: Awards by nomination only for individuals who have enhanced human dignity through the law.
Financial data: Year ended 12/31/87. Assets, $11,684,207 (M); Total giving, $351,736; Grants to individuals, $0; 1986, Grants to individuals, 5 awards totaling $50,000.
Employer Identification Number: 952223738
Applications: Awards are given in even-numbered years.

983
Earhart Foundation
Plymouth Building, Suite 204
2929 Plymouth Road
Ann Arbor, MI 48105   (313) 761-8592
Contact: David B. Kennedy, President

Limitations: Fellowships by nomination only for graduate study in the social sciences or humanities.
Financial data: Year ended 12/31/86. Assets, $39,352,411 (M); Total giving, $1,573,714; Grants to individuals, 212 grants totaling $895,498, high $50,000, low $500; Subtotal for H.B. Earhart Fellowships not specified.
Employer Identification Number: 386008273
Applications: Individual applications not accepted for H.B. Earhart fellowships.
Publications: Annual report, program information.
Program description:
H.B. Earhart Fellowships are awarded to help talented individuals through graduate study in optimum time in order that they may embark upon careers in college or university teaching or in research in the social sciences and humanities. Candidates are nominated by faculty sponsors whose participation is invited annually. Sponsors also monitor the performance of the candidate.

984★
Everett (Mark Allen) Foundation
301 West Eubanks
Oklahoma City, OK 73118   (405) 524-2191
Contact: Alice Allen Everett, Secretary-Treasurer

Limitations: Scholarships by nomination only limited to residents of Oklahoma who are students at the University of Oklahoma or Oklahoma City University, OK, for study in medicine and the fine arts. Prizes and awards by nomination only are also given in various fields at these and other universities.
Financial data: Year ended 12/31/87. Assets, $100,000 (M); Grants to individuals, 10 grants totaling $7,000,

high $1,000, low $100.

Employer Identification Number: 736092127

Applications: Deadline prior to beginning of semester; Completion of formal application required; Interviews usually required; Applications are provided to the student following receipt of nomination by the major professor; **Individual applications without nomination not accepted.**

Program description:

Awards, scholarships and grants are restricted to the State of Oklahoma except in rare instances approved by the board of trustees. The foundation awards grants in a number of fields to enable recipients to improve or enhance their skills and talents. Undergraduate fine arts majors eligible for scholarship consideration are at present limited to those studying violin, cello, piano, and male ballet students. The scholarship in the OU College of Medicine is restricted to an outstanding student at the close of his or her freshman year of the second year (sophomore) of basic sciences. Selection criteria are outstanding ability, performance, and promise. All nominations for consideration are made by the major professor of the student, and not by the student directly.

1. **Prizes and Awards** - Selection of recipients for prizes and awards shall be made by a committee of two or more appropriate authorities named by the trustees of the foundation. (Examples would be two professors of English for literature prizes; a professor of English and a poet for the poetry award, etc.)

2. **Scholarships** - Selection for scholarships shall be made by a committee consisting of one trustee and one or more other appropriate faculty member(s), or by authorities appropriate for selection of a grantee for the scholarship concerned. Selection shall be based upon expectancy for and/or prior demonstration of artistic, scientific, or intellectual excellence, without regard to race, religion, or sex, except where appropriate.

Notification regarding criteria for the award of prizes or scholarships shall be made via media appropriate for the award concerned. (For example, state colleges and universities for the college poetry award; departments of dance for the ballet scholarships, etc.)

3. **Grants** - The criteria used in selecting recipients for grants in order to achieve a specific objective (such as improving or enhancing a literary, artistic, musical, scientific skill or similar talent) will be related to the purpose of the grants. Final selection of the grantee will be made by the board of trustees.

All grantees of scholarships or grants shall be requried to submit a report to the board of the foundation at least once annually (in most cases semiannually), with a transcript of grades received during the academic period to which the scholarship relates, verified by the educational institution attended by the grantee.

985

Fleet Charitable Trust

c/o Fleet National Bank
111 Westminster Street
Providence, RI 02903   (401) 278-6979
Contact: Ms. Nancy L. Langrall, Assistant
Vice-President, Fleet National Bank

Limitations: Work-study scholarships by nomination only for RI high school seniors from minority groups.

Financial data: Year ended 12/31/86. Assets, $9,856,402 (M); Total giving, $176,189; Grants to individuals, 14 grants totaling $12,000, high $1,000, low $500.

Employer Identification Number: 056007619

Applications: Applications accepted throughout the year; Initial approach by letter stating needs; Letter of reference from school and official transcript or grades required.

Program description:

Candidates for the work-study scholarships must be nominated by their high school guidance counselor.

986

Flinn (Peter G.) Estate

c/o First National Bank
Marion, IN 46952
Contact: Bank One, 302 South Washington Street, Marion, IN 46953; Tel.: (317) 662-6611

Limitations: Scholarships by nomination only to Grant County high school seniors who have resided in Grant County, IN, at least one year and have maintained at least a ''C'' average in school.

Financial data: Year ended 12/31/86. Assets, $243,418 (M); Total giving, $16,735; Grants to individuals, 20 grants totaling $16,735, high 1,000, low $360, general range $500-1,000.

Employer Identification Number: 356010860

Applications: Deadline 2nd week of April. Applicants are selected by committees from Grant County, IN, high schools only. Winners are then selected from these applications only.

987

Fort Howard Paper Foundation, Inc.

1919 South Broadway
P.O. Box 11325
Green Bay, WI 54037-1325   (414) 435-8821
Contact: J. A. Prindiville

Limitations: Awards for heroism and for achievement in fine arts, humanitarian activities, or conservation.

Financial data: Year ended 9/30/86. Assets, $13,956,541 (M); Total giving, $373,695; Grants to individuals totaling $18,337; Subtotal for awards totaling $6,000.

Employer Identification Number: 362761910

988★
Fremont Area Foundation, The
108 South Stewart
Fremont, MI 49412   (616) 924-5350
Contact: Mrs. Joyce L. Maynard, Grants Director

Limitations: Scholarships only to residents of Newaygo County, MI.
Financial data: Year ended 12/31/87. Assets, $22,507,751 (M); Total giving, $1,099,427; Grants to individuals, 113 grants totaling $69,220, high $1,500, low $240, average grant $500.
Employer Identification Number: 381443367
Publications: Annual report, informational brochure.
Program description:
Funds will be made available to individuals for scholarships from specific funds of the foundation:
 1. The John K. Rottier Fund, which offers a basketball clinic scholarship. Recipient selection is made by a private advisory committee.
 2. The Bessie B. Slautterback Scholarship are awarded annually to one high school senior from each of the five high schools in Newaygo County. These seniors are chosen by selection committees from each high school.
 3. The Nellie McCarty Fund limited to residents of Newaygo County, MI, for health and medically related scholarships. Completion of formal application required. Final selection is made by an advisory committee at Gerber Memorial Hospital.
 4. The Excellence in Education Scholarships are awarded to the top five percent of the graduating high school seniors in Newaygo County, MI.
 5. The Fremont Public Schools Fund awards college scholarships to top academic high school seniors as selected by a school advisory committee.

989
Frost (The Robert) Teaching Chairs Trust
c/o Shawmut Bank, Trust Division
P.O. Box 2032
Worcester, MA 01613-2032

Limitations: Awards by nomination only to teaching staff at Amherst Regional High School, MA.
Financial data: Year ended 3/31/87. Assets, $67,111 (M); Total giving, $4,054; Grants to individuals, 2 grants totaling $4,054, each grant $2,027.
Employer Identification Number: 046027359
Applications: Deadline June 1st for nominations; **Individual applications not accepted.**
Program description:
Awards are made to encourage excellence in teaching. Candidates must have taught for a period of at least three years. Nominees are selected by secret ballot by a jury of their peers.

990★
Fund for the City of New York, Inc.
419 Park Avenue South, 16th Floor
New York, NY 10016   (212) 689-1240
Contact: Mary McCormick, Deputy Director

Limitations: Public service awards to career public servants in New York City government.
Financial data: Year ended 9/30/87. Assets, $1,527,135 (M); Grants to individuals totaling $30,000, average grant $5,000.
Employer Identification Number: 132612524
Applications: Nominations from all sources are accepted throughout the year. Nominations are investigated by fund staff and consultants to the program. Final selections are made by an independent selection panel whose membership changes every few years.
Publications: Annual report, program information, newsletter.
Program description:
The **Public Service Awards Program**, begun by the fund in 1973, annually presents cash payments to outstanding career public servants of the City of New York. The awards are intended to call public attention to superior work on behalf of the City and its people, raise the morale and effectiveness of the City's municipal work force, and encourage individuals to think of City service as a career. Any employee of the City of New York, including employees of the Transit and Housing Authorities, the Health and Hospitals Corporation, the Board of Education, the Board of Higher Education and the Court System, is eligible for consideration.

991
Garriques (Edwin B.) Trust
c/o Duane Morris & Hecksher
1500 One Franklin Plaza
Philadelphia, PA 19102   (215) 854-6379
Contact: Seymour C. Wagner, Secretary

Limitations: Grants by nomination only to undergraduate students of music performance and music education at specified colleges and universities in the Philadelphia, PA, metropolitan area.
Financial data: Year ended 12/31/85. Assets, $1,717,878 (M); Total giving, $120,000; Grants to individuals totaling $120,000.
Employer Identification Number: 236220616
Applications: Nominations from educational institutions accepted throughout the year; Completion of formal application required; **Individual applications not accepted.**
Program description:
Scholarships are awarded to music students who have the high recommendation of deans or directors of music in privately endowed colleges and universities on an approved list. Selection is based on personal

qualities as well as academic performance and musical talent. Applications must be submitted by the schools.

992
General Motors Cancer Research Foundation, Inc.
13-145 General Motors Building
3044 West Grand Boulevard
Detroit, MI 48202   (313) 556-4260
Contact: J. J. Nowicki, Manager

Limitations: Individual awards to those involved in cancer research. Candidates must be nominated by invited proposers.
Financial data: Year ended 12/31/86. Assets, $2,672,490 (M); Total giving, $356,865; Grants to individuals, 3 grants totaling $356,865, high $130,000, low $100,000.
Employer Identification Number: 382219731
Applications: Candidates for prizes must be nominated by October by invited proposer. Invitations to nominate candidates are sent to individuals holding the rank or its equivalent of Professor or Associate Professor in universities or institutions selected for a given year's nominations. **Personal applications for an award are not considered.**
Publications: Application guidelines.
Program description:
The foundation awards prizes to individuals for "contributions to the prevention, detection, or treatment of cancer in order to stimulate further research in this field."

993★
Golden Nugget Scholarship Fund, Inc.
P.O. Box 610
129 East Fremont Street
Las Vegas, NV 89125   (702) 385-7111
Contact: Elaine Wynn, Vice-Chairperson

Limitations: Scholarships by nomination only to graduates of high schools in Nevada with a GPA of B+ or better, who are planning to enter a post high school program culminating in an associate or baccalaureate degree, or certificate of completion of license.
Financial data: Year ended 5/31/87. Assets, $3,224,113 (M); Total giving, $363,200; Grants to individuals, 148 grants totaling $363,200, high $4,500, low $1,000, general range $1,000-3,500, average grant $2,400.
Employer Identification Number: 942768861
Applications: Deadline March 10th; Completion of formal application through high school guidance office required; **Individual applications not accepted.**

Program description:
A minimum of 20 one-year renewable scholarships are granted each spring for use in the following academic year at any accredited public or private university, college, or community college located in the U.S.
Applicants are nominated by school scholarship committees formed by their high schools who process application forms and select nominees based on the following criteria: outstanding academic performance; good performance on college aptitude tests; personal recommendations; assessment of individuals motivation, character, ability, and potential; and financial need. Each school may select one nominee for each 200 seniors or portion thereof.

994★
Grant (William T.) Foundation
515 Madison Avenue, Sixth Floor
New York, NY 10022-5403   (212) 752-0071
Contact: Robert Johns Haggerty, M.D., President

Limitations: Research grants by nomination only for study to improve the mental health of school age children.
Financial data: Year ended 12/31/86. Assets, $131,258,000 (M); Total giving, $4,628,883; Grants to individuals, 24 grants totaling $699,905.
Employer Identification Number: 131624021
Applications: Deadline for nominations July 1st; Initial approach by letter; Interviews required; Contact foundation for complete application information; **Individual applications not accepted.**
Publications: Annual report, informational brochure.
Program description:
The **William T. Grant Faculty Scholars Program** will support up to five talented investigators for research in the area of children's mental health, especially in the field of stress and coping in school-age children. Award recipients will be called William T. Grant Faculty Scholars.
Awards will be made to the institution for support of a selected faculty member for up to $35,000 per year for five years. This sum includes an indirect cost allowance not to exceed 7.5 percent of total direct costs. This money may be used only for the research efforts of the faculty member. Up to one-half of the faculty member's salary can be met by this grant, but it must not replace current university support for the faculty member's research efforts. In general, it is expected that a portion of this grant would be used for that percentage of the faculty member's salary equivalent to the time spent in research in this program area and the remainder used for support of the actual research. However, each institution will be free to propose how it will use the funds to best achieve the goals of the program.
Criteria for selection are:
1. Faculty at all universities and nonprofit research institutions, both national and international, are eligible.

2. Only one candidate may be nominated from any department or research center of the university.

3. Faculty so nominated usually should be in their first level or rank of appointment (usually at the assistant professor level).

4. Any discipline is eligible, but it is expected that most will come from pediatrics, child psychiatry, education, epidemiology, and the behavioral sciences. Scholars appointed to date have been in the fields of psychology, pediatrics, and child psychiatry.

5. Priority will be given to faculty who are well-trained in research methods and wish to study problems in the area of major program interest to the foundation - problem behaviors in school-age children. They must demonstrate the ability to do sophisticated research in these areas rather than to pursue further training. Research programs in problem areas such as teenage pregnancy, suicide, accidental injuries, substance abuse, delinquency or school failure, with careful evaluation of outcomes, will be encouraged.

6. The university must commit itself to the faculty member for the five-year period of appointment with space, remainder of salary support and the time free to conduct the research.

7. The setting in which the investigator will work should be thoroughly described. A mentor should be available to guide the research. Institutional resources must be available to conduct the research, and the setting in which the investigator can in turn influence colleagues and students should be outlined.

8. Major criteria for selection will be the research record of the candidate (at least one research article in a peer-reviewed journal), the setting, institutional support and the area of proposed research.

A national selection committee will make recommendations for selection to the Board of Trustees.

After initial screening by the Selection Committee, finalists will be asked to come to New York for an interview with the committee. Final selection will be made by the end of March.

995
Gravity Research Foundation
58 Middle Street
Gloucester, MA 01930
Contact: Dr. George M. Rideout, President

Limitations: Awards to individuals for essays on the subject of gravitation.
Financial data: Year ended 6/30/86. Assets, $855,221 (M); Total giving, $3,350; Grants to individuals, 8 grants totaling $2,450, high $500, low $100.
Employer Identification Number: 046002754
Applications: Deadline April 1st.

Publications: Program information.
Program description:
Awards for Essays on Gravitation are given for short essays of 1,500 words or less. The organization holds an annual essay contest on scientific study of gravity for the purpose of stimulating thought and encouraging work on gravitation. Cash awards are made for the best short essays, which are published in the ''Journal of General Relativity and Gravitation.''

996
Grow (Freeman and Emma) Memorial Scholarship Fund
P.O. Box 134
Goldendale, WA 98620
Contact: Frank Knosher, Secretary

Limitations: Scholarships by invitation only to graduating seniors of Goldendale High School, Goldendale, WA, to attend institutions of higher learning in the state of Washington only.
Financial data: Year ended 2/28/87. Assets, $69,331 (M); Total giving, $3,000; Grants to individuals, 6 grants totaling $3,000, each grant $500.
Employer Identification Number: 237123616
Applications: Deadline May 1st; Completion of formal application required; **Unsolicited applications not accepted.**
Program description:
Scholarships must be re-applied for yearly, for up to four years.

997★
Guggenheim (The Harry Frank) Foundation
527 Madison Avenue, 15th Floor
New York, NY 10022-4301　　　　　(212) 644-4907
Contact: Karen Colvard, Program Officer

Limitations: Awards by nomination only to younger scholars and scientists of note to encourage them to undertake studies related to the causes and consequences of dominance, aggression, and violence.
Financial data: Year ended 6/30/87. Assets, $51,705,000 (M); Total giving, $1,556,949; Grants to individuals, 20 grants totaling $469,253, high $35,000, low $5,900, average grasnt $23,000; Subtotal for awards not specified.
Employer Identification Number: 136043471
Applications: Nominations are due once a year on August 1st, with a decision in December and funding to begin July, August, or September of the following year; See program description for more specific application information; **Individual applications not accepted.**
Publications: Multi-year report, application guidelines, program information, newsletter, informational brochure, 990-PF printed copy available upon request.

Program description:

The **Harry Frank Guggenheim Career Development Awards** provide salary support and research expenses in an amount averaging $37,500 a year for three years. Consideration for a Career Development Award can be initiated only by nomination. Candidates may be from any country. Additional criteria is as follows:

1. Candidates must be at least three years beyond the award of a doctoral degree (M.D. or Ph.D.) and not yet forty years of age by the commencement of funding.

2. Candidates must have demonstrated outstanding capability and exceptional promise for significant future achievement, and in their work exhibited quality innovation, and potential to contribute to the foundation's goals.

Forms and guidelines for nominators and candidates are available from the foundation's offices. The nominator should write a confidential letter of support for the candidate and include with it six copies of a proposal prepared by the candidate. This proposal should include:

- an abstract and statement of relevance
- a two-page curriculum vita, including a list of relevant publications
- explicit requests for salary and research
- a project description of no more than five pages
- information about the protection of subjects
- copies of any publications which would contribute to the assessment of the proposal. Two other letters of support are requested by the nominator from persons familiar with the candidate's work and sent directly to the foundaton.

Awards are paid to the recipient's institution with the understanding that suitable space and general facilities will be provided by the institution and that the total amount of the award will be made available to the investigator. The foundation does not contribute to institutional overhead costs. Any amount not required for salary may be allotted to research expenses; however funding awarded for research expenses may be used only for those purposes. The award may be supplemented by other grants or by the home institution with salary, resources, and personnel. Total salary during tenure of the award may not exceed the prevailing range at the particular institution for the rank and position of the grantee. The award may be transferred from the original institution to another, with prior approval by the foundation.

998

Hearst (William Randolph) Foundation

888 Seventh Avenue, 27th Floor
New York, NY 10106   (212) 586-5404
Contact: Robert M. Frehse, Jr., Executive Director (east of the Mississippi River)

Limitations: Awards for undergraduates in journalism and photojournalism and college scholarships for participants in government internship program.

Financial data: Year ended 12/31/86. Assets, $228,918,845 (M); Total giving, $7,475,200; Grants to individuals, 164 grants totaling $336,000.

Employer Identification Number: 136019226

Applications: Deadline November 1st for U.S. Senate Youth Program and beginning of each month of academic year for Journalism Awards Program; Application forms for Journalism Program available from Journalism Departments at accredited schools of journalism and mass communication; Application address for applicants west of the Mississippi River, 90 New Montgomery Street, Suite 1212, San Francisco, CA 94105; Tel.: (415) 543-0400.

Publications: Program information.

Program description:

The Journalism Awards Program: The program, designed to further college education in journalism, comprises a series of six monthly writing competitions and one photojournalism competition. Cash awards are made toward the education of those who place in the top ten for each competition and matching grants are additionally awarded to the winners' colleges. Undergraduates who are currently attending one of the member institutions of the Association of Schools of Journalism and Mass Communication and are majoring in journalism are eligible to enter the writing competitions. Participants in the photojournalism competition must also be journalism majors or be taking a course in photojournalism.

Two articles per month and two photographic portfolios may be selected by the Journalism Administrator of each college or university to be entered in the competitions. All articles and photographs entered must have been recently published in a college, general, or educational publication.

The focus of the writing competition varies each month as listed below:

- October - General News
- November - Features
- December - Editorials
- January - In-Depth Writing
- February - Personality Profile
- March - Sportswriting

Within these categories, the articles may cover a broad range of subjects. Knowledge of the subject, clarity and depth of presentation, flavor, and technical aspects will be important considerations in selection.

Awards are made for the ten best articles as follows:

- First Place - $1,500
- Second Place - $1,000
- Third Place - $750
- Fourth Place - $500
- Fifth Place - $400
- Sixth through Tenth Place - $300

In May, the six first place monthly winners and the next two highest scoring students from any two of the monthly competition participate in a championship and the following awards are made:

- First Place - $2,000
- Second Place - $1,500
- Third Place - $1,000
- Fourth to Eighth Place - $500

Photojournalism portfolios consist of six images, (including a picture story or series considered as one photograph) and three other eight-by-ten photographs covering the following categories: news, features, sports, and portrait/personality. Entries will be judged according to originality, news value, and human interest, as well as photographic quality.

The ten semi-finalists selected in this competition are eligible to compete in the photojournalism championship. Cash awards for the semi-finals will be the same as for the monthly writing competitions.

Three photo finalists will be chosen for additional scholarships after competing in an on-the-spot assignment. The championship awards are as follows:

- First Place - $1,500
- Second Place - $1,000
- Third Place - $1,000
- Best Single Photograph - $350
- Best Photo Series Board - $350.

The United States Senate Youth Program: This program is designed to give high school student body leaders the opportunity to learn about the public issues and the operations of the federal government (particularly the U.S. Senate) at first hand, and to encourage outstanding young people to continue their educational development at the college level. The program is sponsored by resolution of the Senate and completely funded by the foundation, without the use of public funds. All travel and lodging expenses incurred during the week in Washington, DC, are provided by the foundation.

Two high school students (juniors or seniors) from each of the 50 states and the District of Columbia, who hold elective offices in their school, are selected by their chief state school officer to participate in a week's internship program. Two students represent the Department of Defense Dependents Schools. The students are guests of the senators from their respective states, with whom they attend sessions of the Senate and briefings by the House of Representatives and Departments of State, Defense, and Justice. At the end of the internship week, participants receive a $2,000 college scholarship.

999
Heisey Foundation, The
c/o First Bank
P.O. Box 5000
Great Falls, MT 59401   (406) 761-7200

Limitations: Awards for students attending specific public or parochial schools in the Great Falls, MT, trade area.
Financial data: Year ended 12/31/86. Assets, $2,346,488 (M); Total giving, $67,050; Awards to individuals, 321 awards totaling $16,050.

Employer Identification Number: 816009624
Applications: Deadline October 5th for high schools to provide necessary information; Trustees designate eligible schools; Students are recommended to selection committees by their schools.
Program description:
The awards are given to those students making the most improvement in citizenship, effort, and scholarship to the best of his/her ability. The selection committees will give the greatest weight to improvement in citizenship (50 percent); the balance will be divided equally between effort and scholarship.

An award of $50 may be given to one out of each 20 pupils. There are separate selection committees for Great Falls public high school students, Great Falls parochial high school students, and for students attending schools in the approximately 22 other locations in the Great Falls trade area.

1000★
Hemingway (Ernest) Foundation
University of North Dakota, English Society
Hemingway Society, Box 8237
Grand Forks, ND 58202

Limitations: Prizes and incentive awards for best first novel by an American published in the previous year.
Financial data: Year ended 12/31/85. Assets, $118,546 (M); Total giving, $8,500; Prizes to individuals, 3 prizes totaling $8,500, high $7,500, low $500.
Employer Identification Number: 136195832
Applications: For application information, contact P.E.N., 568 Broadway, New York, NY 10012; Tel.: (212) 334-1660.
Program description:
The foundation awards a prize of $7,500 to the novelist whose work is chosen as the best first-time novel published in the preceding year in the opinion of a selection panel composed of members of P.E.N. Upon recommendation of the panel, the foundation may also award small prizes to one or two runners up.

1001★
Hirtzel (Orris C.) Memorial Foundation
Mellon Bank, N.A.
Mellom Bank Center
Pittsburgh, PA 15258-0001

Limitations: Scholarships by nomination only to students attending colleges and universities in NY and northeast PA.
Financial data: Year ended 12/31/85. Assets, $740,543 (M); Total giving, 18,800; Grants to individuals, 43 grants totaling $17,800, high $1,000, low $300.
Employer Identification Number: 256018933

1002
Hodges (Margery Ann and Leland A.) Foundation, Inc.

P.O. Box 1718
Fort Worth, TX 76101   (817) 335-4261
Contact: Leland A. Hodges, President

Limitations: Scholarships by nomination only to high school seniors of Tarrant County, TX.
Financial data: Year ended 12/31/86. Assets, $798 (M); Total giving, $10,350; Grants to individuals, 3 grants totaling $10,350, high $3,600, low $3,150.
Employer Identification Number: 237169387
Applications: Deadline June 1st; **Individual applications not accepted.**
Program description:
High school principals of Fort Worth are requested to submit names of needy students with SAT scores of 1100 or more.

1003
Hyatt Foundation

200 West Madison, 38th Floor
Chicago, IL 60606   (312) 750-8400
Contact: Simon Zunamon

Limitations: Annual award made to an individual for "significant contribution to humanity through architecture.".
Financial data: Year ended 7/31/87. Assets, $830 (M); Total giving, $105,920; Grants to individuals, 1 grant totaling $105,920.
Employer Identification Number: 362981565
Applications: Deadline January 31st.

1004★
Ingersoll Foundation, Inc., The

934 North Main Street
Rockford, IL 61103   (815) 964-3242
Contact: Dr. John A. Howard, President

Limitations: Awards and prizes to writers.
Financial data: Year ended 9/30/87. Assets, $342,029 (M); Total giving, $78,000; Grants to individuals, 2 grants totaling $30,000.
Employer Identification Number: 363211777
Program description:
The foundation awards the two Ingersoll Prizes, which are the **T.S. Eliot Award for Creative Writing** and the **Richard M. Weaver Award for Scholarly Letters**, each with a $15,000 honorarium.

1005
Inland Steel-Ryerson Foundation, Inc.

c/o Inland Steel Industries
30 West Monroe Street
Chicago, IL 60603   (312) 899-3421
Contact: Earl S. Thompson, Director, State and Regional Affairs, Inland Steel Industries

Limitations: Awards to outstanding high school and college teachers.
Financial data: Year ended 12/31/86. Assets, $0 (M); Total giving, $1,310,617; Grants to individuals, 260 grants totaling $244,667; Awards to individuals amount not specified.
Employer Identification Number: 366046944
Program description:
The **Inland Steel-Ryerson Foundation's Outstanding High School Teacher Award** and the **Inland Steel-Ryerson Foundation's Outstanding College Teachers Award** were created to promote excellence in teaching at selected Midwestern educational institutions. Winners are chosen by committees composed of peers, administrators, and student leaders.

1006★
Irwin (The Richard D.) Foundation

1818 Ridge Road
Homewood, IL 60430   (312) 798-6000
Contact: Robert A. Schmitz, Secretary-Treasurer

Limitations: Fellowships by nomination only to doctoral degree candidates in the areas of business, economics, and the social sciences who have completed all work in connection with the degree except writing the dissertation and passing final oral.
Financial data: Year ended 12/31/86. Assets, $157,941 (M); Total giving, $99,594; Grants to individuals, 35 grants totaling $42,394, high $2,500, low $350.
Employer Identification Number: 366074845
Applications: Deadline February 15th; Completion of formal application required, after nomination by dean.
Program description:
Fellowships are available to prospective teachers in the fields of business, economics, and the social sciences. Candidates are nominated by deans of business schools who are invited to submit nominations. Recommendations from the chairman of the applicant's dissertation committee, the director of the doctoral program, or any other individuals who can supply information as to the candidate's promise as a university teacher are also requested.

The foundation asks candidates to outline their career plans, and preference is usually given to those applicants whose contribution to teaching is to be made in the United States and Canada.

The fellowships are considered to be supplemental and no fixed amounts are set for individual grants.

1007★
Jennings (The Martha Holden) Foundation
1040 Huntington Building
Cleveland, OH 44115   (216) 589-5700
Contact: Joan M. Johnson, Program Director

Limitations: Grants and awards by nomination to elementary and secondary educators and students in Ohio.
Financial data: Year ended 12/31/86. Assets, $43,770,541 (M); Total giving, $1,382,530; Grants to individuals, 72 grants totaling $151,906.
Employer Identification Number: 340934473
Applications: Deadline 20th of the month preceding the month in which application is to be considered; Completion of formal application required for grants to teachers; Initial approach by submitting original form and eight copies, signed by the superintendent; Interviews granted upon request.
Publications: Annual report.
Program description:
The foundation seeks to improve the quality of primary and secondary education in Ohio by recognizing excellence in teaching in the elementary and secondary schools and providing opportunity and incentive to teachers and students who desire to improve their skills.

The **Jennings Grants-to-Teachers Program** allocates funds for separate grants of up to $3,000 to Ohio classroom teachers to test new methods, conduct classroom projects, or involve their students in extracurricular, enrichment, or summer programs. Specifically, these grants are awarded for curriculum enrichment, special education, reading, science, fine arts, community interaction, writing, and outdoor education.

Jennings Distinguished Educator Awards honor two outstanding educators, one each in Cleveland and Kent.

The **Jennings Master Teacher Program** attempts to enhance the prestige of the teaching profession by making awards to five classroom teachers of sustained excellence selected from elementary and secondary public schools in northeastern Ohio.

In addition, the foundation sponsors a number of specialized self-improvement workshops, seminars, lectures, and retreats for teachers and administrative personnel in such areas as teacher learning styles, Ohio school law, economics and business.

1008★
Jurzykowski (Alfred) Foundation, Inc.
15 East 65th Street
New York, NY 10021   (212) 439-9628
Contact: Cultural Advisory Committee

Limitations: Awards by nomination only to scholars, artists, and writers of Polish ethnic background for past achievement.
Financial data: Year ended 12/31/86. Assets,

$16,869,762 (M); Total giving, $1,715,207; Awards to individuals, 14 awards totaling $56,000, average award $5,000.
Employer Identification Number: 136192256
Applications: Scholarly and cultural institutions may submit nominations for the consideration of the Cultural Advisory Committee. **Individual applications not accepted.**
Program description:
Alfred Jurzykowski Awards are presented annually to scholars, writers, and artists of Polish ethnic background, regardless of their places of residence or citizenship, for outstanding creative achievements in the sciences, humanities, medicine, creative writing, literary criticism, theater, fine arts and music, as well as for significant contributions to the advancement of Polish culture, and for the best translations of Polish literature into other languages. In this last category, the criterion of Polish background is not applicable. No grants are made to individuals for study, travel, scholarship or publication.

1009★
Kellogg (W.K.) Foundation
400 North Avenue
Battle Creek, MI 49017-3398   (616) 968-1611
Contact: Larraine R. Matusak, Director, Kellogg National Fellowship Program

Limitations: Fellowships to American professionals who are in their early years of professional activity, for personal and professional development. Individuals must be nominated by one of the approved national organizations holding a 501(c)3 tax status, or be self-nominated. Also sponsors awards in excellence to high school seniors of the greater Battle Creek, MI, area and their teachers.
Financial data: Year ended 8/31/87. Assets, $3,581,473,230 (M); Total giving, $88,979,208, Grants to individuals, 159 grants totaling $2,451,056; Subtotal for National Fellowship Program, 116 grants totaling $1,875,984, high $31,768, low $122.
Employer Identification Number: 381359264
Applications: Contact foundation for current application deadline; Completion of formal application in three copies is required, including three recommendations.
Publications: Annual report (including application guidelines).
Program description:
Kellogg National Fellowship Program: The objectives of the fellowship program are as follows:

1. Provide individuals with opportunities and experiences necessary to develop a broadly oriented perspective on human and social skills.
2. Enable Fellows to develop new skills and competencies in fields or disciplines which are different from their chosen career.

3. Establish a network of individuals to become leaders in academic, government, business, industry, and other professional areas.

Applicants must hold an academic or administrative appointment on the staff of a college or university, or a leadership position in a private sector business or industry, a private not-for-profit human service agency or a professional or labor organization. In addition, the endorsement of the applicant's immediate supervisor and the chief executive officer or the president of the institution, agency, or business is required.

Each fellow receives a three-year grant of $35,000 to fund a professionally broadening self-designated plan of study. Fellows must accept responsibility to participate in all fellowship activities over the three-year period. The foundation also supports up to 12.5 percent (or a total of $24,000) of the fellows' salaries for fellows employed by an eligible, nonprofit institution.

Kellogg Excellence in Education Day: The foundation sponsors an **Excellence in Education Day** designed to give academic achievement new meaning and emphasis. Attention is focused on the top five percent of the greater Battle Creek's high school graduating classes and to the teachers who inspired them. The foundation's activities includes a special luncheon with local business and civic leaders honoring the educators, and the final student awards event presented at a dinner attended by teachers, parents and underclassmen.

1010
Kohl (Dolores) Education Foundation
165 Greenbay Road
Wilmette, IL 60091

Limitations: Awards to elementary school teachers "for exemplary teaching."
Financial data: Year ended 6/30/86. Assets, $1,507,764 (M); Total giving, $13,750; Grants to individuals, 22 grants totaling $13,750, high $1,000, low $250.
Employer Identification Number: 237206116

1011
Komarek Charitable Trust
c/o Norwest Bank Nebraska, N.A.
P.O. Box 3959
Omaha, NE 68103   (402) 536-2470

Limitations: Scholarships by nomination only to students pursuing careers in the ministry of the Presbyterian and Methodist faiths and for students at the College of Medicine at the University of Nebraska.
Financial data: Year ended 5/31/87. Assets, $1,322,394 (M); Total giving, $115,683; Grants to individuals, 22 grants totaling $21,500, high $1,800, low $438, general range $438-1,500.
Employer Identification Number: 476141512

Applications: Completion of formal application required; Ministry students must be nominated by delegates of the Presbyterian and Methodist ministries of Omaha, NE; Medical students must be nominated by the University of Nebraska; **Individual applications not accepted.**
Program description:
Scholarship grants-in-aid are made to further the education of deserving students who wish to pursue a career in the ministry of the Presbyterian and Methodist faiths and medical students enrolled in or accepted by the College of Medicine of the University of Nebraska. In making its choice as to persons to be benefited, the trustee is guided by the character, actual financial need, and scholastic record of the individual.

Prospective recipients are nominated annually by delegates of the Presbyterian and Methodist ministries of Omaha and by the scholarship committee of the College of Medicine, respectively. The trustee's discretionary distribution committee selects the recipients on the basis of the nominations received. The scholarships are made payable to the educational institution on behalf of the recipient.

No restrictions are placed on the eligible recipient with respect to age, sex, race, national origin or religion (except for ministerial students who must be of the Methodist or Presbyterian faiths).

1012
Laird (Herbert Frank) and Bertha Maude Laird Oakland Scottish Rite Memorial Educational Foundation
1547 Lakeside Drive
Oakland, CA 94612
Contact: David S. Tucker, President

Limitations: Scholarships by nomination only to public high school students in northern and central California. Preference is given to electrical engineering majors.
Financial data: Year ended 12/31/86. Assets, $590,235 (M); Total giving, $11,700; Grants to individuals, 12 grants totaling $11,700, high $1,620, low $720.
Employer Identification Number: 237047350
Applications: Deadline January for nominations; Selection is made from response of public school superintendents to a questionnaire submitted to them within the area of operation; Personal interview required. **Individual applications not accepted.**
Program description:
Operation of the foundation is confined to university student support.

1013★
Lalor Foundation, The
3801 Kennett Pike, Building B-108
Wilmington, DE 19807   (302) 571-1262
Contact: C. Lalor Burdick, Secretary

Limitations: Postdoctoral research fellowship awards by nomination only in the field of mammalian reproductive physiology and biochemistry, bearing on sterilization and/or prevention or termination of pregnancy.
Financial data: Year ended 9/30/87. Assets, $6,750,552 (M); Total giving, $306,975; Grants to individuals, 15 grants totaling $288,500, high $20,000, low $12,000, average grant $20,000.
Employer Identification Number: 516000153
Applications: Deadline January 15th; Submit proposal from October 1st to January 15th; Initial approach by letter or telephone; Completion of formal application required.
Publications: Informational brochure (including application guidelines).
Program description:
The individual nominated by the applicant institution for the postdoctoral fellowship may be a citizen of any country and should have training and experience at least equal to the Ph.D or M.D. level. Younger people who have held doctoral degrees less than five years are preferred. One nomination is to be made for each project applied for.
  Grant payments are made to institutions on behalf of individuals. Renewal of a grant is possible under special circumstances.

1014★
Lincoln (James F.) Arc Welding Foundation
22801 St. Clair Avenue
Cleveland, OH 44117-1199   (216) 481-4300
Contact: Richard S. Sabo, Executive Director and Secretary

Limitations: Awards to high school students, college undergraduate and graduate students and to professionals working in the fields of arc welding and engineering design.
Financial data: Year ended 12/31/86. Assets, $790,843 (M); Total giving, $116,780; Grants to individuals totaling $114,050.
Employer Identification Number: 346553433
Applications: Deadlines May 1st for Professional Awards and Technicians, Craftsmen, and Users Awards, June 1st for Student Awards, June 15th for Preprofessional Awards.
Publications: Informational brochure (including application guidelines).
Program description:
The purpose of the foundation is to stimulate and encourage educational development in the field of arc welding.

The awards that are made on a competitive basis to students at various educational levels are for projects or papers dealing with problems relating to design or uses of arc welding. The amounts of the awards as well as entry deadline dates vary as noted for each program. In addition to the student awards, each school receives a small amount for each award its students receive. Factors considered in selection, particularly for awards at the post-high school level, are originality and ingenuity, feasibility, practicality, results achieved or expected, engineering competence, and clarity of presentation. For all competitions, students may enter as individuals or in groups of not more than five.

Arc Welding Awards for Students are made to students in three separate noncompeting divisions: Division I includes students 18 years of age or younger in any type of school or training program; Division II includes students over 18 years of age in any type of school or training program; Division III includes students involved in the VICA program. Individual awards range from $75 to $1,000. In 1988, awards will total $25,150.

Arc Welding Awards for Technicians, Craftsmen, and Users of Arc Welding are given to teachers, technicians, shop and business owners, craftsmen, farmers, ranchers, welders, or any other employed or self-employed person. Individual awards range from $150 to $2,000. In 1988, awards will total $7,000.

The **Preprofessional Design Competition** is held for undergraduates and graduates enrolled in engineering and technology programs. Students may submit papers representing their work on design, engineering, or fabrication problems related to structures, machines, or mechanical apparatus or their component parts. They may represent work on problems related to the conservation of materials, labor, and energy, or appearance and performance improvement in any type of building, bridge, or other generally stationary structure; any type of machine, product, or device; or apparatus for research and development, needed to solve the problems. The structure, machine, device, etc. does not have to be actually constructed. Individual awards range from $250 to $2,000. In 1988, awards will total $15,750.

The **Professional Design Competition** is held for U.S. residents who are working, either individually or as a part of a group, in the development or execution of an idea to reduce costs, conserve material, time or energy, increase production or improve quality, function or appearance through the use of welded design, engineering fabrication or research. Subject matter of entries may relate to any type of structure, product, or type of arc welding. Individual awards range from $500 to $10,000. In 1988, awards will total $32,000.

1015
Livingston (Mollie Parnis) Foundation, Inc.
135 Madison Avenue
New York, NY 10016
Contact: C. R. Eisendrath, Executive Director, 2098
Frieze Building, University of Michagan, Ann Arbor,
MI 48109; Tel.: (313) 764-0420

Limitations: Journalism awards to individuals under 35
years of age.
Financial data: Year ended 12/31/85. Assets, $672,888
(M); Total giving, $161,671; Grants to individuals, 3
grants totaling $15,000, each grant $5,000.
Employer Identification Number: 136265280
Applications: Deadline February 1st; Completion of
formal application required.
Program description:
Awards program is for journalists who are not students
and are working for a U.S.- owned publication or
broadcast organization.

1016★
Luce (The Henry) Foundation, Inc.
111 West 50th Street, Room 3710
New York, NY 10020   (212) 489-7700
Contact: Robert E. Armstrong, Executive Director

Limitations: Fellowships by nomination only to
American citizens with a Bachelor's degree who are
no more than 29 years of age as of September 1st of
the year they enter the program.
Financial data: Year ended 12/31/87. Assets,
$245,094,357 (M); Total giving, $12,884,250; Grants
to individuals, 15 grants totaling $290,068, high
$17,000, low $14,000.
Employer Identification Number: 136001282
Applications: Deadline first Monday in December;
Completion of formal application required; Interviews
required. Awards based on nominations submitted by
66 participating colleges and universities. **Individual
applications not accepted.**
Publications: Annual report, informational brochure.
Program description:
The **Luce Scholars Program** makes grants to
individuals in a wide range of professional fields for
participation in internships and job placements in
Asia. The program is aimed at recent college graduates
who are not Asian specialists and would not otherwise
have the opportunity or incentive during the course of
their careers to come to know Asia or their Asian
colleagues. The Program emphasizes experience rather
than purely academic pursuits, and no academic
credit is given.
    Candidates should have a record of the highest
academic achievement and outstanding leadership
qualities, either on campus or off. More important than
any other single criterion is that candidates have a
mature and clearly defined career interest in a specific
field, and that they have evidenced a potential for

professional accomplishment within that field as well
as strong personal motivation.
    The amount of the fellowship is $14,000 for single
and $17,000 for married fellows and is to cover
approximately 11 months. At many locations in Asia,
the basic stipend is augmented by cost-of-living and/or
housing allowances.

1017★
Lyndhurst Foundation, Inc.
701 Tallan Building
Chattanooga, TN 37402   (615) 756-0767
Contact: Jack Murrah, Executive Director

Limitations: Lyndhurst Teachers' Awards provide
grants to teachers in Hamilton County, TN, schools,
grades K-12; Lyndhurst Prizes, which include the
Lyndhurst Young Career Prizes, are awarded solely at
the initiative of the foundation and provide stipends
for individuals, mostly those involved in artistic
endeavors.
Financial data: Year ended 12/31/87. Assets,
$112,402,088 (M); Total giving, $11,028,897; Grants
to individuals, 35 grants totaling $712,152.
Employer Identification Number: 626044177
Applications: Deadline February 15th for Lyndhurst
Teachers' Awards; Completion of formal application
required; Interviews required; **Individual applications,
requests, or nominations not accepted for Lyndhurst
Prizes.**
Publications: Annual report (including application
guidelines).
Program description:
Lyndhurst Teachers' Awards: This program makes
awards to unusually talented and effective teachers to
enable them to carry out projects which can enrich
their understanding of the subjects they teach, support
the intellectual growth which undergirds all good
teaching, and thereby sustain their enthusiasm for
teaching. The projects may entail further academic
instruction, or may consist entirely of travel and study,
individually planned by the teacher.
    A panel of judges, none of them affiliated with the
foundation, review the applications and selects the
recipients of the grants. The criteria used in judging
the applications focus upon the seriousness of the
purpose, the opportunity for growth and the intended
application of the project.
The Lyndhurst Prizes: The foundation awards prizes to
individuals to enable them to carry forth their interests
over an extended period of time without financial
pressure. Recipients have primarily included writers or
artists or individuals who serve special needs in the
southeast.

1018
MacArthur (John D. and Catherine T.) Foundation

140 South Dearborn Street
Chicago, IL 60603   (312) 726-8000
Contact: James M. Furman, Executive Vice-President

Limitations: Fellowships by nomination only.
Financial data: Year ended 12/31/86. Assets,
$2,271,000,000 (M); Total giving, $105,000,000;
Grants to individuals totaling $8,000,000.
Employer Identification Number: 237093598
Applications: Individual applications not accepted.
Publications: Annual report, program information.
Program description:
The **MacArthur Fellows Program** honors a small
number of exceptionally talented individuals who
have given evidence of originality and dedication to
creative pursuits. Nominees are proposed by a group
of specially designated nominators representing a wide
range of academic and professional fields. Nominators
serve for a one-year period and are asked to propose
individuals as recipients when fellowship support
would make a marked difference. No criteria exist for
selection except that the winners be "exceptionally
talented."

The prize is an award of from $24,000 to $60,000
annually for five years. The amount of the prize is
based on the recipient's age at the time the award is
announced. The foundation allows the winners the
freedom to spend the prize money and their time as
they choose. They are not obligated to produce a
scholarly paper or artistic work.

The foundation has said the awards are made in the
hope that the winners would make "discoveries or
other significant contributions to society." Since its
inception in 1981, the **MacArthur Fellows Program**
has provided fellowships to 191 individuals.

1019★
Markey (Lucille P.) Charitable Trust

3250 Mary Street, Suite 405
Miami, FL 33131   (305) 445-5612
Contact: John H. Dickason, Director for
Administration

Limitations: Awards by nomination only to
postdoctoral scholars planning investigative careers in
biomedical research.
Financial data: Year ended 6/30/87. Assets,
$13,423,301 (M); Total giving, $9,800,201; Awards to
individuals, 35 awards totaling $2,051,580, high
$120,000, low $15,500, general range
$43,000-113,000.
Employer Identification Number: 592276359
Applications: Deadline for nominations October 1st;
Individual applications not accepted; See program
description below for information on eligibility,
nomination procedure, and selection.
Publications: Informational brochure, application

guidelines.
Program description:
The **Lucille P. Markey Scholar Awards in Biomedical
Science** go to a maximum of 16 postdoctoral fellows
nominated from medical colleges, universities, and
research institutions. The awards are granted for an
initial period of three years, renewable up to an
additional five years.

Each award has two components:

1. To provide a stipend during the advanced
postdoctoral fellowship years and a salary after the
individual receives a faculty appointment. The stipend
is as follows:

- First-year Ph.D Scholars - $30,000, with an
  increase of $3,000 for one additional postdoctoral
  year.
- First faculty year for Ph.D Scholars - $40,000,
  to be increased by $5,000 per faculty year
  through the fifth year.
- First-year M.D./Ph.D Scholars and M.D.
  Scholars - $35,000, with an increase of $3,000
  per year up to two additional postdoctoral years.
- First faculty year for M.D./Ph.D Scholars and
  M.D. Scholars - $50,000, to be increased by
  $5,000 per faculty year through the fifth year.

Markey Scholars may not receive stipends or salary
supplements from other sources without prior approval
of the selection committee.

2. Support for the Scholar's research. The research
allowance for all scholars is $15,000 per year (up to
two years of postdoctoral training for Ph.D. Scholars,
and up to three years of postdoctoral training for
M.D./Ph.D or M.D. Scholars). All Scholars will receive
the following research funding during their faculty
years:

- Faculty Year 1 - $60,000
- Faculty Year 2 - $50,000
- Faculty Year 3 - $50,000
- Faculty Year 4 - $25,000
- Faculty Year 5 - $15,000

The research allowance may be used for
consumable supplies, equipment, personnel, and
travel to scientific meetings, but may not be used for
fringe benefits for the scholar, nor during the
postdoctoral years for the salary of pre- or postdoctoral
fellows. It may never be used for the salary of junior
faculty.

Eligibility Criteria
1. A maximum of six nominations may come
from any given institution. Of the six nominees,
no more than four may hold M.D./Ph.D, Ph.D., or
M.D. degrees.
2. Since the awards are intended to provide
support for one-to-two years of postdoctoral
training for Ph.D nominees, and one-to-three
years of postdoctoral training for M.D./Ph.D or
M.D. nominees, the following individuals are
ineligible:

- Individuals who have completed four years
  of postdoctoral research training on or before
  July 1st of the year the award is issued; and

- Individuals who already hold a faculty appointment as an assistant professor, or will hold such appointment during the academic year beginning July 1st of the year the award is issued.

3. Ph.D candidates should be nominated in the second or third postdoctoral year. M.D./Ph.D or M.D. candidates must be nominated in the second or third year of postdoctoral research training and must have completed residency training. All nominees must demonstrate aptitude for, and experience in, research; neither residency nor clinical fellowship training will be considered research experience. **All nominees must plan to continue postdoctoral training for at least one additional year after receipt of the award.**

4. Nominations may not be submitted by institutions located outside the country. Outstanding individuals from foreign countries may be nominated by a U.S. institution if they are prepared to make a commitment to remain in the U.S. for their postdoctoral training as well as for their first five years in a faculty position.

Nomination Procedure: An original and twelve copies of the documentation listed below must be submitted for each nominee:

1. The completed face page for the nomination documents.

2. A one-page description of candidate's research and abstract of the work to be conducted during the first three years of the award.

3. The candidate's curriculum vitae, including the institutions attended, years in attendance, and degrees received.

4. A complete bibliography, listing papers published or in press separately from abstracts.

5. A typewritten double-spaced statement (up to ten pages) by the candidate of his/her plan of work and long-term career objectives. The statement should describe the significance of the research planned and the general plan for use of the research support included with the award.

6. A letter from the faculty sponsor under whom the candidate will be working at the time the award is initiated.

7. A letter from the department head or research director, if not the candidate's sponsor.

8. A letter from the senior academic officer of the sponsoring institution.

9. A supporting letter from a Ph.D advisor and/or chief of service for candidates with clincial training.

10. The more than two additional letters from faculty members who know the candidate well. These faculty members will be requested to rank the candidate relative to others they have known at this stage of their careers. These letters are to be submitted by the writers directly to the trust's executive office at 3250 Mary Street, Suite 405, Miami, FL 33133.

One complete copy of the above documentation should be sent to Dr. Robert J. Glaser, Director for Medical Science, Lucille P. Markey Charitable Trust, 525 Middlefield Road, Suite 130, Menlo Park, CA 94025. The original and remaining eleven copies should be sent to the Markey Scholar Selection Committee at the trust's executive office in Miami (see number 10 above).

Selection Criteria

A selection committee of ten independent distinguished scientists hired by the trust selects the Markey Scholars. The committee may schedule interviews with certain nominees. A candidate not selected may be renominated one time in a succeeding year if eligibility requirements are still met.

1020★
McElroy (R.J.) Trust

500 East Fourth Street, KWWL Building
Waterloo, IA 50703   (319) 291-1299
Contact: Linda L. Klinger, Executive Director

Limitations: Fellowships by nomination only to graduates of liberal arts colleges located within the KWWL viewing area in northeast Iowa.
Financial data: Year ended 12/31/87. Assets, $25,728,812 (M); Total giving, $1,144,414; Grants to individuals, 6 grants totaling $22,500, average grant $5,000.
Employer Identification Number: 426173496
Applications: Deadline for nomination February.
Program description:
The president or dean of each college within the KWWL viewing area submits one nomination to the trust. A selection committee chooses two recipients to receive a three-year fellowship. A statement regarding use of the fellowship and the progress being made by the fellow must be submitted to the trust by both the fellow and the dean.

1021
McGovern (John P.) Foundation

6969 Brompton
Houston, TX 77025   (713) 661-1444

Limitations: Honorariums to recognize individuals involved in the research and study of the causes of allergies.
Financial data: Year ended 8/31/86. Assets, $35,633,825 (M); Total giving, $1,042,962; Awards to individuals amount not specified.
Employer Identification Number: 746053075

1022★
McKnight Foundation, The
410 Peavey Building
Minneapolis, MN 55402   (612) 333-4220
Contact: Russell V. Ewald, Executive Vice-President

Limitations: Awards through nomination only to residents of Minnesota who are direct-care personnel with minimum public recognition and minimum financial remuneration.
Financial data: Year ended 12/31/86. Assets, $711,287,900 (M); Total giving, $31,648,302; Grants to individuals, 68 grants totaling $3,541,462; Subtotal for Human Service Awards, 10 grants totaling $50,000, each grant $5,000.
Employer Identification Number: 410754835
Applications: Individual applications not accepted.
Publications: Annual report.
Program description:
McKnight Awards in Human Service were initiated in 1985, to recognize those individuals throughout the state of Minnesota who are making significant contributions in the human service areas by directly assisting others to become productive and participating members of the communities in which they reside. The goal of the program is to reward those persons who are doing the difficult jobs and tasks with a minimum of public recognition and minimum financial remuneration.

Nominees must be direct-care personnel who serve on a voluntary or paid basis, either full-time or part-time, and who are working for a public agency, non-profit making agency, or a profit-making agency. Nominations are made through an organization or by an individual other than the nominee. A review committee, composed of Minnesota citizens, evaluate the nominations and recommend the ten awardees to the foundation's board of directors for ratification. The awards, given annually, are ten in number and provide a $5,000 cash prize to the individual recipient.

1023
Missouri Scholarship Foundation of Phi Gamma Delta, The
911 Main, Suite 2700
Kansas City, MO 64105
Contact: C. Brooks Wood

Limitations: Cash awards only to students who are members of the Phi Gamma Delta Fraternity at the University of Missouri, Columbia, MO.
Financial data: Year ended 6/30/86. Assets, $57,752 (M); Total giving, $3,950; Grants to individuals, 62 grants totaling $2,950, high $70, low $25, average grant $60.
Employer Identification Number: 446006282
Applications: Cash awards are given throughout the year with no formal application required.

Program description:
Cash awards are made to undergraduates whose grade averages are between 3.0 and 4.0, in order to encourage and promote excellence in educational pursuites and development.

1024★
Morehead (The John Motley) Foundation
P.O. Box 690
Chapel Hill, NC 27514   (919) 962-1201

Limitations: Undergraduate scholarships by nomination only to high school students in North Carolina and selected secondary schools in the rest of the United States and Canada, and selected public schools in Great Britain, to be used for attendance at the University of North Carolina at Chapel Hill only.
Financial data: Year ended 6/30/86. Assets, $61,240,000 (M); Total giving, $2,969,000; Grants to individuals, 321 grants totaling $2,406,000, high $10,700, low $6,066, average grant $8,400.
Employer Identification Number: 560599225
Applications: Deadline November 1st for nominations. **Individual applications not accepted.**
Publications: Annual report.
Program description:
The **Morehead Award Program** for undergraduates is the primary focus of the foundation's activities and receives the major commitment of the foundation's resources. The awards are based solely on merit with financial need not a consideration. **No individuals may apply for an award**; awards are made to high school and preparatory school students in the U.S., Canada, and Great Britain who have been nominated by their respective schools to compete for the awards.

Nominations are invited from four sources:
(a) All secondary schools in North Carolina, both public and private;
(b) The following 51 preparatory schools located in the U.S.: Albuquerque Academy, Albuquerque, NM; The Baylor School, Chattanooga, TN; The Bolles School, Jacksonville, FL; Casady School, Oklahoma City, OK; Chatham Hall, Chatham, VA; Choate Rosemary Hall, Wallingford, CT; Cranbrook School, Bloomfield Hills, MI; Culver Academies, Culver, IN; Deerfield Academy, Deerfield, MA; Episcopal High School; Alexandria, VA; Gilman School, Baltimore, MD; Groton School, Groton, MA; Harpeth Hall School, Nashville, TN; Harvard School, Los Angeles, CA; The Hill School, Pottstown, PA; The Hockaday School, Dallas, TX; The Hotchkiss School, Lakeville, CT; Isidore Newman School, New Orleans, LA; John Burroughs School, St. Louis, MO; Kent School, Kent, CT; The Kinkaid School, Houston, TX; Lakeside School, Seattle, WA; The Lawrenceville School, Lawrenceville, NJ; The Loomis Chaffee School, Windsor, CT; The Lovett School, Atlanta, GA; The McCallie School, Chattanooga, TN; Mary Institute, St. Louis, MO;

Milton Academy, Milton, MA; Montgomery Bell Academy, Nashville, TN; National Cathedral School, Washington, DC; New Trier Township High School, Winnetka, IL; Norfolk Academy, Norfolk, VA; The Pembroke Hill School, Kansas City, MO; Phillips Academy, Andover, MA; Phillips Exeter Academy, Exeter, NH; Polytechnic School, Pasadena, CA; Porter-Gaud School, Charleston, SC; San Francisco University High School, San Francisco, CA; St. Albans School, Washington, DC; St. Catherine's School, Richmond, VA; St. John's School, Houston, TX; St. Louis Country Day School, St. Louis, MO; St. Mark's School, Southborough, MA; St. Mark's School of Texas, Dallas, TX; St. Paul's School, Concord, NH; Stuyvesant High School, New York, NY; Tabor Academy, Marion, MA; The Taft School, Watertown, CT; Virginia Episcopal School, Lynchburg, VA; The Westminster Schools, Atlanta, GA; Woodberry Forest School Woodberry Forest, VA;

(c) The following 24 British Public Schools: Bradford Grammar School; Charterhouse; Christ's Hospital; Clifton College; Cranleigh School; Dulwich College; Eton College; Fettes College; Gordonstoun School; Haileybury; Harrow School; Manchester Grammar School; Marlborough School; Radley School; Repton School; Rugby School; Sedbergh School; Sherborne School; Shrewsbury School; Tonbridge School; Uppingham School; Wellington College; Westminster School; Winchester College; and
(d) The following eight sources in Canada: The High Schools of the Toronto Board of Education; Toronto French School; University of Toronto Schools; Cardinal Newman High School; St. Joseph's College School; Don Mills Collegiate Institute; Earl Haig Collegiate Institute; Weston Collegiate Institute.

The program, which is limited to sponsoring undergraduate study at the University of North Carolina at Chapel Hill, has three components. Morehead Scholars receive tuition and an annual stipend of $5,200 to cover tuition and expenses (the out-of-state tuition differential of approximately $3,500 is paid directly to the university for Scholars who are not North Carolina residents). These awards are renewable for four years of study.

The **Summer Enrichment Program** is a four-year optional program designed to balance Morehead Scholars' academic education with real-world experience. Arranged and financed by the foundation, this program is open to all Morehead Award recipients and involves a summer internship prior to each academic year. Prior to freshman year, students participate in an outdoor leadership program, such as Outward Bound or National Outdoor Leadership School; second year student internships are with police departments in major U.S. cities; third year students intern with major American companies; and rising seniors work either in Federal or foreign

governments or on self-devised special projects. A third option prior to the senior year is a travel/study abroad project also of the Scholars' own design.

The foundation's fellowship program for graduate study was discontinued in the summer of 1983.

1025
National Machinery Foundation, Inc.
Greenfield Street
P.O.Box 747
Tiffin, OH 44883 (419) 447-5211
Contact: D. B. Bero, Administrator

Limitations: Awards for good citizenship to children in Seneca County, OH.
Financial data: Year ended 12/31/86. Assets, $6,363,297 (M); Total giving, $278,729; Grants to individuals, 200 grants totaling $36,150, high $1,000, low $58; Subtotal for awards not specified.
Employer Identification Number: 346520191

1026★
Olmsted (The George and Carol) Foundation
(Formerly Olmsted (The George) Foundation)
1515 North Courthouse Road, Suite 305
Arlington, VA 22201 (703) 527-9070
Contact: Barbara S. Schimpff, Executive Vice-President

Limitations: Scholarships by nomination only to career military officers in the Armed Forces.
Financial data: Year ended 12/31/86. Assets, $9,077,883 (M); Total giving, $512,125; Grants to individuals totaling $82,532, average grant $3,500.
Employer Identification Number: 546049005
Applications: Applications handled through Military Services; Funds largely committed; **Individual applications not accepted.**
Publications: Annual report, informational brochure (including application guidelines).
Program description:
The **Olmsted Scholar Program** awards grants for two years of graduate study in a foreign language at a foreign university to individuals from each branch of the military service who are nominated by their departments. Grantees are expected to gain an extensive knowledge of the people, language and culture of their chosen area.

The spouses of married scholars also receive grants to study language as well as to defray other expenses related to their participation in their spouses' educational endeavors.

If an advanced degree has not been earned by the end of two successive years of study abroad, the scholar is eligible for assistance in completing degree requirements at any university in the U.S., under the Advanced Degree Program.

1027
Open Society Fund, Inc.
10 Columbus Circle, Room 1230
New York, NY 10019
Contact: Gary Gladstein, Vice-President and Secretary

Limitations: Scholarships to students who are
financially or culturally deprived or who are members
of racial, religious, or ethnic minorities for study at
educational institutions in the U.S., Europe, Africa or
Asia. Fellowships to individuals for projects involving
scholarly research or analysis or creation of
educational materials, including film and videotape.
Financial data: Year ended 12/31/85. Assets,
$3,192,817 (M); Total giving, $1,211,392; Grants to
individuals amount not specified.
Employer Identification Number: 133095822
Applications: Applicants must be affiliated with an
institution; See program description below for detailed
application information; **Unsolicited applications not
accepted.**
Program description:
Applicants will be solicited through contacts with
educational institutions in the U.S. and foreign
countries, and other public dissemination of grant
criteria. Invited applicants will be required to submit a
complete biographical records, including:
    1. A report on academic and professional careers
    2. A detailed statement of educational or project
plans
    3. A statement of plans and commitments after
the scholarship or fellowship program
    4. Letters of reference (including
recommendations from instructors)
    5. Lists of publications
    6. A demonstrated financial need for the grant
funds.
    There will be a preliminary screening of all
candidates by a selection committee, which will
consist of highly qualified professional, business, and
academic persons who are not employees of the fund.
A committee composed of fund directors will make
the final selection when the number of eligible
candidates is narrowed down to three or four. The
fund pays the scholarship or fellowship directly to the
educational institution on behalf of the individual
recipient.

1028★
Passano Foundation, Inc., The
428 East Preston Street
Baltimore, MD 21202   (301) 528-4000
Contact: E. Magruder Passano, Jr., President

Limitations: Awards by nomination only to
distinguished individuals in science and medicine.
Financial data: Year ended 12/31/87. Assets,
$1,049,662 (M); Total giving, $45,000; Grants to
individuals, 2 grants totaling $45,000, high $30,000,
low $15,000, general range $10,000-30,000.

Employer Identification Number: 526036968
Applications: Deadline October 1st; Nominations by
independent parties accepted throughout the year;
Individual applications not accepted.
Publications: Informational brochure, application
guidelines.
Program description:
Two cash awards are given each year. The recipients
are chosen by the foundation directors with the advice
of the medical community.
    The Passano Award, with an honorarium of at least
$20,000, is presented to an established investigator in
recognition of research which leads to clinical medical
applications. Recipients of this award are called Senior
Laureates.
    The Passano Foundation Young Scientist Award,
with an honorarium of a smaller amount, is conferred
on a young scientist (under 36) who demonstrates
continuing, effective contributions to basic science,
clinical science, and medical education, contributions
which suggest even greater accomplishments in the
future. Recipients are called Junior Laureates.
    The work for which the awards are given must have
been done in the U.S., and preference is given to
outstanding scientists who have not yet received
numerous awards.

1029★
Peninsula Community Foundation
1204 Burlingame Avenue
Burlingame, CA 94011-0627   (415) 342-2477
Contact: Bill Somerville, Executive Director

Limitations: Awards to individuals residing in San
Mateo County and northern Santa Clara County, CA,
in recognition of volunteer leadership.
Financial data: Year ended 12/31/86. Assets,
$14,119,000 (M); Total giving, $1,384,000; Grants to
individuals amount not specified.
Employer Identification Number: 942746687
Publications: Annual report.
Program description:
The **Robert J. Koshland Award** is given each year in
recognition of outstanding volunteer leadership. The
recipient of the award is invited to designate a
Peninsula charitable organization to receive a $10,000
grant given by the foundation.

1030
Pequot Community Foundation, Inc., The
302 Captain's Walk, Room 211
P.O. Box 769
New London, CT 06320   (203) 442-3572
Contact: Thomas T. Wetmore, Executive Director

Limitations: Scholarships by nomination only to
graduating high school students from East Lyme,
Montville, New London, or Waterford, CT.
Financial data: Year ended 12/31/86. Assets,

$1,481,275 (M); Total giving, $66,000; Grants to individuals, 4 grants totaling $5,700.
Employer Identification Number: 061080097
Applications: Interviews required.
Publications: Annual report.
Program description:
The **Marje and Jim Smith Scholarship** provides financial assistance to an outstanding graduating high school student. Candidates for the scholarship are nominated, one each, from East Lyme High School, Montville High School, New London High School, and Waterford High School. The four finalists are interviewed by a committee of area educators and civic leaders which selects the recipient. The award is $2,500 for the first year, with like payments made each year for a maximum of four years, totaling $10,000. The awardee must maintain satisfactory progress toward a baccalaureate degree.

The **Hendel Family Association Scholarship** is awarded annually to a student graduating from New London High School. The purpose of this scholarship is to serve as an encouragement to a student who has had to face obstacles and difficulties and worked hard to overcome them. The award is $450.

1031
Piper (Minnie Stevens) Foundation
GPM South Tower, Suite 530
800 NW Loop 410
San Antonio, TX 78216-5699   (512) 227-8119
Contact: Michael J. Balint, Executive Director

Limitations: Scholarships to students and cash awards to teachers. Both must be residents of Texas and attend or teach at Texas colleges and universities. By nomination only.
Financial data: Year ended 12/31/86. Assets, $17,253,000 (M); Total giving, $604,955; Grants to individuals totaling $230,525.
Employer Identification Number: 741292695
Applications: See program description below for application information on specific programs.
Individual applications not accepted.
Publications: Multi-year report, program information.
Program description:
The **Piper Scholars Program** which makes 10-15 awards annually on a four-year basis to academically promising and superior high school seniors who reside in and plan to attend colleges or universities in Texas. Recipients must maintain a ''B'' average or be dropped from the program.

Upon invitation, nominations are made by principals or counselors for invited high schools throughout Texas. Selection is made by the foundation's Scholarship Committee review of high school record, aptitude and achievement tests, and a personal interview.

The **Piper Professors Program** provides ten annual awards of approximately $2,500 each to professors for excellence in teaching at the college level. Selection is

made on the basis of nominations submitted by each college and university in Texas.

The **Piper Fellows Program** enables former Piper Scholars to attend graduate or professional school. Fellowships are granted to meet financial need while pursuing an advanced degree at an institution in Texas.

1032★
Poetry Society of America
c/o Eisner & Lubin
15 Gramercy Park South
New York, NY 10003   (212) 254-9628

Limitations: Awards and prizes to professional and student poets. Except as noted below for entries in the Cane, Williams, and Di Castagnola contests, all poems must be unpublished. Poems accepted for publication prior to the bestowal of awards must be withdrawn from the publication.
Financial data: Year ended 9/30/86. Assets, $97,819 (M); Total giving, $9,935; Grants to individuals, 17 grants totaling $8,035, high $2,000, low $100, general range $250-500.
Employer Identification Number: 136019220
Applications: Deadline December 31st if sent first-class, November 30th if mailed fourth-class, except as noted below; Completion of formal application required; For all awards, two copies of entries are required. Poems may be of any length unless noted otherwise below. Only one poem may be submitted for each poetry award. Names should not appear on the poem but should be included along with the poet's address and telephone number on an index card. All poems must arrive together with a title page listing all entries. There is a five dollar entry fee per packet of submissions by non-members, with the exception of single entries. Prospective applicants should send a self-addressed, stamped envelope to receive response to inquiries.
Publications: Program information (including application guidelines).
Program description:
The Poetry Society of America grants a number of poetry achievement awards. Competition for some awards is limited to PSA members; open to the general public are the following nine award contests:

The **Elias Lieberman Student Poety Award** in the amount of $100 is given for the best unpublished poem by a high school or preparatory school (grades 9-12) student from the U.S. and its territories.

The **Ruth Lake Memorial Award** in the amount of $100 for a poem of retrospection in any style.

The **Cecil B. Wagner Award** in the amount of $250 is given for the best poem worthy of the tradition of the art, in any style.

The **Robert H. Winner Memorial Award** for $1,000 is for a poem or sequence of poems characterized by delight in language and the possibilities of discovery in ordinary life. Poems should be limited to 150 lines.

The **John Masefield Memorial Award** for $500 is given for a narrative poem in English of up to 300 lines. Translations are ineligible.

The **Melville Cane Award** in the amount of $500 is given in even-numbered years for a book of poems and in odd-numbered years for a prose work on poetry or a poet. Books published in the previous two years are eligible for submission by publishers. Entry forms are available from PSA.

The **Norma Farber First Book Award** for $1,000 is given for a first book of original poetry written by an American and published in either hard or soft cover in a standard edition during the calendar year. Only publishers may submit entries. Entry forms are available from PSA.

The **William Carlos Williams Award** is given for a book of poetry published by a small press, nonprofit, or university press. Only original (no translations or adaptations) work, not previously published, by a poet who is a permanent resident of the U.S. is eligible for consideration. Entries for this award must be submitted by the publishers by December 31st.

The prize for the Williams Award will be the purchase, by PSA, of copies of the winning book (at 40 percent trade discount off the retail price to a total of $1,250) for distribution to PSA members. The publisher will agree to pay the author a royalty of at least ten percent of the retail price and supply the winning book with the logo of PSA and the words, "Winner of the Poetry Society of America's William Carlos Williams Prize 19__."

In addition to the above mentioned awards, PSA administers, **by nomination only**, the **Shelley Memorial Award**, which is given to a living American poet on the basis of the poet's entire work as well as his or her financial need. The amount of this prize, which varies from from year to year is approximately $2,000, and there is no deadline for submission of entries.

The following nine annual awards are open to members of the Poetry Society of America only:

The **Emily Dickinson Award** for $100 is given for a poem inspired by Emily Dickinson, though not necessarily in her style, and not more than 30 lines.

The **Gordon Barber Memorial Award**, for $200 is given for a poem of exceptional merit or character.

Three $250 awards, the **Consuelo Ford**, the **Gertrude B. Claytor Memorial**, and the **Mary Carolyn Davies Memorial**, are given for a lyric poem of 50 lines or less, a poem on the American scene or character, and a poem suitable for setting to music of not more than 30 lines, respectively.

The **Cecil Hemley Memorial Award** gives $300 for a lyric poem on a philosophical theme limited to 100 lines. The society makes two $500 awards, the **Gustav Davidson Memorial** for a sonnet or sequence in traditional forms, and the **Lucille Medwick Memorial** for an original poem on a humanitarian theme in any form or freedom limited to 100 lines; translations are ineligible.

The society offers $2,000 under the **Alice Fay Di Castagnola Award** for a manuscript-in-progress: poetry, prose, or verse-drama. Submissions, in duplicate from a single, well-advanced original work must include a one paragraph proposal stating theme, content, and form, on a title page. Published work must be used. The line limit in 300 lines of sample verse, if poetry; sample chapter if prose; sample scene if verse-drama.

1033★
Racine County Area Foundation, Inc.
818 Sixth Street
Racine, WI 53403   (414) 632-8474
Contact: Helen M. Underwood, Executive Secretary

Limitations: Scholarships by nomination only to residents of Racine County, WI, and grants to teachers in Racine Unified School District.
Financial data: Year ended 12/31/86. Assets, $1,920,336 (M); Grants to individuals, 33 grants totaling $8,556; Subtotal for scholarships, 9 grants totaling $4,500, each grant $500; Subtotal for grants to teachers, 24 grants totaling $4,056, general range $200-500.
Employer Identification Number: 510188377
Publications: Annual report.
Program description:
Scholarship recipients are selected through various advisory groups composed of high school teachers.

The "School Bell Fund" makes grants to individual teachers for innovative programs which are not covered under the district's budget. The school district solicits the funds for the fund.

1034
Rinehart (The Mary Roberts) Fund
George Mason University, English Department
4400 Universtiy Drive
Fairfax, VA 22030   (703) 323-2220
Contact: Professor Richard Bausch

Limitations: Grants by nomination only to unpublished creative writers who need financial assistance to complete works of fiction, poetry, drama, biography, autobiography, or history with a strong narrative quality.
Financial data: Year ended 12/31/85. Assets, $74,000 (M); Total giving, $5,000; Grants to individuals, 2 grants totaling $5,000, each grant $2,500.
Employer Identification Number: 136154182
Applications: Nominations must be submitted by November 1st each year; Grants will be announced by March 1st of the following year; **Individual applications not accepted.**
Publications: Program information.
Program description:
Although most nominations come from writing program faculty around the country, any unpublished

writer is eligible to be nominated by a sponsoring writer or editor. Unpublishhed is defined as being ineligible to apply for a National Endowment Creative Writing grant. If applicants have enough publications to apply for aid from the endowment, they are not eligible for a Mary Roberts Rinehart Fund grant.

Each year two grants of $2,500 will be made to writers who need financial assistance not otherwise available to complete work definitely projected. The grants will be given in two of four categories -- fiction, poetry, drama, and non-fiction -- on an alternate basis, each year. Grants will be given in fiction and poetry in even years, and non-fiction and drama in odd years.

Competition for these grants will take place through nomination by established writers or editors. The decisions of the judges in any given category are final, and will be based on the quality of the nominee's writing. The fund will consider the submission of a candidate's work by any established writer or editor as nomination for a grant; no written recommendations are necessary.

Submitted samples of a nominee's writing may be up to 30 pages in length for fiction, non-fiction and drama, and 25 pages for poetry.

1035
S&H Foundation, Inc., The

c/o Sperry & Hutchinson Company
330 Madison Avenue
New York, NY 10017   (212) 370-1144
Contact: Henry S. Coleman, Coleman Associates, P.O. Box 1283, New Canaan, CT 06840

Limitations: Scholarships to college juniors nominated by colleges which have been selected by S&H to make nominations.
Financial data: Year ended 12/31/85. Assets, $6,916,533 (M); Total giving, $239,450; Grants to individuals, 189 grants totaling $239,450; Subtotal for Beinecke awards, 25 grants totaling $132,500, high $12,000, low $2,500.
Employer Identification Number: 136114308
Applications: Deadline March 15th; College or university must be invited to nominate an applicant; **Individual applications not accepted.**
Program description:
Beinecke Memorial Scholarships are awarded by the foundation to selected students to carry them through their senior year of college and two years of graduate study. Winners are granted an award to cover their financial needs during senior year in college, and full tuition plus additional money for educational expenses during two years of graduate study. Beinecke Scholars may pursue any course of graduate or professional study that they choose.

1036★
Scripps Howard Foundation

P.O. Box 5380
Cincinnati, OH 45201   (513) 977-3035
Contact: Albert J. Schotelkotte, President

Limitations: Awards only to professional print/ broadcast journalists and college cartoonists.
Financial data: Year ended 12/31/87. Assets, $9,361,148 (M); Total giving, $778,148; Grants to individuals, 236 grants totaling $238,050; Subtotal for awards, 14 awards totaling $41,000, general range $2,000-2,500.
Employer Identification Number: 316025114
Applications: Applications and fact sheets, giving rules and deadlines for each contest, are available each fall.
Publications: Annual report, program information, application guidelines, informational brochure.
Program description:
The annual Scripps Howard Foundation National Journalism Awards recognize and award, with plaques and cash prizes, achievement in eight categories of journalistic efforts. They are among the most prestigious in the field.

The Charles M. Schulz Award, a single annual $2,000 award, was established to help further the careers of promising college cartoonists. Cartoonists must still be attending college at time of application.

The Ernie Pyle Awards are given to newspaper writers for outstanding human interest reporting exemplifying "warmth and craftsmanship" in the style of Ernie Pyle. Two awards, of $2,000 and $1,000, are given each year.

The Jack R. Howard Awards are for journalistic achievement in broadcasting, including any program or series of programs designed to promote the public good. Awards are open to any single radio or television stations. Networks may not compete. There are four categories: large market T.V.; small market T.V.; large market radio; small market radio. Four $2,000 awards are given.

The Edward Willis Scripps Awards are given annually to the individual or individuals who contributed the most to that newspaper selected for its outstanding contribution to the cause of the First Amendment guarantee of a free press. Entries may reflect service to the First Amendment in a variety of ways: fighting the growing threat of censorship in America, overcoming public uneasiness with regard to press credibility, combating government secrecy at all levels, and instilling in the public an appreciation of its needs as well as its right to know as guaranteed by the First Amendment. One newspaper is given an award of $2,500.

The Walker Stone Awards for editorial writing are given for outstanding achievement in the field of newspaper editorial writing. Selection criteria will include general excellence in the quality, forcefulness, and importance to the public interest. One annual award for $2,000 is given.

The Edward J. Meeman Awards for newspaper work--news and feature stories, campaigns, editorials, columns, cartoons, and photographic reports or essays--that serves to educate the public and public officials to a better understanding and support of conservation. Two grants are awarded each year: prizes of $2,000 in each of two categories, newspapers with circulation over 100,000, and those under 100,000.

The Roy W. Howard Awards honors newspapers for public service reporting, defined as exposure and contribution toward the alleviation of corruption, crime, health, or other problems. Two annual awards of $2,500 are made in each of two categories, newspapers with circulations over 100,000, and those with circulations under 100,000.

The Charles E. Scripps Award honors leadership shown in fighting illiteracy. There are separate categories for print journalism and broadcasting journalism, with prizes and grants totaling $7,500 in each category.

Competitions for all awards categories are open to daily or weekly journalists in the United States and its territories. To be eligible for consideration, the applicant's work must have been performed during the calendar year of the contest.

1037★
Sloan (Alfred P.) Foundation
630 Fifth Avenue
New York, NY 10111-0242   (212) 582-0450
Contact: Albert Rees, President

Limitations: Fellowships by nomination only to Ph.D. faculty members in colleges or universities in either the U.S. or Canada.
Financial data: Year ended 12/31/87. Assets, $482,920,715 (M); Total giving, $24,079,172; Grants to individuals totaling $3,139,000.
Employer Identification Number: 131623877
Applications: Deadline September 15th; Completion of formal nomination required; **Individual applications not accepted.**
Publications: Annual report.
Program description:
Sloan Fellowships for Basic Research is the foundation's oldest program, and is one of the first fellowship programs in the country. It is aimed at identifying young scientists who show outstanding promise of making creative contributions to scientific knowledge in the early stages of their careers. Their research is expected to advance the frontiers of physics, chemistry, mathematics, neuroscience, and economics.

Candidates must be nominated by department chairmen in a college or university, or other senior scholars, be no more than 32 years of age, and hold a Ph.D. or equivalent degree in the field of inquiry or a related, interdisciplinary field. They must be members of the faculty of a college or university in the U.S. or

Canada, except in neuroscience, in which area postdoctoral fellows with at least one year's postdoctoral experience are also eligible. No formal research proposal is required, and the fellows are free to shift the direction of their research at any time.

Fellowships usually average $25,000 for a two-year period, with extensions granted for a maximum of two years if unexpended funds remain at the end of the first two-year period. The funds may be used for support of predoctoral and postdoctoral research assistants, professional travel, release from teaching where this is compatible with the fellow's department, equipment and supplies, and other related purposes approved by the fellow's institution. About 90 new fellowships are awarded each year to scientists. Funds are administered by the fellow's institution.

In 1986, the 90 recipients were selected from among 450 nominations by a committee of recognized scientists and economists in the fields of chemistry, economics, mathematics, neuroscience, and physics.

1038★
Soren (Madeleine H.) Trust
Boston Safe Deposit & Trust Company
One Boston Place
Boston, MA 02106   (617) 722-7340
Contact: Sylvia Salas, Trust Officer

Limitations: Scholarships by nomination only to female residents of Massachusetts for studies in music and music education.
Financial data: Year ended 8/31/87. Assets, $204,433 (M); Total giving, $10,000; Grants to individuals, 2 grants totaling $10,000, high $2,000, low $1,000.
Employer Identification Number: 046092280
Applications: Deadline April 1st; Completion of formal application required. Applications are sent to participating schools in Massachusetts. The schools then recommend students who meet the above noted limitations. **Individual applications not accepted.**

1039★
State Farm Companies Foundation
One State Farm Plaza
Bloomington, IL 61710   (309) 766-2039
Contact: Dave Polzin, Assistant Vice-President, Programs

Limitations: Fellowships by nomination only to college juniors and seniors majoring in business-related studies. Doctoral awards by nomination only to students at the dissertation stage in insurance or a related field of study. Candidates for both programs must be U.S. citizens.
Financial data: Year ended 12/31/86. Assets, $1,337,699 (M); Total giving, $3,169,817; Grants to individuals totaling $45,000.
Employer Identification Number: 366110423
Applications: Deadline for fellowship program

February 28th, deadline for doctoral program March 31st; Completion of formal application required. **Applications without nominations will not be considered.**
Publications: Annual report, informational brochure, application guidelines.
Program description:
Exceptional Student Fellowship Program: The fellowship program makes awards to encourage young men and women of high potential and to help them prepare themselves for leadership roles in industry and society. The awards are available to juniors and seniors in college majoring in the areas of accounting, business administration, actuarial science, computer science, economics, finance, insurance, investments, marketing, mathematics, pre-law, statistics, and other business-related studies.

Winners are selected by an independent committee of educators on the basis of scholarship and demonstrated leadership in extracurricular activities, as well as character, potential business administrative capacity, and the recommendations of instructors, counselors, and other responsible citizens.

Approximately thirty awards are made annually in the amount of $2,500 each. Candidates must be nominated by the dean of the college or a department head. Nomination and application forms are available in December from business school deans, business departments, and directors of financial aid at colleges, universities and business schools.
Doctoral Dissertation Award Programs: Two awards of $10,000 are made each year under this program. One fellowship is awarded to students who have completed a major portion of their doctoral program in insurance or a related field, to stimulate research and development in the insurance industry and to contribute to the development of qualified teachers of insurance in colleges and universities in the U.S. The other fellowship is awarded to students who have completed a major portion of their doctoral program and are majoring in business or a related field, to stimulate research and development in the business industry.

Candidates must be nominated by the director of the school's doctoral program. Nomination and application forms are available in January from the dean of the doctoral program. Winners are selected by an independent committee of educators on the basis of scholastic achievement, the quality of the doctoral dissertation proposal, and the recommendations of the director of the doctoral program and other faculty members.

1040★
Teagle Foundation, Inc., The
30 Rockefeller Plaza, Room 2835
New York, NY 10112　　　　　　(212) 247-1946
Contact: Richard W. Kimball, Executive Vice-President

Limitations: Welfare assistance by nomination only to needy employees, annuitants and widows of deceased employees of Exxon Corporation and its affiliates.
Financial data: Year ended 5/31/87. Assets, $79,304,320 (M); Total giving, $2,469,666; Grants to individuals, 9 grants totaling $60,151.
Employer Identification Number: 131773645
Applications: Individual applications not accepted.
Publications: Annual report.
Program description:
Welfare assistance is given for special needs not ordinarily met by Exxon Corporation benefit and public welfare plans. Nominations for assistance must originate with the chief executive officer of the appropriate Exxon unit.

1041
Templeton Foundation, Inc.
P.o. Box 563
2223 Highway Nine
Howell, NJ 07731

Limitations: Awards to "the person who has contributed the most to new ideas or methods for widening or deepening man's knowledge of God or love of God.".
Financial data: Year ended 3/31/85. Assets, $573,806 (M); Total giving, $204,000; Grants to individuals, 1 grant totaling $195,000.
Employer Identification Number: 226035108
Applications: Applications accepted throughout the year.

1042
Tiffany (Louis Comfort) Foundation
Five Devon Road
Great Neck, NY 11023
Contact: Angela Westwater, President

Limitations: Awards by nomination only to professionals in the fine arts (painting, sculpture, and graphic arts) and the industrial crafts (ceramics, textiles design, glass design, and metal works).
Financial data: Year ended 12/31/85. Assets, $3,254,853 (M); Total giving, $210,000; Grants to individuals, 14 grants totaling $210,000, each grant $15,000.
Employer Identification Number: 131689389
Applications: Individual applications not accepted.
Publications: Annual report.
Program description:
Awards are granted in alternate years in the decorative arts and crafts fields, and the visual arts. All awards are subject to selection by a jury.

1043★
Tucson Community Foundation
(Formerly Tucson Area Foundation, Inc., Greater)
6842 East Tanque Verde
Tucson, AZ 85715   (602) 772-1707
Contact: Donna L. Grant, Executive Director

Limitations: Scholarships by nomination only to
students graduating from or attending Arizona
educational institutions.
Financial data: Year ended 7/31/87. Assets,
$3,000,000 (M); Grants to individuals, 10 grants
totaling $20,000, high $2,000, low $500, average
grant $1,000.
Employer Identification Number: 942844781
Applications: Deadline February 15th; Contact
foundation for current application deadline;
Completion of formal application required. **Individual
applications without nominations not accepted.**
Publications: Annual report, application guidelines,
financial statement, informational brochure,
newsletter.
Program description:
The **Margaret M. Ingram Scholarship** fund provides
scholarships to students graduating from Pima County
high schools entering postsecondary study for the first
time and are renewable upon reapplication for
successive years of study. Applicants are selected
based on financial need, academic and other
achievements, and potential for postsecondary
educational attainment. Applicants must be nominated
by the high school from which they graduated or are
graduating. Awards are for tuition, required fees, and
textbooks only, and are made to or through the
accredited college or university.

The **Judge Mary Anne Richey Scholarship Fund** is
awarded to full-time first year law students attending
either the University of Arizona College of Law or
Arizona State University are based on financial need,
past and present community service, and potential for
future community service.

The **Arizona Air Force Association Endowment
Fund** assists outstanding and deserving students in
AFROTC and AFJROTC and CAP programs in Arizona.

The **Pete Herder Scholarship Fund** provides
financial aid to students who have the ability or
potential to further the advancement of home building.

The **John and Joan Tedford Scholarship Fund**
provides scholarships to graduates of Pima County
high schools based on financial need and academic
ability.

The **Tucson Music Teachers Association Scholarship
Fund** provides scholarships for high school students
and University of Arizona music students.

1044★
Watson (The Thomas J.) Foundation
217 Angell Street
Providence, RI 02906   (401) 274-1952
Contact: Martin A. Brody, Executive Director

Limitations: Fellowships to graduating seniors of
specified colleges and universities. Applicants must be
nominated by their college.
Financial data: Year ended 5/31/87. Assets,
$52,956,965 (M); Total giving, $3,359,480, Grants to
individuals, 22 grants totaling $556,000, high
$250,000, low $1,000, general range $10,000-30,000,
average grant $10,000.
Employer Identification Number: 136038151
Applications: Deadline 1st Tuesday in November for
nomination; Completion of formal application
required; Interviews required; **Individual applications
not accepted.**
Publications: Informational brochure.
Program description:
The **Thomas J. Watson Fellowship Program** enables
75 college graduates of unusual promise to engage in
an initial postgraduate year of independent study and
travel abroad. Candidates devise a focused and
disciplined plan of travel. The experience is viewed as
a break in which they might explore a particular
interest, view their lives and American society in
greater perspective, and develop a more informed
sense of international concern. It is not intended for
the fellows to engage in extended formal study at a
foreign university. A grant of $13,000 is provided for
each fellow ($18,000 for married students).

The foundation is most concerned with qualities as
integrity, leadership capacity, and potential for
creative achievement and excellence within a chosen
field. The overall academic record of a candidate is
not the principle criterion for selection, nor is an
extensive array of campus activities. However, weight
is given to a candidate's record in his or her field of
special interest, as well as to extracurricular
involvement. A candidate's proposed project should
be realistic, imaginative, and personally significant; it
should be one which could be pursued with
independence and adaptability.

The foundation only accepts nominations from the
following cooperating private colleges and universities
throughout the U.S.: Amherst College, Bates College,
Berea College, Birmingham-Southern College,
Bowdoin College, Brandeis University, Bryn Mawr
College, California Institute of Technology, Carleton
College, Centre College of Kentucky, Claremont
McKenna College, Colorado School of Mines, Colby
College, Colgate University, The College of the
Atlantic, College of the Holy Cross, Colorado College,
Connecticut College, Davidson College, Earlham
College, Grinnell College, Hamilton College,
Haverford College, Harvey Mudd College, The Johns
Hopkins University, Kalamazoo College, Kenyon
College, Lafayette College, Lawrence University,
Middlebury College, Mills Collge, Morehouse College,

Newcomb College of Tulane University, Oberlin College, Occidental College, Pitzer College, Pomona College, Reed College, Rice University (TX), Scripps College, Spelman College, St. John's College (MD), St. John's College (NM), St. Lawrence University, Swarthmore College, Trinity College (CT), Trinity College (DC), Union College, The University of the South, Wellesley College, Wesleyan University, Wheaton College (MA), and Williams College.

1045★
Welch (The Robert A.) Foundation
4605 Post Oak Place, Suite 200
Houston, TX 77027   (713) 961-9884
Contact: Norbert Dittrich, Executive Manager

Limitations: Grants by nomination only for basic chemistry research.
Financial data: Year ended 8/31/87. Assets, $259,179,000 (M); Total giving, $11,921,000; Grants to individuals, 376 grants totaling $11,921,000; Subtotal for awards, 1 award totaling $225,000.
Employer Identification Number: 741216248
Applications: Deadline February 1st for nomination; **Individual applications not accepted.**
Publications: Annual report, program information.
Program description:
The **Robert A. Welch Award in Chemistry** is granted to foster and encourage basic chemical research and to recognize, in a substantial manner, the value of chemical research with respect to the betterment of mankind. The award in the amount of $225,000 can be awarded annually. The award may be omitted in any award period during which the Scientific Advisory Board and the Board of Trustees are of the opinion that truly meritorious nominations have not been received.

Nominations may be made by one of several chemistry and scientific organizations as well as by individuals, and should include a brief biographical sketch of the nominee, list of scientific publications, and an outline of his contributions to research in chemistry, as well as three seconding letters of nomination. No direct application or self-nomination is accepted.

1046★
Whiting (Mrs. Giles) Foundation
30 Rockefeller Plaza
New York, NY 10112   (212) 698-2500
Contact: Robert H.M. Ferguson, Secretary-Treasurer

Limitations: Awards to support emerging writers. Funds are currently committed for the foreseeable future.
Financial data: Year ended 11/30/87. Assets, $18,719,916 (M); Total giving, $1,099,700; Awards to individuals totaling $163,000, average grant $25,000.
Employer Identification Number: 136154484

Applications: Applications are neither invited nor accepted.
Program description:
The **Whiting Writers' Awards** are made to support emerging writers. Candidates are chosen by a committee of selectors chosen by the foundation.

1047★
Whitney (Thomas & Donna) Education Foundation
745 Distel Drive, Suite 5
Los Altos, CA 94022   (415) 961-4245
Contact: Elizabeth H. Curtis, Executive Director

Limitations: Teacher Award for Outstanding Contribution to Education, by nomination only, to elementary middle/junior high school teachers in San Mateo and Santa Clara counties, CA.
Financial data: Year ended 6/30/87. Assets, $988,779 (M); Total giving, $97,556; Grants to individuals, 17 grants totaling $8,100, high $1,500, low $50.
Employer Identification Number: 942775750
Applications: Nominations are accepted in early winter; Completion of formal application required; **Individual applications not accepted.**
Publications: Annual report (including application guidelines).
Program description:
As a means to reward and encourage excellence in the field of education, the foundation annually awards $2,000 each to five elementary and middle/junior high school teachers for their outstanding contribution to education. An award of $50 is also paid to each sponsor of awardees.

Teachers are nominated by certified staff members who have worked with the nominees. Nominees are not to be informed of their nomination. Selection of the finalists and the awardees is made by a five-member selection committee consisting of foundation personnel and local educators. Site visits including classroom observations and interviews with colleagues and supervisors are made in the Spring.

1048
Willo (Veronica) Scholarship Fund
c/o Bank One of Eastern Ohio, N.A.
P.O. Box 359
Youngston, OH 44501

Limitations: Undergraduate scholarships by nomination only to graduating seniors of Mahoning County, OH, high schools.
Financial data: Year ended 12/31/86. Assets, $159,739 (M); Total giving, $5,250; Grants to individuals, 4 grants totaling $5,250, high $1,500, low $750.
Employer Identification Number: 346577619
Applications: Nominations made by Mahoning County high school principals; **Individual applications not accepted.**

Program description:
The fund requests all high school principals in
Mahoning County, Ohio to submit the name of a
graduating student deserving of a scholarship based on
financial need and academic ability. The winners of
the scholarships are selected by a committee
composed of the Bishop of the Catholic Diocese of
Youngston, the President of the Mahoning Valley
Association of Churches, and the President of the
Mahoning County Bar Association.

1049
Wilson (John R.) Scholarship Fund
c/o First Vermont Bank & Trust Company
500 Main Street
Bennington, VT 05201   (802) 447-7533
Contact: Trust Department

Limitations: Scholarships by nomination only to girls
from the Bennington, VT, area.
Financial data: Year ended 12/31/85. Assets, $924
(M); Total giving, $4,500; Grants to individuals, 9
grants totaling $4,500, high, $700, low, $300, average
grant $500.
Employer Identification Number: 036016072
Applications: Deadline May 1st; **Individual
applications not accepted.**
Program description:
Scholarships are awarded to girls recommended by
Bennington County high schools, who would
otherwise have little opportunity for further education.
All funds are paid directly to the institution.

1050
**Wise (Isadore and Selma) Travel Foundation
  Trust**
c/o Connecticut Bank & Trust Company
P.O. 3334
Hartford, CT 06103

Limitations: Awards for travel-related study to
elementary and high school students residing in
Hartford, CT.
Financial data: Year ended 12/31/85. Assets, $433,234
(M); Total giving, $21,339; Grants to individuals, 1
grant totaling $1,300; 1984, Grants to individuals, 1
grant totaling $3,750.
Employer Identification Number: 066030200
Applications: Program information available in
Hartford schools; Recipient selection determined by
Hartford Board of Education. **Individual applications
not accepted.**
Program description:
The trust makes two types of grants to individuals for
travel-related study. Grants to travel abroad are
awarded to members of the junior class of Hartford,
CT, public schools who have shown a proficiency in
the subject of U.S. history. The second grant is to

students in the sixth grade at Barnard Brown School in
Hartford for one-day trips to New York City and
Plymouth, MA.

COMPANY EMPLOYEE GRANTS

This section covers foundations that made grants directly to employees, former employees, and families of employees of specific companies or corporations. In many cases, these foundations have been established by companies to provide assistance only to their employees. Many, although not all, of these foundations bear the company name; however, in some cases, the foundation offering grants to the employees of a particular company is not sponsored or affiliated with the company at all.

To facilitate access to very different kinds of employee-related assistance, the section is subdivided into two alphabetical listings by foundation name:

● **Educational Support -** includes sources of scholarships and loans for children of company employees. **Not listed in this publication are company-sponsored foundations whose scholarship programs for children of employees are administered by outside organizations such as National Merit Scholarship Program, Citizens' Scholarship Foundation of America or College Scholarship Service, since the selection and grant payment process is carried on independently of the foundation.**

● **General Welfare -** lists sources of all types of grants, loans, and in-kind services provided by foundations on an emergency or long-term basis to employees, former employees, or families of employees for personal, living, or medical expenses.

In addition to offering grants to employees, some of the foundations listed make awards to individuals who reside within the geographic area in which the company operates. No assumption should be made, however, about the willingness of a foundation to make such grants unless this is expressly stated in the entry. In all cases, known restrictions on giving are indicated in the limitations statement.

Entries are arranged alphabetically by foundation name in each subsection. Access to grants by specific subject areas, types of support, and geographic focus is provided in the "Subject," "Types of Support" and "Geographic Focus" indexes in the back of the book.

For a complete alphabetical list of companies for which employee-related grants are available, see the "Company Employee Grants" index in the back of this book.

REMEMBER: IF YOU DON'T QUALIFY, DON'T APPLY.

EDUCATIONAL SUPPORT

1051
Abbott (The Clara) Foundation
Abbott Park
North Chicago, IL 60064   (312) 937-3840
Contact: Herbert S. Wilkinson, Sr., President

Limitations: Scholarship grants and educational loans only to employees or retirees of Abbott Laboratories or members of their families.
Financial data: Year ended 12/31/86. Assets, $70,072,866 (M); Total giving, $2,496,529; Grants to individuals, 520 grants totaling $2,496,529; Subtotal for educational support, 488 scholarships and 120 student loans totaling $1,472,327.
Employer Identification Number: 366069632
Applications: Deadline March 16th for scholarships and May 15th for student loans (only for those currently holding a loan; no new loans are being considered); Completion of formal application required.

1052
Aigner (G.J.) Foundation, Inc.
5617 Dempster Street
Morton Grove, IL 60053   (312) 966-5782
Contact: Craig P. Colmer, Treasurer

Limitations: Scholarships only to children of employees of G.J. Aigner Company.
Financial data: Year ended 4/30/87. Assets, $2,148,295 (M); Total giving, $80,565; Grants to individuals, 28 grants totaling $24,367, high $1,000, low $250, average grant $1,000.
Employer Identification Number: 366055199
Applications: Deadline April 15th; Completion of formal application required.
Publications: Annual report.
Program description:
Scholarships in business, the liberal arts, and theology.

1053
Alcoa Foundation
1501 Alcoa Buiding
Pittsburgh, PA 15219   (412) 533-2348
Contact: Earl L. Gadbery, President

Limitations: Scholarships to children of employees of Aluminum Company of America.
Financial data: Year ended 12/31/86. Assets, $198,592,557 (M); Total giving, $10,507,005; Grants to individuals, 232 grants totaling $469,000; high $8,000, low $500, average grant $1,500.
Employer Identification Number: 251128857
Applications: Applications accepted throughout the year; Initial approach by letter; Interviews required.
Publications: Annual report, application guidelines.

1054
Amax Foundation, Inc,.
Amax Center
Greenwich, CT 06836   (203) 629-6901
Contact: Sonja B. Michaud, President

Limitations: Scholarships only to children of employees of AMAX Inc.
Financial data: Year ended 12/31/86. Assets, $2,942,190 (M); Total giving, $775,208; Grants to individuals, 48 grants totaling $80,550, high $4,000, low $250.
Employer Identification Number: 136111368
Applications: Initial approach by letter.
Publications: Program information, application guidelines.
Program description:
The foundation funds an **Earth Sciences Scholarship Program** for children of AMAX Inc. employees.

1055
Amcast Industrial Foundation
3931 South Dixie Avenue
Kettering, OH 45439   (513) 298-5251
Contact: Thomas G. Amato, Secretary-Treasurer

Limitations: Scholarships to children of employees of Amcast Industrial Corporation in areas of company operations.
Financial data: Year ended 8/31/86. Assets, $775,635 (M); Total giving, $205,332; Grants to individuals, 3 grants totaling $2,500.
Employer Identification Number: 316016458
Applications: Applications accepted throughout the year.

1056
American Express Foundation
American Express Plaza
New York, NY 10004   (212) 640-5661
Contact: Mary Beth Salerno, Secretary

Limitations: Scholarships to children of employees of American Express Company and its subsidiaries.
Financial data: Year ended 12/31/85. Assets, $471,921 (M); Total giving, $9,458,987; Grants to individuals totaling $176,048.
Employer Identification Number: 136123529
Publications: Company report.

1057
American Optical Foundation
American Optical Corporation
14 Mechanic Street, P.O. Box 1
Southbridge, MA 01550   (617) 765-9711
Contact: Stephen B. Lewis

Limitations: Scholarships and student loans only for children of employees of American Optical

Corporation.

Financial data: Year ended 12/31/86. Assets, $547,509 (M); Total giving, $51,780; Grants to individuals amount not specfied.

Employer Identification Number: 046028058

Applications: Deadline April 25th; Completion of formal application required, including two letters of recommendation from teacher and business acquaintances, transcripts, 200 word essay on career objectives, and SAT scores.

1058
AMEV Foundation

One World Trade Center, Suite 5001
New York, NY 10048

Limitations: Scholarships to outstanding students who are the natural or adopted children or economically dependent step-children of employees for at least two years of AMEV Holdings, Inc., or its subsidiaries.

Financial data: Year ended 6/30/86. Assets, $718,000 (M); Total giving, $112,294; Grants to individuals, 25 grants totaling $22,575, high $1,500, low $350, average grant $1,000.

Employer Identification Number: 133156497

Applications: Initial approach by letter requesting application information; Completion of formal application, including applicable transcripts, scores on relevant standardized tests, and at least two recomendations from instructors, required; Interviews required.

Program description:

Most grants will be awarded to students planning to pursue a course of study leading to a baccalaureate degree at an accredited college or university. However, the foundation may also award grants that will enable the recipients to attend private school at the pre-college level, or to pursue a course of graduate study. Scholarship recipients may apply for additional grants from the foundation.

Recipients are chosen by a selection committee based on the following criteria:

A. Prior academic performance

B. Performance on tests designed to measure scholastic abilities and aptitudes

C. At least two recommendations from instructors

D. Conclusions which a selection committee might draw from a personal interview as to applicant's motivation, character, ability and performance.

The number of scholarships to be awarded in any year shall not exceed 25 percent of the number of employees' children who were eligible applicants for such awards and were considered by the various selection committees in choosing the recipients in that year. Payments are made directly to the educational institution in which the recipient is enrolled.

1059
Anderson (John W.) Foundation

402 Wall Street
Valparaiso, IN 46383   (219) 462-4611
Contact: Paul G. Wallace, Secretary

Limitations: Scholarships to children of employees of the Anderson Company in Lake and Porter counties in northwest Indiana.

Financial data: Year ended 12/31/86. Assets, $75,189,273 (M); Total giving, $4,097,229; Grants to individuals totaling $161,652.

Employer Identification Number: 356070695

Applications: Applications accepted throughout the year; Initial approach by letter.

1060
Andrew (Aileen S.) Foundation

10500 West 153rd Street
Orland Park, IL 60462   (312) 349-3300
Contact: Richard L. Dybala, Treasurer

Limitations: Scholarships to children of Andrew Corporation employees and to graduates of a local high school in Orland Park, IL.

Financial data: Year ended 11/30/86. Assets, $16,075,546 (L); Total giving, $1,213,547; Grants to individuals, 101 grants totaling $211,209.

Employer Identification Number: 366049910

Applications: Deadline April 1st; Completion of formal application required

1061
Arctic Education Foundation

P.O. Box 129
Barrow, AK 99723   (907) 852-8633
Contact: Flossie Andersen

Limitations: Scholarships only to shareholders and children of shareholders of Arctic Slope Regional Corporation for postsecondary education leading to a two- or four-year college degree. Acceptance at or enrollment in a postsecondary institution is required before inquiry and application are made.

Financial data: Year ended 6/30/86. Assets, $43,305 (M); Total giving, $151,410; Grants to individuals, 59 grants totaling $151,410, high $7,500, low $150.

Employer Identification Number: 920068447

Applications: Applications accepted throughout the year; Initial approach by letter requesting application; Completion of formal application required.

Publications: Annual report, program information, application guidelines, newsletter.

Program description:

Scholarships are awarded to eligible applicants based on need.

1062
ARW Foundation, The
725 Park Avenue
New York, NY 10021   (212) 772-6110
Contact: Joan Colello, Executive Director

Limitations: Scholarships to children of employees of Pinkerton's, Inc.
Financial data: Year ended 12/31/85. Assets, $9,238,733 (M); Total giving, $351,289; Grants to individuals, 94 grants totaling $342,031, high $14,300, low $1,000, general range $1,000-5,000.
Employer Identification Number: 136206601
Applications: Submit applications in March or October; Initial approach by letter.

1063
Austin Powder Foundation, The
c/o Austin Powder Company
3690 Orange Place
Cleveland, OH 44122   (216) 464-2400
Contact: Dr. Walter S. Nosal, Scholarship Committee

Limitations: Scholarships only for children and wards of full-time employees of the Austin Powder Company.
Financial data: Year ended 12/31/86. Assets, $344 (M); Total giving, $20,700; Grants to individuals, 13 grants totaling $9,750, each grant $750.
Employer Identification Number: 237434692
Applications: Deadline January 15th; Initial approach by letter; Completion of formal application required.
Program description:
Scholarships are awarded for full-time study toward an associate or bachelor's degree at any accredited college or university. Grants range up to a maximum of $1,000 a year, and are renewable. However, fifty percent of the total grant must be repaid at the rate of $25 per month starting one year after leaving college.

1064
Austin Scholarship Foundation
P.O. Box 1360
Greeneville, TN 37743-1360
Contact: John S. Waddle, Jr.

Limitations: Scholarships to children of full-time employees and seasonal employees who have worked at least 10 weeks for five seasons. No restrictions on course of study.
Financial data: Year ended 6/30/86. Assets, $175,174 (M); Total giving, $37,104; Grants to individuals, 68 grants totaling $37,104, high $1,200, low $300, average grant $600.
Employer Identification Number: 237030223
Applications: Applications accepted throughout the year; Completion of formal application required.

1065★
Avon Products Foundation, Inc.
Nine West 57th Street
New York, NY 10019   (212) 546-6731
Contact: Glenn S. Clarke, President

Limitations: Scholarships for children of current Avon Products, Inc. employees and for high school seniors who reside in proximity to an Avon location.
Financial data: Year ended 12/31/87. Assets, $58,000 (M); Total giving, $1,936,000; Grants to individuals, 71 grants totaling $179,285.
Employer Identification Number: 136128447
Applications: Deadline November 2nd; Initial approach by letter; Completion of formal application required.
Publications: Informational brochure, application guidelines.
Program description:
The maximum amount awarded is $3,000 per year for tuition and fees, for four years of undergraduate education. Scholarship payments are made directly to the educational institutions on behalf of the individual recipients.

1066★
Bailey Foundation, The
P.O. Box 1276
Clinton, SC 29325   (803) 833-6830
Contact: H. William Carter, Jr., Administrator

Limitations: Loans and scholarships to children of active or retired employees of Clinton Mills, Inc., its subsidiaries, or M.S. Bailey & Son, Bankers, who have completed two years of continuous service at the time the application is made.
Financial data: Year ended 8/31/87. Assets, $3,827,000 (M); Expenditures, $320,170; Grants to individuals, 14 grants totaling $27,000, general range $4,000-8,000; Loans to individuals, 37 loans totaling $61,387, general range $500-7,000.
Employer Identification Number: 576018387
Applications: Deadline April 15th of the applicant's senior year in high school; Completion of formal application required; Application forms available through personnel officers at Clinton Mills and Bailey Bank.
Program description:
Scholarships are limited to $1,000 per semester for four years; loans are limited to $875 per semester for four years.

1067
BankAmerica Foundation
c/o Bank of America Center
Dept. 3246, P.O. Box 37000
San Francisco, CA 94137   (415) 953-3175
Contact: Caroline O. Boitano, Senior Program Officer

Limitations: Scholarships only to employees and their

families of BankAmerica Corp. and their subsidiaries in areas of company operation including communities in California metropolitan areas nationwide and foreign countries.
Financial data: Year ended 12/31/86. Assets, $2,300,000 (M); Total giving, $5,475,000; Grants to individuals, 368 grants totaling $312,510.
Employer Identification Number: 941670382
Applications: Applications accepted throughout the year; Initial approach by letter.

1068
Barco Employees Educational Trust
c/o Michael C. Ferguson
2168 Shattuck Avenue, No. 300
Berkeley, CA 94704   (415) 548-9005

Limitations: Scholarships only to employees of Barco of California, Inc., and their lineal descendents.
Financial data: Year ended 12/31/86. Assets, $1,644 (M); Total giving, $2,500; Grants to individuals, 3 grants totaling $2,500, high $1,000, low $500.
Employer Identification Number: 510163192
Applications: Applications accepted throughout the year; Initial approach by letter requesting application; Completion of formal application required.

1069
Beech Aircraft Foundation
9709 East Central Avenue
Wichita, KS 67201   (316) 681-8177
Contact: Larry E. Lawrence, Secretary-Treasurer

Limitations: Scholarships only to children of employees of Beech Aircraft Corp. in Kansas.
Financial data: Year ended 9/30/86. Assets, $5,508,000 (M); Total giving, $360,041; Grants to individuals, 41 grants totaling $26,000.
Employer Identification Number: 486125881
Applications: Initial approach by letter or telephone.

1070★
Belden (Joseph C.) Foundation
c/o Belden Wire and Cable, Division of Cooper Industries
2000 South Batavia Avenue
Geneva, IL 60134   (312) 232-8900
Contact: James D. Eaton

Limitations: Undergraduate scholarships limited to children of employees of Belden Corporation.
Financial data: Year ended 12/31/87. Assets, $1,291,000 (M); Total giving, $135,000; Grants to individuals, 57 grants totaling $135,000, high $3,200, low $2,700, average grant $1,650.
Employer Identification Number: 366209342
Applications: Deadline December 31st; Applications accepted from September 1st through December 31st.

1071
Beneficial Foundation, Inc.
1100 Carr Road
P.O. Box 911
Wilmington, DE 19899   (302) 798-0800
Contact: John O. Williams, Vice-President

Limitations: Scholarships to children of employees of affiliated corporations of Beneficial Corporation or of the Beneficial Finance System.
Financial data: Year ended 12/31/86. Assets, $6,156,588 (M); Total giving, $546,422; Grants to individuals, 312 grants totaling $218,423.
Employer Identification Number: 516011637
Applications: Deadline December 1st; Initial approach by letter; Completion of formal application required.

1072★
Berwind (Charles G.) Foundation
3000 Centre Square West
1500 Market Street
Philadelphia, PA 19102   (215) 563-2800
Contact: Betty A. Olund, Administrator

Limitations: Scholarships to children of Berwind Corporation employees. Occasional scholarships made to residents of areas of company operations.
Financial data: Year ended 9/30/87. Assets, $983,902 (M); Total giving, $44,800; Grants to individuals, 15 grants totaling $44,800, high $7,300, low $500, general range $1,000-5,000.
Employer Identification Number: 237382896
Applications: Deadline November 30th; Completion of formal application required.
Program description:
Scholarships for undergraduate study are available to high school students or graduates who are children of active, deceased, or retired employees of at least one year's employment with Berwind Corporation or its subsidiaries. Consideration is also given to applicants planning to attend junior colleges, graduate schools, and professional schools. Occasionally, the Selection Committee has publicly invited applications from residents of communities in which a Berwind facility is located, but who are not related to a Berwind employee.

1073
Bibb Foundation, Inc., The
P.O. Box 4207
Macon, GA 31208   (912) 743-3731
Contact: Allan V. Davis, President

Limitations: Scholarships only to employees of The Bibb Company or their children.
Financial data: Year ended 8/31/86. Assets, $1,801,682 (M); Total giving, $95,458; Grants to individuals, 110 grants totaling $71,208, high $2,000, low $100.
Employer Identification Number: 580566140

Applications: Deadline April 30th; Completion of formal application required; Interviews required.
Publications: Program information.

1074
Binswanger (S.E.) Memorial Fund Inc.
P.O. Box 171173
Memphis, TN 38117-1173   (901) 767-7111
Contact: Regina Sisson, c/o Binswanger Glass Company, 965 Ridge Lake Boulevard, Memphis, TN 38117

Limitations: Scholarships to children of employees of Binswanger Glass Company.
Financial data: Year ended 10/31/86. Assets, $253,509 (M); Total giving, $9,900; Grants to individuals, 17 grants totaling $9,900, high $1,500, low $300, general range $200-400, average grant $300.
Employer Identification Number: 546038777
Applications: Deadline April 15th; Completion of formal application, including current transcript, required.
Program description:
Scholarship selection criteria are financial need, grades, attitude, leadership ability, and extracurricular activities.

1075
Blank (Samuel A.) Scholarship Fund
c/o Jeffrey Blank
300 Jenkintown Commons
Jenkintown, PA 19046
Contact: Ruth S. Blank, Trustee or Robert S. Blank, Trustee

Limitations: Scholarships only to children of employees of Continental Bank, Philadelphia, PA.
Financial data: Year ended 11/30/85. Assets, $203,726 (M); Total giving $10,782; Grants to individuals, 33 grants totaling $10,782, high $1,000, low $87, general range $150-500.
Employer Identification Number: 237404722
Program description:
Scholarships are awarded on an objective, nondiscriminatory basis.

1076
Block (The H&R) Foundation
4410 Main Street
Kansas City, MO 64111   (816) 932-8424
Contact: Terrence R. Ward, Vice-President

Limitations: Scholarships only to children of employees of H&R Block, Inc. residing in the 50-mile area around Kansas City, MO, including Kansas.
Financial data: Year ended 12/31/86. Assets, $9,451,516 (M); Total giving, $534,878; Grants to individuals, 35 grants totaling $70,000.
Employer Identification Number: 237378232

Publications: Annual report.

1077
Bohemia Foundation, Inc.
2280 Oakmont Way
Eugene, OR 97401
Contact: Ms. Ardis Hughes, Bohemia Inc., P.O. Box 1819, Eugene, OR 97440

Limitations: Scholarships only to entry-level college students who are employees of Bohemia, Inc., or their children.
Financial data: Year ended 12/31/86. Assets, $42,386 (M); Total giving, $5,500; Grants to individuals, 5 grants totaling $5,000, each grant $1,000.
Employer Identification Number: 936037881
Applications: Deadline April 15th; Initial approach by letter; Completion of formal application required.

1078
Boston Globe Foundation, The
The Boston Globe Building
Boston, MA 02107   (617) 929-2895
Contact: George M. Collins, Jr., Executive Director

Limitations: Scholarships to employees of Affiliated Publications, Inc. and its subsidiaries, their families, and to residents in the area of company operations of metropolitan Boston, MA.
Financial data: Year ended 11/30/86. Assets, $2,737,707 (M); Total giving, $2,716,426; Grants to individuals, 9 grants totaling $10,150, high $2,500, low $750.
Employer Identification Number: 042731195
Publications: Annual report.
Program description:
The foundation's scholarship programs include the L.L. Winship Scholarship, the Frank Freitas Awards, the I. Arthur Siegel Scholarship, and the Boston Globe Cooperative Student Scholarships. The foundation also makes educational grants to winners in the Globe-sponsored Science Fairs, Scholastic Art Awards, and Globe Interscholastic Drama Festival.

Information about these programs is available and the foundation staff will aid Globe employees to contact its scholarship committees.

1079★
Briggs & Stratton Corporation Foundation, Inc.
12301 West Wirth Street
Wauwatosa, WI 53222   (414) 259-5333
Contact: K.K. Preston, Secretary-Treasurer

Limitations: Scholarships only to children of employees of the Briggs & Stratton Corporation, Inc.
Financial data: Year ended 11/30/87. Assets, $3,753,370 (M); Total giving, $680,200; Grants to individuals, 38 grants totaling $36,000.
Employer Identification Number: 396040377

Applications: Deadline January 31st; Interviews required.
Program description:
Ten four-year scholarships are awarded each year. Applicant's parent must have been a company employee for two years as of the January 1st prior to the deadline.

1080★
Brother John Memorial Scholarship Fund
c/o Mont La Salle Vineyards
100 South St. Helena Highway, P.O. Box 391
St. Helena, CA 94574   (707) 963-4480
Contact: Helen Serna, Coordinator

Limitations: Scholarships to children of employees of Mont La Salle Vineyards.
Financial data: Year ended 3/31/87. Assets, $6,924 (M); Total giving, $2,700; Grants to individuals, 8 grants totaling $2,700, high $600, low $300.
Employer Identification Number: 237076185
Applications: Deadline December 1st; Completion of formal application and a copy of current school record required.
Program description:
Applicants must be Mont La Salle Vineyards employees' children who are high school seniors ranking in upper 50 percent of class or currently enrolled in an accredited four-year college, university, or a junior college in the U.S. Applicant's parent(s) must be employed by Mont La Salle Vineyards at the time of application, and have been so employed for at least two full years.

1081
Brown Brothers Harriman & Company Undergraduate Fund, The
59 Wall Street
New York, NY 10005   (212) 483-1818
Contact: Personnel Department, Brown Brothers Harriman & Company

Limitations: Scholarships only to children of employees of The Brown Brothers Harriman & Company.
Financial data: Year ended 7/31/86. Assets, $591,036 (M); Total giving, $20,100; Grants to individuals, 20 grants totaling $20,100, high $1,500, low $125, general range $250-1,500.
Employer Identification Number: 136169140
Applications: Deadline November 1st; Completion of formal application required.
Program description:
Awards are based on the scholastic ability and financial need of each candidate.

1082
Bruder (Michael A.) Foundation
600 Reed Road
P.O. Box 600
Broomall, PA 19008

Limitations: Scholarships only to children of employees of M.A. Bruder and Sons, Inc.
Financial data: Year ended 12/31/85. Assets, $761,680 (M); Total giving, $121,300; Grants to individuals, 7 grants totaling $13,500, high $2,700, low $900.
Employer Identification Number: 236298481

1083★
Brunswick Foundation, Inc., The
One Brunswick Plaza
Skokie, IL 60077   (312) 470-4646
Contact: Wendy L. Fuhs, Director

Limitations: Scholarships only to children of full-time Brunswick Corporation employees who have at least one year of service prior to application due date.
Financial data: Year ended 12/31/87. Assets, $6,500,000 (M); Grants to individuals, 121 grants totaling $244,375, high $2,000, low $875, general range $1,500-2,000, average grant $2,000.
Employer Identification Number: 366033576
Applications: Deadline May 1st; Contact parents' Brunswick personnel office for application; Completion of formal application required; Application to be accompanied by copy of current transcript.
Publications: Application guidelines.
Program description:
The foundation awards four-year scholarships to graduating high school seniors ($7,000 maximum), college undergraduate scholarships ($5,250 maximum) to students who have completed at least one year of college, scholarships to handicapped students ($4,500 maximum, no age or disability limit), and scholarships for minority students. All students must meet eligibility requirements as stated in the limitation statement.

1084★
Butler Manufacturing Company Foundation
P.O. Box 419917
Kansas City, MO 64141-0197   (816) 968-3208
Contact: Barbara Lee Fay, Foundation Administrator

Limitations: Scholarships only for children of Butler Manufacturing Company employees.
Financial data: Year ended 12/31/87. Assets, $3,332,888 (M); Total giving, $93,960; Grants to individuals, 42 grants totaling $67,000; Subtotal for scholarships, 39 grants totaling $61,000.
Employer Identification Number: 440663648
Applications: Deadline March 1st; Initial approach by January 15th; Completion of formal application required; Interviews required.
Publications: Application guidelines, program

information.
Program description:
The foundation provides up to 32 scholarships
annually in the amount of $2,000. An independent
committee of educators and professionals recommends
eight new scholarship winners each year, selected on
the basis of academic achievement, need, character,
and future promise. Scholarships are continued over a
four-year period of study leading to a baccalaureate
degree at an accredited college or university,
providing the student performs in the upper half of the
class academically, maintains conduct acceptable to
the school and to the foundation, and carries a normal
academic load.

1085
Caldwell (James R.) Scholarship Fund
c/o Wayne County National Bank
Public Square, Box 550
Wooster, OH 44691   (216) 264-1222

Limitations: Scholarships only to children of
Rubbermaid, Inc., employees who are full-time and
have at least two years of service with the company.
Applicants must be in the top one-third of their class.
Children of officers of Rubbermaid, Inc., and its
subsidiaries are not eligible.
Financial data: Year ended 12/31/86. Assets, $294,045
(M); Total giving, $17,175; Grants to individuals, 14
grants totaling $17,175, high $2,000, low $1,000.
Employer Identification Number: 346525539
Applications: Deadline March 15th; Initial approach
by postcard requesting application to fund c/o
Rubbermaid, Inc., 1147 Akron Road, Wooster, OH
44691; Tel.: (216) 264-6464; Completion of formal
application required.
Publications: Annual report, program information,
application guidelines.

1086
Carnation Company Scholarship Foundation
5045 Wilshire Boulevard
Los Angeles, CA 90036   (213) 932-6282
Contact: Board of Advisors

Limitations: Scholarships for higher education to
relatives of Carnation Company employees on the
basis of academic merit and financial need.
Financial data: Year ended 12/31/86. Assets,
$3,618,912 (M); Total giving, $188,850; Grants to
individuals, 120 grants totaling $188,850, high
$3,225, low $750, general range $1,000-2,000.
Employer Identification Number: 956118622
Applications: Deadline February 15th; Completion of
formal application required, accompanied by personal
references and college transcripts.

1087
Carter (Amon G.) Star Telegram Employees Fund
400 West Seventh Street
Fort Worth, TX 76102   (817) 332-3535
Contact: Nenetta Tatum, President

Limitations: Scholarships only to children of
employees of the Fort Worth Star-Telegram, KXAS-TV
and WBAP-Radio.
Financial data: Year ended 4/30/86. Assets,
$11,228,488 (M); Total giving, $508,015; Grants to
individuals, 83 grants totaling $235,376; Subtotal for
scholarships, 22 grants totaling $60,000, high $3,000,
low $1,500.
Employer Identification Number: 756014850
Applications: Applications accepted throughout the
year; Initial approach by letter.

1088
Central National Gottesman Foundation, The
100 Park Avenue
New York, NY 10017
Contact: Harold R. Doughty, Central National
Gottesman Foundation, Cooper Station, P.O. Box 909,
New York, N.Y. 10276

Limitations: Scholarships for children of employees of
Central National Corporation, Gottesman & Co., Inc.
for Central National-Gottesman Foundation.
Financial data: Year ended 12/31/85. Assets,
$2,963,759 (M); Total giving, $92,527; Grants to
individuals, 11 grants totaling $43,227, high $8,820,
low $516.
Employer Identification Number: 133047546
Applications: Deadlines vary with academic year;
Contact foundation for current application deadline;
Completion of formal application required.

1089
Central Newspapers Foundation
307 North Pennsylvania Street
Indianapolis, IN 46204

Limitations: Scholarships to children of employees
who have been in continuous employment of
newspapers affiliated with Central Newspapers, Inc.,
for a minimum of three years at the time of student's
application.
Financial data: Year ended 4/30/87. Assets, $179,480
(M); Total giving, $195,615; Grants to individuals, 57
grants totaling $102,500, high $2,000, low, $500.
Employer Identification Number: 356013720
Applications: Deadline mid-February; Completion of
formal application required; Applications processed
first through Personnel Department.
Program description:
Selection is on a competitive basis by a panel of
admission directors.

1090★
Chase Manhattan Foundation, The
(Formerly Chase Manhattan International Foundation, The)
Chase Manhattan Bank
One Chase Manhattan Plaza
New York, NY 10081   (212) 676-5080
Contact: David S. Ford, Secretary

Limitations: Scholarships only to children of employees of The Chase Manhattan Bank.
Financial data: Year ended 12/31/87. Assets, $2,366,004 (M); Total giving, $2,074,000; Grants to individuals, 8 grants totaling $120,000, each grant $15,000.
Employer Identification Number: 237049738
Applications: Applications accepted throughout the year; Completion of formal application required.
Publications: Annual report.

1091
Chatham Foundation, Inc.
c/o Chatham Manufacturing Company
3100 Glen Avenue
Elkin, NC 28621   (919) 723-7802
Contact: David H. Cline, Secretary-Treasurer

Limitations: Scholarships to children of employees of Chatham Manufacturing Company for college education.
Financial data: Year ended 12/31/86. Assets, $1,640,272 (M); Total giving, $30,550; Grants to individuals, 12 grants totaling $15,750, high $1,500, low $750, average grant $1,500.
Employer Identification Number: 560771852
Applications: Applications accepted throughout the year; Completion of formal application required.
Program description:
Applicants must be high school seniors who will graduate in the Spring, must meet entrance requirements of an accredited college or university, and cannot be married.

1092
Chubb Foundation
15 Mountain View Road
P.O. Box 1615
Warren, NJ 07060   (201) 580-3570
Contact: Alice Billick, Secretary

Limitations: Scholarships only to qualified relatives of employees of the Chubb Group Insurance Company, including Chubb and Son, Inc., the Colonial Life Insurance Company of America and the Chubb Corporation.
Financial data: Year ended 12/31/85. Assets, $7,011,986 (M); Total giving, $198,956; Grants to individuals totaling $198,956.
Employer Identification Number: 226058567
Applications: Deadline December 15th; Application

information available from all branches and affiliated companies; Completion of formal application required; Application should include name, home address and zip code; whether student is presently attending high school or college and in what class; employee information - name and relationship to student, employer branch, and date of employment.

1093
Circuit City Foundation
2040 Thalbro Street
Richmond, VA 23230

Limitations: Scholarships to children of employees of Wards Company, Inc., and Circuit City Stores, Inc.
Financial data: Year ended 2/28/87. Assets, $35,293 (M); Total giving, $562,996; Grants to individuals, 49 grants totaling $39,500, high $1,000, low $500.
Employer Identification Number: 546048660

1094★
Citizens and Southern National Bank of South Carolina Foundation
1801 Main Street
Columbia, SC 29222   (803) 765-8251
Contact: Betty Davenport, Secretary

Limitations: Scholarships only to children of employees of Citizens and Southern South Carolina Corporation.
Financial data: Year ended 12/31/87. Assets, $612,879 (M); Total giving, $611,424; Grants to individuals, 15 grants totaling $44,299, high $4,000, low $1,000.
Employer Identification Number: 576024906
Applications: Applications accepted throughout the year; Initial approach by letter.

1095
Comstock (James A.) Memorial Scholarship Trust
c/o Norstar Trust Company
One East Avenue
Rochester, NY 14638
Contact: Joan Edwards, c/o Norstar Trust Company, Wellsville, NY 14895; Tel.: (716) 593-2650

Limitations: Scholarships to children of employees of Acme Electric Company.
Financial data: Year ended 5/31/86. Assets, $1,355,102 (M); Total giving, $101,522; Grants to individuals, 24 grants totaling $50,761, high $3,869, low $875.
Employer Identification Number: 222327403
Applications: Deadline January 31st; Completion of formal application required.

1096
Conwed Foundation
620 Taft Street, N.E.
Minneapolis, MN 55413

Limitations: Scholarships only to children of employees of the Conwed Corporation.
Financial data: Year ended 11/30/86. Assets, $320,309 (M); Total giving, $149,746; Grants to individuals totaling $17,946.
Employer Identification Number: 416038506
Applications: Deadline July 1st.

1097★
Cooper Industries Foundation
First City Tower, Suite 4000
P.O. Box 4446
Houston, TX 77210   (713) 739-5632
Contact: Patricia B. Mottram, Secretary

Limitations: Scholarships only to children of employees of Cooper Industries, Inc. in AL, CA, CT, GA, IL, IN, ME, MI, MO, MS, NJ, NY, NC, OH, OK, PA, SC, TN, TX and VA.
Financial data: Year ended 12/31/87. Assets, $3,852,267 (M); Total giving, $2,046,589; Grants to individuals, 7 grants totaling $10,675.
Employer Identification Number: 316060698
Applications: Applications accepted throughout the year; Initial approach by letter.

1098
CPC Educational Foundation
International Plaza
P.O. Box 8000
Englewood Cliffs, NJ 07632   (201) 894-2249
Contact: Linda Salcito

Limitations: Undergraduate scholarships only to children of past and present employees of CPC International Inc., including its domestic and international subsidiaries. Preference is given to the children of deceased or disabled employees.
Financial data: Year ended 11/30/86. Assets, $2,592,333 (M); Total giving, $149,733; Grants to individuals, 72 grants totaling $149,733, high $8,000, low $200.
Employer Identification Number: 136103949
Applications: Submit applications between August 30th and November 30th; Completion of formal application required.
Publications: Application guidelines, program information.
Program description:
Applicants may be current high school seniors or undergraduate students. Scholarships may be renewed upon submission of renewal application.
   For first-time applicants, the selection committee shall consider the following:
   ● Prior academic performance

● SAT (or equivalent) test scores
● Character and potential, as reflected by applicant's statements, recommendations, and other objective factors
● Financial need.
   With respect to renewal applicants, a grant will be continued if the applicant's prior performance is satisfactory, personal financial resources have not significantly increased, and the applicant has fulfilled all requirements of the selection committee.
   New scholarships may not exceed either 25 percent of the number of eligible new applications received for the year or ten percent of the children who are eligible to apply (e.g., those who are qualified and could be expected to attend college).
   Scholarship payments are made directly to the educational institution, with possible exceptions made in the case of foreign institutions.

1099
Cranston Foundation, The
c/o Administrator
1381 Cranston Street
Cranston, RI 02920   (401) 943-4800

Limitations: Scholarships for two years only to children of employees, but not directors or officers, of the Cranston Print Works Company, its divisions or subsidiaries.
Financial data: Year ended 6/30/86. Assets, $613,691 (M); Total giving, $220,643; Grants to individuals, 32 grants totaling $54,933, high $5,480, low $51, average grant $2,000.
Employer Identification Number: 056015348
Applications: Deadline April 15th.

1100★
Credithrift Financial-Richard E. Meier
Foundation, Inc.
P.O. Box 59
Evansville, IN 47701   (812) 424-8031
Contact: Norb Devine, Vice-President, Administration

Limitations: Four scholarships awarded to children of employees of Credithrift Financial Corp. and their subsidiaries.
Financial data: Year ended 12/31/87. Assets, $1,592,886 (M); Total giving, $216,135; Grants to individuals, 15 grants totaling $45,000.
Employer Identification Number: 356042566
Applications: Applications accepted throughout the year; Initial approach by letter.
Publications: Application guidelines.

1101★
Crosset Family Fund

(Formerly Crosset Charitable Trust, The)
205 Central Avenue
Cincinnati, OH 45202
Contact: Richard B. Crosset, Trustee

Limitations: Scholarships and student loans to children of employees of The Crosset Company, Inc.
Financial data: Year ended 12/31/86. Assets, $3,873,611 (M); Total giving, $224,898; Grants to individuals, 14 grants totaling $7,285, high $625, low $385.
Employer Identification Number: 316037727
Applications: Completion of formal application required; Applicants must submit SAT or ACT scores, record of high school grades, and an itemized budget project for ensuring year's education; Two letters of recommendation as to student's character, abilities, and interests are required.
Program description:
Applicants must: be children of persons who have been employed by The Crosset Company, Inc. for at least one year; graduate from accredited high schools in the upper half of their classes; be seeking at least a bachelor degree; be unable to attend college without outside financial aid; have no sibling already receiving aid from the foundation.

Payments will be awarded directly to the educational institution. Scholarships are awarded during the second semester of the student's senior year. Scholarships are renewable.

The program is not available to the children of officers, directors, shareholders, or those related by marriage. Unsuccessful applicants for the scholarship program may apply to the foundation for a student loan.

1102
Crownlet Foundation, Inc.

225 Park Avenue South
New York, NY 10003
Contact: Nadine Balgley, Crown Publishers, Inc., 34 Englehard Avenue, Avenel, NJ 07001

Limitations: Scholarships only to children of employees who are working or have worked for Crown Publishers, Inc., or Outlet Book Company, Inc.
Financial data: Year ended 12/31/85. Assets, $3,119 (M); Total giving, $61,145; Grants to individuals, 8 grants totaling $56,446, high $14,540, low $1,267.
Employer Identification Number: 237421901
Applications: Applications accepted throughout the year.

1103★
CTS Foundation

905 North West Boulevard
Elkhart, IN 46514   (219) 293-7511

Limitations: Interest-free student loans for undergraduate education to employees and children of employees of the CTS Corporation and its subsidiaries.
Financial data: Year ended 6/30/87. Assets, $2,266,280 (M); Expenditures, $97,358; Loans to individuals, 377 loans totaling $862,561.
Employer Identification Number: 356014484
Applications: Deadline prior to beginning of school term; Completion of formal application required.

1104
Cummins Engine Foundation

MC 60814
500 Jackson Street
Columbus, IN 47201   (812) 377-3114
Contact: Adele J. Vincent, Associate Director, Box 3005, MC 60814, Columbus, IN 47202-3005

Limitations: Scholarships only to children of employees of Cummins Engine Company, Inc.
Financial data: Year ended 12/31/86. Assets, $8,904,603 (M); Total giving, $3,479,026; Grants to individuals, 76 grants totaling $76,551.
Employer Identification Number: 356042373
Applications: Applications distributed internally.
Program description:
The **Cummins Sons and Daughters Scholarship Program** gives four-year awards on a competitive basis to eligible high school seniors or first year college students pursuing undergraduate education.

1105
Dan River Foundation

P.O. Box 261
Danville, VA 24541
Contact: Chairman, Scholarship Committee, Dan River Foundation, P.O. Box 2178, Danville, VA 24541; Tel.: (804) 799-7384.

Limitations: Scholarships to employees, or children of current, deceased, or retired employees of Dan River Inc. in New York, Virginia, or South Carolina.
Financial data: Year ended 12/31/86. Assets, $2,121,763 (M); Total giving, $177,931; Grants to individuals, 3 grants totaling $4,586, high $2,141, low $750.
Employer Identification Number: 546036112
Applications: Deadline last day of February; Initial approach by letter; Completion of formal application required; Interviews required.

1106
Daniel Foundation of South Carolina, The
P.O. Box 9278
Greenville, SC 29604-9278
Contact: Barbara C. Lewis, Secretary-Treasurer

Limitations: Scholarships only to children of employees of Daniel International Corporation.
Financial data: Year ended 12/31/86. Assets, $10,124,242 (M); Total giving, $322,805; Grants to individuals totaling $46,000.
Employer Identification Number: 570673409
Applications: Deadline March 31st; Completion of formal application required.
Program description:
Scholarships are available to children of active or retired employees of Daniel International Corporation and its subsidiaries. Active employees must have been employed at least one year by March 31st of the year of award. Retired employees must be retired under a retirement plan of the corporation or subsidiary.

1107★
DeLong (James E.) Foundation, Inc.
c/o Waukesha Engine Division
1000 West St. Paul Avenue
Waukesha, WI 53188   (414) 549-2773
Contact: Selection Committee on Scholarships, c/o President, Carroll College, 100 North East Avenue, Waukesha, WI 53186; Tel.: (414) 547-1211

Limitations: Scholarships only to children of employees of the Waukesha Engine Division.
Financial data: Year ended 9/30/87. Assets, $128,391 (M): Total giving, $15,000; Grants to individuals, 10 grants totaling $15,000, each grant $1,500.
Employer Identification Number: 396050331
Applications: Deadline first Monday in April; Application forms available from the Waukesha Engine Division; School sends completed application to contact address; Completion of College Boards or ACT required.
Program description:
Two new scholarship recipients are selected each year. Awards are four-year scholarships of $1,500 per year. Applicants must be son or daughter (natural, adopted, or living with an employee as part of household) of an active employee at Waukesha Engine Divisions (any brand or plant) and a senior in high school who ranks scholastically in the upper quartile of the class.

1108
Dettman (Leroy E.) Foundation, Inc.
108 Southeast Eighth Avenue
Fort Lauderdale, FL 33301   (305) 525-6102
Contact: Gregory L. Dettman, Secretary

Limitations: Scholarships primarily to temporary employees (and their children) of Personnel Pool of America, but others may be considered.
Financial data: Year ended 10/31/86. Assets, $2,975,725 (M); Total giving, $173,511; Grants to individuals, 64 grants totaling $110,500, high $3,000, low $500, general range $500-2,000.
Employer Identification Number: 591784551
Applications: Deadline March 15th; Initial approach by letter; Completion of application form required.
Publications: Application guidelines.

1109
DeVlieg (The Charles B. and Charles R.) Foundation
c/o DeVlieg Machine Company
Fair Street
Royal Oak, MI 48068   (313) 280-1100
Contact: H.A. Beyer, Jr., Vice-President

Limitations: Scholarships only to employees of the DeVlieg Machine Company.
Financial data: Year ended 12/31/86. Assets, $2,604,007 (M); Total giving, $222,640; Grants to individuals totaling $10,000.
Employer Identification Number: 386075696
Applications: Applications accepted throughout the year; Completion of formal application required.

1110
Disney Foundation
500 South Buena Vista Street
Burbank, CA 91521   (213) 840-1000
Contact: Doris A. Smith, Secretary

Limitations: Undergraduate scholarships only to children of employees of Walt Disney Productions and its subsidiaries or affiliated companies.
Financial data: Year ended 9/30/86. Assets, $72,184 (M); Total giving, $1,029,164; Grants to individuals, 53 grants totaling $162,479.
Employer Identification Number: 956037079
Applications: Deadline October 1st; Completion of formal application required.
Publications: Application guidelines.
Program description:
Applicant must be a high school senior in the upper one-third of his or her graduating class. Applicant's parent must be a full-time regular employee of Walt Disney Productions or its subsidiaries or affiliated companies on October 1st of the year in which application is made and, on the date on which the scholarship is awarded, must have completed one year of continuous employment service with the company, and must be a resident or citizen of the U.S.

Recipients of scholarships are selected on the basis of SAT results, detailed scholastic and other information obtained from the Educational Testing Service, and other available indications of citizenship, leadership, achievement, and college and career potential.

Scholarship grants are paid directly to the college or university and are continued through normal four-year period of college undergraduate studies, subject to compliance by the grantee with all the terms and conditions of the scholarship program.

1111
Downs Foundation, The
P.O. Box 475
Davisville Road and Turnpike Drive
Willow Grove, PA 19090   (215) 672-1100
Contact: T. George Downs, Trustee

Limitations: Scholarships limited to children of full-time employees of Downs Carpet Company, Inc.
Financial data: Year ended 12/31/86. Assets, $1,231,685 (M); Total giving, $64,090; Grants to individuals, 2 grants totaling $3,540.
Employer Identification Number: 236257328
Applications: Initial approach by letter.

1112★
Dyco Foundation, The
1100 Interchange Tower
Minneapolis, MN 55426   (612) 545-4021
Contact: Alicia E. Ringstad, Director

Limitations: Scholarships to children of employees of Dyco Petroleum Corporation, which has operations in the Minneapolis-St. Paul, MN, area, and Tulsa and Elk City, OK.
Financial data: Year ended 12/31/87. Assets, $1,001,193 (M); Total giving, $114,275; Grants to individuals, 5 grants totaling $8,500, high $2,000, low $1,000, average grant $1,700.
Employer Identification Number: 411390020
Applications: Deadline March 30th; Completion of formal application required.
Publications: Company report (including application guidelines), 990-PF printed copy available upon request.
Program description:
The **Robert H. Johnson Scholarship Program** awards scholarships for postsecondary education to sons and daughters of Dyco Petroleum Corporation employees.

1113★
Eder (The Sidney and Arthur) Foundation, Inc.
c/o Awards Committee
P.O. Box 949
New Haven, CT 06504   (203) 934-8381

Limitations: Undergraduate scholarships to children of present or former employees of Eder Brothers, Inc.
Financial data: Year ended 12/31/87. Assets, $3,510,829 (M); Total giving, $257,463; Grants to individuals, 15 grants totaling $29,050, high $4,500, low $250.
Employer Identification Number: 066035306

Applications: Contact foundation for current application deadline; Initial approach by letter; Completion of formal application required; Interviews required.

1114
Educational Fund for Children of Phillips Petroleum Company Employees
180 Plaza Office Building
Bartlesville, OK 74004   (918) 661-4087
Contact: Bill Dausses, Administrator

Limitations: Scholarships only for high school seniors who are children of present or deceased full-time employees of Phillips Petroleum Company, employed for at least two years (three years in the case of deceased employees).
Financial data: Year ended 8/31/86. Assets, $492,793 (M); Total giving, $264,000; Grants to individuals, 338 grants totaling $264,000, high $2,500, low $250, average grant $1,000.
Employer Identification Number: 736095141
Applications: Deadline March 7th; Completion of formal application required.
Program description:
The fund makes awards of $1,000 per year for four years. Students apply in their senior high school year.

1115
Emerson Charitable Trust
c/o Emerson Electric Company
8000 West Florissant Avenue, P.O. Box 4100
St. Louis, MO 63136   (314) 553-2000
Contact: R. W. Staley, Executive Vice-President, Emerson Electric Company

Limitations: Scholarships only to children of employees of Emerson Electric Company.
Financial data: Year ended 9/30/86. Assets, $1,281,683 (M); Total giving, $4,923,769; Grants to individuals, 206 grants totaling $116,625, general range, $500-625.
Employer Identification Number: 526200123
Applications: Employees are notified directly when and how to apply.

1116
Ensign-Bickford Foundation, Inc., The
660 Hopmeadow Street
Simsbury, CT 06070   (203) 658-4411
Contact: Linda M. Walsh, Secretary

Limitations: Scholarships to children of employees of Ensign-Bickford Industries, Inc.
Financial data: Year ended 12/31/85. Assets, $98,104 (M); Total giving, $231,104; Grants to individuals, 16 grants totaling $23,400, high $5,250, low $500.
Employer Identification Number: 066041097

Applications: Applications accepted throughout the year; Initial approach by letter.

1117
Ettinger Foundation, Inc., The
420 Lexington Avenue, Room 2320
New York, NY 10170
Contact: Richard P. Ettinger, Jr., President

Limitations: Scholarships to children of employees of Prentice-Hall, Inc.
Financial data: Year ended 12/31/86. Assets, $10,914,535 (M); Total giving, $197,500; Grants to individuals amount not specified, average grant $2,000.
Employer Identification Number: 066038938
Applications: Applications accepted throughout the year; Initial approach by letter.

1118
Evans (D.A. & J.A.) Memorial Foundation
Robert Barensfeld
Ellwood City Forge Corporation
Ellwood City, PA 16117   (412) 752-0055

Limitations: Scholarships to children of employees of Ellwood City Corporation.
Financial data: Year ended 12/31/86. Assets, $271,442 (M); Total giving, $27,642; Grants to individuals totaling $25,142.
Employer Identification Number: 256032325

1119
Evans Products Company Foundation
6917 Collins Avenue
Miami Beach, FL 33141   (305) 866-7771

Limitations: Scholarships to children of employees of Evans Products Company or its affiliates and subsidiaries.
Financial data: Year ended 6/30/86. Assets, $4,598 (M); Total giving, $0; 1985, Grants to individuals, 9 grants totaling $25,720, average grant $2,500.
Employer Identification Number: 936032343
Applications: Deadlines January 1st of junior year in high school for Merit Scholarship, February 15th of senior year in high school for Financial Aid Scholarships; Completion of formal application required.
Program description:
Scholarship payments are made directly to the educational institution on behalf of the individual recipient.

1120
Evinrude (The Ole) Foundation
100 Sea Horse Drive
Waukegan, IL 60085   (312) 689-5235
Contact: F. James Short, Vice-President

Limitations: Undergraduate scholarships to children of employees of Outboard Marine Corporation in Wisconsin, Illinois, Tennesee, Mississippi, North Carolina, Georgia and Nebraska only.
Financial data: Year ended 9/30/87. Assets, $795,437 (M); Total giving, $155,337; Grants to individuals, 33 grants totaling $33,000, high $1,000, low $500.
Employer Identification Number: 396037139
Applications: Deadline October 31st; Initial approach by letter.
Publications: Annual report.

1121★
Fairchild Industries Foundation, Inc.
P.O. Box 10803
Chantilly, VA 22021-9998
Contact: John D. Jackson, President

Limitations: Scholarships only to children of employees of Fairchild Industries, Inc. and its subsidiaries.
Financial data: Year ended 12/31/87. Assets, $350,000 (M); Total giving, $197,040; Grants to individuals, 27 grants totaling $27,375, high $2,500, low $1,000.
Employer Identification Number: 526043638
Applications: Applications accepted throughout the year; Initial approach by letter.

1122★
Fansteel Scholarship Foundation
One Tantalum Place
North Chicago, IL 60064   (312) 689-4900
Contact: MaryAnn Maki

Limitations: Scholarships limited to children or, in limited cases, grandchildren of Fansteel employees, retirees, or deceased employees.
Financial data: Year ended 12/31/86. Assets, $136,298 (M); Total giving, $37,750; Grants to individuals, 18 grants totaling $37,750, high $3,000, low $1,000, general range $1,000-1,500.
Employer Identification Number: 362614698
Applications: Deadline April 8th; Completion of formal application including parent's confidential statement, high school counselor's report, transcripts, SAT and ACT scores required.
Program description:
The maximum scholarship grant awarded by the foundation is $3,000.

1123
Fieldcrest Foundation

326 East Stadium Drive
Eden, NC 27288 (919) 627-3126
Contact: Calvin Barnhardt, c/o Fieldcrest Cannon, Inc., General Office, Eden, NC 27288; Tel.: (919) 627-3046

Limitations: Scholarships limited to children of employees of Fieldcrest Mills, Inc.
Financial data: Year ended 12/31/86. Assets, $1,429,797 (M); Total giving, $434,598; Grants to individuals amount not specified.
Employer Identification Number: 566046659
Applications: Deadline May 1st.

1124
Flynn Foundation

80 Boston Street
Salem, MA 01970 (617) 745-4000

Limitations: Scholarships for undergraduate study, including grants to children and other relatives of employees of John Flynn and Sons, Inc., and children of employees of Pownal Tanning Co., Inc.
Financial data: Year ended 6/30/86. Assets, $351,779 (M); Total giving, $44,747; Grants to individuals, 14 grants totaling $36,302, high $7,900, low $58.
Employer Identification Number: 046040377

1125
Founder's Memorial Fund of the American Sterilizer Co.

2222 West Grandview Boulevard
Erie, PA 16509

Limitations: Scholarships to dependents of employees of the American Sterilizer Co.
Financial data: Year ended 12/31/86. Assets, $1,696,154 (M); Total giving, $171,762; Grants to individuals, 16 grants totaling $5,627, high $1,322, low $36.
Employer Identification Number: 256062068

1126
Fox Educational Foundation

P.O. Box 29, Rehoboth Valley
Belle Vernon, PA 15012 (412) 929-7800
Contact: Raphael D. Niccolai, Trustee

Limitations: Student loans to active or former employees and their children of Fox Industries or affiliated retailers.
Financial data: Year ended 12/31/86. Assets, $148,872 (M); Expenditures, $9,600; Loans to individuals, 8 loans totaling $9,600, each loan $1,200.
Employer Identification Number: 256064976
Applications: Deadline July 1st; Initial approach by letter requesting application; Completion of formal

application required.
Program description:
The foundation was formed to offer financial assistance by means of a loan to worthy and needy individuals in furthering their post-high school education at an accredited college or university.

Students who have completed or will complete their high school education in June of any year shall be eligible to apply for a loan for the academic year commencing in the fall of that year, if, as of January, they are natural or legally adopted children of:
- An active or former employee of Fox Industries, Inc. (Headquarters), Fox Grocery Company including Wetterau-Pittsburg Group Headquarters, Wetterau-Pittsburg Division including the Candy Division, and the Wetterau-Butler Division, with at least two years service;
- An active or former employee, with at least two years service, of a retailer affiliated with Fox Grocery Company for at least one year; or
- An individual retailer affiiliated with Fox Grocery Company for at least one year.

Also eligible to apply are former recipients of the Fox Scholarship Loan Award and employees who have two years service with the companies and retailers listed above.

Students who receive loans shall repay them in equal monthly installments over a period to be determined by the Trustees. However, such repayment shall not begin until after completion of the academic course and until procurement of employment. No interest shall be charged on the loans.

The following will be considered by the Scholarship Committee in selecting students to receive awards: scholastic achievement, financial need, moral character, leadership, citizenship, and seriousness of purpose.

1127
Gannett (Frank) Newspapercarrier Scholarships, Inc.

Lincoln Tower
Rochester, NY 14604 (716) 262-3315
Contact: Debra J. Buckett, Scholarships Administrator

Limitations: Scholarships to carriers of Gannett newspapers.
Financial data: Year ended 12/31/85. Assets, $5,025 (L); Total giving, $389,353; Grants to individuals, 457 grants totaling $389,353, high $1,500, low $34, average grant $1,000.
Employer Identification Number: 160766965
Applications: Deadline January 1st of senior year of high school; Completion of formal application required; Application forms available from circulation department of participating newspapers; Interviews granted upon request depending on local committee.
Publications: Program information, application guidelines.

Program description:
College scholarships of $4,000 each for a basic four-year college course are awarded annually on a competitive basis. The award is issued in payments of $500 a semester. Recipients must have been carriers for at least one year as of December 31st preceding the date of the awarding of the scholarships. Up to 100 new awards are made each year, with the number of awards assigned annually to each participating Gannett Co., Inc., newspaper community.

1128
Gemco Charitable and Scholarship Fund
6565 Knott Avenue
Buena Park, CA 90620   (714) 739-6351
Contact: Jim Barnett

Limitations: Scholarship awards to high school seniors in specified communities where the Gemco Corporation operates.
Financial data: Year ended 2/2/86. Assets, $31,775 (M); Total giving, $171,675; Grants to individuals, 106 grants totaling $106,875.
Employer Identification Number: 952497896
Applications: Schools select scholarship entrants and send out application forms; Completion of formal application required.
Program description:
Awards are made to high school seniors in specified communities where the Gemco Corporation operates (Phoenix, AZ; CA; Baltimore, Montgomery, and Prince Georges counties, MD; Houston and Beaumont, TX; and Fairfax County, Richmond, and Arlington Heights, VA). Students with a good understanding of current issues in U.S. economics and the free-enterprise system are nominated by their high schools to participate in oral competitions set up as discussion groups, which are judged by representatives from local business and government.

In the past, finalists from the first round of discussions received $50 in U.S. Savings Bonds; runners-up received $25 in bonds. Finalists participated in a second discussion and first place winners received $1,500 paid over a two-year period. Second place winners received $1,000 over two years, and third place awards were $500.

1129
Georgia-Pacific Foundation, Inc.
133 Peachtree Street, N.E.
Atlanta, GA 30303   (404) 521-5228
Contact: Marion L. Talmadge, President

Limitations: Scholarships only to graduating high school seniors where there are major plants or offices of Georgia-Pacific Corporation.
Financial data: Year ended 12/31/86. Assets, $2,022,297 (M); Total giving, $1,732,157; Grants to individuals totaling $672,928.

Employer Identification Number: 936023726
Applications: Applications accepted throughout the year.
Program description:
The foundation will award annually four-year $3,000 college scholarships to outstanding students from high schools in areas where Georgia-Pacific Corporation has major holdings and operations; if the recipient attends a nontax-supported college in the state where the scholarship is awarded, the grant is for $4,000 for the four-year period.
   1. Scholarships are awarded annually to those schools designated by the foundation.
   2. Awards are based on the student's need, scholastic achievement, intellectual ability, character and promise of future contribution to society.
   3. Recipient selection is made without discrimination as to race, sex, creed, country of origin, or relationship with the company or its affiliates. However, recipients must be U.S. citizens.
   4. Recipients are selected by local school officials.
   5. Recipients may attend any accredited college or university and pursue any course of study, as long as it culminates in a four-year bachelor degree.
   6. Scholarships are paid on a semester or quarterly basis to the educational institution and disbursed to or for the account of the recipient.
   7. Recipients will be selected at least four weeks before year-end graduation to enable the foundation to prepare appropriate certificates to be awarded at graduation.

1130★
Gerber Companies Foundation, The
(Formerly Gerber Baby Foods Fund)
c/o Gerber Products Company
445 State Street
Fremont, MI 49412   (616) 928-2224
Contact: Yvonne A. Lee, President

Limitations: Scholarships only to employees of Gerber Products Company and their children.
Financial data: Year ended 5/31/87. Assets, $16,730,875 (M); Total giving, $746,461; Grants to individuals amount not specified.
Employer Identification Number: 386068090
Applications: Deadline April 1st.
Publications: Program information.
Program description:
Scholarships of $350 per year are awarded, renewable each year for four years of study leading to a bachelor degree (or for a two-year Registered Nursing program). Recipients must have been accepted for full-time attendance at an accredited college or university.

1131
Giles (The Edward C.) Foundation
736 Hempstead Place
Charlotte, NC 28207
Contact: The Edward G. Giles Foundation, P.O. Box 33056, Charlotte, NC 28233

Limitations: Scholarships only to descendants of employees of Carauster Industries, Inc. and its subsidiaries.
Financial data: Year ended 12/31/86. Assets, $11,719,921 (M); Total giving, $105,624; Grants to individuals, 20 grants totaling $65,624, high $5,333, low $1,215.
Employer Identification Number: 581450874
Applications: Deadline February 15th; Completion of formal application required including biographical, scholastic, extracurricular, civic and financial information.

1132
Goldman Sachs Fund
85 Broad Street, Tax Department, 30th Floor
New York, NY 10004

Limitations: Scholarships for the spouses and children of employees of Goldman Sachs & Co.
Financial data: Year ended 6/30/87. Assets, $5,980,823 (M); Total giving, $690,873; Grants to individuals, 32 grants totaling $65,500, high $5,000, low $500.
Employer Identification Number: 237000346

1133
Golub Foundation, The
501 Duanesburg Road
Schenectady, NY 12306
Contact: Scholarship Committee, c/o Golub Corporation, P.O. Box 1074, Schenectady, NY 12301

Limitations: Scholarships only to graduating high school students in areas served by Price Chopper Supermarkets, including New York, Massachusetts, Pennsylvania, and Vermont.
Financial data: Year ended 3/31/86. Assets, $73,894 (M); Total giving, $352,732; Grants to individuals totaling $352,732.
Employer Identification Number: 222341421
Applications: Deadline April 1st; Initial approach by letter requesting application form; Completion of formal application required.
Publications: Program information.

1134★
Gould Inc. Foundation
Ten Gould Center, 9th Floor
Rolling Meadows, IL 60008   (312) 640-4255
Contact: Principal manager of local Gould facility

Limitations: Scholarships based on leadership and merit only to children of employees of Gould, Inc.
Financial data: Year 12/31/87. Assets, $3,033,037 (M); Total giving, $356,408; Grants to individuals, 50 grants totaling $78,921.
Employer Identification Number: 346525555
Applications: Deadline January 31st; Initial approach by letter.
Publications: Financial statement.

1135
Gould Point Sebago Scholarship Fund
Point Sebago
RR 1, Box 712
Casco, ME 04015   (207) 655-7948
Contact: Don Toms

Limitations: Scholarships to employees and children of employees of Point Sebago in Casco, MF, graduates of Lake Region High School, Naples, ME, and graduates of Windham High School, Windham, ME.
Financial data: Year ended 10/31/86. Assets, $26,758 (M); Total giving, $7,750; Grants to individuals, 8 grants totaling $7,750, high $2,000, low $500, general range $1,000-1,500.
Employer Identification Number: 010385138
Applications: Deadline April 15th; Initial approach by letter requesting applications; Completion of formal application required.

1136
Goulds Pumps Foundation
c/o Mrs. M. J. Cator
240 Fall Street, P.O. Box 330
Seneca Falls, NY 13148   (315) 568-2811

Limitations: Scholarships to children of Goulds Pumps, Inc., employees.
Financial data: Year ended 12/31/86. Assets, $19,950 (M); Total giving, $134,240; Grants to individuals, 8 grants totaling $4,000, each grant $500.
Employer Identification Number: 166054041
Applications: Applications accepted throughout the year.

1137★
Graco Foundation, The
P.O. Box 1441
Minneapolis, MN 55440-1444   (612) 623-6679
Contact: David L. Schoeneck, Executive Director

Limitations: Scholarships to dependent children (25 years or younger) of Graco Inc. employees.

Financial data: Year ended 12/31/87. Assets, $1,710,000 (M); Total giving, $792,700; Grants to individuals, 15 grants totaling $35,700.
Employer Identification Number: 416023537
Applications: Deadlines February 15th, May 15th, August 15th and October 31st; Initial approach by telephone or letter.
Publications: Annual report.
Program description:
Scholarships are awarded to help recipients pursue educational and vocational opportunities.

1138
Gregg-Graniteville Foundation, Inc.
P.O. Box 418
Graniteville, SC 29829   (803) 663-7552
Contact: Joan F. Phibbs, Secretary-Treasurer

Limitations: Scholarships only to children of employees of Graniteville Company.
Financial data: Year ended 12/31/86. Assets, $12,886,922 (M); Total giving, $285,413; Grants to individuals, 27 grants totaling $35,858.
Employer Identification Number: 570314400
Applications: Contact foundation for current application deadline; Initial approach by letter.
Publications: Annual report.

1139
Groves Foundation
10,000 Highway 55 West
P.O. Box 1267
Minneapolis, MN 55440   (612) 546-6943
Contact: Elfriede M. Lobeck, Executive Director

Limitations: Scholarships to dependents of employees of S.J. Groves and Sons Company, and its subsidiaries.
Financial data: Year ended 9/30/86. Assets, $10,358,922 (M); Total giving, $554,332; Grants to individuals, 17 grants totaling $25,500, high $2,000, low $500, general range $1,000-2,000.
Employer Identification Number: 416038512
Applications: Applications accepted throughout the year; Initial approach by letter.
Program description:
The number of scholarships awarded in any given year shall not exceed 25 percent of the eligible applicants.

1140
Habig Foundation Inc., The
1600 Royal Street
Jasper, IN 47546
Contact: Douglas A. Habig, Treasurer

Limitations: Scholarships only to children of employees of Kimball International, Inc.
Financial data: Year ended 6/30/87. Assets, $512,929 (M); Total giving, $360,116; Grants to individuals, 33 grants totaling $59,480, high $2,000, low $1,000.

Employer Identification Number: 356022535
Applications: Deadline April 1st; Completion of formal application required; Application address is P.O. Box 460, Jasper, IN 47546; Tel. (812) 482-1600.

1141
Haggar Foundation, The
6113 Lemmon Avenue
Dallas, TX 75209
Contact: Rosemary Haggar Vaughan, Trustee and Executive Director

Limitations: Scholarships for higher and secondary education only to children of employees of Haggar Company and affiliates, who have been actively employed for at least 6 months.
Financial data: Year ended 6/30/85. Assets, $16,976,868 (M); Total giving, $762,408; Grants to individuals amount not specified.
Employer Identification Number: 756019237
Applications: Submit application January through February; Deadline March 31st; Completion of formal application required.
Publications: Application guidelines.

1142
Hall Family Foundations
c/o Charitable and Crown Investment - 323
P.O. Box 419580
Kansas City, MO 64141
Contact: Margaret H. Pence or Wendy Hockaday, Program Officers

Limitations: Scholarships only to children of employees of Hallmark.
Financial data: Year ended 12/31/86. Assets, $215,321,156 (M); Total giving, $5,687,872; Grants to individuals totaling $200,750; Subtotal for scholarships, 120 grants totaling $170,200, high $2,500, low $600.
Employer Identification Number: 446006291
Applications: Applications available to Hallmark employees only.
Publications: Annual report.

1143
Hall Foundation, The
444 South Second Street
Harrisburg, PA 17104   (717) 236-0384
Contact: John N. Hall, President

Limitations: Scholarships only to children of employees and customers of Hall's Motor Transit Company.
Financial data: Year ended 9/30/84. Assets, $4,586,576 (M); Total giving, $209,796; Grants to individuals, 111 grants totaling $105,794, high $1,310, low $189, average grant $1,000.
Employer Identification Number: 236243044

Applications: Deadline at least 3 months prior to fall semester; Completion of formal application required; Interviews granted upon request.

1144★
Halton Foundation
3114 N.W. Verde Vista Terrace
Portland, OR 97210   (503) 288-6411
Contact: Susan H. Findlay, Manager

Limitations: Scholarships only to children of employees of no less than one year, or disabled, retired or deceased employees of Halton Tractor Company and related companies, who are under 28 years of age, and are planning to be full-time students.
Financial data: Year ended 8/31/87. Assets, $780,487 (M); Grants to individuals, 11 grants totaling $37,453, high $10,584, low $133, general range $1,000-2,500, average grant $2,500.
Employer Identification Number: 936036295
Applications: Deadline January 31st; Completion of formal application including copy of current transcript required; Interviews required; Applications available at the personnel office of the Portland store or through the foundation.
Publications: Program information.
Program description:
Scholarship recipients, known as Halton Scholars, must be high school graduates and may attend colleges, junior colleges, technical, mechanical, or nursing schools, but not study through correspondence courses or at night schools. Scholarships may be used to pay for tuition and books. Each award is for one year only but is renewable annually if student continues to show good progress towards his/her academic goal.

Applicants must show evidence of financial need, as well as academic achievement and participation in extracurricular activities, which include athletics, a part-time job, volunteer work, etc. The applicant's ability to demonstrate long-term planning for achievement of his or her educational goal is also considered.

1145
Harris Bank Foundation
111 West Monroe Street
P.O. Box 755
Chicago, IL 60690   (312) 461-6660
Contact: H. Kris Ronnew, Secretary-Treasurer

Limitations: Scholarships for dependents of employees of Harris Trust and Savings Bank.
Financial data: Year ended 12/31/86. Assets, $450,000 (M); Total giving, $1,000,049; Grants to individuals, 16 grants totaling, $16,500.
Employer Identification Number: 366033888
Applications: Initial approach by letter.

1146
Hoffman (Bob) Foundation
c/o York Bar Bell Co., The
P.O. Box 1707
York, PA 17405   (717) 767-6481
Contact: Michael Dietz, Trustee

Limitations: Scholarships for children of employees of the York Bar Bell Co., Inc., and related companies.
Financial data: Year ended 3/31/86. Assets, $1,310,700 (M); Total giving, $26,333; Grants to individuals, 5 grants totaling $8,556, high $5,000, low $500.
Employer Identification Number: 236298674
Applications: Applications accepted throughout the year; Initial approach by letter with relevant school information.

1147
Home Group Foundation, The
(Formerly City Investing Company Foundation)
59 Maiden Lane
New York, NY 10038
Contact: Bob Wood Endowment Fund, 55 Madison Street, Suite 800, Denver, CO, 80206

Limitations: Scholarships to qualified employees, spouses, and children of employees, of City Investing Company.
Financial data: Year ended 12/31/85. Assets, $4,173,754 (M); Total giving, $186,900; Grants to individuals, 2 grants totaling $3,000, each grant $1,500.
Employer Identification Number: 953308551
Applications: Deadline May; Initial approach by letter; Completion of formal application required.

1148★
Hood (Charles H.) Fund
500 Rutherford Avenue
Boston, MA 02129   (617) 242-0600
Contact: Prudence M. Dame, Executive Director and Secretary

Limitations: Scholarships only to children of employees of H. P. Hood Inc. and Agri-Mark, Inc.
Financial data: Year ended 12/31/85. Assets, $1,827,724 (M); Total giving, $78,300; Grants to individuals, 23 grants totaling $61,200, high $3,000, low $900.
Employer Identification Number: 046036788
Applications: Deadline January 15th; Completion of formal application required.
Publications: Application guidelines.
Program description:
Awards shall not exceed $3,500 per year, per student for four years.

1149
Hotchkiss (W.R.) Foundation
1080 West County Road F
St. Paul, MN 55126
Contact: Michael J. Welch, W.R. Hotchkiss
Scholarship Plan, P.O. Box 64399, St. Paul, MN
55164-0399; Tel.: (612) 483-7232

Limitations: Scholarships to children of employees and
ex-employees of Deluxe Check Printers, Inc.
Financial data: Year ended 6/30/87. Assets,
$8,333,370 (M); Total giving, $379,294; Grants to
individuals, 111 grants totaling $331,754, high
$4,500, low $2,000.
Employer Identification Number: 416038562
Applications: Deadline January 31st; Completion of
formal application required.

1150
Housen Foundation, Inc.
c/o Erving Paper Mills
47 East Main Street
Erving, MA 01344   (617) 544-2711
Contact: Ms. Dawn Williams

Limitations: Scholarships for study at U.S. colleges
and universities only to students who are residents of
Massachusetts and children of Erving Paper Mills
employees.
Financial data: Year ended 12/31/85. Assets, $201,081
(M); Total giving, $88,990; Grants to individuals
amount not specified.
Employer Identification Number: 046183673

1151★
Hunt Manufacturing Company Foundation
230 South Broad Street
Philadelphia, PA 19102   (215) 732-7700
Contact: Vice-President of Human Resources

Limitations: Scholarships only to children of
employees who have had one year of employment
with the Hunt Manufacturing Company as of April
15th of the year in which application is made.
Financial data: Year ended 11/28/87. Assets, $1,900
(M); Total giving, $430,957; Grants to individuals, 17
grants totaling $23,250, high $2,000, low $200,
general range $1,000-2,000, average grant $1,367.
Employer Identification Number: 226062897
Applications: Deadline April 15th.
Publications: 990-PF printed copy available upon
request.
Program description:
Scholastic achievement and merit is the primary factor
to be considered in selecting recipients; the
applicant's financial need is the primary factor for
determining the amount of the grant. Selection of
scholarship winners is made by the Admissions Grant
Committee, Chestnut Hill College, Philadelphia, PA.

The number of awards shall not exceed ten percent
of the number of high school graduates eligible in any
one year. Scholarship payments will be delivered to
the individual recipient; checks are made payable to
the educational institution.

1152
Hyde (J.R.) Foundation, Inc.
3030 Poplar Avenue
Memphis, TN 38111   (901) 325-4245
Contact: Margaret R. Hyde, President

Limitations: Scholarships to children of employees of
Malone & Hyde.
Financial data: Year ended 8/31/86. Assets,
$13,881,813 (M); Total giving, $686,850; Grants to
individuals, 10 grants totaling $25,000, each grant
$2,500.
Employer Identification Number: 620677725
Applications: Applications accepted throughout the
year; Available funds are distributed in August.
Program description:
Scholarships are paid to the institution attended by the
scholarship student.

1153
Inland Container Corporation Foundation, Inc.
151 Delaware Street
P.O. Box 925
Indianapolis, IN 46206   (317) 262-0308
Contact: Frank F. Hirschman, President

Limitations: Scholarships only to children of
employees of Inland Container Corporation.
Financial data: Year ended 12/31/86. Assets,
$6,972,609 (M); Total giving, $475,870; Grants to
individuals totaling $95,000.
Employer Identification Number: 356014640
Applications: Deadline November 1st; Initial approach
by letter.
Publications: Program information, application
guidelines.
Program description:
Approximately 12 new scholarship awards are
available each year.

1154
Inland Steel-Ryerson Foundation, Inc.
c/o Inland Steel Industries
30 West Monroe Street
Chicago, IL 60603   (312) 899-3421
Contact: Earl S. Thompson, Director, State and
Regional Affairs, Inland Steel Industries

Limitations: Scholarships to children of employees of
Inland Steel Company and its subsidiaries.
Financial data: Year ended 12/31/86. Assets, $0 (M);
Total giving, $1,310,617; Grants to individuals, 260
grants totaling $244,667; Subtotal for

employee-related scholarships amount not specified.
Employer Identification Number: 366046944
Applications: Applications accepted throughout the
year; Initial approach by letter or telephone.

1155
Inman-Riverdale Foundation
Inman Mills
Inman, SC 29349   (803) 472-2121
Contact: W. Marshall Chapman, Chairman

Limitations: College scholarships only to dependents
of Inman Mills employees.
Financial data: Year ended 11/30/86. Assets,
$3,233,206 (M); Total giving, $455,294; Grants to
individuals totaling $26,521.
Employer Identification Number: 576019736
Applications: Initial approach by letter; Completion of
formal application required.
Program description:
Four new scholarships are awarded each year.

1156★
ITT Rayonier Foundation, The
1177 Summer Street
Stamford, CT 06904   (203) 348-7000
Contact: Jerome D. Gregoire, Vice-President

Limitations: Scholarships only to students graduating
from high schools and residing in areas of company
operations in Nassau County, FL, Wayne County, GA,
and Clallem, Mason, and Grays Harbor counties, WA.
Financial data: Year ended 12/31/87. Assets,
$2,272,000 (M); Total giving, $353,000; Grants to
individuals, 40 grants totaling $59,500, high $1,500,
low $375, average grant $1,000.
Employer Identification Number: 136064462
Applications: Completion of formal application
required; Applications available from principals of
high schools in areas of company operations (see
Limitations above).
Program description:
The **Plant County Scholarship Program** provides
$6,000, four-year scholarships to students graduating
from high schools and residing in counties in which
ITT Rayonier, Inc., has a manufacturing plant or
research operation. Recipients are free to attend any
accredited, degree-granting college and may major in
any subject leading to a degree. Each scholarship
provides the recipient with $1,500 per school year as
long as the recipient maintains a satisfactory
performance.
The **Timber County Scholarship Program** provides
scholarships to students graduating from high schools
and residing in counties where ITT Rayonier, Inc. has
significant timberland ownership. A $750 and a $375
scholarship are awarded in both Georgia and Florida,
and two $750 scholarships are awarded in
Washington. All grants are for one year only.

Recipients are free to attend any accredited university,
college or junior college, and may major in any
subject.

1157★
Jewell (The Daniel Ashley and Irene Houston) Memorial Foundation
c/o American National Bank & Trust Company
P.O. Box 1638
Chattanooga, TN 37401
Contact: Peter T. Cooper, Treasurer

Limitations: Undergraduate scholarships only to
children of employees of Crystal Springs Printwork,
Inc., Chickamauga, GA, and high school seniors
residing in the areas of Dade, Catoosa, or Walker
counties, GA, to attend accredited college in Georgia,
Alabama, or Tennessee.
Financial data: Year ended 6/30/87. Assets,
$2,591,757 (M); Total giving, $116,250; Grants to
individuals, 11 grants totaling $13,500, high $2,000,
low $500.
Employer Identification Number: 586034213
Applications: Applications accepted throughout the
year; Initial approach by letter.
Program description:
Recipients are recommended to the trustees by a
scholarship committee which includes the
superintendent of the Chickamauga public school
system and the principal of the Gordon Lee High
School.

1158
Johnson Controls Foundation
5757 North Green Bay Avenue
P.O. Box 591
Milwaukee, WI 53201   (414) 228-2219
Contact: Johnson Controls Foundation, c/o Johnson
Controls Corporation

Limitations: Scholarships only to children of
employees of Johnson Controls, Inc.
Financial data: Year ended 12/31/86. Assets,
$15,916,804 (M); Total giving, $2,752,847; Grants to
individuals totaling $65,000, average grant $1,500.
Employer Identification Number: 396036639

1159★
Kelly Foundation, Inc.
800 East Sugarland Highway
Clewiston, FL 33440   (813) 983-8177
Contact: Robert Kelly, President

Limitations: Scholarships to children of Kelly Tractor
Company employees and residents of Florida.
Financial data: Year ended 12/31/87. Assets,
$1,044,887 (M); Total giving, $92,791; Grants to
individuals, 26 grants totaling $22,441, high $2,800,
low $250.

Employer Identification Number: 596153269
Applications: Applications accepted throughout the year; Completion of formal application required.

1160★
Kingsbury Fund

c/o Kingsbury Machine Tool Corporation
80 Laurel Street
Keene, NH 03431   (603) 352-5212
Contact: James E. O'Neil, Jr., Executive Trustee

Limitations: Scholarships to high school seniors who are children of employees of the Kingsbury Machine Tool Corporation, or to an undergraduate student in a technical institute, college, or other accredited school.
Financial data: Year ended 12/31/87. Assets, $2,184,665 (M); Total giving, $163,918; Grants to individuals totaling $19,400.
Employer Identification Number: 026004465
Applications: Deadline March 30th; Completion of formal application required; Applicants must submit an essay and transcript of grades.
Program description:
Up to three new scholarships are awarded each year, provided there are at least 12 applicants to sons and daughters of Kingsbury Machine Tool Corporation employees. The money is payable directly to the school.

All applicants must be in financial need; be a student of good standing, or meet college admission requirements; be active in school affairs or have a part-time job; have demonstrated qualities of leadership; and have evidence of good citizenship. The three winners of scholarships are those who have the best combination of high need and good grades, combined with the best over all level of activity for the other factors. A written statement from each applicant is also used as an additional selection factor.

1161
Knapp Educational Fund, Inc.

P.O. Box O
St. Michaels, MD 21663   (301) 745-5660
Contact: Mrs. Antoinette Vojvoda, President

Limitations: Scholarships only to children of employees of Macmillan, Inc.
Financial data: Year ended 12/31/86. Assets, $2,500,000 (M); Total giving, $65,000; Grants to individuals, 55 grants totaling $65,000, high $3,000, low $500, average grant $1,500.
Employer Identification Number: 132970128
Applications: Applications accepted throughout the year; Initial approach by letter.

1162
Koch (The Fred C.) Foundation, Inc.

P.O. Box 2256
Wichita, KS 67201   (316) 832-5404
Contact: George H. Pearson, President

Limitations: Scholarships only to dependents of employees of Koch Industries, Inc.
Financial data: Year ended 12/31/86. Assets, $8,795,595 (M); Total giving, $148,439; Grants to individuals, 20 grants totaling $20,000, each grant $1,000.
Employer Identification Number: 486113560
Applications: Submit application preferably in February; Initial approach by letter.

1163
Kuntz Foundation, The

120 West Second Street
Dayton, OH 45402   (513) 461-3870

Limitations: Scholarships to children of employees of The Peter Kuntz Company.
Financial data: Year ended 12/31/86. Assets, $2,885,503 (M); Total giving, $204,988; Grants to individuals, 6 grants totaling $6,775, high $2,188, low $121.
Employer Identification Number: 316016465
Applications: Completion of formal application required; Submit completed form to Kuntz Foundation Scholarship Committee, P.O. Box 730, Dayton, OH 45402.

1164
Leavey (Thomas and Dorothy) Foundation

4680 Wilshire Boulevard
Los Angeles, CA 90010   (213) 936-5875
Contact: J. Thomas McCarthy, Trustee

Limitations: Scholarships only to children of employees of Farmers Group, Inc.
Financial data: Year ended 12/31/86. Assets, $87,826,586 (M); Total giving, $5,796,617; Grants to individuals, 79 grants totaling $194,243.
Employer Identification Number: 956060162
Applications: Applications accepted throughout the year; Initial approach by letter.

1165
Lee (Arthur K. and Sylvia S.) Scholarship Foundation

5300 Maryland Way
Brentwood, TN 37027
Contact: James B. Ford, Secretary-Treasurer

Limitations: Scholarships primarily to children and dependents of employees (company not specified).
Financial data: Year ended 12/31/85. Assets, $391,288 (L); Total giving, $52,700; Grants to individuals, 77

grants totaling $52,700, high $1,167, low $333.
Employer Identification Number: 366069067

1166
Levi Strauss Foundation
1155 Battery Street
P.O. Box 7215
San Francisco, CA 94106   (415) 544-6577
Contact: Martha Montag Brown, Director of U.S.
Contributions

Limitations: Business Opportunity Scholarships to
disadvantaged high school seniors in U.S.
communities where Levi Strauss & Company has
production or distribution facilities including AR, CA,
GA, NV, NM, TX, and VA. Foundation also awards
international scholarships.
Financial data: Year ended 12/31/85. Assets,
$20,768,057 (M); Total giving, $4,251,606; Grants to
individuals, $840,000; Subtotal for Business
Opportunity Scholarships, 34 grants totaling $33,500;
Subtotal for International Scholarships totaling
$50,558.
Employer Identification Number: 946064702
Applications: Applications accepted throughout the
year; Initial approach by letter requesting application;
Completion of formal application required.
Publications: Annual report.

1167
Levy (Achille) Foundation
c/o Bank of A. Levy
P.O. Box 244
Oxnard, CA 93032   (805) 487-6541
Contact: Robert L. Mobley, P.O. Box 5190, Ventura,
CA 93006, Vice-President

Limitations: Scholarships to graduating seniors from
high schools in the service areas of Bank of A. Levy in
California, to attend four-year colleges or universities.
Financial data: Year ended 11/30/86. Assets, $13,571
(M); Total giving $255,707; Grants to individuals
totaling $21,250.
Employer Identification Number: 956264755
Applications: Deadline March 30th; Initial approach
by letter; Completion of formal application required.
Publications: Application guidelines.
Program description:
Selection of scholarship recipients is made by the
principals or counselors of the various high schools
along with three officers of the Bank.

1168
Marathon Oil Foundation, Inc.
539 South Main Street, Room 4125
Findlay, OH 45840   (419) 422-2121
Contact: J. S. Dimling, Vice-President

Limitations: Scholarships and awards to children of
employees, directors, and retirees of Marathon Oil
Company studying for a B.A.
Financial data: Year ended 6/30/86. Assets, $313,234
(M); Total giving, $2,486,837; Grants to individuals
totaling $178,284.
Employer Identification Number: 346523012
Applications: Applications accepted from October 1st
to January 1st of senior year.
Publications: Application guidelines.
Program description:
Marathon Scholar Awards of $2,000 are made in
recognition of scholastic merit, leadership qualities,
activities and potential for college success to no more
than 50 high school graduates pursuing college
degrees. **Financial Aid Grants** are awarded to students
who evidence financial need as well as merit. Grants
may be renewed for a maximum of four years.

1169
Maremont Corporation Foundation
200 East Randolph Drive
Chicago, IL 60601   (312) 861-4031
Contact: Shari Parker

Limitations: Scholarships to children of present,
retired, or deceased employees of Maremont
Corporation.
Financial data: Year ended 12/31/86. Assets, $905
(M); Total giving, $117,000; Grants to individuals
totaling $24,000.
Employer Identification Number: 366162616
Applications: Deadline January 1st; Completion of
formal applicaiton required; Application information
may be obtained from the foundation.
Program description:
The foundation's **Scholar Program** is available to
employees who have worked for Maremont
Corporation for at least three years. Children of retired
or deceased employees, or employees on long-term
disability are also eligible, provided that the employee
was in good standing, with three years employment, at
the time of his/her retirement, death, or disability.

Eligible children must be seniors in high school,
planning to enroll in an accredited four-year college in
the U.S.

1170
Marley Fund, The
1900 Johnson Drive
Mission Woods, KS 66205   (913) 362-1818
Contact: Betty L. Paine, Vice-President, P.O. Box
2965, Shawnee, KS 66201

Limitations: Scholarships only to dependents of
employees of the Marley Company.
Financial data: Year ended 4/30/87. Assets, $104,918
(M); Total giving, $299,194; Grants to individuals, 104
grants totaling $46,125, high $450, low $300.
Employer Identification Number: 446012343
Applications: Applications accepted throughout the
year; Initial approach by letter.

1171★
Martin Marietta Corporation Foundation
6801 Rockledge Drive
Bethesda, MD 20817   (301) 897-6863
Contact: Donna Price, Contributions Representative

Limitations: Scholarships only to high school
graduates who are children of Martin Marietta
Corporation employees.
Financial data: Year ended 12/31/85. Assets, $227,973
(M); Total giving, $3,739,010; Grants to individuals,
169 grants totaling $476,222, high $3,000, low $500.
Employer Identification Number: 136161566
Applications: Applications accepted throughout the
year; Application guidelines and forms available from
company personnel office.
Publications: Application guidelines.

1172★
Maytag Company Foundation, Inc., The
c/o Maytag Corporation
One Dependability Square
Newton, IA 50208   (515) 791-8216
Contact: Chairman, Scholarship Committee or
Chairman, Career Education Awards Committee

Limitations: Scholarships and career education awards
to graduating seniors of Newton High School, IA, and
children of employees of the Maytag Company
(excluding Jenn-Air) or the Maytag Corporation staff.
Financial data: Year ended 12/31/87. Assets,
$1,622,419 (M); Total giving, $557,082; Grants to
individuals, 164 grants totaling $160,063, Subtotal for
Scholarship Program, 119 grants totaling $112,705,
high $2,800, low $33; Subtotal for Career Education
Awards Program, 45 grants totaling $47,358, high
$2,700, low $383.
Employer Identification Number: 426055722
Applications: Deadlines vary annually; Contact
foundation for current application deadline; Initial
approach by letter or telephone requesting application
forms; Completion of formal application required;
Interviews required for Career Education Award
applicants.

Publications: Informational brochure, financial
statement.
Program description:
The **Scholarship Program** awards undergraduate
scholarships only to qualified students from Newton
High School, Newton, IA, or other schools, if children
of eligible Maytag employees. Winners must enroll as
degree candidates in regionally accredited four-year
colleges or universities in the U.S.

Selection is based on scholastic achievement,
aptitude for college study, record, and character
references. The amount awarded is determined by
financial need, and may range from a $200 honor
scholarship (for one year only) to a full award which
covers tuition and fees up to a maximum of $2,500
per year (plus $300 for books and supplies) and which
is renewable for four years of undergraduate study. In
addition, because of its commitment to preserving and
strengthening the quality of the nation's educational
system, the foundation makes an unrestricted
supplementary contribution of $500 a year ($200 in
the case of an honor scholarship) to the awardee's
institution.

The **Career Education Awards Program** makes
grants only to students from Newton High School,
Newton, IA (or other schools, if children of eligible
Maytag employees living in Iowa) who are attending
Iowa area community colleges to pursue full-time
occupationally oriented career education programs.
The programs may extend in length from one
academic semester (or quarter) to two years or more
and are designed to prepare young people for
employment in their chosen career field immediately
upon completion of course work.

Selection is based on academic and employment
record in areas related to the chosen career program,
aptitude for that career, character references, and
personal interviews. Financial need is not a factor in
selection of winners, and awards cover the full cost of
tuition, fees, books and supplies for the duration of the
individual career education program.

1173
McCain Foundation, Inc.
c/o Erie Concrete and Steel
P.O. Box 10336
Erie, PA 16514-0336
Contact: Fund Manager

Limitations: Scholarships for full-time undergraduate
study to children of nonstockholding employees of the
Erie Concrete & Steel Supply Company, Perry Mill
Supply Company, and Dobi Plumbing and Heating
Supply Company.
Financial data: Year ended 11/30/85. Assets, $113,034
(M); Total giving, $12,112; Grants to individuals, 3
grants totaling $3,000, each grant $1,000.
Employer Identification Number: 256049931
Applications: Applications accepted throughout the
year; Initial approach by letter.

Program description:
A grant of $2,000 per year, payable for up to four years, is made by random drawing held at the end of May.

1174
Mead Johnson & Company Foundation, Inc.
2404 West Pennsylvania Street
Evansville, IN 47721   (812) 429-5000
Contact: Rolland M. Eckels, President

Limitations: Scholarship to recognize and reward excellence in scholastic achievement by children of Mead Johnson & Company employees.
Financial data: Year ended 12/31/86. Assets, $1,749,320 (M); Total giving, $527,254; Grants to individuals, 8 grants totaling $24,000, each grant $3,000.
Employer Identification Number: 356011067
Applications: Deadline February 15th; Completion of formal application required; Submit completed application and five letters of recommendation to high school principal, to be forwarded to foundation with transcript of applicant's grades.
Publications: Program information.
Program description:
Two undergraduate scholarship grants for children of employees consisting of yearly installments of $3,000 to cover four years of attendance at college are awarded annually.

Parents must have been employed by Mead Johnson & Company for three consecutive years prior to January 31st of the year in which awards are made for their children (including natural children, stepchildren, and legally adopted children) to be eligible for scholarships.

The applicant must be a high school senior in the top one-third of his class. Recipients are chosen by a selection committee composed of the:
- President of the University of Evansville;
- Superintendent of the Evansville public schools;
- Superintendent of Schools of the Catholic Diocese of Evansville.

1175★
Meridian Mutual Foundation, Inc.
2955 North Meridian Street
Indianapolis, IN 46207   (317) 927-8266
Contact: Gary D. McCloud, Secretary-Treasurer; P.O. Box 1980, Indianapolis, IN 46206

Limitations: Scholarships only to children of employees or agents of Meridian Mutual Insurance Company and its affiliates.
Financial data: Year ended 12/31/87. Assets, $143,274 (M); Total giving, $14,350; Grants to individuals, 26 grants totaling $14,350, high $600, low $500.
Employer Identification Number: 351093867
Applications: Deadline April 15th; Completion of

formal application and school reporting form required; Interviews requested.
Program description:
High school seniors and students already enrolled in college or universities are eligible to apply. Grants may be renewable each year for up to four years.

One scholarship will be designated specifically for studies leading to a career in the insurance industry.

1176★
Merit Gasoline Foundation, The
551 West Lancaster Avenue
Haverford, PA 19041   (215) 527-7900
Contact: Robert M. Harting, Executive Director

Limitations: Scholarships for up to four years of undergraduate study to children or stepchildren of active, retired, deceased, or disabled full-time employees (with at least two years' service) of Merit Oil Company and its affiliates.
Financial data: Year ended 8/31/87. Assets, $377,968 (M); Total giving, $140,360; Grants to individuals totaling $21,500.
Employer Identification Number: 236282846
Applications: Deadline April 1st; Applications accepted throughout the year; Contact foundation for current application deadline; Completion of formal application required.
Publications: Application guidelines.
Program description:
Scholarships are awarded on a competitive basis. Factors considered in selections are:
- Financial need
- Academic achievement
- SAT score
- Information pertaining to student's character, quality of leadership, work habits, and general interests.

Up to four new scholarships are available each year, to be used only for full-time study in an undergraduate program of at least two years' duration at an accredited U.S. college, university, junior or community college. **Awards will not be made for part-time study or for graduate work.**

Scholarships may be renewed providing recipients remain in good standing and advance toward a designated degree. Payments are made directly to the educational institution with instructions that the funds are to be allocated equally toward each semester.

1177
MFA Foundation
615 Locust
Columbia, MO 65201   (314) 876-5395
Contact: Ormal C. Creach, President

Limitations: Scholarships primarily to Missouri students residing in areas of company operations of MFA Oil Company, MFA Inc., and Shelter Insurance.

Financial data: Year ended 6/30/87. Assets, $3,410,297 (M); Total giving, $237,701; Grants to individuals, 202 grants totaling $179,261, high $1,800, low $210.
Employer Identification Number: 436026877
Applications: Deadline April 15th; Initial approach by letter requesting application; Completion of formal application required.

1178
Midas International Corporation Scholarship Trust
225 North Michigan Avenue, 11th Floor
Chicago, IL 60601   (312) 565-7500
Contact: Carol Jones, Personnel Services Officer

Limitations: Scholarships to dependents of Midas International Corporation employees only.
Financial data: Year ended 12/31/85. Assets, $0 (M); Total giving, $44,911; Grants to individuals, 43 grants totaling $44,911, high $1,300, low $740, average grant $1,100.
Employer Identification Number: 237024814
Applications: Deadline March 1st; Completion of formal application required.

1179
Monroe Auto Equipment Company Foundation
c/o Comerica Bank
Detroit, MI 45275-1022
Contact: Kay Osgood, Trustee, Monroe Auto Equipment Company, One International Drive, Monroe, MI 48161; Tel.: (313) 243-8000

Limitations: Scholarships only to children of Monroe Auto Euqipment Company employees.
Financial data: Year ended 12/31/86. Assets, $1,028,753 (M); Total giving, $103,262; Grants to individuals amount not specified.
Employer Identification Number: 346518867
Applications: Applications accepted throughout the year; Completion of formal application required; Interviews required.

1180
Morris (The William T.) Foundation, Inc.
P.O. Box 5786
New York, NY 10163   (212) 986-8036
Contact: Bruce August, Assistant Secretary

Limitations: Undergraduate student loans for children of employees of American Chain and Cable Company, Inc. or its subsidiaries; in addition, the Thomas J. Morris Scholarship is awarded each year to a resident of West Pittston, PA.
Financial data: Year ended 6/30/86. Assets, $30,261,500 (M); Total giving, $988,150; Grants to individuals, 4 scholarships totaling $8,000; Loans to

individuals amount not specified.
Employer Identification Number: 131600908
Applications: Deadline July 31st; Completion of formal application required; Applications should be sent to Oak Hill, RD 4, Box 500, Dallas, PA 18612; Tel.: (717) 639-5629.
Program description:
Loans of varying amounts up to $1,500 per year are made to needy college students whose parents are employees of American Chain and Cable Company, Inc. or its subsidiaries. These loans are repayable without interest after graduation or prior to termination of education.
  The **Thomas J. Morris Scholarship Program** is an $8,000 grant awarded annually and payable over four years to a resident of West Pittston, PA. The total number of recipients during the year is four.

1181
Mueller (C.F.) Company Scholarship Foundation
180 Baldwin Avenue
Jersey City, NJ 07360   (201) 653-3800
Contact: Edwin J. Geils, Treasurer

Limitations: Scholarships, grants-in-aid, awards, and student loans to C.F. Mueller employees and their children.
Financial data: Year ended 6/30/85. Assets, $53,387 (M); Total giving, $142,518; Grants to individuals, 114 grants totaling $142,518, high $1,750, low $180.
Employer Identification Number: 226100054
Applications: Submit applications between January 1st and April 30th.
Program description:
The purpose of the foundation is to help company employees and their children to continue education on a preparatory, college, university, graduate, or professional level.

1182
Myers-Ti-Caro Foudation, Inc.
P.O. Box 2208
Gastonia, NC 28053   (704) 864-5461
Contact: Albert G. Meyers Jr., President

Limitations: Scholarships to children and eligible dependents of employees of Ti-Caro, Inc..
Financial data: Year ended 9/28/86. Assets, $6,692,236 (M); Total giving, $373,155; Grants to individuals, 37 grants totaling $82,222, high $3,235, low $484.
Employer Identification Number: 560770083
Applications: Deadline in September; Completion of formal application required.

1183★
National City Foundation, The
c/o Corporate Tax Department
399 Park Avenue
New York, NY 10043

Limitations: Scholarships only to high school seniors who are children of employees of Citibank/Citicorp.
Financial data: Year ended 12/31/86. Assets, $2,400,000 (M); Total giving, $30,350; Grants to individuals, 38 grants totaling $30,350, high $1,500, low $250.
Employer Identification Number: 136097628
Applications: Deadline November 31st; Completion of formal application required.
Publications: Annual report.
Program description:
Ten scholarship stipends per year are awarded, renewable for up to four years, contingent upon academic standards.

1184
National Machinery Foundation, Inc.
Greenfield Street
P.O. Box 747
Tiffin, OH 44883   (419) 447-5211
Contact: D. B. Bero, Administrator

Limitations: Scholarships only to high school seniors or first-year graduates who are children of National Machinery employees.
Financial data: Year ended 12/31/86. Assets, $6,363,297 (M); Total giving, $278,729; Grants to individuals, 200 grants totaling $36,150, high $100, low $58; Subtotal for scholarships not specified.
Employer Identification Number: 346520191
Applications: Initial approach by letter; Completion of formal application required.
Program description:
Under the **E.R. Frost Scholarship Program** the foundation annually awards nine scholarships to employee children of National Machinery Company who are seeking either a four-year undergraduate degree or a three- or four-year nursing degree from an accredited institution.

Six of the scholarships, three each for $4,000 and $2,000 respectively, are designated for children of full-time employees with a minimum of three years service. The $1,000 scholarships are available to children of all full-time employees. Grants are made on the basis of an annual written competition. Contestants should be high school seniors. However, non-winners are given a second chance; thus, recent graduates also compete.

1185
Noble (The Samuel Roberts) Foundation, Inc.
P.O. Box 2180
Ardmore, OK 73402   (405) 223-5810
Contact: John F. Snodgrass, President

Limitations: Four-year scholarships limited to children of employees of Noble-affiliated companies.
Financial data: Year ended 10/31/86. Assets, $270,199,503 (M); Total giving, $14,320,314; Grants to individuals, 51 grants totaling $38,450, average grant $1,000.
Employer Identification Number: 730606209
Applications: Initial approach by letter; Completion of formal application required.
Publications: Annual report.
Program description:
The foundation provides a maximum of ten $4,000 a year, four-year scholarships to children of employees of Noble Companies as selected, upon application, by an independent scholarship awards committee.

1186
North American Philips Foundation
100 East 42nd Street
New York, NY 10017
Contact: NAP Scholarship Program Administrator

Limitations: Scholarships for higher education.
Financial data: Year ended 12/31/85. Assets, $12,725 (M); Total giving, $186,235; Grants to individuals, 186 grants totaling $186,235, high $1,500, low $500.
Employer Identification Number: 132961300
Applications: Deadline March 1st; Initial approach by letter requesting application; Completion of formal application required.
Program description:
Scholarship awards are made on the basis of:
- Academic performance and potential as shown by applicant's high school record and college entrance tests
- Participation and leadership roles in extracurricular activities and sports
- Evidence of strong character and motivation as seen in the applicant's life outside of school.

1187★
North American Royalties Inc. Welfare Fund
200 East Eighth Street
Chattanooga, TN 37402   (615) 265-3181
Contact: Gordon L. Smith, Jr., Vice-President, Planning

Limitations: Scholarships for children of North American Royalties, Inc. employees.
Financial data: Year ended 12/31/87. Assets, $202,613 (L); Total giving, $190,495; Grants to individuals, 18 grants totaling, $28,874, high $1,750, low $875.
Employer Identification Number: 626052490
Applications: Deadline March 1st; Initial approach by

letter or telephone; Completion of formal application
required.
Publications: 990-PF printed copy available upon
request.

1188
Oilgear Ferris Foundation, Inc.
2300 South 51st Street
Milwaukee, WI 53219   (414) 327-1700
Contact: C. L. Gosewehr, President

Limitations: Scholarships only to children of active
employees of The Oilgear Company.
Financial data: Year ended 2/31/86. Assets,
$1,024,553 (M); Total giving, $72,428; Grants to
individuals amount not specified.
Employer Identification Number: 396050126
Applications: Deadline March 31st.

1189
Oshkosh B'Gosh Foundation, Inc.
P.O. Box 300
Oshkosh, WI 54902   (414) 231-8800
Contact: William P. Jacobsen, Treasurer

Limitations: Undergraduate scholarships for students
in communities in which Oshkosh B'Gosh, Inc. plants
or facilities are located including, but not limited to,
children of Oshkosh B'Gosh, Inc. employees.
Financial data: Year ended 12/31/86. Assets, $162,826
(M); Total giving, $229,067; Grants to individuals, 19
grants totaling $23,750, each grant $1,250.
Employer Identification Number: 391525020
Applications: Completion of formal application
required.
Program description:
The following requirements pertain to applicants who
are high school students or graduates:
  1. The applicant must be a high school student or
  graduate, and have had no previous full-time
  enrollment at a college. A minimum GPA of 2.5
  (or its equivalent) is necessary to qualify a student
  for evaluation.
  2. Recipients must enroll in a beginning course of
  study at a college within eight months after high
  school graduation.
The following requirements pertain to award
recipients who are continuing students at a college:
  1. The recipient must be pursuing a degree
  program as a full-time undergraduate student and
  must have at least one full year of study
  remaining, while maintaining a minimum GPA of
  2.5.
  2. Recipients must continue their course of study
  at a college within three months after the date of
  notification of continuation of the scholarship
  award.

1190★
Oshkosh Truck Foundation, Inc.
2307 Oregon Street
P.O. Box 2566
Oshkosh, WI 54903   (414) 235-9150
Contact: Peter Mosling

Limitations: Scholarships to local high school students
who are children of Oshkosh Truck Corporation
employees.
Financial data: Year ended 12/31/87. Assets, $332,000
(M); Total giving, $192,311; Grants to individuals, 17
grants totaling, $12,500.
Employer Identification Number: 396062129
Applications: Initial approach by letter.
Publications: Application guidelines.

1191
Pantry Pride Foundation
555 Southwest 12th Avenue
Pompano Beach, FL 33069   (305) 785-4334

Limitations: Scholarships for children of employees of
Food Fair Stores, Inc. and Pantry Pride, Inc. and
others.
Financial data: Year ended 4/30/86. Assets, $509,739
(M); Total giving, $128,775; Grants to individuals, 5
grants totaling $5,050.
Employer Identification Number: 236259906
Applications: Deadline March 1st; Completion of
formal application required.

1192
Pella Rolscreen Foundation
c/o Rolscreen Company
102 Main Street
Pella, IA 50219   (515) 628-1000
Contact: Clifford M. White, Assistant
Secretary-Treasurer

Limitations: Scholarships only to children of
employees of Pella Rolscreen Company.
Financial data: Year ended 12/31/86. Assets,
$7,134,427 (M); Total giving, $944,986; Grants to
individuals totaling $16,695.
Employer Identification Number: 237043881
Applications: Applications accepted throughout the
year; Initial approach by letter.
Publications: Program information.

1193
Pennsylvania Steel Foundry Foundation
c/o Meridian Trust Company
P.O. Box 1102
Reading, PA 19603
Contact: Elizabeth N. Clapper, Secretary, Pennsylvania
Steel Foundry Foundation, Hamburg, PA 19526

Limitations: Scholarships only to employees and

children of employees of Pennsylvania Steel Foundry and Machine Company, Hamburg, PA. Recipients must attend an accredited four-year college.
Financial data: Year ended 12/31/86. Assets, $28,024 (M); Total giving, $1,500; Grants to individuals, 4 grants totaling $1,500; 1985, Grants to individuals, 4 grants totaling $2,600, high $800, low $600.
Employer Identification Number: 236490265
Applications: Applications accepted throughout the year; Completion of formal application required. Foundation Committee meets in May to review applications. Students who are reapplying are notified after their college transcripts have been reviewed.

1194
Pennwalt Foundation
Pennwalt Building
Three Benjamin Franklin Parkway
Philadelphia, PA 19102   (215) 587-7653
Contact: George L. Hagar, Executive Secretary

Limitations: Scholarships only for high school seniors who are children of Pennwalt Corporation employees.
Financial data: Year ended 12/31/85. Assets, $719,593 (M); Total giving, $1,141,807; Grants to individuals, 49 grants totaling $91,305, average grant $1,000.
Employer Identification Number: 236156818
Applications: Applications accepted throughout the year.
Program description:
Scholarships are paid directly to the educational institution on behalf of the individual recipients.

1195
Perini (Joseph) Memorial Foundation
73 Mt. Wayte Avenue
Framingham, MA 01701   (617) 875-6171
Contact: Joseph R. Perini, Jr., Secretary

Limitations: Scholarships only to children of employees of Perini Corp. or its subsidiaries residing in Massachusetts.
Financial data: Year ended 12/31/85. Assets, $8,653,660 (M); Total giving, $453,143; Grants to individuals, 13 grants totaling $31,000.
Employer Identification Number: 046139986
Applications: Deadline October 1st; Initial approach by letter.

1196
Perini Memorial Foundation, Inc.
73 Mt. Wayte Avenue
Framingham, MA 01701   (617) 875-6171
Contact: Election Committee, P.O. Box 31, Framingham, MA 01701

Limitations: Scholarships to children of employees of Perini Corporation or its subsidiaries.
Financial data: Year ended 12/31/85. Assets,

$4,618,395 (M); Total giving, $236,725; Grants to individuals, 11 grants totaling $31,000, high $4,000, low $1,000.
Employer Identification Number: 046118587
Applications: Initial approach by letter.

1197★
Peyton (The Mary L.) Foundation
Texas Commerce Bank Building, Suite 1706
El Paso, TX 79901   (915) 533-9698
Contact: James M. Day, Executive Administrator

Limitations: Assistance only to legal residents or children of living residents of El Paso County, TX. Preference is given to children of needy present or former employees of Peyton Packing Company.
Financial data: Year ended 5/31/87. Assets, $2,797,143 (M); Total giving, $152,496; Grants to individuals, 2,321 grants totaling $152,496, high $90, low $60, average grant $75.
Employer Identification Number: 741276102
Applications: Applications accepted throughout the year; Initial approach by letter explaining economic situation causing the need for assistance for basic services and itemization of those for which assistance is requested; Completion of formal application required; Interviews granted upon request.
Publications: Informational brochure.
Program description:
Grants are given to those legal residents who have no other resources on which to depend and cannot obtain funds elsewhere. Grants are to provide food, clothing, medical attention, education opportunity and other necessities of life to those incapacitated by youth or age or physical or mental disabilities from earning a livelihood.

1198
Pfister & Vogel Tanning Company, Inc. Foundation
c/o First Wisconsin Trust Company
P.O. Box 2054
Milwaukee, WI 53201
Contact: Pfister & Vogel Tanning Company, Inc., 1531 North Water Street, Milwaukee, WI 53202

Limitations: Scholarships to children of employees of Pfister & Vogel Tanning Company, Inc.
Financial data: Year ended 5/31/87. Assets, $265,768 (M); Total giving, $14,225; Grants to individuals, 4 grants totaling $5,625, high $2,500, low $625.
Employer Identification Number: 396036556

1199
Phillips (Frank) Educational Loan Fund
c/o Phillips Petroleum Company
750A Plaza Office Building
Bartlesville, OK 74004
Contact: Bill F. Dausses, Director, Educational Funds,
180 Plaza Office Building, Bartlesville, OK 74004;
Tel.: (918) 661-5630

Limitations: Educational loans for undergraduate study
to children of present, deceased, or retired employees
of Phillips Petroleum Company.
Financial data: Year ended 8/31/86. Assets, $217,125
(M); Expenditures, $33,310; Loans to individuals, 94
loans totaling $33,000, high $600, low $300.
Employer Identification Number: 736095140
Applications: Deadline August 1st; Completion of
formal application required.
Program description:
Applicants must be the children, adopted children,
stepchildren, or fully dependent wards of employees
or former employees of Phillips Petroleum Company.
Current employees must have a minimum of two years
of service and deceased or retired employees must
have had a minimum of three years of service with the
company. Loans must be reapplied for each year.

1200★
Pigott (Paul) Scholarship Foundation
P.O. Box 1518
Bellevue, WA 98009   (206) 455-7400
Contact: E. A. Carpenter

Limitations: Scholarships only to children of
employees of PACCAR, Inc. and its subsidiaries for
freshman college year or grades 10-12 at non-tax
supported secondary school.
Financial data: Year ended 7/31/87. Assets,
$1,043,389 (M); Total giving, $44,312; Grants to
individuals, 26 grants totaling $44,312, high $4,000,
low $750.
Employer Identification Number: 916030639
Applications: Deadline November 1st; Completion of
formal application, including transcript, school report,
and test scores, required; **Scholarships are not
renewable.**

1201
Pittsburgh Forgings Foundation
c/o Mellon Bank, N.A.
Room 151-4040
Pittsburgh, PA 15258   (412) 234-5784
Contact: Barbara Robinson, Vice-President

Limitations: Scholarships only to children of
employees of Pittsburgh Forgings Company and its
subsidiaries.
Financial data: Year ended 12/31/86. Assets,
$2,254,652 (M); Total giving, $144,275; Grants to
individuals totaling $3,000.

Employer Identification Number: 256018926
Applications: Contact foundation for current
application deadline; Initial approach by letter
requesting application; Completion of formal
application required.

1202
Pluta Family Foundation, Inc.
3385 Brighton Henrietta Town Line Road
Rochester, NY 14623

Limitations: Scholarships to General Circuits, Inc.
employees and their families.
Financial data: Year ended 12/31/85. Assets,
$3,554,699 (M); Total giving, $181,800; Grants to
individuals, 38 grants totaling $22,800, each grant
$600.
Employer Identification Number: 510176213
Applications: Initial approach by letter.

1203
Post & Courier Foundation
134 Columbus Street
Charleston, SC 29402
Contact: J. F. Smoak, Secretary-Treasurer

Limitations: Scholarships only to Post & Courier
newspaper carriers with at least two years of service.
Financial data: Year ended 12/31/86. Assets,
$1,694,601 (M); Total giving, $339,679; Grants to
individuals, 14 grants totaling, $17,910, high $4,383,
low $250.
Employer Identification Number: 576020356
**Applications: Applications from individuals who are
not within the stated recipient restriction not
accepted.**

1204
Potlatch Foundation for Higher Education
P.O. Box 3591
San Francisco, CA 94119   (415) 981-5980
Contact: George C. Check, President

Limitations: Scholarships to undergraduates who
reside in areas of Potlatch Corporation operations.
Financial data: Year ended 12/31/86. Assets, $150,624
(M); Total giving, $226,000; Grants to individuals, 177
grants totaling $177,000, each grant $1,000.
Employer Identification Number: 826005250
Applications: Deadline February 1st for new
applications, July 1st for renewals; Request application
no later than October 15th preceding the year for
which the scholarship is sought; Completion of formal
application required.
Publications: Application guidelines, annual report,
program information.
Program description:
The **Potlatch Undergraduate Scholarship Program**
makes awards to individuals graduating from high

schools or having a permanent residence in the immediate service areas of Potlatch Corporation. The majority of Potlatch Foundation scholarships are awarded to students residing near major Potlatch operating facilities in Idaho, Minnesota and Arkansas. Applicants need not be related to a company employee. Recipients are selected on the basis of character, personality, leadership qualities, scholastic achievement and ability, and need. Scholarships are subject to annual renewal during the course of a four-year program leading to the B.A. or other degree approved by the foundation's trustees. Approximately 50 new awards are made each year.

1205
Premier Industrial Foundation
4500 Euclid Avenue
Cleveland, OH 44103   (216) 391-8300
Contact: Morton L. Mandel, Trustee

Limitations: Scholarships only to employees of Premier Industrial Corporation and certain close relatives.
Financial data: Year ended 12/31/86. Assets, $4,816,114 (M); Total giving, $141,780; Grants to individuals, 6 grants totaling $5,350, high $1,250, low $100.
Employer Identification Number: 346522448
Applications: Applications accepted throughout the year.

1206
Presto Foundation
P.O. Box 2105
Wilmington, DE 19899
Contact: Harriet Rose, 3925 North Hastings Way, Eau Claire, WI 54703

Limitations: Scholarships only for children of employees of National Presto Industries, Inc.
Financial data: Year ended 5/31/87. Assets, $12,917,770 (M); Total giving, $556,060; Grants to individuals, 14 grants totaling $49,015, high $4,000, low $1,727.
Employer Identification Number: 396045769
Applications: Applications accepted throughout the year; Initial approach by letter.

1207★
Quaker Chemical Foundation, The
Elm and Lee Streets
Conshohocken, PA 19428   (215) 828-4250
Contact: Karl H. Spaeth, Chairman

Limitations: Scholarships only to employees of Quaker Chemical Corporation.
Financial data: Year ended 6/30/87. Assets, $357,519 (M); Total giving, $380,876; Grants to individuals, 39 grants totaling $88,360.

Employer Identification Number: 236245803
Applications: Deadline April 30th; Completion of formal application required.
Publications: Application guidelines.

1208
R. B. Charitable and Educational Foundation
Lucas and Wentzel Streets
Rochester, IN 46975   (219) 223-2171
Contact: Lalla Heyde

Limitations: Student loans for undergraduate studies, primarily to children of employees of the McMahan-O'Connor Construction Company.
Financial data: Year ended 11/30/86. Assets, $41,474 (M); Expenditures, $8,514; Loans to individuals, 7 loans totaling $2,400, high $400, low $300.
Employer Identification Number: 357095817
Applications: Applications accepted throughout the year; Initial approach by letter.

1209
Rahr Foundation
P.O. Box 130
Manitowoc, WI 54220   (414) 684-5515
Contact: Mrs. JoAnn Weyenberg

Limitations: Scholarships only to children of employees of Rahr Malting Company and affiliates.
Financial data: Year ended 12/31/86. Assets, $2,336,843 (M); Total giving, $172,197; Grants to individuals, 15 grants totaling $20,000.
Employer Identification Number: 396046046
Applications: Applications accepted throughout the year.

1210
Ralston Purina Trust Fund
Checkerboard Square
St. Louis, MO 63164   (314) 982-3230
Contact: Fred H. Perabo, Member, Board of Control

Limitations: Scholarships for children of employees of Ralston Purina Company.
Financial data: Year ended 8/31/86. Assets, $11,967,06l; Total giving, $2,657,131; Grants to individuals amount not specified; 1985, Grants to individuals totaling $128,970.
Employer Identification Number: 431209652
Applications: Applications accepted throughout the year.

1211
Reeves Brothers Foundation, Inc., The
115 Summit Avenue
Summit, NJ 07901
Contact: Paschal Wilborn, Reeves Brothers, Inc., P.O. Box 1898, Spartanburg, SC 29304; Tel.: (803) 576-1210

Limitations: Scholarship loans only to employees or children of employees of Reeves Brothers, Inc., or its subsidiaries, or to students who reside, or attend school, in the geographical area in which Reeves or its subsidiaries' plants are located.
Financial data: Year ended 6/30/86. Assets, $16,703,892 (M); Expenditures, $712,058; Loans to individuals, 84 loans totaling $83,800, average loan $1,000.
Employer Identification Number: 131891781
Applications: Deadlines May 15th for summer school and June 15th for full year; Completion of formal application required; Include (when applicable) final high school transcript, college transcript for all years, financial aid form, college letter of acceptance, and letter of recommendation.
Program description:
The college must be a two- or four-year accredited college or university that grants Associates, Bachelors, Masters, or higher degrees.

1212
Reilly Foundation
1510 Market Square Center
151 North Delaware Street
Indianapolis, IN 46204   (317) 638-7531
Contact: Lorraine D. Schroeder, Trustee

Limitations: Scholarships only to children of employees of Reilly Tar & Chemical Corporation.
Financial data: Year ended 12/31/86. Assets, $782,883 (M); Total giving, $199,577; Grants to individuals, 86 grants totaling $161,625, high $640, low $24.
Employer Identification Number: 352061750
Applications: Applications accepted throughout the year; Initial approach by letter.
Program description:
Successful applicants must submit receipts and grade transcripts to the foundation after the first scholarship award is made.

1213
Rexnord Foundation, Inc.
c/o Rexnord Inc.
350 North Sunny Slope Road
Brookfield, WI 53005   (414) 797-5677
Contact: Robert M. MacQueen, Vice-President, Human Resources

Limitations: Scholarships only to children and wards of Rexnord Inc. employees, including employees of subsidiary companies.

Financial data: Year ended 10/31/86. Assets, $3,840,365 (M); Total giving, $1,503,073; Grants to individuals totaling $34,500.
Employer Identification Number: 396042029
Applications: Deadline May 11th; Submit proof of eligibility via photocopy of test scores.
Program description:
The minimum test score required for eligibility is 20 on the ACT or 1000 on the SAT.

1214
Richardson (Sid) Memorial Fund
309 Main Street
Fort Worth, TX 76102   (817) 336-0494
Contact: Jo Helen Dean, Administrator

Limitations: Scholarships to spouses or descendants of current or former employees of companies in which the late Sid W. Richardson had a major financial interest, or a continuation of such company.
Financial data: Year ended 12/31/86. Assets, $3,776,631 (M); Total giving, $189,623; Grants to individuals, 71 grants totaling $186,623, high $11,000, low $348; average grant $2,600.
Employer Identification Number: 751220266
Applications: Deadline March 31st; Applications available January 1st-March 1st; Applicants should provide name, place, and dates of service of qualifying employee; Initial approach by letter.
Program description:
About 18 new scholarships are awarded annually for a minimum of one year for college or vocational education. Acceptance is based on academic achievement and financial need.

1215
S&H Foundation, Inc., The
c/o Sperry & Hutchinson Company
330 Madison Avenue
New York, NY 10017   (212) 370-1144
Contact: Henry S. Coleman, Coleman Associates, P.O. Box 1283, New Canaan, CT 06840

Limitations: Scholarships to children of employees of S&H Company and children of employees of S&H Retail and Green Stamp Licensees.
Financial data: Year ended 12/21/85. Assets, $6,916,533 (M); Total giving, $239,450; Grants to individuals, 189 grants totaling $239,450; Subtotal for employee children scholarships, 27 grants totaling $38,700, high, $2,500, low $750; Subtotal for merchant employee children scholarships, 137 grants totaling $68,250, average grant $500.
Employer Identification Number: 136114308
Applications: Deadline January 1st; Completion of formal application required; Applications available at parent's place of employment.

Program description:
Employees' Children Scholarship Program awards scholarships to qualified students for undergraduate study in colleges and universities as well as technical and vocational schools and hospital schools of nursing.

Grants are renewable for up to four years of college, and once awarded remain in force regardless of parents' employment status, providing the student maintains a satisfactory academic performance.

Merchant Scholarships are four-year grants of $500 per year awarded to children whose parents own retail businesses that give S&H green stamps or whose parents work for businesses that give S&H green stamps. Recipients select their own places and subjects of study.

1216★
Security Pacific Foundation
333 South Hope Street
Los Angeles, CA 90071   (213) 345-6688
Contact: Mrs. Carol E. Taufer, President, P.O. Box 2097, Terminal Annex, Los Angeles, CA, 90051

Limitations: Scholarships only to children of employees of Security Pacific Corporation.
Financial data: Year ended 12/31/86. Assets, $10,318,557 (M); Total giving, $4,755,581; Grants to individuals amount not specified.
Employer Identification Number: 953195084
Applications: Initial approach by letter.
Publications: Annual report.

1217
SFE Technologies Scholarship Program
420 North Brand Boulevard, Suite 600
Glendale, CA 91203
Contact: Scholarship Committee, San Fernando Electric Manufacturing Company, 1501 First Street, San Fernando, CA 91341

Limitations: Scholarships to employees or family members of employees of SFE Technologies.
Financial data: Year ended 12/31/86. Assets, $17,399 (M); Total giving, $15,150; Grants to individuals, 17 grants totaling $15,150, high $1,500, low $250, general range $500-1,000.
Employer Identification Number: 953650982
Applications: Applications accepted throughout the year; Completion of formal application required; Interviews required.
Program description:
Grants are awarded for higher education with no restriction on courses of study. Thus, eligibility extends to undergraduate and graduate study in degree or certificate programs as well as to study in junior colleges. Undergraduates are, however, required to

carry a minimum of 12 credits a semester; postgraduates must carry sufficient courses to enable them to complete their program within the normal period listed in the institution's program description. Scholarships are renewable as long as the student remains in good standing at his institution.

1218
SmithKline Beckman Foundation
One Franklyn Plaza
P.O. Box 7929
Philadelphia, PA 19101   (215) 751-5149
Contact: William L. Grala, President

Limitations: Scholarships only to children of deceased or disabled employees of SmithKline Beckman Corporation and its wholly owned subsidiaries worldwide.
Financial data: Year ended 12/31/86. Assets, $4,116,323 (M); Total giving, $1,050,962; Grants to individuals, 18 grants totaling $81,222, high $11,350, low $460.
Employer Identification Number: 232120418
Applications: Completion of formal application required.
Publications: Annual report.
Program description:
The **C. Mahlon Kline Memorial Scholarship** provides financial assistance toward college or graduate education. The scholarships are competitive and selection is made by an independent committee.

1219★
Sonat Foundation, Inc., The
1900 Fifth Avenue, North
P.O. Box 2563
Birmingham, AL 35203   (205) 325-7460
Contact: Darlene Sanders, Secretary

Limitations: Scholarships only to children of employees of Sonat Inc.
Financial data: Year ended 12/31/87. Assets, $3,932,070 (M); Total giving, $896,419; Grants to individuals totaling $109,400.
Employer Identification Number: 630830299
Applications: Initial approach by letter.

1220
Sony Corporation of America Foundation, Inc.
Nine West 57th Street
New York, NY 10019   (212) 418-9404
Contact: Kenneth L. Ness, Vice-President

Limitations: Scholarships for children of employees of Sony Corporation of America.
Financial data: Year ended 12/31/86. Assets, $1,763,503 (M); Total giving, $498,603; Grants to individuals amount not specified.
Employer Identification Number: 237181637

Applications: Applications accepted throughout the year; Initial approach by letter; Completion of formal application required.

1221★
Southern States Educational Foundation, Inc.
P.O. Box 546
Savannah, GA 31402   (912) 232-1101
Contact: Board of Trustees

Limitations: Scholarships to children of regular monthly salaried employees of Southern States Phosphate and Fertilizer Company who have been accepted for admission by an accredited college.
Financial data: Year ended 5/31/87. Assets, 127,743 (M); Total giving, $1,400; Grants to individuals, 6 grants totaling $1,400; 1985, Grants to individuals, 9 grants totaling $2,600, high $400, low $100.
Employer Identification Number: 586073809
Applications: Deadline 30 days prior to start of semester or quarter; Initial approach by letter giving name of applicant, educational institution to be attended and period of attendance; Letter of acceptance from educational institution must be enclosed.

1222
Steinman (James Hale) Foundation
P.O. Box 128
Lancaster, PA 17603
Contact: M. Steven Weaver, Eight West King Street, Lancaster, PA 17603

Limitations: Scholarships only to newspaper carriers and children of employees of Steinman Enterprises, primarily in Lancaster, PA.
Financial data: Year ended 12/31/86. Assets, $5,820,587 (M); Total giving, $432,218; Grants to individuals, 24 grants totaling $39,000, high $2,000, low $1,000.
Employer Identification Number: 236266377
Applications: Deadline February 28th of senior year of high school; Completion of formal application required.

1223
Stone Foundation, Inc.
150 North Michigan Avenue
Chicago, IL 60601
Contact: Arnold Brookstone, Administrator

Limitations: Scholarships only to children of employees with two or more years of service at Stone Container Corporation.
Financial data: Year ended 12/31/86. Assets, $785,665 (M); Total giving, $253,500; Grants to individuals, 15 grants totaling $23,000, high $2,000, low $1,000.
Employer Identification Number: 366063761

Applications: Deadline April 1st; Completion of formal application required.

1224
Stop & Shop Charitable Foundation, The
P.O. Box 369
Boston, MA 02101
Contact: Frank Ippolito, Corporate Employee Benefits, The Stop & Shop Companies, Inc.

Limitations: Scholarships only to employees or their children of Stop & Shop Companies, Inc., and its subsidiaries, including Bradlees Department Stores, Medi Mart Drug Stores, Charles B. Perkins Tobacco Shops, Stop & Shop Supermarkets, and Stop & Shop Manufacturing Company.
Financial data: Year ended 12/31/85. Assets, $4,606,044 (M); Total giving, $636,087; Grants to individuals amount not specified.
Employer Identification Number: 046039593
Applications: Deadline January 31st; Completion of formal application required; Submit high school transcript, letter of recommendation from high school, and SAT scores with application.
Program description:
The foundation provides approximately ten scholarships of $2,000 each year ($500 a year for four years). Applicant or parent must have been employed by Stop & Shop Companies, Inc. for at least one year by January 1st prior to application submission.

1225
Superior-Pacific Fund
Seven Wynnewood Road
Wynnewood, PA 19096
Contact: Superior Tube Company Scholarship Committee, P.O. Box 616, Devault, PA 19432; Tel.: (215) 647-2701

Limitations: Scholarships only to children of employees of the Superior Tube Company with over three years service.
Financial data: Year ended 12/31/86. Assets, $6,522,722 (M); Total giving, $331,475; Grants to individuals, 16 grants totaling $11,500, high $1,200, low $250, general range $300-1,000.
Employer Identification Number: 236298237
Applications: Deadlines January 1st for high school certification form and January 3rd for personal data form, both forms are part of the application available through the personnel office of Superior Tube Company; Completion of formal application required; SAT test must be taken no later than the test offered in January and a sealed copy of scores mailed to the company early in the year; Financial Aid Form (FAF) should be mailed to College Scholarship Service no later than January 10th.

1226
Taft (Hulbert) Jr. Memorial Scholarship Foundation
c/o Taft Broadcasting Company
1718 Young Street
Cincinnati, OH 45210
Contact: Dudley S. Taft, President

Limitations: Scholarships only to children of full-time employees of the Taft Broadcasting Company who are graduating from high school.
Financial data: Year ended 12/31/86. Assets, $6,374 (M); Total giving, $12,350; Grants to individuals, 11 grants totaling $12,350, high $3,000, low $137.
Employer Identification Number: 316079591
Applications: Deadline February 27th; Completion of formal application required. Completed application must be submitted to school counselor, who completes last page of application and forwards to the foundation.

1227★
Tektronix Foundation
Y 3-439
P.O. Box 500
Beaverton, OR 97077   (503) 643-8146
Contact: Thomas O. Williams, Administrator

Limitations: Scholarships to children of Tektronix, Inc., employees and students attending high school in Clackamas, Washington, and Multnomah counties, OR, and in Clark County, WA.
Financial data: Year ended 12/31/86. Assets, $1,796,522 (M); Total giving, $2,278,256; Grants to individuals, 27 grants totaling $27,420, average grant $1,000.
Employer Identification Number: 936021540
Applications: Deadline March 15th; Completion of formal application required; Interviews for finalists only are required.
Program description:
Single grants of $2,000 usable during a five year period.

1228★
Temple-Inland Foundation
303 South Temple Drive
P.O. Drawer 338
Diboll, TX 75941   (409) 829-1305
Contact: James R. Wash, Secretary-Treasurer

Limitations: Scholarships only to children of employees who have completed three years of continuous full-time service as of April 1st of the year of application at Temple-Inland, Inc. or its subsidiaries (except Inland Container Corporation).
Financial data: Year ended 6/30/87. Assets, $5,386,086 (M); Total giving, $478,170; Grants to individuals, 13 grants totaling $27,750, high $3,000, low $1,750, average grant $2,135.
Employer Identification Number: 751977109
Applications: Deadline March 15th; Completion of formal application required; Interviews required; Application forms and information can be obtained in the offices of Temple-Inland, Inc. and its subsidiaries as well as from the foundation.
Publications: 990-PF printed copy available upon request.
Program description:
The scholarship committee, consisting of three faculty or administrative representatives selected from two or more fully accredited four-year colleges, reviews all applications, may conduct personal interviews with the candidates, and finally select the winners on the basis of:

- High school scholastic record
- Performance on any required tests
- Leadership and responsibility
- Character
- Aptitude and promise of success
- Financial need
- Motivation
- Seriousness of purpose
- Qualities of citizenship.

Amount of scholarship awards varies depending upon the student's financial need and other factors deemed by the scholarship committee to be pertinent. Special achievement scholarships of $250 each will be made to scholars who attain a grade point average in the top ten percent of their college class for a school year.

Relatives and children of officers or directors of Temple-Inland, Inc., its subsidiaries, the foundation or its substantial contributors are not eligible to apply.

1229
Texas Industries Foundation
8100 Carpenter Freeway
Dallas, TX 75247   (214) 637-3100
Contact: James R. McCraw, Controller

Limitations: Scholarships to dependents of employees of Texas Industries, Inc., to be used at an accredited institution.
Financial data: Year ended 12/31/86. Assets, $473 (M); Total giving, $195,618; Grants to individuals, 5 grants $16,231.
Employer Identification Number: 756043179
Applications: Deadline January 15th; Interviews required.

1230
Thomasville Furniture Industries Foundation
c/o Wachovia Bank and Trust Company
P.O. Box 3099
Winston-Salem, NC 27150   (919) 770-6222
Contact: David C. Taylor, Account Manager

Limitations: Scholarships to children of employees of
Thomasville Furniture Industries.
Financial data: Year ended 12/31/86. Assets,
$3,166,000 (M); Total giving, $223,910; Grants to
individuals, 91 grants totaling $56,010.
Employer Identification Number: 566047870
Applications: Applications accepted throughout the
year; Initial approach by letter. Application address:
c/o Carlyle A. Nance, Jr., Thomasville Furniture
Industries, P.O. Box 339, Thomasville, NC 27360;
Tel.: (919) 475-1361

1231
Thomson (Frank) Scholarship Trust
c/o Fidelity Bank, N.A., Trustee
135 South Broad Street
Philadelphia, PA 19109
Contact: Frank Thomson, Chairman Selection
Committee

Limitations: Scholarships only to high school seniors
who are sons of active, retired, or deceased employees
of Conrail or Penn Central, and Amtrak who were
employed by the Penn Central Transportation
Company or Pennsylvania Railroad Company before
April 1st, 1976.
Financial data: Year ended 12/31/85. Assets,
$1,230,722 (M); Total giving, $44,625; Grants to
individuals, 40 grants totaling $44,625, high $2000,
low $200, general range $600-2,000, average grant
$1,500.
Employer Identification Number: 236217801
Applications: Deadline March 31st for initial
application, May 30th for renewals; Initial approach
by letter requesting application; Completion of formal
application required; Applications and instructions
available at Conrail office only.
Publications: Program information.
Program description:
Scholarship selection is based on financial need and
the applicant's performance on Scholastic Aptitude
Tests. Scholarships may be renewed for up to four
years.

1232
Timken Company Educational Fund, Inc., The
1835 Dueber Avenue, S.W.
Canton, OH 44706
Contact: Thomas E. Grove, Supervisor - Education
Programs

Limitations: Scholarships to children of employees of
the Timken Company.

Financial data: Year ended 12/31/86. Assets, $259,408
(M); Total giving, $343,800; Grants to individuals, 31
grants totaling $307,800.
Employer Identification Number: 346520257
Applications: Deadline is announced each year;
Completion of formal application required.
Program description:
Grants provide money for tuition, fees, books, and
living expenses.

1233
Tiscornia Foundation, Inc., The
P.O. Box 8787
2303 Pipestone Road
Benton Harbor, MI 49022-8787   (616) 962-0812
Contact: Laurianne T. Davis, Secretary

Limitations: Scholarships only to Northern Berrien
County High School seniors and children of
employees of Auto Specialties Manufacturing
Company.
Financial data: Year ended 11/30/86. Assets,
$3,222,767 (M); Total giving, $136,075; Grants to
individuals, 9 grants totaling $15,150, high $2,750,
low $875, average grant $1,750.
Employer Identification Number: 381777343
Applications: Deadline April 1st; Initial approach by
letter requesting application; Completion of formal
application required.

1234
Tractor & Equipment Company Foundation
5336 Airport Highway
P.O. Box 2326
Birmingham, AL 35201-2326   (205) 591-2131
Contact: James W. Waitzman, Sr., President, c/o
Tractor & Equipment Company, Inc.

Limitations: Scholarships only for children of Tractor
& Equipment Company, Inc. employees.
Financial data: Year ended 12/31/86. Assets, $223,692
(M); Total giving, $147,451; Grants to individuals, 6
grants totaling $8,901, high $2,000, low $301.
Employer Identification Number: 630718825
Applications: Completion of formal application
required. **Applications from individuals who are not
within the stated recipient restriction not accepted.**

1235
TRW Foundation
1900 Richmond Road
Cleveland, OH 44124   (216) 291-7164
Contact: Donna L. Cummings, Manager

Limitations: Scholarships to children of TRW Inc.
employees.
Financial data: Year ended 12/31/86. Assets,
$12,000,000 (M); Total giving, $5,441,310; Grants to

individuals totaling $23,200.
Employer Identification Number: 346556217

1236
Union Camp Charitable Trust
c/o Union Camp Corporation
1600 Valley Road
Wayne, NJ 07470   (201) 628-2232
Contact: Harold Hoss, Vice-President & Treasurer,
Union Camp Corporation

Limitations: Scholarships only to employees of Union
Camp Corporation.
Financial data: Year ended 12/31/85. Assets, $702,360
(M); Total giving, $1,422,762; Grants to individuals,
48 grants totaling $79,000, high $1,750, low $1,500.
Employer Identification Number: 136034666

1237
United Conveyor Foundation
300 Wilmot Drive
Deerfield, IL 60015   (312) 948-0400
Contact: Helen O'Donnell, Manager

Limitations: Scholarships for students whose parents
have been employed at United Conveyor Corporation
for at least three years.
Financial data: Year ended 12/31/86. Assets,
$1,656,419 (M); Total giving, $90,725; Grants to
individuals, 3 grants totaling $7,500, each grant
$2,500.
Employer Identification Number: 366033638
Applications: Deadline July 1st; Completion of formal
application required.
Program description:
Requests for scholarships should include:
   1. A certified copy of high school grades
   transcript
   2. Evidence of acceptance in an institution of
   higher learning
   3. A certified copy of college bound test scores
   (SAT or ACT).
Applicants already in college must submit, in
addition to the above, a certified copy of college
grades transcript.
   A letter of recommendation from a high school or
college instructor is required and should be sent
directly to the foundation.

1238
Valspar Foundation, The
1101 Third Street South
Minneapolis, MN 55415
Contact: Joanne Smith, Valspar Scholarship
Committee, Personnel Department, P.O. Box 1461,
Minneapolis, MN 55440

Limitations: Scholarships to children of employees of
the Valspar Corporation.

Financial data: Year ended 9/30/86. Assets, $152,665
(M); Total giving, $300,439; Grants to individuals, 20
grants totaling $19,200, high $1,000, low $200.
Employer Identification Number: 411363847
Applications: Deadline June 1st; Completion of formal
application required.
Program description:
Applicant must be entering a post-high school
educational institution as a full-time student who is a
child of a Valspar Corporation employee. Selection is
based on financial need, record of achievement, and
future goals.

1239★
Wabash Inc. Scholarship Foundation
810 North Cass Street
Wabash, IN 46992   (219) 563-3111
Contact: James K. Calvin, Human Resources Director

Limitations: Scholarships only to children of
employees of Wabash, Inc., its divisions and
subsidiaries, including IPM and Wabash Automotive
Components Division.
Financial data: Year ended 12/31/87. Assets, $5,328
(M); Total giving, $25,000; Grants to individuals, 22
grants totaling $25,000, high $4,000, low $500.
Employer Identification Number: 356205883
Applications: Submit applications betweeen January
1st and March 1st; Contact foundation for current
application deadline; Initial approach by letter;
Completion of formal application required.
Publications: Newsletter, application guidelines,
financial statement, 990-PF printed copy available
upon request.
Program description:
Annual amounts are renewable.

1240
Wal-Mart Foundation
608 Southwest Eighth Street
Bentonville, AR 72716
Contact: High school counselor

Limitations: Scholarships to graduating high school
seniors in areas where Wal-Mart Stores, Inc. are
located.
Financial data: Year ended 1/31/87. Assets,
$3,496,216 (M); Total giving, $1,714,554; Grants to
individuals amount not specified.
Employer Identification Number: 716107283
Applications: Deadline February 20th. Application
forms available at high schools; Completion of formal
application required; Interviews required for finalists.
Program description:
The **Wal-Mart Foundation Community Scholarship
Program** is a competitive program administered by
store managers of qualified Wal-Mart Stores. Schools
located in towns that patronize a store in operation
prior to January 31st are included in the program.

Scholarships are in the amount of $1,000, payable over a two-year period at the rate of $250 per semester. The store will accept two applicants for the first 100 graduating seniors and one additional applicant for every 100 graduating seniors after that.

A panel of judges selected from the community by store managers will evaluate applications and determine a maximum of three finalists. The judges' evaluation of the applicants will take into account the following criteria:

- ACT or SAT scores
- Grade point average
- Curriculum
- Financial need
- Extracurricular activities
- Work activities.

Company employees or their children are not eligible.

1241
West (Herman O.) Foundation
P.O. Box 808
Phoenixville, PA 19460   (215) 935-4500

Limitations: Scholarships only for employees of The West Company and their dependents.
Financial data: Year ended 12/31/85. Assets, $512,806 (M); Total giving, $228,215; Grants to individuals, 36 grants totaling $40,504, high $2,250, low $205.
Employer Identification Number: 237173901
Applications: Deadline February 28th; Contact The West Company for application.

1242
Westinghouse Educational Foundation
Westinghouse Electric Company
Westinghouse Building, Gateway Center
Pittsburgh, PA 15222   (412) 642-6035
Contact: Walter A. Schratz, Executive Director

Limitations: Four scholarship programs, each with different limitations (see Program Description for specific qualifications).
Financial data: Year ended 12/31/86. Assets, $7,291,919 (M); Total giving, $3,579,352; Grants to individuals, 134 grants totaling $549,350.
Employer Identification Number: 256037105
Applications: Deadline August 15th for The Bertha Lamme-Westinghouse Scholarship; September 1st for The 4-H Scholarships; December 15th for The Science Talent Search; and December 1st for The Westinghouse Family Scholarships; Initial approach by letter; Completion of formal application required for The Westinghouse Family Scholarships.
Publications: Company report (including application guidelines).
Program description:
The Bertha Lamme-Westinghouse Scholarship is open to any freshman woman entering the field of

engineering in pursuit of a bachelor's degree in engineering. Three $1,000 scholarships are awarded based on the following: a high school record, three letters of reference and a one page essay written by the applicant. Contact the Society of Women Engineers, United Engineering Center, Room 305, 345 East 47th Street, New York, N.Y. 10017; Tel.: (212) 705-7855 for further information.

The 4-H Scholarships are open to students in the U.S. and Puerto Rico who are 4-H members working under the supervision of the Extension Service and wishing to compete in the 4-H Electric Awards Program. Applicants must by at least 14 and not more than 19 years of age on January 1st of the year in which the competition is held. Selection is based on the applicants report on the 4-H Electric Program Record and the applicant's general 4-H record. Contact the local 4-H leader or National 4-H at 150 North Wacker Drive, Chicago, IL 60606.

The Science Talent Search is open to any student in the U.S. who is in the last year of secondary school and expected to complete college entrance qualifications before October 1st in the year in which the awards are made and who has not competed in any previous Science Talent Search. Selection is based on the following: a report of 1,000 words on an independent research project; a transcript from the applicant's high school and a completed application form. Contact Science Clubs of America, 1719 N Street, Washington, D.C. 20036; Tel.: (202) 785-2255. The scholarship must be used within one year of the date of the award toward a course in science or engineering at an approved, degree granting institution of higher learning.

The Westinghouse Family Scholarships are open only to sons and daughters of current Westinghouse employees and its wholly-owned U.S.A. subsidiary companies who are in their last year of school, or who graduate from high school after November 1st of the school year in which the awards are made. The applicant's parent must by employed by Westinghouse for a period of one year or more as of May 1st of the year in which the awards are made. Sons and daughters of retired, deceased, or permanently disabled employees are eligible provided the employee-parent had met the one-year employment requirement. Selection is based on scholastic aptitude, achievement, general ability and leadership. Contact the Personnel Relations Office where the parent is or was employed for further information.

1243
Westmoreland Coal Company and Penn Virginia Corporation Foundation
2500 Fidelity Building
Philadelphia, PA 19109   (215) 545-2500
Contact: Philip D. Weinstock, Manager

Limitations: Scholarships to children of employees of Westmoreland Coal Company or Penn Virginia

Corporation or their subsidiaries who are employed at a VA or WV division of either company or a coal mining subsidiary of Westmoreland, or reside within the following locations: Lee, Scott and Wise counties, VA; Boone, Fayette, Greenbrier, Logan, Nicholas, Raleigh, and Wyoming counties, WV, and Delta County, CO.
Financial data: Year ended 12/31/86. Assets, $1,625,952 (M); Total giving, $192,532; Grants to individuals, 238 grants totaling $182,532, high $3,000, low $150, general range $500-1,000, average grant $500.
Employer Identification Number: 237398163
Applications: Applications accepted beginning of fall; Deadline December 1st; Completion of formal application required; Interviews required.
Program description:
The purpose of the scholarship award program is to encourage and assist individuals, who live in mining communities where facilities of the sponsoring companies are located, in the pursuit of higher education.
   To be eligible to apply for an award an applicant must:
   1. Be a son, daughter, stepchild, or legally adopted child of an active, retired, or deceased employee of Westmoreland Coal Company or Penn Virginia Corporation who is/was employed at a Westmoreland mining division or subsidiary; or be a resident of one of the mining division or subsidiary areas.
   2. Be a high school graduate or intend to be graduated during the current academic year.
   3. Plan to enter an institution of higher learning not later than the fall term of the year and to carry a full academic load leading to graduation. Included are junior, community, and four-year colleges, universities, and schools of nursing and related fields. Technical schools are ineligible except for those applicants pursuing certificates in fields related to mining and allied activities.
   In addition, eligible individuals who are already attending institutions of higher learning may apply for aid if they find themselves unable to continue their education because of altered financial conditions.
   The annual award is automatically renewed for up to a total of four undergraduate academic years, providing the recipient maintains satisfactory personal and scholastic standards. The amount of the award is paid directly to the school entered with the authorization for the winner to draw on this amount for tuition, room and board at a campus facility, books and other educational expenses.

1244
Whirlpool Foundation
2000 U.S. 33, North
Benton Harbor, MI 49022   (616) 926-3461
Contact: Patricia O'Day, Secretary

Limitations: Scholarships only to children of employees of the Whirlpool Corporation.
Financial data: Year ended 12/31/85. Assets, $10,148,049 (M); Total giving, $2,700,413; Grants to individuals totaling $233,000.
Employer Identification Number: 386077342
Applications: Initial approach by letter or telephone.

1245
Whitaker Foundation, Inc.
476 North Winnebago
Lake Winnebago, MO 64034

Limitations: Scholarships only to Whitaker Cable Corporation employees, including their children or blood relatives.
Financial data: Year ended 5/31/87. Assets, $107,606 (M); Total giving, $11,500; Grants to individuals totaling $7,500.
Employer Identification Number: 436047609
Applications: Deadline November 30th of senior year; Initial approach by letter requesting application from foundation at 1301 Burlington Avenue, North Kansas City, MO; Completion of formal application required, including copy of SAT scores (to be mailed directly to the foundation from the examination board), biographical information, and statement of financial need.
Publications: Program information (including application guidelines).
Program description:
The scholarship award consists of funds for tuition to any accredited degree granting college or university in the U.S., not to exceed $500 per year for living expenses for a period of one or more years. The applicant must have a bona fide senior class standing in the top 60 percent as of his or her senior year and thereby be eligible to complete his or her high school education by no later than August of the following year. Awards are based upon scholastic excellence and secondary school record, financial need, and biographical information furnished by the candidate.
   Scholarship payments for tuition are made directly to the educational institution; payment for living expenses are determined on a case-by-case basis.

1246
Wisconsin Public Service Foundation, Inc.
700 North Adams Street
P.O. Box 19001
Green Bay, WI 54307   (414) 433-1465
Contact: Wisconsin Public Service Foundation, Inc., Scholarship Program, College Scholarship Service,

Sponsored Scholarships Program, CN 6730, Princeton, NJ 08541

Limitations: Scholarships to children of employees or customers of Wisconsin Public Service Corporation in Wisconsin and Upper Michigan.
Financial data: Year ended 12/31/86. Assets, $6,543,131 (M); Total giving, $579,754; Grants to individuals totaling $53,075.
Employer Identification Number: 396075016
Applications: Applications accepted throughout the year; Initial approach by letter; Completion of formal application required.
Program description:
Children of customers must legally reside in the retail territory of Wisconsin Public Service Corporation (Wisconsin and Upper Michigan). Applicants must be graduating high school seniors in the upper 25 percent of their class scholastically who plan to attend one of the 35 listed colleges and universities (all except Michigan Technological University in Wisconsin) or any of 14 two-year campuses of the University of Wisconsin Center System. Scholarships are renewed throughout the normal period of college attendance if satisfactory academic progress is made.

1247
Women's Aid of the Penn Central Transportation Company
c/o Consolidated Rail Corporation
Six Penn Center, Room 1010
Philadelphia, PA 19103
Contact: J. P. Fox, Human Resources Department;
Tel.: (215) 977-4509

Limitations: Scholarships to dependent children of employees of Conrail, employees of its predecessor roads now employed by Amtrak or Penn Central Corporation, and former employees of these companies who have retired because of age or disability or who have died.
Financial data: Year ended 12/31/85. Assets, $885,563 (M); Total giving, $32,217; Grants to individuals, 53 grants totaling $32,217, high $2,250, low $100, general range $250-800.
Employer Identification Number: 236232572
Applications: Deadline April 1st; Completion of formal application required; Interviews granted upon request by mail through a consultant.
Publications: Program information.
Program description:
For their children to be eligible, employees of Penn Central Transportation Company (living, deceased, or retired) must have been employed before April 1, 1976; employees of the Pennsylvania Railroad Company must be presently in active service for Penn Central Company or Amtrak. Applicants should be prospective college freshmen, although consideration is given to students already in college who have had a substantial change in family financial status since

entering college and relate such circumstances when applying. Primary consideration is given to the financial need of those applicants who demonstrate their capacity for success in college by their performance on the Scholastic Aptitude Test.

Scholarships provide assistance toward tuition and additional necessary expenses for undergraduate study at recognized and accepted colleges and universities. Each scholarship provides for four years of study, subject to annual requalification on the basis of good academic standing and continuing financial need.

1248★
Worcester Community Foundation, Inc., Greater
44 Front Street, Suite 530
Worcester, MA 01608   (617) 755-0980
Contact: Ms. Kay M. Seivard, Executive Director

Limitations: Scholarships to students who are residents of Worcester County, MA, or are children of employees of Guaranty Bank or Rothman's Furniture.
Financial data: Year ended 12/31/87. Assets, $10,048,494 (M); Total giving, $603,562; Grants to individuals, 32 grants totaling $62,175, high $5,000, low $50, general range $1,000-4,000, average grant $1,000.
Employer Identification Number: 042572276
Applications: Deadline March 15th; Initial approach by telephone or letter to Scholarship Coordinator; Completion of formal application required; Interviews required for finalists.
Publications: Annual report, informational brochure, application guidelines, financial statement, newsletter, program information, 990-PF printed copy available upon request.

1249
World Carpets Foundation, Inc.
One World Plaza
P.O. Box 1448
Dalton, GA 30722-1448   (404) 278-8000
Contact: Jim Carrier, Chairman, Scholarship Committee

Limitations: Scholarships only to children of employees of World Carpets, Inc.
Financial data: Year ended 6/30/87. Assets, $657 (M); Total giving, $80,820; Grants to individuals, 49 grants totaling $80,820, high $5,286, low $100.
Employer Identification Number: 237248425
Applications: Deadline March 15th; Completion of formal application required.
Program description:
Applicant's parent(s) must have been employed by World Carpets, Inc. for at least three months prior to application. Scholarships are awarded primarily on the basis of academic achievement and potential, character, integrity, and need. Recipients are

recommended to the foundation directors by a scholarship selection committee, a group of professional educators who are not employed or affiliated with World Carpets, Inc.

1250
Yegen (Christian C.) Foundation
Mack Center Drive, Fifth Floor
Paramus, NJ 07652   (201) 262-9300
Contact: Jason W. Semel

Limitations: Scholarships to employees and dependents of employees of Yegen Holdings Corporation and affiliated companies, where the earnings of a family with two or more dependents does not exceed $40,000.
Financial data: Year ended 12/31/85. Assets, $12,114 (M); Total giving, $4,000; Grants to individuals, 3 grants totaling $4,000, high $2,000, low $1,000.
Employer Identification Number: 226071113
Applications: Deadline before commencement of semester; Completion of formal application required.
Program description:
No more than $1,000 per grantee per semester.

GENERAL WELFARE

1251
Abbott (The Clara) Foundation
Abbott Park
North Chicago, IL 60064   (312) 937-3840
Contact: Herbert S. Wilkinson, Sr., President

Limitations: Special relief grants and loans, and aid for the aged and indigent, only to employees or retirees of Abbott Laboratories or members of their families.
Financial data: Year ended 12/31/86. Assets, $70,072,866 (M); Total giving, $2,496,529; Grants to individuals, 520 grants totaling $2,496,529; Subtotal for welfare assistance: 457 relief grants and 507 relief loans totaling $905,442, and 63 grants to aid the aged totaling $118,760.
Employer Identification Number: 366069632
Applications: Applications accepted throughout the year.

1252
AMAX Aid Fund, Inc.
AMAX Center
Greenwich, CT 06836
Contact: David George Ball, Senior Vice-President

Limitations: Relief assistance to needy employees and former employees of AMAX, Inc., and subsidiaries.

Financial data: Year ended 12/31/85. Assets, $89,676 (M); Total giving, $11,070; Grants to individuals, 1 grant totaling $11,070.
Employer Identification Number: 136124362

1253
Bacon (Charles F.) Trust
c/o Bank of New England
28 State Street
Boston, MA 02107   (617) 973-1798
Contact: John M. Dolan, Vice-President, Bank of New England

Limitations: Welfare assistance to former employees of Conrad and Chandler Company who either have retired or resigned due to illness.
Financial data: Year ended 12/31/85. Assets, $1,676,500 (M); Total giving, $99,000; Grants to individuals, 8 grants totaling $30,000, high $5,000, low $2,000.
Employer Identification Number: 046024467
Applications: Deadline November 30th; Initial approach by letter.

1254
Beaumont (Louis D.) Foundation
c/o C.I.T. Financial Corporation
135 West 50th Street
New York, NY 10020   (212) 408-6000
Contact: Michael Fitzpatrick, Director of Benefits

Limitations: Relief assistance, primarily to needy employees or former employees of C.I.T. Financial Corporation and its affiliates and their families.
Financial data: Year ended 12/31/84. Assets, $769,825 (M); Total giving, $35,177; Grants to individuals, 16 grants totaling $35,177, high $12,500, low $374, general range $1,000-1,700, average grant $1,200.
Employer Identification Number: 136083855
Applications: Applications accepted throughout the year; Initial approach by letter stating reason for requesting financial assistance, and demonstrating financial need.
Program description:
The purpose of the program is to provide supplemental income to indigent persons demonstrating continuing hardship and financial need. All applicants in need of financial aid are considered, however, preference may be given to current or former employees of C.I.T. Financial Corporation and its affiliated companies and their families.

1255★
Brown (George Warren) Foundation
8400 Maryland Avenue
St. Louis, MO 63105   (314) 854-4400
Contact: David L. Bowman, Treasurer

Limitations: Pensions for long-term employees of Brown Shoe Company that retired before the implementation of company sponsored retirement plans.
Financial data: Year ended 12/31/87. Assets, $2,742,830 (M); Total giving, $212,414; Grants to individuals, 21 pensions totaling $35,080.
Employer Identification Number: 436027798
Applications: Initial approach by letter.

1256★
Burlington Industries Foundation
P.O. Box 21207
3330 West Friendly Avenue
Greensboro, NC 27420   (919) 379-2515
Contact: Park R. Davidson, Executive Director

Limitations: Emergency aid to employees of Burlington Industries and their families in areas of company operations, primarily in NC, SC, and VA.
Financial data: Year ended 9/30/87. Assets, $8,166,553 (M); Total giving, $1,822,509; Grants to individuals, 52 grants totaling $25,650.
Employer Identification Number: 566043142
Applications: Applications accepted throughout the year; Initial contact by telephone or letter; Interviews granted upon request.
Publications: Program information.
Program description:
Support is granted to employees and their families who have suffered severe loss from disaster.

1257★
Butler Manufacturing Company Foundation
P.O. Box 419917
Kansas City, MO 64141-0197   (816) 968-3208
Contact: Barbara Lee Fay, Foundation Administrator

Limitations: Hardship grants for persons in need, including employees, and former employees of the Bulter Manufacturing Company and their dependents.
Financial data: Year ended 12/31/87. Assets, $3,332,888 (M); Total giving, $93,960; Grants to individuals, 42 grants totaling $67,000; Subtotal for assistance, 3 grants totaling $6,000, high $3,500, low $1,000, average grant $2,000.
Employer Identification Number: 440663648
Applications: Applications accepted throughout the year; Initial approach by letter; Interviews required.
Publications: Application guidelines, program information.

Program description:
Assistance is provided to active and retired employees in financial distress because of serious illness, or loss or damage to property from weather or fire.

1258★
Campeau (Robert & Ilse) Family Foundation, Inc.
(Formerly Allied Stores Foundation, Inc.)
1114 Avenue of the Americas
New York, NY 10036   (212) 764-2574
Contact: Joseph Y. King, Secretary-Treasurer

Limitations: Giving for relief of needy and indigent employees of Allied Stores Corporation and its subsidiaries.
Financial data: Year ended 12/31/87. Assets, $5,262,027 (M); Total giving, $191,352; Grants to individuals, 3 grants totaling $1,310; 1986, Information not available; 1985, Grants to individuals, 4 grants totaling $2,132, high $767, low $413.
Employer Identification Number: 136102820
Applications: Deadline November 15th.

1259
Carter (Amon G.) Star Telegram Employees Fund
400 West Seventh Street
Fort Worth, TX 76102   (817) 332-3535
Contact: Nenetta Tatum, President

Limitations: Pension supplements and medical and hardship assistance only to employees of the Fort Worth Star-Telegram, KXAS-TV and WBAP-Radio.
Financial data: Year ended 4/30/86. Assets, $11,228,488 (M); Total giving, $508,015; Grants to individuals, 83 grants totaling $235,376; Subtotal for welfare assistance, 61 grants totaling $175,376, high $6,822, low $216.
Employer Identification Number: 756014850
Applications: Applications accepted throughout the year; Initial approach by letter.

1260
Cenex Foundation
5600 Cenex Drive
Inver Grove Heights, MN 55075   (612) 451-5105
Contact: Sharon A. Blaiser, Manager

Limitations: Welfare assistance to former employees of Central Exchange Agency and its affiliated companies.
Financial data: Year ended 11/30/85. Assets, $2,064,527 (M); Total giving, $336,316; Grants to individuals amount not specified.
Employer Identification Number: 416025858
Applications: Initial approach by letter; Completion of formal application required.

1261
Clark (Edward) Benevolent Society of The Singer Manufacturing Co.
Eight Stamford Forum
Stamford, CT 06904

Limitations: Grants for emergency aid, with emphasis on medical support, to employees and their families of The Singer Manufacturing Co.
Financial data: Year ended 12/31/85. Assets, $1,622,464 (M); Total giving, $44,493; Grants to individuals, 27 grants totaling $44,493, high $6,000, low $250.
Employer Identification Number: 221712370
Applications: Applications accepted throughout the year.

1262
Crane Fund, The
222 West Adams Street, Room 849
Chicago, IL 60606
Contact: Fern N. Brodie, Senior Caseworker

Limitations: Grants restricted to indigent and needy former employees of Crane Company in the U.S. and Great Britain.
Financial data: Year ended 12/31/86. Assets, $54,193,026 (M); Total giving, $1,466,033; Grants to individuals, 1,371 grants totaling $1,466,033.
Employer Identification Number: 366124341
Applications: Applications accepted throughout the year.

1263★
Crawford (E.R.) Estate
P.O. Box 487
McKeesport, PA 15134
Contact: Francis E. Neish, Trustee

Limitations: Welfare assistance limited to indigent individuals who are former employees of McKeesport Tin Plate Company who meet income requirements.
Financial data: Year ended 12/31/86. Assets, $6,196,055 (M); Total giving, $517,329; Grants to individuals, 31 grants totaling $26,700, high $1,200, low $240.
Employer Identification Number: 256031554
Applications: Applications accepted throughout the year; Completion of formal application required.

1264
Eaton (Georgiana Goddard) Memorial Fund
c/o Welch & Forbes
73 Tremont Street
Boston, MA 02108 (617) 523-1635
Contact: Kenneth S. Safe, Jr., Trustee

Limitations: Pensions to former employees of Community Workshops, Inc. Boston, MA.

Financial data: Year ended 6/30/86. Assets, $6,006,120 (M); Total giving $289,915; Grants to individuals, 6 grants totaling $61,565, high $16,700, low $5,640.
Employer Identification Number: 046112820

1265★
Giannini (A.P.) Foundation for Employees
c/o Bank of America, Personnel Relations Dept. No. 3650
P.O. Box 37000
San Francisco, CA 94137 (415) 622-3706

Limitations: Relief assistance to employees of the Bank of America and its subsidiaries for medical bills or other emergencies.
Financial data: Year ended 12/31/87. Assets, $420,921 (M); Total giving, $32,675; Grants to individuals, 14 grants totaling $25,175, high $4,400, low $550, general range $1,000-4,000.
Employer Identification Number: 946089550
Applications: Applications accepted throughout the year; Application should include reason for grant request, amount requested, and applicant's financial status.

1266★
Giannini (Clorinda) Memorial Benefit Fund
c/o Bank of America, Personnel Relations Dept. No. 3650
P.O. Box 37000
San Francisco, CA 94137 (415) 622-3706

Limitations: Relief assistance to employees of the Bank of America for medical bills or other emergencies.
Financial data: Year ended 12/31/87. Assets, $1,229,786 (M); Total giving $12,953; Grants to individuals, 3 grants totaling $12,953, high $10,977, low $875, general range $1,000-5,000.
Employer Identification Number: 946073513
Applications: Applications accepted throughout the year; Application should include reason for grant request, amount requested, and applicant's financial status.

1267
Gleason Fund, Inc.
1000 University Avenue
Rochester, NY 14692 (716) 473-1000
Contact: James M. Weltzer, President

Limitations: Grants only to former Gleason Corporation employees in poverty and distress.
Financial data: Year ended 12/31/86. Assets, $10,062,838 (M); Total giving, $366,183; Grants to individuals totaling $53,058.
Employer Identification Number: 166023234

Program description:
Regular awards in the form of cash grants are made to individuals to relieve poverty. Special awards in the form of payment of medical insurance premiums and expenses, homeowner's insurance, taxes, repairs, and funeral expenses of families and individuals. All awards are based on the investigation of individual cases.

1268
Hall Family Foundations

c/o Charitable and Crown Investment - 323
P.O. Box 419580
Kansas City, MO 64141
Contact: Margaret H. Pence or Wendy Hockaday, Program Officers

Limitations: Emergency relief assistance only to employees of Hallmark.
Financial data: Year ended 12/31/86. Assets, $215,321,156 (M); Total giving, $5,687,872; Grants to individuals totaling $200,750; Subtotal for relief assistance, 18 grants totaling $30,550, high $4,500, low $400.
Employer Identification Number: 446006291
Applications: Applications available to Hallmark employees only.
Publications: Annual report.

1269★
Hornblower (Henry) Fund, Inc.

Box 2365
Boston, MA 02107   (617) 589-3286
Contact: Nathan N. Withington, President

Limitations: Welfare assistance for needy current or former employees of Hornblower & Weeks.
Financial data: Year ended 12/31/86. Assets, $25,897,311 (M); Total giving, $68,650; Grants to individuals, 2 grants totaling $2,500.
Employer Identification Number: 237425285
Applications: Applications accepted throughout the year.

1270★
Hudson-Webber Foundation

333 West Fort Street, Suite 1310
Detroit, MI 48226   (313) 963-7777
Contact: Gilbert Hudson, President

Limitations: Relief assistance to employees and former employees of the J.L. Hudson Company and their dependents ("Hudsonians").
Financial data: Year ended 12/31/87. Assets, $69,299,282 (M); Total giving, $2,468,156; Grants to individuals, 119 grants totaling $95,480, general range $500-1,000.
Employer Identification Number: 386052131
Applications: Applications accepted throughout the

year; Completion of formal application required; Interviews required.
Publications: Biennial report.
Program description:
The foundation provides the **Hudsonian Assistance and Counseling Program** to help Hudsonians to cope with personal and family problems. The program offers the services of an independent professional counselor who assists Hudsonians in diagnosing their problems and offers referral to public agencies and private resources as appropriate. When financial assistance is a necessary component of crisis resolution, and when personal or family resources, outside commercial resources, and/or assistance available through community, charitable, or public resources is unavailable or inadequate, the program counselor may apply for a grant from the foundation on behalf of a Hudsonian. Such application is made only as a last resort after a thorough screening process.

The foundation's distribution committee reviews each grant application form and written application for assistance, evaluates the circumstances and needs presented, considers pertinent recommendations, makes final judgements, and approves or denies each request. Grants are provided mostly for problems with physical health, emotional health, welfare needs, legal needs, and financial emergencies.

1271
Ittleson Beneficial Fund

c/o The C.I.T. Group Holdings, Inc.
135 West 50th Street
New York, NY 10020   (212) 408-6000
Contact: Michael Fitzpatrick, Director of Benefits

Limitations: Relief assistance primarily to needy current and former employees, and their families, of C.I.T. Financial Corporation and its affiliates.
Financial data: Year ended 12/31/85. Assets, $674,328 (M); Total giving, $25,186; Grants to individuals, 19 grants totaling $25,186, high $4,500, low $30.
Employer Identification Number: 136083909
Applications: Applications accepted throughout the year; Initial approach by letter stating the reason for the request, detailing applicant's financial status.
Program description:
All applicants in need of assistance are considered by the fund. However, preference may be given to current or former employees of C.I.T. Financial Corporation and its affiliates. The purpose of the grants is to provide supplemental income to persons demonstrating continuing hardship and financial need.

1272
Kellogg Company 25-Year Employees Fund, Inc.
One Kellogg Square
P.O. Box 3549
Battle Creek, MI 49016-3599   (616) 961-2000
Contact: D. E. Kinnisten, President

Limitations: Welfare assistance only to 25-year employees and former employees of the Kellogg Company and their dependents.
Financial data: Year ended 12/31/86. Assets, $36,081,776 (M); Total giving, $628,232; Grants to individuals, 119 grants totaling $569,899, high $29,224, low $61, average grant $4,789.
Employer Identification Number: 386039770
Applications: Deadline June 1st; Submit proposal preferably in April; Initial approach by letter; Completion of formal application required.
Publications: Program information, application guidelines.
Program description:
Grants are awarded primarily for living and medical expenses.

1273
Loeb Rhoades Employees' Welfare Fund, Inc.
40 Wall Street
New York, NY 10005

Limitations: Welfare assistance only to employees of Loeb Rhoades, Inc.
Financial data: Year ended 12/31/85. Assets, $272,340 (M); Total giving, $9,170; Grants to individuals, 2 grants totaling $4,220, high $3,500, low $720.
Employer Identification Number: 132618946

1274
Martin (Glen L.) Foundation
c/o Fiduciary Trust Company of New York
Two World Trade Center
New York, NY 10048

Limitations: Welfare assistance to retired employees of the Martin Marietta Corporation suffering hardship.
Financial data: Year ended 12/31/85. Assets, $1,246,504 (M); Total giving, $62,670; Grants to individuals, 46 grants totaling $47,150, high $2,250, low $250.
Employer Identification Number: 136086736

1275
Morrison-Knudsen Employees Foundation, Inc.
One Morrison-Knudsen Plaza
Boise, ID 83729   (208) 386-5000
Contact: J. C. Conway, President

Limitations: Welfare assistance to needy company employees.
Financial data: Year ended 12/31/85. Assets,

$3,276,572 (M); Total giving, $120,880; Grants to individuals, 29 grants totaling $84,880, high $6,780, low $225.
Employer Identification Number: 826005410
Applications: Applications accepted throughout the year.

1276
National Machinery Foundation, Inc.
Greenfield Street
P.O. Box 747
Tiffin, OH 44883   (419) 447-5211
Contact: D. B. Bero, Administrator

Limitations: Relief assistance to former employees and other needy individuals in Seneca County, OH.
Financial data: Year ended 12/31/86. Assets, $6,363,297 (M); Total giving, $278,729; Grants to individuals, 200 grants totaling $36,150, high $1,000, low $58; Subtotal for relief assistance not specified.
Employer Identification Number: 346520191
Applications: Initial approach by letter.

1277
Pfaffinger Foundation
Times Mirror Square
Los Angeles, CA 90053   (213) 237-5743
Contact: James C. Kelly, President

Limitations: Relief assistance to employees and former employees of The Times Mirror Company.
Financial data: Year ended 12/31/86. Assets, $55,122,570 (M); Total giving, $2,126,925; Grants to individuals, 316 grants totaling $1,268,800, high $27,466, low $12.
Employer Identification Number: 951661675
Applications: Applications accepted throughout the year; Initial approach by letter; Completion of formal application required.

1278
Pierce (S.S.) Company Employees Aid Fund
c/o Boston Safe Deposit & Trust Company
One Boston Place
Boston, MA 02106   (617) 722-7415
Contact: Michele H. Gorab, Trust Officer

Limitations: Supplements to retirement income only for needy former employees of S.S. Pierce Company.
Financial data: Year ended 8/31/85. Assets, $174,478 (M); Total giving, $35,900; Grants to individuals totaling $35,900.
Employer Identification Number: 046092670

1279
Plitt Southern Theatres, Inc. Employees Fund
1801 Century Park East, Suite 122
Los Angeles, CA 90067
Contact: Joe S. Jackson, President

Limitations: Welfare assistance to employees of Plitt
Southern Theatres.
Financial data: Year ended 12/31/86. Assets,
$7,881,486 (M); Total giving, $632,201; Grants to
individuals, 70 grants totaling $140,101, high $9,845,
low $156.
Employer Identification Number: 756037855

1280
Richman Brothers Foundation
1600 East 55th Street
Cleveland, OH 44103   (216) 432-7000
Contact: Richard R. Moore, President

Limitations: Relief assistance to needy employees,
pensioners, widows, and children of employees of the
Richman Brothers Company.
Financial data: Year ended 12/31/86. Assets,
$1,640,458 (M); Total giving, $181,450; Grants to
individuals, 278 grants totaling $62,670, high $620,
low $95.
Employer Identification Number: 346504927
Applications: Deadline November 15th; Initial
approach by letter; Completion of formal application
required.

1281
Stockham (The William H. And Kate F.) Foundation, Inc.
c/o Stockham Valves & Fittings, Inc.
4000 North Tenth Avenue, P.O. Box 10326
Birmingham, AL 35202
Contact: Herbert Stockham, Chairman

Limitations: Relief assistance only for needy
employees, ex-employees, and their dependents, of
Stockham Valves & Fittings, Inc.
Financial data: Year ended 12/31/86. Assets,
$3,771,851 (M); Total giving, $468,740; Grants to
individuals, 13 grants totaling $19,090, high $9,555,
low $150.
Employer Identification Number: 636049787
Applications: Applications accepted throughout the
year; initial approach by letter.

1282
Tyler (Marion C.) Foundation
c/o Society National Bank
P.O. Box 6179
Cleveland, OH 44101
Contact: Don Whitehouse, 8200 Tyler Boulevard,
Mentor, OH 44060; Tel.: (216) 946-4100

Limitations: Pension supplements only to retired
employees of W.S. Tyler, Inc.
Financial data: Year ended 12/31/86. Assets, $814,105
(M); Total giving, $76,750; Grants to individuals, 70
grants totaling $76,750, high $2,803, low $137.
Employer Identification Number: 346525274
Applications: Applications accepted throughout the
year; Initial approach by letter requesting application;
Completion of formal application required.

1283
Vang Memorial Foundation
P.O. Box 11727
Pittsburgh, PA 15228   (412) 563-0261
Contact: E. J. Hosko

Limitations: Grants-in-aid only to past, present and
future employees of George Vang, Inc., and related
companies, and their dependents.
Financial data: Year ended 12/31/85. Assets, $482,373
(M); Total giving, $15,593; Grants to individuals, 14
grants totaling $15,593, high $1,808, low $600,
general range $720-1,400.
Employer Identification Number: 256034491
Applications: Applications accepted throughout the
year; Initial approach by letter, including name,
address, and telephone number of applicant and
stating type of grant requested and basis of need.

1284
Walgreen Benefit Foundation
200 Wilmot Road
Deerfield, IL 60015   (312) 940-2931
Contact: Edward H. King, Vice-President

Limitations: Welfare assistance to needy Walgreen
employees and retirees and their families.
Financial data: Year ended 4/30/87. Assets,
$9,740,451 (M); Total giving, $500,451; Grants to
individuals totaling $214,982.
Employer Identification Number: 366051130
Applications: Applications accepted throughout the
year; Initial approach by letter.
Publications: Annual report.

APPENDIX

This appendix lists those foundations that appeared in the Fifth Edition of *Foundation Grants to Individuals*, but were excluded from this Sixth Edition for the reasons stated. Foundations not meeting our criteria of awarding $2,000 in grants to individuals in one of two most recent years for which information is available, of selecting recipients, and of accepting applications directly from individuals, were excluded. Also excluded were foundations that terminated, those whose status has changed, those no longer making grants to individuals, or those for which no recent information could be obtained. **Foundations listed here should not be considered possibilities of funding for individuals.**

Abell Foundation, Inc., The, MD
The foundation's employee-related scholarship program is being discontinued.

Abex Foundation, Inc., CT
The foundation is in the process of terminating.

American Electric Power System Educational Trust, The, OH
The trust makes grants to specified beneficiaries only.

Armco Foundation, NJ
The foundation's scholarship program is administered by College Scholarship Service.

Atlantic Richfield Employees' Emergency Fund, CA
The fund did not make any grants in 1985 or 1986.

Bamberger-Allen Health and Educational Foundation, UT
The foundation will no longer be making direct grants to individuals.

Barra Foundation, Inc., PA
The foundation does not make direct grants to individuals.

Bentley (Alvin M.) Foundation, MI
The foundation's scholarship program has been discontinued.

Boettcher Foundation, CO
The foundation no longer makes grants to individuals.

Boston and Maine Railroad Employees Fund, Inc., MA
The fund did not make any grants to individuals in 1983 or 1984; more recent information was not available.

Bovaird (The Mervin) Foundation, OK
The foundation does not select the scholarship recipients.

Brookville Foundation, The, IN
Grants to individuals totaled less than $2,000 in both 1985 and 1986.

Brown Memorial Foundation, KS
The foundation does not make grants to individuals.

Broyhill Family Foundation, Inc., NC
The foundation is no longer funding new student loans directly to individuals.

Carolina Freight Carriers Scholarship Fund, NC
The fund has been terminated.

Carrier (Robert M. & Lenore W.) Foundation, TN
The foundation makes grants to specified beneficiaries only.

Conway (Carle C.) Scholarship Foundation, CT
The foundation's scholarship program is administered by College Scholarship Service.

Cox (Charles M.) Trust, MA
No grants to individuals were made in 1984; grants to individuals totaled less than $2,000 in 1983; more recent information was not available.

Dedicators, Inc., The, NY
Information since 1983 was not available.

Defenders of Public Safety, The Fund for the, MA
The fund is in the process of terminating.

Djerassi Foundation, The, CA
The foundation is an operating non-grantmaking foundation.

Dravo Corporation & Subsidiaries Charitable Trust, PA
The trust does not make grants to individuals.

Duhamel (Mae L.) Trust, WI
Grants to individuals totaled less than $2,000 in 1985 and 1986.

DuPage Medical Society Foundation, IL
Information since 1983 was not available.

Edmondson Foundation, Inc., The, VA
The foundation does not make grants to individuals.

Farm Foundation, IL
The foundation is now a public charity.

Fermi (Enrico) Educational Fund of Yonkers, Inc., NY
Information since 1982 was not available.

Fiji Foundation of Texas, TX
The foundation has been terminated.

Fluor Foundation, The, CA
The foundation's employee-related scholarship program is administered by an independent scholarship corporation, and its minority scholarship program is being phased out.

Ford Motor Company Fund, MI
The fund no longer makes company-related student loans to individuals.

Frank Family Memorial Scholarship Fund, WI
The fund makes grants to specified beneficiaries only.

Gould (Edwin) Foundation for Children, NY
The foundation does not make direct grants to individuals.

Griswold (Harry E.) Trust, IL
The trust makes grants to specified beneficiaries only.

Gulf Oil Foundation of Delaware, PA
The foundation has been terminated.

Hamilton Community Foundation, Inc., The, OH
The foundation does not make direct grants to individuals.

Helms Foundation, Inc., CA
The foundation does not make grants directly to individuals.

Jacobus/Heritage Foundation, Inc., WI
The foundation has been terminated.

Johnson (The George E.) Foundation, IL
The foundation has been terminated.

Kelly (John B.) Foundation, PA
The foundation is presumed to be in the process of termination.

Keywell (Barney L. and Beatrice) Foundation, MI
Grants to individuals totaled less than $2,000 in 1986 and 1987.

Killough (Walter H.D.) Trust, NY
Grants to individuals totaled less than $2,000 in 1986; 1985 information was not available, and no grants to individuals were made in 1984.

Kohlrausch (Charles H.) Jr. Trust Fund, MA
The fund did not award any grants in 1985 or 1986.

Lewer Foundation, TX
Grants to individuals totaled less than $2,000 in 1987 and 1986.

Lowengard (Leon) Scholarship Foundation, PA
The foundation makes grants to specified beneficiaries only.

Marsden Foundation, The, NY
The foundation no longer makes grants to individuals.

Masonic Foundation of Utah, UT
The foundation does not make direct loans to individuals.

Massachusetts Society of the Cincinnati, MA
The society no longer makes grants to individuals.

McDonnell Douglas - West Personnel Community Services, Inc., CA
The foundation has been terminated.

Moore (W. Gerald) Educational Foundation, MA
The foundation does not make direct grants to individuals.

Mount Vernon Community Trust, The, OH
The trust does not make direct grants to individuals.

Muse (Amy) Trust UA FBO W.H. Muse Scholarship, NC
Grants to individuals totaled less than $2,000 in both 1985 and 1986.

Nabors Foundation, LA
The foundation is in the process of terminating.

Nelson (Victor and Mary D.) Trust, WI
The trust makes grants to specified beneficiaries only.

Oberlin Shansi Memorial Association, OH
The association does not make grants to individuals.

Ohmart (David Marshall) Memorial Fund, ME
Grants to individuals totaled less than $2,000 in 1985; information for 1983 and 1984 was not available.

Olympia-Tumwater Foundation, The, WA
The foundation does not make grants to individuals.

Orentreich Foundation for the Advancement of Science, Inc., NY
The foundation does not make grants to individuals.

Payson (Amanda Caroline) Education Fund For Girls, Inc., MA
The fund has been terminated.

PepsiCo Foundation, Inc., NY
The foundation does not make direct grants to individuals.

Peters (Donald and Evelyn) Foundation, IL
The foundation is in the process of terminating.

Phelps County Community Foundation, Inc., NE
Grants to individuals totaled less than $2,000 in 1986 and 1987.

Philadelphia Award, The, PA
Information since 1983 was not available.

Sawtelle (Virginia Harkness) Foundation, NJ
The foundation's scholarship program has been discontinued.

Scarborough (W.F.) Educational Trust, TX
The trust has been terminated.

Scholl (Dr.) Foundation, IL
The foundation's scholarship program has been discontinued except for scholarship renewals.

Shoemaker (Ray S.) Scholarship Foundation Trust, PA
The trust makes grants to specified beneficiaries only.

Star Foundation, MA
The foundation has been terminated.

Student Aid Foundation of Michigan, MI
The foundation has been terminated.

Tinker Foundation, Inc., The, NY
The foundation has terminated its Postdoctoral Fellowship Program. Final installments of fellowships will be paid out in 1988.

Turn On To America, CA
The foundation is in the process of terminating.

Turney (W.W.) Student Loan Fund, TX
Information since 1982 was not available.

Widows' Society in Boston, MA
The society does not make grants to individuals.

Winn-Dixie Stores Foundation, FL
The foundation no longer makes direct grants to individuals.

Winter Park Community Trust Fund, FL
The fund is in the process of terminating.

INDEXES

INDEX OF FOUNDATIONS

This alphabetical index lists all foundations with full entries in this volume, as well as those which appeared in the Fifth Edition but no longer qualify and are listed in the Appendix. Numbers following the foundation names refer to sequence numbers of entries in the Descriptive Directory section. The letter "A" following a foundation name refers to the Appendix.

SUBJECT INDEX

The numbers under the subject terms in this index refer to the sequence numbers of entries in the Descriptive Directory section of this book. Those foundations which give nationally or regionally are indicated in boldface type following the states in which they are located. Foundations which restrict their giving to particular states are listed in lighter type following the states in which they give.

Accounting
Connecticut: **132**
Florida: **531**
Illinois: **1039**
Indiana: 412
New York: **194**
Ohio: **226**

Actuarial science
Illinois: **1039**
Indiana: 412

Administration
Minnesota: 113
North Dakota: 113
South Dakota: 113
Texas: 615
Wisconsin: 113

Aegean prehistory
New York: **342**

Aeronautics, space sciences
Michigan: 461

Africa
California: 286

Africans
California: 286

Aged
Colorado: 844
Connecticut: 815
District of Columbia: **716**
Florida: **816**, 906

Hawaii: 841
Illinois: 901, **1251**
Indiana: 893
Maine: 874
Maryland: 818, 907
Massachusetts: 790, 819, 843, 881, 885
Michigan: 828
Missouri: 1255
New Jersey: 815
New York: **288**, 789, 815, **914**
Ohio: 824, 832, 892, 1280
Pennsylvania: 820, **894**
Rhode Island: **904**
Texas: 878
Vermont: 809
Washington: 909

Aggression
New York: **288**, **997**

Agricultural sciences
California: 89, 172, 286
Idaho: 651
Michigan: **958**
New York: **244**, **576**, **953**
North Dakota: 495
Ohio: 400, 708
Oregon: **950**
Texas: 421
Washington: 651

Agriculture
Connecticut: 325
Massachusetts: 325, 419
New Jersey: 325
New Mexico: 949
New York: **244**, 325
Rhode Island: 325

Illinois: 74
Kentucky: 500
Michigan: 461, 483
Minnesota: 17
New York: 731
Oregon: **950**
Pennsylvania: **1242**
Washington: 516

Scientific research
Arizona: **564**
Florida: **755**
Maryland: **1028**
New York: **224, 289, 355, 530, 952**

Scientists
Maryland: **1028**

Sculptors
California: 926
Minnesota: 921
New York: **916, 918**

Sculpture
New York: **916, 940, 1042**

Seamen
Connecticut: 775
Maine: **875**
Massachusetts: 397, 885, 891

Secondary schools
Connecticut: **243**
District of Columbia: 780
Iowa: 551
Maryland: **782**
Pennsylvania: 221
Tennessee: 749

Secretarial studies
Maryland: 416

Serbians
Wisconsin: **388**

Singers
New York: **944**

Social sciences
Illinois: **649, 1006**
Kansas: **336**
Michigan: **983**
New Jersey: **318**
New York: **170, 244, 288, 289, 594**
Oregon: **950**

Social work
Florida: **307**
Minnesota: 113
New York: **632**
North Dakota: 113
South Dakota: 113
Tennessee: 141
Wisconsin: 113

Sociology
Illinois: **580**

Solar energy
California: **862**

Southern Baptist Church
South Carolina: 371

Special education
Kansas: 360

Sports
Connecticut: 325
Maryland: **865**
Massachusetts: 325
Michigan: 988
New Jersey: 325
New York: 325
Rhode Island: 325
Texas: **97**

Swiss
Illinois: 685, 901
Indiana: 685
Iowa: 685
Michigan: 685

TYPES OF SUPPORT INDEX

The numbers under the types of support in this index refer to the sequence numbers of entries in the Descriptive Directory section of this book. Those foundations which give nationally or regionally are indicated in boldface type following the states in which they are located. Foundations which restrict their giving to particular states are listed in lighter type following the states in which they give.

Awards
Alaska: 967
Connecticut: 7, 718
Delaware: 975
Florida: **1019**
Arizona: **564**
California: **982**, 1029
Illinois: 637, **1003**, **1004**, **1005**, **1010**, **1039**
Indiana: **527**
Kentucky: 420
Maryland: **1028**
Massachusetts: 989, **995**
Michigan: **992**, 1009
Minnesota: 1022
Missouri: 341, 1023
Montana: 999
New Jersey: **979**, **1041**
New York: 171, **402**, 496, **576**, **632**, **968**, 990, **997**, **998**, **1008**, **1032**, **1042**, **1046**
North Carolina: 972
North Dakota: **1000**
Ohio: 977, 1007, **1014**, 1025, **1036**, **1168**
Oklahoma: 984
Pennsylvania: **973**
Tennessee: 1017
Texas: **97**, **976**, **1021**, 1031
Virginia: **631**
Wisconsin: **987**

Camperships
Pennsylvania: 836
Texas: 899

Company-related scholarships/student loans
Alabama: 1097, 1157, **1219**, **1234**
Arkansas: 1204
California: 1065, **1067**, 1068, **1080**, **1086**, 1097, **1110**, **1164**, **1216**, **1217**
Colorado: 1243
Connecticut: **222**, **1054**, 1097, 1113, 1116, 1180
Alaska: **1061**
Delaware: 1065, **1071**, **1206**
Florida: **1108**, **1119**, 1159, **1191**
Georgia: 1065, **1073**, 1097, 1120, 1157, **1221**, **1249**

Idaho: 1204
Illinois: **1051**, **1052**, 1060, 1065, **1070**, **1083**, 1097, 1120, **1122**, **1134**, **1145**, **1154**, **1169**, **1178**, **1223**, **1237**
Indiana: 1059, **1089**, 1097, **1100**, **1103**, 1104, 1140, **1153**, **1174**, **1175**, **1208**, **1212**, **1239**
Iowa: 1172, **1192**
Kansas: 1069, 1076, 1142, 1162, **1170**
Louisiana: 1229
Maine: 1097, 1135
Maryland: **1161**, **1171**
Massachusetts: **1057**, 1078, 1099, **1124**, **1148**, 1150, 1195, **1196**, **1224**, 1248
Michigan: 1097, 1109, **1130**, 1179, 1233, **1244**, 1246
Minnesota: 595, **1096**, 1112, **1139**, **1149**, 1204, **1238**
Mississippi: 1097, 1120, 1229
Missouri: 1076, **1084**, 1097, **1115**, 1142, **1210**, **1245**
Nebraska: 1120
New Hampshire: 1160
New Jersey: **1092**, 1097, **1098**, **1181**, **1211**, **1236**, 1250
New York: **268**, **398**, **656**, **1056**, **1058**, **1062**, 1065, **1081**, **1088**, **1090**, **1095**, 1097, **1102**, **1117**, **1127**, **1132**, **1136**, 1147, 1180, **1183**, **1202**, **1215**, **1220**
North Carolina: **497**, 1066, 1091, 1097, 1120, **1123**, **1131**, **1182**, 1230
Ohio: **1055**, **1063**, 1065, **1085**, 1097, 1101, **1163**, **1168**, 1184, **1205**, 1226, **1232**, **1235**
Oklahoma: 1097, 1112, **1114**, **1185**, **1199**
Oregon: 1077, **1144**, 1227
Pennsylvania: **1053**, **1072**, 1075, **1082**, 1097, **1111**, **1118**, **1125**, **1126**, **1143**, 1146, **1151**, **1173**, **1176**, 1180, **1193**, **1194**, 1201, **1207**, **1218**, 1222, **1225**, **1231**, **1241**, **1242**, **1247**
Rhode Island: 1099
South Carolina: 1066, 1094, 1097, 1106, **1138**, 1155, 1203
Tennessee: **1064**, 1074, 1097, 1120, **1152**, 1157, **1165**, **1187**
Texas: 1087, 1097, **1141**, 1197, **1214**, **1228**, 1229
Virginia: 1065, **1093**, 1097, **1105**, **1121**, 1243
Washington: **1200**, 1227, 1243
Wisconsin: **457**, **1079**, **1107**, 1120, **1158**, 1188, **1189**, 1190, 1198, **1209**, **1213**, 1246

Company-related welfare
Alabama: 1281
California: **1265, 1266, 1277, 1279**
Connecticut: **1252, 1261**
Idaho: **1275**
Illinois: **1251, 1262, 1284**
Kansas: 1268
Massachusetts: **1253, 1264,** 1269, **1278**
Michigan: **1270, 1272**
Minnesota: 886, **1260**
Missouri: 1255, **1257,** 1268
New York: **1040, 1254, 1258,** 1267, **1271, 1273, 1274**
North Carolina: 1256
Ohio: 1276, 1280, **1282**
Pennsylvania: 1263, 1283
South Carolina: 1256
Texas: 1259
Virginia: 1256

Conferences
District of Columbia: **263**
Kansas: **336**
Minnesota: 470
New York: **170, 576**
Tennessee: 142

Dental expenses
California: 847, 859, 884
Colorado: 812
Florida: **817**
Maine: 874
Minnesota: 826, 827
New Mexico: 840
Texas: 840

Emergency aid
California: 813
Colorado: 812
Connecticut: 802
Illinois: 879
New York: **919, 923, 929, 938, 940**
Pennsylvania: **876**
Virginia: **631**

Exchange programs
New York: **167**

Fellowships
California: 44, **313,** 337, 410, 926, **943, 948**
Connecticut: **146**
Delaware: **1013**

District of Columbia: **263, 372, 517, 927, 954, 957**
Florida: **364, 545**
Hawaii: 19
Illinois: 144, **215, 278, 308,** 613, **637, 1006, 1039**
Indiana: **527**
Kansas: **336**
Kentucky: 616
Massachusetts: **282,** 335, 381, 641
Michigan: **208, 958, 1009**
Minnesota: 113, 921
New Hampshire: **343**
New Jersey: **199, 961**
New York: **193, 194, 244, 289, 387, 393, 423,** 575, **576, 606,** 672, **684, 740, 746, 759, 918, 924, 952, 953, 962, 1016, 1027**
North Carolina: **972**
North Dakota: 113
Ohio: **226, 455, 617,** 721
Pennsylvania: 659
Rhode Island: **1044**
South Carolina: **639**
South Dakota: 113
Tennessee: 142
Texas: 615, **711, 720**
Wisconsin: 113

Graduate student loans
Arizona: 198
California: 269, 570, 599, 726
Connecticut: 751
Florida: 235, **403**
Georgia: 675
Illinois: 456
Indiana: 456
Iowa: 456
Kansas: 456
Kentucky: 456
Massachusetts: **489**
Michigan: 373, 456
Minnesota: 456
Missouri: 456, 648
Nebraska: 456
New Jersey: 354
New York: 354, **962**
North Carolina: 661
Ohio: 629
South Carolina: 169
South Dakota: 456
Texas: 414
Wisconsin: 456

Grants by nomination only
Arizona: **1043**
California: 1047
Connecticut: 925, **969,** 1030
Delaware: **1013**
District of Columbia: **954**

New Jersey: **801**, 815, 900
New Mexico: 840
New York: 789, **795**, 796, 803, 815, 846, **848**, **856**,
   864, **867**, **877**, 888, **896**, **898**, 900, **914**, **917**, **920**,
   934, **938**, **940**, **963**, **1254**, **1271**
North Carolina: **880**
Ohio: 808, 822, 824, 832, 1276
Oklahoma: 849, 900, 913
Oregon: 889
Pennsylvania: 820, 836, 851, 857, **894**, 900
Rhode Island: **904**, 908
South Carolina: 833
Texas: 835, 840, 878, 899, **956**, 1197
Vermont: 809
Virginia: 838
Washington: 909, 910
West Virginia: 837
Wisconsin: 883

Work-study grants
Illinois: **215**
Rhode Island: 985

GEOGRAPHIC FOCUS INDEX

The sequence numbers in this index refer to foundations which restrict their giving to particular states. State listings are further subdivided by broad categories of giving.

INDEX OF COMPANY EMPLOYEE GRANTS

The numbers following the company names in this index refer to the sequence numbers of entries in the Descriptive Directory section.

INDEX OF SPECIFIC EDUCATIONAL INSTITUTIONS

The numbers following the institution names in this index refer to the sequence numbers of entries in the Descriptive Directory section.